Essentials of Public Service

Essentials of Public Service

An Introduction to
Contemporary Public Administration

MARY E. GUY AND TODD L. ELY

Melvin & Leigh, Publishers
IRVINE, CALIFORNIA

Essentials of Public Service: An Introduction to Contemporary Public Administration
© 2018 by Mary E. Guy and Todd L. Ely
All Rights Reserved.

Published by Melvin & Leigh, Publishers
6 Curie Court
Irvine, CA 92617

orders.melvinleigh@cox.net
www.melvinleigh.com

Cover design by Jesse Sanchez
Production by Stacey Victor

ISBN: 978-0-99923590-4

Printed in the United States of America on mixed recycle paper

Visit our home page at www.melvinleigh.com

BRIEF CONTENTS

DETAILED TABLE OF CONTENTS

This book is written as a text for graduate students in Master of Public Administration and Master of Public Policy programs and for upper level undergraduate students. Whether the course is called an introduction to public service/public administration/ public management/public policy/or public affairs, the content is tailored to the sensitivities and knowledge that public service professionals need.

Essentials of Public Service is written for the twenty-first century, employing a governance lens in which the term "public sector" embraces government, public service-minded nonprofits, social enterprises, and for-profit entities that partner with government to provide goods and services. Our purpose is to illuminate the work wherever it occurs in: local, state, or federal government, regional compacts or special districts, nonprofits, partnerships between government and business, and international linkages. In this intersectoral setting, the democratic imperative requires attention to constitutional values, citizen engagement, skilled management, integrity, transparency, and a collaborative state of mind.

THINK GLOBALLY, GOVERN LOCALLY

Ever mindful of the global context, content is sensitive to the fact that practices must be responsive to each nation's traditions and political culture. The book focuses primarily on the U.S. context, which employs a complex governance model that relies on government to set the rules that let markets thrive, relies on nonprofits to unite common interests, and depends on business to create wealth and to deliver services that are necessary but for which government need not provide by itself. It is a system that relies on collaboration between the three sectors of the economy and blends the strengths of each.

The fabric of public service is threaded together by democratic values of equality and equity, paired with a management emphasis on efficiency and effectiveness. This text explains how these values and goals are blended and balanced in the pursuit of public purposes from street-level services to top-level administration. Starting with an overview of constitutional tenets that paint the "lines on the road," chapters explore the role of federal, state, and local governments as they collaborate with citizens, nonprofits, and business; in order to set policy, design and manage programs, deliver services, and evaluate outcomes.

DYNAMIC AND DIVERSE

The profession of public service contains a panorama of career opportunities with a variety of venues in which the work takes place. Cases throughout the chapters reflect the variety of settings and jobs, the diversity of the workforce, and the breadth of public service pursuits.

About one-third of students who enroll in public administration programs are more interested in working in nonprofits than in government and wonder why they should study government. But the nonprofits that hire them are extraordinarily likely to depend on government grants and contracts to fund their operations. This blend is detailed so that students complete the course with a rich understanding of the collaboration that marks the relationship between government, nonprofits, and public/private partnerships. Regardless of their career objectives, our goal is for students to find a place for themselves in this variegated tapestry we call "public service."

The book embraces the circle that public service is: from citizen input to policy formulation to program creation and management to service delivery to evaluation and back to input. Collaboration and citizen engagement are emphasized, as is the role of social media and rapid information flow. A chapter on contracting is included, for most everyone working in public service must now be adept at issuing requests for proposals (RFPs), or responding to RFPs to land contracts, monitoring compliance, or evaluating performance. A chapter on transparency is included because the openness within which public actors operate makes government significantly different from business. A chapter on performance measurement is included because outcomes matter. In other words, each step of this dynamic process is covered.

LEVEL AND ORGANIZATION OF THE BOOK

Crafted to satisfy multiple models for introductory courses, *Essentials of Public Service* fits into curricula that want students to learn about public service as a profession, or want students to learn about the breadth of public administration and the many subject areas it draws upon, or want to address overall interests in public service at any level of government or in combination with nonprofits or public/private partnerships. It is appropriate for students just entering the profession of public service or for those who already have work experience and wish to advance their knowledge.

Mindful of the democratic context within which public service happens, chapters on leading, organizing, budgeting, human resources, finances, and digital democracy accentuate management. Material on constitutional values, citizen engagement, public economics and policy, financial management, administrative law, transparency, contracting, public integrity, and performance management shape the contours. Cases drawn from federal, state, and local contexts provide examples of everyday challenges and opportunities.

Essentials includes coverage of subjects that are often overlooked: citizen engagement, contracting, how administrators intersect with the policy process, the impact of the Internet, how sunshine laws influence what gets done and how it gets done, and administrative law. These are topics that too many practitioners are expected to know but have to learn on the job because they are not covered adequately in traditional coursework. An additional contribution is that we offer a significantly stronger presentation of finance-related subject matter with chapters on budgeting, public economics and policy, and financial management for both government and nonprofits.

Throughout, the book reflects the moral obligation to pursue social justice and to be good stewards of the public weal. And it is mindful of the diversity of students, their career goals, and the many venues in which public service takes place.

CHAPTER DESIGN

Essentials of Public Service is divided into four parts. The first set of chapters focuses on the context within which public service occurs, with chapters on constitutional values and citizen engagement. The second part focuses on the work of public executives, with chapters that focus on leading, managing, organizing, staffing, budgeting, and harnessing the power of the Internet to communicate with the public. The third section focuses on the parameters that govern how policy is transformed into programs, how programs are financed, how law sets the boundaries for administrative action, how contracting works, how transparency requirements function, and the importance of public integrity. The fourth part focuses on performance measurement and meaningful outcomes of public action.

READER-FRIENDLY CONTENT AND FORMAT

Multiple features make the book reader-friendly. Each chapter begins with a timeline that traces important literature and inflection points that shape today's thinking. Then, an opening case for each chapter followed by thought-provoking questions set the stage for the chapter's content. Additional cases are included in the chapters to show how the concepts take shape in real life.

Chapter content covers the gamut of public service, from executive-level decision making (which is where most texts focus) to street-level work (which is where most students gain employment). To help students translate the abstractions of public service into their own lives and to see how their interests fit into the big picture, each chapter concludes with a highlight of an accomplished public service professional. Immediately preceding each chapter summary, a biography and a link to a video of an impressive public servant is included. These are people who have distinguished themselves in their work, are committed to public service, and speak about their views and their careers. The *Ask Me Why I Care* series illuminates the work of public service and what life is like in the trenches. It is our goal that students will read the biographies, watch the videos and conclude, "I could do this!"

Following the summary for each chapter, end-of-chapter discussion questions, and exercises, another special feature is included. At the end of each chapter, a "how to" guide, referred to as a skillbox, gives step-by-step instructions on an essential skill drawn from the subject matter covered. From memo writing to public speaking to manipulating spreadsheets to accounting for inflation in cost forecasts, the skill is described, instructions are provided, and a sample exercise is included that provides an opportunity to practice. These skillboxes focus on the foundational tools that public service professionals need: effective communication, critical thinking, grant writing, program evaluation, conducting cost-benefit analysis, and more. We use the opportunity presented by an introductory course textbook to draw attention to and impart basic competency in the most critical public service skills.

For students wishing to earn extra credit or explore a subject more deeply, there are additional readings and resources listed at the end of chapters 2 through 15. Through coverage of the subject matter, cases, discussion questions, end of chapter exercises, and skillboxes, readers learn the essentials.

PEDAGOGICAL FEATURES

Learning objectives for each chapter

Cases that bring the subject matter to life

Demonstration of how concepts relate to practice

Ask Me Why I Care links to accomplished professionals

Key Terms

Discussion Questions

Exercises

Skillboxes

Additional Resources

SUPPLEMENTS

A companion website delivers support materials for instructors, including a sample syllabus, a chapter-by-chapter elaboration of content that includes an explanation of entries on each chapter's opening timeline, an overview of the chapter, presentation slides, discussion items, exercises, and test questions.

ACKNOWLEDGMENTS

Capturing the panoply of public service requires contributions from many. We are grateful to research assistants Alexis Kennedy and Jennifer Hooker for their assistance editing the manuscript and preparing the instructor manual, and to Leigh Espy and Samantha J. Larson for locating and developing cases. And, two classes of Master of Public Administration students "test drove" the chapters, providing input and feedback on content.

We are grateful for the *Ask Me Why I Care* stories and videos. These were directed by Co-Project Directors Mary R. Hamilton and Rita Paskowitz and produced by the University of Nebraska at Omaha College of Public Affairs and Community Service. Within this series, the videos featuring Rita Paskowitz, Brandy Hodge, Michael G. Massiah, Fred Silva, Bill Ciaccio, Selvi Stanislaus, Dan Ahern, Dewey Harris, Phin Xaypagna, and Rachel Lyon were produced in conjunction with the University of Nebraska College of Public Affairs and Community Service. The videos featuring Edward A. Flynn, Valerie Lemmie, Alan Dean, Howard Messner, and Janet Norwood, were produced by the National Academy of Public Administration. We thank Mary Hamilton, Rita Paskowitz, the University of Nebraska at Omaha College of Public Affairs and Community Service, and the National Academy of Public Administration for permission to use this material.

The text has benefited greatly from the keen eyes and thoughtful style of Stacey Victor on the publishing team. We have special words of thanks to editor and publisher Harry Briggs for his ever-helpful guidance. Like an accomplished equestrian, his firm hands but gentle touch guided this project from beginning to end.

Mary E. Guy and Todd L. Ely

PART I

The Context for Public Service

Chapter 1 Running a Constitution

Chapter 2 Citizen Engagement

Governance is a hallmark of civilization, shaped according to local customs. For it to be lasting and effective, it must fit the political, social, and economic landscape. These chapters focus on the U.S. context by describing how the norms embedded in the Constitution sculpt the American system.

Chapter 1 Timeline: Running a Constitution

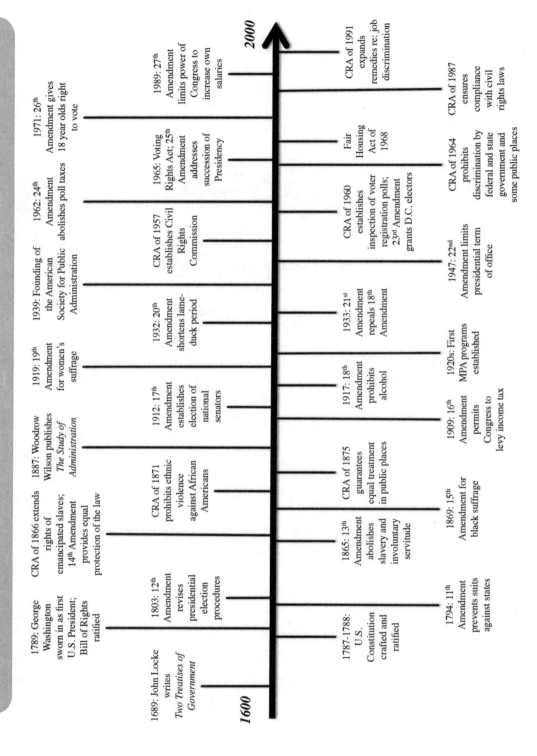

1689: John Locke writes *Two Treatises of Government*

1787-1788: U.S. Constitution crafted and ratified

1789: George Washington sworn in as first U.S. President; Bill of Rights ratified

1794: 11th Amendment prevents suits against states

1803: 12th Amendment revises presidential election procedures

1865: 13th Amendment abolishes slavery and involuntary servitude

CRA of 1866 extends rights of emancipated slaves; 14th Amendment provides equal protection of the law

1869: 15th Amendment for black suffrage

CRA of 1871 prohibits ethnic violence against African Americans

CRA of 1875 guarantees equal treatment in public places

1887: Woodrow Wilson publishes *The Study of Administration*

1909: 16th Amendment permits Congress to levy income tax

1912: 17th Amendment establishes election of national senators

1917: 18th Amendment prohibits alcohol

1919: 19th Amendment for women's suffrage

1920s: First MPA programs established

1932: 20th Amendment shortens lame-duck period

1933: 21st Amendment repeals 18th Amendment

1939: Founding of the American Society for Public Administration

1947: 22nd Amendment limits presidential term of office

1957 CRA of 1957 establishes Civil Rights Commission

CRA of 1960 establishes inspection of voter registration polls; 23rd Amendment grants D.C. electors

1962: 24th Amendment abolishes poll taxes

CRA of 1964 prohibits discrimination by federal and state government and some public places

1965: Voting Rights Act; 25th Amendment addresses succession of Presidency

Fair Housing Act of 1968

1971: 26th Amendment gives 18 year olds right to vote

CRA of 1987 ensures compliance with civil rights laws

1989: 27th Amendment limits power of Congress to increase own salaries

CRA of 1991 expands remedies re: job discrimination

1600

2000

RUNNING A CONSTITUTION

WHAT YOU WILL LEARN

Public administration competencies

The nature and context of public service

Intellectual roots of public administration and the field's enduring debates

How government differs from business

The importance of public integrity and social equity

The interdependence of government and nonprofits

Linguistics of the field

Skillbox: How to write a memorandum

Public service is both an enterprise and a profession. As an enterprise, it is the pursuit of public purposes. As a profession it is a calling committed to the public interest and is referred to as public administration. Although all three segments of the economy—government, business, and nonprofits—play important roles in public service, government and nonprofits are the largest players and the two segments whose values are most closely aligned. Government and many nonprofits work hand-in-glove to deliver services and to engage volunteers toward public ends.

To demonstrate the interplay of many elements, the chapter starts with a case that is an example of public service at the street level in the midst of chaos. The Aurora theater shooting demonstrates the power that public service has to impact the quality of life for individuals, neighborhoods, and communities. Note the collaboration of multiple government agencies, coupled with nonprofit services after the immediate crisis is resolved. There is not one hero in this event. Rather, many people worked together effectively, efficiently, and with caring, to respond to a horrific situation in the middle of the night.

THE AURORA THEATER SHOOTING[1]

On the night of July 20, 2012, a lone gunman opened fire on moviegoers attending the midnight premiere of a Batman movie in the Century 16 Theater complex in Aurora, Colorado. Within minutes, James Holmes had shot seventy people, twelve of whom died, and twelve others were injured as they fled the theater.

Through the combined efforts of the city's public safety agencies—police, fire, communications—with timely assistance from neighboring jurisdictions' agencies, plus federal agencies—the Federal Bureau of Investigation (FBI) and the Bureau of Alcohol, Tobacco, Firearms and Explosives (ATF)—local hospitals, and a nearby public school, these outcomes were achieved:

- Fire department personnel treated over one hundred people at multiple triage centers set up around the theater. All victims with survivable serious wounds were rapidly transported to nearby hospitals and recovered.
- A police unit arrived under two minutes from the first 911 call, and multiple units arrived within three minutes.
- The first fire department unit arrived in five and a half minutes and immediately engaged in patient care near the main entrance of the theater.
- Multiple improvised explosive devices at the shooter's apartment were discovered. Police evacuated residents in the apartment building where the explosives were located and in the surrounding buildings. They contacted two neighboring counties' bomb squads and police department experts, along with the FBI and the ATF and working collaboratively, they disarmed

the devices with no harm done to the residents or first responders. Only minor damage to the apartment where the shooter had rigged the devices occurred.

- Five area hospitals received victims and provided emergency care with only a few minutes' forewarning to prepare for the influx of patients. Because of traffic and pedestrian congestion, ambulances could not get through to several patient triage and treatment locations. Officers transported victims in police vehicles rather than wait for ambulances to get through or for patients to be carried long distances to the ambulances. Of sixty patients treated in hospitals that night, twenty-seven went in police cars and twenty in ambulances. Others were transported in private vehicles. This level of police transport was unplanned and unprecedented. While considered out-of-the-box thinking, the latest emergency medicine research suggests that speed of getting a gunshot wound victim to a nearby hospital is more important than the mode of transport or care en route.
- The 911 call takers handled 6,000 calls instead of the typical 1,500 for an evening. The telecommunicators supported the incident throughout and were instrumental in alerting nearby jurisdictions to render mutual aid.
- Police quickly set up a family reunification center at nearby Gateway High School with cooperation from Aurora public school officials. Police officers and supervisors managed crowd control of the 1,200 people pouring out

of the theater complex into the parking lots. Police separated the crowd into groups by theater and arranged bus transport to the school where they were interviewed.

- Victims and their families were cared for by the Aurora Police Victim Services Unit, supplemented by trained volunteers and professional family assistance personnel from nearby jurisdictions.
- Families of the deceased were given the option of having their own public information officer assigned to them to help with media requests for interviews.
- The coroner's office and Aurora police department sped confirmation of the deceased victims' identities by having a police forensic analyst use an innovative practice—taking just two fingerprints from each deceased victim while still in the theater—and matching them against driver's license records. This approach expedited the process—a concern for loved ones—while meeting legal and professional requirements.
- A series of press conferences and press releases kept the public informed. The governor and the mayor spoke several times in press conferences and public information officers from the police department, federal agencies, and fire departments released information on a regular basis for weeks afterward. As the investigation proceeded, the Public In-

formation Officer for the Aurora police department used Twitter and Facebook to announce upcoming press conferences and alert the press to what topics would be covered.

- Despite the fatigue felt by public safety personnel, they successfully provided security for a prayer vigil for the community and a visit from the president of the United States.
- Supportive counseling was offered early on and over a period of time for theatergoers and first responders who suffered psychological trauma.
- As a result of a trial by jury, the shooter was sentenced to life in prison.

Questions to Ponder

1. Think about the number of public services that were involved in this case. How many levels of government? How many branches of government? What is the role of nonprofits?
2. How does coordination among these entities occur?
3. How is the business community involved in terms of press and hospitals?
4. Where is the nexus between theatergoers and public service?
5. What does it take to have well-trained responders on staff and ready to go at a moment's notice when emergencies like this happen?

PUBLIC ADMINISTRATION COMPETENCIES

The work of public administration is the work of breathing life into the principles embedded in the Constitution. To this end, public administration programs are designed to teach administrative competencies that encompass five essential domains of public service. These include the ability:

- to lead and manage in public governance;
- to participate in and contribute to the policy process;
- to analyze, synthesize, think critically, solve problems, and make decisions;
- to articulate and apply a public service perspective; and
- to communicate and interact productively with a diverse and changing workforce and citizenry.

All of these competencies are demonstrated in the case of the Aurora theater shooting. Leadership was practiced not only at the agency level as the Aurora police department joined forces with neighboring departments and federal agencies to defuse the bombs in Holmes' apartment, but also at the street level, as police officers took the initiative to transport injured victims to nearby hospitals rather than delay treatment by waiting for ambulances. The 911 call takers, deluged with calls during what would usually be a quiet night shift, managed to dispatch services to the crime scene at the same time that they fielded calls from concerned family members, routed calls between police and firefighters when their radios would not communicate with each other, and relayed information to surrounding jurisdictions. Thinking analytically was essential for the responders as well as the call takers.

The public service perspective was brought to bear when neighboring police and fire departments rushed to the scene to help, and when the local school was opened in the wee hours of the morning to provide a staging place for family members and those who had escaped the terror. Victim's assistance counselors were made available by a non-profit association whose mission is to advance fairness and healing for crime victims, their families, and communities. The association collaborates with police departments in the state and provides trained volunteers when needed. Frequent press conferences were held by public information officers to keep everyone in the community informed about the event, its aftermath, and the ensuing investigation. As the judicial branch became involved with Holmes' court proceedings, the district attorney's office reached out to the victims and families. Thus, leadership, management, decision making, communication, and public service mindedness combined to address the crisis and its aftermath.

The work of administrators and the profession of public service is broad in its reach, diverse in its tasks, and must always be at the ready. Cases like this show how public administration occurs at all levels of society—from the local to the state to the federal level—and how they interconnect. Public service has few boundaries; it occurs in planned programs and in instantaneous responses at the spur of the moment. If the capitalist economy forms the bricks of American society, public service is the mortar, filling in the chinks and reinforcing the bonds that hold society together.

Human-made crises such as the Aurora theater shooting occur without warning and mobilize responses from many services. Natural disasters, such as floods, tornadoes, hurricanes, and wildfires, also episodically elicit an outpouring of services. These events bring to the forefront services that are ever present, but when not on stage they function in the background. When not needed, the emphasis is on planning, training, readiness, and performing everyday maintenance routines. Taxpayers often question what their dollars are paying for, but when systems work well, they are almost invisible and taken for granted. When needed, they respond within minutes, coordinated and focused.

Although they grab headlines, emergencies are the exception. On a day-to-day basis, public schools operate; roads and rails transport commuters from home to work and move products to market; caseworkers help families resolve problems of housing, employment, and childcare; water treatment stations operate to ensure clean drinking water; public health departments monitor restaurant cleanliness; the Food and Drug Administration (FDA) regulates food and drug safety; planners collaborate with businesses to secure economic development that will connect job seekers, businesses, and customers and will provide a tax base for the jurisdiction. Social security payments are processed, the military functions smoothly, coins are minted and currency is printed, trade relationships are maintained around the globe, space exploration is ongoing, airline traffic flows smoothly, and federal research dollars spur innovation in universities across the nation. The pieces of this complex quilt are held together by stitches between government, nonprofits, business entities, and civic-minded residents, all of whom collaborate to provide safety, security, and a good life.

THE NATURE AND CONTEXT OF PUBLIC SERVICE

Welcome to the world of public service, where opportunities are endless. Whether the goal is a career in federal, state, or local government, the nonprofit sector, or the private sector supporting government, the needs are many, the work is challenging, and successes are meaningful not only to those who do the work but to all whose lives are improved because of the work done. No other career offers the abundance of opportunities for making a real difference in the quality of life for families, communities, and the broader society, not only today but far into the future.

Context

The context within which public services are delivered has to fit the norms of the political and economic system. Each nation establishes a system of governance that comports with its traditions and expectations. Around the world, the elements of history, customs, cultural values, power, population characteristics, fiscal policy, and natural resources, combine to shape each system of governance. While most nations create a strong central government, the United States uses a weaker model by diffusing power across the federal government, states, and locales, and constraining it at all levels. Americans' suspicion of power is manifested in the capacity for the legislative, executive, and judicial branches each to check the actions of the other. And the requirement to have transparency and citizen engagement throughout all public processes puts an additional check on public actions. Moreover, unlike other countries that categorize organizations as being either governmental or non-governmental (NGO), the United States sectors its economy into three areas: government, nonprofit, and business. Like looking into a kaleidoscope, this combination results in a complex matrix having multiple levels and dimensions of government and an economic sector partitioned into three parts.

Making Democracy and Capitalism Work Together

The American system is unique. So unique, in fact, that it works better in practice than in theory. In the United States, governments are empowered to do only that which is specifically allowed by law. Conversely, businesses are free to do whatever they wish to do, except that which is prohibited by law. This means that businesses have the freedom to extend and expand their enterprises and to take whatever lawful actions they wish in order to pursue their ends. The constraint on government to do only that which it is empowered by law to do, and the fact that its actions are open to scrutiny by the press and the public, accomplishes the intent of preventing government from usurping people's freedoms. At the same time, it allows the pursuit of wealth with minimal checks. Thus, the system comports with the regime values of life, liberty, and the pursuit of happiness, understood to mean the right to be free from government intrusion and the right to own property and to pursue wealth. In utilitarian terms, the American adage, "the right to swing my fist stops where your nose begins"[2] captures the expectation of people to be free of government interference to the extent that is reasonable. And at the same time, government services are on standby for when they are needed. This irony must be understood to comprehend Americans' love/hate relationship with government.

Democratic principles require that each person is equal under the law. Capitalism requires inequality, where the minority own businesses and the majority are employed by them. Despite political equality, with inherent inequalities in earnings there cannot be economic equality. The cement that holds this mosaic together are the paradoxical cultural values that imbue Americans with the belief that a) if they work hard they will earn more and move up the economic ladder so that they become business owners; and, b) regardless of economic inequality, everyone has a right to have their voices heard and their votes counted. These diametrically opposed assumptions guarantee that the third branch of government, the judiciary, always has a full caseload. Courts are the mechanism used to peacefully resolve conflict.

> *"The care of human life and happiness is the first and only legitimate objective of good government."*
>
> —Thomas Jefferson

It is within this context that public administrators function. Despite the paradoxical norms and constitutional constraints, their sphere of influence is huge, multilayered, and nuanced. The constitutional, democratic, and cultural tenets that shape notions of acceptable government action create a uniquely American milieu. Links between public opinion and power create policy, and management transforms policy into programs. This transformation happens through the interaction of managerial, political, and economic forces, as they are exerted via networks of intergovernmental and intersectoral collaboration. Understanding the intellectual roots of the field provides understanding of how the ironies of the American system were built into it in a way that has succeeded.

THE INTELLECTUAL ROOTS OF PUBLIC ADMINISTRATION

When George Washington took office as the first president of the United States in 1789 there were no precedents for him to follow. In essence, he was the nation's first administrator, with no procedure manual and only the Constitution to serve as his guide. There were no models for how to create a successful presidency yet his challenge was to set the "American experiment" on a steady course. Aware that all of his actions would set precedents for the future, he set forth to interpret constitutional tenets in a way that would establish a coherent framework for the fledgling nation. He succeeded. Well over two hundred years have passed, the Constitution remains in force, and the republic continues, though not without continuing debates about how much government is too much, how much is too little, and where the bounds should be.

In an address to Congress in 1791, aware of the importance of creating a system that was acceptable to all, Washington said, "It is desirable on all occasions, to unite with a steady and firm adherence to constitutional and necessary Acts of Government, the fullest evidence of a disposition, as far as may be practicable, to consult the wishes of every part of the community, and to lay the foundations of the public administration in the affection of the people."[3]

The Constitution does not provide guidance on how to administer the government. It was up to Washington to chart the course. With great latitude, an eye over the horizon, and no historical precedent, Washington started the process to establish "a public administration" that would implement the system that was sketchily outlined in the Constitution. The creation of a democratic republic has been in process ever since. Attempts to regularize processes are structured in administrative law. This is what provides interpretation and meaning to constitutional precepts. Attempts to advance political equality are marked by the passage of nine civil rights acts,[4] each extending protections to people categorized by demographic characteristics. In addition to trying to level the playing field for citizens, there have also been ongoing attempts to reconcile the debate about whether patronage or formal, merit-based selection processes should be used to hire civil servants. The latter prevailed and by the late 1800s, Congress approved The Pendleton Act, a bill that standardized the process for recruiting and hiring federal workers and protected them from partisan firing. By the 1930s, parallel processes for recruiting and hiring personnel were being implemented in states and cities.

Couched in the assumptions of the Enlightenment, the Constitution assumes a natural right of people to have a contractual relationship with their government without interference from religion. It provides for a separation of powers between branches of government and creates a system for election of the president and members of Congress. Although it sets fundamental norms about the structure of government and its relationship to the people, the wording is broad, leaving interpretation up to those responsible for implementing it. It is a set of fundamental standards about the structure of government and its relationship with the people. Ratified in 1788, the U.S. Constitution has been unusually successful in that it is the oldest single-document national constitution still in force and has only been amended twenty-seven times; the first ten amendments are called the Bill of Rights and were added in 1789, only one year after ratification.

The Constitution, and the Lockean worldview that serves as its foundation, stabilizes government and steadies its hand. The national government provides for the common defense, a market where businesses can flourish, safety nets for those who find themselves disadvantaged by the market, regulations to ensure fair competition, and political monitoring of the economy. States, often thought of as laboratories for democracy, mirror the executive, legislative, and judicial branches, and provide policy and direction for services within their geographic boundaries. For many programs funded by the federal government, states serve as partners and pass-throughs, funneling and sometimes adding to federal dollars for local programs. Most direct service provision occurs at the local level, managed by cities and counties.

Like a great unfinished symphony, the question of how best to institutionalize citizen engagement and make government work to everyone's satisfaction continues to be partially answered. With Alexander Hamilton's interest in a strong central government and Thomas Jefferson's emphasis on vibrant local communities, Washington grappled with how best to build institutions that would reconcile conflicting views. The debate continues to this day despite the fact that the United States is the longest running democratic republic. But it only succeeds with constant effort put forth by administrators at all levels of government working within constitutional constraints. It is no way to run a business. But it is the way to run a democracy.

The Constitution continues to resonate with Americans because its assumptions comport with deep-seated American values. The American character is one that, like the founders, is suspicious of government power and agrees with strict boundaries on the power of government to encroach into private lives. All public executives—city manager, county administrator, governor, president, agency head—are familiar with the buzz saw they confront when trying to move government too forcefully or extend powers too much. The document is sparing of words, leaving it up to each new generation to interpret its spirit in the context of changing times. For example, the document was written by and for privileged white men who owned property. Women had no right to vote and for purposes of the census, each slave was counted as three-fifths of a person. By now, through amendments and laws, the right to legally participate in governance with the right to vote is not limited by gender or race. And separate is not equal. These changes did not come quickly or easily, but they arrived. More changes will continue to come.

The founders believed in the natural right of the people to enter into a contract that would establish self-government, provide for separation of powers, and create a system for election of the president and members of Congress. The design was put in place in the Constitution and parallel systems have been established at the state and local levels, creating a government for a geographically dispersed nation with a diverse population. The American experiment is still just that, challenged differently with each generation as globalized markets and media affect internal dynamics.

Woodrow Wilson and the Formal Study of Public Administration

The nation's first century saw the institutionalization of administrative processes and government's relationship to citizens. It also developed a workable relationship between elected and career officials within the executive branch and a functioning relationship between the three branches of government. While George Washington asserted his desire to create "a public administration" that would serve the nation's needs, scholarly study of it began a century later.

The processes for public problem-solving that set boundaries between problem identification, policy deliberations, policy making, and implementation are parsed between the legislative and executive functions. Attention to the interconnection between these was first addressed by a young scholar in 1887. While he was an academic and long before he pursued the White House, Woodrow Wilson puzzled over government and concluded that the best way to understand it is to look at it from two perspectives, one being the province and processes of politics (the legislative function) and the other being the province and processes of administration (the executive function). He argued his point in a now classic journal article, "Study of Administration."[5] In the article, which is heralded as the first scholarly attention to public administration in the United States, he argues that to understand government, one must look through two lenses: the policy-making roles of Congress and the administrative roles of the executive branch. Acknowledging that they are inextricably intertwined and overlapping, he nevertheless argues that it is easier to grasp the roles of either by studying them separately in order to comprehend the nuances of each. Like a fulcrum, he modified the leverage point of politics and administration as he viewed the field from different vantages, first as a scholar and later as a politician.

Because Wilson used the linguistic convenience of separating the domains of policy and administration in order to study them, his point has been mistakenly interpreted as arguing that politics and administration are distinctly separate enterprises. It is important to note that, as any city manager or department head knows, effective administration requires active involvement in the policy process. And effective policy making requires close collaboration with those who will implement the policy. Wilson's attention to the subject of government and how it functions marks the beginning of the academic field of public administration, a century after Washington puzzled over the best way to set institutions in place.

Although there had been training in public administration prior to formal graduate programs based in universities, the 1920s marked the beginning of university-based Master of Public Administration (MPA) programs. The Maxwell School at Syracuse University established the first MPA program in 1924. Shortly after that, universities around the nation instituted MPA programs and there are now 192 accredited MPA programs, most of which are in the United States, and more are being developed around the globe.

The Field's Enduring Debates

One way to track the intellectual development of public administration is by observing the positioning on three classic debates: Where are the boundaries between politics and administration? Are decisions made based on facts or values? Where is the dividing line between public and private? Each of these debates provides a perspective on the proper role and function of the public sector. Consensus on each of these three debates is difficult to achieve and changes over time. Like a windsock, discussions illuminate positions on the continuum and reflect the tenor of the times. In real life, they are reflected in clashes over proposed solutions to public problems at all levels of government.

Politics versus Administration

Woodrow Wilson's argument was that the political aspect of governing—the questions and answers pertaining to "who gets what"[6]—is best understood by isolating it from the executive aspect of governing. That thinking prevailed until the latter 1900s. Public administration scholars focused on administrative actions and excluded policy making, to the extent that the acronym POSDCORB[7] was coined to represent these executive responsibilities: planning, organizing, staffing, directing, coordinating, reporting, and budgeting. By the latter 1900s, however, scholars were arguing that one cannot be truly effective as an administrator without also engaging in the policy-making process to shape inputs to legislative deliberations, to construct rules by which policies are transformed into programs, and to make modifications to policies so that they work better. In reality, effective public executives keep the lines of communication open between their offices and lawmakers' offices and work closely with them in the crafting of legislation. This enables them to be persuasive advocates for modifications in laws and funding priorities so that programs for which they are responsible more closely meet the needs of constituents being served. The boundaries between policy and administration are blurred at the edges and remain so, yet they are the responsibility of coequal branches of government.

Facts versus Values

Are public decisions based on facts or values? The popular notion that quantitative analyses produce better justifications than value-based argumentation rises and falls. For example, student testing in public education and data dashboards that enable evidence-based management emphasize the importance of "facts" to guide administrative action. At the same time, deep-seated values give rise to persuasive logic that often sways policy decisions and determines whether the recommendations in quantitatively sophisticated audit reports gather dust or are implemented. For example, when numerical indicators demonstrate that a poor performing school should be closed, neighborhood identification and loyalty with the school may keep the school open despite what the numbers say.

The debate over facts versus values is useful when analyzing decisions that are made both in the policy realm and in the administrative realm. The ideal outcome is that both values and facts inform decision making. As Nobel Prize-winner Herbert Simon[8] said, facts interpreted without values are as useless as a one-bladed scissor.

Public versus Private

The public versus private debate focuses on the difference between government and business. The question pertains to whether a function should be performed by government or by business. And if it is agreed that the function is in the pursuit of the public interest, the question that follows is whether the production should be contracted to a private sector vendor or produced directly by government.

Another way that the debate arises is less a matter of who should deliver a service and more a question of publicness itself, in terms of the degree to which an organization operates in the public domain. From this perspective of public versus private, the debate revolves around discussions of who has authority, both economic and political, over the organization. For example, are public utilities public or private? If provided by a privately-owned company, should the rates be regulated by a body of elected citizens? Compromises in the public versus private debate result in public service commissions in a number of locales where the utility company is privately held but publically restrained in the rates it can charge.

HOW GOVERNMENT DIFFERS FROM BUSINESS

In some ways the work of a public executive is the same as the work of the business executive. Those who manage and lead must know how to articulate a vision, set strategy, organize, communicate, allocate resources, hire and develop staff, and monitor output to ensure that it produces the outcome that is desired. And all this must be done as efficiently and effectively as possible. The difference between public service and business lies in the purpose for which the work is done, the context within which the work must be done, the stakeholders involved, and the constraints that surround work processes. And these make all the difference.

In the American context, any solutions to public problems for which a profit can be made are left to the business sector. When a profit cannot be made and there is sufficient interest from the philanthropic community, the work is left to the nonprofit sector. Government is the body of last resort for those solutions that are too large or too expensive or too unpopular to be addressed elsewhere. In this regard, government provides the safety net. This means that it performs many impossible jobs—jobs that can never eradicate the problem. At best, problems can be ameliorated. Child protective services, crime fighting, disaster response, and environmental protection are examples of such work. The problem can never be erased; it can only be addressed as equitably and effectively as possible.

In 1949, Paul Appleby[9] published a book entitled *Policy and Administration*. In it, he wrote that the purpose of public administration is to "make a mesh of things." Never is that more true than today. The meshing of policy interests, intergovernmental relationships, and intersectoral collaboration creates networks that are funded from a variety of sources. For example, service provision for large programs, such as health insurance enabled by the Affordable Care Act, links businesses, nonprofits, and government together, creating complicated networks that more closely resemble cobwebs than linear relationships. Government is the catalyst that brings entities together.

Other factors that contribute to the difference between public and private include the scope of activities, the type of needs being addressed, electoral cycles, metrics, legal constraints, and nonmission based requirements. All of these occur with regard to fulfilling public values that are extrinsic to the purpose of the agency. Primary among these are transparency and information sharing as well as safeguards for privacy. At times these imperatives are mutually contradictory. For example, as police officers don body cameras for the purpose of accountability, the issue of privacy for anyone being photographed arises.

> *"The business of business is business and the goal of business is to earn a profit in the provision of goods and services. The business of government is service—well managed, one hopes, and not wasteful, but never at a profit. There is no such thing as government money. Governments have no money; they have only what they take from their citizens, either in taxes or by inflation."*
>
> —Mickey Edwards

Scope

Business is the engine of economic growth in the United States and drives personal wealth. Running a business exposes executives to how government affects the private sector. But heading a large corporation is very different from administering a federal government that employs millions of people and spends trillions of dollars while dealing with a vast range of interconnected domestic and foreign policy issues. No business ever comes close to dealing with this breadth of scope and complexity. A congress of 535 members designed as a coequal branch of government dwarfs any sort of oversight that a corporate board could exercise. The checks and balances that Congress and the judiciary exercise, along with requirements for transparency, substantively change the job of the chief executive officer, which in the case of national government is the president of the United States. Although the demands for leadership at the federal level far exceed that of governors or mayors, each level brings a scope that in most cases extends much further than that of any corporation or nonprofit entity.

Moreover, the problems that come to government are interconnected agglomerations of social, economic, and political conditions for which there is no easy answer. Only when the problem cannot be addressed by business or nonprofits does it come to government. This means that problems are already well established and expensive when they get to government. Unlike producing a unique product and creating a market for it, public service delivery is reactive to need, as in the case of law enforcement and emergency response, or proactive in terms of environmental protection and economic

PUBLIC VS. PRIVATE VIEWPOINTS: THE FLINT WATER PROBLEM

The water crisis in Flint, Michigan shows what can go wrong when public executives run government like a business. The problems began in 2013 when the city switched water providers to save an estimated $5 million. Flint discontinued a more expensive service and tapped into the Flint River instead. Water quality tests soon showed the presence of E. coli and residents reported yellow water coming out of their taps. They also reported having rashes and extreme hair loss. The Environmental Protection Agency (EPA) tested and warned of heavy metals in the water. But more than 500 days passed before Governor Rick Snyder declared a state of emergency.[10] By 2016, 102,000 residents were without potable water, 8,600 children were at risk of lead exposure, and ten people had died as a result.[11] How did this happen?

In 2011, Snyder had taken office promising to make Michigan "great again" by zeroing in on government inefficiency. An early act of the former venture capitalist was to appoint an emergency manager for Flint who was empowered to cut public services,

privatize assets, and lay off public employees. Edward Kurtz was appointed to be Flint's emergency manager in 2013 and immediately abandoned the well-established water agreement with Detroit in favor of a less expensive water system that had not been properly vetted.[12] Improving municipal finances was his sole directive.

Prioritizing short-term savings over long-term priorities and democratic processes led to disaster. The governor's corporate philosophy of efficiency at any cost replaced a passion to serve the public interest. While business executives must focus on profit, public executives must utilize bureaucratic means to achieve democratic ends. They are responsible for balancing efficiency (analyzing inputs vs. outputs), effectiveness (accomplishing their mission), and equity (promoting fairness). The viewpoint of public executives must expand beyond the bottom line to citizen-centered public service delivery. The case of Flint, Michigan shows that the alternative can result in logistical, environmental, and public health crises.[13]

development. And size matters. Most public jurisdictions even at the local level are far larger than most businesses. In other words, the size and scope of activities present a far more complex work environment.

Wicked Problems and Long Time Horizons

Quick fixes are rare—it takes a long time for a problem to get to government and sometimes years of bargaining before a consensus is reached by lawmakers that government should address it. The debate centers less on the need for the services and more on the boundaries of how much service. Problems that survive the gamut are complex, multidimensional, and long-standing. And they are problems that no one else wants to address. In other words, they are so complicated that they are called "wicked." Multilayered interdependencies complicate resolution strategies and increase the number of actors who must be involved. Whether problems are of food safety, economic inequality, job development, public safety, or water supply, multiple agencies are involved and all segments of the economy factor into the solution: government, nonprofits, and business. Take the case of commuter rail. By the time people are aware that traffic snarls are getting worse, traffic is already a problem. Add in the years it takes to pass and enact legislation, develop funding sources, and build railways, and traffic has gotten progressively worse. By the time commuter trains are running, traffic jams occur more frequently than when the rail system was first planned.

Elections and Partisan Politics

When people think about government, they picture what the media report: partisan political campaigns and elected officials. Presidents, governors, mayors, legislators, city council members, and county commissioners deserve the attention they get, serving as leaders in federal, state, and local government. But there is so much more to governing: it is the management of public institutions, every day, regardless of electoral cycles. In some ways, government is like football. Elected officials are the franchise quarterbacks and the face of the jurisdiction, while career officials are the receivers and defenders. Without the whole team, there is no game.

Regularly held elections that decide who will hold office present a significant difference between business and government. It would be unthinkable to expect a huge corporation to change boards every two years, require Chief Executive Officers (CEOs) to stand for election every four years, and term limit them at eight years. And yet, because government is to be responsive to citizens, elections are central because they ensure that officials will be responsive to the will of the people. What is less central is expertise in governing, which is why it falls to career officials to carry on programs regardless of election cycles. This provides continuity across time while the face of government—the elected official—periodically changes. The public executive functions within an environment that is rife with cross-cutting pressures. In fact, the Constitution is designed to invite conflict, to slow the actions of any one branch of government, and to ensure that alternative views are heard.

Elusive Metrics

To look beneath the top leadership position is to see still more differences between public and private organizations. Business metrics fail to capture essential elements of governing. While return on investment is easily quantified in for-profit settings, it often defies measurement in public service because important public values of citizen engagement and nonquantifiable public goods cannot be reduced to numbers that are meaningful. Preventive expenditures made to prepare for disasters of unknown extent, preventive health care that avoids expensive future Medicaid procedures, educational programs that benefit graduates years into the future, and bridge repair to prevent decay, are examples that defy meaningful quantitative measures.

Legal Constraints

Legal boundaries differentiate business from government. Business has the freedom to do anything it wishes to do, except that for which it is prohibited by law. Conversely, government is empowered only to do that which is specifically provided for by law. This contrast gives business freedom and flexibility while government works in a corral.

Nonmission-Based Requirements

Another difference is in the necessity for government agencies to perform nonmission-based services. Transparency and information sharing are examples of nonmission-based work. For example, while the mission of the agency may be to manage public lands, the U.S. Bureau of Land Management must also be staffed to comply with Freedom of Information Act requests from media, citizens, and businesses.

Because of information transparency, failures become news, unlike business which is protected by its proprietary interests from revealing its shortcomings. And unlike business, there is no marketing budget to put the best spin on a mishap or to change the agency name and start over. What happens in government is public and is everyone's business. What happens in business is proprietary so information is sealed from public view.

Transparency adds cost to operations but does not translate into mission-based outcomes. Similarly, solicitation of public input requires staffing and procedures that add to the budget but do not align with direct costs for mission achievement. To add the cost of nonmission-based requirements is to escalate the cost of the program itself. In summary, extrinsic public values, like transparency, access to services, equity, representativeness, privacy, security, and safety are elusive to measure but always present.

THE QUALITIES AND WORK OF THE EXECUTIVE

Important traits for executives, whether in business, government, or nonprofits, include intelligence, both cognitive and emotional; self-confidence; decisiveness; a sense of humor, and humility. The ability to communicate; listen and learn, recognize problems, and delegate are also needed. But running a business is very different from heading an agency that employs hundreds to thousands of people, spends millions to billions of dollars, and confronts complex policy issues, many of which demand immediate attention. And while CEO's in business can usually make sure that their orders are carried out, in government the legislative branch—county commissions, city councils, state legislatures and Congress—foil the smooth chain of command.

Most public officials upon taking office, whether elected or appointed, find themselves in the midst of what feels like a rapidly moving stream. Processes are in motion from the past, planning has already occurred for the near future, and it can take years to achieve noticeable change. While newly seated public officials want to turn their rowboat around, they find themselves at the helm of an aircraft carrier. Time horizons become an important variable as they plan for the next budget cycle to rearrange spending priorities.

PUBLIC INTEGRITY

Expectations for how public servants comport themselves is higher than expectations for business officials. Everyone in public service has to be aware of how their actions are interpreted. The term public integrity refers to practicing responsible citizenship, avoiding conflicts of interest or commitment, and conducting oneself honorably with respect for others. It requires moral awareness, moral reasoning, and moral behavior, all in the context of the public interest and laws. The code of ethics for public administrators is explained on the next page. Created by the American Society for Public Administration, it is written broadly in order to be applicable to the great variety of jobs in public service.

In summary, managing public enterprises is different from managing private enterprises because of the purpose of the enterprise, the demands on the services, the power and fragmented panoply of stakeholders, the role of elections, the relationship between elected officials and career administrators, the expectations of how services are provided, how outcomes are measured, the amount of oversight, and the necessity to operate in

CODE OF ETHICS FOR PUBLIC ADMINISTRATORS[14]

1. **Advance the Public Interest.** Promote the interests of the public and put service to the public above service to oneself.

2. **Uphold the Constitution and the Law.** Respect and support government constitutions and laws, while seeking to improve laws and policies to promote the public good.

3. **Promote Democratic Participation.** Inform the public and encourage active engagement in governance. Be open, transparent and responsive, and respect and assist all persons in their dealings with public organizations.

4. **Strengthen Social Equity.** Treat all persons with fairness, justice, and equality and respect individual differences, rights, and freedoms. Promote affirmative action and other initiatives to reduce unfairness, injustice, and inequality in society.

5. **Fully Inform and Advise.** Provide accurate, honest, comprehensive, and timely information and advice to elected and appointed officials and governing board members, and to staff members in your organization.

6. **Demonstrate Personal Integrity.** Adhere to the highest standards of conduct to inspire public confidence and trust in public service.

7. **Promote Ethical Organizations.** Strive to attain the highest standards of ethics, stewardship, and public service in organizations that serve the public.

8. **Advance Professional Excellence.** Strengthen personal capabilities to act competently and ethically and encourage the professional development of others.

the sunshine. These considerations cut to the core of public management, to the point that, while some elements of management may be the same, the overall purpose, processes, stakeholders, and funding streams differ so substantially that they are different enterprises. The delays that are built into public action to ensure that government moves slowly will frustrate anyone who fails to understand that government and business exist for two different purposes and are guided by two very different sets of principles.

ECONOMY, EFFICIENCY, EFFECTIVENESS, AND EQUITY

While business and public service are both interested in economy, efficiency, and effectiveness, equity is a consideration that is of paramount importance in government. It is incumbent upon a democracy that prides itself on equality to attend to the inequality created by the U.S. economic system. The uneven ground puts opportunity out of the grasp of some while advantaging others.

Social equity—the distribution of fairness—is important because of the simultaneous tensions of a capitalist economy. This requires inequality, set within a democratic constitutional system, which assumes equality. It is impossible to simultaneously achieve both but the American myth that hard work is the vehicle to prosperity is a societal motivator and is powerful—so powerful, in fact, that throughout the twentieth century, it propelled economic development and a burgeoning middle class. But by the turn of the century, automation and global competition for low priced goods had stalled wages. The more interconnected the American economy became with the world economy, the less control it had over its own. The middle class, after fueling the economy for decades, began to erode and the erosion continues. This causes multiple problems: it stymies progress for those disadvantaged by the economy; it diminishes the tax base while increasing needs; it amplifies the contrast between high-end earners and low-end earners, causing ripple effects across the economy; and it produces a collective anxiety that is reflected in the nation's politics and the public's frustration that government is unable to make the problem go away.

Equity versus Equality

While equality means that equal parts are identical in size or number, equity is a more adaptable measure allowing for equivalency while not demanding exact sameness. For example, a child entering school who does not speak English is at a substantive disadvantage compared to her native English-speaking classmates. Though the entire class may receive equal instruction in language, the non-English-speaking student requires additional tutoring if her learning is to be equitable with that of her classmates. Despite the importance of equity, government enacts laws that insist on equality, such as in the case of the Fair Housing Act of 1968, which prohibits discrimination in the sale, rental, and financing of dwellings. This is because equality is easier to define than equity, which requires a sophisticated understanding of fairness and the conditions that give rise to unequal opportunity.

Social equity is an implicit rather than explicit constitutional value. It is a term that implies a calculation of fairness, right, and justice, all of which are notions that have both empirical and normative dimensions. It involves determinations of whether administrative systems operate impartially in the delivery of public services and it draws attention to the human factor in terms of economic fairness and advantage. As a concept, it evolved from social contract theory—the notion that people's political obligations are dependent on a contract among them to form the society in which they live. The views of John Locke and other Enlightenment thinkers were used to imbue the Constitution with the values of personal liberty and the pursuit of happiness, often interpreted to mean the right to own property. The Constitution, then, guides how government is to maintain these principles given the primacy of equality within a reality of inequality. The document is explicit about equality but leaves it up to administrative processes to secure equity.

Similar to the question of "who gets what?," social equity is an administrative concern of "who ought to get what?" and "for whom is this program good?" The American dream holds that those who study hard, work hard, and invest well will pull themselves up by their bootstraps and achieve all that is good. However, one study tracked 6,000 individuals born between 1942 and 1972. Almost half—42 percent—who were born into the bottom fifth of the income distribution ended up where they started—at the bottom. Only 7 percent of those born into the bottom fifth rose to the top tier—the rags-to-riches success story of American myth.[15] There are complex reasons why upward mobility is rare, ranging from economic forces too large to alter, poor education, poor job opportunities, and inadequate transportation, among a host of additional constraints, most of which are caused by a confluence of market forces and social forces. Inequality in the United States is significantly more pronounced than in most of its peer nations.[16]

Social equity is now a pillar of public administration alongside economy, efficiency, and effectiveness.[17, 18] As such, it has the capacity to frame deliberations, advance fairness, and monitor outcomes. These are its imperatives:

- procedural fairness, meaning due process, equal protection, and equal rights;
- equity in the availability of services and benefits;
- equity in the process of providing services and benefits;
- an equal level of outcomes for all groups; and
- the right to express views on policies, programs, and service delivery.

All five of these imperatives can be addressed through administrative processes. These concerns belong within the purview of public administration, for government is the entity of last resort when market and social dynamics create problems that do not resolve on their own. Policy debates about public education, access to health care, housing, food, water, and environmental justice all provide examples of the social equity frontier.

THE INTERDEPENDENCE OF GOVERNMENT AND NONPROFITS

In the United States there is an interdependence between government and nonprofit organizations. In the early 1800s Alexis de Tocqueville[19] traveled throughout the United States and observed how Americans governed themselves. In his classic work describing his observations, *Democracy in America*, he noted the frequency with which Americans created organizations to represent their views and to collectively pursue their interests, ranging from hobbies to political lobbying to delivering services. The role of nonprofits in supporting and advancing democracy was as substantial then as it is now.

Nonprofits exist to provide services that address the needs of the people they serve. In doing this, they empower their constituents and they have the potential to influence public policy. Because of their instrumental roles and their contribution to representation and to democracy, it.is in government's interest to encourage their work. It does this through preferential tax treatment that encourages charitable giving. Tax policy makes a distinction between sectors of the economy to differentiate taxpayer-funded entities (public), voluntary organizations (nonprofit), and business (private for-profit).

Government and nonprofits have a hand-in-glove relationship. Nonprofits have become the hands and feet of government in many respects with regard to how they crystallize public interests and represent them to government. Nonprofit think tanks and policy centers analyze data and contribute to policy debates. In addition, a substantial portion of health and human services are delivered by nonprofit organizations and a substantial portion of the funding that supports nonprofits is supplied by government.

Because the value of advancing the public interest aligns closely to the mission of government, there are many similarities between managing nonprofits and managing public organizations. And in contrast to government agencies, which are large and well-established with operating habits that are resistant to change, most nonprofits are small organizations that are nimble and can quickly adapt to changing funding streams and initiatives. Thus, it is in government's best interest to contract with nonprofits to deliver services that would otherwise need to be delivered by large bureaucracies whose processes are not conducive to the unique demands of startup programs or narrowly tailored programs.

LINGUISTICS OF THE FIELD

The language of public administration is nuanced. Throughout this chapter the terms *public service, public administration, public management, government,* and *governance* have been used and their meanings are similar in many respects. For example, the terms public administration and public management are often used interchangeably but in the most formal sense, public administration is a broader term than public management. Like flying at 30,000 feet rather than 10,000 feet, public administration refers to the agglomeration of politics, law, and management that combine to set policy and to implement, manage, and evaluate programs, all within constitutional parameters. Public management is a narrower term that focuses on the managerial work involved to transform policy into program.

Public service denotes the calling that is a profession. It denotes a commitment to public purposes and values. Thus, one studies public administration to pursue a profession of public service. Public service careers are concentrated in government and the nonprofit sector.

The term *government* refers to constitutionally created, taxpayer-funded operations of an executive, legislative, or judicial nature. The actions of government are guided by the rule of law. In contrast, the actions of the private sector are guided by market principles of supply and demand. The term *governance* is a broader term than government. It refers to the combination of authorities and interests that provide direction for communities. It usually involves government and nonprofits and business. For example, governance of cities involves formal government structures—the mayor's office, city council, city manager, and executive departments, joined by the business community—often represented by the Chamber of Commerce, a business-oriented nonprofit—as well as community-minded nonprofits.

Public administration, by its very nature, is contextual. The processes that guide the selection of administrators, the programs authorized, the manner in which they are delivered, and how they are evaluated must be consistent with deep-seated cultural values. This is why *governance* systems vary across nations. This text focuses on the U.S. system and describes the administrative system that results from its unique blend of political philosophy and social, religious, and economic trends.

Public Infrastructure

Government exists to do for people what needs to be done but which they cannot do themselves, either individually, or by voluntarily joining cooperative arrangements. The term *infrastructure* refers to all the systems necessary to ensure that communities thrive: roads, power grids, water lines, policing, education, and more. Building and maintaining the infrastructure is inherently political because of its publicness.

Federalism

The term *federalism* refers to the system of shared governmental powers. The Constitution specifies the powers of the national government and reserves all other powers to the states. This dispersion of power across levels of government creates a complex system but has the advantage of reserving power for the states. Federalism gives rise to *intergovernmental* relations, which refers to the links between governmental levels and jurisdictions encompassing federal, state, local, and regional connections.

Although there are exceptions to the rule, the federal government provides for: the national defense; regulates interstate commerce and monopolies that defy market dynamics; provides assistance to K–12 education; focuses on environmental protection; assists states and locales with transportation systems; cleans up after disastrous chemical pollution left by businesses; regulates the fiscal system and currency so that markets are stable; and provides safety net services to businesses whose failure risks too much economic hardship, among a panoply of other activities. States focus on services and regulatory procedures within their boundaries, serve as a conduit of federal funds to local communities, regulate the activities of local jurisdictions, and maintain a court system. Cities, counties, and school districts provide the predominance of street-level services: police and fire protection; emergency medical services; K–12 education; parks and recreation; public health services; planning and zoning; and economic development, among others.

Special districts are created in local areas to fund and provide services to defined geographic areas that span metropolitan boundaries. They are used primarily for fire protection, water and sewer, parks and recreation, and the arts.

Intersectoral Networks

The term *intersectoral* refers to links between business, government, and nonprofits. To a large degree, networked services derive from intergovernmental and intersectoral collaborations. Terminology changes as the focus shifts from entities, such as jurisdictions and agencies, to the links that connect them. Networks refer to the linkages among entities that are brought to bear to address public problems. They may involve organizations and jurisdictions such as: federal and/or state agencies; cities and/or counties; nonprofit organizations and/or businesses. For example, on the domestic scene, the federal government sends funds directly to states and communities to disperse for specific services. At the same time, foundations and nonprofit organizations match funds and enhance service delivery. This happens in all venues, from the local level to the international scene, such as at the United Nations and the organizations it has created. For example, the World Health Organization (WHO) and United Nations Educational, Scientific, and Cultural Organization (UNESCO) span the globe with programs.

While for-profit firms have contracted with government since the nation's founding, they are predominantly used to provide services that are time-limited, require a special expertise, or require an investment in equipment that is not efficient for government to provide. Examples include garbage collection, information and communication technology (ICT) services, and low-skilled labor such as groundskeepers.

Large forces shape public initiatives. In the early 1900s, urbanization gave rise to urban poverty and the need for housing and employment. Government relied on churches and civic organizations to respond to these needs until the problems became so expensive that nonprofits could not meet the need. At that point, the problems fell to government. The twenty-first century brings the debate about marketization of services to the point that social enterprises are increasing in number. These are hybrid organizations that blend philanthropy with for-profit goals. They differ from business in that the mission has a social good focus and they differ from philanthropy in that they may be structured as a for-profit enterprise. In sum, as problems grow or recede, systems develop to address them. Networks of service providers have done this for over a century and continue to evolve. This develops an ever larger set of intersectoral networks.

Ask Me Why I Care: Rita Paskowitz, professional storyteller and advocate for public service[20]

Rita Paskowitz is a professional storyteller who wrote "Ode to Public Service." It is a story that celebrates the many ways that people in every community rely daily on public service and the diversity of those who deliver it. Watch her perform the story at https://www.youtube.com/watch?v=7OphiwFIc7I.

SUMMARY

Public service has many dimensions. It reaches all aspects of life and involves all kinds of skills. From the engineering skills required in public works projects to the legal skills required in jurisprudence; to the interpersonal skills required of caseworkers to the sharpshooter skills of tactical squads; to the health-care skills of emergency medical response teams to the Information and Communication Technology (ICT) skills necessary to develop and maintain complex information systems; and to the management skills required of county administrators, opportunities in public service are endless. Regardless of one's technical skills, administrative prowess is necessary to coordinate the work of many to produce desired outcomes for the public good. To achieve these ends, running a constitution requires drawing expertise and perspectives from all disciplines, including political science, law, management, sociology, economics, health care, education, engineering, information technology, psychology, and anthropology, all to address the varied problems that come to government and the many programs that it operates.

Just as opportunities are many, so are the challenges. A vision for a better tomorrow relies on trust. For government to function well, the governed must have confidence that their interests are taken into account, tax dollars are spent as intended, public goals are being met, and that help is on the way when an emergency strikes, such as with the Aurora theater shooting. Guided by ideals of shared community and engagement, public administration relies on civic engagement and works broadly across businesses, nonprofits, and government agencies at the national, state, and local levels. Constructive connectedness—not silos—requires responsible self-governance.

The goal is to responsibly facilitate constitutional democracy through resilient governance. The means for doing so resides in a professionally expert workforce and requires confidence in people and public institutions. America's transformation from its founding by the landed gentry into a broadly inclusive society demonstrates the capacity for the field's professionals to be catalysts in a disciplined search for human dignity and reasonableness.

The public infrastructure for this symphony remains a work in progress. How to engage citizens? How to harness the power of the Internet without sacrificing privacy? How to deliver programs economically, efficiently, effectively, and equitably? How to set benchmarks and measure outcomes for program delivery? How to ensure transparency? How to support markets while ensuring fair competition? All these and more are the questions that confront public service professionals. The answers evolve as each generation builds on the strengths of the past while repairing mistakes and nudging the system forward.

KEY TERMS

Capitalism – a system where the economy is maintained by private interests for profit, instead of being controlled by the state; it requires inequality, where the minority who own businesses employ the majority who work for them.

Democracy – government run by the will of the people.

Intergovernmental relations – the links and interaction across governmental levels and between jurisdictions encompassing federal, state, local, and regional entities.

Intersectoral relations – "intersectoral" refers to links between business, government, and nonprofits; intersectoral collaboration creates networks between sectors that are funded from a variety of sources.

Governance – the combination of authorities and interests that provide direction for communities usually involving government, nonprofits, and business.

Government – constitutionally created, taxpayer-funded operations of an executive, legislative, or judicial nature.

Nonprofits – organizations that provide services that address the needs of the public, empower their constituents, and potentially influence public policy.

Public administration – the agglomeration of politics, law, and management that combine to set policy and to implement, manage, and evaluate programs, all within constitutional parameters.

Public integrity – practicing responsible citizenship, avoiding conflicts of interest or commitment, and conducting oneself honorably with respect to others; requires moral awareness, moral reasoning, moral behavior, all in the context of the public interest and laws.

Public management – the managerial work involved to transform policy into program.

Public service – both an enterprise and a profession; as an enterprise, it is the pursuit of public purposes. As a profession, it is a calling committed to the public interest and is referred to as public administration.

Social equity – the distribution of fairness.

DISCUSSION QUESTIONS

1. Explain what "public service" means.
2. Think of an example of how the public versus private debate arises in local government.
3. List three differences between government and business.
4. Why is social equity referred to as the fourth pillar of public administration?
5. Give an example of how government and nonprofits work interdependently.

BUILD YOUR SKILLS

Whether communicating a directive, clarifying a procedural issue, or making policy recommendations, the memorandum is the ideal format. Use these tips the next time you write a memo.

SKILLBOX: HOW TO WRITE A MEMORANDUM

Memoranda are the most frequently used form of formal communication in organizations. A good memo is brief and to the point. The usual elements are heading, opening, context, task, discussion, and closing. Whether the subject is a management directive or a policy recommendation, the structure works equally well. Here is the format:

Heading
TO: (name and job title)
FROM: (sender's name and job title)
DATE:
SUBJECT: (Be specific, concise, and unambiguous)

Opening
State the purpose of the memo. Be direct and explicit. Convey information in a clear, concise manner.

Context

Specify the event, circumstance, or background of the problem being addressed. Use a few sentences to establish the background and state the problem. Calibrate the level of technical detail to the reader's knowledge base.

Task

Describe the specific action without being too wordy. Include only as much information as is needed.

Discussion

The discussion segment includes the details that support the message of the memo. Winnow the material to the key points.

Closing

Close with a courteous ending that states what action the reader should take.

Attachments as necessary

Provide supporting information or detailed findings in appendices.

Editing

Before you send, edit and edit again. Nothing undercuts the message more than careless phrasing and stylistic errors. Ask a colleague to review it. A different perspective will uncover ambiguous statements and unclear assumptions.

Hands-On Activity: Write a Memo to the Professor

Write a memorandum to your professor and explain why it is important for public managers to know how to craft an effective memo.

NOTES

1. For the full report, see TriData Division and System Planning Corporation, *Aurora Century 16 Theater Shooting: After Action Report for the City of Aurora* (April 2014), https://www.courts.state.co.us/Media/Opinion_Docs/14CV31595%20After%20Action%20Review%20Report%20Redacted.pdf.

2. This expression was used by Zechariah Chafee in 1919 to explain the limits of free speech. See Zechariah Chafee, "Freedom in Speech in War Time," *Harvard Law Review* 32, no. 8 (1919): 932–73.

3. Scott A. Cook and William Earle Klay, "George Washington's Precedents: The Institutional Legacy of the American Republic's Founding Public Administrator," *Administration & Society* 47, no. 1 (2015): 77.

4. The Civil Rights Acts of 1866, 1871, 1875, 1957, 1960, 1964, 1968, 1987, and 1991.

5. Woodrow Wilson, "Study of Administration," *Political Science Quarterly* 2, no. 2 (June 1887): 197–222.

6. In 1936, Harold Lasswell argued that the central question of governing is "who gets what?" See Harold D. Lasswell, *Who Gets What, When, How* (New York: Whittlesey House, 1936).

7. POSDCORB was coined by Luther Gulick in 1936 to capture the managerial functions of the executive. See Luther Gulick, "Notes on the Theory of Organization," in *Papers on the Science of Administration,* ed. Luther Gulick and Lyndall Urwick (New York: Institute of Public Administration, 1937), 3–35.

8. Herbert Simon, *Models of Man* (New York: John Wiley & Sons, 1957).

9. Paul Appleby, *Policy and Administration* (Tuscaloosa, AL: University of Alabama Press, 1949).

10. "Flint Water Crisis: A Timeline," *MSNBC* (February 4, 2016), http://www.msnbc.com/msnbc/flint-water-crisis-timeline.

11. Brandi Blessett, "Water: A Privilege or a Right," *PA Times* (February 5, 2016), http://patimes.org/water-privilege-right/.

12. Claire Groden, "How Michigan's Bureaucrats Created the Flint Water Crisis," *Fortune* (January 2016), http://fortune.com/flint-water-crisis/.

13. Dana Milbank, "The Flint Disaster Is Rick Snyder's Fault," *Washington Post* (January 25, 2016), https://www.washingtonpost.com/opinions/the-flint-disaster-is-rick-snyders-fault/2016/01/25/9c77e036-c3b1-11e5-a4aa-f25866ba0dc6_story.html.

14. This code is developed by the American Society for Public Administration. Available at https://www.aspanet.org/ASPA/Code-of-Ethics/ASPA/Code-of-Ethics/Code-of-Ethics .aspx?hkey=5b8f046b-dcbd-416d-87cd-0b8fcfacb5e7.

15. Bernard Wasow, *Rags to Riches? The American Dream Is Less Common in the United States Than Elsewhere* (New York: The Century Foundation, 2004), http://www.tcf.org /assets/downloads/tcf-ragrichrc.pdf.

16. OECDilibrary, *Income Inequality (Indicator)* (2016), http://www.oecd-ilibrary.org/ social-issues-migration-health/income-inequality/indicator/english_459aa7f1-en.

17. Norman J. Johnson and James H. Svara, *Justice for All: Promoting Social Equity in Public Administration* (Armonk, NY: M.E. Sharpe, 2011).

18. James H. Svara and J.R. Brunet, "Social Equity Is a Pillar of Public Administration," *Journal of Public Affairs Education* 11, no. 3 (2005): 253–58.

19. Alexis de Tocqueville, *Democracy in America*, trans. Harvey Mansfield and Delba Winthrop (Chicago, IL: University of Chicago Press, [1835], 2000).

20. Rita Paskowitz, "Ode to Public Service," published October 23 2014, available at https://www.youtube.com/watch?v=7OphiwFIc7I.

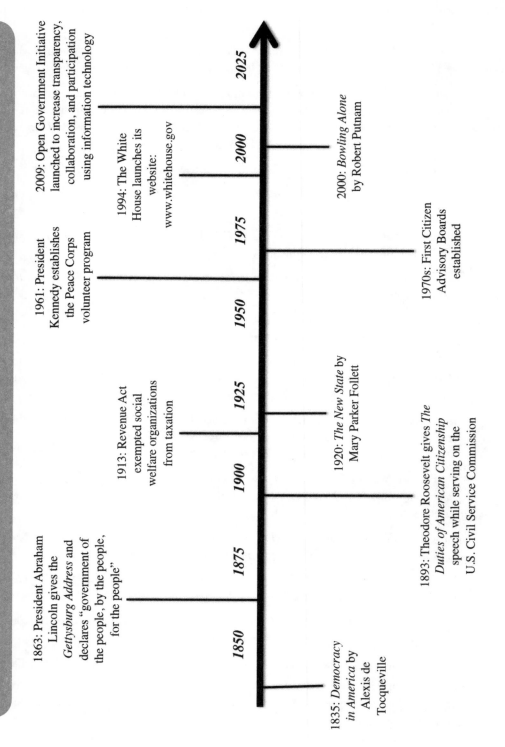

Chapter 2 Timeline: Citizen Engagement

1835: *Democracy in America* by Alexis de Tocqueville

1863: President Abraham Lincoln gives the *Gettysburg Address* and declares "government of the people, by the people, for the people"

1893: Theodore Roosevelt gives *The Duties of American Citizenship* speech while serving on the U.S. Civil Service Commission

1913: Revenue Act exempted social welfare organizations from taxation

1920: *The New State* by Mary Parker Follett

1961: President Kennedy establishes the Peace Corps volunteer program

1970s: First Citizen Advisory Boards established

1994: The White House launches its website: www.whitehouse.gov

2000: *Bowling Alone* by Robert Putnam

2009: Open Government Initiative launched to increase transparency, collaboration, and participation using information technology

1850   1875   1900   1925   1950   1975   2000   2025

CITIZEN ENGAGEMENT

WHAT YOU WILL LEARN

Why citizen engagement matters

Forms of engagement

Coproduction

Soliciting viewpoints

Skillbox: Effective public speaking

Citizen engagement is essential for a democracy to function. When Abraham Lincoln described American government as "of the people, by the people, and for the people," he was emphasizing the active engagement of citizens in the pursuit of public purposes. Although that was in 1863 as he delivered the Gettysburg Address, the words are as true today as then. To own the actions of government, the populace must be engaged in the processes that govern them. A strong democracy relies on active civic engagement. That was the intent of the founders as they crafted the Constitution and it remains an imperative today. Law enforcement cannot enforce unless citizens respect the law; schools cannot educate in the absence of a readiness to learn; government cannot provide services without adequate resources; civil relationships do not develop in the absence of respect for one another.

A century ago, management theorist Mary Parker Follett[1] wrote about the importance of citizen engagement in urban neighborhoods. In *The New State,* she encouraged public participation in governance matters, neighborhood activism, and the development of community spaces as areas to meet, share ideas, and engage in dialogue about issues of common interest. More recently, in his book *Bowling Alone,*[2] Robert Putnam lamented that people are less engaged in public matters than they should be or had been in the past. His argument drew attention to the importance of *social capital,* which refers to the social norms and social structures that emerge and guide individual behavior toward communal ends. Both of these books focus on the importance of social capital as the missing link that cements communities or explains their failure.

Whether at the U.S. Department of Transportation or in neighborhoods across the country, effective public service both enhances social capital and relies on it. The goal is to achieve maximum feasible participation of stakeholders in policy deliberation, program planning and operations, and evaluation of outcomes. This means that as many constituencies as possible should be involved in decision making. But as the following case of the U.S. Department of Transportation demonstrates, each constituency brings with it an added dimension and added complexity.

ENGAGING THE PUBLIC AT THE U.S. DEPARTMENT OF TRANSPORTATION

In response to the 2009 Open Government Directive, a presidential directive to federal agencies to improve transparency and to integrate public participation and collaboration into their activities, the U.S. Department of Transportation (DOT) used web-based online dialogues to engage citizens in the agency's strategic planning process.[3] An example occurred in 2013 when DOT hosted a two-week dialogue as it developed its 2014–2018 strategic plan. To do this, it used a social networking site platform to engage groups and individual citizens in a review of the draft plan. This software provided easy access to documents and enabled site visitors to propose their own ideas, to comment on others, and to vote for ideas they liked.

To encourage participation, the agency announced the dialogue in advance by e-mailing people who were known to have an interest in transportation policy and who had participated in public meetings hosted by the agency in recent years. This target group included more than 1,160 in-dividuals from approximately 900 organizations. Among these were state departments of transportation, metropolitan planning organizations and municipal governments, along with a number of advocacy groups. Invitations to participate were also communicated in the transportation secretary's blog and by administrative units throughout the agency.

During the dialogue, 3,400 individuals visited the site, 993 individuals registered to participate, and 551 registered users cast 3,500 votes for ideas under deliberation. Individuals representing government agencies, advocacy groups, and professional or industry trade associations accounted for 54 percent of registrants. When considered cumulatively, results suggested that participation was widespread and far broader than the original target group. Regardless, individuals affiliated with a few advocacy organizations, such as the Coalition for Recreational Trails and the League of American Bicyclists, submitted about one-third of all the ideas. These intermediaries had mobilized their members to participate in disproportionately high numbers.

While DOT's strategic goals did not substantively change based on the input, a number of corrections and additions to the strategic plan resulted. Additionally, the response from targeted groups was helpful although many of the comments they submitted focused only on a single concern and did not address the entire scope of the plan. The responses from the bicycling and recreational trails communities, as well as advocates for more access to transportation for disabled persons and expanded opportunities for women in the transportation workforce were key contributors to the high number of votes received.

In retrospect, agency managers were unsure the responses reflected a balanced view of all transportation stakeholders despite the large number of participants. The software made it easy for visitors to simply register their vote without taking time to submit comments. "Drive by participation" such as this results when online participants register their votes but do not post comments that explain their views. Managers concluded that the simplicity of merely voting actually hindered dialogue and thoughtful deliberation.

An important lesson was learned by DOT: To overcome the problem of too little deliberation, the focus should be less on increasing the number of participants and more on ensuring representativeness and quality of the dialogue. More usable results would have been yielded by engaging with stakeholders at an earlier stage in the strategic planning process before a first draft of the plan was written and using face-to-face and online venues. Social networking sites are best when complementary rather than substitutes for traditional methods of citizen engagement, such as roundtable discussions or town hall meetings.

The case of DOT's effort to engage the public in its strategic planning process demonstrates the challenges that administrators face as they encourage engagement and responsiveness. By employing social media to maximize its outreach and timeliness, success was achieved in reaching a large number of people who cared about the agency's plans. The case also demonstrates the role of nonprofit advocacy groups as they mobilized members to express their views. At the end of the day, however, the agency was left to ponder questions of representativeness. Who had not participated? Might their views be different from those who expressed views? Determining the best type of engagement—face-to-face versus online—and soliciting views in a way that is representative of all those affected by the agency's actions requires thoughtful choices, because participation is an essential ingredient in public administration.

Questions to Ponder

1. What worked well in this example of citizen engagement?

2. Why is representativeness an important element when soliciting feedback from the public?

3. What are the administrative costs and benefits for agencies as they solicit public opinion?

WHY CITIZEN ENGAGEMENT MATTERS

There are many reasons why citizen engagement is an essential ingredient in good government. These range from issues of social capital to the mechanics of governing and include these purposes:

(1) to practice democratic principles and citizenship behavior;
(2) to create resilient communities;
(3) to build commitment for programs;
(4) to enlist coproduction;
(5) to develop creative solutions to public problems;
(6) to avoid policy failure; and
(7) to keep public processes and services tightly linked to the people being served.

To Practice Democratic Principles and Citizenship Behavior

The theory of democracy states that people involve themselves in decisions that influence public action and they care about the delivery and evaluation of public services. Because the size of the nation and the scope of government is huge, representative rather than direct democracy is used. This means that representatives speak and act on behalf of the public, rather than all citizens making decisions. Acting as agents of the public, representation comes in a number of forms. It includes lawmakers elected to seats on city councils, county commissions, state legislatures and Congress, as well as executives elected as mayors, governors, and the president of the United States. It also includes citizens elected to school boards, public service commissions, and a variety of other boards and commissions. Representation also comes in the form of office-holders who are appointed to their posts by elected officials. Additionally, public interest groups speak with a collective voice on behalf of their members. Within the executive branch, representation is delegated from the elected official to appointed agency heads and then to career officials who manage and deliver public services. These officials are responsible for transforming policy decisions into programs, setting the rules by which services will be administered, and managing and evaluating operations so that they are as efficient, effective, and equitable as possible.

Practicing democratic principles takes many forms. At the least, it involves "drive-by participation" in the form of voting for representatives. At best, it means being a partner in the processes of governing. Active engagement on the part of the public through participation in public deliberations and volunteering in the delivery of public services—coproduction—provides a vehicle for the public to practice citizenship behavior. Compliance with decisions reached through majority votes and coproduction of civil society through compliance with traffic rules, signage, and zoning ordinances, for example, are symbolic of practicing democracy and adhering to the rule of law.

Both action and compliance are part of the American mantra. In 1883, long before he became president, Theodore Roosevelt delivered a speech called "The Duties of American Citizenship." In it, he exhorted listeners to participate in public purposes and to be engaged in civic activities, saying:

> If freedom is worth having, if the right of self-government is a valuable right, then the one and the other must be retained exactly as our forefathers acquired them, by labor, and especially by labor in organization, that is in combination with our fellows who have the same interests and the same principles.[4]

To Create Resilient Communities

Resilience is the capacity for a community to absorb disturbance and rebuild, literally or figuratively, while undergoing dramatic change. The goal of sustainability efforts is to achieve resilience, which requires that communities, states, and the nation have the resources, both social and fiscal, to withstand crises and prolonged periods of stress. When neighbors help neighbors, social bonds are strengthened. When residents trust that government officials are acting on behalf of their best interests, public agencies can pursue their missions unimpeded by wariness. When citizens and their government work hand-in-glove, the coproduction that results is constructive and extends the capacity of government to deliver services that residents want. Trust and a willingness to help—to lean in—creates social bonds; this is the cement in resilient communities. The case of policing in Akron, Ohio provides an example of how engagement with the public leads to positive outcomes.

COMMUNITY POLICING IN AKRON, OHIO

More than 50 percent of black citizens in the United States report that police officers have treated them unfairly, compared to just 3 percent of whites.[5] The case of Akron, Ohio is emblematic of this. Only 40 percent of black residents say they trust the police, compared to 70 percent of whites. The Akron Police Department (APD) has strategically aimed to increase citizen engagement to overcome this trend. They use *community policing*, "a philosophy that promotes organizational strategies that support the systematic use of partnerships and problem-solving techniques to proactively address the immediate conditions that give rise to public safety issues such as crime, social disorder, and fear of crime."[6]

Police–community partnerships are valued. A message from Chief of Police James Nice on the APD's webpage states: "Our mission is to serve the community of Akron in a *collaborative effort* to enhance the quality of life through crime prevention, enforcement of laws, promotion of safety, and reduction of fear" (emphasis added).[7] The APD's core values emphasize positive relations based on six attributes: honesty, integrity, fairness, competence, trust, and respect.

Several programs have been implemented to advance the APD's goal. The Mayor's Office of Community Relations established Akron Peacemakers to engage youth and police. They offer workshops on citizens' rights, emergency resources, and proper conduct with officers. The Peacemakers have had success and received the 2015 American Society for Public Administration's (ASPA) Equal Opportunity/Affirmative Action Exemplary Practices Award.[8]

A related summer initiative called Police and Youth Together enhances relations between officers and young boys and girls of color. Similar adult programs include the "Hoops with Cops" Community Basketball Tournament[9] between officers and citizens, and Community Oriented Policing Services (COPS), which is a collaboration with residents to identify problem areas in the city. Such programs show how police can partner with citizens to build trust and coproduce public safety.

As the case of Akron shows, the bonds of trust created through face-to-face interaction between police and the public build resiliency. As the public and the police develop rapport, there is increased likelihood that the community is better equipped to overcome future problems.

To Build Commitment for Programs

Unlike in business, where customers buy a product and then exit the store, government requires a foundation of engaged citizens. In fact, Cheryl King's book,[10] *Government Is Us 2.0*, reminds readers that commitment and engagement are the qualities that create communities. With citizenship comes responsibilities, including the right to be informed and the obligation to lend a hand when necessary. At the same time, people have a right to expect accessible, navigable systems that work when they need government's help. In other words, citizen engagement is a two-way street. Government is the instrument citizens use to ensure their safety and to secure services that are not provided elsewhere. Because citizens are stakeholders as well as arbiters of government action, their involvement in decisions that will affect them is essential, for they own the outcomes of those decisions. Government programs only work well when the public is committed to them. Otherwise, services lack the support that is necessary for people to have confidence in them and in the workers who deliver them. The commitment of the public is the most important resource that governments have. One of the several advantages of engaging the public in planning processes, such as used by the DOT, is that by the act of their participation, stakeholders are more likely to understand and accept the agency's actions.

To Enlist Coproduction

Government relies on the public not only to fund programs but to help deliver services. There will never be enough financial largesse for agencies to deliver all the services the public would like. But neither is it necessary to do so. Some services lend themselves to voluntary action, such as the work in public education that parent-teacher associations provide in the form of fundraising and sponsored activities. Managing elections is another public activity that lends itself to coproduction. Election offices cannot afford to be staffed year round for services that are rendered only on an annual, biennial, or quadrennial basis. Instead, a few full-time workers train volunteers as each election nears and then precinct polling places and ballot drop-off stations are staffed by volunteer poll workers. Other examples include reliance on volunteer firefighters by small communities, as described below, who cannot afford full-time fire departments. Volunteers work full-time jobs elsewhere but are on call to respond as the need arises. These examples in education, elections, and firefighting show how coproduction extends the work of government by relying on the efforts of the public. On a more widespread basis, compliance with laws is a form of coproduction in which the public, by complying with laws, maintains civic life and safe communities.

VOLUNTEER FIREFIGHTERS

About two-thirds of the approximate 1,134,000 firefighters in the United States are volunteers and of these, 95 percent are affiliated with departments that protect fewer than 25,000 residents. A volunteer fire department is funded by taxes raised in a city, town, county, or fire district, along with donations and grants. With these funds the department acquires and operates the firefighting apparatus, equips and trains firefighters, maintains the firehouse, and covers insurance, worker's compensation, and other post-injury or retirement benefits. Estimates are that reliance on volunteers saves local governments $140 billion annually in pay, benefits, operating, and maintenance costs.[11] The training that volunteer firefighters receive varies by jurisdiction. They may be trained as generalists or as specialists for fighting structure fires, wildland fires, swift water rescue, hazardous materials response, or vehicle extrication.

A volunteer fire department is reached by calling 911, which is the same way as other emergency services are accessed. The dispatcher reaches the firefighters through texting, radioing, or a fire siren. Although the average response times may be a little longer than with full-time services because the members must come from different distances to the incident, the services are present and available and have worked since the nation began.

Table 2.1 lists other coproduction behaviors and notes how they benefit residents individually while at the same time benefiting communities.

TABLE 2.1. How Coproduction Benefits Individuals and Communities

Coproduction Behavior	Policy Area	Individual Benefit	Collective Benefit
Solid waste Recycling	Environment	Raises environmental consciousness	Reduces cost of waste disposal
Vaccinations	Health	Protects individuals from preventable diseases	Diminishes the spread of disease
Exercise	Health	Increases personal health	Reduces health-care costs
Neighborhood watch program	Safety	Protects personal property	Reduces crime rate
Obeying traffic laws without law enforcement presence	Safety	Prevents personal injury from accidents	Reduces rate of accidents

To Develop Creative Solutions for Public Problems

Many public problems are interconnected and do not fit neatly into one agency's mission compared to another's. In these cases, agencies work collaboratively to develop solutions and often creative solutions are achieved by involving as many varied interests as possible. As with the case of DOT engaging the public in its strategic planning process, the goal is to reach beyond agency borders to realize innovation.

Diverse viewpoints are essential. Diversity refers to differentness in race, religion, age, gender, ethnicity, socioeconomic status, and physical ability. Additionally, there are intersections of differentness, such as gender and race and socioeconomic status. All combinations and descriptions bring different life experiences and perspectives to bear on policy deliberations, program design, and evaluations of effectiveness. The case of the greater sage-grouse demonstrates a blend of coproduction and innovation. It sprang from the collaboration of public agencies whose mission is to preserve endangered species and manage public lands; state, county, and city governments whose interest is to preserve their tax base; tribes, ranchers, and farmers whose interest is in economic security and perpetuating life as they have lived it for generations; and businesses whose interest is in maintaining their markets.

As the Bureau of Land Management and the Forest Service transition to the imple-

PROTECTING GREATER SAGE-GROUSE

A chicken-sized bird native to the western plains, the greater sage-grouse was declared to be on a path to extinction because of loss of habitat across an eleven-state area. The usual process is for prescriptive federal regulation to be adopted. However, a diverse group of stakeholders collaborated in a multistate decision-making process with a two-pronged goal: to save the bird from potential extinction while avoiding rigorous federal regulation. Their strategy was to protect the bird's habitat without having to add it to the endangered species list, which would have severely restricted any further development that could impinge on the bird's habitat. Their effort succeeded when, in 2015, the U.S. Fish and Wildlife Service announced that the greater sage-grouse did not warrant listing under the Endangered Species Act (ESA). This decision resulted from extraordinary collaboration across the American West.[12] It was a remarkable and welcome evolution from the agency's determination five years earlier that the species would warrant protection due to the fragmentation of its sagebrush habitat and the lack of regulatory mechanisms to control habitat loss.

The greater sage-grouse is often referred to as a landscape-scale species.[13] This means that it needs large areas of undisturbed habitat to thrive. Current research estimates the minimum necessary area for a lek (mating area) of birds to survive is approximately fifty-square miles, an area roughly the size of the city of Pittsburgh. With an estimated 3,000 active leks in existence,[14] an ESA listing had the potential for significant impacts to the economy because of the amount of land that

would have to be set aside. Ranchers, farmers, and oil and gas drilling would experience significant impacts, upstaging the culture, quality of life, and economy of western communities.

When the Fish and Wildlife Service first declared that the greater sage-grouse warranted protection, workgroups and task forces across the West went to work to forestall such dramatic change. Federal agencies, states, counties, regional interests, and private landowners formed workgroups and task forces to review existing conservation plans. Their goal was to find ways to protect the habitat for greater sage-grouse without placing the bird on the endangered species list and thereby having to remove valuable lands and resources from the economy. This included the establishment of a state/federal Sage-Grouse Task Force in 2011 at the initiative of the Secretary of the U.S. Department of the Interior. The Task Force was co-led by the governors of Wyoming and Colorado.[15] Its charge was to provide coordination and leadership at the federal and state levels across the entire geographic range of the species.

An example of the collaboration that resulted was the updating of ninety-eight U.S. Bureau of Land Management and U.S. Forest Service land use plans in ten western states. Working in concert with each other, the Bureau of Land Management and Forest Service conducted fifteen separate yet coordinated projects to update the plans. The updated plans incorporated greater sage-grouse habitat conservation measures on over eleven million acres of publicly managed lands, which represents approximately 50 percent of the habitat used by the birds.[16] It was through the sustained and multitiered collaborative work of federal agencies, states, counties, tribes, public land users, and private land owners that the planning process was a success.

In a routine land use planning update process, the Bureau of Land Management and Forest Service staff work with a broad array of stakeholders. This includes Resource Advisory Councils, which are comprised of ranchers, environmental groups, tribes, state, county, and city officials, academics, and other public land users;[17] cooperating agencies; tribes that may be affected; and comments from the public at large. Due to the enormous scale of the greater sage-grouse effort, however, the processes were even more extensive. In fact, they were unprecedented. Collectively, they involved approximately fifteen Resource Advisory Councils; roughly 250 cooperating agencies representing federal, state, local, and tribal agencies and governments; formal consultation with approximately seventy-five separate federally recognized tribes; and review of 7,500 comments from the public.[18]

The collaboration was a huge administrative undertaking. To engage all stakeholders and to ensure consistency across the planning efforts and the geographic range of the species, the Bureau of Land Management and Forest Service established several interagency and multistate governance teams that coordinated efforts and provided oversight. Senior managers from the federal Departments of Interior and Agriculture, Bureau of Land Management, Forest Service, Fish and Wildlife Service, and the Natural Resources Conservation Service, formed a combination of hierarchical, geographic, and intersecting teams. The teams provided overall policy, guidance, coordination and consistency to the effort. They also provided technical and scientific advice. And, teams researched, analyzed, and wrote the specific plans.[19] The work of the plan writers was supplemented by specialists across the federal and state agencies as well as a network of contractors.

mentation phase of greater sage-grouse protection, the need for collaboration remains essential. As part of its decision to not list the greater sage-grouse under the Endangered Species Act, the U.S. Fish and Wildlife Service committed itself to conduct a five-year status review of the species. The review in 2020 will provide a test of whether this unprecedented collaboration was successful and whether the political will remains to keep it in force.

Despite the extensive and complicated administrative structure that was required for planning to take place and for consensus to develop, stakeholders agreed to participate because everyone wanted to avoid having to place the bird on the endangered species list. The effort was monumental but is now heralded as a major breakthrough in civic engagement toward a common end: to preserve an animal in danger of extinction while preserving the stakeholders' way of life. The collaboration resulted in the federal government being a collaborator and monitor, rather than a rule-maker.

To Avoid Policy Failure

Even when resources are adequate and plans seem logical, public programs will fail if the public does not accept them. There must be commitment to the goals of the program and public trust in the actions of government. The link between public opinion, prescribed action, and compliance will fail without an engaged public. The next example demonstrates the action that government had to take to fight disease. The goal was to prevent an outbreak of tuberculosis, a contagious and potentially fatal disease thought to have been eradicated.

As the tuberculosis (TB) case in Alabama demonstrates, it is difficult to engage citizens who do not trust government. In this case, government used an innovative practice to encourage people to be tested. Paying citizens was an expensive undertaking, but it was efficient in the long run because it prevented further contagion. The goal of effective

PAYING TO COMBAT TUBERCULOSIS

Since 2014, three people died of TB in the small, poor town of Marion, Alabama. In proportion to the population, this is an outbreak worse than in many developing countries. The state health department met resistance when it investigated the cases. Victims would not reveal with whom they had come into contact so tracking the infection was not possible. And the rest of the 3,500 townspeople did not want to get tested. To entice them, the department held a health fair with free food and drinks. But turnout was small and hostile: townspeople threw bottles at the health workers. Tuberculosis was largely eradicated by the latter 1900s but in recent years it has been reappearing among poor people. In the town of Marion, one-third of its residents live below the poverty line and almost two-thirds are African-American.

When traditional approaches to combatting the outbreak did not work in Marion, health officials had to innovate: They paid people to get tested. Anyone who came for a blood test was paid $20, and then they were paid another $20 for returning to get their results. If they tested positive, treatment was prescribed. Another $20 was awarded for X-ray follow-ups, with $100 for finishing medication treatment. During the pay-for-testing period, more than 2,000 people were tested. Of those, 151 tested positive for TB and three active cases were caught. Alabama has stopped paying people to get tested for TB, but the public health department still offers free testing to anyone who makes an appointment. The state health department funded the project with a grant from the U.S. Centers for Disease Control and Prevention.[20]

engagement is that citizens trust government so that such extreme measures are not necessary. In the absence of trust, innovation—and often additional expense—is required.

To Keep Public Processes and Services Tightly Linked to the People Being Served

Cynicism of the public toward government helps no one. It diminishes trust in government and makes it harder for public officials to work collaboratively with the public. A tight linkage helps to prevent or overcome cynicism, just as the city of Akron's police department knows. The case of the Marion, Alabama health department's efforts to combat an outbreak of tuberculosis demonstrates that policy failure and cynicism go hand in hand. The absence of engagement breeds cynicism, where the public feels disengaged and powerless with regard to government action. Even when government uses its power to help citizens and be responsive to their needs, it is difficult to convince those who are cynical. Good performance and effective communication of that performance will address a cynical public but the effort takes time and consistency.

For all these reasons—to practice democratic principles, create resiliency, build commitment, enlist coproduction, solve public problems, avoid policy failure, and to link public processes to the people being served—government accomplishes its work through public agencies. Known collectively as the bureaucracy, agencies have a checkered image in the public's mind. As a whole, they can seem to be faceless creations over which the public have little authority. For executing the public will, the debate persists about how to reconcile the demands of democracy, which assumes individual autonomy, and hierarchical process-driven agencies. This leads to perennial questions about democracy versus bureaucracy.

DEMOCRACY AND BUREAUCRACY

The relationship between democracy and bureaucracy has been tense since the nation's founding. While democracy requires equality, bureaucracy—the term for hierarchical formal organization—requires deference to authority, lack of autonomy, restricted control, and formalized rules and processes. Moreover, organizational routines tend to cause instrumentalist thinking, focusing more inward than outward. This risks overlooking the perspectives of constituencies they are created to serve. As part of the bureaucracy, public managers are the bridges between their own organization and the public being served. The human face is put on bureaucracy by those who work at the street level—the street-level bureaucrat—who are instrumental in developing a rapport between the state and the citizen. Street-level bureaucrats are those who have face-to-face interactions with residents. In the case of city government, police officers are the face of government to many residents. The case of Akron, Ohio shows how this face is being humanized through personal outreach. A contrasting example occurred in Ferguson, Missouri in 2014.

The case of how citizens experienced law enforcement practices in Ferguson, Missouri shows what can happen when residents of a community feel isolated from those in government. After the tumult that resulted from the police shooting of Michael Brown, an unarmed eighteen-year-old black man, the Civil Rights Division of the U.S. Department of Justice (DOJ) investigated the circumstances of the shooting and the cries of outrage that followed. As the DOJ summary demonstrates, the lack of trust between African American residents and law enforcement had been fermenting for years. The report issued by the department emphasizes the importance of perceived legitimacy on the part of the public being served. Much as a chicken-and-egg problem, residents must trust government before they will constructively engage with it. Engagement is a two-way street, where both residents and officials must work collaboratively to create better communities. When relations are poisonous, as they were in Ferguson and Marion, they are difficult to overcome and make the work of the street-level bureaucrat even more challenging.

In the case of the Ferguson, Missouri police department, only 7 percent of uni-

FERGUSON, MISSOURI: THE IMPORTANCE OF COMMUNITY TRUST

Excerpt from the investigative report of the DOJ: "Since the August 2014 shooting death of Michael Brown, the lack of trust between the Ferguson Police Department and a significant portion of Ferguson's residents, especially African Americans, has become undeniable. . . . Our investigation has shown that distrust of the Ferguson Police Department is longstanding and largely attributable to Ferguson's approach to law enforcement. This approach results in patterns of unnecessarily aggressive and at times unlawful policing; reinforces the harm of discriminatory stereotypes; discourages a culture of accountability; and neglects community engagement. In recent years, FPD has moved away from the modest community policing efforts it previously had implemented, reducing opportunities for positive police-community interactions, and losing the little familiarity it had with some African-American neighborhoods. The confluence of policing to raise revenue and racial bias thus has resulted in practices that not only violate the Constitution and cause direct harm to the individuals whose rights are violated, but also undermine community trust, especially among many African Americans. As a consequence of these practices, law enforcement is seen as illegitimate, and the partnerships necessary for public safety are, in some areas, entirely absent. Restoring trust in law enforcement will require recognition of the harms caused by Ferguson's law enforcement practices, and diligent, committed collaboration with the entire Ferguson community. . . . The City must replace revenue-driven policing with a system grounded in the principles of community policing and police legitimacy, in which people are equally protected and treated with compassion, regardless of race."[21]

formed officers were African-American, despite the fact that two-thirds of Ferguson's residents are African American.[22] Increasing the representativeness of a police force does not necessarily increase community trust but it is more likely to than not. The lack of representation of the neighborhoods being served created a psychological distance between law enforcement officers and residents and contributed to a lack of confidence on the part of residents that police were there to help them, not hurt them. As the distance grew, so did mistrust. As the DOJ report advises, meaningful collaboration between the police department and residents has to exist if trust is to be built. This requires representation in the form of advisory councils or community meetings or the inclusion of influential neighborhood leaders in decision making. It requires citizen engagement and in this case, government is the catalyst to bring one of its services—law enforcement—in closer touch with whom it is charged with helping. The report recommends a citizen-centric service delivery system built on trust and responsiveness.

Both the examples in Akron, Ohio of relations between police and the public and of preserving the greater sage-grouse without formal regulation demonstrate good outcomes. Conversely, the examples of Ferguson, Missouri and combatting the tuberculosis outbreak in Marion, Alabama show the difficulties posed when citizens and government are estranged, rather than engaged.

FORMS OF ENGAGEMENT

There are a number of ways to formalize citizen engagement. These range from advisory bodies for public programs, to volunteers who assist in service delivery, to solicitation of input through public hearings and e-communication, to input on 311 information lines. Some forms are integrated so well into the system that they are taken for granted, such as juries for court proceedings and parent-teacher associations. Throughout, representativeness is important because the life experience of citizens differs based on their personal characteristics. The views of those who are directly affected by public action are the most important to gather. As arbiters of public action, citizens affirm the work of government, or in the worst of circumstances, such as in Ferguson, Missouri, they engage in civil disobedience.

Engagement works in two directions: outward-facing and inward-facing. Outward refers to government reaching out to the public and providing information in such a way that the public is knowledgeable about events. Inward refers to government soliciting information and effort from the public.

FROM GOVERNMENT TO THE PUBLIC

Outward-facing mechanisms include using public information officers to inform the public, strategic planning processes that engage the public, council meetings that are open to the public, citizen advisory boards, task forces and commissions, town hall meetings, coffee-with-the-mayor type meetings, websites, reverse 911 calls, citizen academies, focus groups, and real-time performance data.

Public Information Officers

Public Information Officers (PIOs) are an example of how government provides information, often in times of crisis. PIOs are the first faces that the public sees when learning about a public event. They speak with authority and are the face of the agency. This is, for the most part, a one-way communication. A person in this role must rely on reports from the field because they are outsiders to the actual actions or decisions on which they report. But they must speak as if deeply involved and close to the situation, with trust, compassion, rapport, and credibility. All these attributes hinge on the ability of the PIO to frame a message and convey it in a meaningful, confident, understandable, and tempered way.

The PIO is like the artist who, with a verbal paintbrush, creates the picture for citizens by selecting from a mass array of facts those details that are significant. The goal is to raise citizen consciousness as well as faith, trust, and confidence in government. Expertise translates into credibility, and compassion translates into trustworthiness. When questions arise, the media and other stakeholders demand an immediate, thorough, and unqualified response from their government. A spokesperson for a large municipal fire department explains:

> "I try to paint a picture for viewers and listeners of what is going through the mind of the firefighter or the first responder . . . If that firefighter had such a sorrowful face on I would try to describe the sorrow that I saw on that firefighter the moment he or she was explaining to me what he or she went through. So it was an ability to feel the pain or the suffering or the emotions of that rescuer and being able to translate that to an articulate sentence or paragraph or sound bite that people could associate with."[23]

Strategic Planning

The U.S. Department of Transportation's engagement of the public in its strategic planning process demonstrates how engagement with those who care about public transportation initiatives produced input from many different perspectives. Although its initiative had a positive outcome, the experience taught lessons to agency officials about how to improve engagement in such a way that participation is representative. Representativeness is an important element when collecting input. Without it, officials cannot be certain that the views expressed are generalizable to the population being served.

Council Meetings

Meetings of elected officials, such as city council meetings, county commission meetings, and deliberations in state legislatures and Congress, are open to the public and are often televised. The purpose of this is to ensure that those who are interested in following the deliberations of their representatives can do so. Most cities and counties also have provisions for inviting public comments so that persons may make a personal appearance and speak.

Citizen Advisory Boards

These are most frequently created by city governments and appointments are usually made by the mayor. Some boards operate in only an advisory capacity while others have administrative powers that allow them to make policy decisions. Their powers and the manner of appointment to them is specified in ordinance, resolution, or council motion.

Task Forces/Citizen Review Boards/Commissions

Public entities often create project specific task forces or citizen review boards or commissions to which members of the public are appointed. The purpose of these is to benefit from the diverse views and expertise of stakeholders as well as to coproduce public programs. When volunteers participate, the work of government is expedited, allowing it to achieve more than it could otherwise.

Neighborhood/Town Hall/Public Meetings

Discussion of local issues often occurs in neighborhood or town meetings. These venues provide an opportunity for the public to meet with their neighbors and express concern about issues, propose solutions, plan strategy, or build consensus on a plan of action. Meetings are usually called for a specific purpose, scheduled at a time when most people are available, and notice of the meeting is posted in numerous places to encourage as many people as possible to attend.

Coffee-with-the-Mayor Type Meetings

There are a number of innovative venues for involving the public. One such format is when a public official dedicates a time and place for an informal exchange of ideas. This may be in an office or coffee shop, or may be a virtual meeting via a chat room.

Information and Communications Technology (ICT)

ICT provides many opportunities for informing the public as well as actively engaging them in discussion. It includes telephone and Internet technologies and ranges from elementary to sophisticated. For example, robocalls allow governments to send brief messages to every phone in a jurisdiction. Reverse 911 calls alert neighborhoods to watch for missing children. And television and streaming video make it possible to broadcast public meetings. ICT presents a variety of ways that government communicates with residents and receives input from them. From web-based forms that enable builders to file plans with city planning and zoning departments to online comments solicited by state and federal regulatory agencies as they develop new regulations, ICT expands government's capacity to communicate with the public to make public services more accessible. Moreover, social media, such as used by the U.S. Department of Transportation to involve the public in its strategic planning process, is gaining in use.

Since 1994 when the White House launched its own website, uses for the Internet to increase communication with the public have grown enormously. Jurisdictions use webpages to increase transparency and accessibility by providing information about services and job listings, posting annual budgets, describing city services and providing contact information, and highlighting successes and events. Also since the mid-1990s, dedicated phone numbers have provided easy access to government services. For example, 211 is the universal number that anyone may call to gain general information about health and human service resources.

Citizen Academies

Citizen academies are educational programs conducted by school districts, cities, and counties. They are designed to inform and engage community residents. They may provide general training with regard to government processes or they may be specific to public functions, such as law enforcement or emergency response. Academies provide training that acquaints the public with the processes used and also provides training for volunteers.

Real-Time Performance Data

Many jurisdictions take advantage of widespread access to the Internet to post performance data and live video feeds. Cameras at busy intersections record traffic congestion and make it convenient for traffic apps to guide drivers around problem areas. In Colorado, for example, the state transportation department provides live camera feeds of traffic conditions through mountain passes so that travelers know in advance whether roads are blocked with snow. State governments in Alaska, Arkansas, and Colorado have an "open checkbook" policy in which all checks written by the treasurer are posted online so citizens can follow expenditures. Because of the wealth of information being collected from a wide range of sources, such as the body cameras that police wear, the challenge for government is not so much in collecting information as it is in storing, retrieving, and using the information strategically, making it available to the public in a way that is accessible and interpretable, while still protecting privacy.

FROM THE PEOPLE TO GOVERNMENT

Inward-facing methods of citizen engagement provide ideas and feedback on programs and priorities. Among the mechanisms used to gather input and feedback are community surveys, suggestion boxes on municipal websites, advisory groups, and citizen boards. Another vehicle is the independent voice that public-service-minded nonprofits offer. They represent a number of issue-oriented constituencies and play a large role in bringing issues to government's attention and helping to shape policy.

Soliciting views of the public is a necessary element to citizen engagement, but it is easier said than done, as demonstrated by the experience of the U.S. Department of Transportation. Knowing what public opinion holds is important if a manager is to achieve commitment to public goals and to avoid public outcry. The case of public spaces makes this point. Parks, streets, and town squares that are enjoyed reinforce the civic bond between residents and government. Input at the design stage sets a tone of inclusiveness and reaps rewards in terms of civic bonds and civic pride.

From the High Line Park in New York City, which transformed an abandoned elevated railway into an urban park, to the local parks in Charleston, South Carolina, citizen engagement in the planning process contributes to civic pride. In the case of the High Line, for example, advocates for transforming the abandoned railway formed a nonprofit to speak with a unified voice for the line's repurposing as a public greenway. Public meetings were held in neighborhoods that would be affected by the repurposing and a groundswell of support developed for the project. This approach for developing interest and then commitment by those who would be most affected by the project demonstrates the success of citizen engagement.

In contrast to the High Line, when DOT tried to interpret the feedback it had received from the strategic planning process, the problem was that viewpoints were not representative of all constituencies. Representativeness occurs in one of two forms: passive or active. Passive refers to representation in name only. Active refers to representation in terms of having a voice in deliberations and decision making. On the one hand, an advisory body that reflects the diversity of an agency's constituency and whose deliberations are sought is an example of active representation. Passive representation, on the other hand, occurs when, although a member of a group, one is in a powerless position because decisions have already been made or input will be disregarded. Passive representation contributes to cynicism while active representation contributes to strengthened relationships and ownership.

Focus Groups

Focus groups are used when an initiative is under consideration and decision makers need to learn how the public will react. When problems arise such as in the case of fighting the tuberculosis outbreak, where many of the public are more distrustful than trustful, focus groups of selected opinion leaders in a community can be effective. They can provide insights and perspectives that are otherwise unknown to officials.

Citizen Surveys and E-Communication

A number of cities use annual citizen surveys for strategic planning, for setting program and budget priorities, and to monitor progress. Surveys query residents' attitudes about safety, transportation, environmental issues, economic issues, recreation and wellness, education and enrichment, and overall level of community engagement. Residents report their perceptions about the quality of their community and its services as well as their own level of engagement. Results provide a snapshot in time of how residents are experiencing their community and they can be used to set benchmarks. They also provide a common basis for discussion at public meetings of residents and government officials. When used year after year, survey results show a pattern of areas that are improving or not improving. Issues such as shortage of affordable housing, adequate parking, or issues with K–12 education can be identified. And, areas that receive high marks and deserve congratulations can be identified, such as improvements with the natural environment, economic health, cultural/arts/music activities, parks, libraries, and so forth.

Although public meetings and citizen surveys are the most frequently used methods for securing feedback, multiple forms of e-communication are also effective. For example, idea boards and *Contact Us* pages on agency websites provide a way for the public to give input. And 311 telephone numbers provide a means for residents to alert government to problems that are not emergencies.

Nonprofit Organizations as Vehicles for Participation

Just as de Tocqueville observed in the early 1800s, Americans use nonprofit associations as a means for citizen engagement in causes that interest them. In contemporary parlance, these are called voluntary associations, civic sector organizations, third sector organizations, independent sector organizations, nonprofits, social sector organizations, philanthropies, charities, or nongovernmental organizations. To a large extent, the terms are synonymous. They provide a means for people with a common interest to organize into a group and speak with one voice. In this way, people with similar views have their voices heard in a more potent way than if each person tries to gain access to the policy process individually.

There are a multitude of nonprofits that focus on a variety of interests: the arts, education, environment, health care, human services, international interests, hobbies, and religion. In California alone, there are more than 72,000 public charities. Of these, about one-third have paid staff, over half are of the grassroots, voluntary type, and across the state, one out of every sixteen jobs is at a charitable organization.[24] Each of these represent the visions and values of their members. Most nonprofits in the United States are intricately involved with civic life, providing policy information to lawmakers, direct services to residents, and giving voice to whatever their interest is. In many nonprofits, volunteers outnumber paid staff.

By being part of an organized group, people are able to speak with a louder voice than when they speak individually, as was demonstrated by the groups that participated in the DOT's planning process. Nonprofits engage in the policy process by influencing problem definition, policy formulation, and selection of the best alternative to address the problem, as well as participating in the planning process for programs. Moreover, they provide social capital that public entities call upon. One example is how museums rely on arts groups to supply docents. Nonprofits mediate between the state and the individual. In a principal-agent context, nonprofits are the agents for interests in the community, speaking to government and influencing policy deliberations. They provide a voice, supply volunteers to help deliver public programs, and they create social capital by strengthening social ties in communities.

In addition to aiding collective action, the nonprofit community also provides funding for special purposes. For example, community foundations play an important role not only in the arts and human services, but also in recovery from disasters. They can tap into funding sources that are not available to public agencies, such as corporate

giving, private donors, and large philanthropic foundations. In cases of natural disasters such as floods and tornadoes, time
is critical, and nonprofits can often move
more quickly than government to mobilize volunteers and to supply relief funding.

> *"Nonprofits are the intermediaries be-
> tween generosity and social change."*
>
> — Laura Arrillaga-Andreessen

THE PUBLIC AS PARTNER

Whether acting through membership in voluntary organizations or engaging individually with government, the public is partner with government. From giving input when
regulations are being formed and when neighborhood initiatives are under consideration, to providing feedback about program performance and program outcomes,
there is no time when public managers can reasonably ignore the public voice. And
vice versa. In other words, government and the public coproduce public values and
public goods.

Coproduction refers to citizen participation in the execution of government action. The term can be extended to refer to compliance, that is, if drivers do not obey
traffic laws, safety cannot be ensured. If people do not pay their taxes, there is insufficient revenue. Refraining from littering on sidewalks and streets makes neighborhoods attractive. Government could produce the service by itself, but when residents
chip in, the burden on government is reduced. Residents partner with government to
create public value (traffic safety), to reduce crime (neighborhood watch programs),
to combat eradicable disease (vaccination programs), to enhance literacy (public education), and much more. Unlike the customer model in a sales relationship, where
the exchange is complete once the sale is made, citizens have obligations to contribute to the public weal.

Coproduction occurs in a number of ways, from citizenship activities that support
the law to proactive actions that contribute to the safety and enjoyment of the public.
Picking up litter and putting it in a trash receptacle at a park is coproducing on an individual level as is notifying government of problems via 311. Neighborhood watch
programs and community groups that adopt parks and keep them in good condition
are coproducing public value. Traffic safety, safe streets, better health, good education,
and environmental practices, such as recycling, are all forms of coproduction because
the community is better off by the actions of its members. Civic engagement is fostered
at the same time that service delivery is enhanced when volunteers help in libraries,
zoos, parks, and museums.

The idea of coproduction assumes active and voluntary activity and government
is the catalyst to encourage the activity. Even when the activity is partially subsidized,
such as stipends paid to volunteer poll workers, the payment is not as much as a regular

wage would be, in contrast to the case of contractors performing work for government for compensation. Coproduction extends the hands and feet of government by sharing the workload.

Another form of coproduction occurs every ten years when the federal government performs a constitutionally required function: the census. Originally required to determine the allocation of Congressional representatives, results are used for a myriad of services, including tracking demographic shifts and allocating federal dollars. Data gathering is a massive undertaking with mail-in forms voluntarily submitted, combined with door-to-door canvassing when necessary.

Volunteerism is the primary basis for coproduction. For example, the Peace Corps was created in 1961 by the federal government as a way to use volunteers in outreach programs around the globe. The U.S. Forest Service provides another example. It invites volunteers to help manage campgrounds, meet and greet visitors to national parks, build trails, inventory wildlife and plants, and to serve as fire lookouts. Each person who assists in the work of the Forest Service extends the services that the agency can provide. Another example is how police departments rely on neighborhood watch programs for residents to watch out for each other and alert officials when crime threatens.

> *"A volunteer is a person who can see what others cannot see; who can feel what most do not feel. Often, such gifted persons do not think of themselves as volunteers, but as citizens – citizens in the fullest sense: partners in civilization."*
>
> —George H. W. Bush

Managing for Coproduction

From the public manager's perspective, there are a number of actions that will increase coproduction. The following six principles are demonstrated by the cases described in this chapter.

First, program managers must determine the type of involvement that is most likely to be effective with the stakeholders who care about an issue. It is important to define in advance what assistance is needed and to design the task so that it is as convenient as possible. This is what the U.S. DOT did when it used the social media site to ask people to vote on items in its strategic plan.

Second, agencies may need to use incentives to encourage assistance. These may be financial, such as the case of fighting the TB outbreak or, they may be stipends, as in the case of volunteer poll workers and firefighters.

Third, public officials can appeal to the benefits of participation. For example, avoiding the constraints of federal regulation was a sufficient motivator to cause ranchers, businesses, and land management officials to collaborate in order to preserve habitat for the greater sage-grouse without having to incur constraining regulations. Attractive highways and safe sidewalks are enough to encourage residents and community groups to adopt sections of highway and keep them litter-free and for homeowners to take responsibility for their sidewalks.

Fourth, involvement should not be invited when it is neither wanted nor will be used. The frustration caused by this is expressed by an aggravated resident of Boulder, Colorado. Participation must be real, not theater. Otherwise, residents grow cynical. This news clip demonstrates the point:

> "At a recent Boulder City Council meeting, an angry resident yelled, 'Why did you waste our time?' as the council prepared to vote on an annexation that had been in the works for years but was opposed by many neighbors. It's a sentiment that has been expressed in quieter forms by many city residents who don't feel like their feedback gets incorporated into policy decisions. In an effort to help residents feel more heard and to, in fact, hear them better, Boulder City Council plans to hold periodic town halls and work with consultants to improve the community-engagement processes in every city department."[25]

Fifth, the involvement must be meaningful. Citizen involvement should be initiated in decision making as soon as possible, not after the decision is already made. This is the lesson that the DOT learned. If the public's views are wanted, they need to be included in early stages of planning, rather than simply being asked to ratify decisions already made.

Sixth, boundaries should be clear. The constraints, whether time, money, or feasibility, should be made clear so that participants understand the parameters within which decisions can be made. This, again, reflects the frustration of the Boulder resident.

In sum, citizen engagement and coproduction are parallel processes. Having these six principles in place helps to secure public involvement in a way that uses everyone's contributions best. It results in better information from government to the public and it provides better information from the public to government. Greater involvement of those who care about an issue produces greater commitment to the program and an improved fit between programs and citizen preferences. Moreover, it increases trust on the part of citizens and more constructive relationships between programs and the communities they serve. The success of this is demonstrated by the case of police in Akron, Ohio, and its failure is demonstrated by the problems in Ferguson, Missouri.

There are costs associated with citizen engagement and coproduction. Although many forms of volunteerism save money or time, some do not. The enthusiasm of volunteers may wax and wane and their performance may be unreliable or uneven. Holding public meetings and securing input may increase costs because the more who are involved, the more time will be consumed in planning, scheduling, and conducting meetings. Lengthier deliberations will be necessary and there must be timely, thoughtful communication of decisions. The information gained may interfere with standard operating procedures, but more voices will often have constructive long-term consequences.

COLLABORATIVE RELATIONSHIPS WITH CITIZENS

The need for collaboration exists not only between governmental agencies, nonprofit organizations, and businesses; it also exists between government and citizens. There is always a need to gather citizen input, which helps officials become aware of street-level problems. Such problems range from potholes and graffiti to nuisance problems such as unoccupied buildings that invite criminal mischief to incidents of police brutality which, if not attended to, erode trust, such as the case of Ferguson, Missouri.

To foster collaboration, community indicator projects are used in a number of places to gather data. Neighborhood associations can be enlisted to identify nuisance problems and infrastructure needs. Partnerships between public, private, and nonprofit firms are used to do restorative work in national forests and public lands. The case of the greater sage-grouse is an example of coregulation in public lands. In this case, to avoid what many did not want—strict regulation on the lands native to the threatened bird—a collaborative network of all stakeholders interested in the sage-grouse dilemma came together to develop a strategy that would avoid federal regulatory standards but would still protect sage-grouse.

Ask Me Why I Care: Brandy Hodge, Volunteer Services Coordinator, Johnson County, Kansas[26]

Brandy Hodge has worked as Volunteer Services Coordinator and Catch-a-Ride Program Manager for the Department of Human Services, an agency of Johnson County, Kansas government. The program provides services to vulnerable residents, including those who have restricted incomes, and those who have issues related to aging or disability. Working effectively with volunteers is about building relationships and Brandy explains this in the video. Access it at https://www.unomaha.edu/college-of-public-affairs-and-community-service/community-engagement/pss-brandy-hodge.php.

SUMMARY

A democracy must rely on its citizens while at the same time have the executive machinery in place to provide services, solicit input, and serve as a catalyst to spur coproduction. As the cases demonstrate, the potential of citizen engagement is great but requires management skill. Imperatives for public managers are:

(1) to practice democratic principles,
(2) to build strong communities that are resilient,
(3) to be responsive to the public's needs, and
(4) to work collaboratively with advocacy groups and citizens.

Working together, government and the public join to build stronger communities, such as in Akron, and resolve environmental problems, such as posed by the greater sage-grouse. Conversely, when cynicism reigns, problems such as occurred with the tuberculosis outbreak in Marion result.

Citizen engagement comes in multiple forms—from public meetings to volunteerism to citizen academies—and builds communities. Sustainable collective action takes work to develop and requires an administrative infrastructure that will prevail over time, regardless of personalities, interest groups, and changing public priorities. And this is why public administration is the essential component that keeps the parts of the democratic puzzle glued together.

KEY TERMS

Citizen participation – the process by which citizens engage in public affairs including voting, giving input, evaluating programs, and paying for and receiving services from government.

Collaboration – working together toward a common goal.

Coproduction – citizen participation in execution of government action.

Representativeness – the degree to which a process or workforce reflects the characteristics of stakeholders or the public.

Social capital – social norms and social structures that emerge and guide individual behavior toward communal ends.

Volunteerism – the primary basis of coproduction in which people follow rules or provide services without being monetarily compensated.

DISCUSSION QUESTIONS

1. Explain why citizen engagement is important.
2. Describe three forms of citizen engagement available to you in your community.
3. Describe the challenges to public managers as they solicit community engagement and input.
4. Compare the tuberculosis outbreak in Marion, Alabama, to community policing in Akron, to civil unrest in Ferguson, Missouri. How does citizen engagement, or the lack of it, explain each?

BUILD YOUR SKILLS

Public speaking is an important skill but almost everyone gets nervous. Practice these tips the next time you make a presentation.

SKILLBOX: EFFECTIVE PUBLIC SPEAKING

Almost everyone gets the jitters when speaking before a group. Here are tips for how to prepare and speak effectively, whether a case of the jitters sets in or not. Being an effective speaker requires three things: managing the message, managing body language, and managing the setting. In many ways it is like being an actor on stage. Follow these steps to take command of the stage.

Manage the Message

Know the Audience. Use this information to tailor your choice of words and level of information. Do not make remarks that are too elementary or too detailed for the audience. Time for questions and answers at the conclusion of the speech provides an opportunity for the audience to ask more specific questions if they want greater detail.

Know the Material. Speak about what you know. Avoid the embarrassment of being asked a question that will reveal an inadequate understanding of the topic. At the same time, it is better to say "I don't know" in response to a question than supplying an incorrect answer.

Practice the Speech with a Timer. Alter the speech if it is too brief or too long. If possible, videotape the practice presentation and watch to identify gestures or expressions that are distracting. Ask a friend to critique your performance.

Establish Rapport. Touch briefly on areas of shared experience or shared values that you have with the audience. Begin with areas of agreement before dealing with areas of disagreement.

Present the Material in a Logical Sequence. Open the speech by explaining its purpose. Use the purpose as the focal point for the entire presentation. Outline main points, then give the main points, then conclude with a summary of the main points.

Get the Audience's Attention at the Outset. Start with an attention grabber. Use a dramatic statistic, an interesting anecdote, or concise quotation.

Use the Summary to Emphasize Important Takeaways. The conclusion should close the loop opened by the introduction. Where the introduction gives advance notice of what will follow, the conclusion should review and reiterate the main points.

Do Not Read; Work from an Outline. By looking at the audience rather than your text, you will engage them and keep their focus on you and your message. A brief outline will jog your memory and keep you on task. Do not read from notes for any extended length of time.

Use PowerPoint Slides Wisely. Visuals are effective at holding the audience's attention and amplifying key points. But do not use too many slides or slides that have so much animation or gaudy colors that they distract from your words. And never torture the audience by cramming a slide with tiny print and then reading it to them.

Thank the Audience for their attention when you finish.

Manage Body Language

Nervousness Is Normal. Use It! Think of nervousness as excitement. Let the adrenaline do its job. It may cause a pounding heart and sweaty palm, but it also keeps you on your toes, making you more alert and ready to give your best performance.

Do Not Expect to Be Perfect. Relax! Expect to be good, not perfect. No one expects perfection. Preparing ahead of time and practicing will give you the confidence you need. Be yourself, speak naturally, use eye contact, body language, and tone of voice to connect with your audience.

Present the Proper Image. Dress appropriately. Look pleasant, enthusiastic, confident, but not arrogant. Appear relaxed, even if you feel nervous.

Establish Credibility. The audience will make judgments within the first few seconds of seeing you. Most of these judgments are based on your body language: appearance, speaking style, competence, and confidence. Smile at your audience as you begin. This will relax you and connect you with them.

Let Your Personality Show. Be yourself. The audience will trust what you have to say if they see you as authentic.

Speak Clearly. Sound confident. Do not mumble. When you make an error, correct it, and continue. Do not make excuses.

Make Eye Contact. Have direct eye contact with as many in the audience as possible, and every now and then glance at the whole audience while speaking. This keeps the audience engaged.

Use Tone of Voice and Gestures to Amplify Important Points. Accentuating main points by altering your tone of voice and using physical gestures will hold the audience's attention.

Speak Slowly, Enunciate Clearly, and Show Appropriate Emotion. This combination helps the audience comprehend the message. Do not speak too fast. Allow yourself and your audience time to reflect and think.

Focus on the Audience. Gauge their reactions, adjust your message, and stay flexible.

Restrict Excess Movement and Mannerisms. Control those mannerisms that detract from the message, such as moving around too much, nodding the head excessively, or using too many filler words such as *umm* and *uhh*.

Manage the Setting

Visit the Room Beforehand. Learn how it is laid out and determine whether it is better to speak behind a podium or move freely in front of the audience.

Visualize the Audience. Imagine looking at them and delivering your remarks.

Visualize Yourself. Imagine progressing through your remarks. Think about how you will open your comments.

Arrive Early. This provides time to check the sound system and load the slides.

Have a Backup Plan. Have notes handy so that you can complete the presentation without visuals. Like carrying an umbrella to ward off rain, this ensures that the projector bulb will not burn out, the computer will power up, the presentation file opens, and the projector is aimed correctly.

Hands-On Activity: Prepare a Presentation to the Class

Use this guide the next time you must make a presentation before the class. Prepare your remarks, practice your presentation beforehand, then deliver. Ask classmates for feedback afterward so that you can continue to improve your presentation skills.

NOTES

1. Mary Parker Follett, *The New State: Group Organization, the Solution of Popular Government* (New York: Longmans, Green & Co, 1918).

2. Robert D. Putnam, *Bowling Alone: The Collapse and Revival of American Community* (New York: Simon and Schuster, 2000).

3. J. Woody Stanley, "Citizen Engagement: A Case Study of Participation in Agency Strategic Planning," *PA Times* (January 2, 2015), http://patimes.org/citizen-engagement-case-study-participation-agency-strategic-planning/.

4. Theodore Roosevelt, "The Duties of American Citizenship" (speech, Buffalo, New York, January 26, 1883), http://www.edchange.org/multicultural/speeches/theodore_roosevelt_duties.html.

5. Associated Press, "3 out of 5 African-Americans Experience Unfair Police Treatment," *The Denver Post* (August 5, 2015), http://www.denverpost.com/nationworld/ci_28592956/3-out-5-african-americans-experience-unfair-police.

6. Community Oriented Policing Services, *Community Policing Defined*, U.S. Department of Justice (2014), http://ric-zai-inc.com/Publications/cops-p157-pub.pdf.

7. City of Akron, *A Message from the Chief* (2016), http://www.akronohio.gov/cms/site/10c5e96e7db5b10f/index.html.

8. "H. George Frederickson and Ohio Youth Group Honored at Social Equity Luncheon," *PA Times* (2015), http://patimes.org/h-george-frederickson-ohio-youth-group-honored-social-equity-luncheon/.

9. Colette M. Jenkins, "'Hoops with Cops' to Bring Police and Community Together," *Akron Beacon Journal* (June 18, 2015), https://www.ohio.com/akron/lifestyle/religion/hoops-with-cops-to-bring-police-and-community-together.

10. Cheryl Simrell King, *Government Is Us 2.0* (New York: Taylor & Francis, 2011).

11. National Fire Protection Association, *U.S. Fire Department Profile – 2014* (2016), http://www.nfpa.org/research/reports-and-statistics/the-fire-service/administration/us-fire-department-profile. Additionally, see Jen Fifield, "Volunteer Firehouses Struggle to Find Recruits," *Stateline* (January 11, 2017), http://www.pewtrusts.org/en/research-and-analysis/blogs/stateline/2017/01/11/volunteer-firehouses-struggle-to-find-recruits.

12. U.S. Department of Interior, "Historic Conservation Campaign Protects Greater Sage-Grouse," press release, September 22, 2015, https://www.doi.gov/pressreleases/historic-conservation-campaign-protects-greater-sage-grouse.

13. Steven T. Knick and John W. Connelly, "Greater Sage-Grouse and Sagebrush: An Introduction to the Landscape," in *Greater Sage-Grouse: Ecology and Conservation of a Landscape Species and Its Habitats,* ed. Steven T. Knick and John W. Connelly, Studies in

Avian Biology (Berkeley, CA: University of California Press, 2011), 1–9.

14. Western Association of Fish and Wildlife Agencies, "Greater Sage-Grouse Population Trends: An Analysis of Lek Count Databases 1965–2015" (2015), http://www.wafwa.org/Documents%20and%20Settings/37/Site%20Documents/News/Lek%20Trend%20Analysis%20final%208-14-15.pdf.

15. "A Timeline of Sage Grouse Conservation," *Western Confluence* (2014), http://www.westernconfluence.org/a-timeline-of-sage-grouse-conservation/.

16. U.S. Department of Interior, "Historic Conservation Campaign."

17. Bureau of Land Management, "Resource Advisory Councils" (2017), https://www.blm.gov/get-involved/resource-advisory-council/about-rac.

18. Bureau of Land Management, "National Greater Sage-Grouse Planning Strategy Land Use Plan Amendments and Environmental Impact Statements: Scoping Summary Report" (2012), https://eplanning.blm.gov/epl-front-office/projects/lup/36511/43228/46290/GSG_ScopingReport_508.pdf.

19. Bureau of Land Management, "BLM National Greater Sage-Grouse Planning Strategy Highlights" (2011), http://www.blm.gov/or/news/files/sage-grouse_fact_sheet.pdf.

20. Mattie Quinn, "Amid TB Outbreak, Alabama Pays Resisters to Get Tested," *Governing* (February 24, 2016), 1, http://www.governing.com/templates/gov_print_article?id=369814821.

21. U.S. Department of Justice Civil Rights Division, *Investigation of the Ferguson Police Department* (March 4, 2015), 5–6, https://www.justice.gov/sites/default/files/opa/press-releases/attachments/2015/03/04/ferguson_police_department_report.pdf.

22. Ibid., 88.

23. Sharon H. Mastracci, Mary E. Guy, and Meredith A. Newman, *Emotional Labor and Crisis Response: Working on the Razor's Edge* (Armonk, NY: M.E. Sharpe, 2002), 62.

24. California Association of Nonprofits, *Causes Count: The Economic Power of California's Nonprofit Sector* (2014), http://www.calnonprofits.org/images/downloads/causes-count-808.pdf.

25. Erica Meltzer, "In Effort to Include the Public a Little More, Boulder Council Will Hold Town Hall Meetings," *Daily Camera* (January 22, 2016), http://www.dailycamera.com/news/boulder/ci_29421722/effort-include-public-little-more-boulder-council-will.

26. *Ask Me Why I Care: Public Service Stories*, video, directed by Mary R. Hamilton and Rita Paskowitz (Omaha, NE: Omaha College of Public Affairs and Community Service), available at https://www.unomaha.edu/college-of-public-affairs-and-community-service/community-engagement/pss-brandy-hodge.php.

ADDITIONAL RESOURCES

Thomas, John C. 2012. *Citizen, Customer, Partner: Engaging the Public in Public Management.* Armonk, NY: M.E. Sharpe.

As an example of encouraging volunteerism, this U.S. Forest Service website provides information about volunteering in national parks: http://www.fs.fed.us/working-with-us/volunteers.

PART II

Managing for Performance: Capitalizing on the Power of People, Money, Information

The pursuit of public purposes is achieved by capitalizing on three primary resources: people, money, and information. The efforts require leadership, defining a mission and organizing everyone's work in a way that brings strangers together to accomplish goals that cannot be achieved by acting alone, and allocating financial resources to achieve the mission. Throughout all this, managing information—its flow, its storage and retrieval, and communication strategies—makes the difference in coordination of effort, engagement, and sense of community. These chapters cover each of these endeavors.

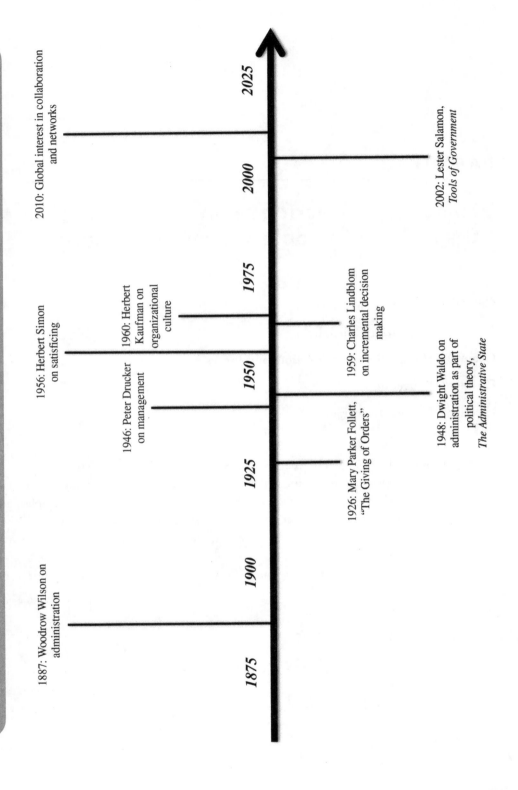

Chapter 3 Timeline: The Savvy Administrator

1887: Woodrow Wilson on administration

1926: Mary Parker Follett, "The Giving of Orders"

1946: Peter Drucker on management

1948: Dwight Waldo on administration as part of political theory, *The Administrative State*

1956: Herbert Simon on satisficing

1959: Charles Lindblom on incremental decision making

1960: Herbert Kaufman on organizational culture

2002: Lester Salamon, *Tools of Government*

2010: Global interest in collaboration and networks

1875 1900 1925 1950 1975 2000 2025

THE SAVVY ADMINISTRATOR

WHAT YOU WILL LEARN

Why collaboration is important

The skills required of effective administrators

The difference between leadership and management

Types of decision making

Skillbox: Running a meeting

The context within which public managers function is a complex, interconnected milieu. In government, their work is directed by elected officials who may have limited experience with agency operations. And the work is performed by career employees with years of experience. In the case of nonprofits, managers are sandwiched between boards of directors and the constituencies being served. In both environments, public administrators are the translators who explain who gets what in real time and real terms, and they are catalysts for the pursuit of public purposes. Whether to advance community action, build economic development collaborations, or deliver direct services, they must work through others to achieve the mission. This requires leadership, astute decision making, and good management skills.

For public managers/administrators/executives, collaboration is imperative because single agencies rarely have the resources or capability to individually address problems as varied as public health crises, workforce development, domestic terrorism, or any of a variety of other challenges. They must have the skills to engage and collaborate with stakeholders from multiple departments, sectors, and levels of government. The case of Gary Cunningham in Hennepin County, Minnesota tells the story of an effective leader who brought a number of different services to bear on a community-wide problem. His work demonstrates collaborative skills, leadership, and a goal orientation that motivated everyone to participate and succeed.

THE AFRICAN AMERICAN MEN PROJECT (AAMP)

The African American Men Project (AAMP) in Hennepin County, Minnesota, offers an instructive example of collaborative leadership. In 1999, Hennepin County Commissioners acknowledged that the unemployment of African-American men was remarkably high despite a thriving economy and labor shortage. They approved a resolution directing the county to: 1) investigate the social and economic barriers that impact African-American males between the ages of 18–30; 2) assess the impact (and outcomes) of current policies, programs, and resource allocations; and 3) recommend actions to improve their quality of life.[1] This task was assigned to Gary Cunningham, director of the county's Office of Planning and Development.

Cunningham was well aware of the problems facing African-American men. Statistics showed a disproportionate number of arrests, higher school dropout rates, and higher mortality than their white counterparts. And Cunningham himself was an African American who had been working for decades on behalf of the community. Based on his personal and professional experience, Gary knew that the solutions would require building a partnership in the community.[2]

The collaboration became known as the African American Men Project. Staff from the Office of Planning and Development coordinated a steering committee comprised of business representatives who valued workforce diversity, well-respected academic researchers, nonprofit executives who served African-American families, educational leaders, elected officials, jour-

nalists, and young African-American men and their families. Cunningham relied on researchers who used systematic stakeholder analysis techniques. This ensured that the final recommendations represented common themes expressed by all the committee members.[3]

Cunningham and his staff capitalized on the networks that steering committee members were a part of to implement the strategic actions included in the report.[4] Many of the recommendations were adopted by organizations throughout the community. For instance, the North Point Health and Wellness Center developed programming focused on health, career services, parenting education, and community engagement. They partnered with several other agencies and instituted a referral system that spans several Hennepin County departments and community organizations, as well as the Minneapolis Police Department.[5]

Cunningham's leadership was vital to AAMP's success. His skills mirrored those of successful executives in all avenues of public service. Effective collaboration depends on a leader with *individual attributes* of an open mind and patience; *interpersonal skills* of being a good communicator and an active listener; *group process skills* of facilitation and collaborative problem-solving; *strategic leadership skills* of big-picture thinking; and *substantive technical expertise,* which includes subject area knowledge and project management.[6]

As the Director of the Office of Community Development and Planning, Cunningham had the will and skill to take advantage of the window of opportunity presented by the Hennepin County Commissioners. His work improved the quality of life for African-American men in the county.

The project demonstrates how multiple agencies worked together for mutual benefit. From the manager's perspective, collaboration is the process of facilitating and operating in multiorganizational arrangements to solve problems that cannot be solved by a single organization. It requires cooperation and coordination, and a balance between autonomy and interdependence. The goal of collaboration is service integration.

Questions to Ponder

1. Why was it necessary for Cunningham to collaborate with so many stakeholders?

2. Is it a coincidence that Cunningham's skills are similar to those of effective administrators at the state and federal levels of government and in well-run nonprofit agencies?

Management is part science and part art. It includes cognitive and emotive skills, analyzing, and sensing; leadership, decision making, building successful teams, and sculpting the culture are all important dimensions. It is the match between the blend of these and the context that determines who succeeds and who fails. Savvy administrators are aware of these elements and put them together well. This chapter distinguishes between administration and management, describes the historical roots for the focus on public administrators' work, contrasts the difference between ideal and practical decision making, and closes with a summary of important administrative skills.

IS IT ADMINISTRATION OR IS IT MANAGEMENT?

Public Executives. Public Administrators. Public Managers. What is the difference, or do the words mean the same? In fact, the terms are used interchangeably, although the words "executive" and "administrator" are sometimes used to connote posts that are higher in the organizational hierarchy than that of managers. As a generic term, however, managers may work at any level in the organization that has responsibility to coordinate the work of others. The term is used to connote anyone from the supervisory level up to the agency director when speaking of their responsibilities to plan, organize, staff, and coordinate the work. Only nuances differentiate *executive*, *administrator*, and *manager*.

The term *executive* suggests an action orientation, that is to execute, and connotes strategic thinking about how to transform public policies into public programs. And the term *administrator* focuses on the responsibilities and tasks associated with guiding the implementation of public policy. While the word "executive" is used more often in business and nonprofits, it is equally appropriate in the public sector. In the case,

Cunningham was the administrator of the agency and he managed its operations and outreach to the community. As a public executive, he was responsible for fulfilling the county commission's charge to address the problems of African-American men and he mounted a successful program. By and large, the terms are interchangeable.

The term *executive* refers to all knowledge workers—managers or professionals—who by virtue of their position, make decisions in the normal course of their work that have a significant impact on the performance of the organization. Regardless of the title used—executive, administrator, manager—the real question is what skills are required to execute the public will, engage stakeholders in the process, and fulfill the mission? This question is as real now as it was a century ago when Woodrow Wilson argued that the work of public administration can best be understood by dividing the process of governing into two segments, the political and the administrative, or in other words, inputs and outputs.

Woodrow Wilson's Prescription

When Woodrow Wilson[7] argued in favor of public administration as its own field of study, he acknowledged the link between the inputs and outputs of government. Inputs come in the form of policy debates while outputs are the programs that breathe life into policy. Treating administrative action as the hands and feet of government, Wilson viewed public administration as "government in action." He realized that the formulation and the execution of policy are substantively different domains and argued that the biggest problems in government are not policy-based but rather, administrative. He noted that "it is getting to be harder to *run* a constitution than to frame one."[8] He distinguished administration's special place within democratic government, asserting that administrative study was a more meaningful way to study governance than focusing on classical institutions and constitutional framing alone. Coming of age during the Progressive Reform era of the late 1800s, he advocated the scientific selection of workers through merit-based processes and urged nonpartisan and efficient administrative systems.

Wilson's prescription was emblematic of the times. People were concerned then, as now, with how best to achieve good government. As the decades progressed, public administration borrowed heavily from industrial business principles that helped improve efficiency of operations. By the mid-twentieth century, it was obvious that there was a need to appreciate the value of administrative principles but the importance of keeping the pursuit of public purposes tightly linked to political philosophy was also apparent. As a student of political theory, Dwight Waldo attempted to do just that.

Dwight Waldo's View

An icon of twentieth century public administration, Dwight Waldo's work urged a balancing act between democratic values, social equity, and administrative prowess. His words ring true today, just as they did decades ago: Public managers must balance priorities and possibilities in the search for effective ways to address intractable problems. His words speak for him:

> My own point of view is that since administration is so large a subject, and still in many ways so dark, we should open upon it all the windows we can find; that all models and idioms have their virtues—and their vices; that as we proceed we exercise as much intelligence and good will as we can command in determining what any particular model can or cannot do for us.[9]

As a student of political theory, Waldo strove to situate public administration within democratic political theory. His pragmatic argument is that there is not "one best way" to administer the state's business. Rather, public executives must use whatever works, as long as the actions contribute to a democratic state.[10] In today's parlance, Waldo embraced mission-driven work.

Similar to Wilson, Waldo emphasized the centrality of public administration to a democratic state, for this is how the public will is executed. He lauded the scientific approach to management methods but argued that merely training public administrators in the mechanics of administration and arming them with a code of ethics is not enough. He believed that public administrators must also be trained in political philosophy. Here lies the seed that differentiates public administration from business administration.

In his argument, Waldo focused on the tension between democracy and efficiency. While autocratic procedures enhance efficiency, democracy slows it down. The search for the golden mean continues today, just as it existed in the mid-1900s. Empowerment of workers, decentralization, and ensuring maximum participation are the hallmarks of good management and democracy. But sunshine laws, open records laws, and accountability demands are the insurance policy that the public insists upon to guard against a government that otherwise could become too powerful, too mighty, in other words, too efficient. To reconcile these opposing demands, Waldo argued that democracy, not efficiency for its own sake, must be the ultimate goal.

Waldo's argument lays out the challenge for public executives: to maximize efficiency but not at the expense of democratic values. Twentieth century reformers during the Roosevelt administration (New Deal) and the Johnson administration (War on Poverty) viewed government as an instrument for achieving community purposes and for improving economic equality. Efficiency was the means but enlivening democratic values was the goal. The juxtaposition of democracy against efficiency accounted then, as it does now, for many of the tensions that exist between business and government.

Both Wilson and Waldo used the term "administration" to refer to public service delivery. The word "management" is now a more popular term and is often used interchangeably with "administration." Regardless of which term is used, the quandary of how to advance democracy remains the same: What should we do? And how should we do it? It is easier to focus on the first, the policy puzzle, than on the second, the administrative question. This was Wilson's point in 1887, Waldo's in 1948, and it was John F. Kennedy's[11] point again in 1962, as he concluded that the biggest problems that the nation faces continue to be administrative problems. Fast forward to now and it remains true.

Public administration is the vehicle for implementing the values of individuals and communities. These values are enduring, but they also compete with each other. At any point in time, one set of values may have to be minimized in order to maximize other, equally important, values. John Rohr's[12] notion of regime values reminds us that administrators are duty-bound to uphold the worth of individual liberties, equality, and the right to own property. And programs must operate within a paradigm of social equity, a concept inserted into the canon of public administration in the 1970s following a conference at Minnowbrook in upstate New York, where Waldo and others met to define the field and accentuate its values.[13]

Managers must think strategically and act democratically while being mindful of three essential ingredients: politics, management, and law.[14] Because responsible administrative practice derives from constitutional principles,[15] legitimacy comes only with an appreciation for how these elements combine in the planning, delivery, and evaluation of public services. Call it administration or call it management, effective public service is measured not only by the outcomes achieved, but also by how the public interest is served, which is the ultimate goal, not the by-product.[16]

CAPACITY BUILDING

From defense contracts to implementation of the Affordable Care Act, to social services funded by government and delivered by nonprofits, management capacity determines success or failure. It is dependent on interwoven elements that result from collaborations across federal, state, and local levels of government and between business, nonprofits, and government. As cities and counties grapple with the growing need to provide housing for the homeless, repair highways and bridges, operate successful school systems, afford amenities such as zoos, parks, and museums, jurisdictions that used to fight with each other now look fondly on the possibility of building regional cooperation. It is challenging to bring diverse entities together to solve problems that are regional in scope but sharing costs builds capacity.

In addition to direct service provision, there are also numerous tools that provide a means for pursuing public purposes. As shown in Table 3.1, these range from contracts with nonprofits, businesses, or other governmental agencies to provide services that the public manager will oversee but not deliver directly; grants to nonprofits to deliver services which government is not equipped to provide but which are within its mission; vouchers to purchase services from for-profit or nonprofit entities such as food stamps or schools or health care; tradable permits such as pollution credits; or government corporations that provide more administrative flexibility than traditional government agencies. There are strengths and weaknesses for each of these tools, but they provide choices to managers as they determine the best means for achieving the mission.

TABLE 3.1 CAPACITY BUILDING TOOLS

Contracts

Grants

Vouchers

Tradable permits

Government corporations

Government is both labor intensive and information intensive. Offices are staffed with knowledge workers, not industrial workers. In this environment, the mission is the organizing principle and productivity is determined by the ability to access and process information. It is the manager's task to build capacity and harness information so that it works for the organization.

An astute observer of contemporary public management, Donald Kettl,[17] recommends what he calls *leveraged government,* a term that relies on building bridges across the boundaries of agencies and levels of government. Strong partnerships are enabled through horizontal collaboration made possible by information systems that connect all the actors in a network of services. Information technology enables these connections where traditional approaches to hierarchy and authority cannot. In this context, leadership and skilled management are of paramount importance, just as management expert Peter Drucker[18] suggested decades ago. Labor is a resource rather than a cost. Knowledge workers are the most important tool in the information age. The combination of this new environment with Dwight Waldo's foresight for the need to preserve the *public* in public administration creates a dynamic workspace for public service.

SKILLS REQUIRED OF EFFECTIVE ADMINISTRATORS

Well-run organizations have a number of attributes. Table 3.2 lists ten, all of which require a management philosophy and approach that combines respect for staff and for the public.

TABLE 3.2 ATTRIBUTES OF A SUCCESSFUL PUBLIC SERVICE ORGANIZATION

1. Unambiguous mission
2. Challenging but achievable goals
3. Meaningful collaboration
4. Respect for worker talents and appreciation for diversity
5. Responsiveness to constituents
6. Reliance on coproduction rather than top-down regulation and enforcement
7. Selection and use of best provider available
8. Focus on public service
9. Effective leadership
10. Resilient systems

Each of these attributes requires a different element of savvy management and is described here:

1. Unambiguous Mission

A clear mission statement helps everyone stay on the same page, regardless of whether the agency is a small nonprofit with only a few staff or a huge federal agency with thousands of employees stationed across the nation. Even when frontline staff are working independently in geographically remote areas, a clear mission provides structure to their priorities and guides their exercise of discretion. A mission that is important, interesting, and understandable makes it easy to set meaningful goals. When managers articulate the mission clearly and compellingly, the priorities of the agency are clear.

2. Challenging but Achievable Goals

Goals link tasks to mission accomplishment. By deliberating with staff to set challenging but achievable goals, both managers and staff know what is expected. When there is shared commitment to stretch goals—goals that are achievable but demanding—staff know what the criteria their performance will be evaluated on and managers have an objective standard on which to base performance appraisals. To the degree that managers remove obstacles to goal achievement, they clear the path for workers to perform.

3. Meaningful Collaboration

To resolve public problems, multiple talents are required. Meaningful collaborations across whatever levels of government are involved and whatever sectors—public, private, and nonprofit—provide mutual benefit and aids in addressing the problem. The traditional "stovepipe" approach of one agency has given way to interconnections expedited by information technology.

4. Respect for Worker Talents and Appreciation for Diversity

The most important asset that any organization has is its people. Regardless of the budget or the physical facility, the human factor is the most important. Having the right people with the right skills in the right jobs is what is required if the mission is to be achieved. Effective managers respect the talents of frontline workers and make them feel appreciated.

Much as an alloy is stronger than a single metal, a diverse workforce is more resilient. It is more capable of adjusting to complexity and new demands than a homogeneous workforce because it brings more perspectives to bear. Moreover, just as democracy promotes equity in the community, diversity promotes equity in the workplace. Managers who skillfully choreograph changes in the workforce with every new hire, promotion, and training opportunity take advantage of the best that the labor force has to offer.

5. Responsiveness to Constituents

Public service agencies have multiple constituencies: oversight authorities (legislative, executive, judicial), policy advocates, clientele, and a workforce. Savvy managers are aware of the various interests and are responsive to them, balancing their often competing demands and communicating clearly with each.

6. Reliance on Coproduction Rather Than Top-Down Regulation and Enforcement

In regulatory matters and in law enforcement, the power of the state is the power to take away freedoms. To the degree that regulated parties comply voluntarily—a form of coproduction—the work of enforcement can be light-handed rather than heavy-handed. Artful persuasion to achieve common objectives is more effective than top-down enforcement and builds support among the regulated.

7. Selection and Use of Best Provider Available

Determining how best to deliver services requires thoughtful decision making. Whether provided in-house (insourcing) or by contract (outsourcing), the best means depends on a number of factors. While some services are best delivered directly by the agency workforce, others may best be delivered by contracts, grants, or vouchers.

Service cost, quality, and accessibility are among the factors to include in the decision calculus.

8. Focus on Public Service

Public work is in service to constitutional tenets and democratic values.[19] This fact frames the mission as well as the factors by which priorities are set and outcomes are measured. Public service means *service*.

9. Effective Leadership

Leadership that is stable and committed to the mission is essential, and it must have the ability to articulate how tasks are linked to goals and how goals are linked to mission accomplishment. Leadership must also work effectively within the constraints presented by political realities, budgetary limitations, and administrative feasibility.

10. Resilient Systems

Resilience is the capacity to bend but not break when crises occur. Being resilient means being flexible, taking risks, and being persistent. A culture that is tenacious—committed to the mission, respectful of workers, responsive to stakeholders—provides the strength to persevere during times of budget cuts and organizational crises.

Figure 3.1 depicts expectations for public managers. The public expects them to be ethical decision makers, who weigh values and maximize as many as possible. They are to be technically skilled, well informed, committed to public service, and experienced. These are high expectations but each is warranted. Public service requires a focus on the public good.

Leading versus Managing

The essence of leadership is to focus followers' attention on a common purpose and to motivate them to pursue it. Some managers are good leaders; some are not. Some leaders are good managers; some are not. But without leadership, organizations do not mobilize themselves effectively enough to accomplish their mission. Leadership is essential because legislatures give agencies missions that are vague and sometimes conflicting, and they often fail to authorize funding that is sufficient to achieve goals. Moreover, only the toughest problems get to government, so there are challenges of scope, size, and severity. Regardless, the manager's task is to make the human machine run smoothly and pursue its purposes with diligence, intelligence, focus, and energy. But human organizations are not machines: they need motivation and inspiration, and this requires leadership.

FIGURE 3.1 EXPECTATIONS OF PUBLIC MANAGERS

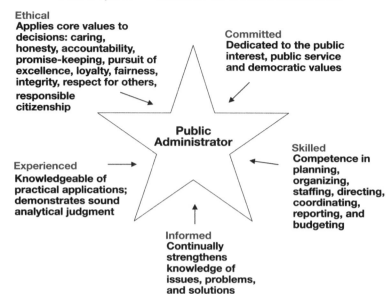

Ethical
Applies core values to decisions: caring, honesty, accountability, promise-keeping, pursuit of excellence, loyalty, fairness, integrity, respect for others, responsible citizenship

Committed
Dedicated to the public interest, public service and democratic values

Public Administrator

Experienced
Knowledgeable of practical applications; demonstrates sound analytical judgment

Skilled
Competence in planning, organizing, staffing, directing, coordinating, reporting, and budgeting

Informed
Continually strengthens knowledge of issues, problems, and solutions

Leaders are responsible for maintaining institutional integrity. They must defend their agency against attacks, avoid any taint of organizational ineptitude, and prevent the agency's resources and authority from being used for unconstitutional, prohibited, or unsanctioned purposes. This

> *"Leadership touches the human spirit, and touching the human spirit has always been the work of art and aesthetics. It's not surprising, therefore, that good leaders have always thought of leadership as more of an art than a science."*
> —Janet and Robert Denhardt

requires not only defensive action but initiative. Values and principles cannot be locked in a vault, only to be used on special occasions. Each public manager's job, whether in public works or public health, has as its end goal to nurture a civic culture and to make manifest the American interpretation of democracy in action. On an everyday basis, this means that leadership skills are necessary for managers to motivate and develop their staff and to breathe life into the mission.

ORDINARY PEOPLE DOING EXTRAORDINARY THINGS

The heralded management expert, Peter Drucker, focused on what he felt were the central questions of organization: the distribution of power and responsibility, the formulation of general and objective criteria of policy and action, and the selection and training of leaders. His focus on human relationships and motivation led him to the conclusion that an organization is like a tune; it is not constituted by individual sounds but by the relations between them.[20] Drucker felt that organizations, like tunes, when in harmony could produce in their members an intellectual and moral growth beyond a person's original capacities.[21] Through decades of his writing, he returned to this notion of ordinary people doing extraordinary things. He believed the ability of an organization to produce leaders is more important than its ability to produce efficiently and cheaply. Efficient and cheap production can always be reached, he argued, given human abilities and human organization. But without an able, responsible and enterprising leadership, willing and capable of taking the initiative, the organization is not sustainable.[22]

It is leadership that causes ordinary people to achieve extraordinary goals. Innovative public managers are entrepreneurial in the way they design and build capacity to achieve ends. Beyond the cognitive skills, however, there is more: Leadership is a blend of technical, social, and emotive skills. Technical skill pertains to concern for production; social skill pertains to the ability to work effectively with subordinates, peers, and superiors; and emotive skill pertains to the ability to sense and regulate one's own emotional state, as well as the ability to sense the emotional state of the other. It is also the ability to exude confidence and optimism.

> *"One of the most important qualities of effective leaders is unwarranted optimism."*
>
> —Alice Rivlin

Social judgment skills involve emotional intelligence, which has three components: social perceptiveness, which is the ability to "take the pulse" of employees to know how they are feeling; self-regulation, the capacity to control and adapt one's own behavior; and self-awareness, the ability to know one's own feelings. People become energized when there is an emotional commitment to their work. This can be spurred by the individual's own interest but it can be enhanced by leadership that triggers, stimulates, and reinforces a positive emotional response on the part of followers. The capacity to energize others through touching the emotions is the art of affective leadership, as described in Table 3.3.

The distinction between exemplary leaders and mediocre ones has little to do with technical knowledge or skill, and much to do with emotive skills. Affective leadership creates an organization's "genetic code," fundamental to motivation and successful job performance. Good leaders encourage the "heart." This is relational work and involves rapport, interaction, compassion, service, and connectedness. The most effective leaders are transformational, which means they engage with others and create a connection that raises the level of motivation in both the leader and the follower.[23] Transformative leaders are "social architects" for their organizations because they redesign how people feel about the mission and their role in its accomplishment.

TABLE 3.3 TO ACHIEVE AFFECTIVE LEADERSHIP

Communicate: Be a good communicator. Engage in active listening, solicit opinions, affirm and embrace the organization's mission and goals, and remind everyone of their role in accomplishing the mission. To be a good listener, watch faces and attend to subtle cues, which gives the ability to communicate at an emotional level. Be willing to engage in crucial conversations. These involve opposing opinions, strong emotions, and high stakes.

Assess and Attune to the Context: Through "artful sensing," appraise the social and emotive environment of a situation, listen to others' perspectives, and anticipate potential reactions/responses.

Perform and Adapt: Given the appraisal of context and anticipated responses, take action and adapt as needed in order to achieve the desired end.

MANAGING PEOPLE, MONEY, AND INFORMATION

Just as leadership is an essential ingredient to organizational performance, so is management. It is up to managers to comprehend the mission and capitalize on the resources that are available to achieve it. Resources include the right people with the right skills doing the right jobs, a budget that covers the costs necessary for goal achievement, enough time to achieve the goals, and the right information. Given these ingredients, savvy managers set strategy, coordinate the work flow, and manage both internal dynamics and external constituencies who affect goal achievement. Strategy establishes objectives and priorities, followed by the development of operational plans. Managing internally involves organizing and coordinating the workforce in a way that capitalizes on strengths. Managing externally involves building and maintaining good communication with stakeholders whose actions directly affect the work that gets done within the organization. It also involves building networks with stakeholders whose collaboration will enable goal achievement, engage the public, and provide accessibility to the media.

There are multiple roles that managers fill. To the external environment, they are the ambassadors who represent the agency to those outside it, explaining its actions and garnering support for it. They are also conveyor belts of information, translating decisions into actions, and providing clarification to workers about decisions that affect their work. They also convey information from workers to those at higher ranks.

To be effective, managers must communicate well. This means that they use feedback as a motivator, alerting workers to good performance as well as to performance that warrants improvement. They are able to deliver messages clearly and are good listeners. They comprehend the varied perspectives that multiple constituencies bring to issues and maneuver through conflict-ridden minefields regarding program priorities.

To balance the interests and rights of everyone, thoughtful, engaged communication with stakeholders is imperative. For example, the problem of homelessness confronts most cities. City managers must balance the interests of business owners who do not want the homeless sleeping in their doorways; against the rights of people to occupy public spaces as long as they are doing no harm; against the concerns of homeless shelters that cannot begin to keep up with the increasing demand for more shelter space. In other words, the role of communicator often becomes the role of negotiator who must balance conflicting points of view and conflicting rights. Maneuvering around the landmines of disagreement requires self-composure, compassion, and sensitivity. The ability to build and mend relationships is important to success.

> *"The single biggest problem in communication is the illusion that it has taken place."*
>
> —George Bernard Shaw

THEORY X VERSUS THEORY Y ASSUMPTIONS

The assumptions that managers hold about workers shape the way they think about motivation and individual performance. Douglas McGregor's[24] depiction of Theory X versus Theory Y assumptions captures two opposing sets of beliefs about what motivates workers to perform. The Theory X manager assumes that workers are indolent, require close supervision, and are only motivated by money. Thus, pay-for-performance systems are thought to motivate workers to produce more. The Theory Y manager assumes that workers are self-motivated, want to develop their skills, and achieve personal satisfaction from their work. Thus, training and development opportunities and self-directed goal-setting are thought to motivate workers. While Theory X managers use top-down management styles, Theory Y managers rely on development techniques and participative decision-making strategies because they view employees not as subjects to be controlled but as assets to be valued.

Although Theory Y assumptions are often thought of as relatively recent in management theory; in fact, Mary Parker Follett[25] based her management advice on such assumptions in 1926. She urged managers not to rely on top-down orders, but rather to engage workers in dialogue about problems to be solved. She believed that managers should foster collaborative decision making, through which supervisors and subordinates would "discover" the most appropriate decision. Follett developed the circular theory of power, distinguishing between "power-over" and "power-with." In today's parlance, this is not surprising, but in its time, it stood in contrast to hierarchical approaches to management that espoused Theory X assumptions.

STABILITY

Another aspect of management is maintaining stability. Routines improve organization performance. When there is stability, disruptions are minimized because unexpected change is diminished. Attention stays focused on the mission rather than on internal dynamics or crises. Keeping turnover as low as possible contributes to stability because it minimizes workflow changes necessitated by retraining and reassignments. At the same time, managers must balance stability with flexibility so that the organization can adapt to changing circumstances, such as when budget cuts occur, or programs are added or changed.

In sum, managers have to manage upward, downward, and sideways within the organization and outward as well. And, they play the role of equalizer. Equity—making room at the table for those traditionally squeezed out—is a benchmark of democratic government. This, as John Rohr reminds us, is because government has the responsibility for running a constitution, just as Woodrow Wilson asserted a century ago. Regime values as embodied by the Constitution must be the guideposts for how public managers behave.

SHAPING THE CULTURE

Managing the organizational culture requires focusing on the intangible dimension of performance. As with the African American Men Project, the collaboration required Cunningham to work with a variety of stakeholders from different organizational cultures, each with its own incentives and goals. By uniting multiple actors, all of whom shared the goal of a better quality of life for African-American men, he succeeded in building a shared purpose that motivated everyone to participate.

Symbols serve to reify values and they become an important motivator. For example, the medals awarded to soldiers are worn with pride, with each color and design taking on a meaning that goes above and beyond the material worth. Similarly, law enforcement officers dress in uniforms not because they are essential to getting the work done. Instead, they symbolize the power of the state and authority that is vested in the institution of policing. Flags and official seals serve a similar function. In other words, popular symbols motivate and strengthen group identity. Office jargon, jokes, slogans, and shared stories also serve to solidify and stabilize the culture. And, shared history provides the narrative by which organization members describe where they work and what they do.

Strengthening the culture is a way to help stabilize the organization, to move it from organization to institution. This buffers it from shocks and helps to coordinate the efforts of disparate units. Why do universities plan huge graduation ceremonies? They do it to celebrate students' achievements but they also do it to provide a time and place for students and their families to celebrate their accomplishments, for faculty and students to mark the passage of time, and to elevate the value of completing a requisite number of courses. They also do it to engage the public and to encourage loyalty in the hope that alumni will give back to the organization in terms of donations and public support. In other words, ceremonies galvanize the most important aspects of the organization in the present as well as into the future.

Culture also strengthens an organization's voice in interorganizational networks because it defines boundaries. In 1960, Herbert Kaufman[26] wrote a study of the U.S. Forest Service because he wanted to learn how an agency as decentralized as the Forest Service could produce such uniform results. Despite hundreds of rangers dispersed across the nation, usually in remote rural areas with limited communication, the agency managed to maintain a coherent, unified program. After interviewing rangers, Kaufman concluded that the culture of the agency was strong, its mission was well understood, its policies were consistent with the mission, and the values of the agency were infused throughout training and in the procedure manual. Thus, rangers held consistent priorities regardless of where they were stationed and regardless of the pressures that local communities exerted on them to make exceptions to Forest Service rules. Kaufman's now classic work demonstrates the power of organizational culture, consistent values, and effective training.

FLATTENED HIERARCHIES, EMPOWERED TEAMS

Organizational change to accommodate today's demands has several basic principles: flattening the hierarchy, empowering workers, and being innovative. The reason that today's managers are flattening hierarchies is that, by reducing the number of ranks between the frontline worker and the director, communication travels faster and the organization is more capable of adapting quicker to changing circumstances. It also expedites collaboration. For example, to prepare a disaster preparedness plan, local government must coordinate the capacity, skills, and resources of first responders and link them with agencies at the state and federal levels. The more direct communication that occurs between management and responders, the faster that decisions are made.

Managers increasingly rely on teams. The advantage over individual assignments is that members of a team combine different levels of expertise and therefore, their response is more comprehensive than one person can produce by acting alone. Teamwork is analogous to the organizational collaboration that Cunningham used in the AAMP program. While organizational collaboration employs multiple agencies, workplace teams employ multiple skill sets, where individuals work collaboratively to solve problems.

Self-managed teams are a synthesis of self-management and teamwork. The teams have autonomy in making decisions, affecting their job performance and this enables agencies to run more efficiently with fewer mid-level managers. They have the added advantage that members experience greater job satisfaction than when working individually. With the teams, members plan, organize, budget, control, staff, and monitor their work. For the best performance, human relations (i.e., the social system) and methods for accomplishing tasks (i.e., the technical system) are in alignment. Members are collectively responsible for their end product and receive feedback and evaluation in terms of team performance rather than on their individual performance. Team leaders function as facilitators rather than controllers, such that the head of the team is a nominal post, rather than a power post. Because "pure" self-managed work teams are rare—they require delegation of both authority and responsibility—it is more likely that teams are blended, with some attributes of self-management and other attributes that comport with traditional hierarchical characteristics.

A sense of teamwork generates identity as part of a group, commitment to its effort, and team spirit. This *esprit de corps* has a direct effect on performance. Consider professional football players, for example. Every player is skilled and has the capacity to play his position. But by the end of the season, there are only two teams remaining to compete in the Super Bowl, whose playing went above and beyond the performance of the others. Teamwork facilitates team members working together, exercising self-determination, owning their objectives, and identifying with organizational goals.

Dividing work processes into teams does not remove the necessity for leadership and coordination between teams. For example, there were tremendous problems with the information technology (IT) system designed to enroll people when the Affordable Care Act was first implemented, as the following case demonstrates. Better coordination between teams could have prevented what occurred.

LACK OF LEADERSHIP AT HEALTHCARE.GOV

HealthCare.gov was created under the Affordable Care Act to enable millions of uninsured Americans to shop for health insurance online. In October 2013, it was launched in the thirty-six states that did not create their own health insurance exchange websites. From the start, serious problems were reported by users. Approximately 250,000 people signed in on the first day—five times the amount expected—and a lack of capacity caused website outages within the first two hours.[27]

A storm of negative media coverage ensued over the next several weeks as staff from the Department of Health and Human Services (HHS), Centers for Medicare & Medicaid Services (CMS), and contractors worked to fix the issues. The Office of the Inspector General later reported that the most critical reason for the breakdown was the lack of clear leadership throughout the website's development and implementation.[28]

In anticipation of the rollout two-and-a-half years earlier, in April 2010, HHS had formed the Office of Consumer Information and Insurance Oversight (OCIIO) to manage the federal exchange program.

However, as the months passed and the scope grew, CMS took over the project because it (CMS) had greater administrative and budgetary resources than OCIIO.

The seeds of impending disaster were sown when the staff and leadership were split into two independent groups: those who worked on policy development and those who handled the technical website building and design components. They were given separate responsibilities and relocated into separate buildings. To travel from one location to the other for face-to-face meetings required a forty-five minute commute. The divide disabled effective communication between the teams.

By late 2011, the lack of leadership was affecting other components of the project. CMS was also responsible for providing guidance for states to develop their own health insurance exchanges. However, because no person was ultimately in charge of making decisions and setting requirements, policies were constantly changing. To avoid the confusion, many states opted for the path of least resistance and joined Health-Care.gov rather than build their own marketplace.

As the countdown to launch neared in early 2013, project staff were reporting potential problems to managers and senior leadership. Among the foreseeable problems were inadequate website capacity, nonconforming information technology standards, and the lack of a single project leader. External technical advisers were also hired to identify problems that could unfold. Assigning a single project leader was a suggestion that HHS and CMS leaders failed to adopt. Fragmentation among decision makers made it impossible to accurately track and address the technical problems and coding defects that were discovered one month before the launch date.

Despite warnings, HealthCare.gov was launched as planned, and problems surfaced immediately. Again, the lack of leadership exacerbated the crisis because there was no one to coordinate the response. The lack of collaboration between health-care policy analysts and website developers further complicated the ability to address system-wide errors. In order to get the site back up and running, there was no clear directive that brought all necessary actors together—including federal staff and contractors—to determine what was causing the breakdowns. For weeks, when users went online, millions were met with the Internet version of a waiting line message that read: "We have a lot of visitors on the site right now. Please stay on this page. We're working to make the experience better, and we don't want you to lose your place in line."[29]

Finally, three weeks after the launch, CMS appointed Jeffrey Zients as the project leader. He was charged with the responsibility to improve the website while finding ways to make the first open enrollment period a success for the uninsured. He partnered with the Secretary of Health and Human Services to gather an ad hoc team of technology experts from public agencies and private companies. Some of the best software engineers in the world worked side-by-side with staff to fix the website. The policy and technical groups were also reunited into one office called the Exchange

Operations Center (XOC). This allowed troubleshooting to occur from both perspectives. Health policy experts were able to work with website developers to design the site so users would navigate to the proper plans based on their eligibility.

Many lessons were learned by CMS and HHS in the implementation phase. The day after the first open enrollment period closed, staff immediately began planning for the second period scheduled for November 2014. Key organizational changes were made, such as identifying a clear scope of work; documenting and tracking all technical improvements that were needed; hiring a team of site reliability engineers to provide guidance and maintain service; and setting an aggressive schedule for improvements. Furthermore, the changes also included formally instituting project leadership in the organizational structure. CMS hired a Chief Executive Officer and agency administrators who could properly coordinate tasks across the various divisions responsible for the long-term implementation and management of HealthCare.gov operations and policy.

Questions to Ponder

1. What went wrong in the planning for HealthCare.gov?
2. How can you reconcile the value of teams with their failure to succeed in the absence of unifying leadership?

DECISION MAKING

Administrators are held accountable for the decisions they make. Decisions shape all aspects of administrative life and they become the markers that outline the rules by which programs will be run, the way services will be delivered, and the way outcomes will be measured. Decisions reflect the values of the decision maker, whether that is a person, team, or an organization. The idealized model of decision making is called the rational model and has six steps, as shown in Table 3.4.

TABLE 3.4 SIX STEPS IN RATIONAL DECISION MAKING

1. Define problem
2. Identify decision criteria
3. Weight criteria
4. Generate alternatives
5. Rate each alternative on each criterion
6. Compute the optimal decision

Defining the Problem Leads to Decision Criteria

Problem definition is the most important phase in decision making because the entire process flows from it. For example, assume that Joe was in an accident and his car is no longer drivable. If the problem is that Joe has no transportation, then decision criteria may focus on how he can get from home to work in an affordable fashion. Alternatives may include commuting by train or bus, using a rental car, or bicycling. These alternatives are different than if he had defined the problem as his car was no longer functional and he needed to buy a new one. In this case, the criteria would focus on cost of the vehicle and its attributes: number of people it will seat, fuel efficiency, cost, size, color, and so forth. In other words, the criteria—those points upon which the ultimate decision will rest—flow from how the problem is defined.

To Weight Criteria Is to Set Priorities

Once criteria are determined, weights are assigned to each in terms of importance. If criteria focus on ways to get from home to work, then the cost and time involved in choosing light rail over bus over bicycling will be used to weight the criteria. If criteria focus on buying a new vehicle, then price, make, and model will be used to weight criteria.

Generating and Rating Alternatives

The alternatives that will provide solutions to the problem are then specified and rated based on each criterion. In the case of selecting a means to commute, cost, convenience, and time will vary based on the respective choice of bike, train, or bus.

Making the Best Decision

To compute the optimal decision, Joe will select the alternative with the lowest cost and highest benefit. In other words, he will select the alternative that maximizes the criteria while costing the least in terms of money, time, or inconvenience.

From a managerial standpoint, strategic decision making is based on this six-step rational model. Strategic decisions are synonymous with mission-driven decisions, in that the mission is the goal to be achieved and the standard by which criteria are listed and weighted, and alternatives are selected and valued. Strategic decision making involves deciding between alternatives based on how each contributes to achieving the mission.

As an ideal, rational decision making assumes that (a) the goal is unambiguous, (b) priorities are stable, and (c) costs and benefits of each alternative are known. It also assumes that decision makers know their preferences and can rank order them. It also assumes that decision makers have the time and willingness to thoroughly examine all alternatives. However, this is rarely the case. Instead, decision makers use heuristics. These are rules of thumb that make decision making faster and less complicated.

Herbert Simon[30] and Charles Lindblom[31] provide two convenient heuristics. Simon argued that people use not full rationality, but rather bounded rationality. He coined the term "satisfice"—a combination of satisfy and suffice—to argue that, rather than considering all elements of a decision problem, people make choices by satisficing. That is, they seek to achieve at least some minimum level of some of the criteria, so they select the alternative that is good enough, even though it may not maximize all criteria. Thus, if Joe is buying a car, he may go to the dealer where he bought his last car, inquire into an updated model, compare the price of that and a couple other models, and base his purchase decision on those few criteria.

Lindblom approached decision making from a different perspective and described a decision-making style that is a form of satisficing, which he called incrementalism. In successive limited approximations, decision makers base today's decision on yesterday's, albeit with a minor adjustment. Thus, the decision is slightly, rather than dramatically, different from the prior decision. The notion of incrementalism is used primarily in the context of budgeting, where next year's budget is based on last year's except for minor adjustments up or down, based on programmatic exigencies. Minor change is easier to adapt to than major reform, so incrementalism produces decisions that are more likely to be within the decision maker's comfort zone.

Another aspect of decision making pertains to who is involved. Participative decision making requires the involvement of everyone who will be affected by the decision's consequences. Unitary decision making means that only one person makes the decision. Self-managed teams make decisions as a group. These variants involve different decision criteria (strategic), different numbers of participants (participative versus unitary), and different dynamics (self-managed teams versus individual).

DYSFUNCTIONAL DECISION MAKING

Although our minds turn to conflict at the thought of problematic decision making, the most deleterious dysfunction arises not from problems of disagreement but rather from problems of agreement. People are often hesitant to speak truth to power. When the boss suggests a course of action, everyone acquiesces, not wanting to be seen as disagreeable or oppositional. Groupthink is the term for uniform agreement without consideration of alternative points of view. It occurs when everyone "goes along to get along" and agrees to a solution despite not actually believing that it is the best. It happens when the reward for agreeing is greater than the reward for laying out alternatives. Thus, the problem is not one of conflict, it is one of too much agreement. Savvy administrators put safeguards in place to guard against this, as described in the next case.

RESILIENT DECISION MAKING

The Regional Transportation District (RTD) is a transit agency that serves the Denver, Colorado metropolitan region. Since forming in 1969, RTD has provided bus, light rail, and special transportation services (e.g., SeniorRide for elderly populations and BroncosRide for professional football games). As RTD grew to keep up with population growth, it expanded to over 9,751 bus stops and forty-six light rail stations, and it continues to expand. RTD currently serves 2.9 million people in forty municipalities.[32]

One of RTD's best practices involves how safety decisions[33] are made. An interdepartmental group was first established in the early 1990s to review the Metro Area Connector (MAC) light rail development. When the Federal Transit Administration (FTA) later mandated that municipal transit providers gather interdisciplinary stakeholders to oversee safety issues, RTD expanded its original scope. The new group was called the Executive Safety and Security Committee (ESSC) and includes representatives from each RTD department, including Bus Operations, Capital Programs, Communications, Facilities, Finance, Rail Operations, Risk Management, Safety, and Security.

All decisions of the ESSC are made at routine, monthly meetings via the consensus and consensus-blocking model. This approach requires that all members must agree on matters that require a vote. If a vote is not unanimous, then the decision is blocked and further work must be done to explore alternative options. This process avoids groupthink and ensures that all dimensions to a solution are carefully examined.

The ESSC's administrative structure has become well-established over the past twenty-five years. The committee also exemplifies a governing body that has institutionalized the flexibility to effectively adapt to ever-changing federal policies while maintaining a balance between standardized practices and adaptable systems.

Questions to Ponder

1. What is the advantage of having each department represented on the ESSC?
2. What is the advantage of allowing a vote to be blocked by only one person rather than deciding by majority vote?

DECISION HEURISTIC: FORCE FIELD ANALYSIS

Change is inevitable but savvy managers have strategies to manage the inherent conflict between comfortable routines of the past versus promising but unproven routines of the future. In any change, there are forces that favor it and forces that will resist it. A convenient heuristic for determining whether to make an administrative change is called a force field analysis. It contains within it the advantages of soliciting multiple points of view and of providing a visible representation of the possibility of success or failure. This field of forces can be examined to determine in advance the degree of success that a proposed change will have.

A force field analysis is a visual depiction of the likelihood of support for the decision. And it can literally be done on the back of a napkin. First, jot down the proposal. Then, think of the forces for and against it and assign a numerical value to the strength of each kind of support. Let the length of the arrow denote the numerical value, such that +5 is longer than +3. Then, do the same for the forces that oppose the decision, and sketch the arrows. By simply looking at the sketched diagram, additional forces may come to mind. And the tally of the numerical values for the pros and cons indicate the likelihood of success or failure. Moreover, a quick glance at the length of the arrows identifies the strongest forces for and against. In addition to yielding a number that indicates success or failure, the forces indicate where more persuasion may be successful at enhancing support or mitigating resistance.

FIGURE 3.2 FORCE FIELD ANALYSIS: TO ADD A REQUIRED COURSE
TO THE MPA CURRICULUM

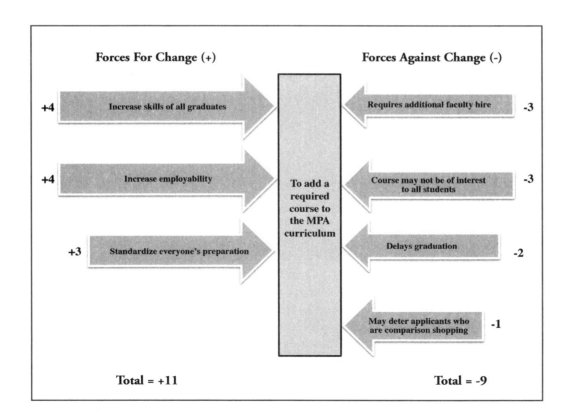

Figure 3.2 provides an example. Assume that the faculty of a Master of Public Administration program are considering whether to add a course to the core curriculum which would require all enrollees to complete this extra course in order to graduate. In deliberations about whether or not to make the change, faculty offer a number of arguments for and against the change. Figure 3.2 depicts the situation. The bar in the middle represents the proposed change. Forces against the change are listed on the right and forces for it are on the left. Based on a scale of 1 to 5, with 5 being most, faculty assign a value that they feel represents the strength of the argument for and against. As a final check, they then examine the proportionality of each force. For example, they determine that the addition could deter applicants from applying to the program, but they believe that is only about a third as strong a force against the cost of hiring another faculty member. After they have determined that they have listed all the forces that will be determinative of success or failure, they then sum the value of the forces for and the forces against. In this case, the forces for the change sum to 11 and forces against sum to 9. This back-of-the-envelope tally indicates that the change will probably succeed, although there will be some active resistance.

The enumeration of forces for and against, and the numerical result of counting values, helps the decision maker decide whether to move forward with the decision. It also provides information about which forces need to be bolstered so that the change will meet less resistance and gain more support. For example, if there is staff resistance to a planned change, training may help to reduce fear of the unknown and increase support for it.

Ask Me Why I Care: Edward A. Flynn, Police Chief in Milwaukee, Wisconsin[34]

Edward A. Flynn is police chief in Milwaukee, Wisconsin, where he has served since 2008. His career in public safety began in the Jersey City Police Department, where he was promoted through the ranks of officer, sergeant, lieutenant, captain and inspector. As chief of police in Arlington, Virginia, he was instrumental in the recovery effort at the Pentagon after the September 11, 2001 terrorist attack. As secretary of public safety under Massachusetts Governor Mitt Romney, he was responsible for the Massachusetts State Police, the Department of Correction, the National Guard, the Department of Fire Services, the Parole Board, and the Massachusetts Emergency Management Agency. Access Flynn's story at https://www.unomaha.edu/college-of-public-affairs-and-community-service/community-engagement/pss-edward-flynn.php.

SUMMARY

Paying attention to management brings us full circle from Dwight Waldo's focus on the state as an administrative body, to Drucker's focus on the mission of the organization, and to John Rohr's fascination with running a constitution. For each of these ways of thinking, management style is contingent on the nature of the work performed, the level of sophistication of the workforce, the size of the workforce, the nature of the mission, and whether the work is performed at the street level, in the office, or by tele-commuting. In addition are the elements that are unique to government, including the simultaneous trust and mistrust that citizens have of government, election cycles that cause turnover at the top, unquenchable demands for accountability, and spend-it-or-lose-it funding rules. To borrow Peter Drucker's words, climbing to the top is less of a steady climb up a ladder and more like a journey through a field of vines where you must bring your own machete.[35] To borrow from Waldo and Rohr, public managers are evaluated not just by the ends they achieve but by the means employed to do so.

The lesson of Kaufman's *Forest Ranger* is that managers control the performance of subordinates by remote control, through identification with the agency culture, and through a thorough grounding in agency policy and procedures. The autonomy and exercise of discretion of street-level bureaucrats, such as caseworkers, patrol officers, food inspectors, park rangers, and teachers, requires that they are well trained and have an unambiguous understanding of the mission and priorities.

Leadership skills are a must for managers both inside and outside of the agency. Often their work requires them to gain cooperation from stakeholders outside of the agency. These may be citizens, other agencies with related missions, and partnerships with businesses and nonprofits. Leadership skills are essential to bringing all actors together toward a common goal. Public administrators must be flexible, take risks, and not give up. In sum, they must be resilient. Leadership and management are related but are not the same. While leaders galvanize followers and motivate them, managers plan processes, coordinate workflows, and ensure that desired outcomes are reached. Some leaders are also good managers. Some managers are also good leaders.

Collaboration is important because only big problems get to government and by the time they get there, multiple resources are necessary for addressing them. This requires building liaisons with citizen groups, other service deliverers, and often other jurisdictions. The work simply cannot be achieved without working with others.

The ability to articulate a clear mission, arrive at a consensus on goals, build bridges with those who can help achieve the mission, and capitalize on the strengths of the workforce are essential ingredients for well-run organizations. Responsiveness to those affected by the actions of the agency, engagement of citizens in the work of the agency, and wise decisions about service providers aid in mission accomplishment. All these require a focus on the publicness of public service, good leadership, and resilience.

KEY TERMS

Capacity building – developing the organizational means to successfully accomplish goals and objectives. It is often accomplished through collaboration or partnerships.

Force field analysis – a convenient heuristic for determining whether to make an administrative change through a visual depiction of the likelihood of support for a decision.

Incrementalism – in successive limited approximations, decision makers base today's decision on yesterday's, albeit with a minor adjustment; the decision is slightly, rather than dramatically, different.

Leadership – the act of focusing followers' attention on a common purpose and motivating them to pursue it.

Rational decision making – the process by which a person proceeds through steps to make a decision. Steps include defining a problem, identifying decision criteria, weighting the criteria, generating alternatives, rating each alternative on each criterion, and computing an optimal decision.

Satisficing – the decision result achieved through bounded rationality. It is a term coined by Herbert Simon that combines "satisfy" and "suffice." Simon's argument is that, rather than considering all elements of a decision problem, people make choices that achieve at least some minimum level of acceptability. They select the alternative that is "good enough."

DISCUSSION QUESTIONS

1. Think about a manager whom you admire. What are the qualities that cause your admiration? Are they similar to the list in Figure 3.1?
2. Think of your choice for selecting this college. What were the decision criteria you employed? How did you weight each? Did you select the alternative that maximized the benefits and cost the least? Was your decision process emblematic of a formally rational process or of satisficing?
3. Think of a situation where you were engaged in solving a problem and everyone but you wanted one alternative and you wanted another. Did you speak up? Did you "go along to get along?" What could you have done differently?
4. Select a problem that confronts you and apply a force field analysis to it. What are your conclusions about the problem after completing the analysis?

BUILD YOUR SKILLS

Being able to run an effective meeting is easier said than done. Here are tips.

SKILLBOX: RUNNING A MEETING

Meetings provide an opportunity for information sharing, problem solving, team building, and dialogue. Do not hold a meeting unless face-to-face communication is the best means for accomplishing the objective. If the purpose is simply to distribute information in a one-way communication, e-mail is just as effective. Two-way communication is the purpose of meetings so set the stage to enable it. Follow these points to get the most out of everyone's participation.

Make the Meeting Matter. Have a clear objective and involve participants in the planning of the meeting and in developing the agenda. Make sure the right people are invited. If discussing a problem, invite those who are good sources of information about it and be sure to invite people with differing points of view. If announcing a change, invite those who will be affected by it.

Stick to the Agenda and Keep Things Moving. Set an agenda and distribute it in advance. Three days is a good rule of thumb. Be thoughtful about the sequence of discussion items. Contentious issues will lead to heated debate and will consume more time. These may be better placed after more routine items. If debate is likely to be prolonged, specify a time allotment for each item. Use language that welcomes people to share their ideas without being belittled or insulted. When someone is monopolizing the conversation, interrupt with "We appreciate your thoughts and now we need input from others." Avoid the temptation to dismiss wild ideas immediately—they may lead to a good idea later.

Start on Time, End on Time. Having a reputation for starting promptly causes people to get there on time. And having a reputation of ending on time encourages people to stay until the agenda concludes.

Close with an Action Plan. Make sure there is consensus for next steps and everyone knows who is responsible for what.

> ***Follow-up.*** To reduce the possibility that people leave the meeting with different interpretations of what transpired, record the minutes, especially the decisions made on action items. Distribute the minutes as soon as possible afterward.
>
> ### Hands-On Activity: Group Meeting
>
> Use this guide when your instructor assigns a group activity. Follow the steps so that the group has a productive session.

NOTES

1. John M. Bryson, Gary L. Cunningham, and Karen J. Lokkesmoe, "What to Do When Stakeholders Matter: The Case of Problem Formulation for the African American Men Project of Hennepin County, Minnesota," *Public Administration Review* 62, no. 5 (2002): 568–84.

2. Barbara C. Crosby and John M. Bryson, *Leadership for the Common Good: Tackling Public Problems in a Shared-Power World,* 2nd ed. (San Francisco, CA: Jossey-Bass, 2005).

3. Bryson, et al. "What to Do When Stakeholders Matter."

4. Sandy Schuman, *Creating a Culture of Collaboration: The International Association of Facilitators Handbook* (San Francisco, CA: Jossey-Bass, 2006).

5. "African-American Men Project," NorthPoint Health & Wellness Center, last modified 2015, http://www.northpointhealth.org/african-american-men-project/.

6. Rosemary O'Leary and Catherine M. Gerard, "Collaboration Across Boundaries: Insights and Tips from Federal Senior Executives," *IBM Center for the Business of Government* (2012), http://www.businessofgovernment.org/report/collaboration-across-boundaries-insights-and-tips-federal-senior-executives.

7. Woodrow Wilson, "Study of Administration," *Political Science Quarterly*, no. 2 (June, 1887): 197–222.

8. Ibid.

9. Dwight Waldo, *Perspectives on Administration* (Tuscaloosa, AL: University of Alabama Press, 1956), 49.

10. Dwight Waldo, *The Administrative State: A Study of the Political Theory of American Public Administration* (New York: Ronald Press Co., 1948).

11. John F. Kennedy, "Yale Commencement Address" (speech, New Haven, Connecticut, June 11, 1962), http://www.jfklibrary.org/Asset-Viewer/Archives/JFKWHA-104.aspx.

12. John A. Rohr, *Ethics for Bureaucrats: An Essay on Law and Values* (New York: Marcel Dekker, 1978).

13. H. George Frederickson, *Social Equity and Public Administration: Origins, Developments, and Applications* (Armonk, NY: M.E. Sharpe, 2010).

14. David Rosenbloom, Robert S. Kravchuk, and Richard Clerkin, *Public Administration: Understanding Management, Politics, and Law in the Public Sector*, 7th ed. (Boston, MA: McGraw-Hill Higher Education, 2009).

15. Anthony M. Bertelli and Laurence E. Lynn, Jr., *Madison's Managers: Public Administration and the Constitution* (Baltimore, MD: Johns Hopkins University Press, 2006).

16. Robert B. Denhardt and Janet V. Denhardt, *The Dance of Leadership: The Art of Leading in Business, Government, and Society* (Armonk, NY: M.E. Sharpe, 2006).

17. Donald F. Kettl, *Escaping Jurassic Government: How to Recover America's Lost Commitment to Competence* (Washington, DC: Brookings Institution Press, 2016).

18. Peter F. Drucker, *Concept of the Corporation* (New York: John Day Co., 1946); ibid., 1972.

19. Janet V. Denhardt and Robert B. Denhardt, *The New Public Service: Serving, Not Steering*, 3rd ed. (New York: Routledge, 2015).

20. Drucker, *Concept of the Corporation*, 26.

21. Ibid., 28.

22. Ibid., 128.

23. Peter G. Northouse, *Leadership: Theory and Practice*, 7th ed. (Thousand Oaks: CA, Sage, 2016).

24. Douglas McGregor, *The Human Side of Enterprise* (New York, NY: McGraw-Hill, 1960).

25. Mary Parker Follett, "The Giving of Orders," in *Scientific Foundations of Business Administration*, ed. H. C. Metcalf (Baltimore, MD: Williams and Wilkins, 1926), 29–37.

26. Herbert Kaufman, *The Forest Ranger: A Study in Administrative Behavior* (Washington, DC: RFF Press, 1960).

27. U.S. Department of Health and Human Services, *HeathCare.gov: CMS Management of the Federal Marketplace*, OEI-06-14-00350 (February, 2016), https://oig.hhs.gov/oei/reports/oei-06-14-00350.pdf.

28. Ibid.

29. Tom Lee, "What Everyone Is Getting Wrong about HealthCare.gov," *The Washington Post* (October 7, 2013), https://www.washingtonpost.com/news/wonk/wp/2013/10/07/what-everyone-is-getting-wrong-about-healthcare-gov/?utm_term=.e0d8f478ce23.

30. Herbert A. Simon, "Rational Choice and the Structure of the Environment," *Psychological Review* 63, no. 2 (1956): 129–38.

31. Charles E. Lindblom, "The Science of 'Muddling Through'," *Public Administration Review* 19 (1959): 79–88; and Charles E. Lindblom, "Still Muddling, Not Yet Through," *Public Administration Review* 39, no. 6 (1979): 517–26.

32. "Facts and Figures," Regional Transportation District, available at http://www.rtd-denver.com/factsAndFigures.shtml.

33. Regional Transportation District, *RTD Best Practices* (2015), http://www.rtd-denver.com/documents/best-practices-2015.pdf.

34. *Ask Me Why I Care: Public Service Stories*, video, directed by Mary R. Hamilton and Rita Paskowitz (Omaha, Nebraska: Omaha College of Public Affairs and Community Service), https://www.unomaha.edu/college-of-public-affairs-and-community-service/community-engagement/pss-edward-flynn.php.

35. Peter F. Drucker, *Managing in a Time of Great Change* (New York: Truman Talley Books, 1995).

ADDITIONAL RESOURCES

Goleman, Daniel. 2006. *Social Intelligence: The New Science of Human Relationships*. New York: Bantam Books.

Hood, Christopher and Ruth Dixon. 2015. *A Government That Worked Better and Cost Less? Evaluating Three Decades of Reform and Change in UK Central Government.* Oxford: Oxford University Press.

Kettl, Donald F. 2016. *Escaping Jurassic Government: How to Recover America's Lost Commitment to Competence.* Washington, DC: Brookings Institution Press.

Rainey, Hal G. 2014. *Understanding and Managing Public Organizations*, 5th ed. San Francisco, CA: Jossey-Bass.

Salamon, Lester M. (ed.). 2002. *The Tools of Government: A Guide to the New Governance.* New York: Oxford University Press.

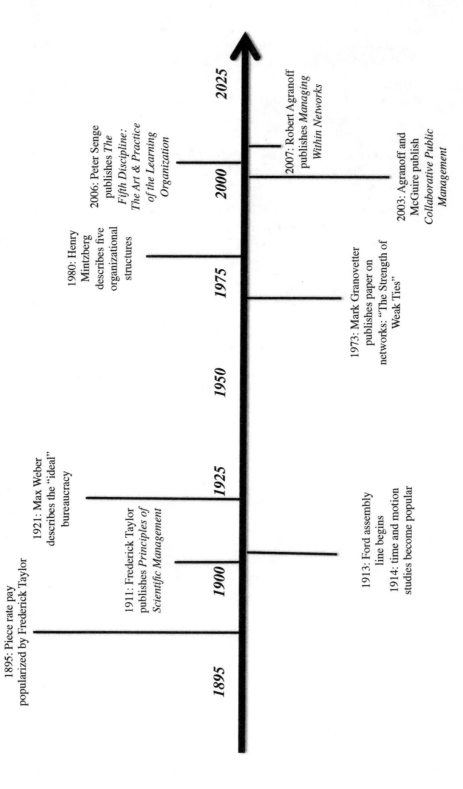

Chapter 4 Timeline: Organizing Principles

1895: Piece rate pay popularized by Frederick Taylor

1921: Max Weber describes the "ideal" bureaucracy

1911: Frederick Taylor publishes *Principles of Scientific Management*

1913: Ford assembly line begins
1914: time and motion studies become popular

1980: Henry Mintzberg describes five organizational structures

2006: Peter Senge publishes *The Fifth Discipline: The Art & Practice of the Learning Organization*

2007: Robert Agranoff publishes *Managing Within Networks*

2003: Agranoff and McGuire publish *Collaborative Public Management*

1973: Mark Granovetter publishes paper on networks: "The Strength of Weak Ties"

1895   1900   1925   1950   1975   2000   2025

ORGANIZING PRINCIPLES

WHAT YOU WILL LEARN

Organization design

Bureaucratic principles

The importance of mission

The difference that age and size make

The learning organization

Skillbox: Starting a nonprofit (or not)

Organizations are the instruments through which public services are delivered. Whether described as machines, organisms, factories, or jungles, they all have characteristics in common. They are the best way humans have found to bring strangers together to achieve a mission that no one can achieve by acting alone. They take various shapes, including: hierarchical to flat, very old to very young, huge to tiny, and loosely formed networks to tightly run machines. Because routines make the actions of organizations predictable and reliable, adapting to change can be difficult. Such was the case with twenty-two separate federal agencies when they became part of the newly formed U.S. Department of Homeland Security.

REORGANIZATION: THE CASE OF THE U.S. DEPARTMENT OF HOMELAND SECURITY

In 2002, fourteen months after terrorists hijacked airplanes and slammed them into the World Trade Center and the Pentagon, killing nearly 3,000 people and injuring another 6,000, President George W. Bush signed into law the U.S. Department of Homeland Security (DHS). The new department—which cobbled together twenty-two existing organizations into one—was the largest reorganization in the federal government in more than fifty years. The change involved 170,000 employees.[1] Among the agencies corralled were the Coast Guard, Secret Service, Customs and Border Protection, Transportation Security Administration, Federal Emergency Management Agency, among others. The new department's mission is to prevent terrorist attacks and enhance security; secure and manage the borders; enforce immigration laws; safeguard cyberspace; and ensure resilience to disasters.

The primary justification for the creation of DHS was the need for a flatter, more decentralized organization that could combat terrorist groups by increasing collaboration across agencies. The 9/11 Commission had found that the Central Intelligence Agency (CIA) and the Federal Bureau of Investigation (FBI) may have had the intelligence to predict the World Trade Center and Pentagon attacks, but the information had been siloed within each individual agency. Had the two been structured in such a way that enabled information sharing, a more robust defense strategy may have been set in motion. The Commission strongly advocated that a central mission of homeland security be delineated within an organizational structure that would enable sharing of information, resources, and decision making across all its parts.[2]

The responsibilities of such an all-encompassing body brought together employees with multiple areas of expertise, ranging from immigration, emergency management, cybersecurity, and transportation administration. Although large at its creation, DHS is now even larger, with about 240,000 employees. Only the Departments of Defense and Veterans Affairs are larger.

The new organizational structure was not a panacea; in fact, it produced its own problems. The loss of autonomy for some of the new department's agencies was a complication that lowered morale and disrupted routines. The goal for the creation of DHS was to develop synergies among the agencies that would lead to effective communication and collaboration. However, blending the diverse missions and activities across the agencies was a challenge. Emblematic of this is the fact that DHS now ranks among the lowest in morale among all of the large federal departments.

Another problem that resulted from the reorganization is that the Federal Emergency Management Agency (FEMA), an organization that must move quickly when disaster strikes, had lost its capacity to respond effectively. When Hurricane Katrina hit the Gulf Coast in 2005, several boundaries that typically existed within centralized organizations were no longer in place. The "authority boundary" defines who is in charge of what. The "task boundary" emphasizes who does what.[3] FEMA's lack of leadership and delegation resulted in a breakdown that made Katrina the most catastrophic hurricane in U.S. history up to that time.[4] Thus, post-Katrina reform has since focused on more formalized interdepartmental coordination.[5]

Size and diverse missions also cause problems. The scale of DHS means that an unmanageable number of congressional committees and subcommittees have jurisdiction over the Department. The number has grown from eighty-four to one hundred since the Department was created. This extraordinary number of hearings and layers of reviews hinders efficiency as well as meaningful oversight.[6]

The DHS mission itself has come into question. The ambiguity of what homeland security entails—from immigration to cybersecurity; from transportation safety to protection from pandemics—has led to mission creep. This makes it difficult for the department's many components to stay focused on the ultimate purpose. The centripetal desire to achieve homeland security competes with the centrifugal forces of each separate unit's mission, whether it is disaster response or fighting cybercrime.

Though few would argue with the logic for creating a department of homeland security, many would agree that it has failed to live up to expectations. The melding of cultures and identity of a department as large as this takes years to develop. Communication across its many components is still problematic. Identification with DHS and its accomplishments has yet to come to fruition. The lessons of the reorganization touch all aspects of organization design: mission, workforce characteristics, financial resources, information and communication channels, structure, coordinating mechanisms, culture, time horizon, decision-making processes, incentive systems, size, partisan politics, public trust, public scrutiny, and policies and procedures.

Questions to Ponder

1. What are the organizational dynamics that complicate a well-intended restructuring?

2. There are cross-cutting tensions in large departments. Did the creation of the Department of Homeland Security reduce or compound the tensions that existed between its components?

3. How does Congressional oversight of executive agencies affect their performance?

ORGANIZATION DESIGN

Organization theorist Henry Mintzberg made these mysterious creations we call "organizations" easier to understand when he defined their various structures and identified the coordinating mechanisms that make them work.[7] There are three essential elements: the strategic apex, the middle line, and the operating core, as depicted in Figure 4.1. Ultimate accountability for the actions of the organization rest at the top, with the director of the agency or board of directors. The middle line are man-

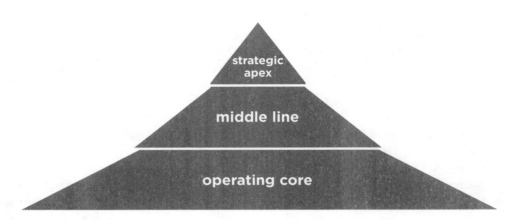

FIGURE 4.1 ORGANIZATIONAL STRUCTURE

agers who serve as a bridge between those who do the work of the organization at the operating core and those who are situated at the strategic apex and set direction.

When depicted in a diagram, organizations are pictured as a pyramid, with those directing the work at the top, those doing the work of the organization pictured at the bottom, and those in the middle serving as the link between the top and the bottom. The hierarchical depiction is used to show that authority flows downward. The higher someone is placed in the pyramid, the more power their position possesses. In government organizations the strategic apex is understood to be the director, but it is understood that the elected executive, whether mayor, governor, or president is the appointing authority and has ultimate authority over the director. And of course, legislative bodies and courts have constitutional authority to provide oversight. Likewise, in nonprofit agencies, those at the strategic apex are the director and the board of directors.

In addition to line positions—those directly responsible for achieving the mission of the organization—there are two types of staff positions: technostructure and support. The technostructure are those employees who usually report to the strategic apex and contribute technical services pertaining to operations and workflow. These may be accountants, legal staff, human resource trainers, and planners. Another category are support staff, who provide services that make it possible for workers to stay focused on the mission of the organization. Support staff may include the public information officer, receptionist, the mail room, those who manage vendors, those who process payroll and benefits, and those who provide support for computer hardware and software. An additional element is intangible. It is ideology and encompasses the beliefs, norms, traditions, and values of the organization.

Mintzberg describes all organizations as having some version of all six parts—strategic apex, middle line, operating core, technostructure, support staff, and ideology—

although the importance of each varies according to the organization's mission, size, age, workforce, environment, and degree of centralization. In order for people in the organization to work in concert with one another and capitalize on the resources available—people, money, information, and time—there are coordinating mechanisms that enable people to work toward a common goal and deliver uniform outputs in pursuit of the mission. These include mutual adjustment, direct supervision, and standardization of work processes, outputs, skills, and norms.

Coordinating Mechanisms

Mutual adjustment achieves coordination by the simple process of informal communication between employees. This is most often used in very small organizations, such as small nonprofits that have only a few employees. There is no need for formal policies because face-to-face communication among the workers is sufficient to coordinate work.

Direct supervision is achieved by managers issuing instructions and monitoring the work of subordinates.

Standardization of work processes is used when a lot of employees perform the same tasks and uniformity of process and output is important. The organization develops procedures that everyone must follow in order for the work to flow predictably and reliably. An example is vocational rehabilitation services, where the ultimate goal is to help citizens receive education, training, or medical services that will enable them to become employed. The ends differ based on each client's needs and skills, but the processes are similar across all clientele.

Standardization of outputs achieves coordination by specifying what the results of work must be. The organization specifies performance targets and workers must achieve them. Workers may vary in how they achieve the outputs, but everyone's outputs must be similar. An example of this method is found in job training programs where the output must be measured competencies or, in the case of colleges, the output is bachelor degrees.

Standardization of skills and/or knowledge is a type of coordination achieved by hiring workers who are already trained to perform their jobs. This form of coordination is found in the military which provides job-specific training to recruits before they are assigned to their duty stations. It is also found in professional organizations, who hire staff already trained, such as schools, universities, health-care facilities, and social services agencies.

Standardization of norms is an intangible coordinating mechanism that is found especially in mission-based nonprofits. The values, traditions, and norms infuse the organization, so that everyone functions according to the same set of beliefs and priorities. Religious organizations are an example.

One or more of these coordinating mechanisms are applied throughout the organization, and especially at the level of operating core. The resulting design resembles one of five basic configurations: simple structure, machine bureaucracy, professional bureaucracy, divisionalized form, and adhocracy. Although each of these types sounds clear-cut, contemporary structures are often a hybrid of these configurations, with features that are primarily of one but which include some features of another.

Structural Types

Simple structure is characteristic of small organizations with only a few employees. There may be no middle line because the director supervises the two or three employees in the operating core. And there will be no technostructure and no support staff other than perhaps a receptionist. This structure is found primarily in small nonprofits. Mutual adjustment is the primary coordinating mechanism because there is no need for more sophisticated processes.

Machine bureaucracy is characteristic of manufacturing firms and relatively small public agencies that operate in a stable environment where standard operating procedures prevail and where the mission is unidimensional and clear-cut. Municipal public works departments provide an example. The primary coordinating mechanisms are direct supervision and standardization of work processes and outputs.

Professional bureaucracy is characteristic of schools, health-care facilities, National Aeronautics Space Administration (NASA), and the U.S. Army Corps of Engineers. These organizations rely on "pre-trained" staff, meaning that employees are hired who received training prior to employment. Once hired, they only need to learn the nuances of the particular community being served before they go to work. The work is sophisticated and relies on worker discretion within the constraints of agency rules. Examples include caseworkers in child welfare agencies, faculty in schools and universities, health-care providers, scientists and engineers in NASA or the U.S. Army Corps of Engineers. The primary coordinating mechanisms are standardization of skills and norms.

Divisionalized form is characteristic of large agencies with multiple missions, such as the U.S. Department of Homeland Security and the American Red Cross. The mayor's office in large cities also provides an example. Coordinating mechanisms vary based on the mission of respective units, but above all, standardization of work processes and outputs are necessary to ensure uniformity. The larger an organization, the more it must rely on formal policies and procedures to guide the work of employees and to standardize work performance and outputs.

Adhocracy is characteristic of innovative organizations that need to adapt quickly to changing circumstances, needs, and worker skill sets. Especially during the race to the moon, NASA embodied this type of structure with its proliferation of project teams, and a network of outsourced services that involved a number of vendors. Contemporary examples in the states involve networks of providers that were convened to meet requirements of the Affordable Care Act. Each state sees variations in its complement of partnerships between insurance companies, medical services, and state and federal government. By definition, standardization is less important in such organizations and mutual adjustment is most important. Workers must communicate and adapt quickly to changing circumstances.

Structural Types and Their Coordinating Mechanisms

Regardless of whether the configuration is a simple structure for a small nonprofit or a huge divisionalized form such as the Department of Homeland Security, each configuration relies on one or more coordinating mechanisms: mutual adjustment, direct supervision, or standardization of work processes, outputs, skills, or norms. Additionally, each organization puts greatest emphasis on one of the five structural elements: strategic apex, middle line, operating core, support staff, or technostructure. For example, in the simple structure, the key part is the strategic apex, which coordinates by direct supervision. The structure is minimally elaborated because the organization is small and highly centralized. This pattern is associated with simple, dynamic environments and strong leaders, and is found in many small nonprofits.

In contrast to the simple structure, the machine bureaucracy coordinates primarily by the imposition of work standards from the technostructure so that the organization works like a machine: jobs are specialized and formalized, operating units are large, and power is centralized vertically at the strategic apex with some horizontal decentralization to the technostructure. There is little discretion allowed to operatives because outputs are standardized. This structure tends to be found in stable environments, especially when mass production of a uniform product is desired.

The professional bureaucracy relies on standardization of skills in its operating core for coordination. Jobs are highly specialized and the work is standardized only insofar as workers' professional training and experience have taught them. Decentralization is extensive in both the vertical and horizontal dimensions and there is little reliance on technostructure, for the professionals in the operating core are the technical experts.

The divisionalized form is found in large government departments or national and international nonprofits. In all these cases, multiple missions—or an overarching mission with multiple subordinate missions—require separate structures within the larger divisionalized form. Power is delegated from the strategic apex to respective divisions in the middle line. There, work is coordinated by the standardization of processes and/or outputs through performance control systems and reliance on policies and procedures.

Adhocracies are young, flexible structures created to achieve a particular purpose. They tend to be small startups, coordinated primarily by mutual adjustment among all of its parts. The structure is decentralized in both the vertical and horizontal dimensions. Liaison devices, such as project leaders and task forces, are used extensively so that communication travels accurately and quickly from one workgroup to another. These structures are found in complex, dynamic environments where work is nonprogrammable.

In addition to coordinating mechanisms, there are additional design parameters that affect how organizations perform. These include how work units are grouped, their size and degree of decentralization, and the sorts of liaison devices that are used, such as teams and task forces. Beyond these basics, additional factors of age, size, and the degree of politicization surrounding the mission affect the application of design features. All of these attributes create the unique architecture of each agency.

Correlates That Affect Design

In addition to the usual characteristics of structure and coordinating mechanisms, there are correlates associated with these. For example, the older an organization is, the larger it is. This is because organizations, like people, seek to survive, build on their capacity, and assume greater responsibilities (sometimes called mission creep). The larger an organization is, the more formalized its structure and processes will be. And, the older an organization is, the more heavily it relies on "tried and true" procedures, which will be captured in extensive policy manuals. Small startups can adapt more quickly to changing circumstances because there are fewer people involved in decision making and fewer historic trappings that govern the paths to be taken.

Herbert Kaufman,[8] an astute student of organizations, studied the forces that differentiate between organizations that survive and those that do not. Those that die, meaning merge with other agencies or simply close their doors, are those whose resources are too few to sustain them or whose missions are no longer relevant. In the case of nonprofits, death comes when the mission is insufficiently attractive to funders or when the mission has been absorbed by a more powerful agency.

In the case of public agencies, death is rare because problems do not get to government until a need is so great that it cannot be addressed by business or the nonprofit sector and yet the public demands a response. Thus, the problem is large and the political consensus is that it must be addressed. The size and scope of the problem ensures longevity for the newly created agency. Changes that may occur with government organizations, however, include the agency's name as it expands, contracts, or clarifications in its mission. For example, the federal Centers for Medicare & Medicaid Services (CMS), an agency within the U.S. Department of Health and Human Services, was previously known as the Health Care Financing Administration (HCFA). The name change was largely symbolic, designed to emphasize service in Medicare and Medicaid programs.

ORGANIZATIONAL ARCHITECTURE

Each organization takes the shape it does because of its architecture. Its elements start with the mission and include a number of variables which, when combined, result in a unique constellation of workers and activities. Managers have at their disposal four sets of resources: people, money, information, and time. How each is allocated is reflected in the priorities, design, and processes of the organization. Although all organizations, whether business, nonprofit, or governmental, have a blend of these resources, government organizations have an additional imperative: They must be transparent and their leadership changes periodically based on results of partisan elections. Election cycles affect the time horizon within which results are expected and electoral politics affect how the mission is achieved as well as the budgetary priorities. Table 4.1 displays the architectural elements of public service organizations.

TABLE 4.1 ARCHITECTURAL ELEMENTS OF PUBLIC SERVICE ORGANIZATIONS

Mission

Workforce characteristics

Financial resources

Time horizon

Information and communication channels

Structure

Coordinating mechanisms

Culture

Decision-making processes

Incentive systems

Size

Partisan politics

Public trust

Public scrutiny

Policies and procedures

As shown by Mintzberg's enumeration of structural elements and the architectural elements listed in Table 4.1, there are a variety of options for how to design public agencies. Organizations that require tight control, standardization of processes and uniformity of output, such as law enforcement and disaster response, employ a classical hierarchy in the form of a machine bureaucracy. In contrast, work that requires discretion on the part of workers and relies on a professionally trained workforce will employ a heterarchy, such as is found in professional organizations. And community arts programs are likely to rely on loosely networked groups that exercise a great amount of discretion and autonomy. In other words, there is not one right way to structure an organization. The best configuration depends on a number of factors, including the nature of the work to be performed, the presence or absence of urgency, characteristics of the workforce, and external forces that constrain the organization.

Whatever configuration results, the architectural elements mix and blend to form a cultural milieu within each organization, whether it is young or old, small or large, politicized or not. Some elements are under the control of management, and some, like partisan politics and public scrutiny, are not. When reorganizations take place, such as with the creation of the Department of Homeland Security, some of these elements are perturbed for better or worse and it takes time for the "new normal" to be accepted. In the case of DHS, the goal of improving cooperation across subunits was achieved at the price of control and autonomy and the blend remains a work in progress more than a decade later.

CENTRALIZATION VERSUS DECENTRALIZATION

The centralization–decentralization continuum is used to describe where decisions are made in an organization. It should not be confused with geographic dispersion. A traditional top-down organization is called that because decisions are made at the top—at the strategic apex—by the director. A flatter organization allows for influential decisions to be made at lower levels. For example, in professional organizations such as universities, decisions are made by the faculty. In health-care facilities, they are made by the clinical staff. Conversely, a geographically decentralized agency, such as a state agency with offices in the counties may or may not employ decentralized decision making. All decisions may be made at headquarters, or they may be made in the local offices.

The issue of decentralized decision making is closely related to the subject of administrative discretion. There is a tension between discretion and control. The more that public managers' choices are constrained, the less likelihood there is for corruption or unfairness to occur. But constraints on discretion also hamper creativity and quick action. The less that managers are constrained, the more capacity they have to consider all aspects of a problem and quickly make the best decision given the exigencies of the moment. The degree of centralization is under management's control and that fact is captured here in the case of a public transit agency as it underwent complicated expansion projects.

DECENTRALIZED DECISION MAKING IN A PUBLIC TRANSIT AGENCY

The Regional Transportation District (RTD) is a public transit agency that has served the Denver, Colorado metropolitan area since 1969. It provides bus, light rail, and other public transportation services to roughly 2.9 million people.[9] With the area's burgeoning population growth in recent decades, additional transit projects emerged to meet ridership needs. In 2001, RTD partnered with the state's Department of Transportation (CDOT) on an expansion project, called T-REX. The project was estimated to cost a hefty $1.7 billion. The magnitude of road, bridge, and transportation engineering decisions required by T-REX concerned officials, who feared that a single project manager would find it challenging to meet every contractor deadline. Unforeseen delays could result in extra fees and the project going over budget.[10]

RTD addressed this issue by decentralizing project management decisions. The board of directors first delegated authority to the general manager, who then delegated contract, purchase order, and other budgetary decisions to the assistant general manager (AGM). Regular updates were then provided to the board. Decisions were further decentralized when the multibillion dollar FasTracks commuter rail program was approved in 2004, adding another 122 miles of light rail, fifty-seven new stations, and 21,000 parking spaces across the district.[11] The AGM consequently pushed authority down to the most appropriate program staff, trusting that those closest to problems would find the best solutions in the timeliest manner.

This decentralized decision-making process worked well and became an RTD best practice. Program managers reviewed quality, schedule, and budgetary aspects while the project manager ensured that T-REX and FasTracks developments were delivered on time and on budget. This type of administrative delegation remains vital to RTD today and helps it meet the needs of the greater Denver transit community.

CONTROL, COOPERATION, AND AUTONOMY

There are three inherent tensions within every organization: control, cooperation, and autonomy.[12] Like the corners of a triangle, they are inevitable comrades who do not like one another (see Figure 4.2). How they are managed and balanced is reflected in the culture and norms of the organization. Control requires subordination and reliance on hierarchy. Cooperation requires integration, while autonomy requires the opposite: separation and delegation of control. The desire to integrate the work of different departments so that everyone is working in concert with one another fights with the desire for autonomy, which allows individuals and departments to pursue their work free from interference from others. At the same time, the desire to control processes and outcomes fights with the desire for autonomy and for the decentralization that is required if workers and departments are to work cooperatively.

FIGURE 4.2 CONTROL, COOPERATION, AND AUTONOMY

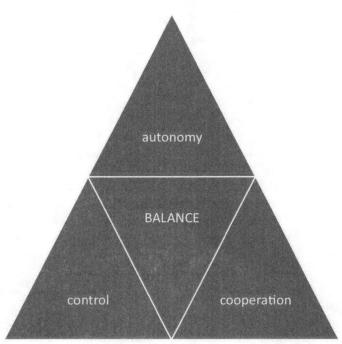

These tensions reside in every organization, large and small, and management sets the tone for how they are, or are not, balanced against each other. In the DHS case, autonomy of individual agencies within the department was sacrificed in order to achieve greater cooperation and control. In the case of the Regional Transportation District, autonomy won over control because management recognized the need to move expeditiously and prevent delays caused by requiring oversight of project managers' decisions. Control was lessened in order to move projects forward more quickly.

ORGANIZATION THEORY

The rise of urbanization and industrialization in the late 1800s and early 1900s heightened attention to formal organizations. Two contemporaries, Frederick Taylor (1856–1915), an American engineer, and Max Weber (1864–1920), a German sociologist, significantly advanced scholarly attention to the workplace. While Taylor crafted a theory of scientific management that focused on the relationship between management and labor, Weber focused on the formal structure of large organizations, whether churches, armies, or businesses.

Scientific Management

An industrial engineer, Frederick Taylor studied the relationship between managers and workers and developed prescriptions for how to improve performance.[13] These are listed in Table 4.2. His work represents the first formal treatment of productivity and was soon named "scientific management" to reflect his rigorous study of how to increase productivity in manufacturing. Although designed with manual labor in mind, Taylor's work was soon applied to service work as well. The principles of scientific management have the goal of improving efficiency through maximizing the productivity of laborers.

A contemporary term for "Taylorism" is process engineering. For example, he studied how manual laborers shoveled coal and then he wrote prescriptions for how they should precisely dig, lift, and empty their shovels in order to be able to move more coal with less effort. He assumed that workers would not be able to identify the best methods for shoveling and that managers, because of their superior cognitive abilities, would be the ones to determine how the work could best be performed. He believed that it was management's responsibility to determine the best way to perform each task and then teach workers.

By systematizing work functions, scientific management emphasized the impersonal nature of the workplace, such that workers were viewed as interchangeable parts. Taylor assumed that, with capable management, any worker could be replaced and trained to perform the same functions. Personality and temperament were thought to be of little importance, and with proper management, each worker could be trained and rewarded for following the exact methods prescribed by management.

Taylor also assumed that workers perform in order to satisfy their economic needs and his work overlooks internally driven social and personal needs. Because of his focus on extrinsic rather than intrinsic rewards, he believed that piece rate pay was the best method for compensation because it linked workers' performance to their pay. The more coal they moved, the more they were paid. Now reviled more than revered, many of today's assumptions about compensation nevertheless continue to be based on Taylorist assumptions. For example, pay-for-performance is similar to piece rate pay. The assumption is that, if someone is to earn more, they must work more. And pay-for-performance assumes that work is measurable. Workers subjected to such pay systems often argue that much of what they do cannot be measured, that quality of work is more important than quantity, and that there is too much subjectivity on the part of supervisors when it comes to judging who is performing well and who is not. Systems developed for manual labor do not transfer well to service work but the concepts remain popular.

Taylorism transferred control from workers to management, taking away worker autonomy. He assumed that managers would know better how each task could best be accomplished. He viewed managers as the thinkers and workers as the doers. Detailed plans were to be formulated by management and communicated to the workers. Close

---

TABLE 4.2. FREDERICK TAYLOR'S PRINCIPLES OF SCIENTIFIC MANAGEMENT

1. There should be a scientific study of tasks and, based on this, rule-of-thumb work methods should be replaced with specific instructions on how to perform a job.
2. Workers should be scientifically selected, and trained, rather than expecting them to train themselves.
3. Managers, based on their scientific analysis of the work to be performed, should provide detailed instruction and supervision of each worker.
4. The work of management is substantively different from the work of laborers. Managers plan the work, instruct workers, and closely supervise them, correcting them when they fail to follow instructions. Workers perform the tasks as instructed.

---

supervision was seen as essential to preventing workers from "soldiering," in other words, being lazy and failing to perform. The development of time and motion studies coincided with Taylor's work on the scientific assessment of the tasks to be performed and are consistent with scientific management principles.

Scientific management assumed that (1) piece rate is the best way to motivate workers to maximize their productivity; (2) employees are motivated by extrinsic, not intrinsic, rewards; (3) employees must be closely supervised and their output monitored because they will only produce when they are being watched; and (4) employees are interchangeable parts, such that new employees, once trained, can replace those who left with no loss of productivity. These assumptions and the principles of scientific management, although still present in part, lose their salience with a more educated workforce, the need for discretion in street-level work, the expectation of personal autonomy that college graduates bring to the workplace, and the convenience of telecommuting.

The value of Frederick Taylor's work is that it drew attention to "regularizing" the workplace and defining the roles of managers versus workers. The principles worked well in assembly line production but public service is a very different environment. Workers are educated, and situations are often ambiguous and best understood by workers themselves. The work relies on knowledge workers—those whose performance is as much self-directed as mandated by one's supervisor. Much of public service requires interacting with multiple constituencies, using discretion, and exercising initiative and public service motivation. Charged with the responsibility to achieve a purpose, public managers require the skill and authority to figure out how best to produce the desired result. In the RTD case, for example, managers have both responsibility and discretion and this serves the agency well.

THE IDEAL BUREAUCRACY

About the same time that Frederick Taylor was puzzling over how to achieve efficiency in manufacturing, a German sociologist, Max Weber, was focusing on organizations from a holistic perspective. His work culminated in a delineation of the elements of formal organizations that contribute to reliability and predictability. An enthusiastic advocate of bureaucracy, Weber noted that it constitutes the most efficient and rational way for human activity to be organized. He believed that its systematic processes and organized hierarchy were necessary to maintain accountability, maximize efficiency, and eliminate favoritism. He argued that bureaucracy is the best design to advance the modern state.

It bears mentioning that at the time Weber was writing, the term "bureaucracy" had a positive connotation. It was seen as a progressive term that stood for good organization, fair processes, and efficient production. In contrast, the term is now more often used as a pejorative to denote the darker side of organization, where delays are extensive, people are treated impersonally, and hierarchy and division of labor is used to place responsibility elsewhere for unpopular decisions. It can be argued that the strengths of bureaucracy are one side of a coin and the problems are the other side and an inevitable consequence. Although imperfect, bureaucracy continues to be the design that endures. From local police departments to public schools, to the Social Security Administration, the Environmental Protection Agency, and the Executive Office of the President, bureaucracy is a distinctive form of social organization whose goal is to regularize and increase the predictability and accountability of government.

MAX WEBER'S DESCRIPTION OF BUREAUCRACY

"Experience tends universally to show that the purely bureaucratic type of administrative organization . . . is . . . capable of attaining the highest degree of efficiency and is in this sense formally the most rational known means of exercising authority over human beings. It is superior to any other form in precision, in stability, in the stringency of its discipline, and in its reliability. It thus makes possible a particularly high degree of calculability of results for the heads of the organization and for those acting in relation to it. . . . It is . . . formally capable of application to all kinds of administrative tasks. . . . This is true of church and state, of armies, political parties, economic enterprises, interest groups, endowments, clubs, and many others. Its development is, to take the most striking case, at the root of the modern Western state."[14]

TABLE 4.3. ELEMENTS OF WEBER'S "IDEAL" BUREAUCRACY

- employment based on education and training rather than patronage or family ties
- scalar chain of command
- hierarchical (top down, pyramid-shaped)
- delegation of authority commensurate with responsibility
- division of labor where jobs are well-defined
- limited span of control
- employees are paid for their work in a systematic salary structure
- reliance on written documentation

Table 4.3 lists the eight Weberian principles to which "ideal" or model organizations should adhere. These principles describe bureaucracy as a formal organization in which relationships are different from those found in informal organizations, such as families. The characteristics that Weber enumerates produce (1) impersonal relationships among workers who are hired on the basis of their technical skills rather than on family lineage or political favor; (2) a clear chain of command in which workers know to whom they are responsible and accountable; (3) a hierarchical authority structure with the person at the top holding the most power; (4) authority and responsibility delegated downward at the director's prerogative; (5) division of labor so that workers know the boundaries of their responsibilities; and (6) limited spans of control for managers so that they can effectively monitor the performance of their subordinates. This number varies based on the homogeneity versus heterogeneity of work performed by subordinates, but a rule of thumb of about seven subordinates persists. The final two principles are (7) employees are to be paid for their work, rather than being expected to volunteer their efforts. And, (8) written documentation is the authoritative form of formal communication. To this day, office procedures and communications that are deemed official are those that appear in print on websites and office manuals, while spoken dictates are informal until formalized in writing.

Hierarchy works because of deference to authority. To elaborate on this, Weber notes that there are three types of authority: traditional, charismatic, and legal-rational. Of these, it is legal-rational that occurs in bureaucracies. In traditional authority, legitimacy is derived by socially scripted roles. For example, in paternalistic societies, the father is ascribed power. In charismatic authority, legitimacy is derived from the personality and leadership qualities of a person, regardless of their family or social roles. The essence of authority in formal organizations—bureaucracies—derives from the legal-rational model, where authority is ascribed based on the rank one holds. In other words, authority in bureaucracies is a function of one's post, not a function of one's family ties or wealth or personality. As clear-cut as these sources of power seem, it is nevertheless true that power actually accrues through blends. For example, the more charismatic that executives are, the more their legal-rational authority is bolstered.

Both Taylor's and Weber's writings are emblematic of their times. Industrial production was skyrocketing and urbanization was driving the need for governments to do more. Both theorists developed models that assumed stable environments, a sufficient supply of educated managers and a ready supply of workers willing to take orders. Their seminal work propelled the industrial revolution and the growth of government as it raced to develop the organizational infrastructure to pursue public purposes.

FORM FOLLOWS FUNCTION

In a departure from Taylor's and Weber's prescriptions, we no longer believe that there is one best way to supervise and one best way to structure an organization. Just as Mintzberg prescribed multiple types of structures, forces surrounding an organization shape and sculpt its outlines. Whether in huge federal bureaucracies or three-person grassroots nonprofit startups, form must follow function. The mission, workforce, workflow, communication channels, and accountability mechanisms drive the type of structure that evolves. And when functions change, so must the form, as in the case of RTD and the move to decentralized decision making. Or when, after the attacks of 9/11, free standing agencies surrendered their autonomy to come under the umbrella of the Department of Homeland Security in order to expedite information sharing and collaboration.

The contemporary workplace is marked by reliance on teamwork, collaboration across agencies and teams, telecommuting, and networks of providers, whether directly employed or whether contracted to provide specific services for specific projects. The recent reliance on more adhocracies—often as units within traditional bureaucracies—results from any number of factors: complicated tasks require the work of multifunctional teams; web-based communication makes it possible for geographically remote persons to collaborate; the complexity of many public problems requires multiple types of expertise so teams perform better than individuals; and contracted services can be quickly brought on line to pursue specific projects and then terminated when the goal is achieved.

Mission Drives the Organization

The smaller an organization, the more likely it is to have one specific mission with clear-cut goals and objectives. Small nonprofits created to pursue a singular goal, such as provide food for the homeless, have an easier job of communicating what it stands for and why it exists than does a larger organization that serves multiple constituencies. The larger an organization, the more likely it is to have multiple missions and ambiguous goals, such as the case with the U.S. Department of Homeland Security.

Organizations strive to survive, even when keeping the doors open requires a change in mission. An example of how one nonprofit transformed itself after its original mission was achieved is the March of Dimes Foundation, a national nonprofit founded by Franklin Roosevelt in 1938 to eradicate polio, a crippling neurological disease. Thanks to the development of an effective vaccine, the organization had achieved its mission by the 1970s. Faced with closing its operations or redesigning itself, the organization chose the latter. In 1976 it changed its mission from fighting polio to combating birth defects. Its new mission is improving the health of mothers and babies and now supplies information and support to families affected by prematurity, birth defects, and other infant health problems.

While a change of mission such as the March of Dimes' is unusual, it happens occasionally among nonprofits. Government agencies take a different tack. Rather than terminate, they often add to their mission by merging or redesigning agencies to expedite, expand, or refocus services, as shown in the case of the Department of Homeland Security.

Unlike nonprofits, government agencies must also perform nonmission-based work. For example, sunshine laws protect the public's right to know about the actions, policies, procedures, successes, and failures of government agencies. This requires sufficient staffing so that requests for documents can be fulfilled. Another example is Public Information Officers, who are on staff in most government agencies at the local, state, and federal levels to provide press briefings and updates on activities.

Networks

As much as bureaucratic structure continues to be the most accountable, efficient mechanism for pursuing public purposes, networks provide a means of collaboration among multiple agencies. Networks arise when multiple organizations are addressing the same problem and realize the value in sharing perspectives, information, and effort. For example, to address problems of unemployment, a job development and training network may consist of representatives from the state department of labor, the city's community development agency, community colleges, and the local Chamber of Commerce. Each entity's representative brings information to share and together they can develop a collaboration and outreach that will generate solutions that no single actor could develop by working alone. Unencumbered by the restrictions of hierarchy, networks are flat organizations, more often informal than formal. With no clear chain of command, each representative is a node in the network, bringing to bear expertise that would otherwise be absent. In this way, networks enable collaboration.

The term collaboration and collaborative networks are often used interchangeably.

Collaboration denotes the importance of interpersonal skill as well as the importance of organizational entities working together by sharing resources, such as staff, information, and services. Collaborations are nonhierarchical and may be formal or informal. They are either self-organizing or organized by someone in a position of authority, such as the mayor. Collaborative networks are collections of organizational entities that work together to provide a public good, service, or value when a single agency is unable to create the good or service on its own.

Form follows function. Organizational designs that worked in one era may need to adapt to changing circumstances. For example, the 9/11 attack and continued terrorist threats gave rise to the creation of the Department of Homeland Security. The need for quick decision making resulted in decentralized processes in Denver's RTD. In the next case, a number of agencies changed their processes in order to deliver services required by the American Recovery and Reinvestment Act, a law passed in response to the Great Recession of 2007–2009.

IMPLEMENTING THE RECOVERY ACT

The Great Recession of 2007–2009 is now considered the worst economic crisis since the Great Depression of the 1930s.[15] The fallout was extensive: 8.4 million people lost their jobs in the United States, more than 10 percent of Americans lost health insurance,[16] and nearly 4 million homes were foreclosed each year.[17] In response, the U.S. Congress passed the American Recovery and Reinvestment Act (ARRA). The legislation specified appropriations for multiple programs across a number of federal agencies. More than $787 billion was dedicated to advancing clean and efficient energy, transforming the economy with science and technology, modernizing infrastructure, overhauling education, dispensing tax cuts to create jobs, expanding access to health care, providing career assistance to disenfranchised workers, saving public sector jobs, and protecting vital public services.[18]

Twenty-eight different departments and agencies were charged with implementing these initiatives. Furthermore, ARRA mandated that at least 70 percent of the funds be disbursed within seventeen months in order to help the American economy recover as quickly as possible. The success of such a rapid, massive endeavor was dependent on effective collaboration, accountability procedures, results, promptness, and transparency throughout each bureaucratic body. A few agencies are highlighted here, illustrating the ability to manage significant budget increases, create new programs with limited capacity, and redesign administrative processes in a condensed timeframe.[19] The U.S. Fish and Wildlife Service (FWS) embodied exemplary financial management strategies after it was awarded a windfall allocation.

With millions more to spend, implementation went to work. FWS is comprised of more than 700 field offices across the eight regions of the U.S. Department of the Interior (DOI). Intergovernmental collaboration was critical to success. Each regional office developed its own implementation team to ensure funds were distributed to local offices on time and projects moved forward as planned. In addition, headquarters established a central reporting tool to track the completion of development phases and provide support to the implementation teams as needed.

Agencies and departments were also challenged with creating new programs, procedures, application forms, and management systems in the first seventeen months. For instance, the U.S. Department of the Treasury was responsible for distributing cash payment programs in place of previous renewable energy tax credit programs. Recipients were rewarded based on the number of kilowatt hours of electricity they produced with renewable energy sources, such as wind turbines or solar panels. Interdepartmental collaboration was key. Treasury quickly partnered with the Department of Energy, which provided the technical expertise necessary to assist with designing an application, website, data collection system, and awarding process. Between July 2009

and September 2010, $5 billion in renewable energy cash payments were distributed.

Finally, many traditional administrative processes were not sufficient to achieve the goals of ARRA. Redesign was a must in each agency. The U.S. Department of Veterans Affairs (VA) underwent a monumental shift in its general business-related procedures. A Recovery Act team was gathered to oversee all strategies, such as shortening the contractor invoice processing time from thirty days to one week. The group also created a method to pre-validate small business contractors in the registration system, developed a reporting tool, and instituted weekly meetings to assess progress toward target goals. These processes were made visible to all VA managers, which simultaneously triggered a healthy bout of competition throughout the department. Teams contended with each other to successfully implement ARRA projects on time and budget across the VA.

These are just a few examples of how bureaucracies adapted to accommodate rapid deadlines, changes in billing and contracting procedures, and staffing needs. The circumstances demanded it. Form followed function. And none of this could have been achieved without formal organization.

POLITICAL CONTROL OF THE BUREAUCRACY

Government bureaucracies are agents working at the behest of elected officials. In a principal/agent relationship, elected administrators, whether president, governor, or mayor, are constitutionally charged with the responsibility of fulfilling the demands of statutes passed by legislative bodies, which are agents of the public at large. Career staff are hired on the basis of their expertise and are expected to perform the duties delegated to them. All this is true in theory. In reality, however, processes are neither as smooth nor as linear.

Experienced public managers may have worked in the same agency across the tenure of a number of elected officials and watched them come and go, along with their unique priorities. The savvy manager knows that there are ways to delay an unworkable order until the next administration takes office. To combat this, legislators may place excessive regulations on administrative discretion, intending to constrain managers' actions. These constraints, in turn, result in workarounds by experienced managers.[20] The reality of this vicious cycle causes elected officials to want to be able to appoint senior executives who share their political goals and are more likely to expeditiously pursue their objectives. On the other hand, savvy political leaders know that respected public managers have the most knowledge about what will, and will not, work. Thus, the tension increases or subsides based on the relationship between elected and career officials.

> *"Bureaucracy is not an obstacle to democracy but an inevitable complement to it."*
>
> —Joseph A. Schumpeter

Reorganization is one means by which newly elected officials attempt to gain control of the bureaucracy. A reorganization strategy has the benefit of giving the appearance of forward-moving change. It also has the potential of shaking up comfortable routines that have outlived their usefulness. Sometimes reorganizations result in positive change but that is not always the case. When change occurs, it results in some people gaining power and prestige and in some losing power and status. It may reconfigure communication channels and improve, or stymie, the flow of information. In the case of the ARRA, reorganization was necessary to adapt to the policy change wrought by the legislation. Reorganization may also be a response to public demands for change, such as in the creation of DHS. In sum, when changes are made in an organization's design, there are ripple effects that affect many. Sometimes they produce good change, sometimes they produce only the appearance of change, and sometimes they gut an organization of its strengths. Reorganizations are more likely to have positive results when there is a consensus within the organization that drives the changes. This is what occurs in learning organizations.

THE LEARNING ORGANIZATION

The case of RTD demonstrates the reliance on decentralized decision making in order to expedite services. As demonstrated by RTD's success, the ideal is for organizations to learn from their performance, identify areas where they fall short, and make adjustments in organizational design, processes or allocation of resources to rectify the shortcoming. Organizations that succeed are called learning organizations, for they have identified a problem and self-corrected, followed by monitoring and subsequent adjustments as needed. Organizations that fail to learn fall behind in performance.

> *"In a learning organization, leaders are designers, stewards, and teachers. They are responsible for building organizations where people continually expand their capabilities to understand complexity, clarify vision, and improve shared mental models—that is, they are responsible for learning."*
>
> —Peter Senge

Learning organizations are characterized by behaviors that are dramatically different from the assumptions of scientific management. Rather than focusing on specific tasks, systems thinking is required. This involves looking at the whole organization and understanding how its various units relate to one another. By seeing the big picture, those within the organization can distinguish patterns that work and those that need improvement.

This way of thinking looks for connections between the units and expects workers to be thoughtful about how they operate, the actions they take, and which of these result in successes or failures. It also requires everyone to be committed to continuous learning, striving to develop themselves and to be open to change. A clear mission that enables a shared vision elicits commitment and binds an organization together.

Sometimes called double loop learning, there is a dynamism in this process that contrasts sharply with the singular focus of each worker on his or her own performance, as prescribed by scientific management. Double loop learning is contrasted with single loop because it includes feedback after the application of a solution is implemented. This continuous feedback enables workers to know what is working well, what is not, and the effect of adaptations. Self-reflection, careful observation, identifying problems, making adjustments, and monitoring them in a continuously iterative process, are the dynamic elements of learning organizations.

To summarize, a learning organization does away with the mind-set that it is only senior management who are responsible for doing all the thinking. It is an empowering notion that trusts workers at all levels to care about the mission and the quality of outputs. Learning organizations challenge all employees to tap into and develop their own resources and potential in order to achieve a shared goal.

SUMMARY

Organizations are fascinating creations. Their goal is to bring together strangers to accomplish a mission that cannot be achieved by individual action. Their design varies based on a number of variables, including mission, size, workforce, age, budget, and environment. Public service organizations range from small agencies of only a few workers to huge organizations that are charged with an overall mission with its units having distinctly different sub-missions, such as the Department of Homeland Security.

The structure is analogous to what can be seen on an X-ray: the formal chain of command is shown and formal communication channels are obvious. What organization charts cannot show are the intangible elements: informal dynamics, norms, traditions, values, and customary workarounds that circumvent the formal processes.

Ask Me Why I Care: Alan Dean, former associate administrator, Federal Aviation Administration[21]

"If you think government is bad, you get bad government."

—Alan Dean

Alan Dean had a long and storied career as an administrator. Starting as a human resource specialist in city government in Portland, Oregon, he then moved to the federal government, where he moved up the ranks. His career included helping to draft the National Aeronautics and Space Act, which was the charter for NASA. In 1960 he joined the Federal Aviation Administration as an associate administrator, where he was a principal adviser on organization and management. Dean was honored in 1965 as a top civil servant by President Lyndon Johnson at a White House ceremony in the Rose Garden. Two years later, President Johnson appointed Dean to be the first assistant secretary of the new Department of Transportation. He retired from government in 1979. He died in 2011 at age 92. Access his story at https://www.unomaha.edu/college-of-public-affairs-and-community-service/community-engagement/pss-alan-dean.php.

Organizations that adapt to changing circumstances are called learning organizations because they identify discrepancies between mission, processes, and outputs and make adjustments. This was the case of the federal agencies that accommodated to the ARRA. Levels of centralization substantively affect the level of discretion that workers have and affect the speed by which work can be completed, as demonstrated in the case of RTD.

The purpose of organizations is to become more than the sum of their parts. By coordinating the efforts of many, the ultimate outcome is the result of a group effort that exceeds the performance of individuals. The conceptual map for how organizations should be structured and how workers should be supervised has grown tremendously over the past one hundred years, from Weber's notion of the best form of organizing and Taylor's conceptualization of management's role vis-à-vis labor, to today's mission-based grassroots nonprofits and megabureaucracies, such as the Department of Homeland Security.

KEY TERMS

Bureaucracy – a system of hierarchical administration with functional specialization and clear rules; the positive connotation of the term denotes good organization, fair processes, and efficient production; the negative connotation denotes extensive delays, impersonal relationships, and hierarchy and division of labor used to place responsibility elsewhere for unpopular decisions.

Coordinating mechanisms – these include mutual adjustment, direct supervision, and standardization of work processes, outputs, skills, and norms. They enable people to work toward a common goal and deliver uniform outputs in pursuit of the mission.

Design elements – the building blocks that construct an organization. These include coordinating mechanisms, reporting channels, unit groupings, and authority structures.

Hierarchy – a graded or ranked series of levels within an organization, with each higher level having more authority than those below.

Learning organizations – organizations that adapt to changes by identifying problems, self-correcting, monitoring, and making subsequent adjustments as needed.

Organizational structure – the shape and contours of an organization. These are created through design elements. In general, structure varies according to how the strategic apex, the middle line, and the operating core are constructed.

Scientific management – a theory of management predicated on industrial norms that emphasize productivity, efficiency, and standardization. The theory assumes that managers closely supervise and direct the work of subordinates.

DISCUSSION QUESTIONS

1. What characteristics differentiate simple organizational structures from machine bureaucracies? Professional bureaucracies? Divisionalized bureaucracies? Adhocracies?
2. Pick a public service organization in your community. What structural type is it most like: simple, machine, professional, divisionalized, or adhocracy? Why?
3. Why do government agencies rarely go out of business?
4. Criticism of bureaucracy centers on its rigidity, slowness, and impersonal nature. Are these characteristics the inevitable consequence of its design features that emphasize predictability, hierarchical chain of command, and reliance on procedures?
5. Learning organizations are those, regardless of type, that learn from their failures and make adjustments. As much as this is the ideal for all organizations, few achieve it. What are the anchors that make it difficult for organizations to change and adapt?

BUILD YOUR SKILLS

There are a number of things to think about when starting a nonprofit organization. Here is a list, along with the major steps to take.

SKILLBOX: STARTING A NONPROFIT (OR NOT)

Nonprofits are a means for organizing around a mission in a way that focuses interest and effort while allowing for favorable tax treatment. As of 2015, there were more than 1.5 million tax-exempt nonprofit organizations in the United States[1] or about one for every 200 people. Of those organizations, nearly 1.1 million were 501(c)(3) public charities.[2] Clearly, nonprofits are widely used to address public-serving purposes. The following steps provide guidance when deciding whether creating a nonprofit is the best route:

Think Long and Hard about Why, Where, and When It Makes Sense to Start a New Organization. Remember: Most start-ups fail, whether for-profit or not-for-profit. Ask these questions:

- Will this organization serve a niche that is already being served? If not,
- Do enough people care about it that funding is likely? If yes,
- What would the elevator speech be? This is a one minute explanation of the organization, its purpose, activities, and its stakeholders. This will be important for enlisting support of funders, volunteers, and staff. If the speech comes easily to mind then,
- What funding sources are possible? If there are enough then,
- What other organizations are already providing a similar service? How would this organization be different? If the answer is obvious, then perhaps it is time to proceed.

Engage a Group of Interested People. A nonprofit is not owned or controlled by any one person, not even the founder. It is accountable to multiple constituencies: its board of directors and officers, the philanthropic community within which it will secure funding, the stakeholders who will benefit from the services rendered, and the volunteers it will engage, among others. Engage representatives from all the constituencies the organization will touch to discuss its creation and what its goals should be.

Develop a Plan. Nonprofits need a plan, just as businesses do. The plan sets forth the vision, mission and goals, the methods or activities that will be used to achieve the goals and pursue the mission, resources needed (financial capital, human capital, and office space), and a timeline with target dates for when key steps will be achieved. These steps include creation of the articles of incorporation and bylaws, legal incorporation, and approval by tax authorities. The plan should also include a description of start-up funding that specifies revenue sources. Additionally, in an evaluation of opportunities and threats, the plan should specify the organizations that have similar missions and it should explain how this one will differ. Threats caused by competition for resources should be delineated and there should be an explanation of how the organization will respond. The plan should also contain an incremental vision for the organization in future years.

Draft the Articles of Incorporation and Bylaws. Bylaws are the organization's rulebook. They specify everything from how officers and directors are selected to when meetings are held to when the fiscal year begins and ends. All bylaws must comply with federal and state laws pertaining to nonprofit status.

Establish Leadership. The board of directors is the governing body of the organization. Board members should be a source of information, commitment, wisdom, and often, financial support.

Create a Budget. Will money come from donations, grants, service fees, contracts, or some combination? Careful planning helps to reveal sources.

Establish Management. Start-ups may rely on the same people to manage the organization as to lead it. As the organization grows, the need for staff will expand. A website and logo will need to be created and maintained that markets the organization, its mission, and its activities.

Think Again. Is a start-up nonprofit the right solution for the problem? Is there a better way to address it? What will be the obstacles that pose the greatest threats? Here are some alternatives:

- If starting a new nonprofit is driven by a desire to make an impact in a certain area, then consider volunteering, serving on the board, or fund-raising for an existing organization with an aligned mission. Such engagement supports the interest while providing visibility into nonprofit operations and whether an unmet need really exists.
- Alternately, establishing a local chapter of an existing global, national, or regional nonprofit, like UNICEF, the American Cancer Society, or Goodwill Industries, can be the best of both worlds. The capacity and name recognition of the larger organization can be leveraged, while still allowing for a local grassroots focus.[3]
- Another alternative is fiscal sponsorship, where an existing public charity "sponsors" a start-up effort or specific project. The arrangement can extend the sponsor's tax-deductibility for donations and qualification for grant funding to the nascent activity, while avoiding the necessity to create an organization that will compete for resources.

- Finally, the boundaries between nonprofit and for-profit organizations continue to blur. An important consideration is whether the identified social purpose can be served more effectively through a private social enterprise unbound by the restrictions placed on nonprofit organizations.[4]

Hands-On Activity: Determining the Need for a New Nonprofit

The goal of this activity is to simulate the early stages of establishing a new nonprofit organization. Document the following tasks in a two-page professional memo written for an audience of potential funders for the new enterprise.

Step 1: Identify a social need in which you are interested. The need could be local, national, or international.

Step 2: Conduct an environmental scan for organizations that work in the identified space. In addition to their name, include some discussion of the geographic areas in which they operate and the level of organizational capacity (size, employees, programs).

Step 3: Determine whether the existing organizations are sufficient to address the selected problem by identifying whether there are gaps in services or programs.

Step 4: Propose either a partnership with an existing organization, an extension of a current program, or justify the need for an entirely new organization.

Notes

1. National Center for Charitable Statistics (NCCS). 2016. "Quick Facts about Nonprofits." Retrieved from: http://nccs.urban.org/data-statistics/quick-facts-about-nonprofits.

2. Ibid.

3. Fritz, Joanne. 2016. "Alternatives to Starting a Nonprofit: You Can Do Good Without Starting a Nonprofit." *The Balance*. https://www.thebalance.com/alternatives-to-starting-nonprofit-2502285

4. Ibid.

For Additional Information

Foundation Center. n.d. "Knowledge Base: Q: How Do I Start a Nonprofit Organization?" http://grantspace.org/tools/knowledge-base/Nonprofit-Management/Establishment/starting-a-nonprofit.

NOTES

1. Donald F. Kettl, "Overview," in *The Department of Homeland Security's First Year: A Report Card*, ed. Donald F. Kettl (New York: Century Foundation Press, 2004), 1–28.

2. National Commission on Terrorist Attacks upon the United States, *The 9/11 Commission Report: Final Report of the National Commission on Terrorist Attacks upon the United States (9/11 Report)* (2004), https://www.gpo.gov/fdsys/pkg/GPO-911REPORT/content-detail.html.

3. Larry Hirschhorn and Thomas Gilmore, "The New Boundaries of the 'Boundaryless' Company," *Harvard Business Review* (1992), https://hbr.org/1992/05/the-new-boundaries-of-the-boundaryless-company.

4. University of Rhode Island, "Katrina Impacts," *Hurricanes: Science and Society* (2015), http://www.hurricanescience.org/history/studies/katrinacase/impacts/.

5. Vicki Bier, "Hurricane Katrina as a Bureaucratic Nightmare," in *On Risk and Disaster: Lessons from Hurricane Katrina*, eds. Ronald J. Daniels, Donald F. Kettl, and Howard Kunreuther (Philadelphia: University of Pennsylvania Press, 2006), 243–254.

6. Michael Coleman, "MISSION CREEP: Homeland Security a 'Runaway Train'," *Albuquerque Journal* (May 12, 2016), http://www.abqjournal.com/390438/homeland-security-a-runaway-train.html.

7. Henry Mintzberg, "Structure in 5's: A Synthesis of the Research on Organization Design," *Management Science* 26, no. 3 (1980): 322.

8. Herbert Kaufman, *Time, Change, and Organizations in a Perilous Environment*, 2nd ed. (Chatham, NJ: Chatham House Publishing, 1991).

9. "Facts and Figures," Regional Transportation District, last modified February, 2017, http://www.rtd-denver.com/factsAndFigures.shtml.

10. Regional Transportation District. *RTD Best Practices* (2015), http://www.rtd-denver.com/documents/best-practices-2015.pdf.

11. "What Is FasTracks?" Regional Transportation District, last modified 2016, http://www.rtd-fastracks.com/main_26.

12. Robert W. Keidel, *Seeing Organizational Patterns* (San Francisco, CA: Berrett-Koehler Publishers, 1995).

13. Frederick Taylor, *The Principles of Scientific Management* (New York: Harper & Brothers, 1911).

14. Max Weber, *Economy and Society*, trans. Guenther Roth and Claus Wittich (Los Angeles: University of California Press, [1921] 1968), 223–226.

15. Russell Sage Foundation, "The Social and Economic Effects of the Great Recession" (2016), http://www.russellsage.org/research/social-effects-great-recession-description.

16. Economic Policy Institute, "The Great Recession," *The State of Working America* (n.d.), http://stateofworkingamerica.org/great-recession/.

17. Institute for Policy Research, "The Great Recession: Over but Not Gone?" (Northwestern University, 2014), http://www.ipr.northwestern.edu/about/news/2014/IPR-research-Great-Recession-unemployment-foreclosures-safety-net-fertility-public-opinion.html.

18. U.S. Office of Justice Programs, "The Recovery Act: Frequently Asked Questions," (n.d.), https://ojp.gov/recovery/pdfs/FAQ_Overview.pdf.

19. Richard F. Callahan, Sandra O. Archibald, Kay A. Sterner, and H. Brinton Milward, *Key Actions That Contribute to Successful Program Implementation: Lessons from the Recovery Act* (Washington, DC: IBM Center for the Business of Government, 2012), http://www.businessofgovernment.org/report/key-actions-contribute-successful-program-implementation-lessons-recovery-act.

20. Carolyn Ban, *How Do Public Managers Manage? Bureaucratic Constraints, Organizational Culture, and the Potential for Reform* (San Francisco: Jossey-Bass, 1995).

21. *Ask Me Why I Care: Public Service Stories*, video, directed by Mary R. Hamilton and Rita Paskowitz (Omaha, Nebraska: College of Public Affairs and Community Service), https://www.unomaha.edu/college-of-public-affairs-and-community-service/community-engagement/pss-alan-dean.php.

ADDITIONAL RESOURCES

Agranoff, Robert. 2007. *Managing Within Networks: Adding Value to Public Organizations.* Washington, DC: Georgetown University Press.

Agranoff, Robert and Michael McGuire. 2003. *Collaborative Public Management.* Washington, DC: Georgetown University Press.

Fry, Brian R. and Jos C. N. Raadschelders. 2008. *Mastering Public Administration: From Max Weber to Dwight Waldo.* Washington, DC: CQ Press.

Granovetter, Mark. 1973. "The Strength of Weak Ties." *American Journal of Sociology* 78 (6): 1360–1380.

Mintzberg, Henry. 1989. *Inside our Strange World of Organizations.* New York: Free Press.

Senge, Peter M. 2006. *The Fifth Discipline: The Art & Practice of the Learning Organization.* New York: Doubleday.

Wilson, James Q. 1989. *Bureaucracy: What Government Agencies Do and Why They Do It.* New York: Basic Books.

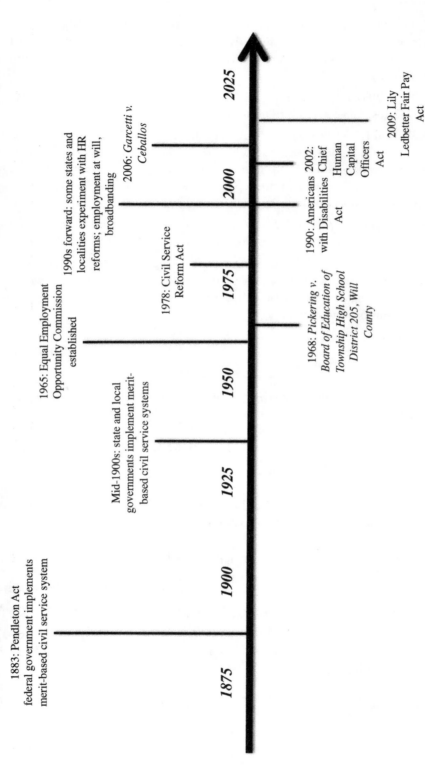

Chapter 5 Timeline: Human Resource Functions and Processes

1883: Pendleton Act
federal government implements
merit-based civil service system

Mid-1900s: state and local
governments implement merit-
based civil service systems

1965: Equal Employment
Opportunity Commission
established

1990s forward: some states and
localities experiment with HR
reforms; employment at will,
broadbanding

2006: *Garcetti v.
Ceballos*

1978: Civil Service
Reform Act

1968: *Pickering v.
Board of Education of
Township High School
District 205, Will
County*

1990: Americans
with Disabilities
Act

2002: Chief
Human
Capital
Officers
Act

2009: Lily
Ledbetter Fair Pay
Act

1875   1900   1925   1950   1975   2000   2025

HUMAN RESOURCE FUNCTIONS AND PROCESSES

WHAT YOU WILL LEARN

Importance of human capital

Human resource functions

Civil service traditions

Representative bureaucracy

Public sector unionism

Theories of motivation

Skillbox: Hiring the right person

The case, "Doing Double Duty," describes a burden similar to that which many public service workers experience. While climactic rescues, military heroism, and scientific breakthroughs are heralded, the day to day work of those at the street level is poorly understood. Especially in work that is more grisly than glittery, public service workers find themselves in emotionally intense interactions. "Doing Double Duty" uses child welfare work to capture the "emotional stew" of street-level jobs.

DOING DOUBLE DUTY

It was a good day. Maria was not sure how she had ended up as a child welfare caseworker, but eight months into the job, she felt really good. After shadowing and training, she had finally been assigned her own caseload at the Department of Children and Families (DCF). Already, she had had the chance to advocate for a child in court, and she also assisted a newly adoptive family in bringing home an eight-year-old special needs child. She was learning about resources in the community and how to help families as she assessed and provided case management. Just today, Maria had attended several tense but productive meetings where families worked out how to create safety for children, and so far, she loved it. She had always been a people person, so this work just made sense. She really believed that she could influence her community in a positive way, and loved using her creativity to problem-solve with families.

When she got home, Maria opened her email and found a note from her mother, "I'm worried about you, honey, call me." The email had a link to a news story. The article led with a splashy title, "DCF failure leads to child's disappearance and murder." Her mother had a flair for the dramatic. Reading the article, however, Maria could not help but feel a twinge of her mother's concern. The case sounded like any of several she had worked this month. The reporter told a story about how a caseworker had knocked on a family's door for three weeks and never reported to the authorities that the family did not answer. Of course the caseworker did not report! Maria laughed. What would you say to the police? A family is avoiding child protective services? Maria knew she would be calling practically every day! Regardless, the article went on to conclude that had the caseworker taken action, a horrible crime against an innocent child would have been prevented.

Years later, Maria reflects on that first realization that stories of casework are rarely fully told in the media. She has developed a strategy for responding to people who ask her about the role of child protection in the lives of families. She defends her profession to relatives who do not understand why a woman with her potential has been "lost to government work." With time, she has managed to reconcile the negative messages from the latest exposé in the media with the realities of her experiences in service to families. But, this takes energy, too, and sometimes she just does not have much at the end of the day.[1]

Questions to Ponder

1. How can the human resource function support workers who must perform unpopular missions?
2. How does public opinion affect morale of workers?
3. What sort of emotional armor is necessary to cope with a critical public?
4. How can human resource (HR) functions improve workers' ability to withstand the emotive rigors of their work?

HUMAN CAPITAL

Organizations have four types of resources: human, financial, information, and time. Of all these, the human factor is most important. Without the right people with the right skills and motivation in the right jobs, all the money, sophisticated information systems, and time spent will be squandered.

Strategic human capital management is the backbone to mission accomplishment. Human capital—analogous to financial capital—includes the collective skills, knowledge, and motivation necessary to do the work of the organization. A capable and well-managed public service workforce is indispensable to the pursuit of public purposes.

The framework pictured in Figure 5.1[2] depicts how human capital is laced through everything that matters, from planning and goal-setting, to operations and organizational culture, and then to outcomes. All inform one another in an interactive loop. These dimensions of human capital systems and processes reside together, whether in small nonprofits with only a few workers or in huge public agencies with thousands of workers. Planning and goal-setting require executive level decision making about the goals of the agency and the objectives necessary to achieve them. These decisions are then used to determine how to align traditional human resource functions in order to get the work done. Once the work is completed, accountability reviews identify processes that need improvement. This information is fed back to planning, which then makes adjustments and the iteration continues.

FIGURE 5.1 INTERRELATIONSHIPS OF HUMAN CAPITAL SYSTEM AND PROCESSES

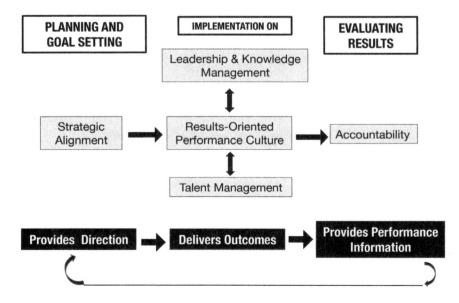

HUMAN RESOURCE FUNCTIONS

Human resource (HR) functions are designed to maximize each organization's human capital. The HR lifecycle begins when strategy is implemented. From the creation of job descriptions, to making hiring decisions, to training and developing the workforce, to separation when workers leave the organization from resignation, retirement, or dismissal, the functions are all in play, all the time. In formal merit systems, they are categorized into seven activities: position management, recruitment, selection, performance appraisal, compensation and benefits, training and development, and grievance and appeals processes.

Position Management

Once the strategic direction is set for the organization, decisions are made about the jobs that must be performed in order for the mission to be achieved. First, this requires job analysis and design. These are processes that define the knowledge, skills, and abilities (KSA) necessary to perform each type of job. Second, job descriptions that specify duties must be written. Third, the job is situated within a classification level, based upon the KSAs. Civil service systems use a hierarchy of job classifications in which higher classifications signify higher levels of KSAs and higher wages.

Recruitment

After a job has been designed, recruitment can begin because the job description is available and the salary range is known. The public workforce should be representative of the constituents being served so there are a number of procedures in place to ensure equal opportunity among all job seekers. Job ads must be widely available so that anyone seeking employment can find the information and there must be sufficient time allowed for potential applicants to submit their applications. Merit system principles are the cornerstone of American civil service and are codified in U.S. law. They govern federal workers and most state and local civil service systems are modeled after these principles. They provide safeguards to workers against discrimination, favoritism, and retribution for whistleblowing. Table 5.1[3] lists the merit system principles that guide the U.S. Office of Personnel Management's HR processes.

Selection

To ensure fairness, lists of finalists are generated through a standardized process so that all applicants are treated the same. Objective measures, such as tests, assessments, education, or résumé review are used to screen applicants. This results in a list of finalists that is sent to the person who will make the hiring decision. After interviews have been conducted, the best candidate is selected.

TABLE 5.1 MERIT SYSTEM PRINCIPLES (5 USC § 2301)

1. Recruitment should be from qualified individuals from appropriate sources in an endeavor to achieve a work force from all segments of society, and selection and advancement should be determined solely on the basis of relative ability, knowledge and skills, after fair and open competition which assures that all receive equal opportunity.

2. All employees and applicants for employment should receive fair and equitable treatment in all aspects of personnel management without regard to political affiliation, race, color, religion, national origin, sex, marital status, age, or handicapping condition, and with proper regard for their privacy and constitutional rights.

3. Equal pay should be provided for work of equal value, with appropriate consideration of both national and local rates paid by employers in the private sector, and appropriate incentives and recognition should be provided for excellence in performance.

4. All employees should maintain high standards of integrity, conduct, and concern for the public interest.

5. The federal work force should be used efficiently and effectively.

6. Employees should be retained on the basis of adequacy of their performance, inadequate performance should be corrected, and employees should be separated who cannot or will not improve their performance to meet required standards.

7. Employees should be provided effective education and training in cases in which such education and training would result in better organizational and individual performance.

8. Employees should be protected against arbitrary action, personal favoritism, or coercion for partisan political purposes, and prohibited from using their official authority or influence for the purpose of interfering with or affecting the result of an election or a nomination for election.

9. Employees should be protected against reprisal for the lawful disclosure of information which the employees reasonably believe evidences a violation of any law, rule, or regulation, or mismanagement, a gross waste of funds, an absence of authority, or a substantial and specific danger to public health or safety.

Compensation and Benefits

This function monitors labor supply and ensures that KSAs are compensated at a level that is competitive in the labor market. Compensation decisions involve equity theory, seek internal consistency across positions, and offer benefits that entice workers to remain on the job. This function also manages annual raise pools, health insurance benefits, retirement benefits, and other offerings.

Performance Appraisal

This is a regularly scheduled monitoring of each employee's performance. In theory, it is an opportunity for the worker and supervisor to engage in a dialogue about expectations and assessment of performance. Most appraisals involve standardized rating forms that require a conversation between the supervisor and the worker and a rating of the worker's performance on a series of job-related items.

Training and Development

For newcomers, training involves instruction in agency-specific work processes. For those already employed, it involves development of job-specific skills. It is often instituted after a needs assessment indicates that workers will benefit from additional skills, often because a job has changed since the worker was hired. Development is a term often paired with "training" because it denotes the interest and effort in helping workers expand their repertoire of skills. In addition to training that is designed to improve technical skills, leadership development within the agency is an aspect of staff development activities.

As workers develop more skills, they become more valuable to the organization and they increase their likelihood of promotion into leadership positions. Succession planning requires that organizations identify staff who embody the values and motivation that reflect well on the organization and will serve as role models for others. Leadership development is an integral part of succession planning and includes training that:

- Develops creativity, innovation, resilience, strategic thinking and vision
- Teaches the importance of team building, developing others, leveraging diversity, and managing conflict
- Emphasizes the importance of accountability, service to the public, decisiveness, problem solving, and technical credibility
- Instructs about how to manage finances, human capital, and information technology
- Sensitizes trainees to the importance of collaborative skills, political savvy, and negotiating skills

- Reinforces resilience, which is the capacity to respond to stress in such a way that goals are achieved at minimal psychological and physical cost

Due Process

Workers who hold permanent positions in most civil service systems have the right to due process. This means that when workers are disciplined or removed for cause, they have the right to file an appeal and have their complaint adjudicated by an appeals board. The rules of the appeals process are governed by the organization's formal procedures and/or by the laws of the jurisdiction. Due process refers to the opportunity—before removal—for the individual to know the charges, present a defense, and appeal a removal decision before an impartial adjudicator. Due process is available for anyone who has permanent status in the job, including the whistleblower, the employee who belongs to the "wrong" political party, the reservist whose periods of military service are inconvenient to the boss, the scapegoat, and the person who has been misjudged based on faulty information. Grievance processes that are transparent and fair help to mitigate legal action.

Attention to Job Satisfaction and Motivation

This aspect of HR management involves monitoring employees' level of job satisfaction, their level of engagement in their work, and their desire to remain in their jobs or to change jobs or employers. The primary means for assessing job satisfaction, engagement, and retention is by employee surveys. The annual Federal Employee Viewpoint Survey, for example, is administered to all federal employees. The results provide a means for agency directors to compare responses of workers in their agencies with those in other agencies, and also provides a way for workers to anonymously report their work experience.

> *"Your work is going to fill a large part of your life, and the only way to be truly satisfied is to do what you believe is great work. And the only way to do great work is to love what you do."*
>
> —Steve Jobs

Many cities and states also conduct employee surveys. The results provide a means for data-based decision making about aspects that warrant improvement and areas that are functioning well.

Other HR Activities

In addition to position management, recruitment, selection, training and development, compensation and benefits, performance appraisal, and grievance processes, additional dimensions to HR management include labor relations and providing a

FIGURE 5.2 HUMAN RESOURCE FUNCTIONS

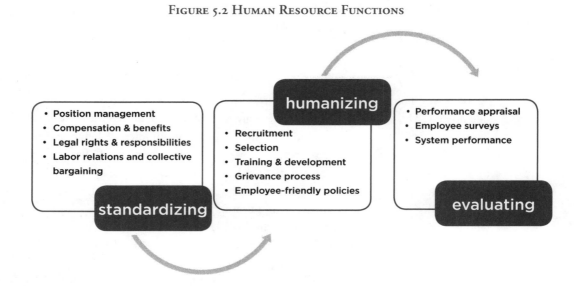

worker-friendly environment. All these add up to the overall attention to human capital.

Figure 5.2 shows how the HR functions relate to one another. They can be categorized into three types: those that standardize functions so that all job applicants and employees are treated similarly and fairly; those that humanize HR processes so that individual differences are taken into consideration; and those that contribute to an evaluation of how well the functions are operating. Collectively, these comprise the HR processes in all organizations, whether nonprofit, governmental, or private sector, although they are more formalized in government agencies and larger nonprofits and businesses.

CIVIL SERVICE TRADITIONS

The history of merit-based civil service begins with the passage of the Pendleton Act in 1883. Prior to its passage, appointments to federal jobs were made on the basis of political partisanship, rewarding loyal campaign supporters, and otherwise giving jobs to family, friends and neighbors. As part of the enlightened reforms designed to produce better government, merit-based civil service came into fashion.

Pendleton Act of 1883

The Pendleton Act established that positions within the federal workforce should be awarded on the basis of merit rather than on political affiliation, personal favor, or subjective whim. The act provides for se-lection of government employees by objective measures designed to assess knowledge and skill. It also made it illegal to fire or demote government workers for political reasons. To manage and enforce the merit system, the law created the United States Civil Service Com-mission, which set the rules, regulations, and implementation of the act's provisions. The

> *"I urge the enactment of a civil service law so explicit and so strong that no partisan official will dare evade it, basing all rewards, promotions and salaries solely on merit, on loyalty and industry in the public service."*
>
> —Arthur Capper

Act also allowed for the president, by executive order, to decide which positions could be subject to the act and which would not. The Pendleton Act remained in force for almost a century, when its provisions were modified by the Civil Service Reform Act of 1978.

Civil Service Reform Act of 1978

The system set forth by the Pendleton Act continued largely unchanged until the Civil Service Reform Act of 1978 (CSRA). Intended not as a complete overhaul but rather to keep pace with the need to refine several key provisions, CSRA explicitly required that the federal workforce be reflective of the nation's diversity. It also streamlined and clarified boundaries between the traditional HR functions, grievance processes, and labor-management relations by abolishing the U.S. Civil Service Commission and distributing its functions into three separate agencies: the Office of Personnel Man-agement (OPM), the Merit Systems Protection Board (MSPB), and the Federal Labor Relations Authority (FLRA). Responsibilities of these three entities are as follows:

- OPM provides management guidance to executive branch agencies and issues regulations pertaining to HR functions
- The MSPB conducts studies of the federal civil service and hears appeals of federal employees who have been disciplined or dismissed from their jobs
- FLRA oversees the rights of federal employees to form collective bargaining units (unions) in order to bargain with agencies

In addition to the creation of the three new agencies, a new grade classification for the top level of government's managers was created—the Senior Executive Service (SES). Members of the SES serve in key positions just below the top presidential appointees. They are the link between these appointees and the rest of the federal workforce. In this capacity, they oversee nearly every government activity in approximately seventy-five federal agencies.

While the federal government's civil service system led the way, most states and municipalities have followed suit. For example, in 1884, New York became the first state to adopt a civil service system for state workers. Massachusetts became the second state when it started a merit system in 1885. In the decades that followed, other states as well as municipalities followed suit, adopting merit-based civil service systems spurred by the requirement in a 1939 amendment to the Social Security Act that required jurisdictions to replace their patronage systems with formal merit systems if they wished to receive federal grants.[4, 5]

Now a common foil for complaints about public personnel systems, formal merit-based civil service systems are challenged to balance the need for a representative, skilled, agile, workforce that functions with transparency and offers equal opportunity for all jobseekers against the changing demands of public service and the whimsies of partisan ideology. Never a perfect compromise, systems continue to experiment with reforms, whether in the form of broadbanded job classifications, removal of job protections, or pay systems that include bonuses. There has yet to be devised a perfect civil service system that can adjust quickly to changing needs. The more process-laden a system is, the more accountability and transparency the system has. But formal processes require delays which are frustrating to managers when time is of the essence.

Representative Bureaucracy and Diversity

Diversity is the collective mixture of differences and similarities that include demographic characteristics such as gender, race, religion, ethnicity, and nationality, along with values, beliefs, experiences, backgrounds, preferences, and behaviors. Diversity traits may be visible or invisible. Visible traits include physical abilities, age, body size, or skin color. Invisible traits include socio-economic status, sexual orientation, level in the organization, military experience, beliefs, thinking styles, education, and training.

> *"One of the things that's beautiful about New Orleans is how culturally rich we are and how well we have worked together. People call us a gumbo. It's really important that we get focused on the very simple notion that diversity is a strength, it's not a weakness."*
>
> —Mitch Landrieu

For the bureaucracy to be representative of the nation's diversity, the workforce must be representative. People of different backgrounds and heritages have different experiences. It is important that their voices be heard in program planning and delivery so that these experiences are reflected. It is also important that their points of view be included in decision making. This is how representative democracy comes to life in the pursuit of public purposes.

Achieving representativeness is difficult, however, because of cross-cutting pressures to give advantage to some applicants over others. For example, in federal hiring, agencies are expected to give preference to veterans. However, only about 10 percent of veterans are women, putting women at a disadvantage in accessing federal jobs. This example shows that achieving one goal—to reward those who have performed military service—becomes an obstacle toward another goal: gender integration in the workforce. Balancing acts are required when competing initiatives get in the way of achieving representativeness.

PUBLIC SECTOR UNIONS AND COLLECTIVE BARGAINING

Although public sector and private sector unions have much in common in terms of providing a collective voice to advocate for issues important to workers, there are significant differences. For instance, the parties for collective bargaining are more or less equal in the private sector. In government, however, the state has much more power than unions. Second, private sector unions and companies are constrained by market forces, while public sector unions are constrained by economic pressures as well as political values. Third, economic issues are distributive in the private sector. Wages and benefits come from the firm's earnings and the question during bargaining is how much of the earnings will be allocated to labor. In public unions, discussions about wages and benefits are dependent on budgeted expenses. And, fourth, in the private sector, disputes may result in labor actions such as strikes or lockouts. In government, strikes in many settings are illegal. Thus, the bargaining clout of public sector unions is less than that of private sector unions.

Despite the differences between private sector and public sector unions, or perhaps because of them, union representation is markedly higher for public workers than for private sector workers. As shown in Table 5.2,[6] union representation is five times higher in government than in business. And the spread is even greater at the local level, where most teachers, police officers, and firefighters are represented by unions. This means that HR directors must be conversant in labor-management negotiations and collective bargaining processes.

TABLE 5.2 UNION REPRESENTATION OF WORKERS BY SECTOR	
Private Sector	7.4%
Public Sector	39.0%
Federal	32.3%
State	33.6%
Local	45.0%

HR IN NONPROFITS

HR management in nonprofits is more similar to human resource processes in business than in government, with a few exceptions. Compared to government's civil service systems, there is more latitude in hiring and setting compensation. There is not an explicit expectation that the workforce be representative of the clientele being served and, except in the largest nonprofits, there will not be standardized sets of job classifications with limits on the pay range within each classification. They have more latitude to offer compensatory time in lieu of a higher salary and to make individual exceptions to procedures. And, all employees are at will, which means they serve at the pleasure of the director and may be terminated at any time for any, or no, reason. As a nonprofit grows and adds employees, however, the more it will find it necessary to develop standard HR processes to ensure that it treats all workers fairly. Standardization of processes prevents charges of favoritism or wage discrimination in large nonprofits just as it does in businesses.

A difference between nonprofits and business is the expectation that business leaders can earn very sizeable incomes but in nonprofits, it is expected that leaders will be paid a reasonable, but not excessive, income. Another difference is at the leadership level, where board members of nonprofits are volunteers while directors of businesses are usually paid. Also, in business, the chief executive officer is often on the board of directors, and sometimes is the president of the board. In nonprofits, the chief executive officer (often called the "executive director") usually does not serve on the board or, if on the board, serves in an ex-officio capacity and does not have a vote.

Another difference between business and nonprofits comes from relying on volunteers to deliver services. This means that motivation is disconnected from salary so managers must rely heavily on the meaningfulness of the job and commitment. Unlike business, where performance is linked to profits, volunteers' contributions are linked to public service and mission achievement. The activities necessary to effectively manage paid staff in nonprofits are similar to those required to manage volunteers. Job descriptions are necessary because they set clear expectations and provide a basis for performance appraisals. On-the-job training is necessary in order to familiarize volunteers with agency procedures. Challenging and rewarding tasks are important in order for the work to be interesting to both staff and volunteers.

Retention of staff is a significant challenge in small nonprofits for two reasons: salary limitations and a low ceiling for upward mobility. In small organizations, there are only a few opportunities for promotion due to there being only a small number of positions. Organizations that are dependent on grants, contracts, and occasional philanthropy often have tight budgets with little room for expansion. All these differences, from recruiting to compensating to directing to motivating, combine to make HR processes in nonprofits sort of like, and sort of unlike, HR in government.

ENGAGEMENT, MOTIVATION, AND JOB SATISFACTION

Employee engagement, motivation, and job satisfaction are human factors that contribute to performance in all work settings. Motivated employees are intent on their jobs and take pride in their accomplishments. Often referred to as person-job fit, having the right person with the right skills in the right job ensures performance. Surveys conducted by the National Research Center confirm that workers in state and local governments value good person-job fit. More than 70 percent report that they are well-suited for their jobs and that they are helping people.[7] Another HR function, however, does not fare as well: less than 50 percent positively rate questions about their performance evaluations. As important as performance appraisals are for providing feedback to workers and for setting expectations, they rarely achieve their goals of being perceived as a fair, objective measure of the worker's performance. This information was revealed through employee surveys, a useful tool for "taking the temperature" of the workforce and proactively identifying areas that need improvement.

Employee surveys provide a basis for managers to assess how workers feel about their jobs and data also provide a means for comparing one agency and one level of government to another. For example, findings from the state and local levels are not the same as for federal workers. The Federal Employee Viewpoint Survey (FEVS) reveals that federal employees rate their compensation and the respect they receive from superiors higher than do local government employees. Conversely, ratings by local government employees show higher levels of satisfaction with their jobs and they report that they are more inclined to know what is expected from them than are federal workers.

Employee surveys in the state of Washington and in the cities of Minneapolis, MN and San Antonio, TX, show that employees in these three jurisdictions rate the level of recognition they receive lower than federal employees do. For example, in Minneapolis, only 49 percent of the city's employees feel like they "regularly receive appropriate recognition." In San Antonio, similar results were found, and in Washington state, recognition was one of the lowest-rated areas in its annual survey despite the fact that 86 percent of employees said they are treated with dignity and respect.[8, 9]

BEST AGENCIES TO WORK FOR IN FEDERAL GOVERNMENT

The FEVS is administered to all federal employees each year by the U.S. OPM. The results are used by agency administrators to track improvements over the years, to flag problems, and monitor where improvements are or are not occurring. The results are also useful to job seekers because they provide a snapshot of the best places to work. Table 5.3[10] shows how the largest agencies rank based on responses to three items on the 2015 survey:

- I recommend my organization as a good place to work.
- Considering everything, how satisfied are you with your job?
- Considering everything, how satisfied are you with your organization?

TABLE 5.3 BEST PLACES TO WORK IN FEDERAL GOVERNMENT, 2015

Rank	Agency	2015
1	National Aeronautics and Space Administration	76.1
2	Intelligence Community	67.1
3	Department of Justice	66.3
3	Department of State	66.3
5	Department of Commerce	66.2
6	Social Security Administration	66.0
7	Department of Health and Human Services	63.9
8	Department of Labor	63.1
8	Department of Transportation	63.1
10	Department of the Air Force	60.0
11	Department of Agriculture	59.4
11	Department of the Navy	59.4
13	Department of the Interior	59.2
14	Environmental Protection Agency	58.5
15	Office of the Secretary of Defense, Joint Staff, Defense Agencies, and Department of Defense Field Activities	58.4
16	Department of the Treasury	57.5
17	Department of the Army	57.0
18	Department of Veterans Affairs	55.1
19	Department of Homeland Security	43.1

Scores range from 100 to 1, with 100 being most positive.

Surveys such as these provide information for managers within each agency and for the Office of Personnel Management, which provides HR services to the entire federal government. They also provide a baseline by which an agency can monitor its progress in making improvements in its work culture. In this case, it is obvious that NASA, a perennially favorite place to work, tops the chart and the Department of Homeland Security, an agency that has struggled with morale problems since its creation, continues to have problems. Feedback such as this is useful in management training because it identifies organizations that are functioning well in terms of mission clarity, job satisfiers, and motivators. It also provides a means for monitoring progress from year to year.

EMPLOYEE SURVEYS[11]

Employee surveys are a means to assess job engagement and satisfaction. Results provide a foundation for making decisions based on data rather than on assumptions. But when managers in King County, Washington, read the results of the 2012 employee survey, they did not address the problems identified. So when employees were asked to complete the same survey three years later, only 36 percent said they thought their responses would lead to changes. To repair the trust deficit, supervisors were trained in how to translate findings into action plans.

Managers and supervisors were divided into groups and assigned specific areas from the survey to focus on. One group focused on "growth and development," for example,

because it had been identified as an area of weakness. To be responsive to the findings, managers started giving more information to employees about online learning opportunities and they created professional development plans for everyone.

Turning survey results into action may be difficult when budgets are tight, but it is necessary in order for employees to know that it is worth their time to complete surveys. The employment relationship is an exchange between employer and employee. Employees must believe they are valued and their work matters before they will be willing to go above and beyond on a task, even when it is simply a case of completing a survey.

In the work setting, there is a progression from being engaged in one's job to being motivated to perform, to feeling satisfaction with one's work. Each of these elements reinforces the other. Engagement and motivation arises from each worker's unique personal needs, which may change over time, either because once satisfied, other needs impel behavior or because other needs become more potent and replace the prior driver of behavior. Figure 5.3 provides a simplistic notion of motivation but this path continues to serve as our basic understanding of why people behave as they do.

FIGURE 5.3 FROM NEEDS TO JOB SATISFACTION

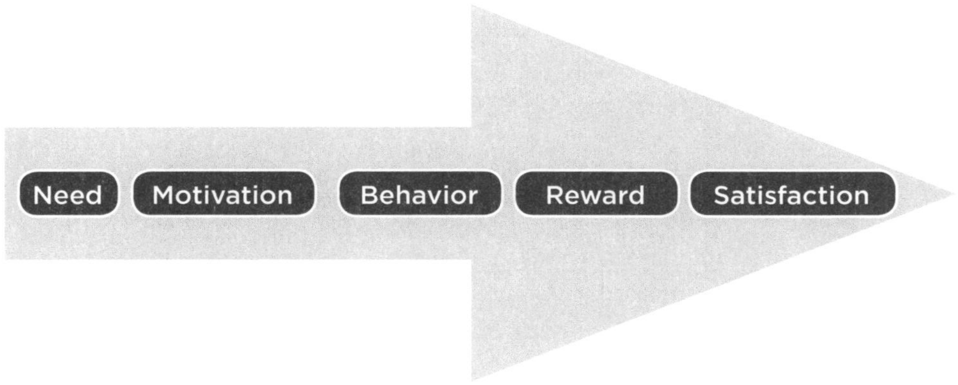

Need Motivation Behavior Reward Satisfaction

THEORIES OF MOTIVATION AND JOB SATISFACTION

The resolution to many morale problems in organizations is deceptively simple: people want to be treated as valuable contributors in the workplace. They are motivated to perform when their work is recognized. To understand this more fully, theories of motivation have been developed and are taught to supervisors in training. These theories can be categorized into several kinds. First are those that assume a hierarchy of needs exists, in which lower needs must be satisfied before higher needs express themselves. Then there are theories that assume people are motivated by a sense of fairness in terms of how they are treated compared to how their peers are treated. Third are theories that assume there are two separate sets of factors—hygiene factors that, when absent, cause workers to quit their jobs, and motivational factors that, when present, cause them to be motivated to perform above minimal expectations.

Maslow's Hierarchy of Needs

Abraham Maslow's hierarchy of needs posits that people are motivated to satisfy primal needs first and, once achieved, they strive to satisfy social needs. After that, they strive to satisfy higher order individual growth needs. As pictured in Figure 5.4, this conceptualization assumes that needs at the bottom are foundational to the needs above in such a way that those lower in the hierarchy must be satisfied before those above become salient.

FIGURE 5.4 MASLOW'S HIERARCHY OF NEEDS

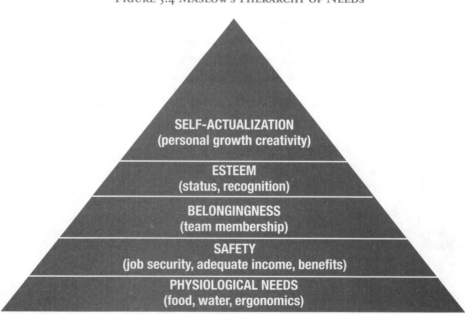

Loftier needs, such as personal growth and creativity rest atop the lower needs. Although this hierarchy is intuitively satisfying, it only captures the complexity of human behavior in the most elementary way. Why do soldiers risk their lives to rescue a fallen comrade when it puts their lives in danger? Why do firefighters run into burning buildings when everyone else is running out? To answer this quandary, variants of needs theories have emerged.

Alderfer's Existence, Relatedness, Growth Theory

To address the limitations of Maslow's hierarchy as a true depiction of motivation, Clayton Alderfer proposed the Existence, Relatedness, Growth (ERG) theory. Similar to Maslow's theory, Alderfer's model describes needs as a hierarchy but broadbands them into Existence, Relatedness, and Growth, as shown in Figure 5.5.

Existence needs are the most basic and focus on physical well-being. Relatedness needs pertain to social needs and interpersonal connections. Growth needs include the development of personal competence and potential. Alderfer's model assumes that as higher order needs are satisfied, they become self-motivating, so relatedness and personal growth become more important the more one gains esteem and additional skills. In terms of work behavior, Maslow's and Alderfer's theories assume that:
- Not everyone is motivated by the same things
- The needs hierarchy mirrors the organizational hierarchy and expects that top managers are more likely to be motivated by self-actualization/growth needs than by lower level needs

FIGURE 5.5 ALDERFER'S ERG THEORY

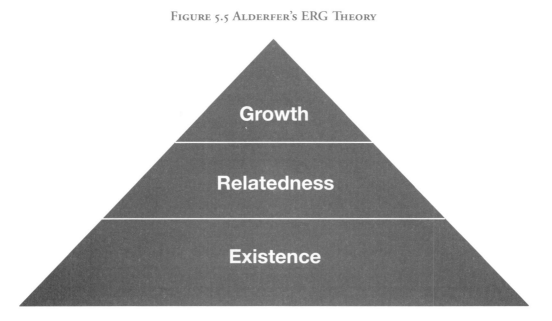

Herzberg's Two Factor Theory

As opposed to hierarchical needs theories, Frederick Herzberg's Two Factor Theory assumes that job satisfaction and job dissatisfaction are two independent factors. Job dissatisfaction results from attributes that Herzberg calls the hygiene factor. These are necessary if a worker is to remain in a job, but they do not impel the worker to be more than minimally productive. Job satisfiers, on the other hand, are motivators. They are those attributes whose presence causes people to be engaged and productive, similar to Maslow's notion of self-actualization. If absent, the worker may remain in the job but is not motivated to perform above minimal levels.

Hygiene factors are those considerations whose absence causes workers to be dissatisfied and to leave their jobs but whose presence fails to motivate productivity. Examples include adequate working conditions, job security, pay, benefits, satisfactory interpersonal relationships, and adequate supervision. In general, these are items lower in the Maslow/Alderfer hierarchies.

Motivators are factors whose presence motivates workers to be engaged and to perform above and beyond minimal accepted performance. They include needs that are higher in Maslow's and Alderfer's hierarchies: recognition, opportunities for personal growth, achievement, advancement, and the ability to make a difference.

Salary and benefits packages are hygiene factors. Workers have a variety of needs so "one size fits all" is not an informed approach. For instance, as organizations design reward systems to enhance retention, cafeteria plans are popular because they allow workers to select the benefits that work for them. While leave days may be the most valued for a parent with small children, health-care benefits may be more important for someone with a chronic health condition. While retirement benefits may be of greatest importance for those in the latter years of their careers, childcare benefits and flextime may be most important for parents of young children. While employers hope that benefits will cause employees to remain with the agency longer, employees anticipate that their choices will enhance their quality of life and work/life balance. Thus, they are hygiene factors.

The absence of hygiene factors will cause workers to seek work elsewhere but the presence of hygiene factors does not necessarily affect productivity. On the other hand, the absence of motivators may not cause workers to look for work elsewhere, but it does not motivate productivity. The presence of motivators, however, causes workers to be more productive.

Adams' Equity Theory

J. Stacy Adams developed the notion of equity theory, which assumes that workers seek to maintain parity between the knowledge, skills, and abilities that they apply in their jobs compared to what their peers apply, and the rewards that they receive compared to what their peers receive. Equity theory says that it is not the actual reward that motivates, but rather the perception of it, and the perception is based not on the reward in isolation, but in comparison with the effort that went into getting it, and in comparison to the efforts of others. For example, if Joe gets a 5 percent raise, he will feel quite pleased until he learns that Ellen—whom he perceives to be a slacker—got an even higher raise. At that point equity theory holds that Joe will be demotivated. In other words, equity theory assumes that people's motivation results from comparing the reward they receive in return for the effort they expend with the comparable ratio of reward to effort for others. Although equity theory is plausible, the realities are difficult. First, people usually do not have complete information about how others perform and how they are rewarded. Thus, they make judgments based on perceptions and inferences. Second, some people's ratios are complicated as they may be willing to ignore short-term inequities as long as they expect things to work out in the long term.

Vroom's Expectancy Theory

Another way of explaining motivation is through expectancy theories. Victor Vroom developed this idea to bring together many of the elements of other theories. It combines the perceptual aspects of equity theory with the behavioral aspects of the hierarchical and two-factor theories. It results in an equation that motivation = expectancy + instrumentality + valence. Motivation is the intensity of one's emotive desire to be productive and is a function of expectancy, instrumentality, and valence. Expectancy is a worker's assessment of the degree to which effort will correlate with performance. Instrumentality is the worker's assessment of how the amount of reward correlates with performance. In other words, an instrumental consideration asks "what is the likelihood I will be rewarded if I do a good job?" For intrinsic considerations, the instrumental query is "how good will I feel if I do this?" And valence is the perceived strength of the reward or punishment that will result from the performance. If the reward is too small, the motivation will be small, even if expectancy and instrumentality are both high. If risk of failure is high, the valence will be negative and will discourage performance.

As with equity theory, expectancy tries to incorporate as much information as possible but the reality is that workers make decisions about their level of motivation with incomplete information. The reason that all these theories of motivation remain of interest is that, even after decades of research, no one has a definitive explanation for what motivates all workers all the time.

McGregor's Theory X and Theory Y

Another approach to motivation addresses it from the assumptions of management. Douglas McGregor proposed two different sets of assumptions about worker motivation. While hierarchical, two factor, equity, and expectancy theories of motivation focus on the worker, McGregor's theory focuses on the assumptions that affect how managers supervise workers. For years, McGregor's Theory X and Theory Y notion of motivation has been a useful training tool as people develop supervisory and management skills.

McGregor's theory differentiates two sets of assumptions about how employees are motivated to perform. Those who espouse Theory X assume that workers are lazy and require constant supervision to ensure that they follow orders. Those who espouse Theory Y assume that workers are self-motivated and work to satisfy intrinsic needs for achievement. These two sets of assumptions represent two very different views about subordinates and result in very different management styles. Theory X managers give direct orders, prefer to closely supervise workers, and expect them to "do as they are told." They assume that workers will only produce when closely supervised and if not supervised, will shirk responsibility. Theory X assumes that extrinsic rewards such as salary are the prime motivator for workers. In terms of Herzberg's Two-Factor Theory, they focus totally on hygiene factors. Theory Y managers, on the other hand, focus on Herzberg's motivators. They see themselves as coaches whose job it is to assist workers in overcoming obstacles so that they can be most productive. Theory Y assumes that intrinsic rewards—self-esteem, pride, and personal accomplishment—are the prime motivator for workers and that workers are self-directed and seek responsibility.

Training and development is an important HR function and the preparation of managers for contemporary organizations focuses on Theory Y notions. If there is one thing that is certain, knowledge workers prefer Theory Y managers to Theory X managers, and most public service workers fall into this category. Their work relies not on physical labor but rather on the application of knowledge. In fact, about twice as many government workers hold college degrees than private sector workers—48 percent to 23 percent.[12] Teachers, social workers, engineers, probation officers, government accountants, public lawyers—all need four years of college if not more.

An example of how Theory X is out of tune with contemporary workers arises in telework, which is defined as any work conducted away from the primary workplace that is facilitated by information and telecommunications technology. For the employer, it improves employee retention, improves employee productivity, increases flexibility because employees can be "two places at once," reduces sick leave, and avoids relocation expenses. For employees, it improves work-life balance, improves job satisfaction, and increases personal flexibility as long as teleworkers are evaluated on work performed rather than on time expended. Telework is on the increase as managers become more comfortable with it. But management resistance continues to be a problem. In 2010, former director of the OPM, John Berry, summed it up this way: "Managers who believe that unless they have the employee in front of them, and are stuck in a sort of nineteenth century, twentieth century mind-set that someone needs to be at their desk to be working, I would put [that] as our largest barrier."[13] Theory X managers have a difficult time letting go of the control that face-to-face supervision affords them.

Public Service Motivation

The subject of public service motivation (PSM) is a valuable dimension to understanding public service workers. It refers to an individual's predisposition to respond to motives grounded in public service. The construct is associated conceptually with four dimensions: attraction to public policy making, commitment to the public interest, self-sacrifice, and compassion.[14] Research shows that those who make a career in

public service are significantly more likely to possess PSM than those who make careers in business.

Although PSM is not a requirement for working in public service, it is a strength and commitment that most who make careers in

> *" 'Public service' is a concept, an attitude, a sense of duty-yes, even a sense of public morality."*
>
> —Elmer B. Staats

public service bring to the job and it is an important characteristic for HR processes to accentuate and reward.

Doing Double Duty Revisited

Think again about Maria's experience in the opening case: Doing Double Duty. What does it take for her to do her job day in and day out? The answer is that it takes both cognitive skill and emotional resilience to deal with the family situations she encounters, and it takes PSM to care enough to keep doing the job. The work also requires her to perform with autonomy, making decisions that blend agency rules and procedures with the exigencies of the individual cases. For her to stay in the job, she will need positive recognition and the opportunity to grow and develop new skills, as outlined by Herzberg's notion of motivators. And she will need a manager who subscribes to Theory Y assumptions. Regardless of the jurisdiction and regardless of the job being performed, the quality of the human resource functions and the quality of supervision will largely determine whether she continues in the job or whether she changes jobs.

RECOGNITION FOR EXCELLENCE IN PUBLIC SERVICE

Public servants are the hands and feet of government. They lead efforts to cure diseases and prevent epidemics. They strengthen the economy by supporting small businesses and struggling communities. They promote student achievement and ensure equal access to quality education. They provide public safety and national defense, environmental protection, and exploration of distant planets. To encourage people to pursue careers in public service, and to honor exceptional ingenuity, persistence, and commitment, there are a number of award programs that celebrate excellence. All the awards described seek honorees whose work manifests public service motivation. The following, although not an exhaustive list, provides examples. Awards such as these are—in Herzberg's Two Factor theory—examples of motivators.

Public Service Recognition Week

Since 1985, the first week of May has been officially designated by Congress as Public Service Recognition Week (PSRW). During the week celebrations are held throughout the nation to honor those who work for federal, state, and local government. The celebration is spearheaded by the Public Employees Roundtable, a nonpartisan coalition of public-service minded organizations whose mission is to:

- Promote government employment and careers
- Educate Americans about the value of public servants and the services they provide
- Recognize excellence in public service and promote the spirit of public service

In 2016, President Obama issued this presidential proclamation:[15]

> During Public Service Recognition Week, we honor those who dedicate themselves to ensuring America's promise rings true in every corner of our country, and we recommit to upholding the values they fight for every day. Civil servants demonstrate resolve and inspire optimism in sectors throughout our country. They are engineers and educators, military service members and social workers, and their individual and collective contributions drive us forward on the path toward an ever brighter tomorrow. Both at home and abroad, they carry forward the notion that as Americans, we are committed to looking out for one another and to working together to forge a bright future for generations to come. . . . Throughout this week, we recognize the tireless efforts of the women and men who strive to make sure ours is a government that stays true to its founding ideals.

ASPA/NAPA National Public Service Award

This award honors contributions of public service practitioners across all sectors of government and is given jointly by two professional public administration associations, the American Society for Public Administration and the National Academy of Public Administration. It honors individuals who make outstanding contributions and whose accomplishments are models of public service. Award winners are selected from all levels of public service—local, state, and federal governments, and domestic and international nonprofit organizations. While winners come from diverse backgrounds, they are individuals who have taken risks to achieve change, have made profound improvements in service to the public, have achieved substantial savings in government operations, have fostered a more democratic society, and/or have served as champions for social equity.

Sammies

Another award is given by The Partnership for Public Service, which is a nonpartisan nonprofit organization whose mission is to help make government more effective through strengthening its human capital. The annual Service to America awards honor public servants who put service to others foremost in their work. Thought of as the "Oscars" of government service, Sammies reward dynamism, innovation, and commitment in response to the needs of Americans.

These three national awards, along with national military honors and civilian awards given in states and locales across the nation, are examples of how public service motivation is rewarded. Without people working on behalf of their communities, there would not be communities. This is why the human factor is so important in public service.

CAREER CHOICES

Of public administration students who graduated in 2015, survey results show that 47 percent are employed by government, 23 percent are employed in nonprofits, and 18 percent work in the private sector (see Table 5.4[16]). But it is likely that, regardless of the sector where they work upon graduation, most will work in another sector before their careers are done, or at least in another agency. This is because people rarely work for the same employer, or at least the same agency, throughout their careers.

TABLE 5.4 WHERE DO MPA GRADUATES WORK?

Sector	% of all MPA Alumni	Cumulative Percentage
City, county government	17	17
State government	17	34
Federal government	13	47
Nonprofit	23	70
Private	18	88
Other	8	96
Obtaining further education	2	98
Military	1	99
Unemployed seeking employment		100

HR training and development provides a valuable service to both the agency and employees by offering job growth opportunities, such as internships, apprenticeships, and job rotations, that are designed to expose workers to new work environments. As employees add skills to their repertoire, they become more valuable to the agency while they also open doors of opportunity for themselves. This serves their personal development well and prepares them for more choices as they seek advancement. An effective HR operation serves the interest of the agency while also serving the interest of workers.

HUMAN RESOURCE REFORMS

From reinventing to reengineering, downsizing to rightsizing, and outsourcing to insourcing, HR functions adapt to fit new programs, new technology, new job demands, and altered budgets. In an attempt to give managers more discretion over job titles and salaries, some jurisdictions have adopted broader classification systems. Some agencies, to avoid increasing the number of full-time employees but to still get the work done, have resorted to using contract workers who have no job protections and leave as soon as the contract terminates. Other agencies have tried outsourcing, only to find that their cadre of managers no longer has the experience necessary to implement new programs. In response, they have reverted to insourcing, relying on full-time employees to perform the work of the agency.

Every change that occurs in the workplace affects human resource management, whether in the development of new job descriptions, training for skill building, or changes to compensation and benefits. Contracting for public services, such as garbage and street maintenance, call upon skills in mediation and negotiation strategies, contract monitoring, and competitive bidding processes. Moving from a geographically centralized face-to-face work environment to telecommuting requires supervision with a Theory Y perspective, rather than Theory X. It also requires changes in communication protocols and systems for setting expectations and monitoring performance.

Modernizing Classification and Compensation Systems

Broadbanding is an example of a reform that has been implemented in some civil service systems. In essence, several bands of job classifications are combined into one, which allows more flexibility on the manager's part in terms of setting job title and salary. The challenge is to achieve a balance between uniformity across agencies while providing flexibility at the agency level. Broader classification systems only work when budget allocations per payband are increased to allow managers to actually use their discretion.

Bonuses to Reward Performance

Another reform used by some jurisdictions is that of allowing managers to award bonuses to reward good performers. The downfall of this is that legislative bodies often fail to allocate enough money to make the bonuses meaningful. Bonuses are only effective when the budget will allow for meaningful increments to all who are deserving. When an arbitrary quota is placed on the number of bonuses that may be awarded, charges of favoritism are soon to be heard.

Job Protection versus Employment At-Will (EAW)

Among the reforms that have been implemented in several states is the removal of job protection for some classes of jobs and its replacement with employment at-will. The assumption is that, if workers know that they may lose their job if they do not please their boss, they will be motivated to perform at a higher level. This is a Theory X assumption that reverts to the pre-Pendleton Act years. It means that, unlike traditional systems that protect workers from arbitrary dismissal after they have completed a probationary period, workers may be removed at any time without due process rights. The only job protections for employees in at-will positions come from federal law that applies to all workers regardless of sector, such as antidiscrimination laws, wage and hour laws, and laws that govern worker safety, family and medical leave, and union activity. Proponents for EAW argue that the threat of losing their jobs prevents workers from taking the job for granted and not performing at their best. On the other hand, public employees have traditionally been paid less than equivalent jobs in the private sector and have less luxurious work environments. The tradeoff has been the security offered by job protections. Employment at-will is now the norm in the state of Georgia, and it has been expanded for selected job classifications in some other states.

There is always a tension between tried and true procedures that offer stability and predictability—and frustration with bureaucratic inertia—versus new procedures that offer cost savings or avoid lengthy delays in hiring and dismissal processes. The important thing to remember is that public HR systems are in place to ensure equal opportunity to jobs and employment based on applicants' knowledge, skills, and abilities, rather than partisanship or personal connection. Transparency in compensation is required. To change one element of the system requires changes in most other aspects.

Debate: Time-Consuming Hiring Processes versus Speedy Hiring?

Although civil service systems have achieved merit-based hiring, equal opportunity for job applicants, and a representative workforce, these positive attributes are not without cost, primarily in the form of time. In order to provide for broad opportunity to apply for jobs, positions must be posted in multiple outlets with sufficient time for prospective applicants to learn of the job and apply for it. Then, objective measures must be used to screen applicants, whether that is a simulation, résumé assessment, or test that is scheduled at such times that applicants may participate. The scoring must be done in a transparent fashion. Once scoring is complete, lists of qualified finalists are forwarded to the hiring authority and interviews must be scheduled. All of this requires months, not days, to complete. Critics say that the time delay is not worth the benefit and that streamlined processes should be used, even if such processes short-circuit equal opportunity and standardized selection processes. Which is better? Hiring processes that achieve important democratic ends or speedy processes that minimize equal opportunity?

BALANCING ACT: PUBLIC EMPLOYEES AND FREE SPEECH

Government employees occupy an interesting space in legal theory: They are both citizens with all the rights that come with constitutional protections and they are also employees obligated to fulfilling employer demands. The U.S. Supreme Court has weighed in on this balance via two decisions: the 1968 *Pickering v. Board of Education*[17] case, followed by the 2006 *Garcetti v. Ceballos*[18] decision. While *Pickering* affirms the first amendment rights of public employees, *Garcetti* sets a boundary around those rights.

In *Pickering*, a high school teacher was fired after publishing a letter in the local newspaper blowing the whistle on how the school district was spending more money on athletics than on academics. The decision noted that employee-employer disputes often present a conflict between the employee's free-speech interests and the employer's efficiency interests. Justice Thurgood Marshall wrote "The problem in any case is to arrive at a balance between the interests of the teacher, as a citizen, in commenting upon matters of public concern and the interest of the State, as an employer, in promoting the efficiency of the public services it performs through its employees."[19] The decision reinstated Pickering to his teaching job and is the foundation of public employee first amendment rights. The court's decision made clear that citizens do not give up their right to speak to matters of public interest just because they are an employee of the state. This line of reasoning was upheld recently in a 2016 case before the Supreme Court, *Heffernan v. City of Paterson*,[20] in which the decision was in favor of Heffernan, a police detective who had been demoted because the police chief thought he was supporting a mayoral candidate who was trying to unseat the incumbent. The ruling affirmed that public employees cannot be penalized for exercising their first amendment freedoms.

In *Garcetti*, on the other hand, a deputy district attorney had criticized a search warrant and the sheriff's affidavit that supported it. He wrote a memorandum communicating his findings to his supervisors, recommending dismissal of the case. The supervisors refused to dismiss the case and afterward he was subjected to a series of retaliatory employment actions, including reassignment to a different position, transfer to another courthouse, and denial of a promotion. In this case the court held that public employees are not speaking as citizens when they are speaking to fulfill a responsibility of their job. The opinion stated that Garcetti was not acting as a citizen when he wrote the memo but rather as an employee and that there could not be constitutional protection for every statement that public employees make in the course of doing their job. The opinion went further to say that it is part of the employment relationship for supervisors to evaluate performance and make employment decisions accordingly.

These cases show the thin line between speaking as a citizen versus speaking as an employee. *Pickering* and *Heffernan* are reminders that public employees do not give up their citizenship rights in the employment relationship. And *Garcetti* is a reminder that workplace policies and procedures trump employees' freedom of speech when within the performance of official job duties.

Careers in human resource management are rich in possibility. The story of Michael Massiah, who once served as Director of Human Resources for the Port Authority of New York and New Jersey, demonstrates this.

Ask Me Why I Care: Michael Massiah, Chief, Capital Planning, Execution and Asset Management, Port Authority of New York and New Jersey[21]

"Public service was a way I could contribute as an individual to try to improve the quality of life for all within a jurisdiction—that's what drove me to it."

—Michael Massiah

Michael Massiah began his Port Authority career in 1981 as a Management Trainee. Over the decades, he worked in progressively more responsible roles including Director of Business and Job Opportunity, where he directed programs that supported the achievement of women, minority, and small business enterprises. As his career progressed, he was promoted to Director of the Human Resources Department and was later named to head the Management and Budget Department. Budgets for the Port Authority are worth billions of dollars. For four consecutive years, the Government Finance Officers Association (GFOA) awarded Mr. Massiah with the Certificate of Recognition for Budget Preparation. These recognitions acknowledged Mr. Massiah's role in the Port Authority achieving the GFOA Distinguished Budget Presentation Award, the highest award in governmental budgeting. Access his story at https://www.unomaha.edu/college-of-public-affairs-and-community-service/community-engagement/pss-michael-massiah.php.

SUMMARY

Human capital is the bedrock of all organizations and all public services. It is the foundation of program planning, staffing, performance, and outcomes. From determining the types of jobs necessary, to recruiting and developing staff, to evaluating outcomes and making strategic changes to improving processes, people are at the heart of the enterprise. Public service workers are both architects and agents. They plan the services and they deliver them.

The terms "human capital" and "human resources" are largely synonymous. Human capital is used to denote the fact that *human* capital is as important as *financial* resources. The differentiation between *capital* and *resources* came about in 2002 with the Chief Human Capital Officers Act, which required federal agencies to designate a Chief Human Capital Officer (CHCO). CHCOs are their agencies' chief policy adviser on all human resource management issues. The CHCO is responsible for selecting, developing, training, and managing a high-quality, productive workforce. Thus, the CHCO is typically the director of the agency's human resource office. The term human capital denotes elevation of human resource management from a purely staff function designed to assist managers in staffing their operations to a strategic element of the organization, essential to all agency planning and operations.

Human resource functions guide the development of job descriptions, recruitment, selection, training and development, compensation, benefits, performance appraisal, and grievance processes. Collectively, they shape what work gets done and who does it. In other words, having the right people with the right skills in the right jobs determines mission accomplishment.

Decades of attention to motivation reveal that there is not one best way to motivate all workers: The same rewards that incentivize some fail to motivate others. For this reason, there are several categories of theories that have proven useful in understanding how to improve human potential. Hierarchical models assume that workers must satisfy their basic needs and their social needs before they are motivated to pursue higher-order ends, such as self-actualization. Equity models use workers' judgments about how fairly they are treated as the key to motivation. Expectancy models pair workers' expectations with outcomes to explain how rewards motivate some and not others. The two-factor model separates workplace characteristics into two types: those that provide sufficient satisfaction that workers elect to remain in the job versus characteristics that motivate workers to perform above and beyond minimal requirements. And public service motivation is an additional element salient in public service jobs. It reflects an interest in the common good and a desire to help advance the common weal.

Management's assumptions about the factors that motivate workers set the tone for the workplace. During the industrial revolution, Theory X assumptions were predominant. In an enterprise that relies on knowledge workers, Theory Y assumptions are more applicable, although Theory X assumptions continue to manifest themselves in HR reforms such as at-will systems.

KEY TERMS

Broadbanding – refers to when several bands of job classifications are combined into one, which allows more flexibility on the manager's part in terms of setting job title and salary.

Classification – a job level within an organization; higher classifications receive higher wages.

Compensation – the inducements, in the form of wages and benefits, that workers receive for their work.

Garcetti – Supreme Court case that set a boundary around first amendment rights of public employees; established that public employees are not speaking as citizens when they are speaking to fulfill a responsibility of their job.

Motivation theories – theories that attempt to explain why workers contribute their effort and energy to an employer.

Pendleton Act – passed in 1883, established that positions with the federal workforce should be awarded on the basis of merit rather than on political affiliations, personal favor, or subjective whim.

Pickering – Supreme Court case affirming the first amendment rights of public employees; the decision made clear that citizens do not give up their right to speak to matters of public interest just because they are an employee of the State.

DISCUSSION QUESTIONS

1. Compare Maslow's and Alderfer's hierarchical theories of motivation, against expectancy, and equity theories. Which one most clearly captures your experience?
2. Do you think McGregor's Theory X or Theory Y better explains worker motivation? Think of supervisors you have had. Did they subscribe to Theory X or Theory Y? Why? Which do you prefer?
3. Compare Herzberg's two-factor theory of motivation to hierarchical, equity, and expectancy models. Which do you think presents a more realistic comprehension of motivation and job satisfaction?
4. Describe public service motivation in your own words. Do you have it?

BUILD YOUR SKILLS

The hiring process is every organization's opportunity to build capacity. Here are steps to follow for recruiting, screening, and selecting the best candidate for the job.

SKILLBOX: HIRING THE RIGHT PERSON

The objective of hiring is to increase the organization's capacity by adding a person who brings needed skills and who is a helpful coworker. Effective hiring occurs in steps:

1) Start with the job description. Make sure it is an accurate reflection of the required knowledge, skills, and abilities so that applicants know what they are applying for and what will be expected.

2) Advertise widely. Post the job in as many venues as possible so that the broadest possible set of applicants will learn about the job and have an opportunity to apply. Do not overlook deserving candidates already within the organization. Leave enough time between when the ad appears and when review of applications begins that applicants have a reasonable timeframe within which to apply.

3) Create a system for acknowledging and reviewing applications that is timely and responsive. Acknowledge receipt of applications as soon as they arrive and inform applicants of the timeframe for the search: When will review begin? When will the selection decision be made?

4) Involve several people in the screening process to ensure balance and use a rating system. Ask the screening team to organize applicants into three categories: Yes, Maybe, No. Use the Maybe category for applicants missing key criteria but show excellence in related fields. Rating candidates can be done using the following procedure:
   - Prepare a matrix that lists candidates and rates them on each of the key elements in the job description. Use a scale of 1 to 3 for each element, with 1 = does not meet, 2 = meets, and 3 = exceeds. Then compare totals for the applicants and use their scores to place them in the Yes, Maybe, or No column.
   - To refine the Yes and Maybe columns, consider these questions:
     a) How similar is the applicant's work experience to the job being advertised?
     b) Are past work settings similar to this job?
     c) Are there red flags on the résumé, such as unexplained gaps in work history or rapid movement from one job to another?
     d) Are there personal or volunteer activities that add breadth and experience?

5) Discuss both the strengths and the development needs of candidates in the Yes column. Then discuss those in the Maybe column and keep the strongest in case those in the Yes column do not look as promising after the reference check and/or interview. Once there is a consensus on which candidates are in the No group, thank them for applying and notify them that they are not among the finalists.

6) Use telephone or video conferences to sort through finalists and determine who to invite for in-person interviews. Discuss basics, such as job expectations, scope of the applicant's work experience, and interest in the job.

7) As the selection of finalists narrows, check references. When speaking with former supervisors, ask open-ended questions about the duties performed by the applicant. Ask about strengths and weaknesses. Describe the vacant position and ask the references how they think the candidate would fit. Always check more than one reference.

8) The in-person interview is a two-way street for determining job fit and work style. It is the opportunity to sell the candidate on the job and to read body language during the give and take of conversation. At the same time, it is the candidate's opportunity to learn about the job and decide if it is a good fit. In preparation for the interview, the selection team should determine the questions to be asked of everyone, as well as questions that are specific to each candidate. Here are tips for an effective interview:
   - Start the interview by describing the job, work environment, facilities, and organizational philosophy.
   - Ask questions that are open ended and that require answers about the situation or environment in prior jobs. For example, a good question is "tell me about a challenging situation you encountered when doing X (one of the experience requirements) in your current job." Or, "tell me about a particularly good experience you had when doing X that gives you pride." If the candidate will be working in teams, request examples of their experiences in teamwork. Ask applicants to elaborate on career plans and aspirations and how they feel about their progress to date. Have them assess their own strengths and weaknesses.
   - Give candidates an opportunity to explain any unusual gaps in employment.

- Restrict the questioning to job specific attributes and remember that questions about personal attributes such as age, race/ethnicity, religion, disability, gender, military status, national origin, sexual orientation, pregnancy, health issues, and marital status are off-limits.
- Listen carefully to what is said and encourage the candidate to ask questions. What they ask will provide insights into what they value. Assess whether the candidate's priorities are compatible with the agency's priorities.
- Close the interview by asking applicants about job-related characteristics that "I should know about you but did not ask" and invite them to ask any questions they wish. Give the applicant the timeframe when the final decision will be made.

9) Select the best candidate. Choose the candidate who fulfills the job description and who will fit best into the organization. Be mindful that there is a balance to be reached between similarity and diversity. In public service, it is important that the workforce is representative of the constituency being served. And it is valuable to have diverse points of view on work teams. While it is most comfortable to hire someone like oneself, growth happens when one's comfort zone stretches to embrace diversity.

10) Make the offer. Extending the offer with enthusiasm sets a positive, welcoming tone. Candidates want to know they will be appreciated. The offer letter should include start date, salary, benefits, and any other details that would make a substantive difference as the applicant decides whether to accept the job. Other items might include coverage of relocation costs, amount of vacation time, office accoutrements, and so on.

11) Onboard the new employee. Make the first day be a welcoming one: Place a welcome note on the new employee's desk, introduce the new employee to co-workers and managers, give a tour of the office, and make sure that office essentials are ready, such as desk, computer, file cabinet, and office supplies. Assign a sponsor who will answer "how do we do . . ." questions. Explain job responsibilities, set realistic expectations, and then periodically provide feedback that links performance to expectations.

Hands-On Activity: Verify These Steps with Someone Who Has Hiring Experience

Interview a public service practitioner who has recently hired an employee. In the interview, review the eleven steps and ask for feedback on each. Were these the steps that were followed? Which steps were most helpful? Are there steps that are missing from this list? Are there unnecessary steps in the list?

NOTES

1. Ida Drury, "Doing Double Duty" (unpublished manuscript, 2015).

2. Illustration from *Federal Register* 73, no. 82 (April 28, 2008): 23012–23049, https://www.gpo.gov/fdsys/pkg/FR-2008-04-28/pdf/E8-8661.pdf.

3. "Merit System Principles," U.S. Merit Systems Protection Board, available at, http://www.mspb.gov/meritsystemsprinciples.htm.

4. Michael M. Ting, James M. Snyder, Jr., Shigeo Hirano, and Olle Folke, "Elections and Reform: The Adoption of Civil Service Systems in the U.S. States," *Journal of Theoretical Politics* 25, no. 3 (2013): 363–387.

5. Olle Folke, Shiego Hirano, and James M. Snyder, Jr., "Patronage and Elections in U.S. States," *American Political Science Review* 105, no. 3 (2011): 567–585.

6. U.S. Department of Labor, Bureau of Labor Statistics, "Union Affiliation of Employed Wage and Salary Workers by Occupation and Industry, 2014–2015 Annual Averages," Table 3, (January 26, 2017), http://www.bls.gov/news.release/union2.t03.htm.

7. Katherine Barrett and Richard Greene, "What Employee Surveys Reveal about Working in Government," *Governing* (June 9, 2016), http://www.governing.com/columns/smart-mgmt/gov-employee-surveys-state-local-government.html.

8. Ibid., par. 13.

9. Employee surveys for Minneapolis, "My Minneapolis Employee Engagement Survey," IGR http://www.ci.minneapolis.mn.us/www/groups/public/@hr/documents/webcontent/wcms1p-128718.pdf; for San Antonio, "2011 City of San Antonio Employee Survey," ETC Institute (September 2011), https://webapps.sanantonio.gov/rfplistings/uploads%5CRFP_1680_201211190125101.pdf; and for the State of Washington, Washington State Human Resource Division, Office of Financial Management (2017, April). *Employee Engagement Survey*. http://hr.ofm.wa.gov/sites/default/files/StateEmployeeEngagementReport.pdf.

10. Adapted from "Best Places to Work in the Federal Government," Partnership for Public Service (2017), http://bestplacestowork.org/BPTW/rankings/overall/sub.

11. Katherine Barrett and Richard Greene, "Public Employee Surveys: Worthwhile or Worthless?" *Governing Magazine* (May 19, 2016), http://www.governing.com/columns/smart-mgmt/gov-employee-surveys.html.

12. Robert Reich, "The Shameful Attack on Public Employees," *Robert Reich* (blog), January 5, 2011, http://robertreich.org/post/2615647030.

13. Scott P. Overmyer, *Implementing Telework: Lessons Learned from Four Federal Agencies* (Washington, DC: IBM Center for The Business of Government, 2011), 13.

14. James L. Perry, "Measuring Public Service Motivation: An Assessment of Construct Reliability and Validity," *Journal of Public Administration Research and Theory* 6, no. 1 (1996): 5–22.

15. U.S. President Barack Obama, Proclamation, "Public Service Recognition Week, 2016," (April 29, 2016), https://obamawhitehouse.archives.gov/the-press-office/2016/04/29/presidential-proclamation-public-service-recognition-week-2016.

16. "Graphs from NASPAA 2015 Alumni Survey," *NASPAANEWS* (May, 2016).

17. Pickering v. Board of Education of Township High School District 205, Will County, 391 U.S. 563 (1968).

18. Garcetti v. Ceballos, 547 U.S. 410 (2006).

19. David L. Hudson Jr., *Balancing Act: Public Employees and Free Speech*, First Reports 3, no. 2 (First Amendment Center, 2002), 11, http://www.firstamendmentcenter.org/madison/wp-content/uploads/2011/03/FirstReport.PublicEmployees.pdf, p. 1.

20. Heffernan v. City of Paterson, 136 U.S. 790 (2016).

21. *Ask Me Why I Care: Public Service Stories*, video, directed by Mary R. Hamilton and Rita Paskowitz (Omaha, Nebraska: College of Public Affairs and Community Service), https://www.unomaha.edu/college-of-public-affairs-and-community-service/community-engagement/pss-michael-massiah.php.

ADDITIONAL RESOURCES

To learn about the federal civil service, visit the OPM website at https:/www.opm.gov.

To learn about merit system principles, studies of federal employees, and the appeal process, visit the Merit Systems Protection Board website at http://www.mspb.gov/.

To learn about a nonprofit that advocates for the federal civil service, visit the Partnership for Public Service website at http://ourpublicservice.org/.

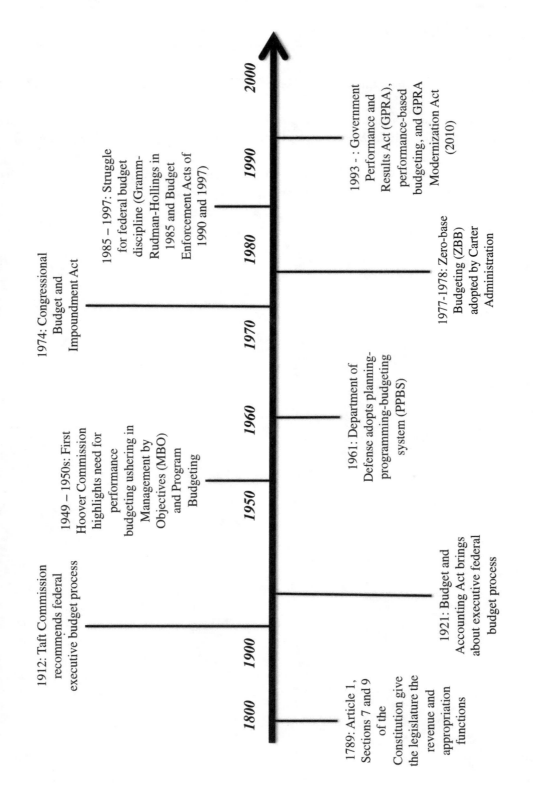

Chapter 6 Timeline: Budgeting

1912: Taft Commission recommends federal executive budget process

1949 – 1950s: First Hoover Commission highlights need for performance budgeting ushering in Management by Objectives (MBO) and Program Budgeting

1974: Congressional Budget and Impoundment Act

1985 – 1997: Struggle for federal budget discipline (Gramm-Rudman-Hollings in 1985 and Budget Enforcement Acts of 1990 and 1997)

1800   1900   1950   1960   1970   1980   1990   2000

1789: Article 1, Sections 7 and 9 of the Constitution give the legislature the revenue and appropriation functions

1921: Budget and Accounting Act brings about executive federal budget process

1961: Department of Defense adopts planning-programming-budgeting system (PPBS)

1977-1978: Zero-base Budgeting (ZBB) adopted by Carter Administration

1993 - : Government Performance and Results Act (GPRA), performance-based budgeting, and GPRA Modernization Act (2010)

WHAT YOU WILL LEARN

Why budgeting matters

The budget process

Approaches and types of budgeting

Skillbox: Data management and presentation with spreadsheets

Regardless of whether governmental or nonprofit, each organization has to budget its resources in order to meet its mission. Reliable budgets are based on reliable estimates of revenue and expenses, but sometimes estimates are only best guesses, as the following case demonstrates.

HAZY FORECASTS OF MARIJUANA TAX REVENUE IN WASHINGTON

In November 2012, voters in Washington State approved Initiative 502 legalizing licensed businesses to engage in the production and sale of recreational marijuana. To make an informed decision on the merits of the initiative, voters needed to understand its budgetary implications. Similarly, the state legislature needed to be aware of its implications for the state budget. The proposal embodied many of the characteristics familiar to government revenue sources. The recreational marijuana revenues were to be based on licensing fees and a 25 percent excise tax on marijuana sales, which would flow directly to a Dedicated Marijuana Fund. Revenue from existing sales and use taxes derived from marijuana sales would support the General Fund. The use of fund accounting in governments is a mechanism to improve control and match sources of revenues to their desired, and typically required, uses. The Dedicated Marijuana Fund would then distribute earmarked shares of tax revenues to a dozen groups for specific purposes, including state departments, universities, and a health insurance trust account. Earmarking is another common government practice supporting accountability by tying the source of revenues to related spending.

The Washington Office of Financial Management (OFM) was tasked with providing fiscal impact estimates of the proposed initiative and provided such a report in August 2012.[1] Unlike existing revenue sources, where historical activity is used to craft a forecast, the recreational sale of marijuana was legalizing a black market activity. In other words, little historical data on demand and pricing was available. The first challenge was, therefore, estimating the volume of recreational marijuana sales to determine the tax base. A complicating factor in the estimation was uncertainty about whether high excise tax rates would keep buyers in the black market or existing medical marijuana market with its lower taxes. The OFM simplified the projection by making the unrealistic assumption that all marijuana purchases would be recreational. Using existing national survey data on drug use, the analysts calculated the share of the state's future population likely to use marijuana. Based on this number of marijuana consumers, the OFM then used estimates

from the United Nations on the frequency of consumption and the average grams per use to find a total projected annual consumption of 85,100,000 grams in 2013. Once the consumption was estimated, figuring out the anticipated excise and sales tax base required a price for marijuana. The analysts looked to the state's existing medical marijuana market for pricing information and used $12 per gram as the estimated retail price in their tax base calculations.

The budgetary implications of the initiative went well beyond state and local tax revenue considerations. The OFM also had to predict fee revenue based on the number of marijuana producers, processors, and retail outlets, account for any loss of federal funding that conflicted with having legalized recreational marijuana sales, and consider the revenues associated with increased arrest activity for driving under the influence. From a spending perspective, the OFM had to predict the implementation costs of establishing, regulating, and monitoring the recreational market. For example, the Washington State Patrol was expected to incur more than $2 million in training expenses related to marijuana-impaired driving. Alternately, the analysts were unable to estimate potentially lower costs for law enforcement, the courts, and correctional facilities due to legalization.

All forecasts, regardless of the sophistication in methodology depend on a series of critical assumptions. The OFM, as is expected in any public forecast, provided extensive disclosure of the assumptions used to determine the revenue and expenditure estimates. The resulting forecast reflected the unusual lack of available information. In fact, the fiscal impact was deemed "indeterminate" given the many legal uncertainties, but "assuming a fully functioning marijuana market" the OFM estimated the Dedicated Marijuana Fund would receive $248.6 million in the first year of legalization. This estimate was presented in the Washington Voters' Guide as background information for the initiative.[2] In reality, only $64.9 million was collected in Fiscal Year 2014. Fiscal Year 2016 saw a dramatic increase in Dedicated Marijuana Fund inflows to $185.8 million, but this was still much less than the $447.2 million originally estimated by the OFM.[3]

The experience of Washington is an extreme example of the uncertainty faced by organizations attempting to look into the future and estimate available resources.

Questions to Ponder

1. In hindsight, how should the anticipated revenue have been calculated?
2. What lessons can be learned from how anticipated revenue was estimated for a newly legalized market?

Thomas Dye famously referred to public policy as "anything a government chooses to do or not to do."[4] The budget is the planning document that translates these choices about an organization's priorities into the necessary resources for implementation. In other words, budgeting is policy making. For example, the outcome of a contentious, year-long debate among city council members and residents over the expansion of a municipal park ultimately appears, or just as important does not appear, in the city's budget as resources allocated to the parks and recreation department. Despite the often unwieldy presentation of public budgets, they are simply a compendium of voter preferences distilled by the budget process and expressed in resource allocations. Behind every dollar amount in a budget, there is a story of political and administrative tradeoffs made between competing demands for limited resources.

This chapter describes the budgeting process, how it affects public managers, and the approaches and types of budgets. Establishing and communicating budget priorities to stakeholders, as well as measuring the related outcomes of the budgeted resources are also reviewed as they represent persistent challenges for public and non-profit managers.

Any discussion of budgeting is grounded in the actual services being delivered and supported by the public sector. The levels of resources dedicated to different functional areas crudely represent our collective public priorities. The activities provide insight into the overlapping roles played in public service delivery by the different levels of government and nonprofits. Table 6.1 presents the functional categories of public sector activity based on shares of spending for governments and revenues for the nonprofit sector.

TABLE 6.1 PUBLIC SECTOR ACTIVITY BY FUNCTIONAL AREA[5]

	Federal Government	State & Local Governments	Nonprofits
General public service	13.9%	15.2%	
National defense	15.4%		
Public order and safety	1.5%	12.6%	
Economic affairs	3.9%	7.7%	
Housing and community services	1.5%	0.4%	3.9%
Health	27.6%	23.6%	48.9%
Recreation and culture	0.1%	1.2%	3.3%
Education	2.7%	32.8%	13.9%
Income security	33.3%	6.4%	
Mutual & membership benefit			7.4%
Human services			5.8%
Philanthropy, voluntarism and grant making foundations			5.8%
Public and societal benefit			4.2%
Total ($ billions)	3,896.7	2,392.7	2,365.0

Sources: Bureau of Economic Analysis, table 3.16. Government Current Expenditures by Function. Revised on November 4, 2015. Internal Revenue Service, Exempt Organizations Business Master File (04/2016). The Urban Institute, National Center for Charitable Statistics, http://nccsweb.urban.org/.

The budgetary prominence of the income security and health-care functions, along with national defense, have resulted in the federal government being called an "insurance company with an army."[6] State and local governments' primary spending area is education, mainly elementary and secondary, followed by health and public safety, the latter of which includes police, prisons, fire, and the courts. Comparison to the nonprofit sector is imperfect due to overlapping functions across activity areas, but the table nevertheless demonstrates the centrality of health and education services across all of public service.

INCREMENTALISM

The budgeting process is frequently characterized as incremental. The term *incrementalism*, popularized by Aaron Wildavsky, refers to the belief that generally, only limited changes are made to existing spending patterns during budget preparation. The "increment" refers to a small increase in resources from the previous period's budget to compensate for changes in the costs of providing existing services that result from inflation and growing populations.

Incrementalism is a frank admission that it is not practically or politically feasible to reassess all budgeted activities every budget period. Instead, shortcuts simplify decision making and reduce conflict over resources, a process that Charles Lindblom called "muddling through."[7] The incremental nature of budgeting is belied both by periods of dramatic as well as gradual change in government activities and the reality that overall spending totals mask variation across time. If current spending decisions are based on existing practice, then it is implicitly assumed that past spending decisions still make sense. Incrementalism is a persistent and useful lens for understanding budgeting even though it is a slap in the face to those who expect a highly rational and analytical approach to prioritizing resource allocation through the budget process.

THE EXECUTIVE BUDGET

Early in the twentieth century, the rising popularity of scientific management and its focus on efficiency demanded a more rigorous approach to budget making than could be accorded by budget requests directly received and considered by legislative bodies.[8] To provide transparency and accountability, the executive budget process came into fashion because it makes the executive accountable for setting the primary policy direction of the organization and for ensuring that spending adheres to the budget. The municipal reform movement, coupled with passage of the federal Budget and Accounting Act of 1921, further institutionalized the executive budget. Despite the centrality of the executive in budgeting, the maxim that "the executive proposes, the legislative disposes" holds true as the branches of government fulfill their roles.

The budget serves a number of purposes for directing the work of the organization. Allen Schick boiled these down to three overarching administrative functions: planning, management, and control, each of which varies in priority over the years.[9] *Planning* captures the goal-setting process inherent in budget preparation and the selection of activities to be supported from the many competing alternatives. The classic question of budgeting is deceptively simple but wrought with political tension. Specifically, V.O. Key asked in 1940, "On what basis shall it be decided to allocate *x* dollars to activity A instead of activity B?"[10] Mikesell and Mullins pragmatically conclude that "public budgeting continues to balance rational decision making and pure politics."[11] *Management* is facilitated because the budget allocates resources to each activity. The budget is a *control* document because it restricts resources to prescribed activities.

Budgeting occurs at many levels. Whether pulling together a program budget for a grant application at a social service nonprofit, contributing to the department's response to the governor's budget call, or working in an executive budget office, the responsible and effective use of funds depends on understanding budgeting. While limited resources are perceived to be the primary budgeting challenge for governments and nonprofits, more relevant concerns are:

1) how to effectively direct the available funds to address the organization's priorities, and

2) how to cope with the inherent uncertainties that accompany the budget.

Although these are commonsense statements, the reality is that the budget process provides competing incentives and limited flexibility for even the most capable managers.

WHY BUDGETING MATTERS

There are many reasons why budgeting matters to both managers and the broader public. First, budgets reflect priorities; second, they are a control mechanism; and third, they are interdependent and prone to uncertainties.

Budgets Reflect Priorities and Necessities

Priorities are rarely universally agreed upon, which makes the budget process a political exercise. Elected officials or nonprofit leaders need to answer fundamental questions about the scope of organizational activities and how resources are distributed across constituencies before the more technical budgeting activities can occur. An organization cannot support its mission if its budget is misaligned with strategic objectives. Strategic planning provides the goals for the organization and a guide for budgeted activities. For example, New York City's FY2016 executive budget of $78.3 billion is by far the largest municipal budget and exceeds the annual budgets of most states. The executive budget presents the areas of growth, fairness, sustainability, and resiliency as components of "Building a Stronger New York".[12] The budget takes these broad, high-level goals and devises a spending plan to support them. In the city's budget, proposed spending ranges in scale from adding 50,000 kids to the pre-kindergarten system in support of fairness, to expanding the service hours of the Staten Island Ferry to promote economic development.

> *"The budget is not just a collection of numbers, but an expression of our values and aspirations."*
>
> —Jacob Lew

The budget comprises many activities, both routine and unorthodox, that when aggregated, represent the capacity of the organization to accomplish both its fundamental and its aspirational goals. Whether it is a citizen receiving public services, an elected official or public manager helping to establish goals and priorities, or an employee delivering services, the budget represents a continuously evolving set of organizational priorities and the resources dedicated to achieving them.

Budgets Are a Mechanism for Control and Accountability

The public nature of the modern budgeting process allows stakeholders, particularly citizens, to monitor and participate in budget-making. While control is a function of guaranteeing that an organization is using its resources as planned and authorized, accountability suggests effective use of resources. To illustrate, a city's residents may be happy to know that the public works department complied with their authorized funding for repairing potholes this year. But, that fact does little to reassure them that the money was well spent. When coupled with evaluation and auditing, the budget can support both improved control and accountability.

Balanced budget requirements are one of the most visible forms of control for government budgets, but exactly what does balanced mean? "Balance" actually means that revenues match or exceed spending over the budgeted period. A balanced budget requirement does not exist for the federal government, but is frequently discussed as a policy option to constrain spending and impose fiscal discipline. All states, with the exception of Vermont, have balanced budget requirements. This is not to suggest that Vermont fails to balance their budget. In fact, Vermont's Governor, Peter Shumlin, has noted that no such requirement is needed since "Vermont has more common sense than the 49 other states . . . We pay our bills, live within our means and hold firm to the tradition of not spending more than we take in."[13] The stringency of statutory and constitutional requirements varies across states with most requiring balance at the end of the budget period rather than simply at the time of budget approval. Local governments, similarly, face balanced budget requirements. Nonprofits do not have such requirements, despite the sector's label that suggests the inability to run budget surpluses.

The subject of balanced budgets is controversial, since the commonsense prescription that a balanced budget is always desirable is contrary to economic rationale under certain conditions. Namely, deficit spending can smooth out spending and reduce disruption to services during economic downturns exactly when countercyclical demand for public services increases. Related, running a deficit can eliminate the need for erratic and inefficient changes in tax rates and revenue sources. Finally, if valuable or long-term investments are being made with the budgeted funds then the spending may be worthwhile when looking beyond the current budget year.

Budgets Are Interdependent and Plagued with Uncertainty

A key reason why understanding budgets is so important is that budgets are interdependent, even across organizations and sectors, and they are prone to uncertainties. Although a city council, governor, or nonprofit executive director may control the composition of their respective organization's budget, the anticipated revenues and proposed spending will reflect the budgeting and administrative decisions of external entities. The availability of federal grants, for example, will trickle down to the budgets of local governments and nonprofits. And a depressed state economy can spike service demands for governments and nonprofits at exactly the time that revenues and support from other sources decline. The degree to which an organization depends on intergovernmental transfers (transfers usually flow downward from higher to lower levels of government), external grants, and contracts, determines its vulnerability to others' budgets. Additionally, mandates from higher levels of government also increase budgetary interdependence. Whether due to interdependency, a shortfall in expected internally-generated revenues, or cost overruns, public and nonprofit managers are commonly called on to rebudget during the budget period and, more formally, to prepare a subsequent budget that accommodates the mismatch between resources and current spending. Conversely, unexpectedly high revenues or low spending will produce unexpected surpluses that also require budgetary adjustments.

Whether shortfall or surplus, both circumstances are fraught with political challenges about how to cut or expand spending. Budget shortfalls are admittedly more painful. There are three possible actions for bringing a projected budget deficit into balance: tap financial reserves, raise revenues, or reduce spending. The response, or combination of responses, depends on the expected duration of the budget gap. For example, the Great Recession, which began at the end of 2007, presented organizations with dramatic revenue declines coupled with spiked service demands. State budget officers softened the impact of the recession by taking multiple courses of action, including across-the-board and targeted cuts to spending, tapping rainy-day funds, spending accumulated operating reserves from prior years, expanding revenue, and benefiting from the availability of federal stimulus dollars.[14]

Raising taxes and fees or introducing new revenue sources is politically unpopular, but can be unavoidable to maintain service levels. A euphemism of budgeters is referring to tax and fee increases as "revenue enhancements." For example, when Brevard Public Schools in Florida proposed measures to reduce a budget gap by nearly $31 million in 2012, they included a number of measures referred to as "revenue enhancements." These included adding fees to existing programs with a "Pay-to-Participate" fee for participation in school sports that reduced the estimated gap by over $400,000.[15]

Decision makers try to avoid raising taxes and fees by turning to the spending side of the budget for reductions. The problem is that public service is labor intensive. This means that budget cuts often require reductions in staff and this is undesirable for both programmatic reasons and employee morale. Additionally, cuts can be complicated and difficult to implement because of reductions-in-force rules in civil service systems. So, how does a manager identify the least damaging way to make budget cuts? The answer is not easy. First, the entire budget is rarely available to be cut. When mandated and entitlement spending is required, only the portion of the budget that allocates discretionary spending may be modified. This limits the activities that can be considered for reductions. Second, decision makers must decide whether across-the-board or targeted spending reductions are preferable.

Across-the-Board Cuts versus Targeted Cuts

While intuitively easy, across-the-board cuts have three main failings: they ignore the relative importance of different activities to the organization; they overlook the fact that some programs are more capable of absorbing cuts without degrading service quality; and they fail to consider organizational priorities. On the other hand, across-the-board cuts have a number of appealing features. Ordering a 3 percent budget reduction for the whole organization is easy to implement and provides a superficial appearance of fairness because everybody receives the same proportional reduction.

Targeted cuts are preferred when the necessary time and effort is available to consider the effects on organizational goals of reducing spending in different program areas. For example, decision makers expecting a relatively short period of budget stress may rationally skimp on routine facility maintenance activities without impacting mission-based services. This may result in higher long-term facility costs, but these are the types of tradeoffs that must be made. The urgency and desired short-term relief from budget cuts often trump a longer-term perspective on the consequences. Following the stock market decline in 2000, state governments most commonly balanced budgets using the diverse set of approaches reported in Table 6.2.

TABLE 6.2 MOST COMMONLY USED BUDGET BALANCING STRATEGIES
REPORTED BY STATE BUDGET OFFICERS

Across-the-board cuts	Program streamlining and reorganization
Targeted cuts	Cut local government aid
Budget stabilization fund/reserve funds	Privatization and contracting-out
Tobacco settlement funds	Tax and fee increases
Revenue transfers	Freeze state spending
Layoffs, furloughs, early retirement, and hiring and salary freezes	Tax increase referenda
Travel freezes	Spending controls

Source: National Association of State Budget Officers. 2002 (December). Budget Shortfalls: Strategies for Closing Spending and Revenue Gaps, 3rd ed.

Gimmicks

Another means of balancing a budget is through the use of gimmicks, which provide only a temporary solution to a budget imbalance. For example, organizations may use one-time funds, those not expected to be available in future years, to address a shortfall in revenue. More obvious gimmicks include delaying payments to employees and suppliers into the next fiscal year. Examples of gimmicks are common. In 2003, Colorado's governor signed Senate Bill 03-197 into law. Referred to as the "payday shift," the law pushed the pay date for state employees and the associated $89.4 million in general fund spending, from June 30 to July 1, the start of the new fiscal year. More than a decade later Colorado state employees, including the authors of this book, continue to be paid a day late due to this budgetary gimmick. More recently, Illinois' state government delayed the repayment of $6 billion in bills from fiscal year 2010 (FY2010) until the following fiscal year to help bridge a budget gap.[16] Arizona addressed a part of its nearly 34 percent drop in state revenues during the Great Recession of 2007–2008 by selling many of its buildings, including the House and Senate buildings of its capitol, for an infusion of cash through a number of sale-leaseback financing arrangements.[17] The use of such budget gimmicks—and this is only a sample—is evidence of the severe pressures faced by public sector managers to maintain services in the face of declining resources. Public and nonprofit managers are often forced to come up with creative solutions to constraints. The problem is that there are long-term financial and reputational costs to temporary fixes.

RULES, NORMS, AND INCENTIVES

Coping with uncertainty is a constant effort for budget professionals. Just preparing a balanced budget as a control mechanism does little to guarantee that funds will be spent effectively or that long-term obligations are being adequately considered. The budget process is guided by rules and institutional norms, which means that *budgets institutionalize incentives*. Incentives can be established to support effective spending behavior, but more frequently budget processes do the opposite. The incremental nature of budgeting means that next year's budget is based on this year's. Incrementalism produces a disincentive to spend less than is budgeted, because this will result in a smaller budget next year. The quandary is how to create incentives rather than reprisals for actual budgetary savings.[18]

If next year's budget is based on last year's, then there is little incentive for program managers to find savings and efficiencies. Those savings would benefit the organization as a whole, but would also conflict with program or department interests by lowering the program's future budget allocations. The incentive to spend all budgeted funds prior to the end of the fiscal year, even if the spending is not needed, has been referred to as a "use-it-or-lose-it" system. In 1965, President Lyndon Johnson commented on end-of-year spending as "an ancient practice—but that does not justify it or excuse it."[19] Systems that incentivize savings in public budgeting exist, but have not been widely adopted.

In 2013, a *Washington Post* story drew attention to the federal government's incentivized end-of-year spending binge. Examples of spending in the last week of the year included $144,000 on toner cartridges for the Agriculture Department and a Department of Veterans Affairs' order of more than half-a-million dollars of artwork. These relatively small purchases pale in comparison to government contracts, which are also disproportionately awarded in the last week of the federal fiscal year. Just because spending occurs at the end of the year does not mean it is inherently poorly planned, but well-publicized examples of wasteful last minute spending have reflected poorly on the federal government. The *Post* highlights an end-of-year Internal Revenue Service conference complete with a "Star Trek" parody video, which drew the ire of Congress. There is also some empirical evidence that end-of-year information technology contracts have poorer outcomes.

Public and nonprofit managers must be cognizant of the perverse incentives imposed by a use-it-or-lose-it annual budgeting cycle. A more serious concern about budget incentives falls on decision makers. Naomi Caiden has raised the paradox that high-performing programs may have their resources cut due to their ability to perform strongly with existing resources.[21] Alternately, what should budgeters do for programs or departments that are not meeting performance expectations? Raising funding to achieve objectives may be called for, but doing so may be rewarding poor performance. This difficulty in determining how to adjust budgeted resources based on results is one of the forces pushing for collecting and integrating better performance measures into budgetary decision making.

The operating budget specifies the availability and use of current resources for the upcoming year or two. Unlike audited financial statements, revenue and spending decisions can be biased toward short-term considerations, especially given the political implications of the budget. In other words, operating budgets can prioritize a short-term focus to the detriment of long-term obligations. The most salient long-term obligations in government include entitlement programs, debt, pension obligations, and other post-employment benefits. The Pew Center on the States' 2010 report on the trillion dollar funding gap for state retirement systems helped focus public attention on long-term obligations.[22] Research shows that state governments address the year-to-year demands of balancing annual and biennial budgets by only partially funding their employee pension systems.[23] The federal government has made an effort to insulate certain funds from these year-to-year budget demands by moving them off-budget. For example, the Social Security trust funds are off-budget, but are still represented in consideration of the unified budget. In other words, many public obligations greatly exceed the time frame of budget cycles, which means that managers must strike an appropriate balance between budgeting fairly for current as well as future needs.

THE BUDGET PROCESS

Budgeting plays a central role in implementing policy priorities and providing a mechanism for control and accountability, but what characterizes the formal process? The traditional budget cycle can be simplified into four major stages (see Table 6.3). Although generalizing the process is helpful, there remains tremendous variation because of the diversity of government and nonprofit organizations.

TABLE 6.3 STAGES AND PRIMARY ACTIVITIES OF THE BUDGET PROCESS

Preparation/ Submission	Approval	Implementation	Review
• Forecast revenues and service demands • Baseline budget • Budget call • Consultation between executive and departments • Departmental budget requests submitted • Requests reviewed and revised by executive • Executive budget assembled and submitted to legislature	• Legislative budget hearings • Budget amendments • Budget approval • Executive veto • Legislative override	• Allotment • Encumbrance • Monitoring • Rebudgeting	• Audit • Evaluation

The timing of the budget cycle stages depends on an organization's fiscal year, which differs across public and nonprofit entities. The federal government's fiscal year begins October 1; most state governments' fiscal years begin July 1 with notable exceptions; and many local governments follow their state's practice or the calendar year. The fiscal year for nonprofits also vary, but typically ends June 30 or matches the calendar year. A new budget is formulated each year in most state governments, but nineteen states continue to adopt biennial budgets.[24] The following sections discuss the stages and activities of the budget cycle with a focus on the relevant actors.

Preparation and Submission

Public and nonprofit organizations never begin a new budget year with a blank slate. At the federal level, a baseline budget is produced by the Congressional Budget Office. The baseline budget determines what the budget would look like in the coming year in the absence of any policy changes, but accounting for inflation, shifts in population and program utilization, and economic activity. The baseline provides the starting point for a dialogue on budget modifications.

The baseline budget may be a less formalized exercise at lower levels of government and in nonprofits, but last year's budget is the common starting point for the budget process and often is the benchmark for determining whether a budget gap exists. Whether the existing spending levels of the baseline budget can be expanded, maintained, or reduced depends on the expected availability of resources and existing commitments.

Revenue forecasts determine the availability of resources for budget development. Forecasting revenues is challenging, especially when governments depend on economically-sensitive tax and fee revenues and fluctuating transfers from higher levels of government. Similarly, nonprofits must predict charitable contributions and the uncertain receipt of grants and contracts. In fact, it is commonly stated that the one certainty in forecasting is that the forecast will be wrong. Of course, the degree to which the forecast is in error and the direction of the error matter critically for organizations. For this reason, revenue projections are periodically updated throughout the budget process as more timely information becomes available. Revenue projections are especially difficult during economic downturns, the launching of new programs, and the adoption of new sources of funds. The case of forecasting marijuana tax revenue at the opening of this chapter is a case in point.

With an approximate idea of the available resources based on forecasts, the executive issues the budget call. The budget call provides instructions for departments to prepare their budget requests based on the executive's priorities and whether available resources will allow for budget expansion through new programs and expanded services, will require a maintained spending level, or will require belt-tightening. At the federal level, the budget instructions are represented by the Office of Management and Budget's (OMB) Circular A-11.

Who is the "executive" who issues the budget call? Foremost, the executive is the individual in charge of the organization. In government, the executive is an elected official, such as president, governor, or mayor, but can also be an appointed municipal manager or superintendent serving at the pleasure of an elected council or board. In nonprofits, the chief executive officer serves this role. The term "executive" also encompasses the staff tasked with managing preparation of the budget. In government, this will be an executive budget staff (commonly referred to as "the budget shop") identified by some acronym reflecting the executive role in budget and management (see, for example, OMB at the federal level, OBM in Ohio, EBO in Alabama, and MBO in Denver).

The budget staff work with the agencies and departments to prepare their budget requests based on the parameters provided in the budget call. They provide budget expertise and the ability to assure that the interests of the overall organization are being met by its subunits. Agency and department managers are most familiar with their day-to-day needs and translate these into the necessary resources to accomplish their goals. Doing so requires identifying activities and projecting costs based on anticipated volume of services. Effectively justifying these estimates and the value of the activities, especially when proposing a new program or expansion of existing services, is critical. The following presents general guidance on formulating budget justifications.

JUSTIFYING A BUDGET REQUEST

Executives depend on program managers to inform the budgeting process, whether in setting budget allocations, considering service expansion, or coping with budget cuts. In the process, managers are frequently called upon to justify their budget request. An inherent tension exists between supporting resource-allocation decisions that are optimal for the organization as a whole, while simultaneously serving as a budget advocate for one's own program. The tendency to look at changes in the budget as a reflection of winners and losers can undermine support for the overall mission. How can managers justify their budget request while serving both the organization and their immediate administrative area? In short, carefully. First and foremost is to be honest and forthright about the need for resources and the consequences of not receiving the requested funds. The State of California's Department of Finance provides helpful guidance for justifying a budget request.[25]

1. Know your audience.
2. Have a succinct, descriptive title.
3. Provide a clear and concise summary.
4. Document needs/problems/opportunities, quantitatively, if possible.
5. Identify benefits to be achieved, quantitatively, if possible.

6. Present and evaluate viable alternatives in terms of costs and benefits.
7. Address history, risks, and uncertainties.
8. Document the required resources needed.
9. Have an independent, skeptical person critically review the proposal before submission.
10. Follow the instructions.

Much of this guidance is common sense, but the elements of a strong budget request combine the need for clear writing and presentation with thoughtful analytics and evidence. As John Mikesell contends, "Bud-geting is logic, planning, justification, and politics, not mathematics or accounting".[26] Present a range of alternatives to give decision makers options for achieving the policy objective.

These tips can help to construct a high-quality budget justification, but the overall confidence of executives in a manager's request is ultimately shaped by the accuracy and reasonableness of their past requests. In other words, managers should not sacrifice their long-term reputation and credibility in the budget process for a short-term gain in resources.

The collaborative budget preparation continues with the submission of department budget requests to the executive budget shop. With the requests in hand, the budget shop reviews the submissions for accuracy and adherence with the guidelines in the budget call. Analysts also use past performance, both financial and operational, to inform their opinion on the reasonableness of the requests. Executive budget hearings may be held so that managers can respond to questions and concerns regarding the requests. Following the hearings and additional consultation, the budget shop uses the latest available revenue and service demand projections to revise requests and aggregate them into a budget proposal referred to as the executive budget. The executive budget's narrative and numbers reflect the priorities that guided the budget formulation and the economic realities that shaped the proposed revenue and spending decisions. Special attention is given to changes in activities from the prior budget period, including new programs and actions taken to balance the budget.

> *"The crucial aspect of budgeting is whose preferences are to prevail in disputes about which activities are to be carried on and to what degree, in light of limited resources."*
>
> —Aaron Wildavsky

Approval

The proposed executive budget is then transmitted to the legislative body for consideration. The body will be Congress, a state legislature, city council, county board of supervisors, or a school board, among others. The legislative body typically holds budget hearings that are open to the public to deliberate the different components of the budget. Similar to the executive, the legislature may have its own budget office with the skills to review and, if necessary, challenge the executive's proposal. The Congressional Budget Office serves this role at the federal level. The relative power of the executive and legislative body dictates the extent to which legislative preferences ultimately appear in the final budget. A vote is required as the legislature uses its power of the purse to appropriate the funds to support the authorized spending proposed by the budget. The budget bill then returns to the executive where, if acceptable, it is signed into law and the budget is adopted. The executive has some recourse when dissatisfied with legislative changes by vetoing the budget bill in its entirety. Many state governors, unlike the president, have the power and flexibility to exercise a line-item veto without rejecting the budget bill as a whole. In the case of a veto, the bill is returned to the legislature where the executive veto can be overridden with a supermajority vote. If the veto is not overridden then the legislature and executive must return to budget negotiations.

This description of the budget preparation process overlooks the political dynamics and external actors that inform and shape the budget. The budget is about allocating resources, so stakeholders that benefit from the resources are also active in the process. Foremost, citizens and interest groups play prominent roles in making their own spending priorities (and revenue priorities in the case of antitax groups) salient for the executive and legislative decision makers. The extent to which interest groups work to influence spending depends on the level of government and the potential benefits to those groups. For these reasons, lobbying activity (efforts to directly influence the policy stance of public officials) is often most intense where the benefits of public spending are concentrated among a small group, while the associated costs are widely dispersed. The following case provides an example of how interest groups surface in response to even fairly minor changes in revenue or spending policy.

A TAXING CONFLICT[27]

The Great Recession battered state tax revenues forcing governors to identify alternative revenue sources or pare back spending. In Colorado, Governor Bill Ritter proposed extending the state's existing sales tax to candy and soda, which were previously exempt, as one piece of a broader plan to help offset the $1 billion gap expected in the 2009–2010 budget. The governor's office noted that the proposed tax change would generate $17.9 million that would otherwise be found through even more extensive cuts to K–12 and higher education spending. Colorado's 2.9 percent rate would mean an additional three cents for each dollar consumers spent on candy and soda.

Health advocates were cited as supporters of the plan, which, in addition to raising revenue, was expected to support healthier diets by making the purchase of sugary foods and drinks slightly more expensive. Such taxes on candy and soda are relatively common across the country. On the other side, some bemoaned the secondary social objectives of the tax. The president of a local libertarian institute suggested that "the governor needs to sit down and watch Willy Wonka a couple of times and stop being such a buzz kill." Not surprisingly, the soft drink industry opposed the expansion of the sales tax to their products and representatives testified at the legislature that job losses might result from the change. A representative of a Colorado candy company also spoke before the legislature in opposition to the change, later commenting that he was "carrying that fight for the National Confectioners Association" since "It just struck us as morally objectionable to fund (state) salaries on the backs of little kids riding their bikes to the 7-Eleven to get a Mars bar." Colorado's House Bill 10-1191 ultimately passed and was implemented. The interest groups that made their opinions known to elected decision makers over this relatively minor tax change are indicative of the vested interests that accompany any change in budgetary policy. As budget scholar Irene Rubin has noted, interest groups are "intensely involved" in revenue decisions.[28]

In addition to interest groups, budget realities are also shaped by voters wielding influence at the ballot box via direct democracy. Tax and expenditure limits are examples of how the initiative power has transformed the discretion of the executive and legislature to expand available resources through tax and fee increases. Most famously, California's Proposition 13, passed in 1978, restricted growth in property tax revenues and continues to influence both the composition and levels of revenue and spending today in the state.

Despite the legislative power over spending, the courts also influence budgets by decisions that require changes in budgeted resources to address constitutional violations. Litigation over inequitable and inadequate support for public education has, for example, forcibly altered spending priorities in more than half the states. The media is another influential actor in public budgeting by drawing public attention to revenue and spending debates, budget preparation, and approval. Despite being a reasonably open process, public budgeting is by no means simple and the media is in the unique position to guide the public dialogue and explain the potential implications of budgetary action to the wider citizenry. Especially at the municipal level, newspapers (yes, they still exist in most places!) assume the responsibility for informing the public about budget issues.

Implementation and Review

The budget cycle continues even after adoption. Periodic monitoring of actual revenues and spending determines whether the adopted budget and its many estimates are proving accurate throughout the period. Adjustments are made as needed in a process referred to as rebudgeting, as funds are periodically transferred to the agencies and departments throughout the year. For example, an unexpected reduction in criminal activity due to a strengthening economy might reduce the demand for corrections and court services. The executive will want to redeploy those savings to other spending priorities or offset higher costs in other areas. The federal government's FY2017 mid-session review and update to Congress, for example, reported that the original deficit expectation for 2016 declined from $616 billion to $600 billion.[29] Revenue shortfalls are also addressed through the rebudgeting process. Audits are traditionally retrospective reviews of the organization's finances as opposed to the prospective view of the budget. The auditing function has expanded over time to also assess organizational performance.

THE FEDERAL BUDGET

In general, the process described earlier holds true for the federal government, but the scale of the federal government and centrality of its budget history and process demand special attention regarding where the process diverges from the norm. After the president submits the proposed budget to Congress on or before the first Monday in February, both houses of Congress review the proposal. The House Ways and Means and Senate Finance committees then separately generate budget resolutions with spending and tax revenue targets for the appropriations committees. Budget resolutions are voted on before moving to a conference committee to work out differences between the House and Senate versions. The resulting Congressional Budget Resolution guides the legislative budget activities with targeted spending amounts for nineteen different budget functions, along with accompanying revenues. The twelve appropriations subcommittees in each house of Congress then receive allocations of the discretionary spending amounts outlined in the budget resolution for programs under their jurisdiction.

The subcommittees hold budget hearings for their respective programs before proposing and voting on an appropriation bill. If passed, the bills from each subcommittee proceed to the full appropriations committee for mark-up (meaning it is reviewed, debated, and amended as needed) before continuing to the full house for a vote. As with the budget resolution, differences between the chambers' appropriations bills are addressed in conference before returning to the House and Senate for a final vote. If approved, the bills are then forwarded to the president where they can be signed or vetoed. The appropriations bills are intended to be signed by October 1, but frequently the deadline is missed. Continuing resolutions must be approved to maintain existing spending levels for discretionary programs in the absence of signed appropriations bills.

Authorizing committees in each house are responsible for creating plans for any changes to mandatory spending programs or tax law if required by the budget resolution. The mandatory programs and tax code otherwise remain unchanged and do not require annual appropriations. Mandatory spending refers to entitlement programs like Social Security, Medicare, and Medicaid. In a process referred to as reconciliation, the budget committees in each house aggregate the plans into an omnibus bill. After each house votes, the approved omnibus bills are reconciled in conference, voted on again in each house, and then forwarded to the president to be signed or vetoed.[30]

DIFFERENCES IN NONPROFIT BUDGETING

The budget process for nonprofits differs in meaningful ways from their government counterparts. Primarily, nonprofit budgeting is less transparent to the public because, unlike government, they are not required to hold public hearings or to produce publicly-available budget documents. With budget documents often unavailable to external parties, nonprofit audited financial statements and Internal Revenue Service filings (Form 990) become after-the-fact sources for revenue and spending information. The budget process may also be more informal with regard to timelines and staff roles depending on the size and sophistication of the organization.

Budgeting practices across the sector reflect the diversity of nonprofits themselves, a sector where nearly 90 percent of spending comes from only 5.3 percent of public charities in 2013.[31] The multitude of smaller organizations differ markedly in management from the giant health insurers, hospital systems, and universities that dominate nonprofit spending. In these large organizations, the players in the budget process parallel those of government, with budget instructions going out to the nonprofit's staff, the executive director formulating the budget priorities often with the board's finance or budget committee, budget approval and strategic guidance by the board, and budget implementation overseen by the executive director.[32]

LOOKING ABROAD

The budget cycle has a logic to its progression of preparation, approval, implementation, and review. The focus on governments and nonprofits in the United States begs the question whether organizations outside the United States budget similarly? The public budget process depends heavily on a nation's political system, traditional practices, and level of decentralization between the national and subnational governments. The underlying logic of the executive budget system, though, translates across borders, but managerial capacity across jurisdictions influences practices just as it does across organizations in the United States. Two groups, the International Budget Partnership (IBP) and The Organisation for Economic Co-operation and Development (OECD), periodically survey international budget practices. The IBP survey analyzes existing budget documents in each country to produce the Open Budget Index, a measure designed to capture the public availability of budget information. The 2015 report presents the index values for 102 countries and ranks the United States fifth behind New Zealand, Sweden, South Africa and Norway in terms of transparency. It concludes that seventy-eight of the 102 countries fail to provide sufficient budget information to the public as defined by IBP.[33]

BUDGETING FORMATS AND APPROACHES

Budgets are formulated and formatted for a number of purposes. This section begins by discussing the various budget formats and approaches. The organization and presentation of budget information dictates its usefulness to managers and how it is perceived by readers. Prominent approaches to budgeting include line-item budgeting and performance, or performance-informed budgeting. The dominant format and approach in budgeting is the *line-item budget*, which groups spending by the specific object of expenditure, such as salaries and benefits or rent and utility costs. This approach and presentation is applauded for providing transparency that holds an organization accountable for the expected use of funds for specific purposes. It is also easy to use, since updating a line-item budget requires only straightforward adjustments to the expected costs of each line-item. When line-item information is broken out at the program, function, or department level, it allows for more granular comparisons of resource use over time, across an organization, and by specific managerial areas of responsibility. The downside of a line-item budget is that it fails to link organizational spending to outcomes. Instead, it provides a narrow view of inputs that provides limited support for managerial decision making.

Alternative approaches to the line-item budget emerged under the banner of *performance budgeting*. Initially, performance budgeting focused on output or efficiency measures. By quantifying public services it was possible to determine the necessary resources to accomplish the expected output. The primary difficulties with applying output-based performance budgeting are the inability to meaningfully quantify many public services and the fact that outputs frequently fail to capture the quality or intended outcome of public services. More modern performance budgeting attempts to connect proposed spending to program or department goals. The difference between inputs, outputs, and outcomes can be demonstrated using a police department as an example. In a traditional line-item budget, readers can observe the amount of dollars, or inputs, available to the department and how much is specifically being spent on police personnel, training, and equipment. Information on the police department's outputs, which might include the number of arrests made or traffic citations issued, can be combined with the existing line-item information or personnel figures to determine the average cost of each action as a crude measure of efficiency. Finally, the goals of the police department are more likely crime reduction and public safety rather than making arrests and writing tickets. An outcome measure for the department might be the effect of its budgeted spending on crime rates, something that is much more challenging to determine than the cost of outputs.

Integrating performance information into budgetary decision making is highly desirable, but has proven challenging due in part to the difficulties of measuring public service outcomes. The history of federal budget reform is one of attempts to inject a more rational planning approach to budgetary decision making. A common practice today is to complement line-item budget information with performance measures at the program or departmental level. Overall, budgeting continues to become more results-oriented by focusing on outcomes rather than inputs.

ADDITIONAL TYPES OF BUDGETS

The previous discussions focus on the operating budget process. Operating budgets are what is generally meant when individuals talk about "the budget," since operating budgets cover the planned revenues and spending to support the day-to-day activities of governments and nonprofits. Cash and capital budgets receive less attention and have less visible and formalized processes, but they are critical elements of a financial management system. *Cash budgets* are all about the availability of cash for the organization at any given point during the budget cycle. A balanced operating budget at the end of the year means little to a nonprofit organization if it has too little cash available to pay its employees on payday. Similarly, government cash flows ebb and flow with tax collection schedules. The cash budget, with its focus on cash receipts and disbursements, helps the organization guarantee that sufficient cash is available at all times to cover planned disbursements. The organization can invest or borrow in the short-term when a mismatch between cash inflows and outflows exists.

Capital budgeting refers to the process of acquiring and financing long-lived assets that maintain value and usefulness to the organization beyond the traditional operating budget cycle. Capital budgeting, along with long-term financing, allows organizations to better match the use and spending on capital assets over time. The public and nonprofit sectors require capital assets to deliver services. Maintaining roads, fighting fires, educating children, providing recreation opportunities, offering temporary housing, caring for health, conveying water and wastewater are examples of public services requiring buildings, vehicles, equipment, and machinery. Organizations establish thresholds for the classification of capital assets that typically depend on how long the asset is expected to last (the useful life) and how much it costs. For capital assets to deserve attention outside the operating budget process they should be both long-lasting and relatively expensive.

Capital budgeting generates long-term plans for the acquisition and financing of an organization's capital assets. Careful planning is essential since capital assets are large investments relative to an organization's operating budget and they usually require long-term financing. Some governments, especially those with voters more averse to public debt, save up over time and use pay-as-you-go financing. Although short-term borrowing occurs frequently to help smooth out cash flows, long-term borrowing enables governments to finance capital assets by spreading out the costs to match the expected benefits over time. In other words, borrowing to construct a bridge makes sense since future drivers, cyclists, and pedestrians benefit from the investment and their future tax payments can be used to service the debt. Borrowing long term for current spending needs, on the other hand, is generally poor financial practice.

An important concept related to capital budgeting is depreciation, which represents the use and reduction in value of an asset over a given period of time and supports explicit planning to replace capital assets. The federal government does not have a separate capital budget, although the use of one is periodically considered. State and local governments tend to use multiyear capital improvement plans to prioritize and schedule capital investments, but the process varies extensively even at the state level. In the end, lists of capital projects are generated often by requesting project needs from departments. The project lists are then prioritized by budget staff based on a set of criteria. The number of capital projects from the list that are approved depends on political support from the executive and legislative bodies, along with the availability of adequate funds (frequently through borrowing). The cash and capital budgets are key tools of management and planning.

When we think of a budget, we naturally consider adequate revenues being raised to support the recommended policies and programs. Frequently, though, revenue decisions embedded in the tax code represent explicit policy decisions that affect the budget in a manner similar to direct programmatic spending. For example, the amount an employer pays for an employee's health insurance is exempt from the employee's taxable federal income despite the fact that such support is compensation. This tax treatment aligns with the government's goal of incentivizing employee-provided health insurance, but it resulted in foregone federal income tax revenue of more than $207 billion in FY2015.[34] *Tax expenditures* are simply taxes that are not collected due to conscious policy decisions. Other tax expenditures are critically important for the nonprofit sector, including the tax deductibility of charitable contributions. The Congressional Budget Act of 1974 requires the federal government to compile a tax expenditure budget so the implications of these revenue decisions are apparent to the public and policy makers. A number of states have subsequently adopted the practice.

CITIZEN ENGAGEMENT IN BUDGETING

The same rationale for engaging citizens in government also applies to budgeting. A budgeting process informed by the public is more democratic because it reflects the public's values and priorities, instills civic responsibility in participants, and can produce different policy alternatives than would emerge from government acting without input. Public participation in the budgeting process, whether during budget preparation or simply communicating the budget document to the public, is also expected to improve the credibility and support for government action. A tension persists, though, between time-intensive efforts to involve citizens in the budget process and the outwardly technical nature of budgeting. This tension is apparent in the acknowledgment that public participation is rarely substantial and tends to have little impact on budget outcomes.[35]

The most common forum for citizen engagement in budgeting is formal budget hearings held during the preparation stage. A number of other practices exist ranging from simply making the budget more accessible and useful to the public (these can be simplified budgets-in-brief or more elaborate citizen budgets that more clearly connect spending to functions rather than departments) to substantial public involvement in budget preparation (for example, the public may be engaged to help identify the government's priorities in a priority-based budget approach). Developments in online interactive budgeting simulations are expanding the options for public participation.

USING TECHNOLOGY TO INFORM CAPITAL BUDGETING PRIORITIES

The potential and shortcomings of using technology to support public participation in budgeting was demonstrated by Arizona's Pima County in 2013. Pima County opted to poll its citizens online to determine the relative support for 144 capital project ideas submitted by local organizations. Almost 17,000 individuals participated over three weeks by ranking the proposed projects by level of perceived importance. The top-ranked projects based on the survey reflect the diverse services provided by the county and popular support for the renowned Arizona-Sonora Desert Museum, a new zoo exhibit, restoration assistance for the historic San Xavier Mission, and a Health Education Campus for the local community college, among others.[36] The survey responses were used as input for the deliberations by the Pima County Bond Advisory Committee, an appointed citizen group, on what projects should be included in a future bond financing referendum. The Advisory Committee ultimately recommended a package of projects to be brought before voters in 2015. The criteria for a project's inclusion in the proposed $653 million list was topped by "broad demonstrated support by public." The Committee touted the "overwhelming" public response to the proposed projects, specifically mentioning that nearly 6,000 open-ended responses were provided during the online survey and "less than 1 percent of these responses were opposed to a bond." The two years leading up to the Committee's recommendation included nineteen public meetings with attendance at each falling between sixty and 320 citizens.[37] Despite the support expressed by online survey respondents, all of the subsequent bond election propositions were defeated by voters in November 2015. One county supervisor commented following the defeat that "maybe the numbers were just too big."[38]

The Pima County experience illustrates that even the thoughtful investment of years of public input into a proposed spending plan can fail to accurately represent the public will. An Achilles heel of citizen participation is that the individuals most benefited (or harmed) by a proposed public activity tend to be disproportionately represented in the engagement activities. The large number of proposed projects and the significant dollar amounts likely generated a similarly expansive number of strong supporters. An online survey may have actually exacerbated the bias in favor of the projects, since individuals had to make an effort to find and complete the survey. Despite the expected benefits of public participation in budgeting, such participation comes with its own resource demands and challenges in capturing representative input.

BUDGETING AS PROFESSION

Most management jobs in the public and nonprofit sectors touch upon budgeting, so gaining deeper skills in the area is strongly suggested. For those beginning a public service career, positions in state and local government budget shops provide a unique opportunity to view and learn about the broader organization across its many departments and agencies. Eugene Bardach goes so far as saying that the government budget analyst is the best professional fit for those wanting to practice policy analysis, since the position must simultaneously "confront tradeoffs and project them into an uncertain future."[39] While some choose to work long term in a budget office, others use the exposure to the inner-workings of the organization to refine communication and analytical skills, and use the relationships developed with different programs and departments as a springboard to other positions.

Budget work can be technical, but most budget offices are looking for individuals with strong communication and critical thinking skills. Being able to communicate complicated information in a clear and succinct manner, both written and verbal, is paramount. The capacity to find, compile, and analyze data for decision making is similarly valued. At a minimum, a comfort with and willingness to use spreadsheets is needed. An analyst with California's Legislative Analyst Office captures the compelling nature of budget work noting that, "A successful budget analyst must be able to compile relevant data and present them in such compelling fashion that legislators and their staff will rethink their policy preferences and consider new policy solutions and/or reconsider previously discounted policy options."[40] In many organizations, the budget office is responsible for providing both budget and management analysis (for example, the federal government's Office of Management and Budget). While the distinction is blurred, management analysts deal less with comparing alternative policies and more with guiding performance improvement efforts to make existing activities more effective and efficient.

The influence and credibility of the budget staff depends upon its independent and objective perspective. The sensitive nature of budget deliberations requires careful consideration of ethical behavior. The National Association of State Budget Officers maintains extensive Standards of Professional Conduct, which include being "scrupulously and consistently honest," using the position "to advance the public interest," and to preserve public trust in government by "avoiding conduct creating the appearance of impropriety."[41] Efforts to support measured consideration of policy alternatives and more effective use of existing resources, all while ensuring accountability to the public, are at the core of the public service profession.

Ask Me Why I Care: J. Fred Silva, Senior Policy Adviser For California Forward, A Nonprofit Organization That Seeks More Effective Fiscal Decision Making[42]

Watch the video as he describes his work as a budgeter and policy adviser in California: http://www .unomaha.edu/college-of-public-affairs-and-communityservice/community-engagement/pss-fred-silva.php. In it, he talks about why he enjoys public service and how the budgeting process ensures a match between public priorities and public revenues. Note his closing comments about the budgeting process and how it connects the public will, service priorities, and finances.

SUMMARY

We return to V.O. Key's classic budgeting question, as it underscores the fundamental challenge of public budgeting: "On what basis shall it be decided to allocate x dollars to activity A instead of activity B?" The budget process determines the seemingly intractable policy tradeoffs being decided each year due to limited public resources: whether to provide more environmental protection but less homeless prevention; better mental health care but more potholes in the streets; or a strong defense but slower response to natural disasters. Much is demanded of public budgeting. The budget process promotes control and accountability, while simultaneously attempting to support improved performance. Each budget necessarily builds upon and is constrained by past decisions even as efforts to better link budget decisions to organizational performance continue. Performing with a fiscal and political environment characterized by uncertainty and interdependence presents constant challenges.

KEY TERMS

Balanced budget requirement – requires that revenues match or exceed planned or actual spending over the budgeted period.

Budget incrementalism – entails using the previous period's budget as the starting point, and making small changes, as needed, to create subsequent budgets based on the availability of revenue.

Capital asset – a long-lived asset that maintains value and usefulness beyond the traditional operating budget cycle; examples include public buildings, vehicles, machinery, and so on.

Earmarking – a common accountability practice that links the source of revenues to related spending in a budget.

Line-item budgeting – a budgeting approach in which spending is grouped by the specific object of expenditure, such as salaries and benefits or rent and utility costs.

Performance budgeting – a budgeting approach that was initially focused on outputs, but more recently has been designed to connect proposed spending to program goals.

DISCUSSION QUESTIONS

1. Do the advantages of incremental budgeting outweigh its limitations? Have you experienced budget environments that reflect incrementalism?
2. How exposed are you to the current budget debates of the different levels of government? Does it take a crisis for the public to care?
3. What are the primary differences between the budget process in governments and nonprofits?
4. Does the increasing budget share of mandatory or entitlement spending influence the ability to budget for current priorities? How?

ACTIVITIES

1. Locate an adopted budget from a state or local government of interest to you (typically available online). Read the opening budget message from the executive and assess whether the budget priorities are presented clearly and align with the described changes to the budget.
2. "Budget Hearing Observation." Observe a state or municipal budget hearing. It is acceptable to virtually "attend" the hearing (or past hearing). Write a one-page memo describing and analyzing the hearing along several dimensions (e.g., the hearing topic, the role of elected officials, staff involvement, public engagement, and the use of evidence for budget justification).

BUILD YOUR SKILLS

Knowing how to manipulate a spreadsheet is an invaluable skill when creating forecasts and budgets. Use the skillbox to learn how.

SKILLBOX: DATA MANAGEMENT AND PRESENTATION WITH SPREADSHEETS

You might think of a spreadsheet as an imposing grid populated with numbers, but today's spreadsheets are more accurately a time-saver, a source of order for complicated information, and a conduit for the effective display of data. As public service embraces evidence-informed decision-making, the spreadsheet is both unavoidable and indispensable for daily work.

Spreadsheet proficiency, like all skills, takes time and exposure to develop. Here, the essentials and some primary shortcuts are conveyed that will make life easier as both a student and public service professional. We use a simple case that, upon completion, allows you to effectively use spreadsheets and more easily develop advanced spreadsheet skills in future courses and work settings.

Spreadsheet Basics

A spreadsheet refers to a collection of data organized in rows and columns. They are created using computer-based software programs that allow for data entry, manipulation, and management. A strength of spreadsheet applications is their ability to perform routine data operations with great efficiency (including sorting and the use of mathematical formulas).

Modern spreadsheet programs also support the display of spreadsheet data through a variety of graphs and charts. Such visual representations of data can be powerful additions to professional writing.

Free spreadsheet programs like Google Sheets are available online, but Microsoft's Excel is the leading workplace application. We therefore focus on Excel, but other software applications provide similar functionality and can be used. The primary uses of spreadsheets in the workplace are to maintain lists (such as contacts or clients), record data (like budget information or service activities), analyze data (the most common use), examine and forecast data trends (for example, by using charts with trend lines), and consider alternative scenarios (by altering parameters in spreadsheet formulas for different possible levels of service activity or costs).[1]

Developing a spreadsheet may sound like a solitary endeavor, but more frequently a spreadsheet is used by more than one individual in a work setting. This is why spreadsheets should be documented well enough so that colleagues can use and understand them. A challenge of spreadsheets is that it can be difficult to identify errors, especially when the errors are caused by formulas applied to the data. For this reason, always validate and double-check spreadsheet findings by sharing work with colleagues for review before using the results to inform decision making. In fact, spreadsheet errors have been credited with causing policy failures:

- In 2012, the State of Utah's Office of Education underestimated student enrollment and the associated costs to the tune of $25 million. The reason: an incorrect cell reference in the state's spreadsheet calculations.[2]
- In 2013, the results of an influential academic study were called into question after researchers reexamined the data and found, in part, a spreadsheet error. The resulting controversy called into question the

relationship between a country's debt level and economic growth. The spreadsheet error reportedly omitted a handful of countries from a calculation of average economic growth rates. The result was a negative—rather than positive—average value being reported.[3]

- MI5, the British national intelligence agency, accidentally surveilled more than 100 of the wrong phone lines in 2010 when the formatting applied to a spreadsheet zeroed out the last three digits of the intended phone numbers.[4]

As the examples show, spreadsheets play a critical role in day-to-day decisions and they need to be correct. The following exercise demonstrates the basics of spreadsheets and commonly used functions in Excel.

Hands-On Activity: Building a Spreadsheet

Imagine that you work for a social services nonprofit organization or local government in Connecticut experiencing rapidly increasing demands for affordable housing. Your supervisor believes expanded collaboration with nonprofit organizations already providing housing services, whether through contracting or partnerships, is necessary to meet the community's rising housing needs.

Tasks

You are tasked with 1) developing an inventory of nonprofits in the state that provide housing services, 2) limiting that pool of potential collaborators to those with substantial assets and experience, 3) prioritizing the potential partners based on income, and 4) presenting an aggregated overview of the identified partners.

Data

- You are provided the Exempt Organizations Business Master File Extract (EO BMF) from the Internal Revenue Service for Connecticut in a format easily imported or opened with a spreadsheet program (.csv, which stands for "comma-separated values").
- The file includes over 6,000 records, each representing an active tax-exempt organization in Connecticut.
- The columns represent a variety of fields describing the organization ranging from identifiers like the name and Employer Identification Number (EIN) to a code representing the focus of the organization's activities and financial information.
- Each row and column combination creates a unique cell in the spreadsheet identified by a letter (representing the column) and number (indi-

cating the row). For example, the first cell in the upper left-hand corner of the spreadsheet is A1 since it is in Column A and Row 1.

- Use these data and the capabilities of the spreadsheet program to satisfy your supervisor's information request by following these steps.

Steps

1) Open the data file in Excel (or another spreadsheet program, but these instructions are specific to Excel on a PC). The first row of the spreadsheet represents column names, so the data start in Row 2. The data file is titled IRS_CT_Data.csv retrievable from the Resources section of: http://essentialsofpublicservice.org[5]

2) In Excel, you can have multiple spreadsheets within the same file. The spreadsheets are referred to as worksheets and reside within the broader file, or workbook.

- Scroll through the data to observe the variety of nonprofits in Connecticut. If columns are not wide enough to view the data, use the cursor to double click the line that separates the columns (at the top of the worksheet next to the column letter) that are cut off and Excel will automatically make them big enough to see the entire contents of the cells in that column. You can also manually drag the column line to widen the cells to see the cell contents.
- Next, limit the observations to those that work in the housing sector. Each organization has a code representing its area of activity found in Column O. The codes for housing nonprofits begin with the letter "L." Columns can be sorted or filtered using the Sort & Filter functions. Here, we will use the Filter function. Select Column O and from within the worksheet, turn on the Filter by selecting Home>Sort & Filter>Filter. Using the Filter dropdown that is visible for the NTEE_.CD column at the top of the column (alternately, you could also use the sort function directly), select Sort A to Z to order the organizations alphabetically by code. A "Sort Warning" box asks if you want to expand the selection. Click Sort. This keeps all the data in each row together as the information is sorted in the spreadsheet.
- Now, delete the organizations that do not have a code that begins with the letter "L." Select Rows 2 through 2544 by clicking on a cell in Row 2 and dragging down to Row 2544. Right click and select Delete to delete the rows.

- Repeat the deletion process for what is now Row 246 to Row 3502. You are left with only housing nonprofit organizations.

3) Next, narrow the list of potential collaborators based on the age of the organization. Your supervisor wants to make sure that the organization has experienced and survived a major economic downturn, so any organization started in 2008 or later is not being considered (EXEMPT_YR less than 2008). You can use the Sort or Filter functions to order the organizations by age and then delete the organizations started in 2008 or later. After sorting, click 'Ctrl + F' to open up the "Find" box and search for 2008 to locate the row in Column G from which to begin deleting.

4) Ensure that the nonprofit organizations are both active and relatively financially secure by limiting the organizations to those with greater than average assets for the group.
- Sort the remaining organizations from largest to smallest by Assets in Column L.
- At the bottom of the data, use a formula, by entering = AVERAGE (L2:L202) in Cell L203, to find the average assets.
  - ➢ Although this formula refers only to cells in the current worksheet, formulas and cell references can also link to cells in other worksheets.
- At the top of Column P, name the column ASSETS_ABV_AVG in Cell P1 and use a formula to determine whether or not each organization has greater than average assets.
- Enter the following formula in Cell P2: = IF (L2 > L$203,1,0), which means "If the value of Cell L2 is greater than the value of Cell L203, a value of 1 is entered or, if not, a value of 0 is entered."
- The formula results in a "1" value when assets are greater than average and "0" otherwise.
- Copy (or drag from bottom-right corner of Cell P2) the formula in Cell P2 to Cells P3 to P202.
  - ➢ Note that the cells referred to in the formula change when you copy the formula to a new cell. The cell reference changes relative to the number of columns and rows away from the original cell. So, for example, the L2 in the original formula changes to L3 when the formula is copied one row below the original cell (the cell is in the same column as the original cell, so the column is not adjusted in the formula).
  - ➢ Note that the copied formulas continue to refer to the average assets in Cell 203. The dollar sign ($) tells Excel that the row location is

fixed (or absolute) and no changes should be made to the row reference when copying the formula. A dollar sign before the column letter will also hold that fixed when copying formulas.

- How many organizations have above average assets? Use the following formula in Cell P203 to sum the "1" values: = SUM (P2:P202)
- Sort the organizations smallest to largest by asset size and delete those with below average assets ("0" values in Column P).
- Delete the formula for average assets now in Cell L60 and delete Column P.

5) Sort the remaining nonprofit organizations by largest to smallest annual income (Column M, INCOME_AMT).

6) Create a table including the top ten identified organizations based on income and report their EIN, name, city, year granted tax exemption (EXEMPT_YR), assets (ASSET_AMT), income (INCOME_AMT), and activity code (NTEE_CD). Delete the unneeded columns.
- Use the following for the remaining column headers: EIN, Name, City, Exempt Year, Assets, Income, NTEE Code.
- Center and bold ("Ctrl + B") the column headers (both formatting options are located in the "Home" toolbar).
- Add borderlines to the table (also located in the "Home" toolbar). You can alter the thickness and style of the table lines and formatting using the toolbar.
- Apply money formatting ($) to the Asset and Income columns (also located in the "Home" toolbar in the "Number" section).

7) Create a bar chart that presents the annual income of the ten identified organizations with the organization name on the horizontal axis and income level on the vertical axis.
- Highlight the income column in your table.
- Insert a chart by clicking on Insert>Bar>2-D Bar.
- Set the horizontal axis labels to the Name column values.
- After the bar chart is created, use the "Design" toolbar above the worksheet to pick the layout you want under "Chart Layouts."

8) Copy the table (from step 6) and chart (from step 7) into a separate word processing document and save the file.

- Highlight the table with your cursor, press "Ctrl + C" to copy the table, and "Ctrl + V" to paste it in the text document (you can also use the "Paste" dropdown from the toolbar). Separately, do the same for the chart.

9) Write a paragraph-long professional memo to your supervisor that describes your work and discusses the table and chart information.

Notes

1. Barry R. Lawson, Kenneth R. Baker, Stephen G. Powell, and Lynn Foster-Johnson, "A Comparison of Spreadsheet Users with Different Levels of Experience," *Omega* 37, no. 3 (2009): 579–590.

2. Utah State Office of Education, "News Release: Utah State Office of Education Identifies Miscalculation in Next Year's Budget; Schools Unaffected" (April 11, 2012), http://www.schools.utah.gov/main/INFORMATION/Online-Newsroom/DOCS/MSPMediaRelease.aspx.

3. Carmen M. Reinhart and Kenneth S. Rogoff, "Debt, Growth, and the Austerity Debate," *New York Times* (April 26, 2013), A31.

4. The Rt Hon Sir Paul Kennedy, 2010 *Annual Report of the Interception of Communications Commissioner* (London, UK: The Stationery Office, June 30, 2011).

5. Source: https://www.irs.gov/charities-non-profits/exempt-organizations-business-master-file-extract-eo-bmf.

NOTES

1. Washington Office of Financial Management (OFM), *OFM Fiscal Impact Statement (I-502)* (August 10, 2012).

2. Bob Young, "A Year In, Taxes on Legal Weed Yet to Yield Big Windfall for State," *The Seattle Times* (July 4, 2015), http://www.seattletimes.com/seattle-news/a-year-in-taxes-on-legal-weed-yet-to-yield-big-windfall-for-state/.

3. Washington State Liquor and Cannabis Board, "Marijuana Sales Activity: Fiscal Year 2016 Sales and Excise Tax by County" (May 30, 2017), http://lcb.wa.gov/sites/default/files/publications/Marijuana/sales_activity/FY16-MJ-Sales-Excise-Tax-by-County.xlsx.

4. Thomas R. Dye, *Understanding Public Policy* (Englewood Cliffs, NJ: Prentice-Hall, 1972).

5. Government figures are based on current expenditures for FY2014 and nonprofit figures are based on revenues. Nonprofit activity is based on NTEE Codes for registered nonprofit organizations and do not align directly with government activities. The Health category includes multiple nonprofit NTEE codes (E, F, G, and H). For comparison purposes, the K-Food, Agriculture and Nutrition, L - Housing and Shelter, and S-Community Improvement and Capacity Building are aggregated as "Housing and Community Services" and the A-Arts, Culture and Humanities and N-Recreation and Sports NTEE Codes are combined as "Recreation and Culture" in the table. The nonprofit areas presented represent nearly 90 percent of sector revenues, but there are an additional twelve NTEE Codes omitted from the table, further illustrating the diversity of the sector.

6. There is some debate over the origins of the statement, but it was widely popularized in the writings of economist Paul Krugman and appears prominently in Jonathan Gruber's *Public Finance and Public Policy* text, see Paul Krugman, "Outside the Box," *New York Times* (July 11, 2001), A17.

7. Charles E. Lindblom, "The Science of 'Muddling Through'," *Public Administration Review* 19, no. 2 (1959): 79–88.

8. Charlie Tyer and Jennifer Willand, "Public Budgeting in America: A Twentieth Century Retrospective," *Journal of Public Budgeting, Accounting & Financial Management* 9, no. 2 (1997): 189.

9. Allen Schick, "The Road to PPB: The Stages of Budget Reform," *Public Administration Review* 26, no. 4 (1966): 243–258.

10. V.O. Key, "The Lack of a Budgetary Theory," *The American Political Science Review* 34, no. 6 (1940): 1137–1144.

11. John L. Mikesell and Daniel R. Mullins, "Reforms for Improved Efficiency in Public Budgeting and Finance: Improvements, Disappointments, and Work-in-Progress," *Public Budgeting and Finance* 31, no. 4 (2011): 1–30.

12. Bill de Blasio, "The City of New York Executive Budget Fiscal Year 2016: Budget Summary," Office of Management and Budget (2015), http://www.nyc.gov/html/omb/downloads/pdf/sum5_15.pdf.

13. Abby Goodnough, "Vermont Exercising Option to Balance the Budget," *New York Times* (April 23, 2011), http://www.nytimes.com/2011/04/24/us/24vermont.html?mcubz=0.

14. National Association of State Budget Officers, *State Budgeting and Lessons Learned from the Economic Downturn: Analysis and Commentary from State Budget Officers* (2013).

15. Brevard Public Schools, *2013-14 Proposed Budget Cuts & Revenue Enhancements* (April 23, 2012), http://documents.brevardschools.org/Updates/Budget/Budget%20 Information%20201213/REVISED%202013-14%20Budget%20Reductions%20 and%20Revenue%20Enhancements.pdf.

16. Yvette Shields, "Illinois Seeks Team for Tobacco Issue," *The Bond Buyer* (August 13, 2010), 9.

17. Richard Williamson, "Arizona Back to Selling Buildings," *The Bond Buyer* (June 8, 2010).

18. Gerald J. Miller, Donijo Robbins, and Jaeduk Keum, "Incentives, Certification, and Targets in Performance Budgeting," *Public Performance and Management Review* 30, no. 4 (2007): 469–495.

19. David A. Fahrenthold, "As Congress Fights over the Budget, Agencies Go on Their 'Use It or Lose It' Shopping Sprees," *Washington Post* (September 28, 2013), https:// www.washingtonpost.com/politics/as-congress-fights-over-the-budget-agencies-go-on-their-use-it-or-lose-it-shopping-sprees/2013/09/28/b8eef3cc-254c-11e3-b3e9-d97f-b087acd6_story.html?utm_term=.3a64218ffe0e.

20. Ibid.

21. Naomi Caiden, "Public Service Professionalism for Performance Measurement and Evaluation," *Public Budgeting & Finance* 18, no. 2 (1998): 35–52.

22. The Pew Center on the States, "The Trillion Dollar Gap: Underfunded State Retirement Systems and the Roads to Reform" (February, 2010), http://www.pewtrusts .org/~/media/legacy/uploadedfiles/pcs_assets/2010/trilliondollargapunderfundedstate retirementsystemsandtheroadstoreformpdf.pdf.

23. Barbara A. Chaney, Paul A. Copley, and Mary S. Stone, "The Effect of Fiscal Stress and Balanced Budget Requirements on the Funding and Measurement of State Pension Obligations," *Journal of Accounting and Public Policy* 21, no. 4 (2003): 287–313.

24. Ron Snell, "State Experiences with Annual and Biennial Budgeting," National Conference of State Legislatures (April, 2011).

25. California Department of Finance, "How to Write an Effective Budget Change Proposal (BCP)" (2000), http://www.dof.ca.gov/budget/resources_for_departments/budget_ analyst_guide/effective_BCPs.html.

26. John Mikesell, *Fiscal Administration*, 9th ed. (Boston, MA: Cengage Learning, 2014), 182.

27. The discussion of the candy and soda tax exemption comes from the following articles: Tim Hoover, "Ritter's Plan to Tax Soda and Candy Gets Cheers, Jeers," *Denver Post* (November 14, 2009), http://www.denverpost.com/2009/11/14/ritters-plan-to-tax-soda-and-candy-gets-cheers-jeers/; and Tim Hoover, "Job Losses Haven't Panned Out, De-

spite Concern over Eliminating Colo. Tax Breaks," *Denver Post* (August 7, 2010), http://www.denverpost.com/2010/08/07/job-losses-havent-panned-out-despite-concern-over-eliminating-colo-tax-breaks/.

28. Irene S. Rubin, *The Politics of Public Budgeting: Getting and Spending, Borrowing and Balancing* (Thousand Oaks, CA: CQ Press, 2009).

29. U.S. Office of Management and Budget, *Mid-Session Review: Budget of the U.S. Government Fiscal Year 2017* (July 15, 2016).

30. The Center on Budget and Policy Priorities, *Policy Basics: Introduction to the Federal Budget Process* (February 17, 2016), http://www.cbpp.org/sites/default/files/atoms/files/3-7-03bud.pdf.

31. Brice McKeever, *The Nonprofit Sector in Brief 2015: Public Charities, Giving, and Volunteering*, Urban Institute (October 29, 2015).

32. Lynne A. Weikart, Greg G. Chen, and Ed Sermier, *Budgeting and Financial Management for Nonprofit Organizations* (Thousand Oaks, CA: CQ Press, 2012).

33. The International Budget Partnership, *Open Budget Survey 2015* (September, 2015), http://www.internationalbudget.org/wp-content/uploads/OBS2015-Report-English.pdf.

34. Office of Management and Budget, *Fiscal Year 2015 Analytical Perspectives: Budget of the U.S. Government* (2014).

35. Carol Ebdon and Aimee L. Franklin, "Citizen Participation in Budgeting Theory," *Public Administration Review* 66, no. 3 (2006): 437–447.

36. Joe Ferguson, "Favorite 25 Pima County Projects ID'd for Possible Bond Money," *Arizona Daily Star* (August 20, 2013), http://tucson.com/news/local/govt-and-politics/favorite-pima-county-projects-id-d-for-possible-bond-money/article_e3a29dd3-89d8-5f84-bf17-ade0ae81e18d.html.

37. Pima County Bond Advisory Committee, "Bond Advisory Committee's Recommended 2015 Bond Package" (March 31, 2015), http://webcms.pima.gov/UserFiles/Servers/Server_6/File/Government/Bonds/2015%20Bond%20Election/Public%20Involvement/Pima-Co-Bond-Advisory-Committee-rec-%20to-Board-2015-Bonds.pdf.

38. Patrick McNamara, "County Bond Plan Might Have Been Too Big to Pass," *Arizona Daily Star* (November 4, 2015), http://tucson.com/news/local/govt-and-politics/elections/county-bond-plan-might-have-been-too-big-to-pass/article_f39b045a-816d-5823-82ff-8a7ed348cbfa.html.

39. Eugene Bardach, "Report from the Trenches: The Life of the Apprentice Budget Analyst," *Journal of Policy Analysis and Management* 24, no. 2 (2005): 419.

40. Jennifer Kuhn, "Going Undercover as a Budget Analyst," *Journal of Policy Analysis and Management* 24, no. 2 (2005): 420–424.

41. National Association of State Budget Officers, "Module 12: Ethics and Standards of Professional Conduct," *Budget Analyst Training Program* (n.d.).

ADDITIONAL RESOURCES

Finkler, Steven A., Daniel L. Smith, Thad D. Calabrese, and Robert M. Purtell. 2016. *Financial Management for Public, Health, and Not-for-Profit Organizations.* Thousand Oaks, CA: CQ Press.

Mikesell, John. 2013. *Fiscal Administration.* Boston, MA: Cengage Learning.

For state and local governments, the Government Finance Officers Association (GFOA) provides a series of Best Practices/Advisories related to budgeting and financial management: http://www.gfoa.org/best-practices.

Chapter 7 Timeline: Digital Democracy

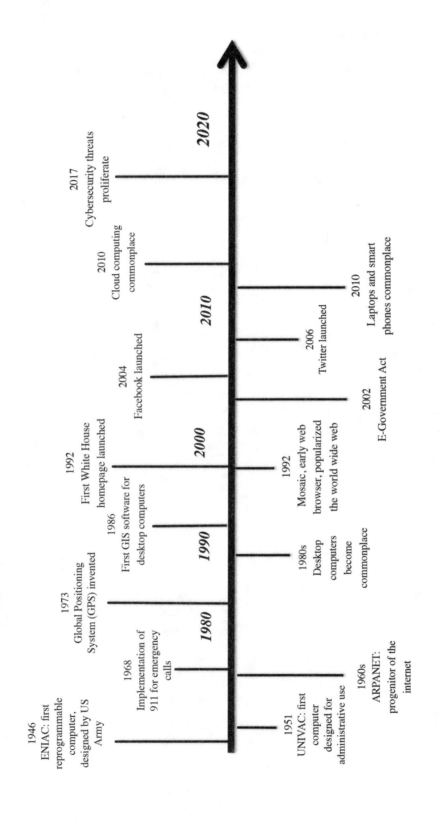

1946
ENIAC: first reprogrammable computer, designed by US Army

1951
UNIVAC: first computer designed for administrative use

1960s
ARPANET: progenitor of the internet

1968
Implementation of 911 for emergency calls

1980

1973
Global Positioning System (GPS) invented

1990

1980s
Desktop computers become commonplace

1986
First GIS software for desktop computers

2000

1992
First White House homepage launched

1992
Mosaic, early web browser, popularized the world wide web

2004
Facebook launched

2002
E-Government Act

2006
Twitter launched

2010

2010
Cloud computing commonplace

2010
Laptops and smart phones commonplace

2017
Cybersecurity threats proliferate

2020

DIGITAL DEMOCRACY

WHAT YOU WILL LEARN

The evolution of information and communication

How digital governance connects government with the public

Multichannel strategies and digital democracy

Marketing via the web

Big data

Cybersecurity challenges

Skillbox: E-mail versus in-person communication

Public service is a labor-intense and information-rich pursuit and digitization is its technology. Information and communication technology (ICT) enables service providers to communicate with the public instantaneously, bringing services to their fingertips. It is not without its challenges, however. The case of the rollout of HealthCare.gov, the website designed to enable millions of uninsured Americans to shop online for health insurance, provides an example.

WEBSITE DEBACLE: WWW.HEALTHCARE.GOV

The 2010 Affordable Care Act offered health insurance to millions of uninsured Americans. With much fanfare, the federal website, HealthCare.gov, was launched on October 1, 2013. It was designed as the online site to sign up for health insurance in the thirty-six states that had not created their own health insurance exchanges. Approximately 250,000 people signed on the first day. This was five times the number expected and within hours there were outages.[1] Web designers scrambled to add capacity.

Over the next week, outages grew worse as millions attempted to sign on. Initial reports were that the persistent glitches were due to an overwhelming crush of users—8.6 million unique visitors in the first week. Technology experts speculated that flaws in system architecture, not traffic alone, contributed to the problems. This was because, when users tried to create an account on HealthCare.gov, the code was written to prompt the computer to load an unusually large amount of files and software, overwhelming the browser.[2]

Hitting "apply" on HealthCare.gov caused ninety-two separate files and plug-ins to stream between the user's computer and the servers that powered the website. Fifty-six of the files were JavaScript files, including plug-ins that made it easier for code to work on multiple browsers (such as Microsoft's Internet Explorer and Google's Chrome) and let users upload files to HealthCare.gov. Because so much traffic was going back and forth between the users' computers and the server hosting the government website, it was as if the system was attacking itself.

A storm of negative media coverage ensued over the next several weeks as staff from the Department of Health and Human Services (HHS), Centers for Medicare & Medicaid Services (CMS), and contractors scrambled to fix the issues. Problems were finally corrected and an after-action report was conducted by the Office of Inspector General of the Department of Health and Human Services. Although the technical design was extraordinarily complex, auditors concluded that the most critical failing was the human factor of clear leadership.[3] There was a disconnect between the policy work of designing the federal marketplace for health insurance and the technical work of web design. This produced delays in decision making, ambiguity in project tasks, and a failure to recognize the magnitude of problems as the project deteriorated. Resistance to warnings of impending problems and a refusal to alter plans and deadlines for launch resulted in an embarrassing start for an ambitious program.

The rollout of the Affordable Care Act website produced these important lessons:[4]

(1) Assign clear project leadership to provide cohesion across tasks and a comprehensive view of progress.

(2) Promote acceptance of bad news and encourage staff to identify and communicate problems.

(3) Make sure that the project and strategies for achieving it align with the resources and expertise available.

(4) Design steps in the execution of the project and continually measure progress.

(5) Identify and address factors of organizational culture that may affect project success.

(6) Ensure effectiveness of information technology contracts by promoting innovation, integration, and rigorous oversight.

(7) Simplify processes as much as possible, particularly for projects with a high risk of failure.

(8) Develop contingency plans that are quickly actionable, such as redundant systems.

(9) Integrate policy and technological work to promote operational awareness.

(10) Promote continuous learning that encourages flexibility and a willingness to change course quickly when needed.

Questions to Ponder

1. Software development must be closely coordinated with the program it will serve. How does the case of Health-Care.gov demonstrate the problems that a disconnect can cause?

2. ICT provides a way for government and the public to connect instantaneously. Because of the scope of public programs, how is public confidence affected when connection problems arise?

FROM PAPER TO CLOUD: THE EVOLUTION OF INFORMATION AND COMMUNICATION

Within decades after Johannes Gutenberg invented the printing press in the mid-1400s, the production of documents flourished throughout Europe. The invention revolutionized the speed with which the written word could be published, and hard-copy documents became the *modus operandi* for formal communication. Paper and print remained foremost for 500 years, until the creation of the Internet and personal computing again revolutionized communication.

As the timeline shows, recent decades brought a proliferation of inventions that have changed how people get information and how they communicate. The transition from paper to cloud is in progress. The speed with which communications can be transmitted globally is now lightning fast. From Gutenberg to gigabytes to terabytes, government races to keep up with the power of the Internet. Storage of documents, which used to consume acres of warehouse space, now resides in the cloud. Handwritten ink-on-paper signatures to prove authenticity are replaced with electronic signatures. The transformation has happened in only decades, analogous to the dramatic revolution heralded by the printing press.

The Internet

When the Defense Advanced Research Projects Agency, the research and development arm of the U.S. Department of Defense, developed ARPAnet—the progenitor of the Internet—the objective was to create a system in which any computers that were online could talk to each other. This created a free flow of communication from anywhere to everywhere. *Wikipedia* provides an example. It is an open source knowledge base to which anyone can contribute.

The Internet is open and collaborative and has these characteristics:[5]

1. No one owns or manages it
2. It cannot be turned off or on
3. Its infrastructure is available for anyone to use, anywhere in the world
4. It is both public and private, global and local, commercial and cooperative
5. It evolves without central coordination in rapid cycles of innovation

The contrast between the Internet and traditional formal organizations could not be greater. The Internet is receptive to contributions, resources, ideas, and direction from anyone, anywhere. In contrast, government agencies and nonprofit organizations are closed entities. Closed projects, such as public service organizations, have internally defined objectives and tightly controlled participation, resources, and information flows. They have clear boundaries, governed by who is, and is not, employed. Their funds are allocated for specific purposes based on mission, and roles and responsibilities are specified for everyone who is a participant. Each organization has a leader who is accountable for its actions. It is ironic that closed systems such as these now rely on an open system to reach their constituencies. This magnifies opportunities at the same time that it brings challenges.

From the mechanics of production and storage, to the ease of communication, to the threat of misinformation, to security breaches, to the increase in networks, and to the reduction of hierarchy, managing information has become an essential component of public administration. One example is the E-Government Act, passed by Congress in 2002. The Act created a Chief Information Officer in the Office of Management and Budget and a Chief Information Officer Council, which is an interagency forum that focuses on practices for information and communication technology (ICT) management. The Council's mission is to improve practices related to the design, acquisition, development, modernization, use, sharing, and performance of federal government information resources. Its objectives include establishing priorities on information technology policy and sharing best practices related to information management. Similar interagency councils exist in some states and municipalities. The interconnectedness that is possible because of e-mail, websites, and shared databases, drives this flattened approach to collaboration between agencies, jurisdictions, and levels of government. It also drives the rising significance of how information is managed.

The E-Government Act of 2002 was enacted to improve the management and promotion of electronic government services and processes. It establishes a framework of measures that require using Internet-based information technology to improve citizen access to government information and services, to promote interagency collaboration in providing electronic government services, to improve efficiency of agency operations, to make government more transparent and accountable, and to promote better informed decision making by policy makers.

Types of Information Flows

Easy and rapid access to information erodes the hierarchical control mechanisms that used to be necessary in organizations, where information would flow up one chain of command, be communicated from one director to another, and then flow down the next chain of command. This has reduced the need for mid-level managers and thinned the ranks of those whose job was primarily to transmit information from those who do the work of the organization to those who direct it, and vice versa. At the same time, the ease of information access has resulted in a new occupational category: information management.

As shown in Figure 7.1, there are three main types of information flows: broadcast, community, and network-of-networks.[6] The Internet facilitates each of these.

Broadcast—in this model, information is disseminated from a central source to others. E-blasts, websites, blogs, Twitter, and amber and silver alerts are examples. (Amber alerts notify the public of child abduction cases and silver alerts notify about missing seniors with dementia). Broadcast communication is a unidirectional strategy for distributing announcements, notifications, calls to action, and warnings without a capacity for the receiver to reply.

FIGURE 7.1 TYPES OF INFORMATION FLOWS

Broadcast

Community

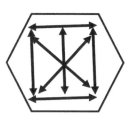

Network

Community—in this model, information flows freely among subscribers within a group. It allows for feedback and exchange of information between senders and receivers. This is effective for keeping those with a common interest informed of events and for soliciting feedback from them. Thus, it is multidirectional. An electronic town hall meeting, homeowner associations, neighborhood centers, and public schools are examples of groups that can use this system to inform their constituencies as well as solicit ideas, opinions, and feedback. Also, this can feature online chats that allow for conversations among everyone.

Network of networks—in this model, information and chats flow freely through any number of networks with exchanges of information as senders and receivers connect. As more users participate, the network grows even larger. This is the Facebook phenomenon. The incredible rate at which communication is diffused across a broad range of users defies any capacity to shape or stop a message. It is this aspect of the Internet that is a double-edged sword. Its advantage is that information spreads globally and instantaneously. Its disadvantage is that it spreads misinformation as rapidly as it spreads authentic information.

INFORMATION AND COMMUNICATION TECHNOLOGY

Keeping up with the power of the Internet is like drinking from a fire hose. E-mail became widely used in the 1980s, web search engines were developed in the 1990s, Mark Zuckerberg launched Facebook in 2004 and social media was born, smartphones—mobile phones that access the Internet—were commonplace by 2010, as was cloud computing. Innovations continue, such as driverless vehicles and package delivery by drone. The year-by-year proliferation of more convenient and more accessible information is a boon to government as it increases engagement with the public and improves services. The adoption of digital strategies to manage public programs, deliver services, and inform residents is affecting every aspect of public service, as the example of "smart cities" demonstrates.

SMART CITIES

The term "smart city" takes various forms, from video sensors that strengthen the brightness of street lights when pedestrians are near, to traffic lights that are programmed to keep traffic flowing, to digital kiosks that make it easy for pedestrians to find directions and attractions. Smart cities are integrating information and communication technology in multiple ways, depending on their needs and capacity. In general, the term implies innovation in which digital technology is used to improve service operations and quality of life. This comes in the form of direct service as well as in the form of gathering data on residential water and energy use, traffic, and crime. This information is then used to provide feedback and encourage conservation, efficiency, and security. Smartness expands government capacity and convenience for the public.

Working hand-in-glove, government and nonprofits ensure the most basic of needs are met—food, shelter, health care, and safety—and these services are enabled through information and communication technologies. While administrative functions organize information around a defined purpose—military strategy, housing, public education—street-level practice applies information in real-life situations. For example, cities use crime data and GIS (geographic information systems) to forecast where crime is most likely to occur. Photographic evidence made available by body cameras aid law enforcement and the public when disputes arise about whether undue force was used during arrests. In other words, governments are learning how to harness digital capacity to advance communication, planning, marketing, and the delivery of services.

Enterprise Architecture and Systems Integration

The public-facing web presence of an organization gets attention based on its appearance and functionality. What is often overlooked is the role of information management systems, which enable online transactions to occur and support critical day-to-day functions such as human resource management, payroll, accounting, customer relationship management (CRM), procurement, asset management, and grants management. The enterprise architecture of an organization is the overall set of processes and technology systems used to support day-to-day operations. The architecture can be carefully crafted or it can evolve over time as technology systems are added or modified in a piecemeal manner to address problems as budgets allow.

A trend for public service agencies is to undertake efforts to integrate existing siloed information technology systems through the adoption of enterprise resource planning (ERP). ERP systems integrate disparate systems and operations, although doing so requires an intense outlay of planning, time, and resources. Agencies usually select ERP software that aligns with their anticipated needs and they hire external consultants to assist existing staff in the design and implementation of the new system. Systems integration through ERP has the potential to streamline operations and allow the organization to focus on its mission-based activities by making information more readily available for analysis and improved decision making. The ability to store data centrally and make it instantly accessible to the different functional areas of an organization is a key benefit of integration.

Such information technology systems are not without challenges. Underperforming technology projects result from the difficulty governments have attracting and retaining employees with up-to-date technical skills. And aging systems means that software and hardware may no longer be supported by the original vendors. Moreover, customization over time makes it more difficult to maintain the systems, and data security becomes more challenging. Regardless, information management systems support, influence, and expedite operations.

HOW E-GOV CONNECTS GOVERNMENT WITH THE PUBLIC

E-gov includes the use of electronic devices and information and communication technology to deliver public services, communicate with the public, and to gather feedback. The term implies digital interactions between people and government, between public agencies and employees, and between government and businesses. The communication channels that are involved range from traditional telephone calling and e-mailing, to websites with information and downloadable forms, to chat rooms and social media.

> *"It's not just a technology problem. It's an attitude. What I keep telling my colleagues in Sacramento is that it's not about e-government; it's about 'we government.'"*
>
> —Gavin Newsom

Jurisdictions use GIS mapping on a daily basis to track everything from sewer lines, flu outbreaks, and crime. They use GPS (global positioning systems) to track navigational routes and city-owned vehicles. Thanks to Federal Communications Commission (FCC) regulations and partnerships with carriers, the use of dedicated phone numbers make it convenient for the public to seek information or help.

Dedicated Call Numbers

211: community information and referral services
311: nonemergency calls for help
511: traffic and transportation information
911: emergency calls for help

While the earliest communication technology was telephones and call numbers, the services and connections made available by ICT now encompass many more options. Jurisdictions use E-gov to post city council minutes, ordinances, downloadable forms, employment information, GIS mapping data, customer relationship management, chat rooms, online requests for services, and payment of taxes, property registration, and much more.[7] Social media is used for late-breaking announcements, and digital recordings are used for accountability.

Websites

Websites enable agencies and jurisdictions to provide up-to-date information and announcements to users. They also provide a place to post public documents such as ordinances, downloadable forms, contact information, emergency announcements, and late-breaking news. The White House launched its first homepage in 1992[8] and such websites are now as much a part of operations for all jurisdictions and departments as are mission statements and budgets.

As digital technology makes it easier for the public to communicate with government, it is also changing the way government presents itself to citizens. For example, public agencies are structured by function—housing, education, transit—but this is not necessarily the best way to organize a webpage that is intended to inform viewers of services. The public knows the services they seek, but they may not know which agency provides them. Rather than listing agencies and then the services provided by them, jurisdictions are listing the most sought after services with a link to the agency. In other words, the focus is changing from an agency-centric presence on the web to a citizen-centric presence.

There are a number of challenges that confront government and nonprofit website developers, ranging from design to maintenance:

Personal Computers versus Mobile Accessibility

While most sites are constructed to run on personal computers, people are increasingly using mobile devices to get information. In 2016, for instance, 40 percent of those who visited federal websites used a mobile device.[9] Because lower income users tend to rely on smartphones as their only device for accessing the Internet, access and information is lost to them unless the site loads well on a mobile device.

Organization

The difference between how citizens view government and how government is structured causes difficulty for web designers. While citizens access websites to learn about a discrete service, regardless of which department offers it, those who input data onto the site do so from their vantage as an employee who works for a particular agency. Thus, input is made by someone whose context is their employer. The public access the site from their vantage as users who simply want to know how and where to get a driver license or learn about zoning laws. The challenge for designers is to craft a site that provides information about services without requiring the user to have prior knowledge of which department does what.

Language

The literacy level and the language(s) for which content is written determine who will read and comprehend the information. For content to be accessible to the widest range of users, it must be written at a reading level that is accessible to all and in the languages of the constituencies for whom it is designed.

Timely, Informative Content

In order to be useful, minutes of public meetings must be posted quickly after a meeting, not months afterward. And, they must be substantive enough to make it worth the time to read. Technology improves disclosure, but only if there is a willingness to disclose it in a user-friendly fashion.

Outdated Information

When data are not continually updated, sites run the risk of failing to keep up with current information. When a user navigates through a complex site to find a person to contact, only to learn that person no longer works there, confidence in the jurisdiction's management falters. From an administrative perspective, the website is a vessel of information. From the user's perspective, the website is an indicator of management competency.

Broken Links

Links must be checked frequently to ensure they are still operable. The more complex and comprehensive the site, such as city websites, the greater the number of people who are continually updating pages. Links may be severed when content changes are made without the data entry person realizing it. Maintenance of complex websites is usually dispersed across many persons in multiple organizational units, rather than it being the responsibility of only one person. When everyone is responsible, no one is accountable, and the likelihood of broken links escalates.

When websites work well and provide information that is timely and accessible, a positive halo extends around the jurisdiction. Confidence in government is enhanced by this 24/7 interface between the served and the servants. When websites fail to reflect well on the jurisdiction, a negative halo contributes to a negative perception of government's ability to manage programs, be responsive, and deliver services.

Social Media

Public officials use social media to communicate directly to constituents and reach mass audiences. For example, Twitter, the 140 character microblog, provides a mechanism for distributing mission-relevant information, emergency alerts, and outreach. It, along with other social media, such as Nextdoor.com, offers opportunity for creative information dissemination and provides an immediacy that is responsive to rapidly changing events. It is an excellent way to alert the public about rapidly changing events, such as the spread of flooding, wildfire, traffic jams, or hazardous road conditions. Its functions are fourfold. It *pushes* information out to the public, it *pulls* feedback from the public, it creates *networks* of constituencies, and it has the effect of improving *responsiveness*.[10]

Push Information out to Constituents

This is the broadcast function. Museums and libraries use Twitter for a number of purposes: to provide real-time assistance to requests posted by researchers, teachers, and students; to provide news on exhibitions; and to solicit interest in their activities.

Twitter feeds during emergencies are particularly effective at keeping the public informed, such as when the sheriff's public information officer posts rapid notices of how a wildfire is spreading. This sort of communication is no longer optional. A government agency that is not doing it is an agency that is failing to live up to its duties and serve the polity. The U.S. Department of Homeland Security uses Twitter feeds to provide rapid updates of department initiatives as well to provide safety alerts and to solicit "see something, say something" reports.

Pull in Information and Feedback

This function relies on the community of users who subscribe to the information. It actively engages audiences and asks them to make comments that will help the sender perform better. For example, the U.S. Geological Survey (USGS) uses Twitter after an earthquake to ask "Did you feel it?" This allows for information about the extent of the quake that extends the value of scientific evidence.[11]

Community Building

As information about services becomes available and the network of consumers increases, outreach becomes more extensive. Moreover, as feedback comes in from the "pull" function, the agency learns who their audience is and this helps them identify constituencies that they are not yet reaching. Twitter can be used strategically to direct messages to influencers in a network as well as to identify other channels where issues relevant to the agency's mission are being discussed.

Responsiveness

As a result of pushing information out, pulling feedback in, and extending outreach, public service agencies are able to be more responsive to needs. This increases their capacity to identify problems in service delivery. In many cases, 140-character messages are too brief to convey a complex communication, so they use a tweet to link to their website where a chat function is possible.

While websites have become the backbone of the ICT strategy for each department and jurisdiction, the capacity of social media to push information out and to solicit feedback make it more useful in terms of engaging the public and being responsive to rapidly

> *"We're moving from e-government to e-democracy . . . The first generation of technology delivered revenue-generating services such as licensing and permitting. Now we're talking about tools that give citizens greater voice in the process."*
>
> —Beth Noveck

changing events. Elected officials now post on Twitter and similar sites, putting them in direct touch with constituents. People are being connected to people whom they otherwise would not be able to reach and in real time, whether celebrities or government officials.

MULTIPLE CHANNEL STRATEGIES AND DIGITAL DEMOCRACY

Multiple channels maximize outreach. Employment of ICT strategies embraces dedicated call lines, GIS, GPS, websites, body cameras, social media, and more. Facebook pages and tweets reach those who may not scroll through websites. Analogous to customer relationship management in business, citizen relationship management is enabled by using a multichannel strategy to connect people to services. Websites, combined with social media, and dedicated call numbers, make it easier for people at all levels of IT sophistication to access the services they seek and to enable their communication with government.[12]

The increasing number of communication channels and tools has increased democratic access, responsiveness, and engagement. Digitization improves access to real-time information and the ability to respond more quickly to urgent needs. It reduces the time needed to complete transactions, improves citizens' ability to control and monitor the transactions, and captures a robust audit trail of all interactions. Information has become "democratized," meaning that easy access to it has shifted power away from centralized control. *Digital democracy* is the term used to capture this phenomenon.

At the same time that digital democracy brings advantages, problems of misinformation, security breaches, and invasions of privacy are challenges of growing proportion. The issue of dashcams and body cameras for law enforcement officers provide an example of how government employs ICT strategies for accountability. Video footage of police actions provides transparency for citizens who are wary of police at the same time that it protects police from accusations of wrongdoing.[13] In fact, some jurisdictions are expanding the use of body cameras to other government officials, such as those who work in code enforcement, parking, and building and fire inspection. In a desire to improve customer service and resolve disputes, videos provide data to disgruntled motorists whose cars have been towed and property owners who are issued code violations.[14] But the question of how jurisdictions treat video footage varies. Some impose outright bans on releasing footage unless there is a court order, while some treat it like any other public record, as open and accessible.

Both Missouri and Georgia have laws that make footage public unless it is taken in a private place or shows victims. Oklahoma has a law that allows for disclosure except in recordings that include nudity, children, criminal informants, victims of sex crimes or domestic violence, and the personal information of innocent people. Under Texas law, footage is only considered public if it will "further a law enforcement purpose." In contrast, in Maryland footage is available under the state's public information law. In Oregon, footage can be released only if it is considered to be in the public interest, but faces must be obscured. In the city of Las Vegas, footage can be viewed at the police department but copies are not given out.[15] As these different responses across the United States demonstrate, the question is one of striking a balance between access and privacy. As in many aspects of ICT and government, the technology of body cameras has outpaced the public policy governing it. The potential of ICT to increase government capacity is great but the age-old tradeoff between individual privacy and government action is ever-present.

MARKETING VIA THE WEB

The Internet has made it possible for governments to have a "market" presence. Unlike business, where marketing is an essential component used to develop desire for a product, marketing in public services takes the form of information distribution and outreach. To this end, businesses build marketing costs into their financial plans. Government and nonprofits, on the other hand, operate on tight budgets and are expected to devote resources to direct service, not marketing. Websites and social media provide a way to override the reluctance to market by making it affordable. Whether encouraging energy conservation or smoking cessation, the Internet has made it possible for each agency to publicize its mission and inform the public about programs and services.

In many offices, the work of public information officers has expanded to include marketing duties. This expansion of their focus extends to branding, in which the jurisdiction/agency's logo and the appearance of each webpage is standardized in order to put forward a uniform look that is easily recognized, just as retailers use recognizable logos as they market products. Each agency sets its own rules for what social media outlets may be used for publicizing events and providing information.

BIG DATA

The conversion from data to information has been enabled by computing, first with mainframe computers that filled a room, to desktop computers, and to networks of computers working simultaneously. This progression results from the profusion of digital data. Geographic information system (GIS) data, body cameras and dashcams, central datafiles of tax returns, utility files of water usage, all contribute to the proliferation of large datasets.

The term "big data" refers to data sets that are too large or too complex for usual storage, retrieval, and computation methods. Uses of big data include spotting trends, identifying terror threats, monitoring use of water and energy resources, and spotting health threats, among many others. The term "informatics" is used to capture the focus on data usage. Megadata is now generated at incomprehensible speeds and administrators are eager for, as well as challenged by, the avalanche.

Data sets grow in number as well as size as it becomes easier and cheaper to collect. Mobile devices, wireless sensors, cameras, and scanners have made collection cheap and easy, but the challenges are many. Traditional relational databases and desktop computing is not powerful enough to manipulate the data. Thus, cloud computing with parallel software running on multiple servers is becoming more common. From terabytes to zettabytes, data size continues to grow.

As big data analytics become more widespread, public administration is drowning in data but starving for certainty. How jurisdictions build capacity to make sense of the data and improve service is a question to be explored as each site becomes its own laboratory in democracy. The goal is for the impact on the public to lead to innovation long thought impossible, add to government effectiveness, and increase citizen engagement.

CHIEF INFORMATION OFFICER

Most public agencies and large nonprofits now have a Chief Information Officer (CIO), also called Chief Innovation Officer or Chief Data Officer. The title continues to evolve as the role for strategic integration of information, communication, and data usage becomes clearer in each organization. This position is responsible for the information and communication portfolio of the agency or jurisdiction. The portfolio includes the information and communication infrastructure of the agency, along with management of ICT projects and contracts.

The CIO is also responsible for aligning ICT objectives and programs with the agency's mission and programs. The alignment involves defining and maintaining performance standards, and ensuring information security at the same time that information and communication strategies enable activities that will achieve the mission. Both the information collected by the agency and the information systems that support the mission are involved.

The challenges for government are for it to invest quickly enough to keep up with ICT innovations and to use ICT to become more transactional with the public, rather than top-down. To meet these challenges requires the continual building of capacity to be transparent in its activities and accessible for everyone. CIOs play an important role in meeting these challenges.

CYBERSECURITY CHALLENGES

ICT offers convenience as it bridges transactions between citizens and government. At the same time, it offers convenience to cyber thieves at all levels, from local to state to federal. If it is true that bank robbers rob banks because that is where the money is, it is also true that cyber thieves attack the Internet because that is where the information is. Government at all levels is dotted with information gold mines.

At the federal level, personnel records kept in the Office of Personnel Management (OPM) database contain information about all federal employees. It is attractive to thieves and in one incident in 2014, the cyber theft of OPM records resulted in the theft of personal data that put 22 million federal employees at risk.[16] Likewise, cyber thieves hacked into 350,000 IRS taxpayer accounts in 2014–2015.[17] The IRS learned that the agency's authentication standards, which were state of the art when online access was initiated, had quickly become inadequate. Information gained from hacks such as these is used to impersonate the victims in identity theft schemes.

As shown in Figure 7.2,[18] the number of reported cybersecurity incidents in federal agencies skyrocketed from 5,503 in 2006 to 77,183 in 2015. These are sobering numbers and show that cybersecurity will be one of the most important challenges in years to come. Threats to security evolve with each advance in technology. Taxpayer data, patents, copyright information, national security data, employment records, medical information, and social security records are all at risk. The number of incidents is deceptively low compared to their actual impact because one incident, such as happened to OPM files, affected 22 million employees.

FIGURE 7.2 CYBERSECURITY INCIDENTS IN FEDERAL AGENCIES 2006–2015

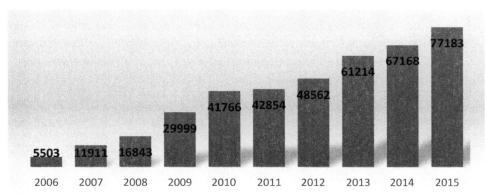

Cyber thieves also operate by creating fake accounts that look like government websites. The proliferation of cybersecurity threats is a challenge that will continue to be a problem as technology outpaces the human capacity to control its dark side. Whether in terms of identity theft, spreading untruths, or threatening the power grid, cyber threats endanger American institutions. The extent of the threat is so large that multiple civilian and military departments are working on the problem. This raises the unanswered question of how government can optimize the capacity of ICT while not being handcuffed by cyber threats.

Propaganda

Disinformation campaigns, long employed by international powers to affect public opinion within nation states, has become more widespread and powerful due to the Internet and social media. Before the advent of the Internet and cyber hacking, such efforts relied on radio and television broadcasts and printed materials to spread propaganda and bias public opinion. With the advent of the Internet, "fake news" has become more widespread, with many more outlets targeting particular constituencies. For example, during the 2016 presidential campaign, hacked e-mails and documents made it easy to distort and accentuate negative information, to the advantage of one candidate—Donald Trump—and the disadvantage of the other—Hillary Clinton. YouTube, Twitter, and Facebook were employed as vehicles that delivered this to millions of voters. In an unprecedented report issued January 6, 2017, the Central Intelligence Agency, Department of Justice, and National Security Agency issued a joint report that explained how the Russian government had used electronic document theft and disinformation to disparage Clinton's presidential campaign and sway public opinion in favor of her opponent, Donald Trump.[19]

Such efforts at disinformation are not new. During the Cold War, the Soviet Union used intelligence officers, influence agents, forgeries, and press placements to disparage candidates perceived as hostile to the Kremlin. What is new is the ease of dissemination to hundreds of millions of "news" consumers via the Internet. Cyber-enabled propaganda brings a threat to the political order that is beyond the ken of the founding fathers, who viewed a free press as a protection against the abuses of government, rather than as a vehicle for direct abuse.

Energy

Cyber hacking of the power grid is a threat to everything from lights in the classroom, a shutdown of transit systems, or a computer blackout in nuclear power plants. Safety of the energy infrastructure is essential for American productivity and is of growing concern to government.

The U.S. Department of Energy issued a warning in 2017[20] about cyber threats to the American energy infrastructure. The warning highlighted interconnections between private businesses, energy generators, and local, state, and federal government. For example, the fact that the natural gas industry and the electricity industry are regulated as separate entities makes it difficult to unify procedures in a way that provides security for electricity that is produced by natural gas. Such interconnections defy the silos of regulation that govern natural gas differently than electricity. This is causing the U.S. Department of Energy to revise its policies and regulations in order to keep up with changes that are necessary to ensure safety of the power grid.

U.S. DEPARTMENT OF ENERGY

"Mitigation and response to cyber threats are hampered by inadequate information-sharing processes between government and industry, the lack of security-specific technological and workforce resources, and challenges associated with multi-jurisdictional threats and consequences. . . . [R]isk factors stem from the increasing interdependency of electric and natural gas systems, as natural gas-fired generation provides an increasing share of electricity. However, coordinated long-term planning across natural gas and electricity can be challenging because the two industries are organized and regulated differently."[21]

Ask Me Why I Care: William "Bill" Ciaccio, Sr., Senior Director of the New York City Metropolitan Transit Authority, Capital Program Department[22]

There is a reason that conversation about Internet technology often turns to the "information highway." In fact, information and transportation are similar in that they are essential and, yet, taken for granted. When trains run on time and buses make their stops as usual, they are part of the urban landscape, a "comes with." Just as with the Internet infrastructure, 911 call systems, and agency websites, no one notices reliable performance. Only breakdowns draw attention. That is a compliment to those who ensure performance reliability. Watch the video as he describes his work as a budgeter and policy adviser in California. In it, he talks about why he enjoys public service and how the budgeting process ensures a match between public priorities and public revenues. Note his closing comments about the budgeting process and how it connects the public will, service priorities, and finances. "Transportation is the lifeblood of New York City. . . . When our system doesn't run, New York City doesn't run, which means the economy of the whole region is at a standstill."

Watch as Bill Ciaccio describes his work managing a $3 billion Infrastructure Program and why it is important: http://www.unomaha.edu/college-of-public-affairs-and-community-service/community-engagement/pss-william-ciaccio.php.

The challenges wrought by security threats to information and to energy demonstrate how the profusion of ICT is forcing a transformation from silos, in which each agency and sector of the economy focused on insular concerns, to collaborative, interdependent networks that foster broad, fast communication among entities that, in past decades, needed little interaction with each other. A hallmark of the information age is that administrative practice is racing to keep up with technological development.

SUMMARY

Whether called the older term, E-gov, or the newer, broader term, digital governance, the fact is that integrating ICT into public service is a work in progress, embracing an ever-growing set of practices and channels that connect citizens and public services. Information and communication technology make it possible for public service organizations to create news, broadcast it, and gather feedback and input from their constituencies. Social media makes it possible for information to spread like wildfire, for agencies like the Department of Homeland Security to be essential information sources, and for the governed and their government to be directly engaged.

Nonprofits use technology for many of the same purposes as governments do: to market their services, to inform the public, and to gather data from constituencies. Additionally, they use it for fundraising through e-blasts and gofundme-type campaigns, and for mobilizing action and protests in the form of marches and boycotts.

ICT has increased the capacity to create and access information at an unprecedented rate. This brings benefits in the form of increased efficiency of daily operations. However, there is a downside that looms ever larger: hacking, transmission of fake news that is not easily identifiable as false, and invasion of privacy. The challenge is to harness technology in a way that benefits everyone, while minimizing the characteristics that threaten civil society.

ICT tools are changing how governments interact with the public and how the public interacts with government. They are also changing the types of work skills that are sought by public employers. At the same time, traditional demands on government remain: to ensure fairness, equity, and safety; to protect people's privacy; and to ensure representativeness in decision making. And, as the problems associated with the rollout of HealthCare.gov demonstrate, no amount of technological sophistication can replace the human factor that is responsible for planning and coordination. Human capacity to lead and coordinate efforts is essential for technology projects to succeed.

KEY TERMS

Big data – refers to datasets that are too large or too complex for usual storage, retrieval, and computation methods.

Chief information officer – the person responsible for the management of an agency's information and communication technology, including oversight of ICT projects, contracts, strategy, and security.

Cyber hacking – the act of hacking, or breaking into, computer systems, networks, websites, and so on.

Cybersecurity – relating to the protection of electronic data (on a computer, network, website, and server) from attack or theft.

Digital democracy – involves the use of modern communication and information technology to support democracy.

E-Gov – refers to the use of electronic devices and information and communication technology to deliver public services, communicate with the public, and gather feedback.

GIS – Geographic Information System; jurisdictions use GIS mapping to map everything from sewer lines to flu outbreaks.

GPS – Global Positioning System; jurisdictions use GPS to track activities and assets, including navigational routes and government-owned vehicles.

Internet – the worldwide network of electronic information that can be accessed with a computer or related device.

Smart cities – cities that incorporate modern communication and information technology into their operations to improve services for their residents.

Social media – refers to web-based platforms that allow users to share content and engage in social networking.

DISCUSSION QUESTIONS

1. Contrast the advantages and disadvantages of websites to the advantages and disadvantages of social media.
2. Describe your most recent use of a public service website. Was your experience positive? Did you achieve your objective?

3. Regardless of technology advances, the human element cannot be removed from IT projects. Discuss how the problems associated with the rollout of HealthCare.gov reflect the human factor in IT initiatives.

EXERCISE

Find one governmental or nonprofit website. If it is governmental it may be a jurisdiction (city, county, state, or federal) or an agency. If it is nonprofit, it may be any organization or association that is nonprofit. Describe the site by including this information:

- The URL
- The site's purpose, intended audience, and message(s)
- Your assessment of the website's effectiveness (Are its goals and purpose clear? Is the communication straightforward and accessible? Is it easy to maneuver through the site?)
- What would it take to make the site better—and what do you mean by "better?"

BUILD YOUR SKILLS

Communication via e-mail, chats, and blogs is fast but lacks the fullness of communication that can only be achieved through in-person exchanges. See the skillbox to learn how to distinguish when e-mail is appropriate versus when an in-person discussion is preferable and how to follow e-mail etiquette.

SKILLBOX: E-MAIL VERSUS IN-PERSON COMMUNICATION

E-mail is the most convenient way to communicate, but it is not always the best. The most meaningful communication is face-to-face and too much reliance on e-mail leads to fewer interpersonal interactions and a disconnected workplace. Tone of voice, facial expression, and body language transmit as much, if not more, information than words. This is why phone calls and face-to-face conversation are more powerful than e-mail and more effective in the following circumstances:

1) When a topic has many parameters that need to be explained or negotiated;

2) When the conversation is emotion-laden and requires sharing and listening to divergent points of view;

---

3) When the message is ambiguous such that the give-and-take of questions and answers is necessary for clarification;

4) When there are subtleties and nuances that become too complicated to communicate in the one-dimensional language of e-mails; and

5) When it is important to show commitment to the work of the team and their concerns.

As items 1 through 5 show, complex issues and conflict-ridden problems are better discussed face-to-face, because in-person discussion provides an instantaneous opportunity to clear up confusion. Tone of voice, facial expression, and body language provide signals in addition to words. And in-person discussion avoids a flurry of back-and-forth e-mails that attempt to clear up confusion. Communicating in person makes it possible to see and sense the reactions of the others and to respond immediately in order to clarify meanings.

E-mail Etiquette

On the other hand, if the message is straightforward and can be communicated in a brief written message, then e-mail is an excellent channel for conveying it. These pointers ensure that the message that is intended is the message that is received.

1) Think of e-mail messages as simple memoranda. Each message should be clear, to the point, and unambiguous.

2) The subject frames the way the reader will interpret the message so use the subject line to state exactly the purpose of the message.

3) Be clear and to the point. Proof the message before sending it to make sure it conveys the desired message. Is it addressed to the correct recipients? Will it be sent to "reply all" or just to the sender?

4) When sharing someone else's idea is the best way to communicate an idea, forwarding the text of another message is appropriate. Before forwarding, remove extraneous material that is not germane to the point at hand.

5) Avoid irony or sarcasm. Something that is funny in person may not be perceived as humorous in an e-mail. The one-dimensional nature of e-mail obscures humor and may cause the message to be misunderstood.

6) Acknowledge receipt of a message so the sender knows it has reached its destination. If no action is required, a simple "thanks" is sufficient. If a lengthy response is called for, acknowledge receipt and give the sender an approximate time to expect a full response.

7) Style matters: make sure spelling and punctuation are correct. A sloppy e-mail reflects badly on the sender and diminishes the message.

8) Do not use your nickname for an e-mail address. Use the name that recipients know and will recognize.

9) When writing a message, add the e-mail address of the recipient last. This prevents sending the message prematurely, before there has been time to edit and proof it.

10) Use a signature that contains contact information. This avoids follow-up e-mails to provide a phone number or address.

11) It is fine to write an e-mail when angry, but do not send it until sufficient time has passed to reconsider the message and edit it.

12) Be careful with confidential information. If it should not be forwarded, think twice before including it in a message. And do not send or forward messages that contain libelous, defamatory, offensive, racist, or obscene remarks. Remember, there is nothing private about e-mail.

E-mail Policies and Best Practices

1) In general, use official e-mail accounts for official business. Personal e-mail account use for official business can conflict with existing laws and policies pertaining to public document retention.

2) Keep official e-mails official by limiting the inclusion of personal communication. Mixing the two can lead to the potential disclosure of personal information and reflect poorly on the organization.

3) Remember that each government has policies related to preserving and archiving e-mail communication. Employees should familiarize themselves with those policies to ensure compliance. Just because an e-mail is deleted by a user does not mean that it no longer exists. It may remain available to internal or external information requests.

Hands-On Activities

1. Examine three e-mail exchanges that you recently had. Do they meet e-mail etiquette standards 1 through 12? Where do they fall short? How could they be improved?

2. Find an example from the popular press where e-mail correspondence was at the center of a government or nonprofit controversy. In a one-page memo addressed to the leadership of the affected organization, describe what happened, the role played by e-mail communication, and the key lessons and best practices, based in part on the guidelines mentioned, that should be communicated to the organization's employees regarding the use of e-mail communication.

NOTES

1. Sharon Begley, "Analysis: IT Experts Question Architecture of Obamacare Website," *Technology News* (October 5, 2013) http://www.reuters.com/article/us-usa-health-care-technology-analysis-idUSBRE99407T20131005?irpc=932; and U.S. Department of Health and Human Services, "HeathCare.gov: CMS Management of the Federal Marketplace" (February, 2016), https://www.actiac.org/system/files/oei-06-14-00350.pdf.

2. Begley, "Analysis."

3. "HealthCare.gov," U.S. Department of Health and Human Services.

4. Ibid.

5. David Witzel, "Designing Open Projects: Lessons from Internet Pioneers," IBM Center for the Business of Government (2012), http://businessofgovernment.org/sites/default/files/Designing%20Open%20Projects.pdf.

6. Ibid.

7. Jooho Lee and B.J. Reed, "From Paper to Cloud," in *Public Administration Evolving: From Foundations to the Future*, ed. Mary E. Guy and Marilyn M. Rubin (New York: Routledge, 2012), 158–191.

8. Ibid.

9. Tod Newcombe, "Dot-Govs Get a Much-Needed Facelift," *Governing* (June, 2016), http://www.governing.com/columns/tech-talk/gov-government-website-updates.html.

10. Ines Mergel, "Working the Network: A Manager's Guide for Using Twitter in Government," IBM Center for the Business of Government (2012), http://www.business

ofgovernment.org/report/working-network-manager%E2%80%99s-guide-using-twitter-government.

11. Ibid.; and Michael E. Milakovich, *Digital Governance: New Technologies for Improving Public Service and Participation* (New York: Routledge, 2012).

12. Akhlaque Haque, *Surveillance, Transparency, and Democracy: Public Administration in the Information Age* (Tuscaloosa, AL: University of Alabama Press, 2015).

13. Sarah Breitenbach, "States Impose Wildly Different Policies in Releasing Police Videos," *Stateline* (October 11, 2016), http://www.pewtrusts.org/en/research-and-analysis/blogs/stateline/2016/10/11/states-impose-wildly-different-policies-in-releasing-police-videos.

14. Mike Maciag, "Police Aren't the Only Public Workers Wearing Body Cameras," *Governing* (June 10, 2015), http://www.governing.com/topics/public-justice-safety/gov-body-cameras-employees-expansion.html.

15. Breitenbach, "States Impose."

16. Joe Davidson, "Federal Cyber Incidents Jump 1,300% in 10 Years," *Washington Post* (September 22, 2016), https://www.washingtonpost.com/news/powerpost/wp/2016/09/22/federal-cyber-incidents-jump-1300-in-10-years/?utm_term=.b81162faa896.

17. Joe Davidson, "Thieves Stole Taxpayer Data from IRS 'Get Transcript' Service," *Washington Post* (September 12, 2016), https://www.washingtonpost.com/news/power-post/wp/2016/09/12/thieves-stole-taxpayer-data-from-irs-get-transcript-service/?utm_term=.95971c785531.

18. Government Accountability Office, *Testimony Before the President's Commission on Enhancing National Cybersecurity: Federal Information Security*, GAO-16-885T (September 19, 2016), http://www.gao.gov/assets/680/679877.pdf.

19. Office of the Director of National Intelligence, "Intelligence Community Assessment: Assessing Russian Activities and Intentions in Recent US Elections" (January 6, 2017), https://www.dni.gov/files/documents/ICA_2017_01.pdf.

20. U.S. Department of Energy, *Transforming the Nation's Electricity Sector: The Second Installment of the QER* (January, 2017), p. 4–2, https://energy.gov/sites/prod/files/2017/01/f34/Chapter%20IV%20Ensuring%20Electricity%20System%20Reliability%2C%20Security%2C%20and%20Resilience.pdf.

21. Ibid.

22. Ask Me Why I Care: Public Service Stories, video, directed by Mary R. Hamilton and Rita Paskowitz (Omaha, Nebraska: College of Public Affairs and Community Service), http://www.unomaha.edu/college-of-public-affairs-and-community-service/community-engagement/pss-william-ciaccio.php.

ADDITIONAL RESOURCES

Haque, Akhlaque. 2015. *Surveillance, Transparency, and Democracy: Public Administration in the Information Age.* Tuscaloosa, AL: University of Alabama Press.

Milakovich, Michael E. 2012. *Digital Governance: New Technologies for Improving Public Service and Participation.* New York: Routledge.

Visit *Building a More Awesome Government Through Technology,* a website of the Executive Office of the President, to learn about digital initiatives in the federal government: https://www.usds.gov/.

Control Mechanisms

There are a number of ways that the boundaries for public action are set. These range from political to managerial to legal to personal. They include policy decisions, restrictions on how finances are managed, how information is disseminated, legal constraints contained within contracts and law, and ethical considerations surrounding personal conduct. These chapters explain each of these means for shaping and controlling public action.

Chapter 8 Timeline: Public Economics and Policy

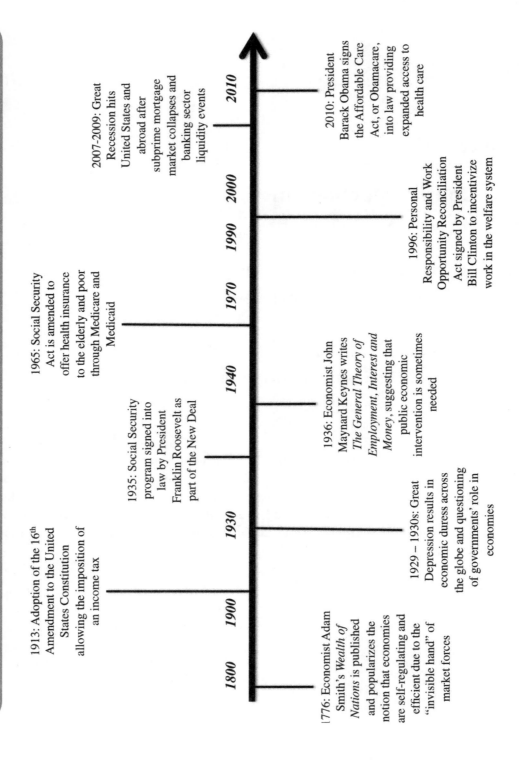

1913: Adoption of the 16th Amendment to the United States Constitution allowing the imposition of an income tax

1965: Social Security Act is amended to offer health insurance to the elderly and poor through Medicare and Medicaid

2007-2009: Great Recession hits United States and abroad after subprime mortgage market collapses and banking sector liquidity events

1935: Social Security program signed into law by President Franklin Roosevelt as part of the New Deal

1800   1900   1930   1940   1970   1990   2000   2010

1776: Economist Adam Smith's *Wealth of Nations* is published and popularizes the notion that economies are self-regulating and efficient due to the "invisible hand" of market forces

1929 – 1930s: Great Depression results in economic duress across the globe and questioning of governments' role in economies

1936: Economist John Maynard Keynes writes *The General Theory of Employment, Interest and Money*, suggesting that public economic intervention is sometimes needed

1996: Personal Responsibility and Work Opportunity Reconciliation Act signed by President Bill Clinton to incentivize work in the welfare system

2010: President Barack Obama signs the Affordable Care Act, or Obamacare, into law providing expanded access to health care

WHAT YOU WILL LEARN

Economic rationale for government intervention

Tools of public finance

How behavior is influenced through public finance

Skillbox: How to compare costs and benefits

Americans express high levels of frustration with government. In 2015, 79 percent of survey respondents reported being either angry (22 percent) or frustrated (57 percent) with the federal government according to the Pew Research Center.[1] This contrasts with only 18 percent of respondents reporting feeling basically content. The negativity is much less apparent when the public is asked about the performance of specific federal government functions. These functions reflect traditional roles of government, particularly stepping in where the market is incapable of effectively providing services. More than 70 percent of respondents believe that the federal government is doing a somewhat good or very good job of responding to natural disasters, setting standards for workplaces, keeping the country safe from terrorism, and ensuring safe food and medicine. The complete list of functions and the perceptions of performance and the appropriate role of the federal government in providing the function are provided in Figure 8.1.

Throughout the chapter, keep in mind how each of these functions address either a market failure or an effort to redistribute resources. The following case describes a public service that came under fire for receiving government support.

FIGURE 8.1 PERCEPTIONS OF PERFORMANCE AND ROLE OF
U.S. FEDERAL GOVERNMENT BY FUNCTION

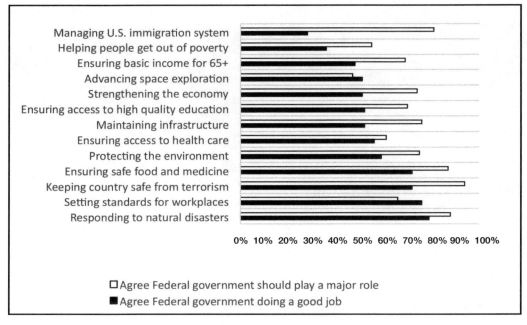

Note: Based on data and charts contained in Pew Research Center's *Beyond Distrust: How Americans View Their Government*, November, 2015.

THE PUBLIC IN PUBLIC BROADCASTING: A STROLL DOWN SESAME STREET

In a 2012 U.S. presidential debate, Republican candidate Mitt Romney called out an icon of public television programming. Romney remarked that "I like PBS [Public Broadcasting Service], I love Big Bird . . . but I'm going to stop borrowing money from China to pay for things we don't need."[2] Cutting federal government support for public broadcasting, and specifically the well-regarded children's program, Sesame Street, was a clear questioning of the scope of government. Should the government, with its many competing demands, provide funds for such television programming?

If the programming is valued and of high quality, then why is public funding needed? A press release from PBS made the case for continued federal support, which amounted to only a fraction of the overall PBS and Sesame Street budgets:

For more than 40 years, Big Bird has embodied the public broadcasting mission—harnessing the power of media for the good of every citizen, regardless of where they live or their ability to pay. Our system serves as a universally accessible resource for education, history, science, arts and civil discourse . . . Each day, the American public receives an enduring and daily return on investment that is heard, seen, read and experienced in public media broadcasts, apps, podcasts and online—all for the cost of about $1.35 per person per year. Earlier in 2012, a Harris Interactive poll confirmed that Americans consider PBS the most trusted public institution and the second most valuable use of public funds, behind only national defense, for the 9th consecutive year . . . Numerous studies—including one requested by Congress earlier this year—have stated categorically that while the federal investment in public broadcasting is relatively modest, the absence of this critical seed money would cripple the system and bring its services to an end.[3]

A few years after the presidential debate, Sesame Workshop (the nonprofit parent of Sesame Street) signed a contract with HBO, a private media company. The agreement, touted as a public-private partnership, funds expanded programming in return for airing Sesame Street to HBO's paying customers nine months before the release to PBS stations. Once again, Sesame Street became a focus when debating the appropriate role of government support for the arts as the public expressed concerns over preservation of the show's original educational mission. The headlines of news stories and opinion pieces reporting the deal say it all: "B Is for Broke: Why 'Sesame Street' Is Moving to HBO,"

"How New Money Has Ruined Sesame Street," "Sesame Street Goes to HBO and Makes It Clear Why We Should Fund the Arts," "Welcome to the New, Gentrified Sesame Street on HBO," and "New 'Sesame Street' Deal Is All About Economics." From another perspective, there was commentary supporting the partnership with HBO, including those that pointed to the deal as evidence that public support of television is unnecessary: "Get the Government Out of Public Broadcasting: The Rest of PBS Should Follow the Lead of Sesame Street," for example.

What is it about Sesame Street that justifies government support? Why is it that the private market cannot provide the show? Sesame Workshop is a nonprofit education organization with a mission "to help kids grow smarter, stronger, and kinder." From its inception in the late 1960s, the organization has had a public service orientation. The creation of Sesame Street was funded by a combination of private foundation and federal government support. Some direct federal funding continued for a number of years before ending in the 1980s. Federal grants and relatively small payments from PBS have continued to support Sesame Workshop, but the importance of product licensing, distribution fees, and royalty revenues grew over time with the popularity of the programming. In 2015, only 31 percent of funding came from government and foundations (both corporate and private).

According to Sesame Workshop, over 1,000 studies provide evidence that Sesame Street supports improved cognitive outcomes for preschool children who watch the show. The impact of Sesame Street on children has been equated to other preschool interventions in terms of effectiveness, but the scale is much greater because it serves over 150 million kids worldwide. In the 1960s, using television for educational purposes was a somewhat radical notion. Support from government and nonprofit foundations allowed for the risk-taking that was necessary to launch such an ambitious noncommercial enterprise. Once launched and proven successful, the argument for public tax-funded support of Sesame Street weakened. The long-term benefits of Sesame Street are difficult to value, but the show's educational focus and broad accessibility reflect characteristics of public goods as well as redistribution.

Questions to Ponder:

1. What are the arguments for and against government investing in public television, and in Sesame Street, in particular? Which reasons do you find most compelling: those for the investment or those against?

2. The Corporation for Public Broadcasting (CPB), a private nonprofit entity created by Congress, "is the steward of the federal government's investment in public broadcasting." In 2014, CPB received a federal appropriation of $445 million[4] or approximately 0.01 percent of federal spending. Does the relative size of the expenditure matter when questioning whether government should be involved in supporting a service?

3. Personal donations to nonprofit public television stations are a significant source of revenue. These donations are tax deductible and represent another source of support for public television. Why can't stations depend entirely on donations from viewers to support programming?

Public service is called upon to respond to social problems and citizen demands, even when the expanded services exceed available capacity and resources. Tempering the responsibilities of the public sector is a view from economics that sets a boundary around the appropriate role of government. It is important to understand this economic perspective and the policy tools—taxation and regulation—that are useful when government intervention is needed.

The broad question of why government should be involved in the free market provides a lens for narrower questions about the appropriate public role in education, health care, safety-net programs, and the optimal level of government capacity to provide and deliver such services. The economic perspective, which at times reflects skepticism toward more growth in the size and scope of government, provides a rationale for focusing resources in the greatest areas of need.

WHEN SHOULD GOVERNMENT INTERVENE?

There are many reasons to doubt that government can effectively provide the appropriate levels of desired services at the right time despite its best intentions. In practice, a number of significant barriers exist to matching public programs with the will of the people. Foremost is the difficulty in making sense of citizen preferences based on their partisan points of view. Further, policy making occurs in an uncertain environment where preferences of voters and social and economic conditions constantly change. Ultimately, the "government" is comprised of human beings (whether elected or appointed) and our natural decision-making biases and limitations.

The mismatch between government actions and citizen preferences is reflected, for example, in the use of direct democracy to limit public sector activities throughout the United States. Representative democracy selects individuals to make decisions that reflect the priorities of their constituents. If elected officials successfully translated voter preferences into government action, then there would be little need for restrictive citizen initiatives like California's Proposition 13 and Colorado's Taxpayer Bill of Rights, which limit state governments' ability to tax and spend.

Based on a combination of economic considerations and social goals, government intervenes in the free market when there is a failure of the pricing system to promote desired outcomes and to maximize social well-being. Called "market failure," these interventions result from a number of factors, each of which is discussed next: public goods, externalities, natural monopolies, information asymmetry, redistribution, and managing the economy.

> *"The legitimate object of government, is to do for a community of people, whatever they need to have done, but can not do, at all, or can not, so well do, for themselves—in their separate, and individual capacities. In all that the people can individually do as well for themselves, government ought not to interfere."*
>
> —Abraham Lincoln

Public Goods

Some goods and services are undersupplied when left to individual choices in a free market. The main characteristic that leads to under-provision is the inability to exclude other individuals from consuming the good or service. Public goods, referred to as *nonexcludable*, are goods and services that are available to all once they are provided. Related, an individual's use of these goods and services does not impede others from using them, meaning that they are *nonrival*. In other words, these goods and services are truly beneficial and available to the public.

Examples of pure public goods are limited, but the classic public good is national defense. Actions of the U.S. military to protect the country from invasion are all or nothing. The Joint Chiefs of Staff would be hard-pressed to defend the nation but leave Topeka, Kansas defenseless. Setting an optional price and charging individuals for national defense would be a fool's errand. Knowing that national defense is already in place, individuals would be unwilling to pay a fair share for the service. In other words, people will "free ride" because they can benefit from the public good without paying for it. The power of government to tax partially sidesteps the free rider problem, although citizens still have an incentive to understate their preference for public goods. More common are impure public goods like sanitation, protection against communicable diseases, national parks and forests, primary and secondary education, and roads and bridges. Although these goods might be *rival* and *excludable* to some degree, since for example, an admission fee can be charged for a park and crowds detract from the experience, they benefit the public broadly and cannot be provided at desired levels by the private sector.

> *"Markets just don't run themselves in delivering public goods, because most of the time they are being asked to do things they aren't used to doing. And because policymakers tend to assume that the markets will take care of themselves, they often don't build governmental capacity to steer the process."*
>
> —Donald F. Kettl

Framing something as a public good is a common strategy to garner support for government provision. Public goods are also delivered regularly by the nonprofit sector. Scholar Dennis Young suggests that nonprofits bolster the availability of public goods by supplementing the levels provided by government, complementing government efforts through partnership, or serving as an adversary working to persuade government support of public goods.[5] The continued justification for preferential tax treatment of nonprofit organizations is, in part, based on the promotion of public goods. The following case considers the public good characteristics of a common local government function.

"FORE" THE PUBLIC GOOD?

Among the more than 15,000 golf courses in the United States, nearly 2,500 are owned by municipal governments. Historically, access to golf came only with membership in expensive private golf courses and exclusive country clubs. The advent of public courses in the late 1800s, including municipally-owned facilities, provided access to the sport without membership requirements. By the late 1990s, more than a third of large city governments operated golf courses.[6] The public sector is typically constrained with limited resources, so why prioritize a golf course? Why would the private market fail to satisfy the demand to golf?

Golf course development boomed in the 1990s and the increased supply of courses was met with flattened and then reduced demand beginning in the 2000s. The evolution of the golf industry is a reminder that the public's demand for services can vary over time. Cities and towns typically operate golf courses as enterprise funds. The enterprise fund is operated as a business within government and charges greens fees and sells concessions to cover its costs. When all goes well, the local government breaks even on the golf course while saving money each year for course improvements.

Municipal governments have, at times, struggled to manage golf courses and alternative operational arrangements have been adopted. When municipal golf courses become financially stressed, elected officials need to decide whether to subsidize the operations with general funds, increase fees, or reduce associated costs. Increasing fees and reducing costs can alienate golfers, especially when cost cutting includes skimping on investment, services, and maintenance. At the extreme, municipal governments must consider closing golf courses.

Once a service is provided by government it becomes expected and reversing the status quo can be politically difficult. Municipal governments turn to outsourcing municipal golf course management to private operators. In this arrangement the local government maintains ownership of the golf courses, but the private operator receives a fee and is incentivized to operate the course more efficiently. Maintaining the initial goals of a municipal course with a private operator presents its own challenges, but effective contracts can help preserve the public values under private operation. Alternately, in the mid-1980s the City of Baltimore opted to create a nonprofit management corporation to operate its municipal golf courses.

Golf may not be at the top of the list for essential government services, but it provides a powerful example of the breadth of public-sector activities. The challenges of managing municipal golf courses have forced governments and citizens to question whether government should play a role in such recreational services. Before embarking on expanded service offerings, decision makers should ask whether a market failure exists and whether the nature of the service has meaningful characteristics of a public good.

Questions to Ponder

1. Does a municipal golf course represent a public good? Carefully consider the characteristics of the service.
2. Assume that you are a city manager tasked with justifying the government provision of a golf course to residents. What reasons will you use? Should government promote golf?

Externalities

Market failure occurs when the price of a good fails to reflect all of the costs and benefits to society. These pricing failures in the private market are referred to as externalities. Consider a beekeeper who cares for beehives to produce honey for sale. The bees provide a benefit, or positive externality, to neighboring lands by pollinating crops as they forage for nectar. Alternately, having more bees in the area results in a higher incidence of bee stings (a negative externality) for neighbors. The beekeeper's price of honey does not reflect the additional benefits and costs of its production, since the buyer in the marketplace is not the party whose crops were pollinated or children who were stung.

The private market, under certain conditions, can internalize externalities when property rights are fully assigned to the affected parties. Otherwise, governments may choose to address externalities by either altering the price or quantity of externality-producing activities in the market. What does this mean? It means that taxes and subsidies are the mechanisms by which prices are changed, while regulation can limit market activity. When property rights are not fully assigned, the government can sometimes create a market for the activity and allow firms to value the rights through a bidding process.

As a prominent example, the impetus for the Clean Air Act Amendments of 1990 was that the cost of electricity failed to account for the damage caused by energy plant emissions. A market-based system of tradable sulfur dioxide emission allowances was created to incentivize electric utilities to curb the emissions causing acid rain in down-wind locations. By creating a market for the pollution, firms that could reduce emissions most cheaply were incentivized to do so. In this way, the federal government's solution supported both a reduction in emissions and a less costly solution than a mandated uniform reduction in emissions across all plants. As an aside, a small number of environmental nonprofit groups, most notably the Acid Rain Retirement Fund, bid for emission rights alongside electric utilities and chose to retire the purchased rights.

Taxes that adjust the market price for goods to reflect the social costs of negative externalities are referred to as Pigovian taxes. The U.S. Congress created the Superfund program in 1980 to clean up hazardous waste and contaminated lands, "that pose an imminent or long-term risk of exposure and harm to human health and the environment." The Superfund itself, formally the Hazardous Substance Superfund Trust Fund, was initially financed through a series of excise taxes on select chemicals, crude oil, and "an environmental tax on corporations."[7] Excise taxes are taxes levied on a specific good or service. The tax authority expired in the mid-1990s, but reflect an effort to recognize the long-term social costs of commercial activities that are not captured by private market pricing.

Subsidies are used to promote private activities that produce positive externalities. For example, cities across the country offer free or low-cost trees to residents through programs like TreeBaltimore; NeighborWoods in Raleigh, North Carolina; City Plants in Los Angeles, California; and One Person One Tree in Orlando, Florida. Even though the trees are planted on private property, they benefit the city through neighborhood beautification (and higher property values), increased shade, reduced runoff, and improved air quality. The subsidized trees are an upfront cost to the government, but the continued maintenance and care for the trees is provided by residents.

Despite the potential to address externalities, the magnitude of corrective taxes and subsidies are often difficult to match with the size of the associated externalities. Instead of taxing undesirable activities, governments can also regulate, or limit, the quantity of an activity. Local zoning codes regulate the location of commercial businesses, the height of buildings, and the ability to construct multifamily housing to reduce conflict over potential negative externalities. The associated negative externalities might include noise from truck deliveries, blocking out light from low-rise buildings, or congestion, respectively. Another example of quantity regulation comes from the National Park Service (NPS) efforts to limit the number of rafts on the Colorado River as it runs through Grand Canyon National Park. Each additional raft worsens congestion on the river and its campsites, while threatening the solitude and immersion in nature sought by rafters. The rafting season is dictated by snowmelt, which limits the times when people can run the river and worsens congestion concerns. The NPS created a wait list for noncommercial permits to raft the canyon. Wait times ballooned to more than two decades. In 2006, the system was changed to a weighted lottery where the chances of a permit improved to one in eight with the addition of more noncommercial spots. Balancing the negative externalities of an additional rafting trip with the pent-up demand for access to the public river is far from simple. Such decisions reflect the challenges governments face when trying to determine the optimal quantity in regulation. The following case focuses on a less obvious example of a production externality.

GOATS, SWEATERS, AND CLEAN AIR[8]

Cashmere sweaters are admired for their softness and warmth. Cashmere wool comes from the fine undercoat of a particular type of goat, historically located in the Kashmir region of South Asia. The hair is collected when the goats molt, then it is dyed and woven to create yarn. Clothing is made from the yarn and shipped all over the world to satisfy consumer demand. As the popularity of cashmere grew, so too did the number of goats being raised on the plains of China and Mongolia. The traditionally high price of cashmere began to fall, spurring even greater desire for the material.

The increasingly large herds of goats have contributed to the degradation of the grasslands in China and Mongolia. One report estimates the goat population of In-

ner Mongolia, a region located just south of the Mongolian border, grew more than tenfold from 1949 to 2004. The resulting dust from the degraded grasslands knows no geographic boundaries and disperses across the globe in more frequent dust storms. In addition to the localized impacts, the dust has combined with other pollutants to contribute to orange skies in Beijing, billions of dollars in economic damages in South Korea, reduced visibility in Colorado, and public health warnings in the northwest United States and British Columbia.

The cashmere sweater is an example of a good whose market price fails to internalize the negative externalities from its production. The president of the Cashmere and Camel Hair Manufacturers Institute admitted that the desertification is "a government problem and a world problem." Indeed, externalities are a common justification for government intervention. The cashmere situation is complicated by the transboundary nature of the negative externalities, but the traditional responses to externalities are still available. First, the producer's government can intervene and regulate the cashmere industry. Limiting the number of goats is one approach to reducing the impacts on the grasslands and promoting recovery. Of course, regulation is hard since there are distributional consequences (winners and losers) and knowing just how many goats should be allowed to graze is uncertain. Second, taxes might be imposed to increase the costs of producing cashmere and to reduce the supply. Taxes imposed by only one government, though, results in a competitive disadvantage and loss of market share. Finally, government might subsidize alternate means of making a living to reduce the number of herders.

Addressing externalities, both negative and positive, is a difficult responsibility that falls to the public sector. When government either fails to act or is incapable of acting, third parties, such as nonprofits, may step in to help offset the externalities. In Mongolia, a partnership between the central government and the Swiss Agency for Development and Cooperation since 2004 (referred to as the "Green Gold" project) has worked to improve the sustainability of grazing lands. Talking about sweaters and externalities may seem like a stretch, but the situation is similar to the complexities encountered when trying to address externalities without fully defined property rights.

Questions to Ponder

1. Should goat herders be held liable for the negative externalities associated with overgrazing?
2. How should governments prioritize which externalities to address? For example, which are more salient: negative or positive externalities?
3. Think about the mission of a nonprofit organization that you know. Do its mission and activities encourage positive externalities or alleviate negative externalities?

Natural Monopolies

A less common but critical justification for government intervention in the private market is the existence of natural monopolies. These monopolies do not result from ruthless business practices intended to eliminate competition and secure market power. Rather, high initial infrastructure investment and scale economies make competition wasteful in industries where a firm's average cost declines as production volume increases. More simply, a single firm is the most efficient outcome. Imagine a large tract of undeveloped land that falls within a city's boundaries. A plan to develop new neighborhoods requires infrastructure services, especially water, electricity, gas, and telecommunications. Multiple firms digging up the ground and burying networks of competing water pipes would be wasteful. A single firm can more efficiently spread the high fixed costs of the distribution system over a higher volume of water customers. In fact, residents are buying from a natural monopoly when they pay their monthly water bill. The water provider is likely a publicly-owned utility or a regulated private utility.

Local public utility commissions regulate natural monopolies to ensure that providers do not take advantage of the absence of competition to charge unreasonably high prices. Public control over natural monopolies also means that development is not stymied by the profit motive of private firms.

Information Asymmetry

The efficient operation of a free market depends on consumers having accurate information on which to base a buy-or-not-buy decision. Governments, nonprofits, and even private firms often step in to correct asymmetries in information between purchasers and sellers. For example, when selecting fruit at the supermarket, how is one to know whether the apples are really organic? A system of certifiers has developed in each locale. Without certification, consumers would have to trust the claims of the supplier and would be less willing to pay the organic price premium.

Charitable nonprofit organizations depend on donations from the public. Unfortunately, news stories surface every year of disreputable organizations that spend more for administration than for the causes for which they are fundraising. For example, from 2003 to 2012 the Kids Wish Network reportedly raised $137.9 million from donors but the vast majority of the donations went to the fund-raisers. Only $3.5 million made it to the organization's beneficiaries.[9] Charity Navigator is an example of a nonprofit response to the information asymmetry that can result in misdirected diversions of charitable giving. Charity Navigator evaluates the financial condition, transparency, and accountability of public charities using a standardized rating system. The need for certification of market participants pervades daily life. Just consider the many professions, ranging from doctors and lawyers to hairdressers and massage therapists that require licensing and certification by state governments.

A primary function for modern governments is the provision of social insurance. The rationale for public involvement in insurance markets is largely based on problems of information asymmetry. Social insurance is a blanket term for programs that attempt to smooth personal consumption over time, particularly during adverse life events. Losing a job, being injured while working, becoming disabled, needing medical care, and maintaining income requirements after retirement are all examples of life events that benefit from insurance. In private insurance markets for health, automobiles, and homes, premiums are paid to the insurer in return for a promise of payment if the insured outcome occurs. Insurance markets get tricky because the buyer of insurance has more complete information about their riskiness than the insurer. The lack of complete information for the insurance company makes it difficult to accurately price the insurance premium.

The information asymmetry can be reduced but not eliminated in some cases by looking at an individual's past experience. For auto insurance, past driving records are influential in determining premiums. The imbalance in information between insurer and insured results in adverse selection, where the individuals most likely to need the insurance (careless drivers and less healthy people, for example) will be more likely to purchase insurance. Their costly claims result in the company raising its premiums to the point where it is too expensive for lower-risk individuals. Low enrollments then force the company out of business.

In the case of health insurance, providing insurance to large groups of people creates a risk pool that is less likely to suffer from adverse selection since the healthy enrollees balance out the unhealthy. By not taxing health insurance benefits as compensation, the U.S. government incentivizes employer-provided health insurance and thereby encourages diverse risk pools, which keeps the cost of premiums lower than they would otherwise be. Similarly, requiring everyone to have health insurance under the Affordable Care Act, or Obamacare, had a similar intent to combat adverse selection.

Solutions often cause unintended problems. In the case of insurance, simply being insured can raise the likelihood of adverse outcomes, a condition referred to as *moral hazard*. Having health insurance that covers medical services can lead to riskier behavior that results in a greater consumption of medical services, just like the availability of flood insurance can result in riskier home location decisions. On a larger scale, government bailouts of financial firms (as experienced in the 2008 financial crisis) reduces firms' desire to limit risk. Social insurance programs should be designed to limit the moral hazard that can result. Economic justifications exist for government provision of social insurance, but the debate over spending for programs that safeguard the public's private lives is deeply ideological. The generosity and breadth of social insurance programs result from fundamental decisions about governments' role in supporting redistribution and acting in a caretaker role for citizens.

Redistribution

The free market economy generates winners and losers despite the allure of efficiency. In fact, there is a direct tradeoff between equality and efficiency (when only economic values are used to measure efficiency.) Many observers worry about record levels of income and wealth inequality in the United States. Economist David Autor points to a number of factors responsible for rising wage inequality in the United States, many of which are relevant across the globe. These include the increasing value of skills received through higher education, a long-term decline in the inflation-adjusted federal minimum wage, fewer jobs for noncollege graduates due to automation, global competition, weakened labor unions, and lower marginal tax rates for high earners.[10]

Inequality takes many forms and solutions depend on whether the focus is at the starting gate or the finish line. Fundamentally, the question is about the role that government should play in guaranteeing equality in opportunity and outcomes. The former justifies providing equal access to safe housing and a quality education, for example, so that each person is given the means to be successful in society. Equality in outcomes is a more stringent standard requiring transfers of income and wealth to create a more balanced distribution across society. Redistribution is a broader concept than the cash payments made by traditional welfare systems. Of greater importance, redistribution includes using revenue from a progressive tax system, where a larger share of income is paid by those with higher income levels, in order to support services to those who are disadvantaged by the status quo.

There are strong economic justifications for attempting to equalize the status quo at both the starting gate and the finish line. Unemployment and the inability to earn a living wage results in negative externalities for the economy, ranging from fewer earnings for government to tax (which raises the tax rate on the rest of society) to stressing the health-care system (think about the use of costly emergency rooms rather than preventive care), to increased criminal activity to decreased purchasing power. Those with lower incomes are less likely than the wealthy to invest and grow the economy.[11]

Enacting redistribution policies presents challenges for a number of reasons captured in the mid-1970s by economist Arthur Okun. Okun illustrated the redistribution of resources from the wealthy to the poor with an analogy, where the money taken from the wealthy is delivered to the poor using a leaky bucket.[12] The sources of the leaks include the administrative costs of government intervention, but more important, the changes in economic incentives for the wealthy and poor. While the wealthy respond to the higher relative taxes needed for redistribution with reduced work and earnings, higher levels of resource transfers may dampen the incentive of the poor to seek training and employment, which would result in their losing the benefits of the redistributive programs[13] that pay only marginally less than the minimum wage job they would be able to secure. This result runs the risk of not substantively improving anyone's lot. Governments play the main role in addressing equity, but designing effective programs that balance competing incentives is a perpetual conundrum.

Managing the Economy

One of the functions of government is to influence the economy through monetary and fiscal policy. Economic cycles, and particularly the experience of the Great Depression, left governments searching for ways to counter unemployment, rapid inflation, and stagnant economies. The active government role in managing the economy is most popularly linked to economist John Maynard Keynes, who argued that the public sector can intervene to smooth out the ebbs and flows of the economy.

Monetary policy, enacted in the United States by the Federal Reserve Bank (the Fed) and respective central banks in other countries, alters the availability of money in the banking system through a number of mechanisms. The Fed has the explicit mandate to maintain stable prices and support employment.[14] The most visible approach to monetary policy is setting the discount rate, which represents the interest rate for short-term borrowing from the Fed by banks. Lowering the discount rate makes it cheaper for banks to borrow, improves bank liquidity, and is a common response to economic recessions because other interest rates tend to follow its lead. For example, in July 2007, the Fed's discount rate sat at 6.25 percent, just as it had for more than a year. As the Great Recession loomed, the Fed initiated a series of nine discount rate reductions intended to combat the downturn. By December 2008, the discount rate was 0.5 percent. Alternately, increasing the discount rate can help apply brakes to an expanding economy and the associated inflation as it creates a disincentive to borrow money to buy a house, a car, or to invest in new business ventures.

The Fed also determines the amount of reserves that banks must maintain in cash. These reserve requirements alter the funds available for lending and are only infrequently changed. The third and most common tool of the Fed is to purchase and sell federal securities. When the Fed buys securities issued by the Treasury Department, such as Treasury bonds, they are deposited in banks, increasing the reserves that are available for lending. A bond is a financial instrument representing a debt between a borrower and lender. In return for the funds, the borrower typically pays the lender interest along with a promise to return the borrowed amount (the principal) at some designated time in the future.

Central governments also use fiscal policy to influence the economy through changes in government revenue and expenditure. In the United States, one of the most famous efforts by the federal government to bolster employment was the Work Projects Administration. The New Deal program employed 8.5 million people between the years 1935 to 1943 to combat the chronic unemployment of the Great Depression, while providing purposeful work that left its physical mark across the country.[15] Fiscal policy is the purview of Congress and the president as they deliberate spending and taxation through the budget process. Although increased government spending can stimulate the economy, so too can tax policy that incentivizes investment and spending. Many government programs also act in a counter-cyclical manner to increase spending when the economy weakens through means-testing (means-tested refers to program eligibility requirements based on levels of income, such as for Medicaid for health care).

FISCAL FEDERALISM

Once a convincing case is made for government intervention, the next question is what level of government should provide it. Monetary policy is the domain of the central government but fiscal policy operates at multiple levels. Globally, many national governments provide the funding for most services even if they are ultimately delivered by local governments. In the United States, the system of fragmented and overlapping governments complicates responsibility for public services. At the same time, the variety of governments—federal, state, city, county, special district—allows for a tailored match between citizen demands and government services.

An especially influential view of how governments determine the types and levels of services to provide comes from Charles Tiebout. Tiebout envisioned the competition among local governments for residents as akin to the competition that results among firms for customers in efficient markets. Tiebout's work highlights the importance of mobility. Residents are free to move and "vote with their feet" if the tax and service bundle is inappropriate in their current location.[16] In reality, the public is not uniformly mobile but those who are provide a competitive force for optimal service provision. The flipside of improved efficiency in the provision of services is that everybody benefits from the diversity of government offerings. If local governments compete for residents, then they need to be especially thoughtful about the services they provide. The notion that different levels of government are better suited to fund and deliver certain types of services falls into an area of study called *fiscal federalism*.

Economist Jonathan Gruber explains the implications of Tiebout's model for optimizing fiscal federalism.[17] With mobile populations, governments should focus on providing the goods and services that directly benefit residents and that have limited spillovers to outside populations. In other words, the recipients of goods and services should be directly connected to that government's own revenue sources. Redistribution and activities with outsized positive externalities are better provided by higher levels of government. Otherwise, residents may leave if the costs of redistributive programs become too high or if their tax dollars are actually benefiting outsiders.

Does this mean that state and local governments should always avoid providing services with large positive externalities or weak links to taxes? Not at all. In fact, some local governments have developed programs to combat climate change despite the fact that such actions would be expected at higher (and more geographically expansive) levels of government. A Climate Action Plan (CAP) tax imposed in 2007 by Boulder, Colorado residents represents a first of its kind. The voter-approved tax is tied to electricity consumption with the proceeds, around $1.8 million annually, supporting efforts to reduce greenhouse gas emissions.[18] A primary tool of fiscal federalism is the use of intergovernmental grants. With grant funding, higher-level governments can provide broad-based funding for the local production of goods and services that are not well-suited to funding through local taxes and fees.

Many public services also benefit from economies of scale where larger operations can function more efficiently. When this is the case, provision by higher levels of government makes good economic sense. Regional consolidation of fire departments is an example where the high cost of fire-fighting equipment and the need for specialized employees makes provision of the service on a larger geographic scale desirable. Countering the desire to expand fire service areas is the stark reality that proximity to the structures at risk for fire and emergency medical services is essential. Saving money by consolidating services might be penny-wise but pound foolish if the firefighting equipment is no longer close enough to respond quickly. This example shows the ever-present tension between providing a service locally versus regionally.

FUNDING GOVERNMENT INTERVENTION

Varied justifications exist for government intervention in a free market economy. From providing public goods to redistributing resources, governments must determine how best to accomplish their goals. Regulations can support a wide range of government objectives, such as environmental protection, affordable housing, and workplace safety, but when government decides to intervene it must also cover the costs. The power to tax is unique to government. The fact that taxes are compulsory means that they operate in a vastly different manner than the forces of supply and demand that dictate prices of private goods and services. The authority to tax has to be handled with care to create an efficient and equitable revenue system. Here, too, tradeoffs between efficiency and equity surface. Governments raise revenue primarily with taxes and fees. Taxes are levied on income, wealth, or consumption and fees are specific amounts attached to the receipt of goods and services. In this section, we present principles pertaining to equity and efficiency that are useful for guiding decisions about how to raise revenue in a fair and efficient manner.

> *"There are major functions of local, county, and state government around education, economic development, and infrastructure investment that matter greatly for the ability of lower-income people to connect to opportunity and achieve economic mobility."*
>
> —Alan Berube

Equity

Fairness is a relative term, but in revenue policy there are some generally agreed upon practices. Fees, rather than taxes, do a great job of linking the benefit received by an individual to the revenue received by the government. This is especially true when fees for goods and services are set to cover the production costs. Some taxes, though, can also be targeted effectively. For example, using a tax on gasoline to fund roads, or using property taxes for essential services creates a strong linkage between the taxes and the public services received. The focus on the connection between the tax or fee and the services received might be characterized as a "you-get-what-you-pay-for" system of fairness.

When we talk about equity of taxes, two primary types—at times conflicting—are discussed by economists. Vertical equity is the notion that parties with greater

PROPERTY TAX INEQUITY IN CALIFORNIA

In 1978 California's property tax system was dramatically altered with the passage of Proposition 13. The proposition capped the property tax rate and established rules limiting annual increases to 2 percent, which typically falls well below the actual increase in home value. When a property is sold it is assigned a new assessed value for taxation based on the sale price. The result is a property tax system that lacks horizontal equity, since neighbors with similar homes (that demand similar municipal services) end up paying dramatically different property taxes based on how long they have owned the property.

To provide a tangible example, we use Zillow to look at homes available for sale in one of the wealthiest zip codes in the United States. In Beverly Hills, California (zip code 90210), two similarly-sized homes were for sale for approximately $1.6 million in January 2017. The houses were built in 1939 and 1941, respectively, and are located less than one mile away from each other on the same street. The first was last sold in 2003 and has an annual property tax bill of $13,903. The other house has not changed hands in decades, so the homeowners pay only $2,653 in property taxes each year due to the limits imposed by Proposition 13. The difference of $11,000 in annual taxes for two homeowners in the same neighborhood is a clear example of horizontal inequity.

We can also consider the implications of Proposition 13 for vertical equity in California. A long-time homeowner might pay a similar or lower property tax on a high-value home than the new owners of much more modest residences. In fact, a foreclosed $350,000 home for sale in East Los Angeles in January 2017 had a property tax bill of $3,351, having been sold recently in 2014. Although this house was worth only a fifth of the Beverly Hills homes' market values, the East Los Angeles homeowner's property tax bill was 25 percent higher than for one of the much more expensive homes (at least prior to foreclosure). Table 8.1 summarizes this comparison of property tax burdens for these three homeowners. A study by California's Legislative Analyst's Office also points out that more mobile homeowners, including those in the military, young families, and with less stable employment, end up with higher property tax rates under the system.[19]

TABLE 8.1 COMPARISON OF PROPERTY TAX BURDEN

	Home #1	Home #2	Home #3
Location	Beverly Hills	Beverly Hills	East Los Angeles
Approximate Market Value	$1.59 million	$1.66 million	$350,000
Annual Property Tax (2015)	$13,903	$2,653	$3,351
Property Tax/Market Value	0.87%	0.16%	0.96%

levels of resources should shoulder a higher tax burden than those with lesser resources. In other words, differently-situated individuals and parties will be treated differently by the tax code. Vertical equity is reflected in progressive income tax systems, like in the United States where marginal income tax rates climb with income. In contrast, horizontal equity presumes that similarly-situated parties should be treated similarly by the tax code even when the parties make different economic choices. The following describes a tax system that is designed counter to these primary equity concepts.

Tax systems are riddled with exemptions, deductions, and credits. These exceptions complicate tax administration and are often thought to benefit special interests. Exceptions are more often intended to address equity concerns or promote certain behaviors. For example, sales tax typically applies to restaurant meals, but not groceries intended for home consumption. The sales tax exemption for most groceries is an attempt to counter the inherently regressive nature of the tax. Lower-income individuals spend larger shares of their income on essential goods, such as food, than high-income individuals. Unfortunately, the tweaks to improve equity in taxation experience the previously discussed trade off with efficiency.

Efficiency

Government has to be careful that costs of administering taxes and fees are kept to a minimum. It partners with the private sector to help collect payroll-based taxes (employers) and sales taxes (retailers). Keeping the administrative burden of a revenue source low for both government and the firms that support the collection process results in improved compliance so that more of the net tax revenue is directed to public programs. Effective collection and monitoring systems reduce tax evasion and result in increased revenues and a reduced need for higher taxes.

Efficiency in the physical collection of public revenues is actually a secondary concern to the behavioral responses induced by the revenue policies themselves. Imposing a tax or fee changes the activities of individuals and firms. An overarching guide for revenue decisions is to raise the necessary revenue in the least burdensome manner to minimize changes, or distortions, in preferred behavior.

Changes to market behavior from the imposition of taxes and fees lead to inefficiencies. For example, price-sensitive car renters may go to great lengths to avoid renting a car at an airport where additional taxes and fees are levied. Avoiding the airport car rental makes sense as long as the value of the renter's time and transport to the lower-cost offsite car rental facility is less than the saved airport taxes and fees. Renting the car at the airport, though, would have been preferred since it is simpler, saves time, and is more convenient.

A car rental decision is just a minor example of the kind of tax-based distortions that exist as a result of revenue policies. Much more substantial are the behavioral responses to income taxes (how much and how hard should I work?), corporate profits (should my company keep its profits overseas to avoid taxation or engage in a corporate inversion to change domicile for tax purposes?), sales taxes (can I get the same item online from an out-of-state seller or a neighboring jurisdiction with a lower sales tax rate?), and taxes on savings and investment (do I keep savings accessible for a future home purchase or direct the savings to a tax-deferred vehicle like a 401(k) plan?). When these changes in behavior are aggregated across society they can have a large impact on the efficiency of markets and the well-being of participants. Economists refer to the distortions caused by these responses to taxes as excess burden or the deadweight loss relative to the preferred outcomes in the absence of the tax. Economist John Mikesell sums up the desire to avoid excessive responses to taxation, noting "that governments should avoid excess burden in structuring their tax systems is an application of the general principle that government should avoid doing things that are economically stupid."[20]

Given the desire to avoid "stupid" revenue policies, how does government reduce behavioral responses to taxes and fees? First, a broad tax base with a low rate lessens behavioral responses. The broad tax base means that individuals are less able to substitute other goods or activities for the taxed good or activity. The low rate, made possible by the broader tax base, is less likely to scare off individuals from the taxed good or activity.

Second, consistency in tax systems and rates over time allows for individuals and firms to adjust incrementally rather than being forced to cope with frequent changes in incentives that result in dramatic changes in behavior.

Third, taxes and fees should be directed to less price-sensitive markets. This is a lesson learned by Republican President George H.W. Bush after enacting a luxury tax in 1991 that applied to expensive boats, cars, aircraft, and jewelry. The "yacht tax" amounted to 10 percent of the purchase price that exceeded $100,000. The tax was repealed in 1993 following reports that nearly 100 luxury boat builders scaled back their businesses, thousands of workers were let go, and a number of builders sought bankruptcy protection due, in part, to the change in demand from the luxury tax.[21] In economic terms, yacht demand is price elastic in that buyers responded to the change in price by not buying. Taxing goods and activities with inelastic supply and demand is preferable because changes in the cost do little to change consumer and producer behavior.

Finally, diversification of revenue sources is desirable for stability. State and local governments depend on a "three-legged stool" of taxes comprised of taxes on income, sales, and property. Some revenue sources vary dramatically with the economy, which can create shortfalls exactly when the funds are needed to provide expanded public services. Although not always an option for governments, diversification reduces the volatility of public revenues. The following section describes how the tax code itself is used to influence behavior in support of public policies.

POLICY INTERVENTION THROUGH THE TAX CODE

The primary use of taxes is to fund government services, but the tax code itself is also used to promote behavior that supports public goods, positive externalities, and economic growth. For example, employer-sponsored health insurance is encouraged by excluding contributions to medical premiums from taxable income. Homeownership, a long-standing national policy goal, is subsidized through the ability to deduct mortgage interest payments from federal taxable income and preferential treatment of the capital gains from selling a house. Contributions to retirement plans defer income taxes to support savings for old age. Investors are given preferential tax treatment when they generate capital gains relative to ordinary income. These tax expenditures represent foregone tax revenue based on intentional deviations from the general tax rules.

Support for nonprofits from government comes in two primary forms. One is direct funding through grants and contracts. The other is tax expenditures embedded in the federal, state, and local tax codes. Most prominent is the deductibility of charitable contributions from federal income tax liability for itemizers. With the deduction, the federal government lowers the price of charitable giving and promotes expanded public-serving activities by nonprofit organizations. Individuals can also dictate the activities supported by their funds through donations, unlike with tax payments. The individual discretion embodied in charitable tax deductions is not without criticism, since the nonprofit sector is diverse and there is no threshold by which a nonprofit demonstrates its worthiness for receiving preferential tax treatment. For example, is a homeless shelter more deserving of tax benefits than an opera company? Such debates were highlighted through social media in 2015 following a $400 million donation to Harvard University's school of engineering by hedge fund manager John Paulson. The size of the gift to an already wealthy institution (with an endowment of $35.7 billion as of the end of fiscal year 2016)[22] was criticized by some as undeserving and wasteful. Probably most visible were a series of tweets from author Malcolm Gladwell who noted, "It came down to helping the poor or giving the world's richest university $400 mil it doesn't need. Wise choice John!"

The tax code is too blunt a mechanism for policing the public benefit of each charitable contribution, but all taxpayers subsidize such giving. And while the discretion embodied in the charitable donation tax deduction is considered a strength, it raises questions about the return received for such breaks. Nonprofits can also benefit from access to lower-cost tax-exempt debt and, at the state and local levels, exemptions from paying property taxes. In sum, the policy decisions embedded in tax codes have tremendous influence over behavior and public policy outcomes. Table 8.2[23] provides the annual federal tax expenditures associated with the policies reviewed here. Some of the leading tax expenditures, particularly the deductibility of home mortgage interest and charitable contributions, are expected to decline in the future, since the Tax Cuts and Jobs Act of 2017 will result in fewer taxpayers itemizing deductions.

TABLE 8.2 COMPARISON OF SELECT FEDERAL TAX EXPENDITURES IN THE UNITED STATES, FISCAL YEAR 2017 ESTIMATES

Provision	Objective	Estimate (in billions)
Exclusion of employer contributions for health insurance	Health care	$220.55
Capital gains (except agriculture, timber, iron ore, and coal)	Investment	$95.87
Deductibility of mortgage interest on owner-occupied homes	Homeownership	$68.61
Defined benefit employer plans	Retirement	$66.76
Defined contribution employer plans	Retirement	$65.62
Deductibility of charitable contributions, other than education and health	Nonprofits	$47.63
Capital gains exclusion on home sales	Homeownership	$43.46
Self-employed plans	Retirement	$30.80
Individual Retirement Accounts	Retirement	$16.97
Deductibility of charitable contributions (education)	Nonprofits	$5.56
Deductibility of charitable contributions (health)	Nonprofits	$5.39
Exclusion of interest on bonds for private nonprofit educational facilities	Nonprofits	$2.76

GRANTS

Grants are revenue that is transferred to lower levels of government and nonprofits and do not have to be paid back. They are a mechanism for redistributing resources and take the form of either block grants or categorical grants. Matching grants represent a variation of categorical grants. Another way to classify grants is based on the presence or absence of conditions attached to the receipt of the funds. A grant with no limits or requirements on its use is referred to as "unconditional," while a grant with binding restrictions on its use is "conditional." Understanding the different types of grants and the circumstances under which they are preferred is essential for public service professionals. Grants are given for a reason. Most of the time, a grant is intended to stimulate a desired activity. The grant maker, therefore, wants to ensure that the funds are used for the intended purpose. Recipients rarely turn down an influx of funds, but bemoan the conditions and reporting requirements that accompany the support. The costs of grant compliance can materially erode the benefits of the grant funds for the recipient.

Block Grants

Block grants represent the granting of funds where the recipient has discretion over how to spend the money. The flexibility of a block grant results in the ability to use the funds for the recipient's most highly-valued purposes and devolves authority to the recipient. Block grants may include conditions that allow the grantee to exercise spending discretion but within a given set of activities. In the United States, the federal Community Development Block Grant Program (CDBG) has been active for more than four decades. The funding is awarded to states and local governments. Although the program allows discretion in the spending of funds, most of the dollars must target low- and middle-income populations and support a stated program objective.

Categorical Grants

Categorical grants, unlike block grants, focus on spending for more specific activities and programs. In this sense, categorical grants are conditional. In contrast with block grants, the categorical grant improves the targeting of grant funds, raises recipient accountability, and increases grantee control at the expense of recipient discretion. Given the different characteristics of block and categorical grants, there are ideological and partisan differences over the two grant-making approaches:

> Overall the conservative attitude is basically favorable toward the block grant on the issues of large versus small bureaucracies and centralized versus decentralized government, but favoring the categorical approach for purposes of fiscal accountability. Liberals seem more clearly disposed to favor categoricals because of their lesser trust in state and local governments and their greater desire to target federal funds on national objectives.[24]

Categorical grants come with a major concern for grant makers. Because the grant is required to be spent on a certain function, a recipient might simply reduce existing spending on that function by the grant amount. The categorical grant can crowd-out and replace current spending rather than creating additional spending. Recipients are undeniably better off, since they can now direct the displaced spending to other valued purposes. The grant maker, on the other hand, has given funds for a specific purpose but has achieved no change in spending levels on the desired activity. Conditions sometimes explicitly require grant funds to supplement rather than supplant current spending on the prescribed activity, but such verification is difficult.

Matching Grants

Matching grants use subsidies to lower relative prices of desirable activities. They tie the amount of funds to the level of spending by the recipient. The generosity of the match rate, usually expressed as a ratio, can be altered to incentivize the recipient to devote more internal resources to the activity. A match lowers the cost of the supported activity relative to other uses of the grant recipient's funds.

Colorado's Building Excellent Schools Today program (BEST) provides an example of a matching grant. It helps school districts build and renovate schools. The match percentage depends on the wealth of the school district seeking the funds. The wealthier the school district, the lower the state share of funds provided to the project and the higher the local matching rate.

In 2015, La Junta Schools received a grant of more than $1 million to renovate school kitchens and mechanical, electrical, and plumbing systems. With more than three-quarters of La Junta students qualifying for federal free and reduced lunch programs, the matching rate was 9:1, meaning the BEST program contributed $9 for every $1 provided by the school district. Also in 2015, the program awarded a grant to the wealthier Estes Park School District to replace a middle school roof. The district was required to contribute over $460,000 in matching funds to receive $189,000 in grant funds for a matching rate of 0.4:1. Estes Park contributed nearly 2.5 times the grant amount.[25] In other words, grant makers set matching rates to leverage limited funds, prioritize recipients based on need or strategic objectives, and ensure that the recipient is committed to the supported activity.

NON-PRICE ECONOMICS

This discussion has reviewed how the public sector responds to market failure through regulation and taxation and how it addresses redistribution with grants and publicly-funded programs. The focus on prices and markets remains dominant in economics, but the following discussion describes the increased consideration given to non-price policy interventions by governments.

Policy by Nudging

Behavioral economics reminds us that markets are composed of people who, for a host of reasons, do not behave as economic models predict. The notion that government can craft seemingly minor changes to public programs and help shift individuals' behavior is compelling. President Obama embraced the potential lessons from behavioral science with an executive order in September 2015 that directed executive departments and agencies to "identify policies, programs, and operations where applying behavioral science insights may yield substantial improvements in public welfare, program outcomes, and program cost effectiveness." The order also created a Social and Behavioral Sciences Team (SBST).[26]

Behavioral science teaches that "non-price levers" can be effective in changing individual behavior.[27] The SBST used pilot studies to make design changes in federal programs that have been credited with significantly improved outcomes. Examples include a switch to automatic enrollment for a military retirement plan that resulted in a 53 percent jump in the enrollment rate, sending outreach letters to family farmers that increased the number receiving microloans by more than 60 percent, and communicating the negative consequences of student loan defaults that led to a 41 percent increase in borrowers contacting a default-resolution representative.[28] Economist Richard Thaler, the coauthor of the popular and influential book *Nudge*, provides three general guidelines for the appropriate use of nudges as non-price levers for changing behavior:

- All nudging should be transparent and never misleading.
- It should be as easy as possible to opt-out of the nudge, preferably with as little as one mouse click.
- There should be good reason to believe that the behavior being encouraged will improve the welfare of those being nudged.[29]

Ask Me Why I Care: Selvi Stanislaus, Executive Officer, California Franchise Tax Board[30]

"I was born in Sri Lanka. My father was a tax accountant. He helped indigent people with their tax returns. I remember sitting on his lap when he was compiling and completing tax returns. . . . One of his key phrases when he looked out the door of our house at the line of people waiting for assistance was 'Without a vision, the people perish.' Remembering his words drew me to public service." – Selvi Stanislaus

The California Franchise Tax Board is the second largest tax department in the nation. Selvi Stanislaus oversees 6,000 employees and $60 billion in annual revenue. Ms. Stanislaus immigrated to California in 1986. She earned a law degree then joined the Board of  Equalization's legal staff in 1996. Ms. Stanislaus became the Acting Assistant Chief Counsel of the Tax and Fee Programs Division where she formulated legal policies affecting every tax and fee program administered by the Board of Equalization. Ms. Stanislaus has been instrumental in improving the Franchise Tax Board's transparency and customer service in addition to expanding its use of e-services. Watch her tell her story at https://www .unomaha.edu/college-of-public-affairs-and-community-service/community-engagement/pss-selvi-stanislaus.php.

SUMMARY

The public sector has no shortage of good works to tackle with its limited resources. Sesame Street's evolution highlights the increasing role of partnerships between the government, nonprofit, and private sectors to provide public-benefiting goods and services. Although there are many instances where government intervention in the market is justifiable and obvious, there are many where collaboration with the private sector, or reliance on the private sector, are possible and preferable.

The primary economic justifications for government intervention are market failure and the desire for redistribution. The forms of intervention are through altering prices or regulating quantities of targeted activities. Alternately, governments raise funds to directly or indirectly deliver programs. They do so in a manner intended to maximize equity and fairness, while minimizing unintended consequences, such as deleterious changes in behavior due to taxes and fees.

KEY TERMS

Adverse selection – consequence of information asymmetry, in which the more-informed party knowingly makes a higher-cost decision for the other party (for example, when a risky and aggressive driver purchases full auto insurance coverage on a rental car).

Block grant – grant funding that gives the recipient general discretion over how to spend the money.

Categorical grant – grant funding that is conditional in that it is given to fund specific activities and programs.

Efficiency – related to using the fewest resources possible to achieve a desired end.

Externalities – consequences resulting from an activity (positive or negative) that are not accounted for in the market price of what is produced by that activity.

Fiscal federalism – relating to the notion that different levels of government are better suited to fund and deliver certain types of services.

Fiscal policy – policy used by governments to influence the economy through changes in government revenue and expenditure.

Horizontal equity – the notion that similarly-situated parties should be treated similarly even when the parties make different economic choices.

Information asymmetry – refers to when one party has more complete information about a market transaction than the other party involved in the transaction.

Market failure – this occurs in the free market when there is a failure of the pricing system to promote desired outcomes and to maximize social well-being. Primary sources of market failure include public goods, externalities, natural monopolies, and information asymmetry.

Matching grant – grant funding that is tied to the level of spending, or resources raised, by the recipient.

Monetary policy – policy enacted by a country's central bank that alters the availability of money through the banking system.

Moral hazard – refers to the risky behavior that is incentivized by being protected from the full cost of the consequences of that behavior (for example, with insurance).

Natural monopoly – a monopoly that occurs in industries in which high initial infrastructure investment and scale economies make competition wasteful. In a natural monopoly, a single firm is the most efficient outcome (for example, public utilities).

Public goods – nonrival goods and services from which no member of society can be excluded. They are typically provided by the public and nonprofit sectors.

Redistribution – the process of dividing resources in a different way, as with the redistribution of wealth with a progressive tax system.

Tax expenditure – taxes that are foregone, or not collected, due to intentional policy decisions.

Vertical equity – the notion that parties with greater levels of resources should shoulder a higher tax burden than those with lesser resources.

DISCUSSION QUESTIONS

1. Why is it important for public service professionals to understand the economic justifications for government intervention in the free market?
2. Explain the challenges to improving both the equity and efficiency of the economy through government intervention.
3. From a societal perspective, are the benefits received from higher education primarily private? How would you justify additional public funding for higher education to decision makers?
4. What is an example, not mentioned in the chapter, where the public sector intervenes to address a potentially harmful information asymmetry?

EXERCISES

1. Investigate the entity responsible for regulating public utilities in your state. How are the responsible individuals selected? What services do they oversee?
2. Access the most recent federal budget through the White House or Office of Management and Budget websites. Examine the tax expenditures listed and described in the *Analytical Perspectives* section. Select a tax expenditure of personal interest and explain the economic justification for the deviation from the tax code.

BUILD YOUR SKILLS

Cost-benefit analysis is a useful tool for determining whether to move forward with a project. Here is an illustration of an analysis and steps in the process.

SKILLBOX: HOW TO COMPARE COSTS AND BENEFITS

Comparing costs and benefits in public service is challenging because the anticipated outcomes are rarely denominated in monetary terms and there is uncertainty when new programs are implemented. Nevertheless, the logic of cost-benefit analysis provides a way to value non-monetary costs and benefits so they can be incorporated in decision-making alongside more obvious economic outcomes. The following provides an example of cost-benefit analysis and then each step is described in greater detail.

Example: Comparing Higher Education Policy Interventions

The following table[1] provides an example of how an evaluation of costs and benefits can be used. The Washington State Institute for Public Policy ("the Institute") conducts cost-benefit analysis for policies of interest to the state's legislature. The assumption of cost-benefit analysis is that a program is economically justified when benefits exceed costs. In this example, the Institute examined seven programs used to improve post-secondary educational outcomes. The Institute communicates the ratio of estimated benefits to costs in the column "Benefit to cost ratio." This represents the return on each dollar spent on a program and provides an estimate of program effectiveness. For example, college advising provided by counselors is estimated to return $74.56 of value for each one dollar that is spent. The rows of information in the table educate policy makers about the relative net benefits of different programs and the probability that, in practice, benefits will be larger than costs.

HIGHER EDUCATION PROGRAM BENEFIT-COST ANALYSIS

Program Name	Total Benefits	Taxpayer Benefits	Nontax-payer Benefits	Costs	Benefits Minus Costs (Net Present Value)	Benefit to Cost Ratio	Chance Benefits will Exceed Costs
College advising provided by counselors (for high school students)	$24,510	$5,623	$18,888	($329)	$24,182	$74.56	100%
Dual enrollment (for high school students)	$20,431	$6,175	$14,256	($1,509)	$18,922	$13.54	86%
Summer outreach counseling (for high school graduates)	$18,802	$4,381	$14,421	($96)	$18,706	$195.39	90%
Performance-based scholarships (for high school students)	$8,457	$1,928	$6,529	($1,507)	$6,950	$5.61	74%
Text message reminders (for high school graduates)	$978	$49	$929	($7)	$971	$135.71	53%
College advising provided by peer mentors (for high school students)	$1,617	($348)	$1,965	($784)	$833	$2.06	50%
Opening Doors advising in community college	($1,377)	$303	($1,680)	($811)	($2,188)	($1.70)	22%

An example of how information in the table is useful is demonstrated by summer outreach counseling.[2] A major policy concern in higher education is referred to as "summer melt." Summer melt represents high school graduates who fail to enroll in a higher education institution in the subsequent fall semester despite stated intentions of doing so at the time of graduation. A promising policy intervention is for counselors to "provide support and outreach on financial aid tasks, informational barriers, and social or emotional challenges related to the college transition" during the summer after high school graduation through outreach counseling.[3]

As shown in the Costs column, summer outreach counseling is fairly inexpensive, at $96 per participating student, based on the direct costs of counselor and peer mentor time and communication materials. These cash costs are easy to tabulate, while an array of other costs and benefits are more complex. For example, the benefits of reducing summer melt by using summer outreach counseling will not be felt until the student graduates with a college degree and becomes employed. Then benefits, in the form of higher earnings, will aid the state of

Washington's tax coffers as well as civil society, because it is known that more educated populations have lower crime rates, greater productivity, and reduced dependence on public programs. But these positive consequences take years to materialize and are difficult to quantify.

The summer melt example illustrates that simply looking at the cash costs associated with a program misrepresents the actual costs and benefits to society. At the same time, accurately estimating costs and benefits involves assumptions that are little more than educated guesses. Thus, successful use of cost-benefit analysis acknowledges both its potential and its limitations. The following sections outline the steps of cost-benefit analysis.

Basic Steps of Cost-Benefit Analysis

1) Define the project or policy being considered and understand the existing conditions expected to persist without its implementation. The current environment is referred to as the status quo.

2) Determine the study area, based largely on geography or targeted population that will be served by the program. For example, a city considering a new open space initiative might limit the costs and benefits considered to those within the city limits, even though the effort will impact neighboring jurisdictions. In other words, the focus on benefits and costs is targeted based on the perspective of the group conducting the analysis. Changing the relevant physical area or included parties can dramatically alter the findings of cost-benefit analysis.

3) Create a comprehensive list of associated costs and benefits. This is similar to a pro and con list related to the project.

Begin with the cash or directly attributable costs of the project or policy. These are the tangible upfront and recurring costs of implementation.

Then quantify the intangible costs and benefits in monetary terms. Use evidence from existing evaluations of similar programs to inform the estimates. Where evidence is unavailable, conservative estimates should be used for valuing benefits.

4) Create a schedule of the identified costs and benefits. The timing of the costs and benefits matters, since future costs and benefits are valued less than those in the current time period. Why? Because there is an opportunity cost

associated with dedicating resources for the project when they could be invested elsewhere and earn a positive return. All of the future costs and benefits are discounted to the present value based on a selected discount rate.

The importance of discounting future costs and benefits is demonstrated by President Jimmy Carter's contentious effort to revisit cost-benefit analyses for federal water projects. In 1977, President Carter recommended the cancellation of eighteen water projects—primarily dams—and modification of five others, asserting that a more realistic interest rate should be used in calculating the costs and benefits of projects.[4] Specifically, already authorized projects had been assessed using a low discount rate of 3.25 percent, which was well below the then-current rate of 6.37 percent used in federal cost-benefit analysis. At the time, some in the Carter administration even considered 10 percent to be a more realistic rate. President Carter argued that, "even though we are building the projects today, we are pretending that the cost of capital is still the same as it was many years ago."[5]

Dams are expensive to build. The high up-front construction costs are offset by many decades of benefits in the form of electricity generated by hydropower, flood control, water storage and delivery for farming and residential use, lake and river recreation created and regulated by the dam, and, in some cases, navigation. There are also serious environmental and social costs to dams, but those were not necessarily prioritized in the past.

A fictional example demonstrates the use of discounting and present values in cost-benefit analysis. The initial cost of construction for a proposed dam is $200 million, with annual operating costs of $10 million thereafter for fifty years. The electricity generated by the dam is sold for $10 million annually. Flood control benefits are estimated at $3 million each year in avoided property damage. Water storage creates economic benefits of $5 million per year, while the reservoir created by the dam provides $2 million in recreational benefits annually.

Ignoring the timing of the costs and benefits allows a simple comparison of the summed costs and benefits to determine whether the project is economically viable. Total benefits of $20 million per year for fifty years totals $1 billion. Costs total only $700 million over the fifty-year life of the dam for a net benefit of $300 million. Recognizing that a dollar in the future is not the same as a dollar today alters the cost-benefit calculus. The discount rate is used to bring the future costs and benefits into present value terms. The process is called discounting and determining the discount rate is critical.

The next table presents the discounted costs and benefits of the proposed dam project based on the range of rates used by the Carter administration. The present value of the costs and benefits are significantly lower than the original values once the time value of money is reflected.

EXAMPLE COST-BENEFIT ANALYSIS WITH VARIOUS DISCOUNT RATES

	Year(s)	Cost or Benefit (millions, $)	Present Value (PV) of Cost or Benefit (millions, $) by Discount Rate		
			3.25%	6.37%	10.0%
Construction costs	0	200	(200.00)	(200.00)	(200.00)
Operating costs	1–50	10	(245.52)	(149.83)	(99.15)
Total Costs in PV			(445.52)	(349.83)	(299.15)
Electricity generated	1–50	10	245.52	149.83	99.15
Flood control	1–50	3	73.66	44.95	29.74
Water storage	1–50	5	122.76	74.91	49.57
Recreation	1–50	2	49.10	29.97	19.83
Total Benefits in PV			491.04	299.65	198.30
Benefits less Costs (PV)			45.52	(50.17)	(100.85)

Present value (PV) is calculated by using the following formula:
$$PV = FV / (1+i)^n$$
where FV represents the future value (such as the $3 million benefit from flood control), i is the discount rate (3.25 percent), and n is the number of periods in the future the FV is to accrue (10 years, for example). The PV of the $3 million flood control benefit to be received 10 years in the future at a discount rate of 3.25 percent is therefore:
$$PV = \$3 \text{ million} / (1+0.0325)^{10} = \$2.18 \text{ million}.$$
In practice, spreadsheets provide easy-to-use functions for finding present values of one-time future values and recurring future values, which are referred to as annuities. In Excel, the PV function is used.

To select the discount rate, there are informal guidelines. For private entities, the discount rate is often set to the expected rate of return that can be achieved through other investments or activities. Nonprofit organizations frequently use their cost of borrowing as a proxy for the discount rate. Governments, similarly, look to borrowing costs for setting the discount rate used in cost-benefit analysis.

5) Subtract the present value of the estimated costs from the present value of the estimated benefits. A positive net present value suggests the project or policy is economically viable, whereas a negative value means that the rate of return for the investment is lower than the discount rate (see the bottom row of the previous table).

In the dam example, the economic viability depends on the selected discount rate. At 3.25 percent, the net benefits of the dam in present value terms are positive at more than $45 million because the long-term benefits are discounted less. The net benefits turn negative by nearly $50 and $100 million as the discount rate rises to 6.37 percent and 10 percent, respectively.

6) Stress test the finding by conducting a sensitivity analysis. Use a higher and lower discount rate to determine whether the cost-benefit analysis is consistent with various assumptions. Also, alter the magnitude of any especially subjective costs or benefits, usually benefits, to observe how the results change.

7) Craft a recommendation on moving forward with the project or policy by combining the cost-benefit finding with any qualitative or distributional factors absent from the analysis.

Valuing Hard-to-Value Costs and Benefits

Often, the costs and benefits of public projects are not naturally valued in monetary terms. A number of techniques have been advanced to address this challenge. A frequent benefit, particularly for transportation projects, is saved time for the public. The value of the saved time can be estimated based on a community's average wage rate. Projects focused on improving safety are even forced to assign values to avoided injuries and deaths using similar approaches.

Amenities, like neighborhood parks or better schools, or disamenities, such as a garbage dump or factory, are sometimes valued by examining the response of nearby property values. Using contingent valuation, or willingness-to-pay method, cost-benefit analysis may resort to surveys to help value nonmonetary costs and benefits.

Being a Critical Consumer of Cost-Benefit Analysis

Cost-benefit analysis rests on a variety of assumptions. Consumers of cost-benefit analysis need to be critical and question assumptions that may bias the finding in favor of, or against, a project or policy. Main concerns include incorrectly counting benefits, double-counting benefits, and failing to recognize that cost-benefit analysis does not consider whether costs and benefits are distributed in socially-desirable ways.

Improper counting of benefits happens when a government attempts to claim, for example, that the employment associated with a project is a benefit rather than just a cost. Alternately, the accurate counting of benefits requires that any shift in positive activity, such as jobs or property values, does not come at the expense of another area of the jurisdiction.[6]

Double-counting of benefits occurs when a project generates a benefit that manifests in multiple ways. For example, transit-oriented development expands foot traffic for local retail stores and leads to greater sales. The desirability of the location for retail activity is simultaneously reflected in higher property values for store owners. The benefit should not be counted both ways, as higher retail sales and as increased property values.[7]

Finally, the cost-benefit analysis approach is based on the net change in social welfare, but how that welfare is distributed is not weighed. In other words, a project with positive net benefits does not guarantee social or political desirability if the gains accrue to, for example, a small group of people or organizations.

Hands-On Activities

1. Find an example online of a completed cost-benefit analysis. Review the report and write a professional memo to the leadership of the organization for whom the analysis was conducted. Be critical and address the following dimensions of the analysis:
   - Does the analysis make clear the geographic area or population for whom benefits and costs are being considered?
   - What costs and benefits are most challenging to value in dollar terms and are the estimates believable?
   - Are there costs and benefits that were overlooked in the analysis?
   - What discount rate was applied, and how was it justified, to future costs and benefits?

- Did the authors perform sensitivity analyses to see how changes in assumptions alter the findings?
- Was there any mention of distributional concerns over the program or policy?
- Do the findings convincingly align with the final recommendation about the project or policy?

2. Pick a project or policy, real or hypothetical, and outline the associated costs and benefits. Provide ideas for how to measure the costs and benefits. Explain whether cost-benefit analysis appears worthwhile for assessing the project or policy. If not, why not?

Notes

1. Washington State Institute for Public Policy (WSIPP), "Benefit-Cost Results: Higher Education," last modified May, 2017, http://wsipp.wa.gov/Benefit-Cost?topicId=11.

2. WSIPP, Benefit-Cost Results: Summer Outreach Counseling (for High School Graduates), last modified May, 2017, http://wsipp.wa.gov/BenefitCost/Program Pdf/692/Summer-outreach-counseling-for-high-school-graduates.

3. Ibid.

4. Jimmy Carter, "Water Resource Projects— Statement Announcing Administration Decisions, April 18, 1977," in The American Presidency Project, by John T. Woolley and Gerhard Peters, http://www.presidency.ucsb.edu/ws/?pid=7364.

5. Margot Hornblower, "Carter Tries to Stem Hill Flow of Largess into River Projects," *Washington Post* (December 19, 1977).

6. Jonathan Gruber. 2012. *Public Finance and Public Policy*, 4th ed. (New York: Worth Publishers).

7. Ibid.

For Additional Information

Boardman, Anthony, David Greenberg, Aidan Vining, David Weimer. 2010. *Cost-Benefit Analysis*, 4th ed. (Upper Saddle River, NJ: Pearson).

The Pew-MacArthur Results First Initiative, States' Use of Cost-Benefit Analysis: *Improving Results for Taxpayers* (July, 2013), http://www.pewtrusts.org/~/media/legacy/uploadedfiles/pcs_assets/2013/pewresultsfirst50statereportpdf.pdf.

The Washington State Institute for Public Policy is a recognized leader in conducting cost-benefit analysis for a wide range of policy areas. The analyses and a detailed description of the methodology can be found on their website at: http://wsipp.wa.gov/.

NOTES

1. Pew Research Center, "Beyond Distrust: How Americans View Their Government" (November, 2015), http://www.people-press.org/2015/11/23/beyond-distrust-how-americans-view-their-government/.

2. Commission on Presidential Debates, "October 3, 2012 Debate Transcript" (debate, Denver, Colorado, October 3, 2012), http://debates.org/index.php?page=october-3-2012-debate-transcript.

3. Public Broadcasting Service, "PBS Statement Regarding October 3 Presidential Debate" (October 4, 2012), http://www.pbs.org/about/blogs/news/pbs-statement-regarding-october-3-presidential-debate/.

4. Corporation for Public Broadcasting, "Proposed FY 2014 Operating Budget" (September 11, 2013), http://www.cpb.org/files/aboutcpb/financials/budget/FY2014-Operating-Budget.pdf.

5. Dennis R. Young and John Casey, "Supplementary, Complementary, or Adversarial?: Nonprofit-Government Relations," in *Nonprofits and Government: Collaboration and Conflict*, ed. Elizabeth T. Boris and C. Eugene Steuerle (Washington, DC: Urban Institute Press, 2016), 37–70.

6. Beverly S. Bunch, "Changes in the Usage of Enterprise Funds by Large City Governments," *Public Budgeting and Finance* 20, no. 2 (2000): 15–29.

7. United States Government Accountability Office, *Superfund: Trends in Federal Funding and Cleanup of EPA's Nonfederal National Priorities List Sites*, GAO-15-812 (September, 2015).

8. Evan Osnos, "How Your Cashmere Pollutes the Air," *Chicago Tribune* (December 24, 2006), http://articles.latimes.com/2006/dec/24/news/adfg-cashmere24.

9. *Tampa Bay Times* and Center for Investigative Reporting, "America's Worst Charities" (December, 2014) http://www.tampabay.com/americas-worst-charities/.

10. David H. Autor, "Skills, Education, and the Rise of Earnings Inequality Among the 'Other 99 Percent'," *Science* 344, no. 6186 (2014): 843–851.

11. "How Inequality Affects Growth," *The Economist* (June 15, 2015), http://www.economist.com/blogs/economist-explains/2015/06/economist-explains-11.

12. Arthur M. Okun, *Equality and Efficiency: The Big Tradeoff* (Washington, DC: Brookings Institution, 1975).

13. For a discussion of these "leaks" with regard to welfare programs, see Jonathan Gruber, *Public Finance and Public Policy*, 4th ed. (New York: Worth Publishers, 2013).

14. The Federal Reserve provides a friendly overview of their operations in: Federal Reserve Bank of St. Louis, "In Plain English: Making Sense of the Federal Reserve" (n.d.), https://www.stlouisfed.org/~/media/Images/Education/In%20Plain%20English/PDFs/In_Plain_English.pdf.

15. "WPA Pays Up and Quits," *New York Times* (July 1, 1943), 9, http://graphics8.nytimes.com/packages/pdf/topics/WPA/43_07_01.pdf?mcubz=0.

16. Charles M. Tiebout, "A Pure Theory of Local Expenditures," *Journal of Political Economy* 64, no. 5 (1956): 416–424.

17. Gruber, *Public Finance*.

18. City of Boulder, "CAP at a Glance: Boulder's Climate Action Plan (CAP)" (n.d.), https://www-static.bouldercolorado.gov/docs/CAP_document_FINAL-1-201603211302.pdf?_ga=1.156663032.295232681.1483480597.

19. Legislative Analyst's Office, "Understanding California's Property Taxes" (November 29, 2012), http://www.lao.ca.gov/reports/2012/tax/property-tax-primer-112912.aspx.

20. John Mikesell, *Fiscal Administration*, 9th ed. (Boston, MA: Cengage Learning, 2014).

21. Agis Salpukas, "Falling Tax Would Lift All Yachts," *New York Times* (February 7, 1992).

22. Harvard Management Company, "Annual Endowment Report" (September, 2016), http://www.hmc.harvard.edu/docs/Final_Annual_Report_2016.pdf.

23. Advisory Commission on Intergovernmental Relations, "Categorical Grants: Their Role and Design" (1978), U.S. Government Printing Office, Washington, DC, 66.

24. Office of Management and Budget, "Analytical Perspectives, Budget of the United States Government, Fiscal Year 2017" (2016), https://obamawhitehouse.archives.gov/sites/default/files/omb/budget/fy2017/assets/spec.pdf.

25. Colorado Department of Education, "Building Excellent Schools Today (BEST) Annual Report," by Scott Newell, Division of Capital Construction (February, 2016), https://www.cde.state.co.us/cdefinance/ccabestlegislativereportfy14-15.

26. Executive Order 13707 of September 15, 2015, Using Behavioral Science Insights to

Better Serve the American People, Code of Federal Regulations, FR Doc. 2015-23630: 56365-56367, https://www.federalregister.gov/documents/2015/09/18/2015-23630/using-behavioral-science-insights-to-better-serve-the-american-people.

27. Jeffrey R. Kling, William J. Congdon, and Sendhil Mullainathan, *Policy and Choice: Public Finance Through the Lens of Behavioral Economics* (Washington, DC: Brookings Institution, 2011).

28. Press Secretary Josh Earnest, "Fact Sheet: New Progress on Using Behavioral Science Insights to Better Serve the American People," The White House Office of the Press Secretary, September 15, 2016, https://obamawhitehouse.archives.gov/the-press-office/2016/09/15/fact-sheet-new-progress-using-behavioral-science-insights-better-serve.

29. Richard H. Thaler, "The Power of Nudges, for Good and Bad," *New York Times* (October 31, 2015), http://www.nytimes.com/2015/11/01/upshot/the-power-of-nudges-for-good-and-bad.html?_r=0; and for a thorough consideration of behavioral science and public finance, see Jeffrey R. Kling, William J. Congdon, and Sendhil Mullainathan, *Policy and Choice: Public Finance Through the Lens of Behavioral Economics,* (Washington, DC: Brookings Institution, 2011).

30. *Ask Me Why I Care: Public Service Stories*, video, directed by Mary R. Hamilton and Rita Paskowitz (Omaha, Nebraska: College of Public Affairs and Community Service), accessed May 26, 2017 at https://www.unomaha.edu/college-of-public-affairs-and-community-service/community-engagement/pss-selvi-stanislaus.php.

ADDITIONAL RESOURCES

Gruber, Jonathan. 2013. *Public Finance and Public Policy,* 4th ed. New York: Worth Publishers. (This is one of the standard texts used in MPA and MPP programs to provide a deeper introduction to the microeconomics and finance of public policy.)

Mikesell, John. 2014. *Fiscal Administration*. Boston, MA: Cengage Learning.

Chapter 9 Timeline: Public Financial Management[1]

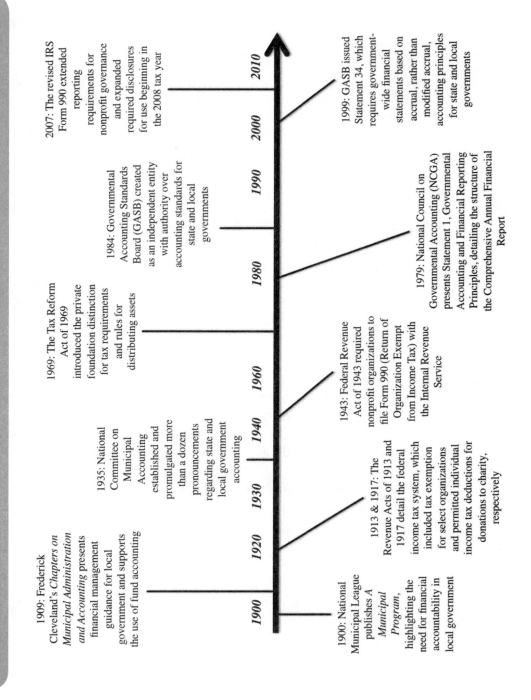

1900: National Municipal League publishes *A Municipal Program*, highlighting the need for financial accountability in local government

1909: Frederick Cleveland's *Chapters on Municipal Administration and Accounting* presents financial management guidance for local government and supports the use of fund accounting

1913 & 1917: The Revenue Acts of 1913 and 1917 detail the federal income tax system, which included tax exemption for select organizations and permitted individual income tax deductions for donations to charity, respectively

1935: National Committee on Municipal Accounting established and promulgated more than a dozen pronouncements regarding state and local government accounting

1943: Federal Revenue Act of 1943 required nonprofit organizations to file Form 990 (Return of Organization Exempt from Income Tax) with the Internal Revenue Service

1969: The Tax Reform Act of 1969 introduced the private foundation distinction for tax requirements and rules for distributing assets

1979: National Council on Governmental Accounting (NCGA) presents Statement 1, Governmental Accounting and Financial Reporting Principles, detailing the structure of the Comprehensive Annual Financial Report

1984: Governmental Accounting Standards Board (GASB) created as an independent entity with authority over accounting standards for state and local governments

1999: GASB issued Statement 34, which requires government-wide financial statements based on accrual, rather than modified accrual, accounting principles for state and local governments

2007: The revised IRS Form 990 extended reporting requirements for nonprofit governance and expanded required disclosures for use beginning in the 2008 tax year

1900 1920 1930 1940 1960 1980 1990 2000 2010

PUBLIC FINANCIAL MANAGEMENT

WHAT YOU WILL LEARN

Diversity of nonprofit organizations

Fund-raising and philanthropy

Addressing cash needs

Financial reporting and accounting

Understanding financial statements

Public sector retirement plans

Skillbox: How to calculate inflation adjustment

Budgeting translates community and organizational priorities into a financial plan for future activities. The budget, as a planning document, is inherently prospective and forward-looking. Alternately, public finance and economics help provide the overall framework for establishing an organization's scope of activities and determining how to raise needed revenue. Financial management, the focus of this chapter, broadly encompasses the day-to-day financial tasks, decisions, and operations of public service organizations, both government and nonprofit. While budgeting and public finance are closely tied to financial management, financial management represents a set of ongoing responsibilities to maintain the viability of an organization.

This chapter weaves together the critical financial management functions, including philanthropy and fund-raising, cash management, financial accounting, financial reporting, use of financial statements, and an overview of retirement plans. While public service missions may overlap between government and nonprofits, their financial management has meaningful differences.

The prominence of philanthropy and fund-raising in supporting many nonprofits is different from government's traditional dependence on taxes as a source of revenue. Donations and grant funds often are accompanied by restrictions on the use of funds, and this requires special treatment by managers. Day-to-day financial management, as well as long-term planning, is dominated by the need for cash to support operations and investment, so borrowing and cash management activities are detailed.

Financial accounting and reporting represent the retrospective counterpart to budgeting, but are no less important for preserving accountability to the public and stakeholders. The variety of financial reports for government and nonprofit organizations are reviewed with a focus on knowing where to find needed information. Financial reports provide managers and external parties a window into an organization. The ability to use financial information to assess the fiscal health of a government or nonprofit agency is essential whether acting as a citizen, grant-maker, potential collaborator, or jobseeker.

Retirement plans for employees are a salient policy and management concern in the public sector. Governments struggle to maintain well-funded pension plans and nonprofits know that retirement plans are an important component to attracting high quality employees. Financial management is public management, since it determines the credibility and effectiveness of government and nonprofit organizations. The following case highlights the pervasive role of financial management, while detailing the rapidly changing fortunes of a nonprofit organization in response to fund-raising.

TOO MUCH OF A GOOD THING? ALS AND THE ICE BUCKET CHALLENGE

In summer 2014, fund-raising went viral with the Amyotrophic Lateral Sclerosis (ALS) Ice Bucket Challenge in which people poured ice water over themselves to raise money for the ALS Association. The ALS Association is a national nonprofit created in 1985 with a mission "to discover treatments and a cure for ALS, and to serve, advocate for, and empower people affected by ALS to live their lives to the fullest." ALS is more commonly known as Lou Gehrig's disease, named after the New York Yankees' baseball great who was afflicted by the progressive neurodegenerative disease.

The ALS Ice Bucket Challenge received unrivaled attention as millions of individuals took the Challenge. It consisted of people having buckets of ice water poured on themselves, recording and posting the act online, and then donating to ALS-related organizations. How big a deal was the Ice Bucket Challenge? Well, celebrity after celebrity participated, ranging from ex-presidents to movie stars and professional athletes. Over 17 million videos appeared on Facebook and they were viewed in excess of 10 billion times. Google searches for the term "ALS" in 2014 exceeded the number of similar searches during the prior ten years combined.

The Challenge provided an unexpected financial windfall to the ALS Association, along with dramatically increased awareness of the disease. The publicity and exposure is difficult to value, but one executive at the ALS Association remarked that the Challenge, "really changed the face of A.L.S. forever."[2] The financial statements of the ALS Association provide a glimpse into the impact of the Challenge. Annual contributions jumped more than 1,300 percent from $8.41 million in fiscal year 2014 to $121.36 million in fiscal year 2015 (see Figure 9.1 for details). The net assets of the ALS Association, which represent the organization's wealth, similarly swelled due to the influx of contributions and the inability to immediately deploy the new funds in support of the mission. Although contributions typically represented just over a third of the ALS Association's annual support and revenue, they provided nearly 90 percent during the year of the Challenge.

FIGURE 9.1 ALS ASSOCIATION FINANCIAL TRENDS, FISCAL YEARS 2012–2016[3]

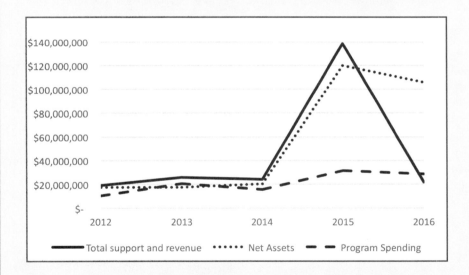

The sensational nature of the Ice Bucket Challenge attracted unexpected criticism. Observers bemoaned the very nature of the fund-raiser. Labeled by some as "slacktivism," the Ice Bucket Challenge allowed individuals to benefit from the warm glow of altruistic behavior without actually engaging the cause in more meaningful ways. Concerns surfaced that the Challenge reduced the intentionality of giving and fears arose that it would cannibalize charitable giving to other nonprofits with, possibly, greater or more dire needs. Some critics even complained that the Challenge wasted water. Possibly more salient was the belief that a massive influx of donations might overwhelm a relatively small nonprofit organization. Would the ALS Association have the capacity to effectively manage the newfound resources and act in accord with donor expectations (even if those expectations were not explicit due to the nature of the fund-raiser)?

In hindsight, criticism of the Ice Bucket Challenge and concerns about organizational capacity at the ALS Association appear to have been overblown. Author James Surowiecki embraced the "slacktivist" nature of the Challenge arguing that, "it took tools—the selfie, the hashtag, the like button—that have typically been used for private amusement or corporate profit and turned them to the public good."[4] Journalist Nicholas Kristof describes the Ice Bucket Challenge's "armchair activism as a gateway drug" that "exposes people to causes and sometimes gets them hooked."[5] Charitable giving actually increased nationally in 2014, which is preliminary evidence that the Challenge did not harm other nonprofits' revenues.

At the organization level, the ALS Association scrambled to react to the fund-raising success by using temporary staff and volunteers to help full-time employees respond to calls and process donations.[6] Program spending by the ALS Association doubled, totaling more than $31 million in the 2015 fiscal year, as the Challenge contributions flowed into the organization. Program spending continued at that elevated level the year after the challenge (see program spending in Figure 9.1). The ALS Association produced a series of infographics, maintains a blog, and issues frequent press releases to communicate to donors the impact and planned uses of the funds generated by the Challenge (see Figure 9.2 for an example). Indeed, the organization's financial statements suggest substantially more resources are flowing to research grants than prior to the Challenge. Specifically, an average of $15.4 million has been spent on research grants annually since the Challenge compared to $6.9 million in the two preceding years. The additional resources for research come from the organization's net assets, comprised largely of contributions from the Challenge.

FIGURE 9.2: ALS ASSOCIATION INFOGRAPHIC ON ICE BUCKET CHALLENGE SUPPORT[7]

The Ice Bucket Challenge dollars have already contributed to meaningful progress in the fight against ALS. A scientist at Johns Hopkins University believes the funds from the Challenge "certainly facilitated" a breakthrough in their ALS-related research.[8] The ALS Association cites other outcomes of the Challenge, including the discovery of at least one gene related to ALS, funding for over 150 research projects, and providing community-based services to 15,000 individuals per year.[9]

Questions to Ponder

1. What approaches work best for managing finances when using nontraditional fund-raising techniques (or new revenue sources) for which there is no track record?
2. Are innovative fund-raising efforts like the Ice Bucket Challenge problematic?
3. Is it correct to think of fund-raising, particularly among charitable nonprofits, as a zero-sum game? In other words, do donors really weigh the merits of multiple organizations before contributing?

The Ice Bucket Challenge experience highlights a number of prominent financial management concepts and lessons. First, revenues from different sources are often difficult to predict. In the case of the ALS Association, the unexpected level of revenue from contributions was favorable, but organizations, both public and nonprofit, must be prepared to cope with revenue fluctuations in either direction.

Second, one-time financial events should be treated differently than those that are expected to continue. The Board of the ALS Association had to determine how and when to use the contributed funds. The organization's mission and the short life span of those afflicted with the disease deterred the organization from thinking of the fund-raising windfall as a long-term savings account. The ALS Association's chief chapter relations and development officer noted "this is a disease that requires urgency."[10] Although the organization has elevated spending, such increases can be spread out over time to guarantee that investments remain worthwhile and within the capacity of the organization to monitor.

Third, public sector organizations are frequently restricted in how funds can be used based on the law or donor requirements. The spontaneous nature of the Ice Bucket Challenge donations meant that the majority of the contributed funds are unrestricted. The flexibility in using such funds is a boon for public sector organizations.

Financial management is a core function. As the ALS Association illustrates, providing adequate financial transparency to stakeholders, proper stewardship of resources, addressing operational uncertainty, and connecting spending to mission-based outcomes are ongoing activities of public service. The following section highlights the variety of organization types among nonprofits, particularly those focused on charitable nonprofit activities and private foundations.

NONPROFIT ORGANIZATIONS

The nonprofit designation masks a surprising amount of diversity within the sector. Most generally, nonprofits are organizations "allowed to make a profit but that are prohibited from distributing their profits or earnings to those in control of the organizations."[11] Legally, there are nearly thirty different classifications of nonprofit organizations that are referred to by the relevant section of the federal tax code (26 U.S. Code § 501). The different classifications cover organizations as diverse as Fraternal Societies, 501(c)(8) and Cemetery Corporations, 501(c)(13), but most people envision a 501(c)(3) organization when they refer to nonprofits. As described in the code itself:

> (3) Corporations, and any community chest, fund, or foundation, organized and operated exclusively for religious, charitable, scientific, testing for public safety, literary, or educational purposes, or to foster national or international amateur sports competition (but only if no part of its activities involve the provision of athletic facilities or equipment), or for the prevention of cruelty to children or animals, no part of the net earnings of which inures to the benefit of any private shareholder or individual, no substantial part of the activities of which is carrying on propaganda, or otherwise attempting, to influence legislation (except as otherwise provided in subsection (h)), and which does not participate in, or intervene in (including the publishing or distributing of statements), any political campaign on behalf of (or in opposition to) any candidate for public office.[12]

There is even a critical distinction made between organizations with the 501(c)(3) classification. Private charities are more common and represent organizations that typically receive donations. Alternately, a 501(c)(3) organization can be either an operating or nonoperating private foundation. Private foundations are characterized by financial support from a "small group of donors, usually members of the same family (a family foundation) or a corporation (a corporate foundation)," although community foundations are supported by a broader public.[13] Whether a foundation is an operating or nonoperating private foundation is determined by the recipients of the foundation's grant-making. If the grants are made to external organizations, then the foundation is nonoperating, whereas an operating foundation directs support to internal charitable programs.

Regardless of the specific classification, nonprofit financial management revolves around supporting the organization's mission. Despite the sector's label, nonprofit organizations strive to do more than simply break even each year. The prominence of financial management is apparent in the saying that "finance sustains mission"[14] and in the prominent role of the nonprofit board of directors, the organization's governing body, in monitoring finances. Finance and audit committees, whether combined or separate, are comprised of a subset of board members to oversee financial management alongside staff and they act with a "fiduciary duty to the public."[15]

Fund-raising and Philanthropy

A distinctive financial feature of the nonprofit sector is the prevalence of fund-raising as a source of support. Fund-raising is the term broadly used to capture the solicitation of external funds from private contributions. Although less important to the sector than many suspect, charitable giving represented more than 13 percent of revenues for public charities in 2013.[16] For some nonprofits, voluntary support from the public is the primary source of funding. This is particularly true for those organizations referred to as voluntary health and welfare organizations (VHWOs), whose missions support health, welfare, or social services functions. Donations to nonprofits take a number of forms. Individual contributions are most prominent providing over two-thirds of giving, followed by support from foundations (16 percent), bequests (9 percent), and corporations (5 percent).[17]

In addition to monetary contributions, nonprofits benefit from in-kind donations of time and materials. Individuals who donate their time are called volunteers and reduce the need for the nonprofit to expand paid personnel. Along with the benefits of volunteers come the demands of managing and training the individuals, so volunteers are not without cost.[18] For example, Habitat for Humanity International, which provides home construction and repair services for those in need, benefited from more than 1.8 million volunteers, received over $180 million in contributions, and $37 million of in-kind donations to support their work during 2016.[19] Given the importance of donations, the following section describes an effort to formalize a set of best practices for donors.

SUPPORTING STEWARDSHIP: ADOPTING A "DONOR BILL OF RIGHTS"

Donors, and the public via the tax code, contribute to charitable organizations with certain expectations about the use of donated resources. For charitable organizations to recognize the seriousness of this stewardship responsibility, many believe they should adhere to a well-defined list of best practices related to donations. Adopted in 1993, "A Donor Bill of Rights" was developed by four leading philanthropic professional associations. Noting that "philanthropy is based on voluntary action for the common good,"[20] the rights of donors should include:

1. To be informed of the organization's mission, of the way the organization intends to use donated resources, and of its capacity to use donations effectively for their intended purposes.
2. To be informed of the identity of those serving on the organization's governing board, and to expect the board to exercise prudent judgment in its stewardship responsibilities.
3. To have access to the organization's most recent financial statements.

4. To be assured their gifts will be used for the purposes for which they were given.

5. To receive appropriate acknowledgment and recognition.

6. To be assured that information about their donations is handled with respect and with confidentiality to the extent provided by law.

7. To expect that all relationships with individuals representing organizations of interest to the donor will be professional in nature.

8. To be informed whether those seeking donations are volunteers, employees of the organization or hired solicitors.

9. To have the opportunity for their names to be deleted from mailing lists that an organization may intend to share.

10. To feel free to ask questions when making a donation and to receive prompt, truthful and forthright answers.

These rights of donors were established nearly twenty-five years ago and some commentators suggest that they should be updated. Philanthropic strategist Bruce Deboskey presents an updated bill of rights for donors, renamed "strategic partnership principles," that reflects contemporary nonprofit organizations' expanded use of technology, improved transparency, and utilization of collaborative partnerships focused on outcomes.

To paraphrase, Deboskey asserts that: 1) the relationship between donor and nonprofit is a partnership, as opposed to a one-way giving transaction; 2) transparency extends to impact and outcomes; 3) organizational failures should be recognized and leveraged for future improvement; 4) financial information is readily accessible on websites (including Form 990s); 5) donor information is safeguarded, including adopting adequate cybersecurity measures; 6) nonprofits engaging external fund-raisers should disclose such spending; 7) full disclosure of potential conflicts of interest should be provided to potential donors by parties engaged in soliciting philanthropy; 8) contributors should understand "and respect" the mission of the charities to which they donate; 9) donors should acknowledge existing capacity constraints in nonprofits related to personnel and overhead support when making contributions; and 10) donors' goals, needs, and expected commitment should be made clear at the start of the relationship with the charitable organization.[21]

Questions to Ponder

1. Which of the rights in the original "Donor Bill of Rights" is most critical to safeguarding a donor's intent? For which right is compliance by the nonprofit likely to be most challenging?

2. Are any of Deboskey's updated "strategic partnership principles" especially critical changes to the original list? Are there any other "rights" or "principles" that should be added to strengthen stewardship of donor support?

Fund-raising is a component of a nonprofit's revenue portfolio, but can also serve to connect supportive members of the public to the organization's goals and social purpose.[22] Fund-raising activities are typically undertaken for a handful of reasons. For some nonprofits, fund-raising is an ongoing effort to support the organization's annual operations. In other cases, nonprofits reach out to donors to provide resources for discrete purposes such as new or developing programs, capital campaigns to support facilities or infrastructure investment, or to establish or grow an endowment fund. Raising funds for specific purposes means that nonprofit managers become stewards of the funds and must ensure that they are deployed as intended by donors. The restrictions that accompany donations are fundamental to nonprofit financial management, as illustrated in the following cases.

A BALANCING ACT: HONORING DONOR INTENT AND MISSION

"Donor intent" refers to a philanthropist's expectations for the use of donated funds, large or small, by an organization. In other words, are gifts spent in accordance with the wishes of the contributor? Restrictions frequently accompany gifts and at times, they can make the donation a double-edged sword. While a restricted donation provides additional funds for the organization, restrictions may not be aligned with the mission or they may overly influence the direction and subsequent activities of the organization. The following vignettes illustrate the complicated nature of restrictions and the quandaries they cause.

Supporting or Swaying Mission: The Salvation Army's Kroc Centers

Joan Kroc, heiress to the McDonald's restaurant fortune, left more than $1.5 billion upon her death in 2003 to the Salvation Army, a venerable religious charity with a mission of "Doing the Most Good." The bequest, one of the largest charitable gifts ever, came at a time when the Salvation Army already provided an extensive network of social services including thousands of community centers, thrift stores, medical centers, rehabilitation programs, daycare and senior centers, homeless shelters, soup kitchens, and disaster support activities across the country.[23]

The gift came with strings attached, or donor-imposed restrictions. Specifically, half of the dollars were to support the construction of twenty-five to thirty community centers divided across the Salvation Army's four regions. The other half of the funds would serve as an endowment whose earnings are used to offset the operational expenses of the Centers. Despite the size of the gift, the funds for construction and the endowment earnings both fell short of the spending requirements to initially build and then operate the Centers. The Salvation

Army, by accepting the gift, committed to extensive ongoing fund-raising, hiring, and training to make the Centers a sustainable reality. At the time, it was reported that the endowment earnings would offset less than half of the Centers' cost of operation.[24] The bequest is unavailable to support the Salvation Army's other programs or general administrative costs.

The size of the gift and the fact that it supported an apparent shift in spending priorities contributed to apprehension by the Salvation Army and outside observers. For one thing, the Salvation Army famously raises a majority of its funds through small donations exemplified by the red kettles that appear for contributions around the holidays. Would the publicity surrounding the massive gift crowd out potential donors who might assume the Salvation Army does not need their coins and dollars to support core activities? One reporter highlighted the tension raised by the new Centers, noting that "the gift has always rested uncomfortably with some Salvation Army officials who have a hard time reconciling the elaborate centers with the Army's image as a frugal church that serves the needy."[25] A spokesman for the Salvation Army was quoted saying "What have we gotten ourselves into?" following receipt of the bequest.[26]

A couple years after receiving the gift, the Salvation Army's Commander observed the organization was "at a crossroads, and the challenge for us is to remain true to our mission . . . The whole idea is to build on what has been accomplished, not to build something completely different."[27] Benefiting from donor-restricted gifts, while pre-

serving and enhancing a nonprofit mission is no easy task. Evidence of how well the Salvation Army has dealt with the bequest and its restrictions is apparent in the twenty-six Kroc Centers established by 2017.[28]

Antiquated and Inappropriate: The Lydia C. Roberts Graduate Fellowships at Columbia University

A donor's wishes, and the associated restrictions, may become outdated or downright illegal over time. In 1920, Lydia (Roberts) Chamberlain made a bequest of $509,000 to Columbia University to endow a graduate student fellowship. An Iowa native, Chamberlain attached a number of specific restrictions for the receipt of a Lydia C. Roberts Graduate Fellowship:

> Open to persons born in Iowa who have been graduated from an Iowa college or university . . . Special provisions: holders may not concentrate their studies in law, medicine, dentistry, veterinary medicine, or theology, and each holder must, when accepting the award, state that it is his or her purpose to return to Iowa for at least two years after completing studies at Columbia.[29]

Another restriction is that the "fellowships shall be awarded only to persons of the Caucasian race." A flurry of attention surrounded an effort initiated in 2013 by Columbia University, with the help of JP Morgan Chase, to have the original donor terms altered in a 150-page legal filing with the New York Supreme Court.[30] At the time of the filing, the trust account had grown to $840,000.

Columbia University stopped awarding the fellowship in 1997 after twenty-seven students received awards but media reports seized on the fact that "an Ivy League university had awarded a racist scholarship for 77 years."[31] Past recipients of the fellowship claimed the university never informed them of the race-based criterion. A spokesperson for Columbia University commented that "it has long been the University's practice to disregard donor restrictions that violate either the law or our policies," but was unable to determine "exactly when the University stopped adhering to the race-related terms of the gift."[32] It is unclear whether all of the recipients over the years met the "Caucasian" requirement.

The "Caucasian" requirement clearly violated federal antidiscrimination laws[33] but a number of more mundane reasons for trying to alter the fellowship rules existed. For example, the requirement of Iowa birth means that applicants are being screened for nationality, which is similarly discriminatory. Other requirements of the fellowship mandated that recipients could not pursue other financial assistance or employment, something that is increasingly infeasible given the growth in tuition costs. The original $750 fellowship amount no longer comes close to covering annual tuition and fees. Also, the investment options available for the funds are limited to Treasury and municipal bonds. The University is also petitioning to loosen the investment restrictions to adopt modernized investment standards for trustees.

The university began the protest process following a review of existing gifts that were no longer benefiting the university or its students. It is a challenge for donors to craft gifts that serve their own goals, benefit the recipient organization without onerous administrative burden, and stand the test of time. As a spokesperson for Columbia University noted, donor restrictions can become "impossible or impractical for a variety of reasons, generally related to changed circumstances over time."[34]

Intent Met?: Conflict Over the Career Paths of Graduates from Princeton's Woodrow Wilson School

An extreme example of conflict over how to comply with donor intent comes from the world of public service higher education. Princeton University received a $35 million gift in 1961 from the heirs to the A&P grocery store chain, Charles and Marie Robertson, to prepare graduate students for government service.[35] The gift provided the funds for an endowment benefiting the Woodrow Wilson School of Public and International Affairs.

In 2002, family members of the Robertsons filed suit against Princeton for failing to comply with the original intent of the gift because Wilson School graduates frequently pursued careers outside of government. The battle over the appropriate use of the funds came to a head in 2008, months after the value of the endowment funds had swelled to greater than $900 million. With a trial looming, the parties settled the dispute at significant cost. The lawsuit had already racked up legal bills exceeding $40 million for each side.

Princeton University, in return for gaining complete control over the existing Robertson funds,[36] agreed to reimburse the family for $40 million in legal fees and to provide $50 million to establish a new foundation controlled by the Robertson family focused on the intent of the original gift. The highly-visible legal battle was cast as "an embarrassment to Princeton, and a worst-case scenario to university development officers."[37] In response to the agreement, the Council for Advancement and Support of Education's president remarked that "the donors' intent was not a full employment act for attorneys."[38]

Princeton University officials cast the resolution in a positive light and reiterated that the Wilson School had honored the donors' intent. University President Tilghman highlighted a universal quandary in foundations: the challenges associated with interpreting donor intent after the death of the original donors. She commented that guiding the use of funds through a foundation is effective "as long as the original donor is alive and can sit at the table and can express his intent clearly."[39] On the other side, the Robertson family argued that the massive transfer of funds back to the donor family sent "a message to nonprofit organizations of all kinds and throughout our country that donors expect them to abide by the terms of the designated gifts or suffer the consequences."[40]

Circumventing Restrictions to Sustain Donor Intent: Building the Clyfford Still Museum in Denver

Clyfford Still, an early abstract expressionist painter, passed away in 1980 in Maryland. More than two decades later, his public-facing legacy was determined by the particulars of his will. Still's artwork, 95 percent of his lifetime output,[41] would be left to a city willing to fund and build a single-artist museum to house his collection. Known as an iconoclast of the art world, the restrictions on receiving Still's collection did not stop at the inability to display other artists' work in the museum. Nearly twenty museums and cities from across the country submitted proposals to receive Still's collection.

The proposals were reviewed by his wife, Patricia, and, after a previous denial, Denver was selected in 2004. The complexity of the bequest and the artist it memorializes raised many questions. *The Washington Post* asked, "Will a one-person museum devoted to an abstract painter hardly anyone knows become a cultural destination or an expensive white elephant? Will an institution shackled with restrictions find a way to evolve when everyone associated with its creation is dead?"[42]

True to the terms of the deal, Denver raised $33 million to build the museum and support operations. The subsequent decision to sell four of Still's 825 paintings destined for the museum attracted national attention from the art and philanthropy communities. To avoid violating restrictions on the museum's ability to sell any of the willed paintings, the museum asked a Maryland court to allow the paintings' sale prior to the estate legally passing to the museum. One observer noted that "officially, they're not doing anything wrong. But obviously, it is problematic."[43]

Museum officials argued, essentially, that the ends justify the means. The proceeds from the sale were directed to an endowment fund to ensure the sustainability and range of desired activities for the museum itself. The proceeds from the four paintings far exceeded modest expectations and generated $114 million, providing nearly $100 million after commissions for the museum endowment.

The museum opened in 2011 and operates annually with substantial contributions from the endowment fund. In 2014, for example, the museum earned just over $300,000 in admission revenue, which accounted for 11 percent of total revenue and support. A little more than half of the museum's revenue and support came in grants from the endowment-holding foundation. The Philanthropy Roundtable's president addressed the tension museums face with donor restrictions when remarking that "respect for donor intent is essential for philanthropic integrity," but "you're not serving donor intent if you go bankrupt."[44]

Questions to Ponder

1. Did the Salvation Army make the right decision to accept the Kroc bequest?
2. What are the primary lessons from the Columbia University fellowship experience?
3. Were there any winners, aside from lawyers, in the Princeton University-Robertson family lawsuit? What side would you pick? How much discretion should Princeton be able to exercise in fulfilling the donors' intent?
4. Do you buy the perspective of The Clyfford Still Museum that circumventing the will in order to sell the paintings was necessary to meet the long-term goals of the donor? Was it ethical even if legal?
5. What common-sense strategies are available to nonprofits to reduce long-term acrimony over donor restrictions?

ADDRESSING CASH NEEDS

The importance of cash for an organization cannot be overstated. Cash is needed for paying staff and for investing in assets that will serve the organization for years to come. Organizations, government and nonprofit, either accumulate reserves or take on debt through borrowing when cash levels are inadequate to satisfy short- or long-term needs. These options are discussed in the following sections.

Operating Reserves and Rainy Day Funds

Government and nonprofit organizations often set aside annual surplus funds to establish formal or informal operating reserves. Former New York Budget Director Dall

Forsythe advises that "financial managers can cushion the stresses of the business cycle by the same simple strategy Joseph recommended to the pharaoh—prepare for the lean years by filling up the granaries during years of good harvest."[45] Operating reserves provide resources for new investments, special projects, or a cushion for unexpected events, such as an economic downturn or natural disasters. In a nonprofit, the board might designate a portion of unrestricted reserves for specific future purposes. Although the designation by the board is not binding, it adds formal structure to the intended purpose of the reserve funds. The level of targeted reserves should reflect the volatility of risk associated with the organization's revenues and expenses.

State governments have relatively well-defined policies around "rainy day funds." The targeted level of reserves is usually set relative to past general fund expenditures; rules for funding and spending down the reserves are explicit policy decisions often written into law.[46] Doing so is intended to inject discipline into funding decisions and the appropriate use of rainy day funds. Local governments vary widely in the level of reserves maintained and the formality of a reserves policy. As a point of reference, a best practice from the Government Finance Officers Association (GFOA) recommends maintaining at least two months of "unrestricted budgetary fund balance" based on general fund operating revenues or expenditures.[47] Two months of reserves represents around 17 percent of annual spending. Importantly, reserves should be prudently invested with a level of risk commensurate with the source and expected use of funds. Most organizations have existing investment policies that guide and restrict such decisions.

Borrowing and Debt

The time horizon for which funds are borrowed distinguishes whether debt is classified as short- or long-term debt. Debt service—in the form of principal and interest—refers to the payments made in return for the borrowed funds. Principal represents the original amount of funds borrowed, while interest payments are the compensation paid by the borrower to the lender for use of the funds.

Short-Term Borrowing

Short-term debt is typically repaid within a year and is used to address a mismatch between when an organization receives cash and needs cash. In governments, spending levels are often more consistent throughout the year than cash inflows from taxes, which are collected only periodically (like semiannual property tax collections) or with seasonal variation (like sales tax spikes around the holidays or income tax payments around filing deadlines). Nonprofit organizations experience similar short-term cash needs. For example, donations are often concentrated at the end of the calendar year and capital campaigns require upfront payments for pledges to be collected over time.

The ways in which government and nonprofits borrow in the short term differ. Governments have easier access to capital markets and borrow through short-term debt broadly referred to as notes (as opposed to bonds for longer-term borrowing). State and local governments issue an array of notes referred to by acronyms that describe the ultimate source of repayment. For example, TRANs are tax revenue anticipation notes, BANs are bond anticipation notes, and GANs are grant anticipation notes. Governments also, when allowed, borrow from other idle internal funds or higher levels of government. Nonprofit organizations tend to be more dependent on established lines-of-credit from local banking institutions. These are established and then called upon as needed.

Long-Term Borrowing

Long-term borrowing, where repayment of principal extends beyond a year, is conducted for fundamentally different reasons than short-term borrowing. Long-term borrowing is most frequently undertaken to finance capital, or infrastructure, investment, such as buildings, heavy equipment, or vehicles. Organizations finance capital spending for long-lived assets with either a "pay-as-you-go" or "pay-as-you-use" approach. Pay-as-you-go financing avoids borrowing by deploying an organization's existing resources from current revenues and support or accumulated savings to purchase the capital assets. This approach appeals to organizations that are either averse to borrowing for ideological reasons or unable to borrow due to poor credit quality or legal constraints. It is best suited for purchases of relatively small capital assets.[48]

More common, and arguably more appropriate, is the pay-as-you-use approach. Organizations borrow to finance capital spending and roughly match the financing period to the useful life of the capital asset. The debt service is, therefore, spread out over time and is paid for in the period in which the asset is used. As with short-term borrowing, the sources of long-term debt differ across the government and nonprofit sectors. For state and local governments, long-term debt primarily takes the form of bonds, which are financial instruments that represent a promise by the issuer (borrower) to repay the borrowed amount (the principal) at set times in the future, along with interest payments.

Long-term bonds of state and local governments are usually tax-exempt, where the interest paid to debt holders is untaxed as income at the federal and, in most cases, state levels. The tax exemption lowers the cost of borrowing as lenders are willing to accept lower interest rates in return for not having to pay taxes on the interest income. Tax-exempt bonds are often classified by the source of credit backing the repayment of the debt. General obligation (GO) debt represents a "full faith and credit" pledge to repay the borrowed funds. In other words, the government will raise taxes or fees as needed to satisfy the debt service requirements. Alternately, the repayment of revenue bonds is tied to a specific revenue source like water utility payments, airport fees, or sales taxes.

Nonprofit organizations, just as government, often require significant capital assets to provide services to the public, whether dorms for a university, medical equipment for a clinic, a building for a nonprofit charter school, or a kitchen for a homeless shelter. Nonprofits adopting the pay-as-you-go approach might use existing reserves or "funding from nonlending institutions (individuals, other nonprofits, governments, foundations, and corporations)" in the form of grants or contributions.[49] Fund-raising is a prominent internal strategy to raise the necessary resources for capital investment.

In 2013, 501(c)(3) organizations used a combination of approaches to borrow funds. In order of dependence, these included issuing tax-exempt bonds through conduit issuers, secured mortgages and notes payable (meaning they are backed by the organization's assets as collateral), unsecured notes and loans payable, and loans from officers and directors.[50] Access to the tax-exempt bond market is generally limited to larger, more established nonprofits. So, even though tax-exempt debt is prominent in dollar terms for the sector, it is less commonly used by medium and small nonprofits for long-term borrowing.[51]

Just like homeowners with a mortgage, government and nonprofit borrowers refinance (or refund, in bond terminology) long-term debt when interest rates fall and debt service savings can be achieved. Managing the borrowing function, which entails minimizing the cost of borrowing, incurring debt only for responsible uses, and avoiding overly risky leverage, is a primary function of public service financial managers.

Hands-on Activity

Examine a bond issuance by a state or local government of your choosing. Access the Official Statement by searching for the government on Electronic Municipal Market Access (EMMA).[52] Which government did you select? What was the intended purpose for the borrowed funds? How much was borrowed? For how long? And what revenues are pledged to repay the debt?

FINANCIAL REPORTING AND ACCOUNTING

Governments and nonprofits have distinct demands for accountability to the public. Government derives its power and authority from the people and nonprofits receive support from the public, including donations and favorable tax treatment. For these reasons, financial reports should be readily available to the public and provide transparency into the responsible use of funds.

Users of Financial Reporting

Who uses the financial information assembled by government and nonprofits? Users are commonly divided into external and internal groups as displayed in Table 9.1. There are many similarities between users of financial information across all public service organizations, but the focus on taxpayers for government differs from that of the individual donor for charitable organizations. Grant funding is significant in both sectors and grant-makers, most visibly private foundations, use financial information to better understand the capacity and needs of grant applicants. Financial statements allow peer organizations to benchmark their own financial condition and performance against similar organizations or assess the potential for strategic partnerships or contracting relationships.

Watchdog groups and regulators depend on timely financial reporting to fulfill their monitoring roles and ensure that public trust is maintained. Government and nonprofit organizations frequently borrow funds to satisfy short-term cash flow needs or finance long-term capital investments. Lenders depend on financial statements to determine creditworthiness and adjust borrowing terms based, in part, on such information. Financial reports provide researchers at universities and think tanks an opportunity to look inside an organization's operations and test propositions related to different management and policy alternatives. Internally, directors and senior management use financial reports to gauge performance in the most recent time period, over time, and relative to peers. Employees are wise to examine and understand the financials of their employer, since they provide insight into critical questions about organizational capacity. For example, is funding available for new or expanded programs? Similarly, financial statements allow potential employees to determine whether the organization is a financially stable employer.

TABLE 9.1 EXTERNAL AND INTERNAL USERS OF GOVERNMENT AND NONPROFIT FINANCIAL REPORTING

	Government	**Nonprofits**
External Users	Individual taxpayers Grant makers (e.g., higher-level governments) Other governments and nonprofits Watchdog groups (e.g., citizen groups) Regulators (e.g., higher-level governments, auditors) Lenders (e.g., banks, credit rating agencies) Researchers (e.g., universities, think tanks) Prospective employees	Individual donors Grant makers (e.g., foundations) Governments and other nonprofits Watchdog groups (e.g., Charity Navigator) Regulators (e.g., state attorneys general) Lenders (e.g., banks, credit rating agencies) Researchers (e.g., universities, think tanks) Prospective employees
Internal Users	Elected officials (e.g., city council, school board) Managers (organization and program) Employees	Board of directors Managers (organization and program) Employees

Financial Reports

Government and nonprofit organizations report financial information in a number of different forms in response to varied requirements. Knowing where to find information is almost as important as knowing how to use it. Table 9.2 presents the primary financial reporting venues based on the type of organization and information of interest. The following sections describe in greater detail the main sources of financial information for state and local governments and nonprofit organizations.

TABLE 9.2 FINANCIAL REPORTING CHEAT SHEET (OR "WHERE DO I LOOK FOR FINANCIAL INFORMATION ABOUT PUBLIC SERVICE ORGANIZATIONS?")

Organization Type	What are you looking for?	Where will you find the information?	How do you get the information?
Federal Government	President's budget	Budget of the United States Government	Office of Management and Budget
	Borrowing and debt, tax expenditures, aid to state and local governments, credit and insurance, trust funds and federal funds, comparison of actual to estimated totals	Analytical Perspectives, Budget of the United States Government	Office of Management and Budget
	Current financial position, long-term fiscal outlook, audit results	Financial Report of the United States Government	Bureau of the Fiscal Service, U.S. Department of the Treasury
State and Local Government	Management's discussion and analysis, audited financial statements (governmentwide and fund), required supplementary information	Comprehensive Annual Financial Report (CAFR)	State or local government website or request from specific budget/finance department
	Annual spending plan	Annual operating budget	
	Guide to planned capital investments	Capital improvement plan	
	Program performance and compliance	Performance audits	State and local auditors' offices/websites
	Federal grant activity and compliance (for organizations with greater than $750,000 in annual federal support)	A-133 Audit	Federal Audit Clearinghouse Image Management System or organization website
	Details of a municipal bond offering (debt issuance)	Official statement	Municipal Securities Rulemaking Board's (MSRB) Electronic Municipal Market Access (EMMA) website

Nonprofit	Reader-friendly overview of the previous year's activities and achievements	Annual Report	Nonprofit organization website or request directly from organization
	Mission and program descriptions, officers and directors, compensation information, compliance information, financial information	IRS Form 990	Nonprofit organization website, request directly from organization (required to be shared and available to public), or public repository (e.g., Foundation Center, GuideStar, ProPublica). Extracts of Form 990 data are also available through the IRS Statistics of Income (SOI)
		IRS Form 990-EZ (for smaller nonprofits, gross receipts are less than $200,000 or total assets less than $500,000)	
	Private foundation details, grant-making activity, assets	IRS Form 990-PF (for private foundations)	
	Audit opinion, financial statements	Audited Financial Statements	Nonprofit organization website, request directly from organization (required to be shared and available to public), or oversight office (state-dependent)
	Federal grant activity and compliance (for organizations with greater than $750,000 in annual federal support)	OMB A-133 Audit (Single Audit)	Federal Audit Clearinghouse Image Management System or organization website
	Federal nonprofit (tax-exemption) status	Form 1023 Application for Recognition of Exemption	Request from nonprofit organization or search for status at Urban Institute's National Center for Charitable Statistics (NCCS)

Government Reporting

State and local governments, including counties, cities, towns, and school districts, issue a Comprehensive Annual Financial Report (commonly referred to as a CAFR). The CAFR serves as an annual report and includes, among other things, audited financial statements for the previous year. Unlike budgets, which represent planned financial activities, the CAFR is largely a retrospective look at the government's activities. The CAFR has a standard format guided by the Governmental Accounting Standards Board (GASB). The CAFR begins with the Management's Discussion and Analysis, which presents a reader-friendly summary of the past year along with high-level financial information. Next, the audited financial statements are included, beginning with the government-wide financial statements followed by the fund-specific financial statements (the distinction is detailed in the following section). After the financial statements, the CAFR includes Required Supplementary Information. This section is a treasure trove of historical information ranging from lists of principal taxpayers and government employment trends to indebtedness and pension liabilities.

Nonprofit Reporting

Nonprofit organizations have more varied financial reporting requirements. Closest to a uniform financial report is the informational filing required by the Internal Revenue Service (IRS) for tax-exempt nonprofit organizations. Despite limitations, including sometimes inaccurate self-reported information, the IRS Form 990 is the primary source for nonprofits' annual financial data. If not available on a nonprofit organization's website, then the completed Form 990 can be requested directly from the organization or retrieved from a public repository (e.g., Foundation Center, GuideStar, ProPublica). Small nonprofits complete an abbreviated form, referred to as the Form 990-EZ, and private foundations complete the Form 990-PF. Of note, many religion-based nonprofit organizations are exempt from the IRS filing requirements.

Unlike governments, most nonprofits are not required to complete publicly-available financial audits.[53] Rather, producing and disseminating audited financial statements is influenced by a patchwork of regulatory authority and demands from grant-makers and donors. State governments, typically through the attorney general's office, play the primary role in mandating financial audits for nonprofits. Nonprofits with significant federal grant support must comply with greater audit requirements to satisfy the Office of Management and Budget (OMB) Circular A-133.

Financial Accounting

Financial accounting refers to the systematic approach to recording and aggregating financial transactions within an organization. A set of rules referred to as Generally Accepted Accounting Principles, or GAAP for short, guides financial accounting. GAAP are determined by a small number of standard-setting organizations. The Financial Accounting Standards Board (FASB) sets the accounting rules for nonprofits, as well as for for-profit publicly-held companies (meaning that they have shareholders) in the United States. The government counterpart is the Governmental Accounting Standards Board (GASB), which establishes standards for state and local governments. Standards and guidance for federal government financial accounting and reporting comes from the Federal Accounting Standards Advisory Board (FASAB). Internationally, financial reporting standards from the International Accounting Standards Board (IASB) are frequently adopted.[54]

A chart of accounts provides the framework for an organization to classify and record accounting transactions. The chart of accounts is comprised of different buckets, identified by codes, representing the organization's assets, liabilities, net assets, revenues, and expenses categories. These different buckets are detailed later in the chapter. An accounting basis is the set of rules that determines when and how financial transactions are recorded.

Cash Basis of Accounting

The cash basis of accounting records financial transactions based on cash flows. Just as in personal finance, a revenue transaction is not recognized until cash has been received and expenses are not recognized until a cash payment has been made (whether by cash, check, or direct withdrawal). Cash accounting is not considered a sophisticated approach to accounting, since profitability (revenues less expenses during a period) can be easily manipulated. For example, an organization might choose to delay a payment due to a supplier until after the reporting period to reduce outflows. The cash basis is still used by some nonprofit organizations, but they represent a small proportion of the sector's total revenues.[55] The cash basis is not compliant with GAAP.

Accrual Basis of Accounting

The accrual basis of accounting is widely used by for-profit businesses, nonprofits, and state and local governments (for a portion of their financial reporting). The City of New Orleans, Louisiana, in its CAFR, describes the economic resources measurement focus of accrual accounting, noting that, "Revenues are recorded when earned and expenses are recorded when a liability is incurred, regardless of the timing of related cash flows . . . Grants and similar items are recognized as revenue as soon as all eligibility requirements have been met."[56] For state and local governments, accrual accounting is used for government-wide financial statements and business-like funds. Accrual accounting is widely perceived to be more representative of an organization's profitability and less prone to manipulation because it matches revenues and expenses to the associated time periods.

Modified Accrual Basis

Modified accrual accounting, with a focus on current financial resources, is used only by state and local governments in reporting the activities of governmental funds. The City of New Orleans explains that revenues "are recorded when considered both measurable and available" where "available means collectible within the current period or soon enough thereafter to pay current liabilities" (typically within sixty days).[57] Expenditures, as expenses are called in governmental funds, "generally are recorded when a liability is incurred, as under accrual accounting"[58] with some noteworthy exceptions.

Comparing the Accounting Bases

An illustration of the different accounting bases details how the approaches can tell varied stories of financial activity. Three social service organizations provide transitional housing services for the homeless. One is a small nonprofit that keeps the books using cash accounting, since it is easier than adopting accrual accounting. The second is a larger nonprofit that adopted accrual accounting to respond to the financial reporting expectations of donors and grant-making organizations. The third is a county housing authority, which operates as a governmental fund and therefore uses modified accrual accounting. Last year, the three organizations partnered to apply for a grant from a foundation to purchase and rehabilitate a mobile home park. The six units will provide a much-needed addition to the area's limited transitional housing stock.

The grant proposal was successful early in the year and the foundation awarded $100,000 to each of the partners. The funds were distributed to the partners as follows: $50,000 midyear of the current fiscal year, $25,000 at the beginning of the next fiscal year, and the remaining $25,000 in the second quarter of the second fiscal year. Each organization independently purchased a third of the mobile home park for $90,000 in cash. The remaining $10,000 from each partner was due to the Realtor that brokered the deal, with half paid upon the closing of the transaction and the remainder at the beginning of the next fiscal year.

The recognition of the funding and expenses (expenditures for the government housing authority) for the current fiscal year differs across the partners, as seen in Table 9.3. The basis of accounting determines whether the partner reports a substantial deficit (cash and modified accrual bases) or a large surplus (accrual accounting basis). Why the differences in the reported financial activity? The accounting basis determines the timing of revenue and expense (expenditure) recognition. Even though the transactions are identical for the three partners, the timing of the payments from the foundation and to the Realtor dictate differences in recognition and influence the bottom line profit or loss.

TABLE 9.3 ILLUSTRATION OF DIFFERENT RECOGNITION RULES BY BASIS OF ACCOUNTING

	Partner 1: Cash Basis	Partner 2: Accrual Basis	Partner 3: Modified Accrual Basis
Revenue and support			
Grant support	$50,000	$100,000	$75,000
Subtotal	$50,000	$100,000	$75,000
Expenses (Expenditures)			
Acquisition (mobile homes)	$90,000	-	$90,000
Realtor fees	$5,000	$10,000	$10,000
Subtotal	$95,000	$10,000	$100,000
Surplus/(Deficit)	($45,000)	$90,000	($25,000)

The small nonprofit, Partner 1, only recognizes the support and the expenses when cash is either received or disbursed. The delay in receiving half the grant funds until the next reporting period reduces the recognized revenue by $50,000, whereas the delay in paying half the Realtor fees into the next year reduces expenses by $5,000. The cash basis results in a $45,000 loss for the fiscal year.

Partner 2, the nonprofit using accrual accounting, matches all of the grant support to the current period in which it was earned despite receiving only half the cash payments. Under accrual accounting, Partner 2 does not recognize an expense for the purchase of the mobile homes. An accrual expense represents the use of resources and the organization simply swapped cash for physical assets (the mobile homes) of equal value. Each year thereafter, Partner 2 will recognize a depreciation expense to match the use of the mobile homes to the appropriate time period. Depreciation is an accounting convention that recognizes the use of long-lived assets over their useful lives. The accrual basis finds a $90,000 profit for the fiscal year.

Partner 3, the government partner, recognizes only the revenue and support that is measurable and available. Although measurable, the third and final payment of the grant funds falls more than sixty days past the end of the current fiscal year, making them unavailable under modified accrual accounting. With the focus on current available resources, the entire cost of the mobile homes is recognized immediately by the government and the entire obligation to the Realtor is also recognized in the current period. The modified accrual approach results in an annual loss of $25,000 for the fiscal year.

Fund Accounting

Fund accounting is a practice utilized by government and nonprofit organizations to bolster accounting control. Separate funds are used to divvy up the organizations' resources, largely "based on legal requirements, donor-imposed restrictions, or special regulations."[59] Each fund acts as its own accounting entity. As an example, voters have approved dedicated sales taxes to support open space acquisition by municipal governments. Governments create a special revenue fund into which the earmarked sales tax dollars are deposited and managed. The fund structure ensures that the taxes intended for open space activities are spent in accordance with requirements.

Nonprofits may use fund accounting internally to deal with the sometimes complicated restrictions attached to support and assets, but must report on the entity as a whole in audited financial statements to comply with GAAP. State and general-purpose local governments continue to use fund accounting, but financial statements are now presented from both government-wide and fund-based perspectives in response to GASB Statement No. 34. GASB Statement No. 34, passed in 1999, created significant new reporting requirements for governments, including the presentation of the accrual accounting-based government-wide statements to supplement the existing fund financials. Understanding government financial management requires a familiarity with the main types of funds. In fact, discussions of government finances assumes a widespread understanding of fund accounting that does not actually exist among the public.

Funds within government are divided into three main categories, governmental, proprietary, or fiduciary. Each reflects the nature of the supported functions. Governmental funds support public functions. The most important is the general fund, which controls general tax revenue and the associated daily operations of government. Governmental funds differ across entities, but often include special revenue funds for earmarked taxes and fees, grant funds with restricted grants serving as the source of funds, capital project funds that operate as savings accounts for future infrastructure projects, debt reserve funds that hold resources dedicated to paying outstanding debt principal and interest, and permanent funds where the funds are invested and held in perpetuity but the earnings (or a portion of the earnings) can be spent.[60]

Governments, at times, operate like businesses and provide similar services. These business-like activities operate as two types of proprietary funds. Enterprise funds deliver services like water, power, transit, parking, golf courses, and health care, where operations are typically funded by sources other than taxes. Internal service funds are also businesslike, but provide services like payroll, motor pool, information technology, accounting, or legal within the organization and typically on a cost-reimbursement basis. Finally, fiduciary funds recognize governments' role as caretaker of resources that belong to other parties, such as pension plans (a trust fund) and collecting taxes for lower level governments (agency funds). The term fiduciary refers to a relationship where one party is required to act on behalf of, and in the best interests of, another party.

A debate exists about the need for divergence between government financial accounting practices and those of the private sector. The primary variations include the use of fund accounting and applying the modified accrual basis of accounting to governmental fund financial statements. GASB makes the case that the differences between governments and private for-profit entities are substantial, as are the needs of the users of the financial information across the sectors. So, how do governments differ from private enterprise? Some of the primary differences, according to GASB, include contrasts in purposes, revenue generation (the role of taxes in particular), stakeholders (citizens and voters), the role of the budget (as a policy and accountability instrument), and lifespan. The prominent use of funds and modified accrual accounting "emphasizes control and accountability over the raising and spending of public moneys."[61]

Financial Statement Analysis

The primary financial statements for government and nonprofit organizations have enough similarities to discuss together, but the distinctions across organization type (including within the nonprofit sector) are substantial and important for practitioners. There are three core financial statements that, respectively, 1) focus on the financial position of the organization at a single point in time (the balance sheet), 2) present the revenues and expenses of the organization over the reporting period (the activity, or income, statement), and 3) demonstrate the sources and uses of cash during the period (the cash flow statement). These building blocks of the financial statements are the same for the biggest of for-profit entities, so a basic understanding makes it possible to investigate the finances of nearly any organization.

Financial statements, by themselves, are an important component of public sector transparency and accountability, but the information can be transformed to answer critical questions about an organization's financial health and operations. Financial statement analysis represents the use of different measures, primarily ratios of figures in the statements, to address various aspects of financial health. For governments, analysis often looks beyond the financial statements and incorporates other relevant political, economic, and demographic information.

Financial statement analysis is a cumulative exercise, where different aspects of an organization's finances are considered individually and then combined for an overall assessment. Each ratio, or measure, focuses on a specific area of financial health, much like different tests performed at the doctor's office examine different parts or systems of the body. A medical doctor would never determine a patient's overall health after only examining their blood pressure. Similarly, financial statement analysis uses a range of ratios to build a case for an organization's financial strengths and weaknesses. The financial ratios are interpreted based on rules-of-thumb for optimal values, through comparisons to ratio values in years past for the organization, or by benchmarking with peer organizations.

A series of steps guide financial statement analysis and are described in the following sections. The Sierra Club Foundation's audited financial statements are used to illustrate the structure and usefulness of the different audited financial statements. The Sierra Club Foundation "promotes efforts to educate and empower people to protect and improve the natural and human environment."[62] The Foundation's history and founding highlight the limitations on lobbying activity by government and nonprofit organizations.

TENSION BETWEEN POLITICS AND PUBLIC FUNDS

Managers of public and nonprofit, specifically 501(c)(3), organizations need to be aware of restrictions on using resources for political purposes. The Hatch Act, at the federal level, is the most widely recognized law limiting the political activity of government employees.[63] Hatch Act provisions can extend to state, local, and nonprofit workers under certain circumstances, such as when a position is fully funded by federal grant funds. Lesser attention has been paid to the state and local government equivalents, sometimes referred to as mini-Hatch Acts.[64]

Although the list of allowed and disallowed political activities is lengthy, a safe rule-of-thumb is that a government employee should not engage in political activity when on duty in an official capacity or on-site at the place of employment. Limitations exist to avoid conflicts of interest and the use of taxpayer dollars for political activities. As an example, Long Beach Unified School District provides employees with guidance on "Protected and Prohibited Political Activities by School District Employees" based on California law. Taxpayer resources include both time and materials, as seen in the following prohibition:

> Photocopy machines, supplies, mail services, e-mail, telephones, computers, duplication services, district vehicles, employee work time and various electronic media are examples of taxpayer-provided assets which may not be used for political purposes.[65]

Restrictions on political activity can be especially critical for 501(c)(3) organizations that depend on attracting donations with the promise of tax-deductible contributions. The next discussion of financial statements, uses the Sierra Club Foundation as an example and the organization's very existence is a byproduct of political limits on certain nonprofit organizations. The Sierra Club Foundation was established in 1960 when its better-known sister-organization, the Sierra Club, ramped up its political lobbying efforts.

The clash between the political objectives and charitable status of the Sierra Club came to a head in 1966 as a public relations battle raged over the proposed construction of federal dams in the Grand Canyon. The Sierra Club placed high-profile ads in national newspapers asking the public to contact elected officials in opposition to the planned dam construction. In the midst of the ad campaign, the IRS "hand-delivered a letter to the Club stating that its charitable status was in jeopardy." Today, the Sierra Club Foundation is a 501(c)(3) charita-

ble organization and "fiscal sponsor of the Sierra Club's charitable environmental programs." Donations to the Sierra Club, classified as a 501(c)(4) social welfare organization, are not tax-deductible due to the extent of the organization's political lobbying.

The distinction between advocacy and lobbying is critical to charitable nonprofits. Lobbying is acting to influence legislation at any level of government, whereas advocacy is not tied to the formulation, passage, or defeat of specific legislation. Lobbying itself is comprised of two distinct activities from the perspective of the IRS. Direct lobbying refers to communication between the charitable organization and legislative party, including legislators and other government employees involved in the legislative process, related to specific legislation. Grass roots lobbying, alternately, entails the nonprofit using its influence to direct members of the public to lobby on behalf of specific legislation.[66]

Charitable nonprofits have no limits on advocacy work, but lobbying is limited based on one of two existing tests. Organizations that elect the "expenditure test," based on section 501(h) of the Internal Revenue Code, must limit lobbying activity based on the size of the charity with a maximum of $1 million in lobbying-related expenditures for the biggest organizations. Only a quarter of the lobbying spending limit can be carried out in the form of grassroots lobbying.[67] Nonprofit managers must pay close attention to the restrictions on lobbying activity to avoid the risk of losing the organization's charitable status or paying an excise tax on excessive lobbying spending.

The National Conference of State Legislatures (NCSL) maintains a helpful resource that catalogues state-level statutes governing political activity of government employees (see Staff and Political Activity–Statutes, updated February 2015, at http://www.ncsl.org/research/ethics/50statetable staffandpoliticalactivitystatutes.aspx).

Auditor's Opinion

Financial statement analysis begins with the examination of a report card on the quality of the information in the financial statements. This is referred to as the auditor's opinion letter. Auditors are individuals, either internal or external, who examine an organization and its activities from an impartial perspective. Although most commonly associated with financial auditing, performance and information technology audits are common in the public sector.

An external accounting firm provides the opinion letter, which precedes the actual financial statements. The letter communicates whether the financial statements are prepared according to GAAP, free of material (meaningful) misstatement, and fairly represent the organization's finances. The auditor's opinion ranges from unqualified, meaning the opinion does not require any qualifications for identified issues, to qualified or adverse. In other words, an unqualified opinion means that the statements comply with GAAP, whereas a qualified opinion may identify some instances of noncompliance. An adverse opinion reflects material misstatements discovered in the financial reporting.

With regard to The Sierra Club Foundation's financial statements, the accounting firm Grant Thornton LLP writes "In our opinion, the financial statements referred to above present fairly, in all material respects, the financial position of The Sierra Club Foundation as of December 31, 2015, and its changes in net assets, functional expenses and its cash flows for the year then ended in accordance with accounting principles generally accepted in the United States of America."[68] So, The Sierra Club Foundation complied with GAAP and received an unqualified opinion. Significantly, the audit opinion does not convey an opinion about an organization's financial health. Rather, the opinion is about the quality of the accounting information used to generate the financial statements themselves.

Audited Financial Statements

Table 9.4 provides an overview of the main financial statements, the type of organizations that produce the statements, and the associated accounting basis. As can be seen, there are differences in the statements required by organization type and also within an organization's reporting. The names of the financial statements also vary across organization types and accounting approach.

TABLE 9.4 FINANCIAL STATEMENTS BY SECTOR

	Accounting Basis	State and Local Governments	Nonprofit Organizations
Balance Sheet	Accrual	Governmentwide Financial Statements (balance sheet is referred to as Statement of Net Position), Business-Type Activities	Audited Financial Statements
Activity Statement			
Cash Flow Statement		Business-Type Activities	
Functional Expenses		None	
Balance Sheet	Modified Accrual	Governmental Fund Financial Statements	None
Statement of Revenues, Expenditures, and Changes in Fund Balances			
Reconciliation Statements	Reconciles modified accrual with accrual-based statements		

Financial Position (The Balance Sheet or Statement of Financial Position)

The balance sheet is a snapshot of the organization's finances as of the last day of the reporting period (typically a fiscal year). The balance sheet is organized based on the fundamental equation of accounting, where assets equal liabilities plus net assets. Assets, items owned by and of value to the organization, are reported at the top or left-hand side of the statement. The total assets must be "balanced" with the organization's combined liabilities and net assets, which are reported at the bottom or right-hand side of the balance sheet. Liabilities represent claims against the organization or what the organization owes external parties. Net assets are the difference between assets and liabilities and represent the worth of the organization. In other words, net assets are the share of assets that belong wholly to the organization.

The balance sheet has rules that guide the presentation of information. Generally, assets are listed in order of declining liquidity (the ease of converting the asset to cash) and liabilities are ordered based on how quickly they are due to be paid. Both assets and liabilities are often categorized as current or long-term depending on whether they are expected to be received or due within the following year, respectively. The balance sheet also presents last year's information for comparison purposes.

The balance sheet for the Sierra Club Foundation (Table 9.5), illustrates substantial growth in assets ($23 million) from 2014 to 2015, driven primarily by increases in "contributions receivable, pledges and bequests," "cash and cash equivalents," and "money market mutual funds." The Sierra Club Foundation's end-of-year net assets in 2015 reflect the positive change in assets and reduced liabilities. The balance sheet allows the reader to determine whether restrictions accompanied the increase in net assets. Indeed, the vast majority of the change is attributed to temporarily-restricted net assets. The balance sheet presents net assets classified based on the degree of restrictions on their use. New accounting rules will simplify presentation of net assets for nonprofits into two classes, net assets with donor restrictions and net assets without donor restrictions.[69]

TABLE 9.5 THE SIERRA CLUB FOUNDATION BALANCE SHEET (DECEMBER 31, 2015 WITH SUMMARIZED FINANCIAL INFORMATION AS OF DECEMBER 31, 2014)[70]

	As of December 31,	
	2015	**2014**
Assets		
Cash and cash equivalents	$ 15,299,493	$ 12,228,138
Money market mutual funds	11,615,397	4,706,786
Contributions receivable, pledges and bequests, net	19,248,886	5,505,583
Contribution receivable, in-kind gift	2,010,902	2,764,120
Contributions receivable, charitable trusts, net	5,994,039	6,814,307
Investments	62,183,328	60,500,732
Assets held under split-interest agreements	13,835,168	14,753,841
Other assets	1,516,361	1,395,358
Total assets	$ 131,703,574	$ 108,668,865
Liabilities and net assets		
Liabilities:		
Accounts payable	$ 376,758	$ 624,333
Grants payable	4,761,642	5,610,073
Accrued software hosting services	579,400	706,600
Liabilities under split-interest agreements	12,756,763	12,644,350
Total liabilities	18,474,563	19,585,356
Net assets		
Unrestricted:		
Undesignated	15,750,012	15,097,755
Board-designated	15,226,881	13,354,156
Total unrestricted	30,976,893	28,451,911
Temporarily restricted	68,563,020	46,946,050
Permanently restricted	13,689,098	13,685,548
Total net assets	113,229,011	89,083,509
Total liabilities and net assets	$ 131,703,574	$ 108,668,865

Importantly, the Sierra Club Foundation financial statements note, "The accompanying footnotes are an integral part of this financial statement." The notes to financial statements contain the details about the balance sheet (and other financial statement) line items that cannot be represented in the high-level statements. For example, the notes would be consulted to learn the composition of the Sierra Club Foundation's investments (assets) or the nature of the limits on the use of temporarily restricted net assets. The related note is referred to directly from within each financial statement line item.

As mentioned earlier, state and local governments report both accrual-based financial statements that are government-wide and fund-level financial statements using modified accrual accounting. The government fund-based statements refer to net assets as fund balance.

The following section discusses endowment funds, which have restrictions that parallel those captured on the balance sheet for net assets.

WHAT IS ENDOWMENT?[71]

The term "endowment" is used most frequently in discussions of colleges and universities, both nonprofit and public. In fact, the majority of endowment assets are owned by higher education nonprofits.[71] Endowments are assets invested to produce a stream of income for the organization. In other words, an endowment represents a pot of money whose growth and earnings are used to support varied activities of the organization. Speaking generally about endowment funds is complicated by the fact that the funds often carry different restrictions on their use.

Traditionally, an endowment referred to funds that cannot be spent by the organization. Rather, it is the earnings of the fund that can be spent. The "corpus" or body of the endowment is permanently restricted by the donors. Today, these permanently restricted funds are referred to as "true endowment." Alternately, an endowment fund may hold assets that are only temporarily restricted. These "term endowment" funds can be deployed after certain donor-imposed conditions are fulfilled or a certain amount of time has passed. Finally, nonprofit boards of directors frequently act to designate a portion of unrestricted net assets as "quasi-endowment" usually for specific purposes. Unlike "true" and "term" endowment funds, board-designated "quasi-endowment" is not really restricted.

As an example of the different categories of endowment, Table 9.6 represents the endowment fund for The Metropolitan Museum of Art (the Met) in New York City at the end of fiscal year 2016:[72]

TABLE 9.6 ENDOWMENT FUND FOR THE MET (2016, IN THOUSANDS OF DOLLARS)

	Unrestricted	Temporarily Restricted	Permanently Restricted	Total
Donor-restricted endowment funds		$808,561	$959,997	$1,768,558
Quasi-endowment funds	$755,132			$755,132
Total funds	$755,132	$808,561	$959,997	$2,523,690

With more than $2.5 billion in its endowment, the Met used the endowment and its earnings to offset more than a quarter of its operating expenses ($114.4 million in endowment support for operating expenses of $398.0 million in 2016). Note that over $755 million of the endowment is board-designated quasi-endowment and therefore legally free to be used at the organization's discretion. Endowed nonprofits establish payout policies to guide the portion of the endowment that is paid out each year. The Met, specifically its Board of Trustees, adopted a payout rate of 5.75 percent during 2016. Dependence on endowment for operations varies widely across nonprofit organizations, but annual endowment payouts averaged 4.1 percent of total expenses in 2012.

For private foundations, there is a minimum requirement in the tax code that 5 percent of endowment assets are distributed to outside organizations annually or the foundation is penalized. For charitable organizations the payout policy is typically set at a rate that will preserve the endowment in perpetuity, while still providing consistent support of the organization's mission-based activities. The Uniform Prudent Management of Institutional Funds Act (UPMIFA) provides guidance to nonprofits on responsible investing, payout rates, and management of the endowment.[73]

Financial Activity (Activity Statement or Income Statement)

If the balance sheet gives the reader a cumulative overview of the organization's finances at one point in time, then the activity statement explains what happened during the past year. The activity statement documents the revenue and support earned over the course of the year (displayed at the top of the statement) minus the expenses required to operate (displayed at the bottom of the statement). The resulting figure represents the change in net assets, commonly thought of as a profit/surplus or loss, for the period. The word profit can make public sector professionals uncomfortable, but whether referred to as profit or surplus it is imperative that organizations generate sufficient revenues to maintain existing services in an inflationary environment, replace depreciating infrastructure, and provide reserves for emergencies.

TABLE 9.7 THE SIERRA CLUB FOUNDATION STATEMENT OF ACTIVITIES (FOR THE YEAR ENDED DECEMBER 31, 2015 WITH SUMMARIZED FINANCIAL INFORMATION FOR THE YEAR ENDED DECEMBER 31, 2014)[75]

	Year ended December 31, 2015				Year ended December 31, 2014
	Unrestricted	Temporarily Restricted	Permanently restricted	Total	Total
Revenues, gains, and other support:					
Contributions	$ 8,208,059	$ 69,386,038	$ 162,435	$ 77,756,532	$ 45,283,012
Contributions related to split-interest agreements	529,272	113,981		643,253	6,724,789
Bequests	7,574,532	1,889,025		9,463,557	6,362,612
Total contributions	16,311,863	71,389,044	162,435	87,863,342	58,370,413
Net gains (losses) from investments	(699,967)	(186,689)	(26,807)	(913,463)	2,197,568
Interest and dividends	854,730	298,594		1,153,324	1,003,018
Net change in value of split-interest agreements	(401,082)	(1,233,967)	(132,078)	(1,767,127)	373,214
Other income	1,225,970	7,991		1,233,961	757,311
Net assets released from restrictions	48,658,003	(48,658,003)			
Total revenues, gains, and other support	65,949,517	21,616,970	3,550	87,570,037	62,701,524
Expenses:					
Program services	54,312,411			54,312,411	51,977,153
Support services:					
Administrative	1,076,599			1,076,599	974,950
Fundraising	8,035,525			8,035,525	6,521,048
Total expenses	63,424,535			63,424,535	59,473,151
Change in net assets	2,524,982	21,616,970	3,550	24,145,502	3,228,373
Net assets, beginning of year	28,451,911	46,946,050	13,685,548	89,083,509	85,855,136
Net assets, end of year	$30,976,893	$68,563,020	$13,689,098	$113,229,011	$89,083,509

As a charitable nonprofit, the Sierra Club Foundation's revenue and support are displayed in the activity statement based on whether restrictions on spending apply (see Table 9.7). The activity statements for state and local government differ in presentation. The government-wide activity statement breaks out revenues and expenses by primary government programs and component units, while the statement of revenues, expenditures, and changes in fund balances for governmental funds presents revenues and expenditures by fund. Component units are "legally separate organizations for which the elected officials of the primary government are financially accountable."[74]

Net losses from the Sierra Club Foundation's investments, portrayed as negative amounts on the activity statement, are more than offset by revenue from interest and dividends. The change in net assets for the period is positive and is the primary focus of the activity statement. The 27 percent increase in net assets from 2014 to 2015, $24,145,502, means that the organization has more financial resources to put toward its mission and operations. The change in net assets is also the difference between the 2014 and 2015 net assets reported on the balance sheet, $89,083,509 and $113,229,011, respectively.

Some noncash expenses appear when using accrual accounting. The most prominent example for the public sector is depreciation, which is an accounting convention to recognize the gradual use or degradation of long-lived assets. The basic formula to find annual depreciation expense places the cost of the capital asset less any salvage value at the end of the asset's useful life in the numerator and then divides by the estimated useful life in years. For example, if a county government built a new bridge for $5 million and it is expected to last twenty-five years then the annual depreciation expense is $200,000 based on the simplest form of depreciation, the straight-line method, and no residual value of the bridge materials.

Cash Flows (Cash Flow Statement)

The activity statement presents the profitability of an organization over the past year, but tells little about the cash flow over the same time period. Without access to cash, even the most profitable organization would cease to exist. Cash flows are related to three primary types of activities: operations, investment, and financing. Operating activities of governments and nonprofits generate cash through payments from taxes, contracts, and donations, while simultaneously disbursing cash to deliver goods and services to citizens and clients. The cash flow statement begins with the change in net assets found on the activity statement, which is then adjusted to reflect cash rather than accrual accounting.

Organizations also generate and use cash in investing activities, including the purchase and sale of financial instruments like stocks and bonds, as well as investments in capital assets such as a building or equipment. Cash flows from investing activities are presented in the cash flow statement after those from operating activities. Finally, the need for cash often leads to borrowing by public sector organizations. Financing, which appears at the bottom of the statement, results in cash inflows in the form of funds raised through borrowing or cash outflows when paying back the financed amounts. Summing the net cash from operating, investing, and financing activities determines the net change in cash and cash equivalents for the period.

Why is a separate statement needed for cash flows when the activity statement already represents an organization's profitability? The answer is that accrual accounting focuses the activity statement on revenues earned and expenses used during the year, which often differ dramatically from the cash flows experienced by an organization. For example, as seen in Table 9.8, using cash reserves to purchase investments, like Sierra Club Foundation did with $10 million in 2015, reduces the organization's cash but does not show up as an expense since the organization has just swapped one asset (cash) for another of equal value (investments). In other words, there was no expense. Similarly, an organization that borrows money by issuing a bond or receiving a mortgage from a bank has not earned those funds so they do not appear on the activity statement despite providing cash to the organization. The cash flow statement also accounts for, or undoes, noncash revenues and expenses appearing on the activity statement like depreciation expense, in-kind (material or time) donations, and unrealized investment gains or losses.

The cash flow statement therefore provides much needed transparency for an organization's cash position. Cash flow statements are not included in government financial statements, except for businesslike proprietary funds. The Sierra Club Foundation's cash flow statement in 2015 shows a dramatic increase in cash flows from operating activities compared to 2014: $9,497,732 versus a negative $9,422,922, respectively. The positive cash flow from operations are offset by an outflow of cash from investing activities of $6,461,612, but the net cash flow for the year remains positive, $3,071,355, compared to the negative cash flow in 2014 of $1,903,999. The net change in cash and cash equivalents is also the difference between the 2014 and 2015 cash and cash equivalents reported on the balance sheet.

TABLE 9.8 THE SIERRA CLUB FOUNDATION STATEMENT OF CASH FLOWS
(FOR THE YEAR ENDED DECEMBER 31, 2015 WITH SUMMARIZED FINANCIAL
INFORMATION FOR THE YEAR ENDED DECEMBER 31, 2014)[76]

	Years ended December 31,	
	2015	**2014**
Cash flows from operating activities:		
Change in net assets	$ 24,145,502	$ 3,228,373
Adjustments to reconcile change in net assets to net cash provided by (used in) operating activities:		
Depreciation	8,463	4,399
Noncash gifts	(168,773)	(101,888)
Contributions of investment securities	(1,933,354)	(1,382,759)
Contributions restricted for long-term investment	(162,435)	(154,960)
Net (gain) loss on investments	913,465	(2,197,397)
Change in in-kind contribution receivable	(753,217)	711,956
Changes in operating assets and liabilities:		
Contributions receivable, net	(11,416,600)	(8,588,656)
Other assets	(106,245)	(370,564)
Accounts payable	(247,575)	134,715
Grants payable	(848,431)	(378,655)
Liabilities under split-interest agreements	66,932	(327,486)
Net cash provided by (used in) operating activities	9,497,732	(9,422,922)
Cash flows from investing activities:		
Proceeds from sale of investments	9,480,999	13,791,607
Purchase of investments	(10,143,706)	(19,022,333)
Proceeds from sale of money market funds	4,458,797	37,130,476
Purchase of money market funds	(11,367,408)	(24,829,627)
Purchase of property and equipment	(6,423)	(6,646)
Change in other assets - software hosting services	127,200	469,000
Change in assets held under split-interest agreements	988,929	300,487
Net cash provided by (used in) investing activities	(6,461,612)	7,832,964
Cash flows from financing activities:		
Payments of software hosting services obligations	(706,600)	(469,000)
Software hosting services obligation	579,400	-
Contributions restricted for long-term investment	162,435	154,960
Net cash provided by (used in) financing activities	35,235	(314,040)
Net change in cash and cash equivalents	3,071,355	(1,903,999)
Cash and cash equivalents, beginning of year	12,228,138	14,132,137
Cash and cash equivalents, end of year	$ 15,299,493	$ 12,228,138

Program Services (Statement of Functional Expenses)

The statement of functional expenses presents nonprofit spending broken out by program services and support services. Program services include the delivery of directly mission-supporting activities. Support services are further divided into administrative and fund-raising expenses. The statement allows for an examination of the balance between program and support spending. The influence of the statement in the charitable nonprofit sector cannot be overstated. Historically, the statement was required of only a particular charitable subset of nonprofit organizations. Beginning with financial statements for fiscal years following December 15, 2017, functional classification of expenses is required of all nonprofits but can be presented in a statement of functional expenses, within the activity statement (Sierra Club Foundation does both), or as part of the notes.[77]

Nonprofit boards and donors use the statement to determine a very crude approximation of the organization's efficiency. The Sierra Club Foundation, for example, classified $54.3 million of spending for program services, while $9.1 million went to administration and fund-raising activities (see Table 9.9). Program services spending represents 85.6 percent of total spending, or 85.6 cents of every dollar, for Sierra Club Foundation in 2015. The Sierra Club Foundation touts the functional spending information noting:

> We're proud of our solid reputation for stewarding charitable contributions and assets responsibly. We've earned a rare seventh consecutive four-star rating from Charity Navigator. In the final analysis, we spend nearly 90 cents of every dollar directly on environmental and conservation programs.[78]

This use of financial statement information to characterize an organization's performance is a first look at the application of ratios in financial statement analysis, which is discussed in the following sections.

USING FINANCIAL STATEMENT INFORMATION

The audited financial statements and completed Form 990s of nonprofit organizations and the CAFRs of state and local governments provide the necessary information to examine an organization's financial activity over time and to compare it to peers. General techniques are described here, followed by approaches specific to nonprofits and governments, respectively.

TABLE 9.9: THE SIERRA CLUB FOUNDATION STATEMENT OF FUNCTIONAL EXPENSES (FOR THE YEAR ENDED DECEMBER 31, 2015 WITH SUMMARIZED FINANCIAL INFORMATION FOR THE YEAR ENDED DECEMBER 31, 2014)[79]

| | Year ended December 31, 2015 | | | | | Year ended December 31, 2014 |
| | | Support services | | | | |
	Program services	Administrative	Fundraising	Subtotal	Total	Total
Grants	$54,013,133	$	$	$	$ 54,013,133	$ 51,677,704
Reimbursement for fundraising services			5,500,000	5,500,000	5,500,000	5,300,000
Fund-raising– other			1,650,983	1,650,983	1,650,983	882,980
Salaries	166,678	541,274	49,300	590,574	757,252	713,776
Employee benefits and taxes	42,692	155,447	13,798	169,245	211,937	206,079
Professional services	37,577	187,494	-	187,494	225,071	173,953
Rent	17,694	52,791	2,632	55,423	73,117	72,521
Board of directors meetings	-	30,150	-	30,150	30,150	25,447
Office equipment and supplies	6,960	14,129	788	14,917	21,877	14,785
Software hosting services	-	-	815,159	815,159	815,159	279,762
Depreciation	3,951	4,207	305	4,512	8,463	7,918
Travel	4,772	12,707	653	13,360	18,132	19,519
Insurance	5,367	16,012	798	16,810	22,177	21,995
Bank charges	10	12,292	-	12,292	12,302	1,979
Printing and copying	1,386	4,136	206	4,342	5,728	10,636
Regulatory compliance fees	-	14,496	-	14,496	14,496	15,365
Postage and shipping	977	2,917	145	3,062	4,039	3,672
Publications	-	11,321	-	11,321	11,321	11,680
Miscellaneous	11,214	17,226	758	17,984	29,198	23,380
	$ 54,312,411	$ 1,076,599	$ 8,035,525	$ 9,112,124	$ 63,424,535	$ 59,473,151

Percent Change and Standardized Percentages

A simple, but effective use of financial information is to examine the growth or decline of financial line items over time or as a share of total financial activity. For example, balance sheets provide information from the current and previous fiscal year and allow the use of percent calculations to assign a relative magnitude and direction to changes. Similarly, each line of a financial statement can be divided by the same denominator to create a proportional measure of importance. The most frequently used denominators in these common size ratios are total revenues or expenses.[80] To demonstrate the approach, an abridged balance sheet for the Sierra Club Foundation is included in Table 9.10, displaying only liabilities. Two columns are added to show the percent share of total liabilities for each liability category and the percent change of the liabilities from 2014 to 2015. Although simple, these techniques help establish trends and standardize financial information for comparison. For example, Sierra Club Foundation's accounts payable fell 40 percent in 2015 (Step 1: $376,758 minus $624,333 = –247,575; Step 2: $247,575 divided by $624,333 = –0.396, Step 3: –0.396 multiplied by 100 = –39.6%), but they only represent 2 percent of total liabilities for the organization (Step 1: $376,758 divided by $18,474,563 = 0.020; Step 2: 0.020 multiplied by 100 = 2.0%).

TABLE 9.10 EXCERPT FROM THE SIERRA CLUB FOUNDATION BALANCE SHEET
(DECEMBER 31, 2015 WITH SUMMARIZED FINANCIAL INFORMATION
AS OF DECEMBER 31, 2014)[81]

	% of Total Liabilities	% Change from 2014	As of December 31,	
			2015	2014
Liabilities:				
Accounts payable	2%	–40%	$ 376,758	$ 624,333
Grants payable	26%	–15%	4,761,642	5,610,073
Accrued software hosting services	3%	–18%	579,400	706,600
Liabilities under split-interest agreements	69%	+1%	12,756,763	12,644,350
Total liabilities	-	–6%	18,474,563	19,585,356

Financial Ratios

Transforming financial statement information into various ratios allows the user to address a range of financial questions. The most prominent financial topics addressed by ratios for public sector organizations include profitability, asset turnover, liquidity, leverage, and coverage. Best practice is to use multiple ratios to validate findings in financial statement analysis.

Profitability refers to whether an organization experiences a positive financial return from its activities. Even public service organizations need to be profitable in order to support their missions. The total margin is a common measure of profitability. The ratio, expressed as a percentage, divides the annual surplus or deficit (total revenues less total expenses) by total revenue and support. For the Sierra Club Foundation, the statement of activities provides the total revenue and support ($87.57 million) and total expenses ($63.43 million) required to calculate the total margin. The total margin is just less than 28 percent, meaning that for every dollar of revenue received in 2015, the organization retained or profited 28 cents. Profitability for public sector organizations should be positive over time, but organizations with surpluses are expected to reinvest in the organization to maintain services, expand programs, or even reduce taxes and user charges when feasible. *Asset turnover* is another profitability measure that compares profits with assets or net assets to find the return on organizational resources.

Liquidity ratios provide evidence of an organization's capacity to cover short-term financial obligations. The current ratio is a straight-forward comparison of current assets to current liabilities, where current refers to assets that include cash and those that will be converted to cash within a year and liabilities due within the year.

Leverage ratios measure an organization's degree of dependence on borrowing. Leverage can be quantified as the proportion of total debt to total assets. The higher the proportion, the greater the organization's financial leverage.

A related measure are *coverage* ratios, which indicate how easily the organization can make its obligated debt service payments from current net revenues or cash flows.

A separate class of ratios measure efficiency. So-called *turnover* ratios measure the efficiency with which receivables, like payments due and pledges, are collected, or with which inventories are used.

Nonprofit Financial Assessment

For nonprofit organizations, the program services ratio represents the spending division between program and support services. The information for the program services ratio is found in the activity statement or statement of functional expenses. Higher program services ratios are considered better, with the rule-of-thumb being that 70 to 75 percent or more of each dollar should be spent on program services.

> *"The percent of charity expenses that go to administrative and fund-raising costs—commonly referred to as 'overhead'—is a poor measure of a charity's performance."*
>
> —Art Taylor, Jacob Harold, and Ken Berger

Although the program services ratio provides a convenient measure of the resources directed to mission-based activities, the ratio simultaneously pushes nonprofit managers to reduce spending on management functions. Over the long-term, the fixation on increasing program service ratios can undermine efforts to improve management capacity. In other words, overhead (central administrative costs) should not be a dirty word. Three leading charity watchdog groups even started a website in 2013 to counter "The Overhead Myth."[82]

Similarly, users of financial information should avoid the simplicity of a single benchmark value for comparing program service ratios across the nonprofit sector (like the range presented earlier). A thoughtful use of the ratio should, at a minimum, develop a benchmark specific to the nonprofit's field of work for comparison. Some subsectors simply have higher administrative demands than others. Examining the program services ratio over time for a single organization is also a potentially useful exercise, since changes in program spending suggest strategic shifts or changes in efficiency. More generally, ratio measures including the program services ratio should be adopted in combination with other measures of financial performance and effectiveness.

Third-party organizations play an important role in producing and disseminating financial accountability information for nonprofits. Examining the methodology of Charity Navigator, a prominent rater of charitable nonprofits, reinforces the previous points about analyzing financial health. First, Charity Navigator distinguishes between charities that are primarily fund-raisers (like Sierra Club Foundation) and other charities, since function matters for finances. Second, the rating methodology uses multiple measures of financial efficiency and capacity, with criteria specific to different subsectors, such as museums, food banks, or community foundations.

The financial efficiency measures used by Charity Navigator are program service expense-related indicators, including Program Expense Percentage, Administrative Expense Percentage, Fund-raising Expense Percentage, and Fund-raising Efficiency. Financial capacity is represented by Program Expenses Growth, Working Capital Ratio (a comparison of unrestricted and temporarily restricted net assets to expenses), and Liabilities to Assets Ratio. Each of the seven measures is scored and adjusted based on the subsector, where appropriate, before being summed and calibrated to a 100-point scale. The resulting Financial Health Score translates to a four-star rating system, where four stars is considered exceptional and zero stars is exceptionally poor relative to peers.[83]

Financial analysis for nonprofits can be based on either audited financial statements or completed IRS Form 990s, but certain questions, such as levels of executive compensation, can only be addressed using data from the Form 990.[85] In addition to compensation levels, the share of income earned rather than donated, and diversification of revenue sources, are measures of particular interest.[86]

Table 9.11[84] presents the key financial criteria used by leading watchdog groups to evaluate financial health and suitability of charitable nonprofit organizations for donors.

TABLE 9.11 SELECT CHARITY WATCHDOG GROUP FINANCIAL MEASURES AND STANDARDS

	Better Business Bureau (BBB) Wise Giving Alliance (www.give.org)	CharityNavigator (www.charitynavigator.org)	CharityWatch (www.charitywatch.org)
Program Expenses (higher is better)	Spend at least 65% of its total expenses on program activities.	Charities spending more than 85% of their budget on program expenses receive the maximum score.	A charity is classified as "highly efficient" when the program spending percent is 75% or greater.
Administrative Expenses (lower is better)		Charities spending 15% or less of their budget on administrative expenses receive the maximum score.	
Fund-raising Expenses (lower is better)	Spend no more than 35% of related contributions on fund raising.	Charities spending 10% or less of their budget on fund-raising expenses receive the maximum score.	
Fund-raising Efficiency (lower is better)		Charities spending 10 cents in fund-raising expenses or less to raise $1 receive the maximum score.	Cost to Raise $100 is equal to or less than $25 to be classified as "highly efficient."
Available Reserves (not too high and not too low)	Accumulation of Funds—The charity's unrestricted net assets should be no more than three times the past year's expenses or current year's budget, whichever is higher.	Working Capital—Represents how many years a charity can sustain spending using net available assets. Charities with a working capital ratio greater than 1 receive the maximum score.	Years of Available Assets—If a charity's "available assets in reserve" are greater than three years' of spending, then the CharityWatch letter grade is downgraded.

Government Financial Assessment

Assessing state and local government finances is complicated. Standardizing key financial information based on population (e.g., using per capita figures) makes comparisons easier across jurisdictions or across time for a rapidly growing government. A chart of a city's full-time employees per capita over time is a simple metric for illustrating how the size of government has changed with population.

The complex intergovernmental system suggests that a focus on a government's financial independence from higher-level government support is critical for understanding financial health. Government financials, specifically the government-wide

Statement of Activities, allow users to compare the associated revenues and expenses for specific programs or functions. In other words, financial statement users can determine the degree to which different programs or functions are self-supporting versus dependent on general tax revenue.

Credit rating agencies provide information on a government's financial condition. They act as a third party intermediary to mitigate the problems associated with information asymmetry between lenders and governments. Three agencies continue to dominate municipal bond ratings: Standard & Poor's (S&P), Moody's, and Fitch Ratings. General obligation bond ratings, which are representative of the government's overall creditworthiness, are a crude measure of financial condition. Letter-based credit ratings are applied to either a government issuing general obligation debt or a revenue bond supported by a specific source of backing.

More frequently, understanding a government's financial health requires digging into the financial statements for state and local governments. Such efforts are assisted by the work of Maher and Nollenberger[87] who revisited a classic set of ten financial indicators for governments.[88] The resulting indicators (listed in Table 9.12) look beyond the general fund to a government's businesslike enterprise funds and consider the all-important unfunded liabilities related to pension funds. Their work also provides benchmarks for each indicator based on the size of the municipal government.

The final of the ten financial indicators focuses on unfunded liabilities, particularly the adequacy of funding for post-employment benefits. The inclusion of a measure related to retirement plans highlights their influence on a government's financial condition. The following section provides an introduction to public sector retirement plans and the differences in employer responsibilities across plan types.

PUBLIC SECTOR RETIREMENT PLANS

Managers of public sector organizations constantly make tradeoffs between short-term and long-term financial obligations. The most visible and pressing long-term financial obligation for state and local governments is ensuring adequate funding for retirement promises already made to current and past employees. In addition to salary, benefits are a significant part of total compensation and the public sector has historically offered generous benefits and job security as a tradeoff for lower wages. Benefits range from health insurance to tuition reimbursement, but the financial demands of retirement systems became especially salient following the 2008 financial crisis. Investment losses resulted in a growing shortfall between state pension fund assets and future obligations. An influential report by the Pew Center labeled this shortfall "The Trillion Dollar Gap."[89]

Focus of Measure	Measure	Formula
Revenue	Total Revenues per Capita	Total Revenues for all Governmental Funds (Excluding Capital Project Funds) Divided by Population
	Intergovernmental Revenues/ Total Revenues Percentage	Intergovernmental Revenues for the General Fund Divided by Total General Fund Revenues
	Property Tax or Own Source Tax Revenues/Total Revenues Percentage	Total Tax Revenues Levied Locally for the General Fund Divided by Total General Fund Revenues
Expenditure	Total Expenditures per Capita	Total Expenditures for all Governmental Funds (Excluding Capital Project Funds) Divided by Population
Operating Position	Operating Surplus or Deficit/ Operating Revenues Percentage	General Fund Operating Surplus or Deficit Divided by Total General Fund Revenues
	General Fund Balance/General Fund Revenues Percentage	General Fund Unreserved Fund Balance Divided by Total General Fund Revenues
	Enterprise Funds Working Capital Coverage Percentage	Current Assets of Enterprise Funds Divided by Current Liabilities of Enterprise Funds
Debt	Long Term Debt/Assessed Value Percentage	Long-Term General Obligation Debt Divided by Assessed Value
	Debt Service/Operating Revenues Percentage	General Obligation Debt Service Divided by Total General Fund Revenues
Unfunded Liabilities	Postemployment Benefit Assets/ Liabilities Percentage	Funded Ratio (i.e., Actuarial Value of Plan Assets/Actuarial Accrued Liability)

A retirement plan sets aside and invests resources during an individual's working years to provide support for post-employment years. Retirement plans take two primary forms regardless of whether in the private or public sector: defined benefit and defined contribution.

Defined Benefit (DB) Plans

A defined benefit plan guarantees that employees receive a set amount of annual income throughout retirement. The guarantee is based on an employee's number of years working for the organization and a salary measure, often the employee's average wages over some period of time. A percentage multiplier, set by the plan, is multiplied by the years worked and salary amount to find the annual retirement benefit paid under the system. The percentage applied in the formula determines what share of an employee's salary is replaced in retirement by the benefit. For example, consider an employee who worked for the state of Arizona for thirty years and earned an average salary of $60,000 annually. A 2.3 percent multiplier is applied to estimate the monthly retirement benefit. On a monthly basis, the employee can expect to receive $3,450 in pension plan payments after retirement for a wage replacement ratio of 69 percent (30 years * 2.3% * $5,000 = $3,450).[90]

Defined benefit plans, like all retirement plans, often include vesting requirements where an employee must work for a certain number of years before qualifying for the earned benefits. The security of a defined benefit plan is appealing to workers, since they cannot outlive the retirement benefit. Alternately, the defined benefit plan can limit professional mobility as the contributions are not portable unless the new employer is also a participant in the same pension system. In other words, employees are incentivized to stay within a defined benefit plan to maximize the retirement benefits. Continuing the example of a public employee in the state of Arizona, the percent of wages replaced after ten years of service is 21 percent and grows more than three-fold to 69 percent with thirty years of service. The employer, rather than the employee, bears the risk of ensuring that there are sufficient funds to honor current and future retirement benefits under a defined benefit plan.

Defined benefit plans are increasingly less common, but still more prominent in government than in business. Actuaries determine the pension obligations and the needed funds that must be set aside during employees' working years. Pension contributions are split, with the employer and employee each paying a given percentage each month. Despite the best actuarial estimates, the sufficiency of contributions to a pension fund is uncertain due to market fluctuations of the investments.

Higher investment returns, all else constant, mean lower required contributions to satisfy the pension funding requirements. To ensure sufficient funds for the promised retirement benefits, employers make annual contributions to the system to cover the plan costs for benefits accrued in the current year, referred to as the "normal cost," and for "supplemental costs" representing an estimate of the unfunded portion of liabilities spread out over time.

The sufficiency of a defined benefit plan's assets to satisfy promised obligations, or liabilities, is best summed up in the "funded ratio" measure. The funded ratio indicates the plan's assets as a share of promised liabilities. A higher ratio indicates a better ability to meet current and future obligations without increasing contribution rates. As of 2014, state pension systems averaged a 75 percent funded ratio. The average masks a great deal of variation ranging from Illinois and Kentucky with 41 percent of liabilities funded, all the way to Oregon, South Dakota, and Wisconsin with greater than 100 percent funded.[91] Defined benefit plans for governments are frequently operated at the state level, like the behemoth California Public Employees' Retirement System (CalPERS). Such systems allow smaller governments to benefit from lower relative administrative costs.

Defined Contribution (DC) Plans

A survey of nonprofit employees found that more than three-quarters are offered an employer-sponsored retirement plan. Defined

> *"Retirement benefits are an important part of how states can attract and retain a high-caliber workforce for the twenty-first century—and the bill coming due for these promises is an increasingly crucial issue affecting states' fiscal health and economic competitiveness."*
>
> —Susan Urahn

contribution plans represented two-thirds of the plans in the nonprofit sector, while defined benefit plans represented the remaining third.[92] In contrast, as of 2014, 16 percent of state and local government workers participate in defined contribution retirement plans.[93] The prominence of defined contribution plans in the nonprofit sector and the growing presence in government mean that understanding such plans is essential as both an employer and an informed employee. Employers with defined contribution plans pay a set amount to an employee's retirement account, expressed as either a percentage of salary or a fixed dollar amount.

Often, the employee must make a contribution in order to receive a matching contribution from the employer. To illustrate, Reinvestment Fund, a Philadelphia-based community development nonprofit, offers employees a defined contribution retirement plan with up to a 4 percent employer match and immediate vesting. The defined contribution plan allows the employee to contribute their own funds, up to a limit prescribed in the tax code, and take advantage of deferred income taxes on the contributions and earnings until withdrawn in retirement. Once vested, the defined contribution plan is portable with employees able to move on to different jobs without sacrificing their existing contributions to the plan.

Unlike the defined benefit plan, the employer does not guarantee a certain level of retirement income with a defined contribution plan. Rather, the employer simply contributes the relevant amount to the retirement plan each year based on the organization's policy. Unlike with defined benefit plans, the responsibility to manage the retirement funds and ensure that the savings are sufficient for retirement falls on the employee. A point of confusion with defined contribution plans is that they are often referred to by the number of the tax code provision. This means that public and nonprofit employers and employees can be overwhelmed by discussion of 401(k) and 403(b) plans, in addition to 457(b) plans.

The 401(k) is a common retirement plan option in for-profit organizations and is increasingly seen in the nonprofit sector. Although some differences persist between the plans, the 403(b) was the traditional equivalent to the 401(k) in nonprofit organizations until 1996 when 501(c)(3) nonprofits were able to offer either type of plan. The

457(b) is a deferred compensation plan offered by some government and nonprofit organizations. Employees can elect to "defer" paying taxes on retirement contributions, like all defined contribution plans, until the withdrawal of the savings in the future.

Retirement plans are a critical component of financial management in government and nonprofit organizations. Both defined benefit and defined contribution plans require regular contributions by the employer, but a recent movement away from defined benefit plans to defined contribution or hybrid plans is an attempt to limit the size and uncertainty of long-term obligations to employers.

Ask Me Why I Care: Dan Ahern, financial manager and performance auditor[94]

"I have a real belief in the contributions government makes in society. I went into public service because I wanted to make sure government accomplished what it could and did it in ways that would serve the public interest." – Dan Ahern

Dan Ahern, President of Clarus Group, has spent his career devoted to strengthening performance, integrity, and accountability in the public and nonprofit sectors. Prior to co-founding Clarus Group, Dan served as the First Assistant Inspector General for Man-

agement in the Massachusetts Office of the Inspector General, an independent state agency mandated to prevent and detect fraud, waste, and abuse in government. He has also served as performance auditor for the Virginia General Assembly and an independent consultant to state agencies in Massachusetts and Virginia.

Dan is a Certified Government Financial Manager, Certified Inspector General, Certified Fraud Examiner, and Massachusetts Certified Public Purchasing Official. Watch his story at https://www.unomahaedu/college-of-public-affairs-and-community-service/community-engagement/pss-dan-ahern .php.

SUMMARY

Financial management broadly encompasses the day-to-day financial tasks, decisions, and operations of public service organizations, both government and nonprofit. Financial management transcends its operational importance because financial reporting provides a rare glimpse into the workings of an organization. Financial management *is* public management as it helps determine the effectiveness of, and public support for, government and nonprofits.

As described at the beginning of the chapter, the Ice Bucket Challenge provided a windfall for the ALS Association. The fund-raising inflow was accompanied by increased scrutiny into the use of the donations and a short-term stretching of the organization's capacity. Financial reporting requirements and practices enhance public accountability and transparency in such situations, specifically the IRS Form 990 and accounting rules that guide audited financial statements. More common issues found in the public sector are organizations coping with too few resources, often with strings attached, to fully support their mission.

Financial reports and statements provide the information needed for both internal and external parties to understand the financial health and trends of organizations. Using simple techniques of analysis, including percent changes and ratios, can improve decision making by managers, potential partners, taxpayers, and donors.

Government and nonprofit organizations operate under sometimes onerous restrictions on the use of funds. Fund accounting provides a framework for segregating funds to guarantee they are used for intended purposes. Nonprofits are extremely diverse, ranging from businesslike hospitals and universities to grassroots arts and volunteer-supported organizations. This means that the financial management skills that are needed range from relatively simple to extraordinarily complex.

Philanthropy and fund-raising are critical financial management topics for charitable nonprofits. Proper stewardship of donated resources and fulfilling donor intent are foremost considerations for nonprofit financial managers. Endowment funds exist in government, most notably public universities and states with trust lands, in addition to being a defining characteristic of certain nonprofit subsectors.

Public sector organizations, both government and nonprofit, are unable to tap the equity markets to raise capital. Instead, they depend on planning in the form of reserves and rainy day funds, as well as debt, to address liquidity and cash requirements. Public service motivation helps attract talented people to public service, and retirement plans are a key part of total compensation considered by potential employees. Traditional defined benefit retirement plans offered by state and local governments have become increasingly stressed, while many younger employees prefer the flexibility and portability of defined contribution plans.

KEY TERMS

Accounting basis – the set of rules that determines when and how financial transactions are recorded.

Activity statement – the document showing an organization's revenue and support earned over the course of the year minus the expenses required to operate.

Assets – property or anything of value that an organization possesses.

Balance sheet – a snapshot of an organization's finances as of the last day of the reporting period (typically a fiscal year).

Board-designated funds – a portion of unrestricted net assets, designated by a nonprofit's board of directors as "quasi-endowment"; usually set aside for specific purposes.

Cash flow statement – statement that adjusts the change in net assets found on the activity statement to reflect cash, rather than accrual, accounting.

Comprehensive Annual Financial Report (CAFR) – serves as an annual report for state and local governments and includes, among other things, an organization's audited financial statements for the previous year.

Donor intent – a philanthropist's expectations for the use of donated funds, large or small, by an organization.

Endowment – assets invested to produce a stream of income for the organization; in other words, a pot of money whose growth and earnings are used to support an organization's activities.

Financial ratios – comparison formulas that allow for a range of financial questions to be addressed from an organization's financial statement information.

Fund-raising – broadly, this refers to the solicitation of external funds from private contributors to support an organization.

IRS Form 990 – form filed by most tax-exempt nonprofits to report financial information; primary source for nonprofits' annual financial data.

Liabilities – claims against the organization or what the organization owes external parties.

Operating reserves – surplus funds set aside to provide resources for new investments, special projects, or a cushion for unexpected events like an economic downturn or natural disasters.

Philanthropy – the charitable act of giving to help others, typically in the form of financial donations.

Proprietary funds – government funds that exist for the businesslike activities of government.

Rainy day fund – reserve funds maintained by governments that have relatively well-defined policies, including rules on target reserve levels and spending.

Donor restrictions – a philanthropist's formally-established rules for the use of donated funds by an organization.

Statement of revenues, expenditures, and changes in fund balances – for government funds, a statement that presents revenues and expenditures by fund.

Tax-exempt bonds – bonds in which the interest paid to debt holders is untaxed as income at the federal and, in most cases, state levels.

Third-party watchdog organizations – groups that monitor the financial activity of public or nonprofit organizations.

DISCUSSION QUESTIONS

1. Discuss the fundamental differences between government and nonprofit organizations and whether financial reporting practices seem to recognize those differences.
2. Review the list of traditional users of government and nonprofit financial information presented in Table 9.1. Identify and justify the two most important user groups for each organization type. Are there other users that are missing?

EXERCISES

1. A key to comparing governments based on financial ratios is selecting the appropriate benchmark or comparison group based on distinguishing features, such as size or revenue structure. An alternative approach is to compare a government's current financial condition to its past condition. Assume that a finance office decides to benchmark its most recent year's financial condition based on the previous year's financials. Pick a local government (county, city, or town) and collect the most recent CAFR. Pick three of the ten measures in Table 9.12. Apply the indicators to the selected government and compare the most recent year's indicators to the previous year values. Write a sentence explaining each of the selected indicators, the value of the indicator, and whether the indicator suggests an improved or degraded financial health compared to the previous year. Based on the three indicators, add a sentence that conveys the overall trend in financial health for the government.

2. Assume that you work for a grant-making foundation considering proposals from several nonprofit organizations for funding. The review committee has tasked you with collecting a couple of key metrics for one of the applicants. Select a nonprofit organization that interests you and collect the organization's most recent IRS Form 990 from their website or a third-party provider. The committee has asked for the program services ratio (divide "Program service expenses" by "Total expenses" found on 2016 IRS Form 990, Part IX, Line 25, Columns B and A, respectively) and a list of the five highest compensated individuals and their salaries (2016 IRS Form 990, Part VII, Sec-

tion A). Provide the name of the selected organization, the requested information, and a sentence or two explaining potential limitations to the program services ratio.

3. Locate the audited financial statements of a nonprofit of interest on its website. Examine the balance sheet or statement of financial position for debt listed under the liabilities section. Which nonprofit did you select? How much debt does the organization carry? Can you tell if it is short-term or long-term based on the balance sheet or by looking at the notes to the financial statements? How does the total debt compare to the organization's net assets, or worth, also presented on the balance sheet?

BUILD YOUR SKILLS

The value of a dollar changes over time. Use this skillbox to learn how to account for the effect of inflation.

SKILLBOX: HOW TO CALCULATE INFLATION ADJUSTMENT

The growth in prices of goods and services is referred to as inflation, whereas deflation is a decline in prices over time. The old saying that "a dollar isn't what it used to be" captures the fact that a dollar today has less purchasing power, the ability to buy goods and services, than it did in the past. Inflationary pressures mean that an organization can maintain stable revenues and still fall short of the resources needed to continue providing services at past levels. Understanding the impact of price changes over time is essential for financial managers in the public sector.

Government and nonprofit financial reporting is in nominal (or current) dollars, so figures are not adjusted for inflation. Justifications for new or additional spending, investigating financial trends, or setting prices are just a few activities that benefit from inflation adjustment. Without doing so, policy makers operate with the implicit assumption that purchasing power remains constant over the years, which it does not. A variety of indices capture month-to-month and year-to-year price changes and serve as the basis for adjusting revenues and spending from nominal (current) dollars to real (constant) dollars. The most commonly used index for inflation adjustment is the Consumer Price Index (CPI), available from the Bureau of Labor Statistics.

To demonstrate the effects of inflation and its relevance for public sector financial decisions, consider the case of the Port Authority of New York and New Jersey (PANYNJ). The public authority spans two states and "builds, operates, and maintains critical transportation and trade assets" including an extensive "network of aviation, rail, surface transportation and seaport facilities."[1] The PANYNJ opened the George Washington Bridge in 1931, which crosses the Hudson River to link Fort Lee, New Jersey to New York City in northern Manhattan. More than 51 million vehicles crossed the nearly mile-long bridge in 2016. The toll to cross the bridge into New York has increased since 1931 (there is no toll heading into New Jersey), but it is difficult to judge how much that increase has been because a dollar in 1931 was worth much more than a dollar today.

In fact, the cash toll for a passenger vehicle climbed from 50 cents in 1931 to $15 in 2015. Here, the process for adjusting for inflation in the historic financial information is presented for years where cash toll changes took place. This exercise allows us to determine how the toll in 2015 compares in real, inflation-adjusted terms, to the original 1931 toll. The first step is to arrange the toll data in a spreadsheet by year (see column A in Table 9.13[2, 3, 4, 5]). The second step requires collecting price index values for each year represented in the toll data (see column B). The annual CPI specific to the New York–Northern New Jersey area is used in this case. The CPI value in 1931 was 16.1 and grew to 260.6 by 2015, reflecting the rise in consumer prices.

The third step is to calculate an inflator based on the current year CPI value (referred to as the base year and 2015 in this example). The inflator equals the base year CPI of 260.6 divided by the CPI from the year of the observed toll rate (column C). Since the most recent year's CPI is typically larger than prior years, the inflator is usually a value greater than 1. The amount greater than 1 represents the relative price increase (or inflation) since the earlier year. The final step is to multiply the nominal toll rate by the inflator (Column A × Column C) to find the real, inflation-adjusted toll rate, which is now stated in constant dollars of the base year (see Column D). The following table represents these steps in inflation adjustment.

As seen in the table, the 50 cent toll from 1931 is more than $8 in 2015 terms. Current 2015 fares, though, are nearly double that inflation-adjusted amount from 1931. Graphically (see figure), inflation adjustment tends to flatten a financial trend line because past values increase. If tolls tracked inflation perfectly, the inflation-adjusted toll line would be flat. The actual line, despite the gaps in years, tells a story that tolls did not keep up with inflation until the mid-1990s. More recently, tolls have seen substantial real growth. Inflation adjustment is a useful technique for financial managers in the public sector to understand the actual changes in resources dedicated to different functions over time and to assist in adjusting prices and fees.

The George Washington Bridge Cash Tolls for Passenger Vehicles in Current and Constant (2015) Dollars

	(A) Toll Amount (current dollars)	(B) Annual Consumer Price Index (CPI-U)	(C) Inflator	(D) Toll Amount (constant dollars, 2015)
			C=260.6/B	D=A*C
1931	$0.50	16.1	16.18	$8.09
1975	$1.50	57.6	4.52	$6.79
1984	$2.00	104.8	2.49	$4.97
1987	$3.00	118	2.21	$6.62
1991	$4.00	144.8	1.80	$7.20
2001	$6.00	187.1	1.39	$8.36
2008	$8.00	235.8	1.11	$8.84
2011	$12.00	247.7	1.05	$12.62
2012	$13.00	256.8	1.01	$13.19
2014	$14.00	260.2	1.00	$14.02
2015	$15.00	260.6	1.00	$15.00

The George Washington Bridge Cash Tolls for Passenger Vehicles in Current and Constant (2015) Dollars

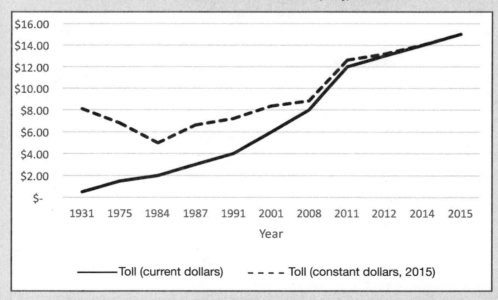

Hands-On Activity

Locate financial data of interest to you that span at least a ten-year period. Possibilities include the overall revenues or spending for a government or nonprofit, individual revenue sources (for example, property tax or donations), spending on specific activities (such as parks and recreation or compensation), or prices and fees (like museum memberships). Promising sources of such data include CAFRs for state and local governments, completed IRS Form 990s for most nonprofit organizations, or open data websites for governments. Once the data are acquired, follow the previously described steps to inflation adjust the financial figures using the CPI-U from the Bureau of Labor Statistics for the appropriate years.[6] In a spreadsheet, report both the nominal and real values along with a chart comparing the two series. Provide a couple sentences describing the story that can be told with the inflation-adjusted data. In short, have the values kept pace with inflation?

Notes

1. The Port Authority of New York and New Jersey (PANYNJ). n.d. "The Port Authority Moves the Region." http://www.panynj.gov/.
2. The Port Authority of New York and New Jersey (PANYNJ). n.d. "The Port Authority of NY & NJ 2012 to 2015 TOLL RATE TABLE." http://www.panynj.gov/bridges-tunnels/pdf/toll-table-2012-2015.pdf.
3. PANYNJ. 2016. Monthly Traffic and Percent of E-ZPass Usage (2017). http://www.panynj.gov/bridges-tunnels/pdf/traffic-e-zpass-usage-2016.pdf.
4. Steve Strunsky, "How the George Washington Bridge Toll Has Risen Through the Years," *NJ.com* (December 5, 2014), http://www.nj.com/traffic/index.ssf/2014/12/tolls_going_up_at_bridges_tunnels_to_nyc_a_look_at.html.
5. U.S. Department of Labor, Bureau of Labor Statistics. Consumer Price Index. n.d. https://www.bls.gov/cpi/.
6. See https://www.bls.gov/cpi/.

For Additional Information

David N. Ammons. 2009. *Tools for Decision Making: A Practical Guide for Local Government*, 2nd Ed. Washington, DC: CQ Press.

NOTES

1. Dean Mead, "The Development of External Financial Reporting and Its Relationship to the Assessment of Fiscal Health and Stress," in *Handbook of Local Government Fiscal Health*, ed. Helisse Levine, Eric A. Scorsone, and Jonathan B. Justice (Burlington, MA: Jones & Bartlett Learning, 2012), 77–124; and Paul Arnsberger, Melissa Ludlum, Margaret Riley, and Mark Stanton, "A History of the Tax-Exempt Sector: An SOI Perspective," *Statistics of Income Bulletin* (Winter, 2008).

2. James Surowiecki, "What Happened to the Ice Bucket Challenge?" *The New Yorker* (July 25, 2016), http://www.newyorker.com/magazine/2016/07/25/als-and-the-ice-bucket-challenge.

3. The Amyotrophic Lateral Sclerosis Association, Audited Financial Statements, multiple years.

4. Surowiecki, "What Happened to the Ice Bucket Challenge?"

5. Nicholas Kristof, "Payday for Ice Bucket Challenge's Mocked Slacktivists," *New York Times* (September 3, 2015), A31.

6. Rachel Emma Silverman and Lindsay Gellman, "Ice Bucket Challenge: When Success Creates Problems of Its Own," *Wall Street Journal* (September 16, 2014), https://www.wsj.com/articles/ice-bucket-challenge-when-success-creates-problems-of-its-own-1410810931.

7. ALS Association, "Your Ice Bucket Dollars at Work," last modified 2017, http://www.alsa.org/fight-als/ibc-infographic.html.

8. Kristof, "Payday for Ice Bucket Challenge's."

9. The ALS Association, "Progress Since the Ice Bucket Challenge," http://webga.alsa.org/site/PageServer/?pagename=GA_edau_ibc_progress_infographic.

10. Claire Zillman, "A Different #icebucketchallenge: How Will the ALS Association Spend All That Money?" *Fortune* (August 22, 2014), http://fortune.com/2014/08/22/ice-bucket-challenge-als-charity/.

11. John T. Zietlow, Jo Ann Hankin, and Alan G. Seidner, *Financial Management for Nonprofit Organizations: Policies and Practices* (Hoboken, NJ: John Wiley & Sons, 2007), 2.

12. *Exemption from Tax on Corporations, Certain Trusts, etc.*, U.S. Code Title 26 Subtitle A Chapter 1 Subchapter F Part I (Year), § 501.

13. Joseph Cordes, and Richard Sansing, "Institutional Philanthropy," in *Financing Nonprofits: Putting Theory into Practice,* ed. Dennis R. Young (Lanham, MD: AltaMira Press, 2007).

14. Zietlow, Hankin, and Seidner, *Financial Management,* 17.

15. Woods Bowman, "Tools and Techniques of Nonprofit Financial Management," in *The Jossey-Bass Handbook of Nonprofit Leadership and Management,* 4th ed., ed. David O. Renz (Hoboken, NJ: Jossey-Bass, 2016), 588.

16. Brice S. McKeever, "The Nonprofit Sector in Brief 2015," Urban Institute Center on Nonprofits and Philanthropy (October, 2015).

17. Giving USA Foundation, *GivingUSA: The Annual Report on Philanthropy for the Year 2015* (Chicago, IL: Giving USA Foundation, 2016).

18. Dennis R. Young and Jung-In Soh, "Nonprofit Finance: Developing Nonprofit Resources," in *The Jossey-Bass Handbook of Nonprofit Leadership and Management,* 4th ed., ed. David O. Renz (Hoboken, NJ: Jossey-Bass, 2016), 509–535.

19. Habitat for Humanity International, *Annual Report FY2016: July 1, 2015–June 30, 2016.*

20. Association of Fundraising Professionals (AFP), Association for Healthcare Philanthropy (AHP), Council for Advancement and Support of Education (CASE), and Giving Institute, *A Donor Bill of Rights* (2015), http://www.afpnet.org/files/content documents/donor_bill_of_rights.pdf.

21. Bruce Deboskey, "On Philanthropy: Rethinking and Revising the 'Donor Bill of Rights'," *Denver Post* (September 11, 2016), http://www.denverpost.com/2016/09/11/on-philanthropy-donor-bill-of-rights-bruce-deboskey/.

22. Sarah K. Nathan and Eugene R. Tempel, "Philanthropy and Fundraising: The Comprehensive Development Program," in *The Jossey-Bass Handbook of Nonprofit Leadership and Management,* 4th ed., ed. David O. Renz (Hoboken, NJ: Jossey-Bass, 2016), 488–508.

23. Jacqueline L. Salmon, "For Salvation Army, Bequest Brings Challenges," *Washington Post* (January 26, 2004), https://www.washingtonpost.com/archive/politics/2004/01/26/for-salvation-army-bequest-brings-challenges/ee6382e0-b0de-4f91-808f-60366449b836/.

24. Stephanie Strom, "Salvation Army Receives $1.5 Billion from Estate Built on McDonald's Franchises," *New York Times* (January 21, 2004), A13.

25. Stephanie Strom, "Big Salvation Army Project Falls Short of Donor's Vision," *New York Times* (June 15, 2009), A13.

26. Salmon, "For Salvation Army."

27. Stephanie Strom, "New Wealth Leaves the Salvation Army with Worries Concerning Its Mission," *New York Times* (August 4, 2006), A14.

28. For details see http://www.kroccenter.org/.

29. Columbia University, "Endowed Fellowships" (May 3, 2017), http://bulletin.engineering.columbia.edu/endowed-fellowships.

30. Devin Kelly, "Columbia University Moves to Modernize Trust Fund," *Los Angeles Times* (June 6, 2013), http://articles.latimes.com/2013/jun/06/nation/la-na-columbia-race-fellowship-20130607.

31. J.K. Trotter, "How Columbia's 'Illegal' White-Only Scholarship Disappeared," *The Atlantic* (May 16, 2013), https://www.theatlantic.com/national/archive/2013/05/columbia-white-scholarship/315166/.

32. Ibid.

33. Sharyn Jackson, "Whites-only Scholarship at Columbia Challenged," *USA Today* (May 15, 2013), https://www.usatoday.com/story/news/nation/2013/05/15/whites-only-scholarship-challenged/2164815/.

34. Kelly, "Columbia University."

35. Tamar Lewin, "Princeton Settles with A. & P. Heirs Over Use of an Endowment Gift," *New York Times* (December 11, 2008), A29.

36. W. Raymond Ollwerther, "Robertson Lawsuit Settled," *Princeton Alumni Weekly* (January 28, 2009), https://paw.princeton.edu/article/robertson-lawsuit-settled.

37. Lewin, "Princeton Settles."

38. Ibid.

39. Ollwerther, "Robertson Lawsuit Settled."

40. Ibid.

41. "About the Museum," Clyfford Still Museum, last modified 2017, https://clyffordstillmuseum.org/about-the-museum/.

42. David Brown, "All-to-His-Own Museum for America's Greatest Unknown Painter, Clyfford Still," *Washington Post* (April 6, 2012), https://www.washingtonpost.com/

entertainment/museums/all-to-his-own-museum-for-americas-greatest-unknown-painter-clyfford-still/2012/04/05/gIQAHnd5zS_story.html.

43. Kyle Macmillian, "Denver Museum's Plan to Sell Four Clyfford Still Paintings Has Art World Watching," *Denver Post* (November 11, 2010), http://www.denver-post.com/2010/11/11/denver-museums-plan-to-sell-four-clyfford-still-paintings-has-art-world-watching/.

44. Patricia Cohen, "Museums Grapple with the Strings Attached to Gifts," *New York Times* (February 5, 2013), C1.

45. Dall W. Forsythe, "Financial Management and the Reinvention of Government," *Public Productivity & Management Review* 16, no. 4 (1993): 415–423.

46. Justin Marlowe, "What's the Point of Rainy Day Funds?" *Governing* (June, 2013), http://www.governing.com/columns/public-money/colpoint-of-rainy-day-funds.html.

47. Government Financial Officers Association (GFOA), "Appropriate Level of Unrestricted Fund Balance in the General Fund" (2017), http://www.gfoa.org/appropriate-level-unrestricted-fund-balance-general-fund.

48. Todd Ely, "Capital Financing for Education," in *Encyclopedia of Education Economics and Finance*, ed. Dominic J. Brewer and Lawrence O. Picus (Los Angeles, CA: Sage, 2014), 101–105.

49. H.P. Tuckman, "How and Why Nonprofit Organizations Obtain Capital," in *Nonprofit Organizations in a Market Economy*, ed. David C. Hammack and Dennis R. Young (San Francisco, CA: Jossey-Bass, 1993), 207.

50. Internal Revenue Service (IRS), "Statistics of Income Division, Exempt Organizations (Except Private Foundations), Form 990 Returns of 501(c)(3) Organizations: Balance Sheet and Income Statement Items, by Asset Size, Tax Year 2013," Table 1 (July, 2016).

51. Thad D. Calabrese and Todd L. Ely, "Borrowing for the Public Good: The Growing Importance of Tax-Exempt Bonds for Public Charities," *Nonprofit and Voluntary Sector Quarterly* 45, no. 3 (2016): 458–477.

52. See https://emma.msrb.org/.

53. Thad D. Calabrese, "Public Mandates, Market Monitoring, and Nonprofit Financial Disclosures," *Journal of Accounting and Public Policy* 30, no. 1 (2011): 71–88.

54. Bowman, "Tools and Techniques," 588.

55. Calabrese, "Public Mandates."

56. Finance Department of the City of New Orleans, *City of New Orleans, Louisiana Comprehensive Annual Financial Report December 31, 2015* (2016), 36.

57. Ibid.

58. Ibid.

59. Martin Ives, Terry K. Patton, and Suesan R. Patton, *Introduction to Governmental and Not-for-Profit Accounting*, 7th ed. (Upper Saddle River, NJ: Pearson Higher Education, 2012), 8.

60. Steven A. Finkler, Daniel L. Smith, Thad D. Calabrese, and Robert M. Purtell, *Financial Management for Public, Health, and Not-for-Profit Organizati*ons, 4th ed. (Thousand Oaks, CA: CQ Press, 2016).

61. Governmental Accounting Standards Board (GASB), "Why Governmental Accounting and Financial Reporting Is—and Should Be—Different" (April, 2013), http://www.gasb.org/cs/ContentServer?c=Document_C&pagename=GASB%2F-Document_C%2FGASBDocumentPage&cid=1176162354189.

62. Sierra Club Foundation, "History," last modified 2017, https://www.sierraclub-foundation.org/about-tscf/our-values/history; and Sierra Club Foundation, "FAQs," last modified 2017, https://www.sierraclubfoundation.org/faq.

63. U. S. Office of Special Counsel, *Political Activity and the Federal Employee* (2005).

64. James S. Bowman and Jonathan P. West, "State Government 'Little Hatch Acts' in an Era of Civil Service Reform: The State of the Nation," *Review of Public Personnel Administration* 29, no. 1 (2009): 20–40.

65. Christopher J. Steinhauser, memorandum, September 2, 2016, Long Beach Unified School District, "Protected/Prohibited Political Activities by School District Employees," http://www.lbschools.net/Asset/Files/District/Political%20Activities%20September%202016.pdf.

66. Center for Nonprofits, "Non-Profit Organizations CAN Lobby" (2017), http://www.njnonprofits.org/NPsCanLobby.pdf.

67. Internal Revenue Service (IRS), "Lobbying," last modified February 24, 2015, https://www.irs.gov/charities-non-profits/lobbying.

68. Financial Accounting Standards Board (FASB), *FASB No. 2016-14 Not-for-Profit Entities (Topic 958): Presentation of Financial Statements of Not-for-Profit Entities* (August, 2016).

69. Ibid.

70. Grant Thornton, *Financial Statements (with Report of Independent Certified Public Accountants): December 31, 2015 (with comparative financial information for December 31, 2014)*, The Sierra Club Foundation (2016), https://www.sierraclubfoundation.org/sites/sierraclubfoundation.org/files/uploads/SCF%202015%20Audited%20Financial%20Statements%20-%20Public_0.pdf.

71. Thad D. Calabrese and Todd L. Ely, "Understanding and Measuring Endowment in Public Charities," *Nonprofit and Voluntary Sector Quarterly* 46, no. 4 (April 5, 2017).

72. The Metropolitan Museum of Art, *Audited Financial Statements 2015–2016*, Note O. Disclosure for Endowment Funds and Net Asset Classifications, 121.

73. National Conference of Commissioners on Uniform State Laws, "Uniform Prudent Management of Institutional Funds Act," last modified 2017, http://www.uniformlaws.org/shared/docs/prudent%20mgt%20of%20institutional%20funds/upmifa_final_06.pdf.

74. GASB, *Statement No. 14 of the Governmental Accounting Standards Board: The Financial Reporting Entity (No. 078-B)* (June, 1991), 8.

75. Thornton, *Financial Statements*.

76. Ibid.

77. FASB, *FASB No. 2016–14*.

78. Sierra Club Foundation, "Financial Management," last modified 2017, http://www.sierraclubfoundation.org/about-tscf/financial-management.

79. Thornton, *Financial Statements*.

80. Finkler, et al., *Financial Management*.

81. Thornton, *Financial Statements*.

82. See http://overheadmyth.com/.

83. Charity Navigator, "How Do We Rate Charities' Financial Health?" (2016), https://www.charitynavigator.org/index.cfm?bay=content.view&cpid=35.

84. BBB Wise Giving Alliance, *Standards for Charity Accountability* (2003), https://www.bbb.org/us/storage/0/Shared%20Documents/Standards%20for%20Charity%20Accountability.pdf; and Charity Navigator, "How Do We Rate?"; and Charity-Watch, "Criteria & Methodology," last modified 2017, https://www.charitywatch.org/charitywatch-criteria-methodology.

85. Elizabeth K. Keating and Peter Frumkin, "How to Assess Nonprofit Financial Performance" (October, 2001), https://nasaa-arts.org/wp-content/uploads/2007/12/READING5.pdf.

86. For more details see Nonprofits Assistance Fund, *Analyzing Financial Information Using Ratios Guidelines for Nonprofits* (2014), https://www.nonprofitsassistance-fund.org/sites/default/files/publications/analyzing_financial_information_using_ratios_2014.pdf.

87. Craig S. Maher and Karl Nollenberger, "Revisiting Kenneth Brown's '10-Point Test'," *Government Finance Review* (October, 2009).

88. K.W. Brown, "The 10-Point Test of Financial Condition: Toward an Easy-to-Use Assessment Tool for Smaller Cities," *Government Finance Review* (December, 1993).

89. The Pew Center on the States, "The Trillion Dollar Gap: Underfunded State Retirement Systems and the Roads to Reform" (February, 2010), www.pewtrusts .org/~/media/legacy/uploadedfiles/pcs_assets/2010/trilliondollargapunderfunded stateretirementsystemsandtheroadstoreformpdf.pdf.

90. Arizona State Retirement System, "Estimate Your Benefits," last modified 2016, https://www.azasrs.gov/content/estimate-your-benefits.

91. The Pew Charitable Trusts, *The State Pension Funding Gap: 2014* (August, 2016).

92. TIAA–CREF Institute and Independent Sector, *Financial Security and Careers in the Nonprofit and Philanthropic Sector: Key Findings from a Joint Study by the TIAA–CREF Institute and Independent Sector* (2012), https://www.tiaainstitute.org/sites/default/files/presentations/2017-02/A68420-212906_JointStudy_Bro_vs2_final5 .pdf.

93. Matthew Hoops, Irina Stefanescu, and Ivan Vidangos, *FEDS Notes: Defined-Contribution Pension Plans for State and Local Government Employees in the Financial Accounts of the United States* (April 20, 2015), https://www.federalreserve.gov/econresdata/notes/feds-notes/2015/defined-contribution-pension-plans-for-state-and-local-government-employees-20150420.html.

94. *Ask Me Why I Care: Public Service Stories*. Co-Project Directors: Mary R. Hamilton and Rita Paskowitz. Stories and videos available courtesy of the University of Nebraska at Omaha College of Public Affairs and Community Service, https://www .unomaha.edu/college-of-public-affairs-and-community-service/community-engagement/pss-dan-ahern.php.

ADDITIONAL RESOURCES

Finkler, Steven A., Daniel L. Smith, Thad D. Calabrese, and Robert M. Purtell. 2016. *Financial Management for Public, Health, and Not-For-Profit Organizations.* Washington, DC: CQ Press.

Peng, Jun. 2008. *State and Local Pension Fund Management.* Boca Raton, FL: CRC Press.

Renz, David O., ed. 2016. *The Jossey-Bass Handbook of Nonprofit Leadership and Management*, 4th ed. Hoboken, NJ: Jossey-Bass.

Weikart, Lynne A., Greg G. Chen, and Ed Sermier. 2012. *Budgeting and Financial Management for Nonprofit Organizations.* Washington DC: CQ Press.

Young, Dennis R., ed. 2006. *Financing Nonprofits: Putting Theory into Practice.* Lanham, MD: Altamira Press.

Zietlow, John T., Jo Ann Hankin, and Alan G. Seidner. 2007. *Financial Management for Nonprofit Organizations: Policies and Practices.* Hoboken, NJ: John Wiley & Sons.

For state and local governments, the Government Finance Officers Association (GFOA) provides a series of Best Practices/Advisories related to financial management: http://www.gfoa.org/best-practices.

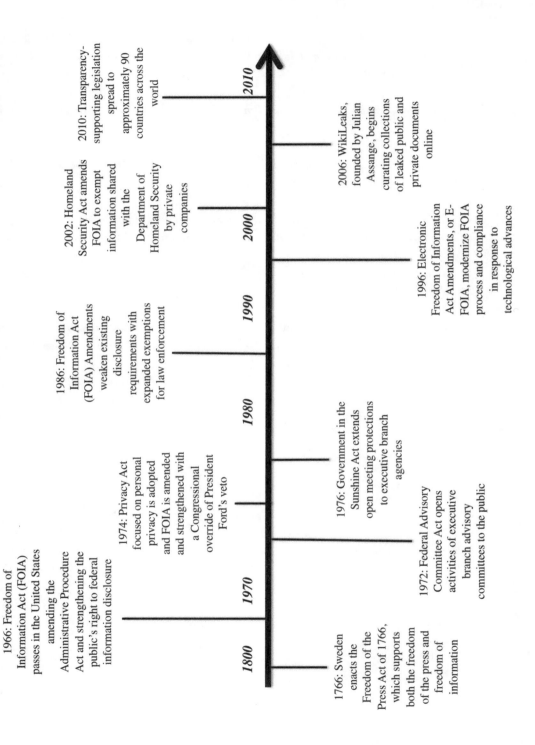

Chapter 10 Timeline: Transparency

1966: Freedom of Information Act (FOIA) passes in the United States amending the Administrative Procedure Act and strengthening the public's right to federal information disclosure

1974: Privacy Act focused on personal privacy is adopted and FOIA is amended and strengthened with a Congressional override of President Ford's veto

1986: Freedom of Information Act (FOIA) Amendments weaken existing disclosure requirements with expanded exemptions for law enforcement

2002: Homeland Security Act amends FOIA to exempt information shared with the Department of Homeland Security by private companies

2010: Transparency-supporting legislation spread to approximately 90 countries across the world

1766: Sweden enacts the Freedom of the Press Act of 1766, which supports both the freedom of the press and freedom of information

1972: Federal Advisory Committee Act opens activities of executive branch advisory committees to the public

1976: Government in the Sunshine Act extends open meeting protections to executive branch agencies

1996: Electronic Freedom of Information Act Amendments, or E-FOIA, modernize FOIA process and compliance in response to technological advances

2006: WikiLeaks, founded by Julian Assange, begins curating collections of leaked public and private documents online

1800   1970   1980   1990   2000   2010

WHAT YOU WILL LEARN

Transparency defined

Forms of transparency

Why transparency?

Open government laws

Limits to government transparency

Transparency of nonprofit organizations

Skillbox: How to file a Freedom of Information Act (FOIA) request

Transparency is about access to information. Often viewed as a panacea for corruption and disengaged or mistrustful citizens, it is a hallmark of good government reform efforts. While transparency has blossomed with developments in technology, its impact on public sector operations and its relationship with the public is complicated and still evolving.

Democracy is anchored in transparency. As founder and fourth president of the United States, James Madison wrote, "A popular Government, without popular information, or the means of acquiring it, is but a Prologue to a Farce or a Tragedy; or, perhaps, both."[1] Transparency for nonprofit organizations is rooted in fiduciary and stewardship obligations to the public and to donors.

This chapter begins by defining transparency followed by a survey of approaches. The range of outcomes associated with increased transparency is reviewed along with the drivers. Key laws and practices are then reviewed with a focus on the Freedom of Information Act. Circumstances where transparency is problematic are reviewed because the positive connotation of transparency can obscure its limitations. Finally, transparency in nonprofit organizations is explored with a review of current and emerging trends.

Occasionally public sector transparency emerges in a way that is out of government's control. The following case describes how WikiLeaks launched a new era of government transparency, raising a number of fundamental lessons for traditional efforts to promote open government.

TRANSPARENCY BY LEAK: THE CASE OF WIKILEAKS

Leaks are nothing new in government. Philosopher Sissela Bok observes that "Leaking has a symbiotic relationship with secrecy. Without secrecy there would be no need to leak information."[2] The unofficial, and often surreptitious, release of information is traditionally carried out through the media. Leaks range from casual tips from unnamed government sources to the systematic sharing of sensitive information for broad dissemination. Leaks are an extreme, but prominent, form of public transparency.

One of the most famous leaks in U.S. history is referred to as The Pentagon Papers. A classified Department of Defense report on military activities in Vietnam was photocopied and passed to the *New York Times* and other newspapers. In 1971, the resulting publication of damning excerpts from the report seriously damaged White House and military credibility. In subsequent decades, leaks have remained a prominent informal venue for transparency.

Leaking public information has grown easier with advancements in information technology, particularly the ability to copy, transfer, and disseminate information through online venues. The most visible and active repository for leaked information is WikiLeaks, a nonprofit organization founded by Julian Assange and launched in 2006. More than 10 million documents have been anonymously released through the WikiLeaks website. Assange describes the organization as "a giant library of the world's most persecuted documents."[3] An editor and journalist for WikiLeaks justifies the need for the organization, noting:

> The world is connected by largely unaccountable networks of power that span industries and countries, political parties, corporations and institutions; WikiLeaks shines a light on these by revealing not just individual incidents, but information about entire structures of power.[4]

The site played a central role in a series of information releases related to the federal government. In 2010, a video of a deadly encounter between a U.S. Apache helicopter with civilians and reporters in Iraq was posted, along with hundreds of thousands of classified documents related to the wars in Afghanistan and Iraq. Nearly a quarter of a million U.S. state department diplomatic cables followed. WikiLeaks released damaging e-mails from the Democratic National Committee and candidate Hillary Clinton's campaign chairman in the lead up to the 2016 presidential election. In 2017, a trove of Central Intelligence Agency documents were posted.

Unsurprisingly, the information released by WikiLeaks has been applauded by some and denounced by others. Former Director of the Federal Bureau of Investigation James Comey candidly discussed WikiLeaks during his 2017 testimony to the U.S. Congress, commenting that "To my mind, it crosses a line when it moves from . . . trying to educate the public and instead becomes about intelligence porn, quite frankly."[5] Other critics include military leaders who worry about potential operational dangers resulting from the release of classified information. Even some proponents of transparency in government have expressed concern over the WikiLeaks approach, suggesting that the organization places sensationalism above individuals' right to privacy and regard for existing legal structures.[6]

Despite the examples provided here, WikiLeaks is not solely focused on government activities or information from U.S. activities. From a transparency perspective, scholar Alasdair Roberts argues that the WikiLeaks model is hardly as transformational as it appears. Roberts notes that the steps to radical transparency, "leaking, publishing, and waiting for the outrage that will precipitate political change," are insufficient and have "only created the illusion of a new era in transparency."[7]

The prominence of WikiLeaks demonstrates that keeping secrets in a digital world is increasingly difficult for public entities. And government must balance the need for openness with the need to protect privacy when dealing with personal information.

Questions to Ponder

1. Is WikiLeaks a protector of the public's right to know or scofflaw causing irreversible harm to government operations?
2. As a public service professional, is it ever a moral necessity to leak information?
3. Go to the WikiLeaks website and review a selected leak. Does the posted information serve the public good? Does the ability to selectively release information cause concern over potential bias in such third-party transparency efforts?

TRANSPARENCY DEFINED

Something is considered transparent if it allows light to pass through so objects beyond are clearly visible. The reference to light evokes the famous statement written over a hundred years ago by future Supreme Court Justice Louis D. Brandeis that, "Publicity is justly commended as a remedy for social and industrial diseases. Sunlight is said to be the best of disinfectants; electric light the most efficient policeman."[8] The notion that information should be out in the open—or in the sunlight—is why rules that support openness are called sunshine laws.

The meaning of transparency is further refined "as the extent to which an (public) organization allows external actors to monitor and assess its internal workings and performance."[9] This ability to view and evaluate an organization is why transparency is frequently subsumed under the broader notion of accountability. The definition of transparency is extended to different types of information: 1) administrative and political decision making, 2) operations, and 3) performance.[10]

Alternately, transparency can be viewed from the perspective of information flows. The directional nature of transparency focuses on the recipient. Within an organization, information flows upward through the hierarchy from staff to managers or downward from managers to staff. In government, information flows are complicated by the presence of both elected and appointed decision makers.

> *"Transparency of information breeds self-correcting behavior."*
>
> —Thad Allen

The internal flow of information receives less attention from a transparency perspective than external, or horizontal, flows of information. These flows, too, are classified based on the direction that information travels. Outward transparency captures the ability of individuals within an organization to view and receive outside information. Most prominent in discussions of public sector transparency is inward transparency, which represents the ability of outsiders to view the activities occurring within an organization.[11]

Forms of Transparency[12]

Transparency is either passive or active. The distinction is important. *Passive transparency* is reactive; it requires an action by an outsider who requests information from an organization. Passive transparency is characterized by the use of freedom of information laws. Alternately, *active transparency* occurs when an organization makes information accessible to the public in the absence of a specific request. Active transparency includes actions such as posting videos of city council meetings, maintaining up-to-date municipal websites, or timely publication of Congressional hearing transcripts. Online platforms have enabled an explosion in active transparency.

Targeted transparency is a type of active transparency. It occurs when mandated disclosures of information, usually driven by government regulation, are made to alleviate information asymmetries.[13] For example, New York City required restaurant chains to post calorie counts on menus beginning in 2008 despite strong opposition from restaurant owners. The forced transparency of nutritional information was a response to public health concerns over rising rates of obesity. Indeed, transparency compelled by government is considered by some to be just another type of regulation rather than an alternative approach to influencing behavior.[14]

Transparency also has a time element that reflects how the information is used. Timing is either "*in retrospect*" or "*in real time.*"[15] Real-time transparency suggests an urgency in the need to disseminate information. Retrospective transparency, on the other hand, is used to present aggregated information, such as annual reports, statistical digests, and investigative findings. These are issued either on a regular schedule or in response to specific events.

Another distinction between approaches to transparency relates to the usefulness of provided information. The "transparency illusion" refers to the disparity between the disclosures made, referred to as *nominal transparency*, and the ability to actually use and learn from the information, or *effective transparency*.[16]

Why Transparency?

The assumption is that transparency is not only desirable, but that it results in improved outcomes for governance. Although intricately related, its effects can be considered separately for citizens and for government.[17] Following are the outcomes most often associated with increased transparency.

Increased transparency is thought to affect government through (1) improved accountability to the public, (2) reduced corruption, (3) better decision making, (4) greater operational efficiency, (5) upgraded financial management, and (6) strengthened democracy.

Greater transparency is also expected to benefit citizens through (1) improved government legitimacy, (2) a more civically-engaged populace, (3) enhanced trust in government, and (4) higher levels of satisfaction with government. Before considering whether evidence supports these expected outcomes, the following describes a transparency-enhancing effort in California and its associated outcomes.

UNINTENDED CONSEQUENCES OF PUBLICIZING CITY MANAGER PAY IN CALIFORNIA[18]

City managers are the chief executive officers (CEOs) of municipal governments. Publicly reporting compensation for city managers seems logical and akin to a shareholder's right to know how much a corporate CEO is getting paid. The state of California launched the Local Government Compensation Reporting Program (LGCRP) in the summer of 2010 after a *Los Angeles Times'* story exposed excessive city manager compensation in Bell, California. The LGCRP posted salary information on the State Controller's Office website and also required that compensation amounts be disclosed on

municipal websites. Although a majority of California cities already made such information available on their own websites, the state's action brought compensation information further into the sunshine.

The improved disclosure of city manager compensation might be linked to many of the expected outcomes of transparency, including enhanced accountability, reduced possibility of corruption, better decision making, and upgraded financial management. Citizens armed with better information may be more civically engaged. But knowing how much the city manager is compensated might reduce trust in government and citizen satisfaction if the disclosed pay is deemed unfair or excessive.

Economist Alexandre Mas studied the effects of California's disclosure rule by examining changes in the compensation of city managers. He found that increased transparency resulted in a roughly 7 percent decline in city managers' compensation. To reach this conclusion, he compared cities that already disclosed compensation information to those whose behavior changed with the new law. The reductions in compensation were concentrated in cities with highly-paid city managers earning more than $200,000 per year.

The analysis determines that "wage cuts were not the result of the discovery of managers who exploited secrecy to inflate their wages."[19] Rather, the increased transparency appears to have forced cities to respond with lower compensation, especially for high earners, in response to general "public aversion to salaries perceived as excessive."[20] The expanded transparency also affected the turnover of city managers. Those with compensation newly disclosed by the change in rules had a 75 percent higher "quit rate."

The lesson from this is that transparency efforts, despite best intentions, can lead to unexpected outcomes, such as increased turnover among city managers or reducing salaries that were not out of line for the responsibilities of the job. Such outcomes are weighed against the right of the public to know about their government's operations. The nearly 6 million views of California's new transparency website in a little more than two years demonstrates that the wages and benefits of public employees are of interest to citizens.

The diversity of government settings in which transparency efforts are conducted makes it challenging to generalize the effects. As shown in Table 10.1,[21] a review of the literature demonstrates that lessons from research on the subject are inconsistent. There are a handful of findings, though, where evidence supporting the outcomes rests on an increasingly solid foundation. In particular, greater transparency is associated with reduced levels of corruption and improved financial management. Satisfaction with government from the citizen perspective also appears to be enhanced with transparency. Evidence on the remaining outcomes is more mixed.

Drivers of Government Transparency

Given the mixed evidence for benefits of transparency, one might ask what the forces are that drive public transparency efforts. There are a long list of actors who serve formal and informal roles of monitoring and oversight to preserve government accountability.

From the perspective of Congressional oversight, there are two primary forms. The first, and less utilized, is labeled "police-patrol oversight" where regular systematic monitoring of government activities is conducted akin to a routine police presence in neighborhoods looking for improper conduct. Alternately, "fire-alarm oversight" refers to the decentralized reactive process where "instead of sniffing for fires, Congress places fire-alarm boxes on street corners, builds neighborhood fire houses, and sometimes dispatches its own hook-and-ladder in response to an alarm."[22] In other words, fire-alarm oversight responds to newly identified and urgent problems.

TABLE 10.1 EMPIRICAL SUPPORT FOR RELATIONSHIPS BETWEEN TRANSPARENCY
AND GOVERNMENT/CITIZEN OUTCOMES

	Evidence for Relationship with Transparency
Government:	
Accountability	Mixed
Reduced Corruption	Supported
Decision making	Mixed
Performance/Efficiency	Mixed (Positive)
Financial Management	Supported
Citizens:	
Legitimacy of Government	Mixed (Positive)
Public Participation	Mixed (Positive)
Satisfaction with Government	Supported
Trust in Government	Mixed

Source: Based on table 4 in Cucciniello, et al. (2017: 40).

Mechanisms for spurring transparency in the federal government range from the active "police-patrol oversight" of Inspectors General in executive branch agencies, to the "fire-alarm oversight" of focused investigations and commissions, to mixtures of the two approaches by entities like the U.S. Government Accountability Office. Transparency is also a byproduct, both intentional and unintentional, of standard operating procedures, such as publicly available transcripts of Congressional hearings. Externally, interest groups like the Sunlight Foundation and the media play active roles in publicizing government activities.

Technological change has proven to be a profound driver of increased transparency. The ability to make information available online to the public reduces the level of effort required for citizens to learn about their government. Another driver is open government laws, which receive the greatest attention for promoting transparency. The primary open government laws in the United States are detailed in the following section.

OPEN GOVERNMENT LAWS

The movement to greater transparency is global and permeates all levels of government. The first open government law is thought to be Sweden's Freedom of the Press Act of 1766, which supported both freedom of the press and freedom of information. In the United States, transparency is guarded by a series of federal, state, and local laws. These laws typically focus on (1) providing public access to information contained in existing government records; (2) ensuring that public business is conducted in view of the public, primarily through open meetings; and (3) safeguarding personal information held by government.

Freedom of Information Act (FOIA)

The workhorse of transparency in government is the Freedom of Information Act, or FOIA, which passed in the U.S. in 1966. FOIA provides a legal framework within which the public can request access to existing government records. The law also requires federal agencies to regularly disclose certain information in the *Federal Register* and maintain reading rooms that house a set of prescribed documents.[23] The *Federal Register* is the federal government's daily newspaper containing regulations, proposed rules, public notices, executive orders, and proclamations. State-level open records laws exist, separately, across the United States and FOIA-like policies have proliferated across the globe in recent years.[24]

The legislative history of FOIA demonstrates an ebb and flow of protections for the public's ability to access government information. The Act's passage in 1966 actually represented an amendment to the Administrative Procedure Act of 1946 and followed nearly eleven years of congressional activity surrounding the idea of FOIA. Although President Lyndon Johnson (LBJ) signed the law, he did not do so with enthusiasm. According to Johnson's press secretary, "LBJ had to be dragged kicking and screaming to the signing ceremony. He hated the very idea of the Freedom of Information Act; hated the thought of journalists rummaging in government closets; hated them challenging the official view of reality."[25]

Given this inauspicious beginning, it was no surprise that the original FOIA law struggled to accomplish the goal of disclosing information to the public. Congressional hearings in the early 1970s documented ways in which executive agencies were actively resisting compliance with FOIA records requests. High costs and long delays plagued the process. FOIA success stories often came only when the requester was willing and able to engage in litigation. The fallout from the Watergate scandal under President Nixon accompanied the effort by Congress to revisit and strengthen FOIA. Despite a veto from President Gerald Ford, an override by Congress passed the 1974 amendments and bolstered the Act's operational effectiveness.[26]

Further amendments weakened and then modernized FOIA in 1986 and 1996, respectively. The 1996 amendments are popularly known as the Electronic Freedom of Information Act, or E-FOIA, which embraced the role of the Internet to provide documents to requesters electronically and in online reading rooms. A new and broad exemption to the fulfillment of FOIA requests accompanied the Homeland Security Act in 2002 and was considered by some to be a threat to FOIA's core objectives.[27] The exemptions under which agencies can deny fulfillment of FOIA requests include the categories shown in Table 10.2.[28]

TABLE 10.2 FOIA EXEMPTIONS FROM DISCLOSURE

Number	Description
1	Information that is classified to protect national security.
2	Information related solely to the internal personnel rules and practices of an agency.
3	Information that is prohibited from disclosure by another federal law.
4	Trade secrets or commercial or financial information that is confidential or privileged.
5	Privileged communications within or between agencies.
6	Information that, if disclosed, would invade another individual's personal privacy.
7	Information compiled for law enforcement purposes.
8	Information that concerns the supervision of financial institutions.
9	Geological information on wells.

Who Files FOIA Requests and for What Purposes?

A popular misperception is that journalists are the most frequent users of FOIA requests. Although the media is most visible, a recent review of FOIA logs across eighty-five federal agencies found nearly 40 percent of information requests filed by businesses, 20 percent by individuals, 16.7 percent from law firms, and only 7.6 percent from news media organizations.[29] The prominence of requests from businesses and law firms suggests that most records requests are for information that is used for commerce. Other FOIA requests run the gamut from exposing instances of abuse of power to what might be deemed as fodder for popular entertainment.

At one extreme, the FOIA was the tool used by a freelance journalist in the late-1970s to uncover details about a fourteen-year Central Intelligence Agency (CIA) research program in behavioral modification referred to as MKULTRA. The records of the program, which included experiments giving LSD to unknowing civilians, were destroyed by the CIA in 1973 except for financial records uncovered by the later FOIA request. Then-CIA Director Admiral Stansfield Turner testified in a Senate hearing that "the employee who located this material did so by leaving no stone unturned in his efforts to respond to FOIA requests . . . and, thus, discovered the MKULTRA-related documents which had been missed in the previous searches" to comply with earlier Congressional investigations.[30]

In 2007, on the other end of the spectrum, a private website that houses federal government documents asked the Federal Communications Commission (FCC) for any informal complaints made regarding the *South Park* cartoon program on television. In response, the FCC provided more than sixty pages of complaints with redacted personal information. The complaints, sometimes handwritten, provide insight into public outrage over the perceived inappropriate language and content of the show. Ironically, the show is broadcast on cable television, which is beyond the regulatory authority of the FCC.[31]

Costs of Openness Through FOIA

The large number and variation of FOIA requests translates into a labor intensive process for public officials. The Electronic Frontier Foundation raises awareness about the continuing challenges encountered when accessing government information. Each year, the Foundation humorously awards "The Foilies" to not-so-successful FOIA requests. The "Outrageous Fee Award" in 2017 was given to the Missouri Department of Health and Senior Services for a request to receive state vital statistics data—birth and death records—filed by an organization called Reclaim the Records. The Department initially determined that fulfillment of the request would cost $1.5 million for approximately 35,000 labor hours, despite the filer's expectation that the information could be gathered from a basic database query.[32] Such an extreme cost of disclosure is the exception, but there are real and substantial costs to openness that are worth consideration.

In fiscal year 2016, nearly 800,000 FOIA requests were submitted to the federal government. More than 4,000 workers were dedicated to fulfilling these requests at an estimated cost of $514,614,589. The $4 million in fees collected and associated with the FOIA requests accounted for less than 1 percent of the incurred costs.[33] Half-a-billion dollars a year is a lot of money; taxpayers are left to judge for themselves whether the costs of FOIA are worthwhile. Relative to other federal government spending, though, the annual amount spent on FOIA compliance is roughly equivalent to less than half-a-day's interest expense on the national debt in 2016[34] and comparable to the purchase of five-and-a-half F-35A fighter jets at a recently reduced unit cost of $95 million per plane.[35]

Open Meeting and Privacy Laws[36]

FOIA's focus on existing records and documents misses much of the face-to-face activity of government decision making. In particular, meetings where elected and appointed officials deliberate and set policy are critical public venues. While FOIA opened government records to the public, it also raised the specter of concern over privacy for personal information. Congress responded by enacting a series of laws to guarantee open meetings and safeguards for personal privacy during the decade following passage of FOIA.

*Federal Advisory Committee Act (1972) and Government in the
Sunshine Act (1976)*

Federal open meeting laws share similar requirements but are targeted at different organizations. The Federal Advisory Committee Act, or FACA, applies to the more than one thousand federal advisory committees that give advice to the executive branch. These advisory committees range alphabetically from the Assembly of the Administrative Conference of the United States to the World War I Centennial Commission.[37] Unlike the FACA, the subsequently enacted Government in the Sunshine Act, commonly shortened to the Sunshine Act, applies to the executive branch agencies, themselves, that fall under FOIA. This means that the court system, legislative branch, and the White House are not included. Open meeting laws also exist in state and local governments, although the particulars may differ.

Under both the FACA and Sunshine Act, meetings must be open to the public. Importantly, open meeting laws do not mandate that meetings be conducted to make decisions. A meeting under the Sunshine Act is defined as:

> The deliberations of at least the number of individual agency members required to take action on behalf of the agency where such deliberations determine or result in the joint conduct or disposition of official agency business.[38]

The Supreme Court later clarified that dialogue that essentially decides future official actions of an agency represents a meeting under the Sunshine Act.

"Open" means that a number of steps must be taken to ensure the public is adequately informed that the meeting will take place and the events of the meeting are documented and available. Notice and details of an upcoming meeting are provided through the *Federal Register* under FACA at least fifteen days before the meeting is scheduled. The Sunshine Act is less clear about the method of public notification and has a shorter, week-long period needed before the meeting itself takes place.

As with FOIA, exemptions exist that allow advisory committees and agencies to avoid compliance with the open meeting laws. Specifically, ten exemptions exist allowing for closed, or partially closed, meetings. Under FACA, the decision to close a meeting must be reflected in the public notice along with the exemptions being claimed. For agency meetings under the Sunshine Act, the decision to close a meeting requires a supporting majority vote. The vote must be publicized in a timely manner along with certification that the claim of exemption is reasonable by the agency's general counsel or chief legal officer. Most exemptions require that a transcript of the meeting be kept by the agency, although minutes satisfy the requirement in certain cases.

A sample of exemptions include when an open meeting would disclose secret or classified information, violate personal privacy, release trade secrets or privileged information, conflict with an investigation or related proceedings, or release information that would "significantly frustrate implementation of a proposed agency action."[39] The use of exemptions can be challenged. Compliance with FACA has been enforced by litigation under the Administrative Procedure Act, while filing suit in federal court is pursued for perceived violations of the Sunshine Act.

Open meeting requirements exist at all levels of government and are intended to ensure that dialogue and decisions about public policies are indeed public. Open meetings are generally perceived as a common sense form of transparency, but that does not mean that such laws are without controversy. Public officials sometimes get tripped up by the requirements, which can be strict. In Colorado, as a typical example, a meeting between two or more members of a state body (including boards, commissions, and other decision-making entities) qualifies as an open meeting requiring advanced notice to the public if public business is discussed.[40] The following case describes a common tension between preserving openness and efforts to cultivate a collegial working environment.

DINNER OR A MEETING: CONTROVERSY AT THE WISCONSIN DEPARTMENT OF NATURAL RESOURCES[41]

On the evening prior to formal board meetings, Wisconsin's Department of Natural Resources (DNR) traditionally held "social dinners" for members of its Natural Resources Board (NRB). The dinners became a thing of the past following a citizen complaint filed under Wisconsin's open meeting law. The complaint argued that a January 2016 dinner constituted a public meeting, since a pending decision related to Blue Mound State Park was allegedly discussed.

Although the DNR asserts compliance with the law due to the social nature of the dinners, the decision to temporarily halt the practice of the dinners was made to satisfy "a desire for the utmost transparency." According to the DNR, future social events for board members will be publicized in advance and board members and staff "are expected to avoid DNR or NRB business discussions during any purely social gathering."[42]

The Privacy Act (1974)

With the Watergate scandal as backdrop, Congress passed the Privacy Act in 1974. Despite being categorized as an open government law, the Privacy Act differs because its focus is on protections for individual privacy. The policy objectives, as described by the U.S. Department of Justice, include balancing "the government's need to maintain information about individuals with the rights of individuals to be protected against unwarranted invasions of their privacy stemming from federal agencies' collection, maintenance, use, and disclosure of personal information about them."[43]

In practice, this means that the federal government is obligated to limit disclosing "personally identifiable records" that it maintains. Most visible, the Act allows individuals to request access to "records maintained on themselves" by government agencies and to address inaccuracies in those records. Similar to the FOIA process, individuals can write a letter to any federal agency asking for records about the requester. Such letters typically refer to both the Privacy Act and FOIA as a basis for the request.[44] Finally, the Privacy Act established a set of "fair information practices" related to government records.[45]

LIMITS TO GOVERNMENT TRANSPARENCY

Future Supreme Court Justice Antonin Scalia once famously referred to FOIA as "the Taj Mahal of the Doctrine of Unanticipated Consequences, the Sistine Chapel of Cost-Benefit Analysis Ignored" to highlight the law's primary use by private businesses and the high costs of fulfilling requests.[46] Then-Professor Scalia's critique is summed up in the following paragraph:

> "The act and its amendments were promoted as a means of finding out about the operations of government; they have been used largely as a means of obtaining data in the government's hands concerning private institutions. They were promoted as a boon to the press, the public interest group, the little guy; they have been used most frequently by corporate lawyers. They were promoted as a minimal imposition on the operations of government; they have greatly burdened investigative agencies and the courts . . . In short, it is a far cry from John Q. Public finding out how his government works."[47]

Critics of transparency raise a number of concerns about openness in addition to the costs and the fact that the primary use of open government laws is not actually by the public. Moreover, there are generally acknowledged limits to transparency when dealing with a number of sensitive government topics, like military strategy.

Beyond the areas incompatible with openness, there is the potential for misinterpretation of government information. The risk of misinterpretation is due to the complex nature of government activities and an unbalanced focus on negative information by the media. Scholar Amitai Etzioni points out that, "transparency, unlike other forms of regulation, has a major disadvantage: it assumes that those who receive the information released by producers or public officials can properly process it and that their conclusions will lead them to reasonable action."[48]

Another issue with transparency is that it may impede thoughtful policy making if decision makers are less likely to speak freely and less likely to compromise under the bright lights of open government that demand posturing and hardline stances.

Although occasionally mentioned as a solution to legislative gridlock, reducing government transparency is a contentious and unpopular policy shift.[49] Finally, greater transparency is frequently at the expense of cherished privacy.

An emerging concern over transparency is that it may be less compatible with evolving forms of governance. The public's right to transparent government has resulted in a broad set of legal protections for citizens to monitor government information and activities. The burgeoning partnership between government and the nonprofit sector to provide public services has, maybe unexpectedly, complicated expectations of transparency.

A recent example comes from Texas where a private nonprofit organization, the Alamo Endowment and the Alamo Complex Management Company, operates the historic Alamo attraction on behalf of the state. Efforts to review the organization's meeting minutes by a Houston newspaper were rebuffed with the explanation that the nonprofit is not a government, but rather a state contractor. Concerned legislators and open government advocates caution that contracting out "could create essentially a shadow government, opaque to outside scrutiny by taxpayers, for operations that once were public and transparent."[50] To bore more deeply into this conundrum, the following section details transparency among nonprofit organizations.

> *"So does transparency really promote accountability? Some of the time it does, of course . . . . But there's reason to worry that transparency is reaching the stage of faddish excess, distracting public managers and citizens alike from a better-balanced portfolio of governance measures."*
>
> —John D. Donahue

TRANSPARENCY OF NONPROFIT ORGANIZATIONS

The transparency of government is often guided, or even dictated, by laws that empower citizens. Nonprofit organizations operate in a very different environment as, technically, private organizations. Are the expectations for transparency in nonprofit organizations fundamentally different than for government?

In 2004, the Panel on the Nonprofit Sector was assembled to conduct "a thorough examination of the nonprofit sector's governance, transparency, and ethical standards."[51] The Panel asserts that the nonprofit sector has certain responsibilities to government and the public derived from the receipt of (1) preferential tax treatment imbued by federal and state laws and (2) contributions of time and resources by citizens. These responsibilities include that "charities and foundations operate transparently, prevent fraud and the enrichment of insiders and other abuses, and serve the purposes for which they have been created."[52]

While celebrating the independence of the nonprofit sector from government as a virtue, the Panel presents principles for improving accountability in the sector. One of the principles expresses the need for comprehensive and accurate information "about the programs, activities, and finances of all charitable organizations" available to the public in a timely manner.[53] The following sections detail the areas where nonprofit transparency exists, where it is needed, and the particular trade-offs of nonprofit transparency.

Current Practices in Nonprofit Transparency

For some, transparency is seen simply as an approach to management reform across the government and nonprofit sectors. Scholar Paul Light refers to these transparency-oriented practices as the "Watchful Eye," with the assumption that "making financial and performance information visible will allow competition to weed out inefficiency."[54] In his 2000 report on nonprofit management, however, Light suggests that the availability of information, alone, will not improve trust.

Without major laws to support nonprofit openness to the public, like the federal government's Administrative Procedure Act, transparency of the nonprofit sector has fallen to a piecemeal set of actors that includes nonprofit watchdogs (like Charity Navigator), data providers (like GuideStar and the National Center for Charitable Statistics), state attorneys general, and federal agencies (the Internal Revenue Service). The fact that the primary federal agency dealing with nonprofits is a tax collector is ironic given the general lack of tax liability.

Even in the presence of these formal and informal actors that support transparency, Light argues that it is citizens who implement the Watchful Eye by being thoughtful and informed donors. Indeed, transparency has come to mean the timely posting of key pieces of organizational information online for easy access by anyone who wishes to review it.

Bob Carlson, then-Assistant Attorney General of the State of Missouri, provides wise counsel to nonprofits on transparency: First, nonprofits should be as open as possible to the public. At a minimum, financial information should be prominently available online. Second, expectations for transparency from the public and from donors grows each year and already exceed most state disclosure requirements. In other words, nonprofit organizations need to do more than just comply with legal transparency standards to satisfy the demands of the public and donors.[55]

In 2006, GuideStar asked readers to answer the question, "what does nonprofit transparency mean to you?"[56] The responses focused on either "financial accountability" or "openness about missions and programs." The bifurcated answers highlight the sector's historical focus on making financial information public, along with the desire to improve visibility into how, and how effectively, those resources are used.

The financial accountability comments focused on compliance, including discussions of "adherence to federal and state regulations, annual financial audits, timely submission of reporting documents, and clear accounting methods and record keeping." Alternately, respondents focused on mission and program transparency and emphasized the need to demonstrate that a nonprofit's actions directly enhance fulfillment of the organization's mission.

The following anonymous response was highlighted for broadly capturing the meaning of nonprofit transparency and its implications across an organization:

I think of the acronym DWYSYWD (do what you say you will do). Do the actions of the organization reflect the core values and mission it promotes? Is there genuine evidence of the agency's high regard for integrity across all core aspects of the agency— from program operation and hiring practices, to evaluation and communications as well as the financial practices (where most media attention often gravitates)? Examples of evidence may include recognizing and abiding to all applicable state and federal laws, exploring appropriate accreditation opportunities, completing regular annual reports/audits and making that information readily available to funders, using independent researchers to conduct program evaluations, maintaining open lines of communication between donors and the like.[57]

Doing what you say you will do sounds simple, but the following case shows that transparency of operations sometimes is at odds with efforts to generate support.

OPENNESS AND MARKETING: THE CASE OF MICROFINANCE THROUGH KIVA[58]

At times, nonprofit marketing and transparency can appear conflicted. The nonprofit Kiva allows individuals to engage in microfinance by loaning funds to borrowers engaged in a wide range of activities across the world. A couple of current microfinance opportunities include contributing to a $450 loan for a woman in Togo to buy seventeen sacks of onions or a loan of $1,475 in support of a grandson's eye operation in Mexico. The marketing of Kiva focuses on lenders selecting projects to support based on their personal preferences.

A heavily-trafficked blog post in 2009 called into question this person-to-person lending experience. The author explained that Kiva users do not actually make direct loans to the selected people and projects. In reality, the portrayed individual borrowers online have existing loans from secondary microfinance institutions. The Kiva lending helped to "backstop" these microfinance institutions, something that was explained, albeit not prominently, on the Kiva website.

Kiva, apparently in response to the publicity, shifted the tag line on its website from "Kiva lets you lend to a specific entrepreneur, empowering them to lift themselves out of poverty" to a less specific "Kiva connects people through lending to alleviate poverty." Kiva's model has developed since this initial controversy and, with lending closing in on $1 billion in 2017, now offers both direct loans to borrowers and partner loans made to other microfinance organizations.[59]

IRS Form 990

The IRS Form 990 remains the primary source of public information on nonprofit organizations. The IRS called the informational filing "the key transparency tool relied on by the public, state regulators, the media, researchers, and policymakers to obtain information about the tax-exempt sector and individual organizations."[60] In 2007, the IRS engaged the nonprofit community in a major redesign effort of the Form 990. After decades of tinkering with the form, the popular perception was that it lagged the development of the nonprofit sector. The first guiding principle of the redesign effort was "enhancing transparency," meaning that the form should clearly describe the nonprofit organization and allow for meaningful comparisons with peer organizations.[61]

The redesigned form was adopted for the 2008 tax year and it enhanced transparency and accessibility of information by providing a summary page presenting key details of the filing. On the revised form, financial information for the current filing year is presented with last year's numbers for comparison purposes. Program accomplishments prominently follow the summary section and present the organization's mission and descriptions of its largest programs.[62]

The redesigned Form 990 increases the amount of detail provided on governance, management, and disclosure. Questions cover, for example, the independence of the board, the existence of written policies on conflicts of interest, how executive compensation is determined, and whether family or business relationships exist between individuals in the organization. The provided information delves into the structures that are intended to limit fraud and abuse of the nonprofit status. Questions are included about how the organization makes the Forms 1023 (Application for Recognition of Exemption) and 990, governing documents, conflict of interest policy, and financial statements accessible to the public, along with the staff contact responsible for possessing those documents.

Despite the usefulness of annual updates, depending solely on the Form 990 to meet the transparency needs of nonprofit organizations is limited by two main shortcomings. As an informational form collected by the IRS, little rigorous insight into program outcomes can be conveyed. The Form 990 also falls into the category of retrospective transparency. The delay in public access to the filings can be lengthy and reduces the timeliness of the information. The filing of the average Form 990 comes around eight months after the nonprofit organization's fiscal year ends. Many organizations delay filing and use multiple extensions, which can push the timing to more than ten months after the end of the fiscal year.[63]

Guidance on Achieving Nonprofit Transparency

A GuideStar report on voluntary disclosure practices among nonprofits presents steps for them to strengthen their transparency practices.[64]

First, periodically update the organization's website to stay current with changes. Provide any available program evaluations and the organization's underlying theory of change to the public online.

Second, include information on the nonprofit organization's board and staff members including names, titles, and background.

Third, the website is a repository of both required and desired information. Make current and past annual reports, audited financial statements, and the IRS letter of determination available online. Form 990 filings should also be made available, especially in the absence of audited financial statements for smaller organizations.

Executive Compensation

Compensation is a touchy subject for nonprofit organizations, particularly executive compensation. This is because there is tension between the expectation that nonprofits will be led by capable, experienced individuals who are compensated fairly, and the expectation that compensation rates will be consistent with the organization's nonprofit mission. According to Charity Navigator, compensation at nonprofits is the leading topic of complaints they receive.[65]

A by-product of making the Form 990 publicly available is that compensation information is included for board members, who are usually unpaid, and the most highly-compensated employees. Nonprofit organizations have been lambasted by members of Congress for perceived excesses in executive compensation. Nonprofit organizations and their boards should not approve executive salaries unless they are comfortable releasing and defending the compensation to the public.

In 2015, a member of Congress alleged that nonprofit "Planned Parenthood is an organization with massive salaries" as an additional critique in an already contentious debate over continued federal funding for the organization. The primary focus of this claim was the compensation package for the organization's president, Cecile Richards, which totaled $590,928 in 2014. Richards' salary was $427,597 with the remaining compensation coming from bonuses and contributions to a retirement plan. The press looked into the claim that Richards was overpaid by comparing her compensation to two comparison groups: large nonprofits and nonprofit health-care organizations. Using the publicly available executive compensation information on the Form 990 and reports from watchdog organizations, reporters demonstrated that her compensation fell nearly 17 percent below the average for large nonprofits and that it greatly lagged behind the salaries for nonprofit hospital chief executives, which ranged from $1.2 to $1.5 million annually.[66] This is an example of how required transparency in nonprofit compensation can be viewed as either a threat or an opportunity to justify salary levels.

Fund-raising Practices and Expenses

Fund-raising is another nonprofit topic that receives scrutiny from the public and deserves adequate transparency. Foremost, nonprofit organizations should be honest in calculating and reporting fund-raising expenses to the public rather than disguising the costs by shifting them to programs. Related, the practice of compensating professional fund-raisers based on a percentage of the funds raised is strongly discouraged by professional associations. Fund-raising arrangements should always be communicated to potential donors so they know where and how their gifts are being used.[67]

Best Practices in Nonprofit Transparency

In response to reports of financial improprieties in charities and the increasing influence of private foundations, some observers argue that the nonprofit sector is possibly the least "accountable to outsiders."[68] This lack of transparency is inconsistent with the global trend of increasingly accessible information in government and business.

In some countries governments have taken a renewed interest in providing oversight to the nonprofit sector. For example, the Charity Commission for England and Wales was formed in 2007 "to ensure that the public can support charities with confidence," in part by collecting nonprofit organization information, issuing transparency reports, and providing support to whistleblowers on nonprofit misconduct.[69]

At about the same time, in the United States, the Panel on Nonprofits developed recommendations to strengthen accountability. A number of these foreshadowed the direction of today's transparency efforts that encourage disclosure of performance data in addition to financial data. While financial disclosure and audits preclude corruption, performance metrics based on the share of spending directed towards programs offers little information about the effectiveness of those programs. In response, the Panel calls for each charitable organization to "provide more detailed information about its operations, including methods it uses to evaluate the outcomes of programs, to the public through its annual report, website, and other means."[70] The focus of transparency, thus, is moving in the direction of disclosure of mission-based effectiveness.

Focusing on transparency in public charities obscures the increasing prominence of private foundations. The role of citizen-donors in demanding transparency and putting that information to use is less clear for the latter. Philanthropy has become less open as a majority of private foundations refuse to even consider unsolicited funding proposals.[71] Despite this, some foundations have acted to improve the transparency of their grant-making activity. The Foundation Center, for example, has taken a leadership role in promoting transparency. It identifies the following benefits: strengthens credibility, increases public trust, improves grantee relationships, reduces duplication of effort, facilitates greater collaboration, and builds a community of shared learning.[72] The following case presents a glimpse at such efforts by The David and Lucile Packard Foundation.

FOUNDATIONS OF TRANSPARENCY: THE DAVID AND LUCILE PACKARD FOUNDATION

Contributors to private foundations receive upfront tax benefits in return for the promise of future grant-making activity to charitable organizations. Efforts to be transparent by The David and Lucile Packard Foundation were showcased as best practices for foundations more than a decade ago in a 2005 report to Congress:

> The David and Lucile Packard Foundation is a 40-year-old family foundation that has long provided information about the impact of its grantees. As part of its commitment to transparency and effectiveness, it recently added extensive information on governance to its online presence. The foundation's website now offers grant-seekers, media, and the public access to its bylaws, committee charters, code of conduct and statement of values, conflict of interest policy, and whistleblower policy. It also features the foundation's 990-PF for the previous five years and results from its two most recent surveys of grantees about the foundation's performance. An easily accessible place for public access to these policies, financial information and grantee perceptions, the website has helped educate the public about the foundation's operations, ensured greater accuracy in media reports, and saved staff time in responding to requests from reporters or other interested people.[73]

The Foundation continues to provide detailed information to the public on its grant-making activity and, maybe more important, on the efficacy of the giving. A visitor to the website can now search past grant-making activity by keyword, program, award amount, or year. For example, a search for grant-making in Colorado returns information on a $150,000 grant made to the Denver Foundation in 2012. The grant supported the Colorado Fire Relief Fund, which helped victims of wildfires in Pueblo, El Paso, and Teller counties.

While public access to grant-making activity is useful to agencies that seek funding, citizens also have the ability to learn about projects supported by the Foundation. The Foundation also publicly provides evaluations, toolkits, and research that can inform and support activities beyond its own grantees.

Trade-offs of Nonprofit Transparency

Greater transparency in the nonprofit sector is desirable as a means to maintain and enhance the public trust. At the same time, transparency is costly and causes additional management burdens for already underresourced enterprises. The former president of Charity Navigator, a nonprofit watchdog organization, captured this trade-off when he said "Greater transparency will mean more work for charities, no doubt about it."[74] In particular, concerns over mandated costs of transparency are greatest for the sector's many small organizations.

Ask Me Why I Care: Valerie Lemmie, Director of Exploratory Research, Kettering Foundation[75]

"I never fully appreciated how much courage one has to have to step into a position of trying to lead a community with differing views, opinions and voices."—Valerie Lemmie

Valerie Lemmie is currently director of exploratory research for the Kettering Foundation, a position she has held since 2014. In 2005, she was a scholar-in-residence at the foundation and wrote about the value of public administrators working collaboratively with citizens in naming, framing, and acting on wicked community problems.

Valerie served as city manager for the cities of Petersburg, Virginia and Dayton and Cincinnati, Ohio; commissioner on the Public Utility Commission of Ohio; and district director and acting chief of staff for Congressman Mike Turner (Ohio's 10th District). Most recently, Lemmie directed the Eastern Interconnection States' Planning Council, an initiative designed to evaluate transmission grid development options throughout the Interconnection. Learn more about her at https://www.unomaha.edu/college-of-public-affairs-and-community-service/community-engagement/pss-valerie-lemmie.php.

SUMMARY

Transparency in public service organizations is a powerful concept where best practices for openness are continuously challenged by a blend of expanding expectations and advancing technology. This chapter began with a look at WikiLeaks and the emergence of less conventional forms of transparency being imposed on governments around the world. More than two decades ago, Senator Daniel Patrick Moynihan made a prescient statement on government secrecy, the speed with which information now travels, and the role of the public sector in presenting and using its information. In 1997, Senator Moynihan observed:

> In one direction we can reach out and touch the time when the leaders of the Soviet Union thought that the explosion at the nuclear reactor in Chernobyl could be kept secret from the rest of the world. In the other direction we can see a time—already upon us—when fourteen-year-old hackers in Australia or Newfoundland can make their way into the most sensitive areas of national security or inter-

national finance. The central concern of government in the future will not be information, but analysis. We need government agencies staffed with argumentative people who can live with ambiguity and look upon secrecy as a sign of insecurity.[76]

Openness in government cannot automatically prevent public sector shortcomings because the success of transparency is context-dependent. Its defenders argue, however, that "there is no reason to abandon transparency or the hard-won advantages it has gained us: empowering citizens to hold government accountable, preventing crises and safeguarding communities, increasing effectiveness while reducing waste, and engaging the public in democratic decision-making."[77] Both government and nonprofit transparency are experiencing an important shift from simply providing information for accountability purposes, which is now expected, to using information for demonstrating program effectiveness.[78]

KEY TERMS

Active transparency – exists when an organization makes information accessible to the public in the absence of any specific request.

Exemptions – with regard to the requirements of the Freedom of Information Act (FOIA), these refer to the categories of information for which agencies can deny fulfillment of FOIA requests.

Federal Advisory Committee Act (FACA) – law requiring the more than 1,000 federal advisory committees giving advice to the executive branch to hold open meetings.

Freedom of Information Act (FOIA) – law that provides a legal framework within which the public can request access to existing government records, requires federal agencies to regularly disclose certain information in the *Federal Register*, and requires agencies to maintain reading rooms that house a set of prescribed documents.

Fund-raising disclosure – refers to when nonprofit organizations accurately disclose fund-raising expenses and practices to the public.

Government in the Sunshine Act – law requiring the executive branch agencies that fall under the FOIA to hold open meetings.

Inward transparency – represents the ability of outsiders to view the activities occurring within an organization.

IRS Form 990 – form filed by tax-exempt nonprofits to report financial information; primary source for nonprofits' annual financial data.

Leaks – intentional releases of information that had previously been maintained with secrecy.

Open meeting laws – laws requiring various organizations to hold meetings that are publicized and open to the public.

Passive transparency – exists when an organization is reactive and requires an outside request for information to be provided from the organization.

Privacy Act – law that protects individuals from invasions of privacy related to the collection, maintenance, usage, and disclosure of personal information by federal agencies.

Public notice – notice providing details of an upcoming meeting in the *Federal Register* in accordance with the applicable open meeting laws.

Real-time transparency – the continuous and timely release of information to the public, particularly when there is urgency in the need to disseminate information.

Targeted transparency – refers to mandated disclosures of information, usually driven by government regulation, that are made to alleviate potential information asymmetries.

Transparency – in organizations, refers to the presence of open processes, actions, and documents that are subject to public scrutiny.

DISCUSSION QUESTIONS

1. With more information easily accessible, what are the challenges to achieving effective transparency by governments and nonprofit organizations?

2. Consider the perspective that today's high levels of transparency are at least partially responsible for degraded policy making because elected officials have less freedom to make compromises through back-room deals. Is this perspective credible? And if so, where is the balance between the fundamental merits of openness and the need to get things done?

3. Identify and describe an instance, either from personal experience or from news accounts, where government or nonprofit transparency changed your perception of an organization. Was the resulting change positive or negative?

BUILD YOUR SKILLS

Seeking information under the Freedom of Information Act is a straightforward task. Follow the steps to learn, first, whether the information is already available without having to file. If filing is necessary, proper actions are described.

SKILLBOX: HOW TO FILE A FREEDOM OF INFORMATION ACT (FOIA) REQUEST[1]

The Freedom of Information Act (FOIA) "is the embodiment of the public's right to know about the activities of its government."[2] The following steps provide guidance to filing a FOIA request once the need for federal records is established.

1) Before filing a FOIA request, make sure that the desired information is not already in the public domain. Filing a request requires time and effort. Remember that federal agencies maintain FOIA reading rooms online in an attempt to provide common and recently requested information. FOIAonline houses previously-released records for more than a dozen federal agencies and offices. Ask this question:
- Can the desired information be acquired through an existing online repository? If not:

2) Begin the request process and do not be intimidated. Filing a request "is as simple as writing a letter."[3] The FOIA process is designed to encourage requests. It assumes that requesters have a "right to know" and that the federal government must justify keeping records out of the public's hands.

3) Consider whether the desired records are likely to exist and are subject to FOIA. Remember that FOIA applies only to existing records of the federal government's Executive Branch. So, federal agencies, offices, and the military comply with FOIA, but elected officials and the judiciary do not. Ask these questions:
- Does the information already exist in a record? If not, agencies do not have to collect requested data under FOIA. If so:
- Are the records held by state or local governments? If so, use the respective state or local government open records process to access the information. If not:
- Is the information maintained by the White House, Congress, or the Courts? If not:

4) Determine whether the requested information is likely to fall under one of the nine exemptions for disclosure. Uncertainty about exemptions should not dissuade record requests, but many requests are denied or only partially fulfilled based on exemptions after vetting by agency personnel.

5) Identify where to direct the FOIA request based on the likely source of the desired records. The request must be submitted to an individual federal agency or to multiple agencies because FOIA requests are not centrally administered.

6) Draft the written FOIA request. A sample FOIA request letter is shown on the next page. The following components are required in the written request:
- Direct the letter to the director of the agency or the FOIA officer.
- Make clear that "the request is being made pursuant to the Freedom of Information Act."[4]
- Describe the desired records clearly and with sufficient detail to be located. Use the name and date of a document when available or, alternately, describe the intent of the request to make sure that the request is broad enough to identify the relevant records. Often, communication between the requester and agency representative helps to clarify the needs of the record request.
- Include contact information containing, at a minimum, name and address.

The inclusion of the following information is optional, but helps the agency proceed with record collection in a timely manner:
- Be clear about the maximum amount of fees the requester is prepared to pay to fulfill the records request. Ask to be contacted if the fees will exceed the stated amount. Fees differ by agency and based on the type of requester. For example, businesses are charged higher fees than individuals, employees of news organizations, education institutions, and nonprofit organizations.
- Ask that any fees be waived if the information request serves the public, rather than commercial, interest.
- Explain the preferred format, for example electronic files or as hardcopy, of the retrieved records.
- If the urgency of the request justifies expedited processing, then explain the "compelling need" for the FOIA request. Expedited processing is applicable when a delay in receiving the requested records may result in "an imminent threat to an individual's life or physical safety" or the requester is "primarily engaged in disseminating information" with an "urgency to inform the public concerning actual or alleged Federal Government activity."[5]

7) Submit the FOIA request. The written request can be transmitted in a variety of ways, including by mail, e-mail, online form, or fax.

8) Wait. Within twenty working days, the agency should provide an initial response with a determination on the ability to comply with the records request. The status

of the request can be viewed online for some agencies. If the response time exceeds twenty working days, then contact the agency. The records, if granted, are delivered shortly after this determination. If the request is denied, then ask these questions:

- Did the agency adequately explain the reasons for denying the information request? If not:
- File an appeal of the determination to the agency or contact the Office of Government Information Services (OGIS) for mediation with the agency. Has the agency response to the appeal or OGIS mediation satisfactorily detailed the rationale for denial or delay of the request's fulfillment? If not:

9) File a FOIA lawsuit in U.S. District Court.

Sample Freedom of Information Act Request Letter:[6]

Agency Head [or Freedom of Information Act Officer]
Name of Agency
Address of Agency
City, State, Zip Code

Re: Freedom of Information Act Request

Dear:

This is a request under the Freedom of Information Act.

I request that a copy of the following documents [or documents containing the following information] be provided to me: [identify the documents or information as specifically as possible].

In order to help determine my status for purposes of determining the applicability of any fees, you should know that I am (insert a suitable description of the requester and the purpose of the request).

[Sample requester descriptions]:

a representative of the news media affiliated with the _____ newspaper (magazine, television station, etc.), and this request is made as part of news gathering and not for a commercial use.

affiliated with an educational or noncommercial scientific institution, and this request is made for a scholarly or scientific purpose and not for commercial use.

an individual seeking information for personal use and not for commercial use.

affiliated with a private corporation and am seeking information for use in the company's business.

[Optional] I am willing to pay fees for this request up to a maximum of $__. If you estimate that the fees will exceed this limit, please inform me first.

[Optional] I request a waiver of all fees for this request. Disclosure of the requested information to me is in the public interest because it is likely to contribute significantly to public understanding of the operations or activities of the government and is not primarily in my commercial interest.

[Include specific details, including how the requested information will be disseminated by the requester for public benefit.]

[Optional] I request that the information I seek be provided in electronic format, and I would like to receive it on a personal computer disk [or a CD-ROM].

[Optional] I ask that my request receive expedited processing because _____. [Include specific details concerning your "compelling need," such as being someone "primarily engaged in disseminating information" and specifics concerning your "urgency to inform the public concerning actual or alleged Federal Government activity."]

[Optional] I also have included an e-mail address and a telephone number at which I can be contacted, if necessary, to discuss any aspect of my request.

Thank you for your consideration of this request.

Sincerely,

Name
Address
City, State, Zip Code
Telephone number [Optional]
E-mail Address [Optional]

Hands-On Activities

1. Select a federal agency and draft a FOIA request for documents of interest based on the example letter given. For example, someone with an environmental policy focus might draft a FOIA request for documents containing any communication between the Bureau of Land Management and oil and gas lease-holders related to greater sage-grouse habitat preservation. Housing policy advocates could submit a FOIA request to the Department of Housing and Urban Development for a list of all multifamily housing currently receiving federal housing assistance payment (HAP) subsidies in a specific city. A state health-care director could request a list of all employees working in the nearest Department of Health and Human Services office, along with their position titles, grades, and salaries.

2. Investigate a state or local government open records law. To do this, collect the text of the law and write a one-page memo detailing key examples of how the state or local open records law differs from the federal law. For example, how do the state or local government exemptions from document disclosure differ from the federal FOIA? What are the stated document fees and are fee waivers available?

3. Select an existing FOIA request and document the details of the request, its fulfillment, and the available materials in a one-page memo to the professor. Background information: Federal agencies maintain E-FOIA reading rooms. The reading rooms usually post Frequently Requested Materials. A federal website also serves as a multi-agency repository for existing FOIA request materials (see https://foiaonline.regulations.gov/foia/action/public/home). You can select a FOIA request from an agency of interest or one used as the source material mentioned in a news story.

Notes

1. This skillbox draws heavily from the U.S. Congress, House of Representatives, Committee on Oversight and Government Reform, *A Citizen's Guide on Using the Freedom of Information Act and the Privacy Act of 1974 to Request Government Records*, September 20, 2012, https://oversight.house.gov/report/committee-report-the-citizens-guide-to-using-the-freedom-of-information-act-and-the-privacy-act-of-1974-to-request-government-records/, which serves as an essential resource for generating a FOIA request.
2. Ibid., 1.
3. Ibid., 4.
4. Ibid., 8.
5. Ibid., 9.
6. Ibid., 37–38.

NOTES

1. James Madison, "James Madison to W. T. Barry, 4 Aug. 1822," *The Founders' Constitution* vol. 1, ch. 18, doc. 35, http://press-pubs.uchicago.edu/founders/documents/v1ch18s35.html.

2. Sissela Bok, *Secrets: On the Ethics of Concealment and Revelation* (New York: Vintage Books, 1989).

3. WikiLeaks, "What Is WikiLeaks" (November 3, 2015), https://wikileaks.org/What-is-Wikileaks.html.

4. Sarah Harrison, "Why the World Needs WikiLeaks," *New York Times* (November 17, 2016), https://www.nytimes.com/216/11/17/opinion/why-the-world-needs-wikileaks.html.

5. Devlin Barrett and Karoun Demirjian, "FBI Director Says He Feels 'Mildly Nauseous' About Possibility He Affected Election, but Has No Regrets," *Washington Post* (May 3, 2017), https://www.washingtonpost.com/world/national-security/fbi-director-james-comey-begins-testimony-to-congress/2017/05/03/9e3244bc-3006-11e7-9534-00e4656c22aa_story.html?utm_term=.0b4c44a46546.

6. Eric Schmitt, "In Disclosing Secret Documents, WikiLeaks Seeks 'Transparency'," *New York Times* (July 26, 2010), A11.

7. Alasdair Roberts, "WikiLeaks: The Illusion of Transparency," *International Review of Administrative Sciences* 78, no. 1 (2012): 117.

8. Louis D. Brandeis, "What Publicity Can Do," *Harper's Weekly* (December 20, 1913), 10.

9. Stephan Grimmelikhuijsen, "Transparency," in *Encyclopedia of Public Administration and Public Policy*, 3rd ed., ed. Domonic Bearfield and Melvin Dubnick (New York: Taylor & Francis, 2015), 3277.

10. Maria Cucciniello, Gregory A. Porumbescu, and Stephan Grimmelikhuijsen, "25 Years of Transparency Research: Evidence and Future Directions," *Public Administration Review* 77, no. 1 (2017): 32–44.

11. David Heald, "Varieties of Transparency," in *Transparency: The Key to Better Governance?*, ed. Christopher Hood and David Heald (Oxford, UK: Oxford University Press, 2006).

12. Grimmelikhuijsen, "Transparency," 3277–3278.

13. Archon Fung, Mary Graham, and David Weil, *Full Disclosure: The Perils and Promise of Transparency* (Cambridge, UK: Cambridge University Press, 2007).

14. Amitai Etzioni, "Is Transparency the Best Disinfectant?" *Journal of Political Philosophy* 18, no. 4 (2010): 389–404.

15. Heald, "Varieties."

16. Ibid., 34–35.

17. Cucciniello et al., "25 Years."

18. Alexandre Mas, "Does Transparency Lead to Pay Compression?" Princeton University and NBER (February, 2016).

19. Ibid., 6.

20. Ibid., 3.

21. Cucciniello et al., "25 Years."

22. Mathew D. McCubbins and Thomas Schwartz, "Congressional Oversight Overlooked: Police Patrols Versus Fire Alarms," *American Journal of Political Science* 28, no. 1 (1984): 166.

23. Suzanne J. Piotrowski, "Freedom of Information Act (FOIA): Federal," in *Encyclopedia of Public Administration and Public Policy*, 3rd ed., ed. Domonic Bearfield and Melvin Dubnick (New York: Taylor & Francis, 2015), 1532–1535.

24. Sheila S. Coronel, "Measuring Openness: A Survey of Transparency Ratings and the Prospects for a Global Index" (October 30, 2012), http://www.freedominfo.org/2012/10/measuring-openness-a-survey-of-transparency-ratings-and-the-prospects-for-a-global-index/.

25. Dan Lopez, Thomas Blanton, Meredith Fuchs and Barbara Elias, ed., "Veto Battle 30 Years Ago Set Freedom of Information Norms," *National Security Archive Electronic Briefing Book No. 142* (November 23, 2004), http://nsarchive.gwu.edu/NSAEBB/NSAEBB142/index.htm.

26. Ibid.

27. Piotrowski, "Freedom."

28. United States Department of Justice, "What Are FOIA Exemptions?," FOIA.gov, https://www.foia.gov/faq.html#exemptions.

29. Max Galka, "Who Uses FOIA?—An Analysis of 229,000 Requests to 85 Government Agencies" (March 13, 2017), https://foiamapper.com/who-uses-foia/.

30. U.S. Congress, Senate, *Project MKULTRA, the CIA's Program of Research in Behavioral Modification: Joint Hearing Before the Select Committee on Intelligence and the Subcommittee on Health and Scientific Research of the Committee on Human Resources*, 95th Cong., 1st sess., August 3, 1977, M-408.

31. Federal Communications Commission, *Informal Complaints About South Park Television Show Made to the Federal Communications Commission*, January 27, 2008, http://www.governmentattic.org/docs/FCC_Complaints_South-Park_2004-07.pdf.

32. Dave Maass, Aaron Mackey, and Kate Tummarello, "The Foilies 2017," Electronic Frontier Foundation (March 13, 2017), https://www.eff.org/deeplinks/2017/03/foilies-2017.

33. U.S. Department of Justice, Office of Information Policy, *Summary of Annual FOIA Reports for Fiscal Year 2016*, (2017), https://www.justice.gov/oip/reports/fy_2016_annual_report_summary.pdf/download.

34. "Interest Expense on the Debt Outstanding," TreasuryDirect, last modified June 5, 2017, https://www.treasurydirect.gov/govt/reports/ir/ir_expense.htm.

35. Aaron Gregg, "Lockheed Martin, Pentagon Announce F-35 Contract Deal That Shaves $728 Million in Costs," *Washington Post* (February 3, 2017), https://www.washingtonpost.com/news/checkpoint/wp/2017/02/03/lockheed-martin-pentagon-announce-f-35-contract-deal-that-shaves-728-million-in-costs/?utm_term=.8f6368988f58.

36. Corinna J. Zarek, ed., *Federal Open Government Guide*, 10th ed., (Arlington, VA: Reporters Committee for Freedom of the Press, 2009).

37. General Services Administration, "Agency/Committee List for FY 2016" (April 27, 2017), https://facadatabase.gov/acr/2016_committee_list.pdf.

38. *The Government in the Sunshine Act* (1976), 5 U.S.C. § 552b.

39. Ibid.

40. State of Colorado Office of Legislative Legal Services, *Open Meeting Requirements of the Colorado Sunshine Law* (September 30, 2013), https://www.colorado.gov/pacific/sites/default/files/Open%20Meeting%20Requirements%20of%20the%20Colorado%20Sunshine%20Law.pdf.

41. Lee Bergquist, "DNR Ends Board Dinners Under Open Records Scrutiny," *Milwaukee Journal Sentinel* (October 19, 2016), http://www.jsonline.com/story/news/politics/2016/10/19/dnr-ends-board-dinners-under-open-records-scrutiny/92418924/.

42. Associated Press, "Wisconsin Officials Plan Informal Meeting After Backlash" *US News* (May 15, 2017), https://www.usnews.com/news/best-states/wisconsin/articles/2017-05-15/wisconsin-officials-plan-informal-meeting-after-backlash.

43. U.S. Department of Justice Office of Privacy and Civil Liberties, *Overview of the Privacy Act of 1974* (2015), 4, https://www.justice.gov/opcl/file/793026/download.

44. For greater detail on submitting a Privacy Act request, see, Zarek, *Federal Open*.

45. U.S. Department of Justice Office of Privacy and Civil Liberties, *Overview*, 4.

46. Antonin Scalia, "The Freedom of Information Act Has No Clothes," *Regulation: AEI Journal on Government and Society* (March/April 1982): 15.

47. Scalia, "The Freedom," 16.

48. Etzioni, "Is Transparency."

49. Francis Fukuyama, "America in Decay: The Sources of Political Dysfunction," *Foreign Affairs* (September/October 2014).

50. Mike Ward, "Shifting More State Functions to Nonprofits Raises Transparency Questions," *Houston Chronicle* (May 23, 2017), http://www.houstonchronicle.com/news/houston-texas/houston/article/Shifting-more-state-functions-to-non-profits-11168368.php.

51. Panel on the Nonprofit Sector, *Strengthening Transparency, Governance, Accountability of Charitable Organizations* (Washington, DC: Independent Sector, 2005).

52. Ibid., 21.

53. Ibid.

54. Paul C. Light, *Making Nonprofits Work: A Report on the Tides of Nonprofit Management Reform* (Washington, DC: Brookings Institution, 2011).

55. Bob Carlson, "Transparency Can Keep a Nonprofit out of Trouble," *The Chronicle of Philanthropy* (March 4, 2011), https://www.philanthropy.com/article/Transparency-Can-Keep-a/227803.

56. Suzanne E. Coffman, "What Nonprofit Transparency Means to You: October Question of the Month Results," GuideStar (November 2006), https://www.guidestar.org/Articles.aspx?path=/rxa/news/articles/2006/what-nonprofit-transparency-means-to-you.aspx.

57. Ibid.

58. Stephanie Strom, "Confusion on Where Money Lent via Kiva Goes," *New York Times* (November 9, 2009): B6.

59. Kiva, "Frequently Asked Questions," last modified 2017, https://www.kiva.org/about/how#faq-hkw-section.

60. Internal Revenue Service Tax-Exempt & Government Entities Division, *Background Paper: Redesigned Draft Form 990* (2007), 1.

61. Ibid.

62. Internal Revenue Service, *Overview of Form 990 Redesign for Tax Year 2008* (December 20, 2007).

63. Robert Ottenhoff, "Letter to Lois Lerner, Director, Exempt Organizations Division, Internal Revenue Service re: Form 990 Redesign" (September 14, 2007).

64. GuideStar, *The State of Nonprofit Transparency, 2008: Voluntary Disclosure Practices* (2009), https://cdn2.hubspot.net/hubfs/733304/Docs/State_of_Nonprofit_Transparency_2008.pdf.

65. Stephanie Strom, "Lawmakers, Tightening Belts, Question Nonprofit Salaries," *New York Times* (July 27, 2010), A12.

66. Margot Sanger-Katz and Claire Cain Miller, "Is Planned Parenthood's President Overpaid?" *New York Times* (September 30, 2015), https://www.nytimes.com/2015/10/01/upshot/is-planned-parenthoods-president-overpaid.html.

67. Elizabeth Schmidt, "How Ethical Is Your Nonprofit Organization?" GuideStar (November, 2004), https://www.guidestar.org/Articles.aspx?path=/rxa/news/articles/2004/how-ethical-is-your-nonprofit-organization.aspx.

68. David Callahan, "Who Will Watch the Charities?" *New York Times* (May 31, 2015), 4.

69. Charity Commission for England and Wales, "About Us," https://www.gov.uk/government/organisations/charity-commission/about.

70. Panel on the Nonprofit Sector, *Strengthening Transparency*, 5.

71. Rick Cohen, "10 General Guidelines for Greater Foundation Transparency," *Nonprofit Quarterly* (November 14, 2014), https://nonprofitquarterly.org/2014/11/14/10-general-guidelines-for-greater-foundation-transparency/.

72. Glasspockets, "How Foundations Benefit from Greater Transparency," Foundation Center, http://glasspockets.org/why-transparency/how-foundations-benefit-from-greater-transparency.

73. Panel on the Nonprofit Sector, *Strengthening Transparency*, 19.

74. Strom, "Lawmakers," A21.

75. *Ask Me Why I Care: Public Service Stories* video, directed by Mary R. Hamilton and Rita Paskowitz (Omaha, Nebraska: College of Public Affairs and Community Service), https://www.unomaha.edu/college-of-public-affairs-and-community-service/community-engagement/pss-valerie-lemmie.php.

76. U.S. Congress, Senate, The Commission on Protecting and Reducing Government Secrecy, *Report of the Commission on Protecting and Reducing Government Secrecy,* 103rd Cong., 1997 S. Doc. 105-2, XXXIX.

77. Gary D. Bass, Danielle Brian, and Norman Eisen, *Why Critics of Transparency Are Wrong,* Center for Effective Public Management at Brookings (November 2014), 2.

78. Light, *Making Nonprofits*; and, Grimmelikhuijsen, "Transparency."

ADDITIONAL RESOURCES

Fung, Archon, Mary Graham, and David Weil. 2007. *Full Disclosure: The Perils and Promise of Transparency*. Cambridge: Cambridge University Press.

Roberts, Alasdair. 2006. *Blacked Out: Government Secrecy in the Information Age*. Cambridge: Cambridge University Press.

U.S. House of Representatives Committee on Oversight and Government Reform. 2012. *The Citizen's Guide to Using the Freedom of Information Act and The Privacy Act of 1974 to Request Government Records,* (September 20). Available at https://oversight.house.gov/report/committee-report-the-citizens-guide-to-using-the-freedom-of-information-act-and-the-privacy-act-of-1974-to-request-government-records/.

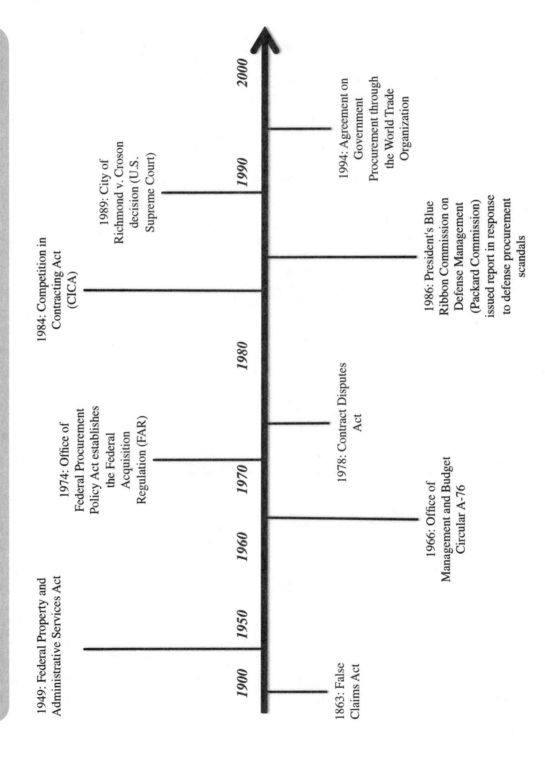

Chapter 11 Timeline: Contracting

1900 · 1950 · 1960 · 1970 · 1980 · 1990 · 2000

1863: False Claims Act

1949: Federal Property and Administrative Services Act

1966: Office of Management and Budget Circular A-76

1974: Office of Federal Procurement Policy Act establishes the Federal Acquisition Regulation (FAR)

1978: Contract Disputes Act

1984: Competition in Contracting Act (CICA)

1986: President's Blue Ribbon Commission on Defense Management (Packard Commission) issued report in response to defense procurement scandals

1989: City of Richmond v. Croson decision (U.S. Supreme Court)

1994: Agreement on Government Procurement through the World Trade Organization

CONTRACTING

WHAT YOU WILL LEARN

The role of contracting in the public sector

Criteria for deciding to contract out

How to responsibly award and oversee contracts

Skillbox: Grant-writing essentials

Contracting in the public sector is ubiquitous. Governments contract with private companies, nonprofits, and other governments to provide public services. Although most contracting decisions are routine, the decision whether to contract often reflects an ideological position to intentionally limit the size of government. In fact, some cities even operate primarily by contract. The most famous of these "contract cities" is Lakewood, California, which contracted out its basic public services to Los Angeles County in 1954.[1] The degree of dependence on contracting by government, though, is not always clear. Responding to a 2015 request to determine the size of the federal contractor workforce, the Congressional Budget Office (CBO) was forced to admit, "Regrettably, CBO is unaware of any comprehensive information about the size of the federal government's contracted workforce."[2]

Public contracting activity has received a great deal of attention for both its advantages and disadvantages. Professor Paul C. Light focused on the federal government's contracted personnel to discover the "true size of government."[3] In 2002, Light reported that a startling 8 million jobs were supported by federal contracts and grants while total federal personnel counted less than 4.2 million employees (includ-

"Over the last several decades, in governments at all levels throughout the world, the public sector's role has increasingly evolved from direct service provider to that of an indirect provider or broker of services; governments are relying far more on networks of public, private and nonprofit organizations to deliver services."

—The New Jersey Privatization Task Force

ing civilians and military).[4] In fiscal year 2016, federal government contracts totaled $464.7 billion dollars, or around 12 percent of federal outlays.[5] These figures reinforce the central role of contracting in the federal government, but contracting pervades all levels of government and is similarly critical for nonprofit organizations.

For modern governance, the contracting relationship is an essential ingredient, to such a point that one line of scholarship suggests that government has evolved into a "hollow state" where its bureaus are dependent on networks of private parties to enable government to function.[6] From this perspective, no public sector role is untouched by contracting and citizens are often interacting directly with contracted third parties rather than government employees. In this way, government potentially loses institutional knowledge as third-party providers are responsible for most aspects of program functioning. If contractors fail or quit, government agencies are left without the organizational intelligence to know how to continue services.

Contracting rarely receives attention when it works well, but watchdog groups, presidential commissions, and the media have repeatedly drawn attention to contracting failures. The following case highlights the dependence of the federal government on contractors and the public perception of waste.

YOU'RE FIRED: PERCEPTIONS OF WASTE IN GOVERNMENT CONTRACTING

From assertions in the 1980s that the Pentagon purchased three-cent screws for $91 apiece and the infamous, if exaggerated, $435 cost of a hammer, to more recent cases of 100-hour workdays by federal contractors and cost-overruns, federal government procurement draws criticism for its excesses.[7] In 1985, the navy's contract for $640 "toilet cover assemblies" (toilet seats) with Lockheed-California Company became a focal point of procurement waste in government. Senator William S. Cohen humorously raised classic issues in government contracting when he remarked, "What I don't understand about this procurement is why we have an aircraft manufacturer making toilet covers . . . Would we ask a toilet company to build a C5 [military transport aircraft]?"[8] Cohen later commented that due to these high costs, "the Pentagon may have to go in-house for its outhouse."[9]

The rationale for contracting out, the decision to forgo producing a good or service internally, is primarily based on the efficiencies gained from specialization.

The Congressional Budget Office (CBO) provides the following guidance for officials who must make "make-or-buy" decisions:

> When deciding whether the best way to perform a function is with its own employees or with contractors, a government agency must take a number of factors into account: whether the function is inherently governmental (as high-level policy decisions, contract administration, criminal prosecutions, and command of military forces are); the feasibility and legality of writing and managing a contract for the function; and the relative cost of different methods of performing the function.[10]

Given the checkered history of federal procurement and the repeated efforts to improve government contracting, it was not a surprise when recently-elected President Donald Trump took to social media to broadcast his dismay at the costs of a contract for Air Force One (the official plane of the U.S. president). Trump wrote, "Boeing is building a brand new 747 Air Force One for future presidents, but costs are out of control, more than $4 billion. Cancel order!"

When fact checkers reviewed Trump's claims, like most things in contracting, the reality proved to be much more complicated.[11] First, Boeing to date had only received a contract worth $170 million to design the new Air Force One. Second, the program was early in its development so there were no cost overruns. The actual contract to build the updated Air Force One (and two planes are required) had not even been put out to bid. Rather, the project is included in the five-year plan of the Defense Department and has an estimated cost of $2.9 billion "for design and development."

The design standards for Air Force One are unusually demanding including the need for in-air refueling, security measures, and the ability to "survive a nuclear war." Even though Air Force One is a Boeing 747-8 jet, there are many "one-time expenses" peculiar to the needs of the president. Such a specialized product that lasts a few decades means that Boeing cannot spread the development and production costs over a large production run. According to press reports, Boeing does not even anticipate making money on the Air Force One upgrade. Although an order that has not been made cannot be cancelled, the ability to influence specific awarded government contracts is dictated by a series of federal regulations and a Congress that authorizes spending for those contracts.

The top 100 federal government contractors in the United States received $238.5 billion in contracts in fiscal year 2015. Leading defense industry firms dominate the top-ten contractor list and represent $120 billion of the total contract obligations. The top five, all with more than $10 billion in obligations, include Lockheed Martin Corporation, The Boeing Company, General Dynamics Corporation, Raytheon Company, and Northrop Grumman Corporation. While most public sector professionals will work in areas outside of defense, approximately two-thirds of all federal contracts are defense-related.[12]

Questions to Ponder

1. Why is the defense function so dependent on contracts with private firms? Is there information asymmetry in such engagements?

2. Which is the more damaging consequence to government of faulty contracting: the waste of tax dollars or the loss of trust in government by the public?

WHAT IS CONTRACTING?

A contract is formally defined as "an agreement that is legally enforceable and reflects the relationship between two or more parties for a specific time period."[13] The purpose of a contract is to align the interests of the parties and lessen principal-agent conflict. Contracting, or contracting-out, broadly represents the use of contracts by governments to either acquire materials or services from the private or nonprofit sectors or from other governments. Steven Kelman distinguishes between the final recipient of the goods and services delivered by public sector contracts. The goods or services are either consumed "directly" by the contracting government in the case of payroll services, for example, or delivered to external parties, such as to citizens as they receive mental health services delivered by a contractor.[14]

PRINCIPALS AND AGENTS: THE TENUOUS RELATIONSHIP OF CONTRACTING

Upon first consideration, government appears to have the upper hand in the contracting relationship. The contracting officials get to specify the contract, determine the pricing approach, and select the awardee based on criteria reflecting the government's own priorities. In reality, contracting represents a principal-agent problem where the contractor (the agent) is in a position to make decisions that take advantage of the government (the principal).

This scenario occurs for reasons related to information asymmetries between the principal and the agent. The contractor is an expert and, therefore, knows more about the contracted activity than the government. If the government already had equal expertise, they would likely produce the good or service internally. The agent may use this information to forward its own interests, such as maximizing profits by incurring additional reimbursable costs, rather than supporting the objectives of the principal and delivering a high-quality product on time and within budget.

An overarching goal of the contracting process for government is to benefit from the contractor's expertise while limiting the principal-agent problem. One way to reduce information asymmetry is through the selection process. Background checks and performance histories provide an early opportunity to discover whether prospective awardees have abused their role in previous contracting relationships.

The agency problem can also be addressed, but not eliminated, using well-designed incentives or penalties that align the interests of the agent with the principal and help guarantee achievement of performance objectives. After the award of the contract, the government can also increase monitoring of the agent to increase the flow of information between agent and principal. Unfortunately, these "solutions" are not costless or entirely effective at eliminating self-interested behavior by agents.

CONTRACTS: FROM SIMPLE TO COMPLEX

A contract for materials is fairly straightforward, especially when the goods are common and do not require customization. This type of material contract, referred to as buying "off-the-shelf," is best represented in the purchase of office supplies. In fact, the number of purchase orders to Staples and Office Depot represented nearly 8 percent of all state and local government purchase orders in 2015.[15] The best price often guides the decision for material contracts, since there is limited product differentiation. Copier paper from Staples is likely to be similar, or even identical, to that from Office Depot.

Contracting for specialized goods and services is more complex and demands additional attention from public sector decision makers. Services are intangible, so cost becomes only one consideration in selecting a contractor.[16] Yong Woon Kim and Trevor Brown provide examples of simple and complex products from a contracting perspective. Routine services like landscaping, laundry, solid waste disposal, and storage are considered simple, while advertising, engineering, information technology development, and legal services are complex.[17] The primary elements of any contract include a description of the material or service to be delivered, the timing of delivery for the material or service, and the compensation for the material or service.

THE CONTRACTING CONTINUUM

In most cases, governments and nonprofits support their respective missions by directly delivering services to their public and beneficiaries, respectively. In other cases, governments and nonprofits provide services by funding the production of those services by a third-party entity. Using the example of mosquito abatement, scholars more than half a century ago highlighted this critical distinction between provision and production:

Government provision need not involve public production—indeed, at some stage in the sequence from raw materials to finished products virtually every public good, not already a natural resource, is of private origin. So, a public agency by contractual arrangements with private firms—or with other public agencies—can provide the local community with public services without going into the business of producing them itself.[18]

Before delving into the details of contracting, it is useful to discuss the relationship of contracting to other commonly-used terms. A handful of labels are used, often interchangeably, by practitioners and researchers to represent how the public sector engages third parties to provide public services. The concepts overlap each other, but a crude continuum beginning with simple purchases of off-the-shelf goods and services helps conceptually relate the broad notion of contracting to these related strategies: contracting-out, relational contracting, public-private partnerships, and privatization.

Contracting-Out or Outsourcing

Governments frequently contract-out or outsource service functions. The terms are used interchangeably. Unlike complete privatization, contracting-out a service maintains public provision and control despite delivery by a third party. Unlike a simple contractual purchase of goods by a government, contracting-out is complicated by competing objectives. Government wants to reduce costs and maintain or improve quality without sacrificing control over the service, while it preserves public values. Public values refer to a commitment to transparency, quality, and equity in addition to efficiency. Although governments contract-out public-facing services, third-party firms are also used to produce internal services on an ongoing or discrete project basis, such as for legal or information technology services. Emmanuel Savas (1989) classifies contracting-out as the most frequent privatization strategy in the United States that "delegates" an activity to a third-party. Government remains active throughout the contract period to provide oversight and ensure that the conditions are met.[19]

Relational Contracting

Business agreements have always been based on relationships. The "handshake deal" is the classic example. Half a century ago, researchers noted that the transactional, or discrete, nature of modern contracts is sometimes inadequate for delivering complicated services.[20] In fact, the ability to craft a "complete" contract (a contract that fully specifies the contracted activity) is unlikely due to unforeseeable challenges and circumstances. Some service areas demand more of a collaborative relationship between the government and the contractor. Nowhere is this more prominent than when a government contracts with a nonprofit to deliver a social service.

The increasing prominence of public service delivery through networks of organizations, both public and private, makes relational contracting especially important.[21]

Relational contracting refers to the central role of relationships in supplementing the formal contract as the public sector cedes authority to third parties. Government, in relational contracting, depends on a mutually beneficial relationship with the contracting entity to align the interests of both parties. For example, consider a city that contracts with a local nonprofit to design and implement a program to address homelessness. The nonprofit mission prior to receiving the contract is aligned with the city's goal to find housing solutions for individuals living on the streets or in transitional housing arrangements. Traditional contracting would re-bid the contract every few years to minimize costs through contracting. Relational contracting relies on the trust and mutual understandings between contractor and contractee to continue the relationship and deal with exigencies that arise.

The threat of periodic competition is often perceived to be counterproductive when addressing chronic social problems in need of long-term solutions. In these cases, the public manager is called on to develop productive relationships outside of a contract's fine print. Scholars Bertelli and Smith focus on the "self-enforcing" nature of a relational contract as both sides understand the longer-term gains of the relationship.[22] Ian Macneil, who coined the term relational contracting, prominently referred to contracts as "instruments for social cooperation."[23]

Those who regularly work with nonprofits might rightly question the distinction between a contracting relationship and a collaboration. Similar missions and close partnership blur the lines between contractor and partner when jointly delivering public services. Scholar Beth Gazley provides a helpful overview of the relationship between governments and nonprofits. Some of the basic characteristics of collaboration, including autonomy for each of the entities, the sharing of resources as well as risks, and mutual determination of approach, are sometimes counter to a traditional contracting approach. Although Gazley notes that "collaboration has been offered as an alternative to purchase-of-service contracts," the distinction is blurred among public and non-profit professionals especially in an age of networked governance.[24]

Relational and transactional contracting are not mutually exclusive. Relational elements shift the bidder's focus from winning a contract to fulfilling commitments and continuing a contracting relationship. An award-winning example comes from down under, where the Australian Navy in 2014 paired an overarching relational contract with performance contracts for the delivery of guided missile frigates by its private sector partners. The relational contract broadly guides the collaboration between the navy and third-party contractors.[25] Relational contracting is unlikely to displace traditional transactional contracts, but embedding relational concepts into contracts is recommended as a step toward long-term programmatic success. This is particularly true when services are complex and there are a limited number of third-party producers.

Public-Private Partnerships

Public-private partnerships, abbreviated as P3s or PPPs, are contractual relationships between government and private firms to deliver either existing or newly-developed public services. What distinguishes a P3 from contracting-out or outsourcing? The P3 is typically long term, infrastructure-based, financed in part by the private partner, and spreads the risk of the project across the public and private partners. When should a P3 be considered? It is especially appealing when the public sector is constrained by debt limitations, would benefit from the expertise of the private sector, where a rigorous comparison (referred to as a Value for Money analysis) provides evidence of savings relative to traditional procurement methods, and the project involves assets that are not inherently governmental.[26] Worldwide, P3s have been used for a wide variety of infrastructure needs including building and maintaining highways, airports, rail systems, solid waste disposal infrastructure, water treatment and supply systems, and public buildings.

Although P3s are regularly touted, a number of challenges exist for successful design.[27] The long-term benefits of the project need to be prioritized over short-term gains, which is often difficult to accomplish in highly political contexts. Another prominent criticism of P3s is the loss of public values that can accompany the partnerships. Public control and accountability are often sacrificed when long-term authority is ceded to a private-sector partner. Transparency and public engagement are necessary during the creation of the P3 but are difficult to maintain during negotiations and implementation.

A visible example where public values were not preserved comes from Chicago's seventy-five year lease of its 36,000 parking meters to a private partner in 2008. The city received a payment of more than a billion dollars for the lease, but an inspector general report found that the transaction lacked adequate public input and focused on the short-term financial gain to the detriment of long-term considerations of value and impact on residents. The report presents a cautionary tale about P3s:

> It is a momentous decision for a government to give a private company control over a major public asset for three generations. And when this decision has a significant impact on the everyday lives of its citizens (here, through a large increase in parking meter rates), the government's decision is even more important.[28]

Privatization

Privatization, broadly speaking, encompasses activities supporting "greater private sector involvement in the delivery of publicly funded services."[29] More narrowly, privatization represents the complete removal of a function from the public sector. Although less common in the United States, one example of privatization of a government entity is the SLM Corporation, or Sallie Mae. Created in 1973 as a government-sponsored entity tasked with servicing federal loans for higher education, the former Student Loan Marketing Association is now a private firm with shareholders.[30]

Such privatization of government entities takes place more frequently in countries where state-owned enterprises have been the norm. For example, a wave of privatization accompanied the fall of communism in Eastern Europe as state-run enterprises transitioned to private ownership and operation. Privatization activity continues across the globe. Between 2000 and 2008, The World Bank reported over 1,800 privatizations in developing countries ranging from utilities, ports, and railroads to oil companies, mills, and banks.[31] In these cases, complete privatization severs the connection between government and the service being provided, although governments maintain a regulatory role for some activities.

Figure 11.1 shows the continuum of contracting activity from the most basic purchase of simple goods and services (where government maintains complete control of the activity) to complete privatization at the other end (where government control is relinquished to the third-party). For each type shown in the continuum, the nature of the relationship between government and the third-party is listed below the line.

FIGURE 11.1: CONTINUUM OF PUBLIC-SECTOR CONTRACTING ACTIVITIES

Simple Purchase	Contracting-out/ Outsourcing	Relational Contracting	Public-Private Partnership	Privatization
Transactional relationship	Oversight relationship	Collaborative relationship	Shared risk and monitoring relationship	Regulatory relationship

THE CONTRACTING PROCESS

The act of contracting is broken into a series of discrete steps beginning with the decision to contract and ending when the contract is closed-out. The process is presented in Figure 11.2 and explained next.

FIGURE 11.2: BASIC CONTRACTING PROCESS

Make-or-Buy Decision	Structure Contract	Choose a Contractor	Contract Administration
Consider Whether to produce good or service in-house or to contract	Specify needs and establish pricing approach	Establish evaluation criteria, issue and publicize a Request-for-Proposal/solicitation, assess proposals, negotiate, award contract	Monitor performance and costs, manage changes to scope and schedule closeout or renew agreement when completed

Make-or-Buy Decision

The first step of the process is the decision whether or not to contract the good or service. The economic and political value of contracting informs this make-or-buy determination and can be controversial. Essentially, decision makers ask whether contracting will bring about some combination of lower costs and higher quality compared to public sector production. The expectation that contracting to the private sector is more efficient is traced back to the existence of a profit motive absent in public sector organizations.[32] For-profit firms depend on the straightforward objective of profit maximization to drive down costs and to make a competitive bid. Public sector objectives are more complex.

Given these expectations of the potential for cost savings, how does a public sector employee know when contracting is desirable? A former mayor of Indianapolis and proponent of outsourcing famously used the "Yellow Pages test" to identify services

COMPETITIVE SOURCING: IN-SOURCING VERSUS OUTSOURCING

The President's Management Agenda of George W. Bush, launched in 2001, included an initiative referred to as competitive sourcing. Competitive sourcing called for existing federal employees and private sector firms to compete for the right to perform commercial activities currently provided by federal employees. The notion of contracting out federal positions that supported commercial activities was nothing new.

According to the Government Accountability Office (GAO), the executive branch was favorably inclined since at least the 1950s toward using the private sector to perform federal roles. The policy was institutionalized in 1966 as part of the Office of Management and Budget's (OMB) Circular A-76, which provides contracting guidance. The process of privatizing existing public jobs was spelled out in detail by the OMB over the years, with the two options being direct conversion or cost comparison.[33]

President Bush's competitive sourcing initiative called for cost comparisons where the existing federal jobs were not "inherently governmental." After creating a detailed overview of the activity, a study was conducted to determine the most efficient organization (MEO) available to continue delivering the activity internally by government employees. The MEO pricing was then competed against in a traditional bid-award process open to the private sector. Private sector bidders could be awarded the work only if the price was a minimum of 10 percent below that of the MEO.[34]

So, what happened when public sector employees competed with the private sector for the jobs they were already performing? Between 2003 and 2006, the competitions resulted in 83 percent of the nearly 47,000 jobs remaining with government employees.[35] That is not to say that the competitions failed to bring about change in the delivery of commercial activities. Even when the activity remained in the hands of federal employees, the MEOs responded to the competition by crafting and implementing proposals that reflected improved business processes and more efficient staffing.

The achievements of President Bush's competitive sourcing effort are unclear. The media and critics pointed to worsened federal employee morale and a huge shortfall in the expected number of federal positions competed for through 2006, while the GAO suggests the resulting savings were inflated. The cost to run the competitions reportedly averaged $4,800 per federal position. Professor Paul C. Light reflected "the competitive sourcing initiative did little to improve management, produced a ton of worthless paper, demoralized thousands of workers and cost a bundle, all to prove that federal employees are pretty good after all." Alternately, the White House claimed savings exceeding a billion dollars annually from the competitions.[36]

Question to Ponder

1. Is it surprising that federal employees were so successful at competing with the private sector? Why or why not?

with the potential to be contracted out to a private firm. If a search in the phone book could identify at least three companies delivering an existing city-county service, then the function would be considered for contracting out.[37] Although phone books are outdated, the logic of the test raises two critical considerations for contracting public goods and services. To benefit from competition, there needs to be a sufficient number of potential producers. For many public services, the firms need to already be physically located in the area. Firms already producing the service locally suggest that the activity is not inherently governmental and routine.

Kelman provides a more comprehensive inventory of conditions that, when present, support the use of contracting over in-house production.[38] Among these are that the nature of the contracted activity must allow for it to be specified clearly; successful fulfillment of the contract can be evaluated effectively; and competition must exist for the initial award and subsequent awards. The decision to contract becomes more convincing if the contracted activity is not closely related to the mission of the organization; the need for the good or service is erratic over time; the private sector has ready access to the required expertise; or, the production benefits from an economy of scale (where average costs of production decline with increased volume) that cannot be captured by the public sector organization.

If the decision is made to contract, then public sector employees are wise to fulfill Kelman's three goals of public contracting: 1) get a good deal, 2) prevent corruption and promote integrity, and 3) fairness.[39] These goals ensure that the economic rationale of contracting is realized, while they preserve the hallmarks of good government. Issuing the contract requires a series of activities that occur within an established legal framework. For example, in the federal government, the Federal Acquisition Regulation (FAR) governs the process.

The centrality of contracting and procurement in the federal government is apparent from the long list of statutes that govern the process of acquiring goods and services: The primary statutes governing federal procurement are the codifications in Titles 10 and 41 of the U.S. Code of the Armed Services Procurement Act and the Federal Property and Administrative Services Act, which, respectively, govern the procurements of defense and civilian agencies. However, a number of other statutes also apply, including:

- the Anti-Kickback Act
- Brooks Act of 1972, as amended
- Buy American Act
- Buy Indian Act
- Contract Disputes Act
- Contract Work Hours and Safety Standards Act
- Davis-Bacon Act
- Defense Production Act
- Economy Act
- Federal Activities Inventory Reform (FAIR) Act
- Miller Act
- Office of Federal Procurement Policy Act
- Prompt Payment Act
- Service Contract Act
- Small Business Act

- Trade Agreements Act
- Truth in Negotiations Act
- Walsh-Healy Public Contracts Act

In addition, there are a number of provisions within other statutes (e.g., national defense authorizations acts, appropriations acts) that address procurement.[40]

IS IT ALL GARBAGE? COST-EFFECTIVENESS OF CONTRACTING OUT

The presumption of private sector supremacy in efficient service delivery is not universally supported by research. Despite the broad appeal of contracting out, the majority of empirical studies of the practice focus on solid waste collection and disposal, rather than more complex social services. It is difficult to determine whether contracting out actually saves money.

First, researchers attempting to compare public and private production of services encounter a serious challenge. The outsourced services being studied were contracted out largely based on an expectation of financial savings, so finding lower average costs is unsurprising. Second, an accurate comparison of public and private costs needs to account for the public resources used in the contracting process itself. The associated transaction costs, such as contract monitoring, offset a portion of the financial benefits of private production. Third, allocating costs to specific functions can be problematic in the public sector when employees, equipment, and capital assets frequently serve multiple purposes.[41]

A classic, albeit minor, example is equipping garbage trucks with plows for snow removal. When calculating the public expense of snow removal for comparison to private

options, arguments can be made for allocating the direct costs of the garbage trucks. The reality, though, is that the government will retain the garbage trucks for their primary function even if the snow removal function is contracted out. The same difficulty of allocating unavoidable costs pervades government and can mislead about potential cost savings from contracting services.

So, what is known about the cost-effectiveness of contracting out? It is safe to say that there is little consensus.[42] Evidence of cost savings is inconsistent and context-dependent, particularly across service areas. Where savings are identified, the magnitudes frequently differ. Meta-analyses, where a collection of studies on a subject are rigorously reviewed, present a more nuanced picture of savings from contracting out services. An international meta-analysis reported cost reductions of 8 to 14 percent for certain routine services, and warned of the importance of reducing estimated savings more in order to account for contract monitoring. Moreover, the report detailed the inability to distinguish between the levels of savings derived from contracting with public versus private third-party organizations.[43]

A more recent meta-analysis focuses on studies of outsourced solid waste and water services. The authors find continued inconsistency in the evidence supporting cost savings from contracting out, although solid waste remains a promising setting. They conclude that achieving cost savings through contracting out depends "on service characteristics, geographic area, and time period of the study."[44]

An overall takeaway from researchers is this: Do not presume that there will be financial benefits to contracting out public services to third-party providers. Rather, each contracting decision should be judged on its merits after a complete comparison of costs and quality between in-house production and outsourcing. Less quantifiable are the political factors that influence decisions to contract out. On one side, contracting can leave public employees feeling vulnerable and devalued. On the other side, elected officials are looking for ways to slow the growth of government, potentially cut costs, or support local private firms. Ultimately, competition is the key to unlocking cost savings for services that are suitable for contracting out, but the actual production can be carried out by existing public employees, a neighboring government, a nonprofit with aligned mission, or a for-profit firm.

CONTRACT STRUCTURE

Designing a contract requires a clear and adequately detailed explanation of the desired deliverable, along with a timeframe for delivery. Elements of timing depend on whether the contracted activity occurs only once or is recurring. The conditions and details are initially conveyed during the solicitation process when the request for bids is issued.

The form of compensation for the contracted activity is a key decision. Although many variations exist, the pricing of a contract falls into two main categories. The simplest is a "fixed price" contract where the contractor is paid a set amount for delivering the products or services. Fixed price contracts are used primarily when there is certainty about the specifications or requirements of the contracted activity.

An alternate pricing approach is cost reimbursement, where the contractor is paid based on the actual costs incurred satisfying the contract requirements. Incentives are incorporated into contracts to further align the contractor's behavior with the needs of the contracting party. When certain conditions are met, such as the early completion of an information technology system, then the contract provides additional compensation.

Addressing Risk Through Contracting Innovations

Contracting is fundamentally about controlling risk in achieving the desired outcome. Contracts are structured to ensure that the activity is completed and the contracting party is protected. Achieving an ideal outcome is easier said than done given the uncertainty that pervades the delivery of complex products and services. Incentives embedded within contracts have long been used to promote positive contracting outcomes. Performance contracting and pay-for-success are considered here to highlight the potential of contracts to align incentives and promote socially desirable outcomes.

> *"We've all had nightmare procurements with IT (information technology). It's truly an exception that an IT project proves to be as good as we claim it to be. There's hundreds of millions of dollars wasted, and it's a miracle we get away with it."*
>
> —Gavin Newsom

Performance Contracting

Performance contracting explicitly links the terms of a contract to the performance level of the contracted activity. Although closely tied to the presence of performance-based incentives in traditional contracting, modern performance contracts are often used to shift risk to contractors and more clearly delineate successful outcomes. Behn and Kant (1999) describe how traditional contracting approaches pay contractors for "inputs, processes, and technologies," while performance contracting pays for "results."[45]

Energy performance contracting is used by governments to fund infrastructure improvements in public facilities instead of depending on reserves, capital budget appropriations, or general borrowing. Performance contracting allows governments to pay for improved energy efficiency with the operational savings generated from the projects themselves. Investment grade audits are conducted of public facilities to identify potential savings in utility and maintenance costs. The government then determines whether the projected savings are substantial enough to support the financing of the project. The contract between the government and the energy service company (ESCO) details the expected improvements in efficiency that will be delivered by the project. These savings are then guaranteed and redirected in future years to pay the financing used for the project.

The State of Colorado, like many states and local governments, actively uses energy performance contracting. In 2003, the state signed a multiphase energy performance contract to improve energy efficiency in government buildings. The first phase included a series of energy conservation measures focused on improvements in lighting, water, and HVAC systems to accompany improved insulation and adoption of an Energy Resource Conservation Program. The projected annual savings from the projects was $631,009. The savings, measured and verified each year as part of the performance contract, are used to pay down the nineteen-year loan of nearly $9 million.[46] At the end of the loan period, the state will have more efficient buildings with lower ongoing operating costs. The performance contract makes the facility improvements feasible without any up-front investment from taxpayers.

Energy performance contracts utilize a clear and measurable change in the use of electricity as the primary indicator of performance. Applying performance contracts in many public sector domains is more difficult when the outcomes are less tangible. One of the challenges to performance contracting in the public sector is that the results used to measure performance may be proxies for the more complex outcomes of public programs. Performance contracting is less promising where high-quality measures of program outcomes are unavailable.

Pay-for-Success

Like performance contracting, an emerging form of contracting similarly attempts to support public sector goals while limiting government liability if programs are unsuccessful. Pay-for-success, also referred to as Social Impact Bonds, differs from traditional and performance contracting. Investors provide the upfront funding for the program, nonprofits deliver the services, and an evaluator assesses the success of the efforts over time. The original contract and the performance of the program, based on the outcome measures collected by the evaluator, determine whether government payments are made to reimburse and reward the investors. The public sector leverages private financing to implement social programs that are unlikely to be supported by current operating budgets.

Pay-for-success projects, to date, focus on social services such as prisoner reentry, housing for the homeless, and early childhood education. Any payments made to investors by government represent a share of the government's cost savings resulting from the project, such as lower rates of recidivism, reduced demand on emergency services from the chronically homeless, and fewer elementary students with special needs. Pay-for-success is being used in Utah to improve access to high-quality preschool programs and, ultimately, to reduce special education enrollments.[47] The Utah High Quality Preschool Program was financed with a $4.6 million loan by investment bank Goldman Sachs and $2.4 million from the J.B. Pritzker Foundation. The five-year program administered by the nonprofit United Way of Salt Lake will serve 3,500 children using local preschool providers.

Utah State University personnel serve as the evaluator for the program's effectiveness in diverting at-risk children from requiring future special education services. Salt Lake County and the State of Utah are the client governments and make outcome payments to the investor of $2,589.70 each year for students not enrolled in special education services due to the program. Determining the causal impact of a program on social outcomes, like the need for special education, is fraught with challenges. Such accurate and defensible measurement of "success" is the linchpin of pay-for-success projects, but public sector outcomes are notoriously difficult to measure.

CHOOSING A CONTRACTOR

The level of competition varies for a specific contract depending on the selection process used by government and the number of potential contractors in the marketplace. The process of selecting a contractor can be situated on a continuum of competition ranging from sole-source procurement on one end (where negotiations take place with only one contractor) to full and open competition on the other.[48]

Sole-source contracting is criticized for its lack of competition, but in some cases the technical requirements of a contract or the need for expediency dramatically limit the number of potential firms. Without competition among multiple firms, the fear is that the sole contractor will use its bargaining power to the government's detriment. Sole-source contracting is especially common during wartime, natural disasters, and where the specialization required for the activity limits the number of potential contractors. If sole-source contracts are required, then public sector officials should proceed with caution and provide prudent justification of the decision.[49]

With an open competition, the solicitation should encourage multiple proposals. Disseminating the opportunity online and with a reasonable amount of time to assemble a proposal has become the norm for the public sector. Typically, the opportunity is in the form of a request-for-proposal (RFP). Personally reaching out to possible contractors to make sure they are aware of the opportunity is also an effective strategy, but responding to a public solicitation is a significant and uncertain investment of time and resources for many smaller firms.

Once proposals are submitted, they are reviewed based on the stated selection criteria reflecting the government's needs. The basis for awarding a contract is a combination of cost and quality. The degree to which cost and quality matter in the competition depends on the use of either a "low-bid" or "best-value" approach.[50] One might say that the public sector should always select the lowest cost option in contracting, but such a perspective is shortsighted.

Awarding a contract to the low-bidder can be conditioned upon the proposal being technically acceptable. The low-bid approach may be warranted for simple products and services where government is confident that the contract is well specified. A major limitation of the approach is that a low-cost bid might indicate a contractor that has "intentionally or through ignorance" underestimated the demands of the contract.[51] Coupled with the inability to incorporate past performance of the contractor, there is the potential for greater risk shouldered by the public sector.

Alternately, the best-value approach has become increasingly common since it allows decision makers to weigh the relative merits of "price," "technical capability," and "past performance" when awarding a contract.[52] The relative weights assigned to the criteria are modified to reflect the priorities for the contracted activity.

Public sector contracts also integrate public values. Bid preferences, or set-asides, are frequently coupled with traditional selection criteria by governments to improve the odds of a contract award for smaller firms and those owned by traditionally disadvantaged groups. Bid preferences broaden the pool of firms receiving contracts and support the growth of firms that might have trouble competing with larger, more established bidders. Set-asides earmark a specific share of the available contracting activity to types of firms deemed socially desirable.

Other techniques for broadening and diversifying the contractor pool include setting specific goals for awarding contracts to preferred groups, providing targeted technical assistance to those groups during the proposal process, or offering loan guarantees to strengthen bids.[53] The most common preferences are targeted at small firms and firms owned by women, minorities, and veterans. Contracting in the public sector may trade some of the potential efficiencies of larger firms for improved equity through these programs, but government contracting is sometimes about more than just cost savings.

The city of Seattle has embarked on an ambitious agenda to pursue social equity throughout its operations. To advance contracting equity, the women and minority business enterprise program (WMBE), uses a variety of strategies to improve the diversity of firms that are awarded city contracts. Diversity of a firm is judged based on its ownership. Solicitations by the city require the completion of the WMBE Inclusion Plan, which is scored as part of the proposal assessment. The plans require the bidder to detail the anticipated roles of WMBE-classified firms as core or noncore project members and to explain how the contractor will support WMBE firms throughout the engagement. Despite voter-imposed restrictions on "race-conscious programs in public purchasing," Seattle has been able to support its program goals by requiring that bidders put forth "a good faith effort" to use WMBEs in city contracts.[54] The city tracks and regularly reports on the share of procurement spending directed to WMBE, with 15 percent directed to WMBE firms in 2016.[55]

Contracting officers assess and score the submitted proposals based on the established criteria. The integrity of the selection process is protected through transparency and by making award decisions using groups of employees.[56] Depending on the type of solicitation, the award may commence a period of negotiation with the selected contractor to finalize the contract specifications.

Responding to an RFP can be burdensome for small businesses and nonprofits because the process requires staff time and expertise and the effort is frequently for naught. Some of the difficulty is mitigated when, after the contract has been awarded, contracting authorities hold a debriefing opportunity for firms with unsuccessful proposals. The debriefing serves multiple purposes. Officials can explain how the selection criteria were fairly applied and provide recommendations for improvements in future proposals. The debriefing process respects and recognizes the investment by the applicants and helps maintain a pool of qualified bidders for future solicitations. Firms that do not secure the contract have recourse if the selection process is deemed faulty. One such process is described next.

CHALLENGING DECISIONS: AN EXAMPLE OF A FEDERAL BID PROTEST

Award protests are handled for the federal government by the Government Accountability Office (GAO). In fiscal year 2016, more than 2,600 bid protest cases were filed with the GAO.[57] The protests provide insight into the contractor selection process used and the sometime subjective nature of contracting criteria. In 2014, California's RQ Construction, LLC (RQC) protested a contract awarded to competitor Stronghold Engineering, Inc. to repair heating, ventilation, air conditioning, and ductwork systems for the Department of the Navy's Naval Medical Center in San Diego, California.[58] Specifically, RQC argued that Stronghold's past performance was considered too favorably and the resulting best-value decision for the fixed-price contract was invalid.

Table 11.1 presents the evaluation factors and scoring for the top three proposals. As can be seen, the factors used as selection criteria included technical approach, experience, past performance, safety, technical solution, energy and sustainable design, small business utilization, and price. Although no weights for each factor are apparent in the matrix, the bidders received information "that the non-price factors, when combined, were equal in importance to price."

Compared to Stronghold's ratings, the RQC proposal rated favorably in Safety and Energy/Design. Both proposals had "Acceptable" technical approaches and overall ratings deemed "Good." The winning proposal from Stronghold was priced nearly $6 million, or 11 percent, below the RQC price. As this case demonstrates, even with clear decision criteria, balancing non-price and price factors is a persistent challenge in contracting. The protest by RQC was, in part, focused on the belief that the selection decision "was inconsistent with the RFP's best-value basis for award."

TABLE 11.1 CONTRACTOR SELECTION DECISION

Bidder	Stronghold	Offeror C	RQC
Technical Approach	Acceptable	Acceptable	Acceptable
Experience	Good	Outstanding	Good
Past Performance	Substantial Confidence	Substantial Confidence	Substantial Confidence
Safety	Good	Good	Outstanding
Technical Solution	Good	Acceptable	Good
Energy / Design	Acceptable	Marginal	Good
Small Business Utilization	Good	Acceptable	Good
OVERALL RATING	GOOD	ACCEPTABLE	GOOD
Price	$46,557,217	$47,372,314	$52,491,931
OVERALL RANKING	1	2	3

> The navy's selection of Stronghold came after determining "that although RQC's proposal met or exceeded requirements in many areas, its technical advantages did not overcome its higher price." The GAO reviewed the selection process and denied the protest, noting that it is acceptable in a best-value assessment to "select a lower-rated, lower-priced proposal." The ability to protest contract award decisions provides discipline and integrity to the public process.

Contract Administration

Once the contract is awarded, public sector employees remain responsible for monitoring the contracted activities. The level of oversight depends on the nature of the work and generally increases:

1) with the complexity of the contracted tasks,
2) with the amount of direct contact between the contractor and the public, and
3) with the use of cost-reimbursement pricing.

Completely specifying a contract is difficult so changes frequently take place after the contract is awarded. Change orders are used to manage departures from the scope of the original agreement. The intention is that the contractor is held harmless for unknown additional requirements at the time of bidding. Change orders can also be a source of cost escalation after the competitive forces of the selection process are absent.[59] Performance of the contracted activity, as well as costs for cost-reimbursement contracts, is monitored through contract completion and closeout.

Contracts can be extended, re-bid, or terminated. Existing awardees have a profound advantage in subsequent contracting activity because they intimately know the work and the people who are monitoring the contract, and they have a record of performance.

ETHICS OF CONTRACTING

Government contracts for a variety of legitimate reasons, including acquiring skills, flexibility, and savings.[60] Yet contracting activity suffers from a disproportionate amount of scandal because, by definition, government explicitly differentiates winners and losers through the procurement process. Large dollar amounts are involved and selection criteria are often subjective despite best efforts. Public sector employees must avoid even the appearance of impropriety when involved in contracting decisions. Ethical dilemmas in public contracting center on bribery, exchange of confidential information that favors one bidder over another, and paybacks in the form of the revolving door between public and private sector employment. "Revolving door" rules are put in place by the public sector to address concerns over post-employment relationships. The re-volving door between government and the private sector, left unchecked, raises doubt about the integrity of the contracting process. The federal government has rules that are designed to lessen such conflicts. The rules are tailored to the nature of the position held by the employee (e.g., executive branch, legislative branch, procurement person-nel) and the subsequent type of work performed for private firms.

Increasingly, individuals' careers expand beyond the borders of a single type of employer. Government employees move to the private sector and vice versa, which raises ethical quandaries particularly for individuals that work in contracting. Why should the government care if a current employee leaves for a private firm with which it contracts? The short answer is that private firms might receive preferential treatment from government employees if such treatment results in the promise of a more lucrative job in the future outside government. In 2006, for example, 1,581 former Department of Defense officials "who had previously served as generals, admirals, senior executives, program managers, contracting officers, or in other acquisition positions" worked for one of seven private contracting firms.[61]

Corruption occurs when the contracting process is illegally influenced to favor a specific firm's proposal. Although typically associated with bribes for the favorable treatment of a bidder, corruption might also include public officials sharing procure-ment information selectively with preferred firms. Alternately, elected officials with authority to select vendors can be influenced by political contributions. Referred to as "pay-to-play," private firms seeking government contracts sometimes perceive that campaign contributions are an informal requirement for receiving an award.

A transparent selection process for procurement of goods and services, along with the ability of losing parties to protest awards, helps limit corruption in public contracting. Rules for public sector employees complement a transparent contracting process and are intended to limit or disclose conflicts-of-interest, the receipt of gifts, and nepotism.

The rules consist of bans and restrictions on "switching sides" for representational, lobbying, or advocacy activities. In particular, these restrictions prohibit former gov-ernment employees from representing private interests on activities they previously worked on in the public sector. "Cooling off" periods are also put in place to create a temporal buffer between individual employees' government and private sector work experiences with the intent that they will reduce any unfair influence or insider knowl-edge that persists.[62] More than two-thirds of state governments use cooling off periods to limit the lobbying activity of outgoing legislators.[63] These rules help limit unethical contracting behavior, but it is important that public sector employees are trained and familiar with contracting rules and with codes of ethics for procurement officials in order to avoid conflicts of interest.

The government also has tools to identify unethical behavior by contractors. The False Claims Act of 1863 incentivizes individuals, referred to as whistleblowers or rela-tors, to file lawsuits on behalf of the federal government if there is knowledge of "false or fraudulent claims" made to the government. Between fiscal years 2009 and 2016, the federal government recovered more than $31 billion under the False Claims Act.

An example of an action under the False Claims Act comes from the software sector.[64] In 2011, Oracle Corporation settled a whistleblower-initiated suit for $200 million. The claim alleged that the firm overcharged the government in its contract with the General Services Administration (GSA). The whistleblower, an Oracle employee, received a $40 million share of the settlement. The GSA's Inspector General at the time commented on the settlement, "It's more important now than ever before to make sure that taxpayer dollars are not wasted on higher prices . . . We will not let contractors victimize the taxpayers by hiding their best prices."[65]

Ask Me Why I Care: Dewey Harris, Assistant County Manager, Catawba County, North Carolina[66]

Dewey Harris began his career in business but soon sought more meaningful work. Switching to a career in public service, he started as a budget analyst and progressed up the ranks. He has now served in local and state government for over twenty-five years. He describes his work as being a practitioner of community capacity building. Along with his job, he volunteers for local nonprofits that focus on improving quality of life. Watch Dewey explain how his career progressed at https://www.unomaha.edu/college-of-public-affairs-and-community-service/community-engagement/pss-dewey-harris.php.

SUMMARY

Contracting allows governments and nonprofits to focus on their missions and core competencies, while benefiting from external expertise. Contracted activities range from simple off-the-shelf products to complex long-term services. Anyone working in public service will undoubtedly encounter the promise and perils of contracting, either as a contractor if working for a nonprofit or as a procurement official if working for the government department that awards the contract.

The decision to contract is, at times, ideological with contracting-out a leading strategy for limiting the growth of government despite mixed empirical evidence about its effectiveness or cost savings. Modern governance, though, looks to contracting for more than cost savings, as nonprofit providers support service delivery in an increasingly "hollow state."

Contracting is a process that begins with the make-or-buy decision, a decision heavily influenced by a desire to inject competition into public sector activities. Choosing a contractor is a rigorous process with proposals weighed against a set of criteria. Government's role in contracting continues through monitoring even after the award of a contract. Relational contracting and public-private partnerships have helped support collaboration and shared risk, respectively, as compared to traditional "transactional" contracting.

The contracting relationship represents a principal-agent problem and contracts are structured to best align the incentives of the contractor with those of the contracting entity. Those involved in the contract process must be sensitive to the potential ethical conflicts inherent in contracting and be mindful of the best interests of the public.

KEY TERMS

Bid protests – claims filed by a contractor against a government organization to dispute a contract awarded to a competitor.

Contract – an agreement that is legally enforceable and reflects the relationship between two or more parties for a specific period of time.

Contracting-out – in government, refers to the decision to forego producing a good or service internally, instead opting to contract with a private/nonprofit sector entity while maintaining government oversight; see *outsourcing*.

Cooling-off period – a time frame during which a former government employee cannot be employed as an industry lobbyist in the private sector after leaving a government job; put in place to reduce any unfair influence or insider knowledge that persists.

Cost-reimbursement contracts – contracts that agree to pay a contractor based on the actual costs; these contracts can use incentives to further align the contractor's behavior with the government's needs.

Fixed-cost contracts – contracts that agree to pay a contractor a set amount; these contracts are used when little uncertainty exists about the specifications or requirements of the contracted activity.

Make-or-buy decision – the consideration of whether to produce a good or service in-house or to contract out; influenced by cost, required expertise, and commercial nature of the work.

Outsourcing – in government, refers to the decision to forego producing a good or service internally; instead, opting to contract with a private/nonprofit sector entity while maintaining government oversight; see *contracting-out*.

Principal-agent theory – describes the problematic scenario in principal-agent relationships in which the agent (e.g., a contractor) can potentially take advantage of the principal (e.g., the government) due to information asymmetries between the parties.

Privatization – the complete transfer of a function from the public sector to the private sector, often establishing a formal, regulatory relationship with government.

Production – refers to the actual generation of a good or service.

Provision – refers to the obligation to deliver a good or service.

Public-private partnerships (P3s) – contractual relationships between government and private firms to deliver either existing or newly-developed public services.

Relational contracting – refers to the central role of relationships in supplementing the formal contract as the public sector cedes authority to third parties.

Request-for-Proposal (RFP) – in contracting, refers to the document that formally solicits proposals/bids from potential contractors.

Revolving door – refers to the relative ease with which government employees move to private industry lobbying positions, and industry lobbyists move to government positions.

Set-asides – specific shares of the available contracting activity that are earmarked for smaller businesses and those that are owned by traditionally disadvantaged groups; also referred to as "bid preferences."

Sole-source contracting – a noncompetitive process in which there are negotiations with only one contractor; in government contracting, this process is common during wartime, natural disasters, and when the specialization required limits the number of potential contractors.

DISCUSSION QUESTIONS

1. What criteria would you use to identify an "inherently governmental" versus "commercial" activity? Provide two examples of roles that you consider "inherently governmental" and two that are carried out by government but appear "commercial."

2. Is it appropriate for public sector contracting to give preference to certain types of firms, such as women and minority-owned businesses, rather than focus entirely on the cost and expected quality of a bid?

3. Are there strategies you can think of that might help retain a competitive environment when the initial winner of the contract is seeking renewal?

4. Nonprofits depend on government contracts just as governments depend on nonprofits to produce many social services. How can governments encourage a collaborative relationship, as opposed to a purely contractual relationship, with nonprofit service providers?

EXERCISES

1. As governments increasingly depend on contracted services, the definition of public service similarly expands. Look at the Federal Procurement Data System—Next

Generation "Top 100 Contractor Report" (https://www.fpds.gov). The report also provides the top contractors for each federal agency. Identify a top contractor for a federal agency whose mission aligns with your career interests. Research the contractor and write a paragraph summarizing the primary expertise of the firm, the size of the firm, an example project (from the contractor's website or news stories), and a selected job posting. Would you consider working for the public sector through such a private partner?

2. Explore the FedBizOpps.gov website (https://www.fbo.gov/) to familiarize yourself with the elements of a federal contract solicitation. Conduct a search of opportunities posted in the last ninety days for your current state of residence. How many opportunities are available? Select an opportunity of interest and scan the posting. Write a one-paragraph overview of the opportunity and tell:

a) the length in pages of the posting,

b) the duration of the opportunity (how long a time period the contract covers),

c) the federal organization issuing the solicitation,

d) whether the contract is for a product or service,

e) whether the contracted activity is routine or specialized,

f) the type of criteria used for the award decision,

g) the form of pricing (e.g., cost reimbursement or fixed cost), and

h) any set-aside codes included in the solicitation (e.g., Woman-Owned Small Business, Veteran-Owned Small Business).

3. Make-or-Buy Decisions: The competing ideological viewpoints that accompany make-or-buy decisions are illustrated with a look at a municipal service provided internally by the city and county of Denver, Colorado. Denver owns and operates an asphalt plant whose mission is to produce low-cost, high-quality asphalt for resurfacing and maintaining the City's streets and alleys. After the local newspaper ran a story on the city's budget woes, the following two letters to the editor demonstrate opposing views about the appropriateness of the city producing its own asphalt. Read them and then respond to the questions that follow.

Denver Should Sell City-Owned Asphalt Plant[67]

Your editorial pointed out that long-term solutions are needed to fix Denver's budget problems. One solution is to sell the Denver-owned and -operated asphalt plant. This would put a stop to the city competing with private industry on a nonessential government service. It would bring in $2 million to $3 million and provide a long-term revenue opportunity by leasing the land.

Denver is the only city in Colorado with its own asphalt plant and is at the epicenter of competition for asphalt materials. The city could easily buy asphalt from one or more of the twenty-two privately-owned asphalt plants in the area. If Denver was truly committed to increasing economic opportunities for local businesses, it would reconsider its current mind-set of being more efficient than private industry and consider one solution that would reduce cost and increase revenue.

Thomas Peterson, *Centennial*
The writer is executive director of the Colorado Asphalt Pavement Association

Within a few days, an opposing point of view was aired:

Why Should City Privatize an Efficient Entity?[68]

According to Thomas Peterson, head of the Colorado Asphalt Pavement Association, Denver should sell its asphalt plant and buy its street-paving products from the private sector even though, according to Peterson, the city-owned asphalt plant is more efficient, meaning it saves the city money.

Apparently this is another case of ideology trumping common sense. In the interest of privatization, Peterson wants Denver to pay more for asphalt from an industry which, I can only guess, uses non-union workers and pays poor if any benefits, thereby forcing the city to lay off workers who receive good pay with health benefits and who bolster their local economy.

The rhetoric from self-serving organizations benefiting from the cover of a much-hyped popular ideology—in this case, a total free-market economy will solve our problems—have pushed us to the mess we're in.

Tom Parsons, *Broomfield*

a) The decision to contract out is heavily influenced by the existing service arrangement. In this case, Denver already publicly produces asphalt. Should that influence the decision to privatize production?
b) Based on the letters, how would you advise the mayor's office to address the publicity the asphalt plant received?
c) What factors are most relevant in the decision whether to retain the asphalt plant as a public asset?

BUILD YOUR SKILLS

Responding to a Request-for-Proposal (RFP) involves proposal writing that is responsive to the elements in the RFP. Use this Skillbox to learn how to be a successful grant writer.

SKILLBOX: GRANT WRITING ESSENTIALS

On June 26, 2006, renowned investor Warren Buffett wrote a letter to Bill and Melinda Gates, formerly of Microsoft fame and, more recently, the driving force behind the namesake Bill & Melinda Gates Foundation. The letter praised the Foundation's operations and described a series of forthcoming stock gifts to the Foundation from Buffett, valued at more than $30 billion, to "materially expand its future capabilities."[1] The recipients were left "speechless" upon word of the "the biggest single gift anyone ever gave anybody for anything."[2]

Without the support of people like Warren Buffett, many government and nonprofit organizations are forced to look to outside organizations for support. A key lesson from Buffett's gift for those seeking grant funding is that external resources flow to effective, capable, focused, and well-managed organizations that demonstrate results. Or, as Buffett wrote to Gates, "both of you have applied truly unusual intelligence, energy, and heart to improving the lives of millions of fellow humans who have not been as lucky as the three of us."[3]

The Basics of Grants

Grants are a primary mechanism for redistributing resources from one organization to another. Major categories of grant makers include foundations (independent, operating, corporate, and community), charitable nonprofit organizations, and governments (federal, state, and local). Grant making occurs from governments to other governments, governments to nonprofits, nonprofits to other nonprofits, and nonprofits to governments. The focus here is on grant writing, but the process for responding to a nongrant Request for Proposal (RFP), like those associated with contracting work, is very similar.

An example of a grant from a nonprofit to government comes from the Bloomberg Philanthropies effort to support "temporary public art projects that engage communities, enhance creativity, and enrich the vibrancy of cities." In June 2015, Bloomberg Philanthropies awarded up to $1 million to four winning cities out of 237 applicants for the Public Art Challenge.[4] The Public Art Challenge demonstrates that grant making tends to focus on specific activities and receipt of funding is highly competitive. There were 233 losing cities that dedicated substantial time and effort to apply for the grant funds.

The following describes the steps and considerations associated with grant writing.

Understand the role of grant funding in your organization.

The uncertainty associated with grant funding means that it is frequently complementary to core revenue sources such as fees for services or donations. In fact, the philanthropy-supporting Foundation Center's "most important things you need to know about finding grants" begins with this warning: "you can't survive on grants alone."[5] Grants are used to kick-start new projects, expand existing activities, or support capital campaigns, but are less frequently awarded for general operating support.

Scan grant-funding opportunities for appropriate fit.

There are three primary strategies for identifying grant-funding opportunities:

- Search. Organizations need to stay up-to-date on funding opportunities from governments and foundations, who release both periodic and regular calls for proposals. Funding opportunities are publicized online. Although not exhaustive, federal government and foundation funding opportunities can be found in the Catalog of Federal Domestic Assistance (http://www.cfda.gov) and Foundation Center (http://www.foundationcenter.org) websites, respectively.[6]

- Focus. Although monitoring all funding opportunities is useful, most organizations quickly get to know the primary funders in their area of operations. Get on the e-mail and social media lists for those key organizations to stay informed of opportunities.

- Interact. Use professional networks to establish a positive reputation for your work and develop working relationships with funders. Get to know foundations' priorities and interests. Do not pester, but seek out brief informational meetings with funders to better understand if your organization's work is aligned with funder interests and to become acquainted with their specific proposal process.

Once a specific funding opportunity is identified:

- Determine whether existing projects, or ideas for projects, align with the call for proposals. Most organizations have more project ideas available than funds. Fit works both ways. Do not let a grant opportunity divert attention and effort away from the organization's existing mission.

- Check for similar projects already underway in the targeted geographic area. If duplication exists, a funder will want to know what distinguishes the proposed activities from the existing projects.

- Consider partnering with another organization for the proposal, particularly when additional expertise or capacity is needed to credibly carry out the proposed activities. Collaboration is perceived positively by funders and can often help scale up a project.

Decide whether to apply for the grant funding.

- Seek input. Internally, involve all of the relevant parties in the organization in the determination to move forward with a proposal. It is not unheard of for different departments of the same government to unknowingly prepare, and even submit, proposals for the same grant funding. Colleagues may have experience with the funder that informs the decision to apply. Externally, reach out to the contact at the funder for a brief call or meeting about the proposal. A discussion prior to embarking on a complete grant proposal can save both parties a great deal of time and effort if the project is not a good fit with the funder's priorities.
- Invest (time) wisely. Applying for a grant is a significant investment of time and resources. For that reason, organizations should be selective in applying for grants. On the other hand, sometimes even an unfunded grant pays dividends by increasing a funder's awareness of an organization for future consideration.

Assign an owner of the grant proposal.

Applying for grant funding is a team effort, but it is a good idea to put someone in charge of the process. This means that at least one person is keeping an eye on the overall proposal requirements and ensuring that deadlines are met.

Follow directions, customize, and sell the proposal.

Proposal requirements vary dramatically in formality and depth. Give the funder what they want. As one foundation program officer notes, rules exist for a reason so "when we say ten pages, we're really serious about that."[7] Track the grant requirements in a spreadsheet to ensure that directions are followed, all components are present at submission, and the organization qualifies for the funding.

Learn from and model the proposal after strong and successful examples available online through sites like Grantspace (http://grantspace.org/tools/sample-documents). Understand the funder's goals and frame the proposal in a way that reflects those goals. In addition to being well written, be careful to avoid technical jargon and acronyms without explanation. Detail the proposed activities. Graphical representations are a plus. Thinking through the inputs, outputs, and outcomes is critical and also helps with development of the narrative and budget.

A great piece of advice is to make the proposal honest and accurate, but also interesting for the funder.[8] Ask a colleague who is not involved in assembling the grant proposal to read it and provide feedback. This helps guarantee that the proposal makes sense to an outsider and presents a compelling case for funding.

An organization should maintain centralized electronic records of all previous grant applications. These records avoid duplication of effort, provide boilerplate language specific to the organization, document any past history with the funder, and allow for learning about the characteristics of successful proposals.

Letters of support from partners and related organizations are often required as part of the proposal. These can be used to demonstrate the need for the project, quantify resources to be contributed by partners, and signal credibility and competence to prospective funders. An organization should have a standard list of partners that can be counted on for providing letters of support.

Be reasonable.

A grant proposal should be realistic. Make sure that the proposed activities can be carried out successfully by the organization in the presented timeframe and for the budgeted resources. A funder should be able to review a proposed budget and understand why the amounts are being requested. In other words, clearly justify expenses, including accurate indirect costs that meet the requirements of the funder.

A foremost consideration of funders is how a proposed ongoing project will be sustained after temporary grant funding concludes. For this reason, include a discussion of the post-grant plan for the project.[9] One foundation director suggests that "proposals most likely to catch a foundation's attention are those that convey plans to use the grant money to bring in other money."[10]

Include an evaluation plan.

Even if it is a minor part of the proposal, having the capacity to measure the effectiveness of the project and demonstrate outcomes is critical to funders.

Responding to a rejected proposal.

Most grant proposals are not funded, but that does not mean that the time and effort of grant writing was wasted. Do not take the rejection personally. Consider asking the program officer to share constructive feedback about the proposal either through a brief meeting or e-mail. This can both strengthen future proposals and establish a professional connection with the funder.

Hands-On Exercises

1. Select an area of interest and use online grant-funding search tools to identify two to three related opportunities. In a professional memo (addressed to leadership of an agency that might pursue the funding), provide an overview of the opportunities and compare and contrast the different application requirements for each. Are there more similarities than differences in the funding processes? How specific are the funders about the focus of proposed projects? Based on the review, is this an area with ample grant-funding opportunities?

2. Select an example of a successful grant proposal online. Review the proposal and compile an inventory of the "best practices" exhibited. First, briefly describe the applicant organization and the funder. For example, are they local, national, or international organizations? Do their missions overlap? Second, based on your judgment, comment on the effective elements of the application for funding. The steps and tips described earlier can be used as guidance.

Notes

1. Warren E. Buffett, "Letter to Mr. and Mrs. William H. Gates III" (June 26, 2006), http://www.berkshirehathaway.com/donate/bmgfltr.pdf.
2. Bill Gates and Melinda Gates, "Our 2017 Annual Letter: Warren Buffett's Best Investment" (February 14, 2017), https://www.gatesnotes.com/2017-Annual-Letter.
3. Buffett, "Letter."
4. Bloomberg Philanthropies, "Public Art Challenge," https://publicartchallenge.bloomberg.org/.
5. Foundation Center, "Introduction to Finding Grants," http://grantspace.org/content/download/717995/17421904/version/1/file/IFG-handout.pdf.
6. U.S. Library of Congress, Congressional Research Service, *How to Develop and Write a Grant Proposal*, by Merete F. Gerli, RL32159 (June 9, 2009).
7. Marilyn Dickey, "Grant Makers Reveal the Most Common Reasons Grant Proposals Get Rejected," *The Chronicle of Philanthropy* (April 24, 2003), https://www.philanthropy.com/article/Grant-Makers-Reveal-the-Most/183799.
8. U.S. Library of Congress, *How to Develop*.
9. Ibid.
10. Dickey, "Grant Makers."

Further Reading

U.S. Library of Congress, Congressional Research Service, *How to Develop and Write a Grant Proposal*, by Merete F. Gerli, RL32159 (June 9, 2009).

NOTES

1. Werner Z. Hirsch, "Contracting out by Urban Governments: A Review," *Urban Affairs Review* 30, no. 3 (1995): 458–472.

2. Congressional Budget Office, "Re: Federal Contracts and the Contracted Workforce," by Douglas W. Elmendorf (March 11, 2015), https://www.cbo.gov/sites/default/files/114th-congress-2015-2016/reports/49931-FederalContracts.pdf.

3. Paul C. Light, *The True Size of Government* (Washington DC: Brookings Institution, 1999).

4. Paul C. Light, *Fact Sheet on the New True Size of Government*, Center for Public Service, Brookings Institution (September 5, 2003), https://wagner.nyu.edu/files/faculty/publications/lightFactTrueSize.pdf.

5. "Overview of Awards by FY 2008 2017," USAspending.gov, last modified 2017, https://www.usaspending.gov/Pages/TextView.aspx?data=OverviewOfAwardsByFiscalYearTextView.

6. Brinton H. Milward and Keith Provan, "Managing the Hollow State: Collaboration and Contracting," *Public Management Review* 5, no. 1 (2003): 1–18.

7. Sandra Salmans, "Preaching Thrift: J. Peter Grace; A Budget Cutter Who Won't Quit," *New York Times* (February 24, 1985), http://www.nytimes.com/1985/02/24/business/preaching-thrift-j-peter-grace-a-budget-cutter-who-won-t-quit.html; Sydney J. Freedberg Jr., "The Myth of the $600 Hammer," *Government Executive* (December 7, 1998), http://www.govexec.com/federal-news/1998/12/the-myth-of-the-600-hammer/5271/; and U.S. Department of Defense Inspector General, *Northrop Grumman Improperly Charged Labor for the Counter Narco-terrorism Technology Program*, DODIG-2014-073 (May 13, 2014).

8. Fred Hiatt, "Now, the $600 Toilet Seat," *Washington Post* (February 5, 1985), A5.

9. Michael Weisskopf, "Firm Backs $544 Price on Toilet Seat Covers," *Washington Post* (November 27, 1985), A3.

10. Elmendorf, "Re: Federal Contracts."

11. Glen Kessler, "Fact Checker: The Inaccuracies in Donald Trump's Air Force One Tweet," *The Washington Post* (December 6, 2016), https://www.washingtonpost.com/news/fact-checker/wp/2016/12/06/the-inaccuracies-in-donald-trumps-air-force-one-tweet/?utm_term=.c86607982bff.

12. National Contract Management Association (NCMA) and Deltek, *Annual Review of Contracting, 2016 Edition* (2016), http://www.ncmahq.org/docs/default-source/default-document-library/pdfs/exec16---book---annual-review-of-government-contracting_lowres.

13. William Sims Curry, *Contracting for Services in State and Local Government Agencies*, 2nd ed. (New York, NY: Routledge, 2016), 4.

14. Steven J. Kelman, "Contracting," in *The Tools of Government: A Guide to the New Governance*, ed. Lester M. Salamon (New York: Oxford University Press, 2002), 282–318.

15. NCMA and Deltek, *Annual Review.*

16. Curry, *Contracting for Services.*

17. Yong Woon Kim and Trevor Brown, "The Importance of Contract Design," *Public Administration Review* 72, no. 5 (2012): 687–696.

18. Vincent Ostrom, Charles Tiebout, and Robert Warren, "The Organization of Government in Metropolitan Areas: A Theoretical Inquiry," *American Political Science Review* 55, no. 4 (1961): 834.

19. Emmanuel S. Savas, "A Taxonomy of Privatization Strategies," *Policy Studies Journal* 18, no. 2 (1989): 343–355.

20. Stewart Macaulay, "Non-Contractual Relations in Business: A Preliminary Study," *American Sociological Review* 28, (1963): 55–67.

21. Anthony M. Bertelli and Craig R. Smith, "Relational Contracting and Network Management," *Journal of Public Administration Research and Theory* 20, no. 1 (2010): i21–i40.

22. Ibid.

23. Ian R. Macneil, *Contracts: Instruments for Social Cooperation* (Hackensack, NJ: F. B. Rothman, 1968).

24. Beth Gazley, "Beyond the Contract: The Scope and Nature of Informal Government-Nonprofit Partnerships," *Public Administration Review* 68, no. 1 (2008): 141–154.

25. Kate Vitasek, "Relational Contracting on the Rise with the Success of the Australian Navy," *Forbes* (November 30, 2016), http://www.forbes.com/sites/katevitasek/2016/11/30/relational-contracting-on-the-rise-with-the-success-of-the-australian-navy/2/#bf4d609522ae.

26. Patrick Sabol and Robert Puentes, *Private Capital, Public Good: Drivers of Successful Infrastructure Public-Private Partnerships* (Washington DC: Brookings Institution, 2014).

27. Justin Marlowe, William C. Rivenbark, and A. John Vogt, *Capital Budgeting and Finance: A Guide for Local Governments* (Washington, DC: ICMA Press, 2009).

28. City of Chicago Office of the Inspector General. *Report of Inspector General's Findings and Recommendations: An Analysis of the Lease of the City's Parking Meters* (June 2, 2009), http://chicagoinspectorgeneral.org/wp-content/uploads/2011/03/Parking-Meter-Report.pdf.

29. Jeffrey L. Brudney, Sergio Fernandez, Jay Eungha Ryu, and Deil S. Wright, "Exploring and Explaining Contracting Out: Patterns Among the American States," *Journal of Public Administration Research and Theory* 15, no. 3 (2005): 393–419.

30. Richard C. Brooks, "Privatization of Government Services: An Overview and Review of the Literature," *Journal of Public Budgeting, Accounting & Financial Management* 16, no. 4 (2004): 467.

31. The World Bank, "Private Participation in Infrastructure (PPI) Database," last modified 2016, http://ppi.worldbank.org/.

32. Jonas Prager, "Contracting out Government Services: Lessons from the Private Sector," *Public Administration Review* 54, no. 2 (1994): 176–184.

33. United States General Accounting Office, *DOD Competitive Sourcing: Results of A-76 Studies over the Past 5 Years* (December, 2000).

34. U.S. Congress, Senate, Subcommittee on Oversight of Government Management, The Federal Workforce and the District of Columbia, *An Update on the Bush Administration's Competitive Sourcing Initiative,* testimony by Paul C. Light (July 24, 2003), https://wagner.nyu.edu/files/faculty/publications/lightCompetitiveSourcing.pdf.

35. Christopher Lee, "Bush Plan to Contract Federal Jobs Falls Short," *Washington Post* (April 25, 2008).

36. Ibid.

37. Jon Jeter, "A Winning Combination in Indianapolis; Competitive Bidding for City Services Creates Public-Private Success Story," *Washington Post* (September 21, 1997), A3.

38. Kelman, "Contracting."

39. Ibid.

40. U.S. Library of Congress, Congressional Research Service, *The Federal Acquisition Regulation (FAR): Answers to Frequently Asked Questions,* by Kate M. Manuel, Elaine L. Halchin, Erika K. Lunder, and Michelle D. Christensen, R42826 (2015).

41. Daniel R. Mullins and C. Kurt Zorn, "Is Activity Based Costing Up to the Challenge When It Comes to Privatization of Local Government Services?" *Public Budgeting & Finance* 19, no. 2 (1999): 37–58.

42. Brudney, Fernandez, Ryu, and Wright, "Exploring and Explaining"; and Germà Bel, Xavier Fageda, and Mildred E. Warner, "Is Private Production of Public Services Cheaper Than Public Production? A Meta-Regression Analysis of Solid Waste and Water Services," *Journal of Policy Analysis and Management* 29, no. 3 (2010): 553–577.

43. Graeme A. Hodge, *Privatization: An International Review of Performance* (Boulder, CO: Westview Press, 2000).

44. Bel, Fageda, and Warner, "Is Private Production?"

45. Robert D. Behn and Peter A. Kant, "Strategies for Avoiding the Pitfalls of Performance Contracting," *Public Productivity and Management Review* 22, no. 4 (1999): 470-489.

46. State of Colorado Office of the State Architect, *FY 2014/2015 Annual Report Presented To The Capital Development Committee* (December, 2013).

47. United States Government Accountability Office, *Pay for Success: Collaboration Among Federal Agencies Would Be Helpful as Governments Explore New Financing Mechanisms*, GAO-15-646 (September, 2015), http://www.gao.gov/products/GAO-15-646.

48. Kelman, "Contracting."

49. Emmanuel S. Savas, "A Taxonomy of Privatization Strategies," *Policy Studies Journal* 18, no. 2 (1989): 343–355.

50. Kelman, "Contracting."

51. Ibid.

52. Ibid.

53. Maria E. Enchautegui, Michael Fix, Pamela Loprest, Sarah C. von der Lippe, and Douglas Wissoker, *Do Minority-Owned Businesses Get a Fair Share of Government Contracts?* Urban Institute (1997), http://webarchive.urban.org/publications/307416.html.

54. Department of Finance and Administrative Services, *City of Seattle Contracting Equity Report* (September 16, 2015), http://www.seattle.gov/Documents/Departments/FAS/PurchasingAndContracting/WMBE/Contracting-Equity-2015-Report.pdf.

55. City of Seattle, *Payment Information by WMBE (Combined) 1/1/2016 to 12/31/2016* (December 31, 2016), http://www.seattle.gov/Documents/Departments/FAS/PurchasingAndContracting/WMBE/1-3p_c.pdf.

56. Kelman, "Contracting."

57. United States Government Accountability Office, *Re: GAO Bid Protest Annual Report to Congress for Fiscal Year 2016*, B-158766 (December 15, 2016), http://www.gao.gov/assets/690/681662.pdf.

58. United States Government Accountability Office, *Decision (Matter of: RQ Construction, LLC)*, B-409131 (January 13, 2014), http://www.gao.gov/assets/670/660174.pdf.

59. Kelman, "Contracting."

60. Light, *An Update.*

61. United States Government Accountability Office, *Defense Contracting: Post-Government Employment of Former DOD Officials Needs Greater Transparency*, GAO-08-485 (May, 2008), http://www.gao.gov/products/GAO-08-485.

62. U.S. Library of Congress, Congressional Research Service, *Post-Employment, "Revolving Door," Laws for Federal Personnel,* by Jack Maskell, R42728 (2014).

63. National Conference of State Legislatures (NCSL), "Revolving Door Prohibitions: Rules Against Legislators Lobbying State Government after They Leave Office" (January 18, 2017), http://www.ncsl.org/research/ethics/50-state-table-revolving-door-prohibitions.aspx.

64. Department of Justice, *Fact Sheet: Significant False Claims Act Settlements & Judgments Fiscal Years 2009-2016* (n.d.), https://www.justice.gov/opa/press-release/file/918366/download.

65. Department of Justice Office of Public Affairs, "Oracle Agrees to Pay U.S. $199.5 Million to Resolve False Claims Act Lawsuit" (October 6, 2011), https://www.justice.gov/opa/pr/oracle-agrees-pay-us-1995-million-resolve-false-claims-act-lawsuit.

66. *Ask Me Why I Care: Public Service Stories*, video, directed by Mary R. Hamilton and Rita Paskowitz (Omaha, Nebraska: College of Public Affairs and Community Service), https://www.unomaha.edu/college-of-public-affairs-and-community-service/community-engagement/pss-dewey-harris.php.

67. Tom Peterson, "Denver Should Sell City-Owned Asphalt Plant," *Denver Post eLetters* (blog), July 23, 2010, http://blogs.denverpost.com/eletters/2010/07/23/denver-should-sell-city-owned-asphalt-plant/9912/.

68. Tom Parsons, "Why Should City Privatize an Efficient Entity?" *Denver Post eLetters* (blog), July 27, 2010, http://blogs.denverpost.com/eletters/2010/07/27/why-should-city-privatize-an-efficient-entity/9954/.

ADDITIONAL RESOURCES

Brown, Trevor, Matthew Potoski, and David Van Slyke. 2013. *Complex Contracting: Government Purchasing in the Wake of the US Coast Guard's Deepwater Program* (Cambridge, UK: Cambridge University Press).

Cohen, Steven and William Eimicke. 2008. *The Responsible Contract Manager: Protecting the Public Interest in an Outsourced World* (Washington, DC: Georgetown University Press).

Hood, Christopher and Ruth Dixon. 2015. *A Government That Worked Better and Cost Less?: Evaluating Three Decades of Reform and Change in UK Central Government* (Oxford, UK: Oxford University Press).

Kettl, Donald F. 1994. *Sharing Power: Public Governance and Private Markets* (Washington, DC: Brookings Institution Press).

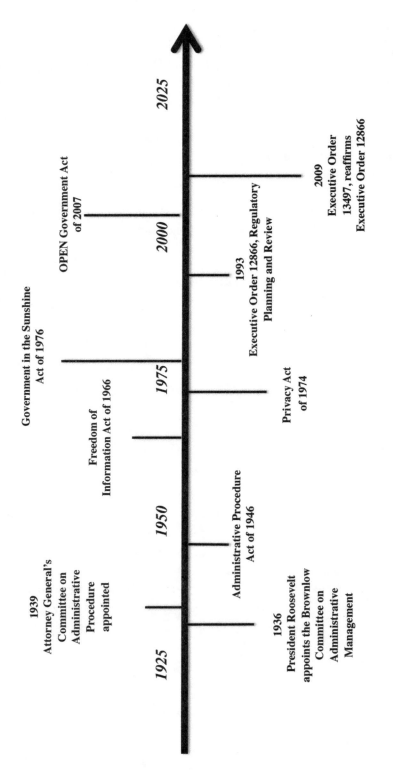

Chapter 12 Timeline: Legal Dimensions of Public Administration

1925

1936
President Roosevelt appoints the Brownlow Committee on Administrative Management

1939
Attorney General's Committee on Administrative Procedure appointed

1950

Administrative Procedure Act of 1946

Freedom of Information Act of 1966

Government in the Sunshine Act of 1976

1975

Privacy Act of 1974

OPEN Government Act of 2007

2000

1993
Executive Order 12866, Regulatory Planning and Review

2025

2009
Executive Order 13497, reaffirms Executive Order 12866

WHAT YOU WILL LEARN

Constraints on administrative action

The rulemaking function

The adjudicatory process

Skillbox: How to dissect a legal opinion

The three branches of government—legislative, executive, and judicial—are separate and they each play significant but different roles in the pursuit of public purposes. The legislative function authorizes programs while the executive function designs and manages them. The judicial function reviews programs to ensure they comport with constitutional and administrative law. The quandary of how best to treat people with mental health conditions provides an example of how the three branches work in collaboration and, sometimes, in opposition to one another.

A TANGLED WEB: DEINSTITUTIONALIZATION FOR PEOPLE WITH MENTAL HEALTH CONDITIONS

Like pulling one string of yarn and unraveling the entire sweater, legislation pertaining to one issue can affect a seemingly unrelated policy, and litigation intended for one purpose can have effects that change programs everywhere. For example, when the Alabama state legislature decided to cut its cigarette tax in 1970, the change set in motion a series of events that culminated in the landmark *Wyatt v. Stickney* case.[1] This court decision drove dramatic changes in the treatment of institutionalized patients with mental health problems. It ultimately resulted in deinstitutionalization across the country.

Because the proceeds from the cigarette tax were earmarked for mental health services, the cut caused reductions in the state's mental health system, including elimination of nearly 100 staff members at Bryce State Hospital, the state-run facility that served patients involuntarily committed for mental health conditions. Twenty professionals, including psychologists, were among those fired. On October 23, 1970, the fired staff members filed a lawsuit in the U.S. District Court against the Alabama Department of Mental Health. They sought reinstatement on the grounds that patients would receive inadequate treatment due to a shortage of treatment staff. To strengthen their position, the group included a patient, Ricky Wyatt, as a plaintiff. Wyatt, a fifteen-year-old, had been placed in the state hospital by the courts in an attempt to correct his delinquent behavior. The staff members' case gradually expanded to include patients of another state hospital for people with mental health illnesses as well as a state-owned facility for people with developmental disabilities. With this expansion, the focus of the litigation shifted from the rights of employees to the rights of residents.[2] The court decision held that people who are involuntarily committed to state institutions because of mental health conditions or developmental disabilities have a constitutional right to treatment that will afford them an opportunity to return to society.

The ruling led to sweeping reforms in mental health treatment and the creation of minimum standards of care for people with mental illness and developmental disabilities. The court found that patients were entitled to individualized treatment plans and to being held in the least restrictive environment necessary. Thus, from a political decision in the legislature to authorize a tax cut, to mental health staff who lost their jobs and sued for reinstatement, and the judgment of the court to compel the Department of Mental Health to change its processes, national treatment for people with mental health conditions changed. From legislature to executive agency to federal court and back to executive agency, the string of events demonstrates how public administrators—the professionals who were fired to cut costs—used the court to dictate to the executive agency about services that must be delivered. Across the nation, large state hospitals closed and patients were discharged and returned to their local communities for care.

The story does not end there. Solutions to one problem create another. Fast forward to now and communities are struggling with the problem of what to do with the large number of people with mental health conditions who need treatment but for whom no facilities exist. In 1955, state psychiatric facilities cared for 560,000 patients. Post *Wyatt v. Stickney*, state facilities now care for only 45,000[3] and patients are being boarded in emergency rooms and jail cells, a situation not unlike the early 1800s, before states began building and operating psychiatric hospitals as a progressive, humanitarian initiative. The Washington State Supreme Court has ruled that boarding is unlawful.[4] Similar rulings in more states are soon to follow. It will be a combination of judicial prodding, political resolve, and administrative expertise to address the problem.

Questions to Ponder

1. What was the chain of events from legislation to administration to judicial decision making to administration in this case?
2. "A Tangled Web" demonstrates how humanitarian programs of one century become inhumane in the next. And now the question of how the state should treat people with mental health conditions is back on the table. Are public programs always a work in progress?
3. Public service workers often play multiple roles, from client advocate to deciding whether an applicant is eligible for services (adjudicating), to delivering the service (administration), and then determining whether the person is entitled to future services (rulemaking). How do public service professionals prevent these roles from colliding with one another?

Administrative actions are subject to review by all three branches of government. The judicial branch reviews actions when they hear suits alleging violation of constitutionally protected rights. The agency itself may submit actions for review to its administrative law judges to ensure that its procedures are consistent with statute. The legislative branch reviews the operation of agencies through committee reviews, public hearings, and in the course of providing constituent services. As demonstrated by the *Wyatt v. Stickney* decision, these reviews have the capacity to significantly alter the way that an agency functions and the way public purposes are pursued.

PUBLIC LAW

Public law focuses on the organization and processes of government, the relations between the state and its citizens, the responsibilities of government officials, and the relations between political jurisdictions. It is concerned with the powers, rights, capacities, and duties of government and government officials and includes both constitutional and administrative law. It can also extend into torts, (an act or omission that causes harm to another and amounts to a civil wrong) and contract law. In other words, it provides the foundation, authority, and boundaries that frame the work of public administration. Whether the question is one of agency rulemaking, application of administrative rules, compliance with statutes, public employee speech, or a question of immunity from prosecution, legal dimensions touch all the corners, nooks, and crannies of public service.

Although public law extends to contracts, torts, and sometimes criminal proceedings, the term primarily refers to constitutional law and administrative law. The objective of executive agencies—the bureaucracy—is to achieve constitutional goals through transparent means, as prescribed in administrative law. The decision in the *Wyatt v. Stickney* case focused on the constitutional rights of inpatients in mental health facilities and it had ramifications for the administrative procedures in every state's department of mental health. The case demonstrates the legal nexus between constitutional principles and administrative process.

Public administrators need not be trained in law but they must be sensitive to the legal ramifications of their work. The public's right to know must be balanced against privacy rights in constitutional law and the search for reasonable principles of organizational justice. And nonprofit organizations are not exempt. When they receive grants and contracts from government to deliver public services, they become a public service provider and, to some degree, fall within the purview of public law as well.

ADMINISTRATIVE PROCEDURE ACT

A common ground joins public administration and administrative law. It is through administrative law that abstract constitutional tenets of delegation of legislative authority and procedural due process are translated into action. This serves as the foundation for government to function fairly and to ensure due process rights for citizens, applicants for services, public employees, and entities that collaborate in service delivery.

> *"In fact, the vast majority of 'laws' governing the United States are not passed by Congress but are issued as regulations, crafted largely by thousands of unnamed, unreachable bureaucrats."*
>
> —Jonathan Turley

Relative to constitutional principles, rulemaking is the most important function performed by agencies because it is delegated lawmaking.[5] Administrative law provides a framework for the rulemaking process, hearing grievances, and enforcement of rules and laws. It regulates what agencies do and how they do it, not by dictating how to manage but by governing the rules by which they operate and by which their outcomes may be appealed. In essence, it puts the brakes on administrative power and makes it accountable by ensuring a means of dispute resolution for stakeholders of government action.

Since its enactment in 1946, the Administrative Procedure Act (APA),[6] has (1) governed the process that administrative agencies follow in adjudicating, rulemaking, and adopting policies; (2) controlled their authority to enforce laws and regulations; and, (3) governed the extent to which administrative action is open to public scrutiny. Although passed long ago, it remains the federal government's basic administrative manual. While the Act applies to federal agencies, similar laws for similar purposes are in effect in the states and locales.

Attention to administrative process grew during the late nineteenth and early twentieth centuries, as demands on government grew and agencies proliferated. In the absence of legal parameters that set boundaries on how agencies could set rules and pursue their operations, great variability arose. In the 1930s, as it became obvious that setting policy is an easier task than making it happen, President Franklin Roosevelt turned his attention to administrative matters. In 1936, he established the President's Committee on Administrative Management, called the Brownlow Committee, and charged it with the responsibility to come forth with recommendations on how to improve management in the executive branch. The committee recommended a number of improvements to administrative structure, urging better coordination of executive agencies and a coordination of their powers.

To further refine recommendations for improvements in how agencies operated, in 1939, President Roosevelt established the Attorney General's Committee on Administrative Procedure and instructed it to ascertain the need for reform in agency procedures. The committee was charged with the responsibility of reviewing criticisms of the federal administrative processes and with formulating recommendations for improvement. The committee's recommendations resulted in passage of the APA in 1946. Its purpose was to clarify and regularize the judicial actions of administrative agencies. Since then, a number of additional laws have been passed to ensure open meetings, reduce intrusiveness of government action in people's lives, ensure the quality of government data, and strengthen freedom of information.

These additional laws further define and ensure public access to government information and operations, while protecting the privacy of citizens. The Freedom of Information Act of 1966 greatly increased the amount of government information that is available to the public. To safeguard individual privacy, the Privacy Act of 1974 was passed to govern the collection, maintenance, use, and dissemination of personally identifiable information that is maintained in federal records. The Government in the Sunshine Act of 1976 was passed to ensure greater transparency in government by requiring open meetings. The OPEN Government Act of 2007 requires agencies to designate chief information officers. Among their duties is the responsibility to promote timeliness in processing information requests from the public. These laws ensure that public administration embraces the core values of democratic constitutionalism and keeps the bureaucracy accountable to the public.

SCOPE OF REVIEW OF AGENCY PROCEDURES

Section 706 of the APA specifies the reasons for reviewing procedural decisions of agencies.[7] They include:

(A) arbitrary, capricious, an abuse of discretion, or otherwise not in accordance with law;

(B) contrary to constitutional right, power, privilege, or immunity;

(C) in excess of statutory jurisdiction, authority, or limitations, or short of statutory right;

(D) without observance of procedure required by law;

(E) unsupported by substantial evidence;

(F) unwarranted by the facts.

The purpose of the APA is to provide minimum procedural standards that federal administrative agencies must follow. It distinguishes between two major forms of administrative functions: agency rulemaking and agency adjudication. Rulemaking is analogous to legislative acts, while adjudication is analogous to judicial procedure. This distinction represents the two processes that coincide with how administrative agencies perform their substantive functions, whether it is providing services to veterans, regulating air standards, or collecting taxes.

The minimum rulemaking requirement is called notice-and-comment. Under notice-and-comment rulemaking, agencies are required to give the public advance notice of a proposed rule and the opportunity to express their views about it before it is finalized. Proposed rules are posted in the *Federal Register,* the daily journal of the federal government. (Find it at https://www.federalregister.gov/.) Adjudicatory provisions govern judicial review of agency actions and public access to agency-created law. For example, in the 1984 case of *Chevron U.S.A., Inc. v. National Resources Defense Council, Inc.,*[8] the Supreme Court ruled that administrative agencies are entitled to substantial judicial deference in their interpretation of laws that are ambiguous or vague. By making this decision, the judicial branch affirmed the authority of agencies to interpret legislation and not be second-guessed by the courts.

In summary, the APA requires administrators to embrace the values of accountability, public participation in rulemaking, and procedural due process. To legal scholars, the APA is more like a constitution than a statute because it provides for flexibility in decision making. Its provisions are written broadly enough that they allow for interpretation without the need for formal amendment. Its fundamental role is to shape the relationship between the people and their government and it gives government considerable leeway in carrying out the laws that Congress enacts. At the same time, it provides the governed with procedural protection.[9]

THE RULEMAKING PROCESS

Rulemaking is the process that executive agencies use to transform statute into programs. It is a legislative function delegated by Congress to the executive branch. From determining the provisions of Medicare to determining when coins can be melted to setting minimal environmental standards, these activities are bounded by administrative rules. Legislatures cannot be expected to have the technical expertise to set standards for air quality or water safety. That function is performed by the Environmental Protection Agency, an agency staffed with scientists who are experts in the field. And lawmakers cannot be expected to understand how best to structure a program so that it has maximum outreach to those being served. Experts in the agency that provides the program to the public make those decisions. The delivery of public services to millions of citizens would be impossible without this delegation of authority.

There are three general categories of rules that agencies write: (1) legislative, which have the force of law; (2) procedural, which specify how operations are to be conducted; and, (3) interpretive, which explain terms and guidelines.[10] These rules provide transparency to the agency's stakeholders and guidance for employees as they pursue the agency's mission. Service providers will still exercise discretion but it exists within the confines of rules. Rules govern which drugs go to market, who gets to live in public housing, and how contracts are awarded. They even govern who can gather plants in national parks. For example, the *Federal Register* publishes proposed and final rules such as the following about the gathering of plants by Indian tribes. It is a rule issued by the National Park Service in 2016.[11]

Gathering of Certain Plants or Plant Parts by Federally Recognized Indian Tribes for Traditional Purposes

"The National Park Service is establishing a management framework to allow the gathering and removal of plants or plant parts by enrolled members of federally recognized Indian tribes for traditional purposes. The rule authorizes agreements between the National Park Service and federally recognized tribes that will facilitate the continuation of tribal cultural practices on lands within areas of the National Park System where those practices traditionally occurred, without causing a significant adverse impact to park resources or values. This rule respects those tribal cultural practices, furthers the government-to-government relationship between the United States and the tribes, and provides system-wide consistency for this aspect of National Park Service-tribal relations."

The following path detailed in Figure 12.1 shows the steps that were followed to bring this rule to fruition.[12] First, there was an initiating event, which could have been an agency initiative, a court decision, or a required review. Then there

FIGURE 12.1 HOW RULES ARE MADE

was debate about whether a rule was necessary. Once decided in the affirmative, the rule was drafted, a notice was posted in the *Federal Register* that planning was underway, and the proposed rule was reviewed and approved by the Office of Information and Regulatory Affairs (OIRA), a part of the Office of Management and Budget (OMB). Per Executive Order 12866, OIRA has ninety days to review the rule. This includes an interagency review to ensure that it is not inconsistent, incompatible, or duplicative of other rules. A cost/benefit analysis is also conducted and a determination must be reached that the benefits of the regulation justify the costs. After approval by OIRA, the proposed rule is posted in the *Federal Register* for public comment. The comments are then reviewed by the agency and revisions are made to the rule as necessary. The revised rule is then reviewed again by the OIRA before being published in the *Federal Register*. The process takes a year or more from beginning to end.

THE ADJUDICATION PROCESS

Under the APA, the adjudicatory process is used to rule on matters pertaining to procedural due process. The first step in the adjudicatory process is at the street level when, on behalf of government, a public service worker makes a decision to provide or deny a service. The second stage occurs when administrative law judges hear appeals made by those exercising their right to appeal the decision.

Administrative Law Judges

The Administrative Law Judge (ALJ) function was created by the APA to ensure fairness in administrative proceedings before federal agencies. They function much like trial court judges when they hear a case without a jury. Rather than individual proceedings or constitutional and civil rights cases, ALJs hear cases that involve federal laws and regulations in such areas as admiralty, advertising, antitrust, banking, communications, energy, environmental protection, food and drugs, health and safety, housing, immigration, interstate commerce, international trade, labor management relations, securities and commodities markets, transportation, social security disability, and other benefits claims.

The APA outlines the general duties and powers of ALJs. They have the power to issue subpoenas, enter or exclude evidence, and execute various powers comparable to a federal trial judge. They may be called upon to evaluate agency rules, resolve disputes, assess and improve procedures, and assign penalties. They have qualified decisional independence in that they must follow their agency's policies and procedures when making adjudicatory decisions but they may not be influenced by the agency as they make decisions. For example, a rule published by the Social Security Administration (SSA) defines the role of the ALJ this way:

> "Qualified decisional independence" means that ALJs must be impartial in conducting hearings. They must decide cases based on the facts in each case and in accordance with agency policy as laid out in regulations, rulings, and other policy statements. Further, because of their qualified decisional independence, ALJs make their decisions free from agency pressure or pressure by a party to decide a particular case, or a particular percentage of cases, in a particular way. The agency may not take actions that abridge the duty of impartiality owed to claimants when ALJs hear and decide claims.[13]

The work of ALJs ensures that claimants against an agency's actions have due process rights. For example, an ALJ may rule on disputes over penalties that a mine inspector has levied against a mine operator, or on disputes between a Medicare claimant and the Centers for Medicare/Medicaid Services (CMS), or between an applicant for social security disability benefits and the SSA.

At the federal level, a legal background is required of ALJs. At the state and local levels, a law degree is usually but not always required and their function and duties conform to the APA to a large degree.

Qualifying Experience for Federal ALJs[14]

Applicants must have a full seven (7) years of experience as a licensed attorney preparing for, participating in, and/or reviewing formal hearings or trials involving litigation and/or administrative law at the Federal, State or local level.

ALJs hear cases brought before adjudicatory boards, such as the Equal Employment Opportunity Commission and the Mine Safety and Health Review Commission, as well as in administrative agencies that deliver services and make decisions about eligibility for services, such as the SSA.

ADMINISTRATIVE LAW JUDGES IN THE SOCIAL SECURITY
ADMINISTRATION[15]

Within the SSA, the Office of Disability Adjudication and Review (ODAR) holds hearings, issues decisions, and reviews appeals as part of the agency's process for determining whether or not a person may receive benefits. Headquartered in Falls Church, Virginia, ODAR is one of the largest administrative adjudication systems in the world. There are approximately 1,400 ALJs whose job it is to hear Social Security Disability cases.

ODAR directs a nationwide field organization of administrative law judges who conduct impartial hearings and make decisions when applicants for services are initially denied and they wish to appeal the decision. Such services include survivors' benefits, retirement, disability, and supplemental security income benefits. SSA's hearing operation is one level in a four-level administrative review process within the SSA.

Administrative law prescribes the path that disputes take. The case of Brian Jackson, an employee, versus Alan Ritchey Materials, a sand mining company, demonstrate how administrative law benefits both parties in a claim under the Mine Act (Federal Mine Safety and Health Act of 1977).

BRIAN JACKSON V. ALAN RITCHEY MATERIALS CO., LC, (JULY 1, 2016)

Brian Jackson, who worked as a ground hand for Alan Ritchey Materials Company, filed a discrimination complaint with the Federal Mine Safety and Health Review Commission (MSHA). When Jackson showed up for work on November 17, 2015, he was told that he would be assigned to work on a boat on the river in the dark that night to repair a cable used in a dredging operation. He refused, explaining to his supervisor that he had worked on a boat several months prior and it sank. He had to be rescued and, based on this experience, he was convinced that the work was not safe. When he was

told that he had to work on the boat anyway, he declined and said that he would return to work the next day. When Jackson returned the following day, he was told that he was terminated. Jackson claimed that his discharge was due to refusing to work in unsafe conditions coupled with discrimination against him because he was a Choctaw Nation Tribal member. The complaint said discrimination and harassment included being called a "f**king Injun" and "damn Indian." He went on to say that he was also subjected to sexual harassment by his supervisor, who had thrown feminine hygiene products at him while telling him "this is for your bleeding p***y."

The Federal Mine Safety and Health Act of 1977 (Mine Act) provides for making a complaint for a danger or safety violation. Protected activity does not encompass all types of discrimination. The ALJ's review of the filing explained that the purpose of the Mine Act is to encourage miners to play an active part in the enforcement of mine safety. It requires that they must be protected against any possible discrimination which they suffer as a result of their participation. Accordingly, Mine Act discrimination claims may not entertain other types of discrimination, regardless of how egregious. And, thus, Jackson's complaint about being fired because he refused to work in unsafe conditions was allowed to go forward and be heard, while his complaints about ethnic discrimination and sexual harassment were disallowed.

The ruling was made by an ALJ employed by the Federal Mine Safety and Health Review Commission, an independent adjudicative agency that provides administrative trial and appellate review of legal disputes arising under the Mine Act.[16]

Administrative law has a major impact on everyday administrative activities. In the case of *Brian Jackson v. Alan Ritchey Materials Co., LC,* the focus of concern was on the question of whether Brian Jackson's dismissal was prohibited action as covered by the Mine Act. The employer argued that the dismissal was a function of an employee who failed to perform as requested while the employee argued that the dismissal was a result of his refusing to work in unsafe conditions, as protected by the Mine Act. The complaints of discrimination may be actionable under the rules of the Equal Employment Opportunity Commission but that would be a different filing than entertained by the Mine Safety and Health Review Commission.

In this example, the Mine Safety and Health Review Commission plays an adjudicatory role whose public purpose is to advance mine safety. Similarly, the public purpose of the Equal Employment Opportunity Commission is to advance equal job opportunity regardless of demographic characteristics. ALJs are constrained by the agency for whom they work in that their decisions are narrowly tailored to conform to the specific rules and laws that govern their decision making.

In summary, rulemaking and adjudication regularize administrative processes, rendering them transparent and accountable. Administrative law is applied in three primary ways. The first is when government determines the eligibility of persons to receive benefits, such as in the case of the rule allowing Indian tribes to gather plants on national park lands while others cannot. It is also applied when government regulates the behavior of entities, such as in the case of requiring that mental health facilities allow those being treated for mental health conditions to live in the least restrictive environment and to have an individualized treatment plan. The third way is when law is applied to provide a benefit and to achieve regulatory goals, which happens when licenses are granted to utilities to operate utility plants or, in the case of Brian Jackson, when the law allowed him to move forward with a complaint about mine safety.

IMMUNITY FOR PUBLIC OFFICIALS: ABSOLUTE VERSUS QUALIFIED

Another aspect of legal considerations for public administrators arises not in terms of how the agency pursues its mission but rather what liability is incurred by performing one's job? Immunity is in place so that public employees can perform their responsibilities without fear of being sued.

While the legal concept of sovereign immunity protects public entities to some degree from liability arising from the actions of government, the application of sovereign immunity is not clear-cut. Laws vary by state in terms of what kind of claims against government can be made. Similar ambiguity surrounds the questions of whether public officials have absolute or qualified immunity from claims that arise as a function of the work they perform. The law is also uneven in how it treats private sector workers who are employed in a contractual arrangement with a public entity, such as in the case of privately operated prisons. Guidance on this issue is provided by a 2015 Supreme Court decision, *State Board of Dental Examiners v. Federal Trade Commission*,[17] in which the court ruled that private contractors must act in a way "clearly articulated and affirmatively expressed as state policy" and the policy must be actively supervised by the state in order to be afforded immunity.

The grant of immunity can range from absolute to limited, based on job duties. While absolute immunity is more likely to be afforded to high level officials, qualified immunity is more likely for lower level officials. This is because high ranking officers, such as prosecutors, must exercise broad discretion in order to do their jobs, while those at lower ranks, such as police officers, must perform within the boundaries of written procedures that provide for less discretion. The general understanding is that public officials can be held personally liable and be levied money damages when they violate well-established statutory or constitutional rights of which a reasonable person would have known. Emphasis is on the interpretation of the word "reasonable." Qualified immunity shields officials from damages for civil liability as long as they do not violate an individual's rights and the claim arises from employees simply performing their job in good faith and with due care. It does not protect against the incompetent or those who knowingly violate the law. Although qualified immunity provides public officials with a legal cushion, it is not absolute protection and is considered on a case-by-case basis.

Ask Me Why I Care: Howard M. Messner, creator of the Environmental Protection Agency[18]

"We created (the Environmental Protection Agency) out of bits and pieces from a dozen federal agencies. We brought together about 5,000 people."—Howard Messner

Have you ever wondered how a federal agency gets started? Howard Messner chaired the Environmental Protection Agency task force in the late 1960s that led to the creation of the agency in 1971 and tells how it happened.

Mr. Messner had a thirty-seven-year federal career, working in a variety of capacities for NASA, the Office of Management and Budget, the Congressional Budget Office, the Energy Department, and the Environmental Protection Agency. In 1986 he was awarded the Presidential Distinguished Executive Rank by President Ronald Reagan. Watch the video to hear Messner tell how the EPA came to life. Access the interview at https://www .unomaha.edu/college-of-public-affairs-and-community-service/community-engagement/ pss-howard-messner.php.

SUMMARY

The purpose of administrative law is to harmonize public administration with constitutional democracy—to balance bureaucracy and democracy. The path to solid administrative performance comes from an understanding of political, economic, psychological, sociological, AND legal dimensions. From the protections afforded by the Civil Rights Acts, to Equal Employment Opportunity Commission procedures, to Mine Safety prohibitions, to employment caselaw, to contracts let to private sector vendors, there are legal dimensions to all of public administration.

Public administration is the instrument by which public purposes are pursued. To ensure that cost effectiveness does not overrun individual liberties in the pursuit of them, the APA was crafted. It reminds everyone that individual liberties have priority over administrative protocols. Administrative law prevents administrators from trampling on individual rights and it ensures accountability and transparency. The APA has continued to be relevant over the decades because its focus is procedural rather than substantive. It is couched in the philosophy of natural rights that people form governments in order to act collectively and that people have inalienable rights that government must protect, not diminish. Thus personal freedoms are protected at all costs and government must tread lightly around them.

There are three types of tools that public executives have at their disposal: policy tools, management tools, and legal tools. Policy tools include executive orders, rules, and regulations. Management tools include administrative procedures. Legal tools include contracts and adjudication, such as performed by administrative law judges. While public law scripts the actions of government, public managers have the awareness of what is administratively feasible. Thus, the courts and agencies work hand in glove to breathe life into constitutional values. For example, the decree in *Wyatt v. Stickney* is only as good as mental health agencies' capacity to effectively treat mental illness.

Like skilled jugglers, public service professionals must often switch tools as they pursue their mission, switching rapidly from policy making to administrative to adjudicatory. They are part of the great constitutional drama of America, translating constitutional principles into everyday actions, all within the confines of the law. Doing so requires standing on a balance beam, balancing the desire to advocate with the responsibility to be a compassionate service deliverer and a neutral arbiter.

KEY TERMS

Adjudicatory procedures – relating to the administrative adjudication process, wherein an executive agency's administrative law judge (ALJ) rules on claims brought before or against the agency, typically pertaining to matters of procedural due process.

Administrative law – body of law that translates constitutional principles regarding the delegation of legislative authority and procedural due process into action; provides a framework for the rulemaking process, hearing grievances, and enforcement of rules and laws.

Administrative law judge – a judge whose function is to hear cases involving laws and regulations pertaining to the agency for which they work; they ensure fairness in administrative proceedings by preserving the due process rights of claimants against the agency.

Administrative Procedure Act – passed in 1946 to clarify the rulemaking and adjudication processes of administrative agencies, control their authority to enforce laws and regulations, and make their activities more open to public participation.

Constitutional law – body of law that establishes the powers and responsibilities of government, and the rights and responsibilities of citizens, rooted in the Constitution.

Delegated lawmaking – refers to the administrative process of rulemaking, wherein executive agencies design the implementation of a law by establishing rules and regulations, as delegated by the legislature.

Public law – body of law pertaining to the organization and processes of government, the relations between the state and its citizens, the responsibilities of government officials, and the relations between political jurisdictions.

Qualified immunity – a form of immunity that shields public officials from liability for civil damages as long as they do not violate an individual's rights and the claim arises from the performance of their job duties in good faith and with due care.

Rulemaking – the process by which executive agencies transform laws into programs by establishing the rules and regulations for their implementation.

DISCUSSION QUESTIONS

1. Why is it important for public administrators to be aware of administrative law?
2. How is the rulemaking function of agencies similar to the legislative branch's lawmaking function? How is it different?
3. Discuss the difference between jobs in business and jobs in government with regard to administrative law.
4. Both constitutional law and administrative law shape the work of public administrators. What is the difference between the two categories of law?
5. Revisit the case of *Brian Jackson v. Alan Ritchey Materials Co., LC* and then answer these questions:
    a. How does the work of ALJs enable the operations of agencies that employ them?
    b. Stakeholder interests are served by administrative law. How was Brian Jackson's interest served? How were the Ritchey company's interests served? How were the government's interests served?

EXERCISE

Access the *Federal Register* at https://www.federalregister.gov/. Click on "Rules," find one of interest, and read the posting that describes the rule and the explanation for it.

BUILD YOUR SKILLS

Understanding seminal court decisions is helpful when a legal case has a significant impact on what an agency does and how it does it. Use the skillbox to learn how to dissect a legal decision.

SKILLBOX: HOW TO DISSECT A LEGAL OPINION

Public service professionals must be sensitive to the legal ramifications of their work. In addition to statutes and regulations, legal cases offer concrete examples of how laws are interpreted. Here is a framework that offers a convenient way to understand the essential elements of a legal opinion. Use the following steps to pick out what is important in a case in terms of its facts, rules, holding, and reasons for the holding.

Overview. First, get an overview of the case by reading through it to understand the big picture. Identify the Who, What, Where, When of the case: Who are the parties? What is the dispute about? Where did the dispute take place and what court heard the case? What was the decision? Why did the court reach the decision it did? When was a decision rendered?

Procedural history. If the case was decided by an appellate court, what happened in the lower courts? Explain how the case got to the court now hearing the case. What was the decision of the lower court(s)? Who appealed and why? What is the appealing party (appellant) claiming the lower court did wrong?

What are the facts? Next, reread the case and take note of the facts: What is the relationship between the parties? Regulator/regulatee? Citizen/public official? Interest group/public agency? What happened that set the dispute in motion? Look for the material facts that are relevant to the outcome of the case.

Action? Who sued whom and what relief was requested? What law does the plaintiff claim was broken? What defense does the defendant put forth?

What is the legal issue? The court will base its decision on the legal issue(s) in question and will make its determination based upon the material facts of the case and the arguments of the parties. If the case involves several issues or questions, state each one. What is the point of law that is in dispute? What are the legally relevant facts for each point of law?

What did the court hold? For each issue, determine what the court held, or how it resolved the legal issue or answered the question. Was one party the clear winner?

Legal reasoning. What was the reasoning that the judges used? What law guides the decision? Laws may be derived from the Constitution, statutes, ordinances, regulations, or precedent based on case law. How did the court analyze the issues and apply the legal principles to the facts of the case?

Judgment. What was the court's final decision? An appellate court will affirm or reverse the prior decision, or remand the case to the lower court with instructions. The judgment will be found at the end of the opinion.

Concurring/Dissenting Opinions. Review any concurring or dissenting opinion for additional insight into how the case was viewed. One judge on a panel may not agree with the majority's decision and will write a separate opinion explaining the dissent. Another judge may agree with the decision but not with the majority's (or plurality's) reasoning. In this case, a concurring opinion may be written.

Appealed? Check to see if the case has been appealed to a still higher court. If it has, who appealed and on what grounds? If a decision has been overturned, it is no longer valid.

Hands-On Activity

Find a court decision that is of interest to you and read it. Follow the steps given earlier to write an analysis of the case. To locate a case by the court that heard the case, the website http://www.uscourts.gov/courtrecords/find-case-pacer provides assistance. Also, http://www.wikihow.com/Find-Court-Cases gives helpful hints for general searches. And, your college librarian will be able to point you to databases where you can access cases.

NOTES

1. *Wyatt v. Stickney, 325 F. Supp. 781 (M.D. Ala. 1971).*

2. "Wyatt v. Stickney," *Disability Justice*, last modified 2017, http://disabilityjustice.org/wyatt-v-stickney/.

3. J.B. Wogan, "Restraining Orders," *Governing* (December, 2015), 44.

4. Nicholas K. Geranios, "State Supreme Court: Psychiatric Boarding Illegal" (August 7, 2014), http://www.courts.wa.gov/content/publicupload/eclips/2014%2008%2008%20State%20Supreme%20Court%20Psychiatric%20boarding%20illegal.pdf.

5. Cornelius M. Kerwin, "Negotiated Rulemaking," in *Public Law and Administration*, ed. Philip J. Cooper and Chester A. Newland (San Francisco, CA: Jossey-Bass, 1997), 225.

6. Administrative Procedure Act, U.S. Code 5 (1946) §§ 501 et seq.

7. Administrative Procedure Act, U.S. Code 5 (1946) § 706.

8. *Chevron U.S.A., Inc. v. National Resources Defense Council, Inc.*, 467 U.S. 837 (1984).

9. Alan B. Morrison, "The Administrative Procedure Act: A Living and Responsive Law," *Virginia Law Review* 72, no. 2 (1986): 253–270.

10. David H. Rosenbloom, *Administrative Law for Public Managers* (Boulder, CO: West-view Press, 2015).

11. U.S. Department of the Interior, National Park Service, "Gathering of Certain Plants or Plant Parts by Federally Recognized Indian Tribes for Traditional Purposes," *Federal Register* 81, no. 133 (July 12, 2016): 45024, https://www.federalregister.gov/articles/2016/07/12/2016-16434/gathering-of-certain-plants-or-plant-parts-by-federally-recognized-indian-tribes-for-traditional#h-31.

12. ICF Consulting, "The Reg Map" (2003), http://www.reginfo.gov/public/reginfo/Regmap/regmap.pdf.

13. U.S. Social Security Administration, "Setting the Time and Place for a Hearing Before an Administrative Law Judge," *Federal Register* 75 (July 8, 2010): 39154–39156, https://www.gpo.gov/fdsys/pkg/FR-2010-07-08/pdf/2010-16549.pdf.

14. "Qualification Standard for Administrative Law Judge Positions," U.S. Office of Personnel Management (n.d.), https://www.opm.gov/policy-data-oversight/classification-qualifications/general-schedule-qualification-standards/specialty-areas/administrative-law-judge-positions/.

15. "Information About SSA's Office of Disability Adjudication and Review," U.S. Social Security Administration (n.d.), https://www.ssa.gov/appeals/about_odar.html.

16. Federal Mine Safety and Health Review Commission, "Order on Motion in the Case of Brian Jackson v Alan Ritchey Materials Co., LC" (July 1, 2016), https://www.fmshrc.gov/decisions/alj/ALJo_7012016-CENT%202016-178.pdf.

17. *North Carolina State Board of Dental Examiners v. Federal Trade Commission*, 574 U.S. 135 (2015).

18. *Ask Me Why I Care: Public Service Stories*, video, directed by Mary R. Hamilton and Rita Paskowitz (Omaha, Nebraska: College of Public Affairs and Community Service), https://www.unomaha.edu/college-of-public-affairs-and-community-service/community-engagement/pss-howard-messner.php.

ADDITIONAL RESOURCES

Asimov, Michael and Ronald Levin. 2014. *State and Federal Administrative Law*, 4th ed. St. Paul, MN: West Academic Publishing.

Kerwin, Cornelius and Scott Furlong. 2010. *Rulemaking: How Government Agencies Write Law and Make Policy*. 4th ed. Washington, DC: CQ Press.

For information about administrative law judges, visit Association of Administrative Law Judges at http://www.naalj.org/.

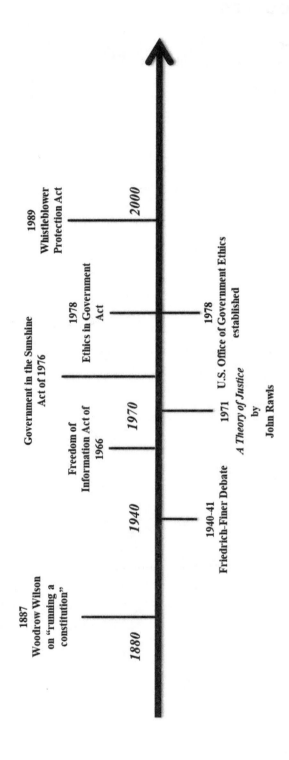

Chapter 13 Timeline: Public Integrity

1880

1887
Woodrow Wilson
on "running a
constitution"

1940

1940-41
Friedrich-Finer Debate

Freedom of
Information Act of
1966

1970

1971   U.S. Office of Government Ethics
A Theory of Justice   established
by
John Rawls

Government in the Sunshine
Act of 1976

1978
Ethics in Government
Act

1978

1989
Whistleblower
Protection Act

2000

WHAT YOU WILL LEARN

Ethics in public service

Regime values

Ethical decision making

Laws that advance ethical expectations of government

Skillbox: Tips for ethical decision making

As guardians of the public weal, public service professionals are held to a high standard of conduct. The term "public integrity" conveys the spirit of responsible professionalism, adherence to constitutional values, and commitment to ethical principles. The next case demonstrates the conflict a newly-hired law enforcement officer experienced when confronted by norms that challenged this imperative.

Doing the right thing, or doing the thing right? These two phrases contain the same words but have different meanings and produce different results. In "Doing the Right Thing," New Jersey state trooper Justin Hopson had to choose between getting along with his fellow officers by going along with a false arrest (doing the thing right, from the viewpoint of his peers), or speaking out (doing the right thing). He chose to do the right thing and, as a result, suffered repercussions.

DOING THE RIGHT THING[1]

In 2002, after only eleven days on the job, Justin Hopson, a rookie New Jersey state trooper, witnessed the arrest of a woman for drunken driving by his training officer. Hopson knew the charge was unlawful and refused to corroborate it because she was not the driver. She was a passenger in the backseat. Over the next several years he was harassed and threatened by the "Lords of Discipline," a secret society of fellow troopers, whose mission it was to keep peers in line. Fellow officers drove by his home in the wee hours of the morning, shining spotlights through his bedroom window or breathing deeply into the loud speaker. At the end of his work shift, he would find his car door covered in chewing tobacco and spit. When he finally reported the "Lords," it sparked the largest internal investigation in state police history. In 2007, the state of New Jersey agreed to a $400,000 settlement with Hopson. Justin Hopson tells the story in his book, *Breaking the Blue Wall: One Man's War Against Police Corruption.*

Questions to Ponder

1. When the norms of a work culture support unethical behavior, doing the right thing brings scorn and harassment. Why?
2. What are the ethical issues in this case?

Sometimes organizational norms create a "go along to get along" culture.[2] When this happens, the problem is one of too much agreement rather than one of disagreement. When the majority agree to take an action, even if it is a wrong action, it is easier to agree than to disagree, especially when doing so will result in being ostracized. It takes courage to use one's own moral agency and defy the norm to conform, which is what Justin Hopson did. He was right to do so, because no job and no position in the organizational hierarchy provides a moral holiday. Ethical action is an imperative in public service. And no organization is a moral sanctuary. One's integrity is always on call. Just as Senator Douglas said decades ago, public service reaches into everybody's lives.[3] For this reason, every decision is important and every action has consequences.

There are a number of governmental structures that are designed to bolster public integrity. These include ethics laws, the Office of Government Ethics (OGE), state ethics commissions, codes of conduct, ethics training, and channels designated for reporting infractions. Although unethical behavior has many sizes and shapes, ethics laws focus on conflicts of interest for they are easiest to define in leg-

> *"Our government is now so huge and affects our lives so directly that we cannot be content with merely a moderately decent level of behavior on the part of our public officials. For even a small percentage of misbehavior on the part of these officials can do a vast amount of harm."*
>
> —Paul H. Douglas

islation. Ethics laws warn against conflicts of interest because it can be difficult to do what obligation requires when personal interests point in a different direction. Conflicts are problematic not because they are automatically unethical but because they may lead to conduct that is unethical.

VALUES, MORALS, ETHICS

The "shoulds" of behavior are couched in three terms: values, morals, and ethics, all of which are almost interchangeable. *Values* are core beliefs about what is desirable. They serve as the foundation for choices in the world of work just as they do in one's private life. These values give rise to ideals that are called *ethics* or *morals*. These personal codes of conduct are the criteria each person uses to distinguish between right and wrong.

While the word *ethics* is derived from Greek, *morals* is derived from Latin. They are synonyms that refer to ideas of character and conduct. In contemporary English, a subtle difference has evolved between the two terms. *Morals* is the term used to describe one's personal code of right and wrong, while *ethics* is used to describe the situational application of a moral code, such as "business ethics" or "professional ethics."

The words *obligation, duty, ought, should, rights*, and *virtue* are the coinage of moral discourse and they invoke a moral frame of reference. Ethical inquiry requires the decision maker to consider moral values as well as the facts of the case. The conclusions reached are often stated as judgments, such as "bribery is wrong," and "caring about others is good." In other words, moral judgments use the language of good versus bad and right versus wrong. Their scope varies, from life and death consequences to everyday actions, such as treating others with respect, keeping promises, and being loyal to friends.

TELEOLOGY VERSUS DEONTOLOGY

Philosophers distinguish two frameworks within which ethical decisions are made. One is teleological and the other is deontological. A teleological point of view, also referred to as a utilitarian point of view, is the belief that the moral worth of an action is determined by its consequences. In other words, even though the process may violate some values, it is acceptable if the outcome will maximize more important values. Ends justify means. For example, if telling "a little white lie" will cause a team member to contribute effort toward a team's goal rather than abandon it, the utilitarian decision is to skirt around the truth in order for the team's output to reach its goal.

The deontological point of view is that there are universal truths and that actions should be taken based on those truths, regardless of the consequences. In everyday terms, that means that the concept of duty is independent of the concept of good. Acts have significance regardless of whether or not good comes of them. A deontological approach demands that absolute principles should be obeyed, regardless of the consequences. An example of an absolute principle would be honesty regardless of how much it hurts the person being told. Another example is found in the world's major religions, each of which is defined by deontological rules about how to treat others.

CODE OF ETHICS FOR PUBLIC SERVICE

Codes of ethics provide guidance by embodying important values in a statement of principles that is public and easily accessible. For example, the Code of Ethics of the American Society for Public Administration[4] is listed next. Its eight principles embody the aspirations and high expectations for those who serve the public interest. The Code lists prescriptions for personal behavior in the context of work-related behavior. It is written in broad language because the work of public service embraces an enormous range of professions and endeavors across all levels of government and public interest organizations. To breathe life into the principles, recommended practices are summarized for each.

Principle 1. Advance the Public Interest

This requires promoting the interests of the public and putting service to the public above service to oneself. Examples include taking current and long-term interests of society into account when making decisions, subordinating personal interests and institutional loyalties to the public good, and treating everyone with courtesy and respect.

Principle 2. Uphold the Constitution and the Law

This requires respecting and supporting the nation's laws and the Constitution. It includes understanding the constitutional, legislative, and regulatory framework of the work; fulfilling professional responsibilities; and promoting principles of equality, fairness, due process, representativeness, and responsiveness. All of this is to be done in the context of respecting the right to privacy by safeguarding confidential information.

Principle 3. Promote Democratic Participation

This requires actively encouraging engagement in governance and being respectful of persons in their dealings with public entities. Examples include being open and transparent while protecting privacy rights and security; involving stakeholders in the development, implementation, and assessment of policies and public programs; promoting timely dissemination of information; and ensuring fair and transparent processes.

Principle 4. Strengthen Social Equity

This is achieved by treating all persons with fairness, justice, and equality while respecting individual differences, rights, and freedoms. Examples include ensuring that all persons have access to programs and services to which they are entitled, and opposing all forms of discrimination.

Principle 5. Fully Inform and Advise

This is achieved by providing accurate, timely information to elected and appointed officials, governing board members, and staff members. Examples include providing information and advice based on an impartial review of circumstances, goals, and objectives, even when the information and recommendations may not be welcomed by colleagues or superiors.

Principle 6. Demonstrate Personal Integrity

This requires adhering to the highest standards of conduct in order to inspire public confidence. This is done by exercising courage and compassion and refusing to compromise honesty for advancement or personal gain. This also requires accepting individual responsibility for the consequences of one's actions. Avoiding conflicts of interest or commitment requires disclosure of interests that may affect objectivity in decision making. The conduct of official acts must be without partisanship or favoritism and others should receive credit for their work and contributions.

Principle 7. Promote Ethical Organizations

Examples include holding individuals accountable for their conduct; being good stewards of public funds by regularly reexamining the efficacy of policies, programs, and services; ensuring that there are administrative channels for dissent and protecting the rights of employees to report wrongdoing; supporting merit principles that promote competence and professionalism in the selection and promotion of employees; and promoting the representativeness of the public workforce.

Principle 8. Advance Professional Excellence

This is achieved by keeping up-to-date on emerging practices, and by allocating time and resources to the professional development of students, interns, beginning professionals, and other colleagues.

Principles one through eight are designed to guide individual behavior in ways that advance the public interest, preserve the freedoms and rights of citizens, and reflect regime values.

REGIME VALUES

Every constitutional order is based on a set of values that shape how people think about government and its proper powers. These values serve as lampposts to illuminate priorities. In the United States, these lampposts are found in the Constitution, laws, and court decisions. The values are what John Rohr labeled *regime values*: equality, personal freedoms, the right to one's property, and due process (due process is the principle that persons cannot be deprived of life, liberty, or property without appropriate legal procedures and safeguards).[5]

Regime values form the bedrock of American political and legal culture. Laws and court decisions reflect and operationalize these into norms that are built into the structure of public programs. As Woodrow Wilson reminded readers when he wrote about the importance of public administration over a century ago, it is getting harder to run a constitution than to create one.[6] For this reason, preserving regime values in public policy decisions, service delivery, and performance outcomes, is paramount.

Constitutional competence is required of everyone in public service. When administrative procedures embody regime values, they provide the framework for the proper way to engage citizens, design programs, deliver services, and evaluate performance. Vigilance about equality, personal freedoms, the right to one's property, and due process is expected so that program priorities reflect these values.

Administrative Environment

The administrative environment of public service requires ethical conduct and priorities that reflect regime values. There are tools available to provide guidance, such as codes of ethics and ethics laws, but no code or law can anticipate the many "gray" areas where conflicting values must be weighed against one another. The shortcoming of ethics laws is that, rather than prescribing priorities, they prescribe actions that should NOT be taken. This approach does not provide a standard for thoughtful decision making that brings consideration of the values at stake nor does it provide guidance in how to make the inevitable trade-offs.

Decisions that are black and white, where the choice is simply between good and evil or right and wrong, are easy because the answer is obvious. Many more decisions must be made in the gray areas where there is no right or wrong answer. This is because, in the pursuit of public goals, the administrative environment is replete with complexity, ambiguity, and conflicting points of view. The number of stakeholders is large and their perspectives are diverse. While some have similar ideas, others see things differently.

Even when it comes to program evaluation, ethical considerations arise. Despite an avalanche of performance data, the decision environment is ambiguous because, for many programs, outcomes defy easy categorization into successes or failures. The solution requires consideration of multiple values, judicious decision making, and the reality that the decision will result in a trade-off where some important values are sacrificed to maximize others.

Any one of three competing justifications may be used to claim the moral high ground of an administrative action. The first is the rationale that, as a *neutral agent* of policy implementation, one is simply following orders. This justification abrogates the responsibility of a thinking professional to make hard decisions. In the case of Justin Hopson, for example, this sort of reasoning would have resulted in his making an unlawful arrest and concealing the truth. A second rationale revolves around *seeking the best compromise* among competing interests, making trade-offs as necessary between mutually important but competing values. The third involves a long-term perspective that looks beyond the immediate issue to focus on the *long-term public interest*. These justifications demonstrate what is hard about ethical decision making. Decisions are not straightforward. Instead, they require thoughtful consideration of multiple values and trade-offs.

The realities of everyday administrative practice reflect the contradictions that are inherent in a culture that prizes individual liberty while also seeking the pursuit of common interests. It is for this reason that traditions have developed that embrace continuities of conflict as well as of agreement. As an example, the Administrative Procedure Act of 1946 embodies due process rights so that any citizen has the opportunity to comment on rules that govern service delivery. Moreover, grievance processes before administrative law judges provide an avenue for aggrieved parties to have a fair hearing when they believe they have been treated unjustly. These procedures acknowledge the fact that parties will view the same rules and decisions differently, some seeing processes as fair while others see them as unfair and seek redress.

ADMINISTRATIVE ETHICS

Administrative ethics refers to the application of moral principles to work-related conduct. Although taught in both business administration and public administration classes, it is of heightened importance and visibility in public service because the work is always in pursuit of public goals. Priorities with regard to ethical values are evident in decisions and procedures.

Ethical decision making is the practice of judgment that includes consideration of moral values. Every organization has an ethical climate that guides—or fails to guide—priorities. The ethics climate refers to the intangible norms that set expectations for what is "normal" and expected. These conditions influence an employee's ethical decision making, and just as Hopson encountered, climates may set the bar high or low on honesty as well as any other value, including regime values.

Due process prescriptions mushroomed in the mid-twentieth century as part of a broad movement to define constitutional rights and protections in the context of the administrative state. The ethicist John Rawls put forward the idea that justice is fairness.[7] This caused public administrators to think about criteria by which administrative decisions, and the procedures used to reach them, could be used to advance fairness. Administrative procedures that are transparent help to ensure fairness. And representativeness serves to embrace differing perspectives because when a broad array of viewpoints are brought to bear on a problem, the values of wider communities factor into the decision. This contributes to social equity.

TRANSPARENCY

From the 1960s onward, there have been efforts to make government more transparent. The adage that "sunshine is the best disinfectant" holds true in government action just as it does in public health. When it comes to government operations, transparency is the best protection against bribery, corruption, conflicts of interest and commitment, and the appearance of impropriety. When actions are open to public scrutiny, they are more likely to be consistent with regime values. For this reason, there are a variety of sunshine laws, all designed to open government action to public view. Federal laws include the Freedom of Information Act, Government in the Sunshine Act, and Ethics in Government Act, among others. Most states have passed similar laws.

When the Administrative Procedures Act of 1946 was passed, federal agencies had broad discretion in terms of what documents they published and did not publish. Concerns soon arose that the provision to make documents public had become more of a withholding than a disclosure mechanism. To rectify this, Congress passed the Freedom of Information Act (FOIA) in 1966 to implement a general philosophy of full agency disclosure. FOIA requires agencies to publish their rules of procedure in the *Federal Register* and to make available to the public in other ways their opinions, working policies, interpretations, staff manuals, and instructions that are not published in the *Federal Register*. The Act also requires agencies to make available any existing records that are requested.

> *"Fighting corruption is not just good governance. It's self-defense. It's patriotism."*
> —Joseph R. Biden, Jr.

Transparency extends beyond documents to the meetings where decisions are made. The Government in the Sunshine Act of 1976 requires open meetings of executive public agencies. An additional check on secrecy is provided by The Ethics in Government Act of 1978, which is a federal law that established the U.S. Office of Government Ethics (OGE). It created mandatory public disclosure of financial and employment history of public officials and their immediate family. It also placed restrictions on lobbying efforts by public officials for a set period of time after leaving public office. The OGE provides leadership, guidance, and training for the ethical dimension of operations in the federal executive branch. Similar laws and offices are mirrored in state governments.

SOCIAL EQUITY

The imperative to advance social equity requires representativeness in decision making bodies and reexamination of usual and customary procedures, even those that are thought normal and noncontroversial. This is because systems put in place for one purpose may have the unintended consequence of exacerbating inequity. Although unbiased and uncontroversial on their face, they may actually disadvantage a segment of the population. Consider the example of Seattle Streetlights.

SEATTLE STREETLIGHTS

When then-mayor of Seattle, Greg Nickels, toured a neighborhood notorious for fatal shootings in 2008, he noticed that a lot of streetlights were burned out, many more than in other areas of the city. When he asked why, he learned that the city waited for residents to report nonworking streetlights before they would replace them. In this neighborhood, the majority of residents were people of color, almost half were refugees, and more than half lived below the poverty line. Residents avoided interacting with government whenever possible. They were less likely to trust government and many did not speak English well enough to report burned-out lights.

Here is the solution that the city put in place: Instead of waiting for complaints, the public works office solved the problem. Each time they replaced bulbs, they noted the bulb's life expectancy and began the process of replacing them on a schedule. Not only did residents in southeast Seattle get better lighting, the more affluent neighborhoods benefited because they no longer had to call to report outages.[8]

In this case, Seattle's high crime neighborhoods—the places where good lighting is needed most—had the least light. The reason lay in the assumption that anyone and everyone would routinely contact the city when streetlights were burned out. In fact, that was not the case. The socioeconomically disadvantaged neighborhoods—the politically powerless segment of the population—did not contact the city.

Social equity is the active commitment to fairness, justice, and equality in all aspects of public service. This requires equity not only in streetlights but in programs, outcomes, and the processes by which the outcomes are produced. Inclusiveness, cultural competence, fairness, and being alert to the consequences of programs, help to ensure that social equity is achieved.

Being inclusive means making sure that representatives from all groups of stakeholders are included in deliberative bodies. This ensures that multiple points of view are considered. Practicing cultural competence means making sure that services are designed and delivered in a culturally sensitive manner. Insisting on fair processes is necessary even when it may be an inconvenience or require a delay in decision making. And, finally, a consideration of consequences should include thoughtful reflection on how program impacts affect all constituencies.

GOVERNMENT VERSUS BUSINESS

As sunshine laws make evident, constraints on public action are much greater than that which exists in the nonprofit or business sectors. This is by design. When the Constitution was crafted, the framers were wary of governmental authority. They crafted a Constitution that puts constraints on government action at every juncture, ensuring checks, balances, debates, and delays, all of which protect citizens from government becoming too strong or too quick to act.

Preparing for the transition from the Obama administration to the Trump administration, the OGE director said, "the rules are really a lot more strict in the federal government than in the private sector, and things that they've been allowed to do before they came to government, like accepting gifts or lunches or trips, are not going to be acceptable in the federal government in their new positions."

—Walter M. Shaub

The purposes of business and of government are different and, for that reason, the rules that affect them are opposite. The purpose of business is to create wealth and to do so as efficiently as possible. The purpose of government, on the other hand, is to pursue public goals. The difference between these purposes means that business is free to do whatever it pleases except that which is prohibited by law. Government, on the other hand, is empowered to do only that which it is allowed by law to do.

Executives whose experience is nongovernmental have to make significant changes in their behavior when they accept a government post. Accustomed to the free-wheeling world of business, adjusting to the constraints of public service and the requirements for transparency are a significant departure from usual business practices. When administrations change, the OGE provides training to acquaint new appointees with laws and expectations.

LEGAL VERSUS ETHICAL

An act that is legal may or may not be ethical. Laws are compromises to which the majority of lawmakers agree. Beyond the agreement of 51 percent necessary for a law to be passed, however, are many questions with ethical implications. In other words, ethical judgment occurs on a higher plane than legal judgment, guided by awareness of the moral values that are maximized or minimized by a decision. Legal compliance is the lowest common denominator for actions and, above that, ethical decision making that balances values, standards, and priorities is the goal.

EXPECTATIONS FOR FEDERAL EMPLOYEES

It is impossible to prescribe enough guidance via statutes and codes of ethics to anticipate every situation. Effective administrators have to rely on their personal moral judgment. To this end, codes of conduct serve an important function. They sensitize decision makers to the importance of ethical decision making, they define the bottom line of acceptable behavior, and they set the tone for expectations. The code of conduct shown in Table 13.1[9] provides guidance for federal employees.

TABLE 13.1 CODE OF CONDUCT FOR FEDERAL EMPLOYEES

Title 5: Administrative Personnel, Chapter XVI, Subchapter B, Part 2635
PART 2635—STANDARDS OF ETHICAL CONDUCT FOR EMPLOYEES OF THE EXECUTIVE BRANCH

§2635.101   Basic obligation of public service.

(a) Public service is a public trust. Each employee has a responsibility to the United States Government and its citizens to place loyalty to the Constitution, laws and ethical principles above private gain. To ensure that every citizen can have complete confidence in the integrity of the Federal Government, each employee shall respect and adhere to the principles of ethical conduct set forth in this section, as well as the implementing standards contained in this part and in supplemental agency regulations.

(b) General principles. The following general principles apply to every employee and may form the basis for the standards contained in this part. Where a situation is not covered by the standards set forth in this part, employees shall apply the principles set forth in this section in determining whether their conduct is proper.

(1) Public service is a public trust, requiring employees to place loyalty to the Constitution, the laws and ethical principles above private gain.

(2) Employees shall not hold financial interests that conflict with the conscientious performance of duty.

(3) Employees shall not engage in financial transactions using nonpublic Government information or allow the improper use of such information to further any private interest.

(4) An employee shall not, except as permitted by subpart B of this part, solicit or accept any gift or other item of monetary value from any person or entity seeking official action from, doing business with, or conducting activities regulated by the employee's agency, or whose interests may be substantially affected by the performance or nonperformance of the employee's duties.

(5) Employees shall put forth honest effort in the performance of their duties.

(6) Employees shall not knowingly make unauthorized commitments or promises of any kind purporting to bind the Government.

(7) Employees shall not use public office for private gain.

(8) Employees shall act impartially and not give preferential treatment to any private organization or individual.

(9) Employees shall protect and conserve Federal property and shall not use it for other than authorized activities.

(10) Employees shall not engage in outside employment or activities, including seeking or negotiating for employment, that conflict with official Government duties and responsibilities.

(11) Employees shall disclose waste, fraud, abuse, and corruption to appropriate authorities.

(12) Employees shall satisfy in good faith their obligations as citizens, including all just financial obligations, especially those—such as Federal, State, or local taxes—that are imposed by law.

(13) Employees shall adhere to all laws and regulations that provide equal opportunity for all Americans regardless of race, color, religion, sex, national origin, age, or handicap.

(14) Employees shall endeavor to avoid any actions creating the appearance that they are violating the law or the ethical standards set forth in this part. Whether particular circumstances create an appearance that the law or these standards have been violated shall be determined from the perspective of a reasonable person with knowledge of the relevant facts.

(c) Related statutes. In addition to the standards of ethical conduct set forth in this part, there are conflict of interest statutes that prohibit certain conduct. Criminal conflict of interest statutes of general applicability to all employees, 18 U.S.C. 201, 203, 205, 208, and 209, are summarized in the appropriate subparts of this part and must be taken into consideration in determining whether conduct is proper. Citations to other generally applicable statutes relating to employee conduct are set forth in subpart I and employees are further cautioned that there may be additional statutory and regulatory restrictions applicable to them generally or as employees of their specific agencies. Because an employee is considered to be on notice of the requirements of any statute, an employee should not rely upon any description or synopsis of a statutory restriction, but should refer to the statute itself and obtain the advice of an agency ethics official as needed.

Just as the federal government has an office of government ethics and a code of conduct for employees, most states have similar instruments that are designed to set expectations and define legal limits on gifts from vendors and lobbyists.

STATE ETHICS COMMISSIONS

Most state governments have mechanisms in place to address or prevent ethical lapses. These are in the form of ethics laws and state ethics commissions—similar to the federal OGE—that are charged with enforcing the ethics laws. These commissions are both instruments and symbols because they both enforce the law and consult with public officials.[10] They interpret ethics laws and to some extent, are prisoner to them. Commissions are usually a bipartisan board appointed by the governor and the legislature. They provide policy direction and render judgments to cases that come before them.

Ethics commissions usually have jurisdiction over appointed and elected officials, monitor conflicts of interest and commitment, collect financial disclosure forms for state officials, undertake investigations, issue advisory opinions, impose penalties when breaches are identified, and provide educational activities designed to train officials about compliance. When the state law is too vague or imprecise or fails to specify prohibited behavior, commissions offer interpretations of intent.

Just as at the federal level, laws and codes cannot anticipate the variety of ethical quandaries that public officials will encounter. Beyond codes and laws, everyone in public service must be sensitive to the ethical nuances of decisions and be vigilant to how social justice will be influenced by outcomes.

THE MANAGERIAL, POLITICAL, AND LEGAL NEXUS

Examining a problem from three perspectives—managerial, political, and legal—helps to reveal its ethical dimensions. This is particularly important when making decisions that have social equity ramifications. Take the case of the county clerk who, because she was opposed to same-sex marriage, decided not to issue marriage licenses to anyone. This response treated everyone the same but denied everyone the privilege of marrying.

THE CASE OF THE COUNTY CLERK AND MARRIAGE LICENSES

When the U.S. Supreme Court issued its decision in the case of *Obergefell v. Hodges* in 2015 decreeing that same-sex couples are entitled to marriage equality, much of the nation cheered, rainbow flags flew, and wedding planners awaited a flood of business. But not wanting to issue licenses to same-sex couples, Kim Davis, a county clerk in Rowan County, Kentucky, ordered her subordinates to stop issuing marriage licenses altogether,[11] a decision that resulted in her being sentenced to five nights in jail.

While this is an extreme case, those who work in public service take an oath to uphold the nation's laws. Ethical analysis that parses public administration into its managerial, political, and legal dimensions[12] demonstrates competing considerations and shows that decisions are often complicated.

According to the Rowan County Clerk's website, the Clerk's office is responsible for providing clerical services of the county court to the people of Rowan County.[13] The managerial lens suggests that Davis' subordinates should do as she directs because she is the boss. Using the political lens, however, brings accountability to the public, representativeness, and responsiveness to the forefront and requires subordinates to defy Davis' decision. Policy is delivered at the street-level, in this case at the county courthouse, and street-level officials are responsible for following the laws of the land.

Using a legal lens makes this unambiguous: Davis' policy violates constitutional law. The legal approach considers substantive due process, procedural due process, and principles of social equity. Substantive due process refers to the fundamental liberties inherent in the Fourteenth Amendment of the Constitution, which declares that no state shall "deprive any person of life, liberty, or property, without due process of law."[14] Substantive due process refers to the liberties in this clause. In the *Obergefell* decision, the Supreme Court extended these liberties to include "certain personal choices central to individual dignity and autonomy, including intimate choices that define personal identity and beliefs." Marriage has long been included among fundamental rights and the Court held that the right to marriage extends to same-sex couples as well as opposite-sex couples. Public managers are bound by constitutional law in their dealings with constituents. In the Rowan County case, Davis violated the fundamental rights of both same-sex and opposite-sex couples when she refused to issue marriage licenses. Administrators have a duty to follow the law and they are also ethically bound to support citizens' rights.

Social equity is an essential element in public administration and administrators have a duty to promote it. It is defined as "the fair, just, and equitable management of all institutions serving the public directly or by contract, and the fair, just and equitable distribution of public services, and implementation of public policy, and the commitment to promote fairness, justice, and equity in the formation of public policy."[15] While Davis' refusal to allow her subordinates to issue any marriage licenses was equal in that it denied both same-sex and opposite-sex couples the right to marry, equity is a more flexible concept that addresses less tangible rights, such as fairness. Thus, from the legal dimension of their work, Davis' subordinates acted both illegally and in violation of principles of social equity by following her policy.

In this case, each dimension to public administration—managerial, political, and legal—are relevant. Under a strictly managerial approach, a subordinate might adhere to Davis' edict. From a political perspective, considerations of representativeness and responsiveness to the public indicate the need to use discretion and not follow Davis' policy. Finally, from a legal perspective, subordinates must adhere to federal law and protect the rights of citizens.

Decisions such as those made by Kim Davis raise the topic of individual discretion and its limits. A classic debate many years ago, the Friedrich-Finer debate, illuminated two distinct points of view on public officials and their exercise of discretion. The debate arises whenever discussion of "how much discretion is too much?" occurs. While Carl Friedrich argued that well-trained public servants should be trusted to exercise their judgment, Herman Finer argued that the state is better served when public servants are closely supervised, make decisions based on rules, and do not rely on their own discretion.

THE FRIEDRICH-FINER DEBATE

In the latter 1930s, two scholars debated whether public servants should be trusted to rely on their discretion or whether formal controls such as close supervision and written procedures should be substituted for personal and professional judgment. Referred to as the Friedrich-Finer debate, the question remains salient today. Carl Friedrich argued that public administrators must rely on an "inner check" that guides them in democratic principles. He believed that relying on the judgment of well-trained administrators results in the balanced and judicious use of discretion and accounts for the exigencies of the moment. In contrast, Herman Finer argued that external controls, such as rules, procedures, and threat of penalty, are necessary to guide workers' decisions. While Finer argued that public servants should be clearly directed so that they do not exercise their own discretion, Friedrich argued that only those with high ethical standards should be hired in the first place. But once hired and trained in agency procedures, they must be trusted to exercise their discretion wisely. Friedrich believed that codes of ethics and professional values would provide the lampposts necessary to light the way toward the right decision. Finer saw such guides as being too easily manipulated, distorted, or circumvented.[16]

As the Friedrich-Finer debate makes obvious, public servants have two types of responsibility and they are interlocked.[17] One type is objective and refers to accountability. As the expressed will of the people, public programs must be carried out regardless of whether the administrator agrees with them or not, contrary to Kim Davis' decision not to follow the law. The other type is more internal, calling upon personal integrity and professional norms. The responsible administrator is guided by both. The result of this enduring debate is the combination of formal training that emphasizes the importance of public service values, coupled with codes of ethics, professional norms, and ethics laws and commissions.

DEVELOPING YOUR ETHICAL COMPETENCE

Regardless of the number of principles in codes of ethics, the variety of ethics laws, and the presence of ethics commissions, decisions that must balance ethical values are personal and require hard thinking. Such quandaries test one's integrity. Making the right decision is often not the easy decision. Character is defined by the choices that the person makes, for this is how one's values are revealed.

As a child, everyone learns basic moral rules from family, teachers, peers, churches, and personal experiences. These become the individual's moral bank upon which ethical analysis is based. For example, assume that Hopson learned as a child that deference to superiors is important and at the same time learned that honesty is important. When he experienced a superior arresting a woman for a crime she did not commit, he was torn between deference to his superior and to honesty. Can anyone disagree with his decision to put honesty first in order to serve the public good, rather than putting deference first in order to serve his superior? Here are four steps to use when determining what action to take when confronted with an ethical dilemma:

1) Describe the problem and then define the values involved. This drives the ethical question.

2) Identify alternative courses of action and which values will be maximized and minimized in each.

3) Consider the possible consequences for each alternative from a moral standpoint.

4) Find the fit. The appropriate solution is a balance of several elements: elemental moral rules; comparison of the reasonable alternatives with accepted professional norms; and justifiability for the values that will be maximized versus those minimized.

The decision must withstand scrutiny and ensure accountability. In the case of Hopson, for example, the culture was unethical, so relying on his peers to scrutinize his decision was not a reasonable test of his decision. He had to rely on his own moral compass.

A moral center of gravity for public service involves honesty, conformity to law, a service orientation, procedural fairness, a sense of democratic responsibility, and an ethic of compromise and social integration.[18] This center helps to ground decisions in important priorities, but it is still easier said than done. Tough decisions require trade-offs among important but competing values.

> *"We often make the mistake of believing that what happens at the bottom makes no difference. As a matter of fact, it is what we do at the bottom which decides what eventually happens at the top."*
>
> —Eleanor Roosevelt

The organizational context adds complexity to otherwise personal decision making because of the interface between personal and organizational values. This requires a blend of organizational reality and individual judgment. While managers are the catalysts who set the stage with common frames of reference for all employees, individuals still make their own decisions. Ethical beacons serve as guideposts as people balance organizational goals and routines with personal priorities.

ETHICAL SATISFICING

Ethics is the everyday application of a standard of relating to one another. When personal and organizational values clash, ethical satisficing results. This produces a compromise that permits satisfaction of ethical parameters at least at a minimally acceptable level.

The process of ethical decision making involves defining the problem, generating alternatives, and choosing among them so that the alternative selected maximizes the most important ethical values while also achieving the intended goal. In satisficing, some values are compromised in order for others to be maximized. This does not necessarily result in an unethical decision but it produces decisions that are only as good as circumstances permit.

Ethical decision making requires that the ethical nuances and trade-offs in each alternative are considered. For some decisions, there is no winning solution where all important values are preserved. In fact, some decisions require tragic choices where no feasible alternative advances the best values. Juries in capital murder cases where the death penalty is an option, for example, are confronted with such scenarios in which they must decide not between good and bad but between the lesser of evils: life in prison or execution. And caseworkers in child protective services must decide whether it is better to allow a child to remain with parents who may be abusive or remove the child to the care of strangers who may, or may not, provide a loving home.

Maximizing one value may require the minimization of another. For example, personnel actions emphasize objectivity and uniform procedures to maximize accountability and reliance on process, but it comes at the expense of caring about an individual's unique circumstances. While human service agencies may want to emphasize caring and timely service, to do so may require sacrificing accountability and fairness to everyone else who is higher on a waiting list for services.

Complex ethical decisions may confront a no-win situation: Two or more values are affected by the decision; a comparison between the values is inevitable, such that a greater return on one can be obtained only at a loss to the other; and, consequences can be predicted in terms of probabilities, not certainties. To complicate matters further, the decision may be dispersed among multiple people and departments and the choice might not be able to be made directly between values. It must derive from among alternatives that differ in the extent to which each embodies particular values or emphasizes some values in relation to others. For example, consider how to distribute an annual bonus to a work team. Four possibilities are:

To each person an equal share

To each person according to individual effort

To each person according to individual need

To each person according to usefulness of his or her contribution

Each rule maximizes different values. The first maximizes accountability because it is easy to justify. It assumes parity on everyone's part. But it does so at the expense of caring about individual contribution and distinguishing between excellence and mediocrity. The second maximizes caring for each person's extent of effort and respect for each participant. But it does so at the expense of rewarding excellence, since less productive workers may devote hours to a task without making a substantive contribution to it. The third maximizes loyalty to individual workers in an appreciation of their unique circumstances but minimizes fairness to others and pursuit of excellence. It rewards people in proportion to what they need rather than what they contribute to the effort. The fourth maximizes the pursuit of excellence while minimizing a respect for everyone's individual skills and abilities. While each of these alternatives is designed to achieve distributive justice, each results in different forms of distributions and sends different messages about what values are most important and which work characteristics are rewarded.

Each alternative for the bonus allocation problem sends a different message around the organization with regard to what work characteristics will be rewarded. This is why it is important for beacons to be present in the organizational culture to help define the problem, steer the debate, and guide the selection of alternatives. The final choice should send a message consistent with expectations for personal performance, the overall mission, and the objectives for achieving it. Beacons become heuristics—rules of thumb—for employees to use.

Ethical satisficing preempts the single-minded pursuit of either deontological or utilitarian ethics by blending the promotion of both means and ends. Institutional controls in the form of rules, rigid procedures, and close supervision cannot serve as a substitute for individual judgment. In the words of Herbert Simon, reason is instrumental: it cannot tell us where to go; at best it can only tell us how to get there. "It is a gun for hire that can be employed in the service of whatever goals we have, good or bad."[20] It is for this reason that organizations must emphasize which values are most important and to rely on individuals in the organization to maximize them without unduly minimizing other important ones.

Choices must be made amid a complex array of pressures and alternatives, and people must come to the best decision they can, given the constraints of the situation. Decision making requires a balance among competing demands from superiors, peers, and subordinates while simultaneously pursuing organizational goals. Thus, strong organizational norms, reliance on individual judgment, and personal accountability for the welfare of the whole is necessary.

CORE VALUES

Ten values that capture that which is good are deeply embedded in American culture and in spheres of influence, from personal standards to interpersonal to organizational.[20] They include:

Personal standards
- Honesty: being truthful and not deceiving or distorting
- Integrity: using independent judgment and being faithful to one's deepest beliefs

Interpersonal standards
- Fairness: being open-minded, willing to admit error, not taking undue advantage of others, and avoiding arbitrary favoritism
- Promise keeping: keeping one's commitments

- Loyalty: being faithful to those with whom one has dealings
- Caring for others: treating people as ends in themselves, not means to an end
- Respect for others: recognizing each person's right to privacy and self-determination and respecting human dignity

Organizational standards

- Responsible citizenship: acting in accord with regime values
- Pursuit of excellence: striving to be as good as one can be, being diligent, conscientious, and industrious
- Accountability: accepting the consequences of one's actions and accepting responsibility for one's decisions

These ten values are unquestioned and form the foundation for the regime values of equality, property, and individual freedoms. The profound acceptance of integrity and respect for others (to afford everyone the right to own property and remain free and equal) and responsible citizenship (to obey the laws of the land) serves as the substrate for regime values.

It is impossible to construct an inflexible value scale that always sets these values in an ordered progression. All situations play out in the crucible of organizational traditions, norms, problem-solving style, time-sensitive pressures, and organizational beacons. Every agency has a mission statement that boasts the good things it does. But employees ferret out the meaning of the words by watching for which behaviors are rewarded, ignored, and discouraged. Differences in beacons produce different behaviors on the part of workers. In a given circumstance, however, it is possible to set priorities on values by thoughtful deliberation. As depicted in Figure 13.1, what is helpful about including all these when making decisions is that it forces everyone to think about everything they want instead of focusing on only one or two values at the expense of the others.

FIGURE 13.1 TEN CORE VALUES

The Personal Check

A handy ethics test to assess whether a decision is the right one is the 3M test: How would you feel telling your <u>m</u>other? How would you feel as you look at yourself in the <u>m</u>irror and explain your choice? How would you feel if your decision was broadcast via the <u>m</u>edia? If the answer to any of these is problematic, that is a good indicator that the decision is wrong.

EXIT, VOICE, OR LOYALTY?

Sooner or later, every employee will be faced with a hard choice: to provide information that superiors do not want to hear, to dissent from the majority point of view, to blow the whistle on actions that are organizationally sanctioned but wrong, or to simply resign and find employment elsewhere. The decision is one of exit, voice, or loyalty[21] and can be anguishing because it tests one's moral fiber and the outcome has punishing trade-offs, regardless of the choice. To exit is to give up the security of one's predictable routines in exchange for the unknown. Open dissent may incur the wrath of coworkers and superiors. But to "go along to get along" is to deny important values, as Janet Norwood explains in the Ask Me Why I Care video at the end of this chapter. Each of these options involves ethical choices and ranks priorities differently.

Dissent

To dissent is to use one's voice to express disagreement with the status quo. Norwood provides an example when she described the need to adjust calculations for the Consumer Price Index. Her personal decision was to be prepared to exit if her recommendation had not been accepted, although that turned out not to be necessary.

Alternate ways to express dissent include protesting within the organization but still fulfilling the obligation to implement the policy. Another way is to seek reassignment to different duties, so as not to have to fulfill the objectionable obligation. Another form is civil disobedience, which requires that citizens act publicly, commit no violence, appeal to principles shared by others, direct their challenge against a substantial injustice, exhaust all normal channels of protest before breaking the law, and plan the disobedience—such as a protest rally—so that it does not disrupt the stability of the democratic process. Peaceful protests to denounce the disproportionate number of police shootings of unarmed African Americans provides a contemporary example.

The dissent that county clerk Davis chose was none of the above. Instead, she chose to withhold a service—marriage licenses—from all constituencies. Because her dissent violated the law and deprived residents of their civil rights, she was arrested. A more constructive action would have been to resign her position since she could not fulfill the responsibilities of the job.

WHISTLEBLOWING

Whistleblowing is used to describe a particular kind of dissent to organizational processes. A whistleblower is an employee or former employee who discloses information that one could reasonably believe is evidence of wrongdoing, such as a violation of law, gross mismanagement, an abuse of authority, or a substantial and specific danger to public health or safety. In other words, the information is not trivial. Whistleblowing usually happens after a loyal employee has noted the problem and reported it through internal channels, only to find that the problem is not corrected. After exhausting internal reporting channels, the person goes public with the information, "blowing the whistle" so that forces outside the organization will cause the problem to be corrected.

Public employees wear two hats: that of employee and that of citizen. This dual role was affirmed by the 1968 case, *Pickering v. Board of Education of Township High School District 205, Will County* (391 U.S. 563) and reaffirmed in 2016 by *Heffernan v. City of Paterson*, 136 S. Ct. 790 (2016). While the employment relationship requires workers to perform as instructed and be loyal to the employer, citizenship requires that workers consider what is best for the jurisdiction, whether it is national, state, county, or city. The ethical question of loyalty is less a matter of disloyalty than a question of loyalty to whom? To one's peers who have covered up a long-standing problem? To the agency, which even after the problem is reported, takes no action to correct it? Or to the public who expect accountability that government is acting for the right reasons? To whom loyalty is owed determines the course of action.

Organizations strive to ensure that internal channels are available, so the whistleblowers do not have to go public to have their complaint heard. Hotlines, also called fraud lines, have been established in many agencies. These provide a means to bypass usual reporting channels and report wrongdoing directly to an inspector general who is empowered to investigate.

Because whistleblowing challenges the status quo and sheds an unwelcome light on programs, it is often damaging to the program's reputation and to the whistleblower's career. The personal cost to those who blow the whistle can be enormous. They are often ostracized by their peers and it is not unusual for them to receive lower performance appraisals, be passed over for promotion, be assigned to unpleasant jobs, or reassigned to another unit. At the federal level, the Whistleblower Protection Act of 1989 was crafted to provide protections from retaliation such as this. Most states have similar laws.

The question of exit, voice, or loyalty forces examination of a range of issues. Weighed as a moral responsibility, it pits the worker's loyalty to the organization against principles of right and wrong. To dissent publicly involves questions of fairness: fairness to one's coworkers, to the agency, to the public. Have all internal reporting routes been exhausted before going public? Does the public have a right to know? Because the implications are significant, questions such as these require serious reflection.

ADMINISTRATIVE EVIL

In the absence of ethical awareness, it is possible to succumb to acts of what Adams and Balfour[22] call administrative evil. Inhumane acts result when an amoral organizational culture overrules individual conscience. Reliance on routines and succumbing to peer pressure leads to moral inversion. A classic example occurred at Abu Ghraib prison and came to light in 2003. U.S. Army personnel and Central Intelligence Agency staff were committing a number of human rights violations against Iraqi detainees who were imprisoned there. The abuses came to public attention when photographs were made public via the news media. Administrative evil occurred because ordinary people performed their duties in a way that wrong became right. Their justification was that "everybody did it." Moral inversion happens when individual responsibility is overlooked, workers lose sight of the consequences of their actions, and fail to give voice to wrongdoing.

The organization's culture is the shared understanding that employees have. Beliefs, values, norms, and philosophies determine how things get decided and what is considered acceptable behavior. In cases of moral inversion, acceptable standards of behavior violate norms of right and wrong. Secrecy propels moral inversion and administrative evil because accountability measures do not have to comport with public expectations.

WHAT HAPPENED AT ABU GHRAIB PRISON?

Physical and sexual abuse, torture, rape, and sodomy, occurred as the U.S. Army and the Central Intelligence Agency used the Iraqi prison as a site to hold and interrogate prisoners of war in a manner that was in violation of the Geneva Conventions. The Red Cross, Amnesty International, and Human Rights Watch reported that the abuses were not isolated incidents but rather a pattern of abuse. After an international outcry, the United States responded by modifying its interrogation techniques.

EASIER SAID THAN DONE

Ethical decision making is easier said than done. Moral deliberation is a sort of calculus, of working out which course of action is supported by the best moral reasoning. Weighing values against one another has to be done for each problem faced, and the outcome varies according to everything that must be considered at the time.

Even in the context of large bureaucracies, ethical responsibility is personal responsibility. Those acting in the public interest must act based on ethical principles that withstand public scrutiny and the principles must embrace transparency, fairness, and equity. Ethical behavior is an accountability standard by which the public judges the work of those providing public services.

Ask Me Why I Care: Janet Lippe Norwood, an economist, was the first woman to be Commissioner of the U.S. Bureau of Labor Statistics (BLS)[23]

"President Nixon felt that the Bureau of Labor Statistics was interpreting the data in a way that he didn't like. He said 'Don't they know they work for us? They should say what we want them to say.' We never did that. . . . This is a scientific agency and that means that objectivity is essential."—Janet Norwood

As Commissioner, Janet Lippe Norwood was responsible for the Bureau's work in compilation, publication, and interpretation of statistics on employment and unemployment, prices, compensation, industrial relations, productivity, and economic growth. She testified monthly before the Joint Economic Committee and frequently before other Congressional Committees, where it was not unusual for her to be challenged for speaking truth to power.

The ethic of administrative neutrality does not suppress independent moral judgment. Watch this video to learn how Norwood faced a big decision about how to calculate the Consumer Price Index properly. She explains how she prepared by making the most compelling argument she could, justifying her viewpoint, and being prepared to accept the decision, whichever way it went. For more of Norwood's story, go to http://www.unomaha.edu/college-of-public-affairs-and-community-service/community-engagement/pss-janet-norwood.php.

SUMMARY

Personal integrity requires that individuals walk their talk. In other words, it requires that people's actions support their values. Similarly, public integrity requires that regime values are upheld in the pursuit of public purposes. Equality, personal freedoms, the right to one's property, and due process are essential priorities. The eight principles of the ASPA code of ethics honor these values with its principles to advance the public interest, uphold the constitution and laws, promote democratic participation, strengthen social equity, fully inform and advise, demonstrate personal integrity, promote ethical organizations, and advance professional excellence. Transparency, as required by sunshine laws, ensures that these values and principles are upheld and that the public is informed about government action.

The cases in this chapter demonstrate how these elements combine. In the case of Justin Hopson, he was forced to choose between following the law and following the dictates of his training officer. He chose the former, but was harassed by his colleagues for doing so. In the case of the Seattle streetlights, the unintended consequence of assuming that all residents will report needed repairs resulted in crime-ridden neighborhoods that were dark. Changing a routine to automatically replace lights on their expiration date overcame the problem. In the case of Kim Davis, the Kentucky county clerk who was opposed to same-sex marriage, her refusal to follow the law resulted in a constitutional violation and she was arrested. Each of these cases demonstrates the connection between decisions and how they affect individual action.

Ethical decision making is easier said than done. Though choices between right and wrong are straightforward, choices that force trade-offs between important values are not. As desirable as it is to maximize all values, that is not always possible. Thus, ethical satisficing is required. This means honoring as many values as possible while understanding that not all can be realized. The decision maker's obligation is to be sensitive to the values that are being minimized and be able to justify the choice made.

KEY TERMS

Administrative evil – refers to inhumane acts that occur when ordinary public administrators perform their duties in a way in which wrong becomes right (moral inversion); this results when an amoral organizational culture overrules individual conscience.

Ethical satisficing – a compromise that satisfies ethical parameters at a minimally-acceptable level, resulting from a clash of personal and organizational values.

Friedrich-Finer Debate – a debate regarding the exercise of discretion by public servants; Friedrich argued that well-trained public servants should be trusted to exercise their judgment, while Finer argued that public servants should be closely-supervised and make decisions based on rules rather than relying on their own discretion.

Regime values – the set of values—upon which a constitutional order is based—that shape how people think about government and its proper powers.

Social equity – refers to the presence of fairness, justice, and equitable outcomes in public administration.

Sunshine Acts – laws designed to open government action to public scrutiny.

Transparency – in organizations, refers to the presence of open processes, actions, and documents that are subject to public scrutiny.

Whistleblowing – refers to when an employee or former employee of an organization discloses evidence of wrongdoing, such as a violation of law, gross mismanagement, an abuse of authority, or a substantial and specific danger to public health or safety.

DISCUSSION QUESTIONS

1. Think of a situation where you had to make a decision and ethical values were at stake.
   a. What were the values?
   b. What decision did you make?
   c. What values did you maximize in your decision?
   d. What values did you minimize?
   e. If confronted with the same situation now, would you make the same decision?
2. The insurance industry is regulated in each state by an insurance commissioner. In many states there is a cozy relationship between insurance regulators and the business they regulate.[24] The Center for Public Integrity, a nonprofit, nonpartisan investigative media organization, found for example, that many regulators have accepted thousands of dollars in trips to conferences that are sponsored by insurance companies. The National Institute on Money in State Politics found that insurance companies and their employees were among the top donors to commissioner candidates in the several states that elect regulators.
   a. Who wins and who loses when the industry being regulated by a state official provides gifts and financial benefits to the state official?
   b. Why are conflicts of interest problematic?

BUILD YOUR SKILLS

Ethical decision making requires consideration of all the values that are at stake[8] and then making the best decision possible. Here are tips for how to do this.

SKILLBOX: TIPS FOR ETHICAL DECISION MAKING

Obvious questions of right and wrong are easy. Tough decisions are not black and white; they are gray. To achieve one thing of importance requires giving up something else of importance. This is what trade-offs are—maximizing one set of values while knowingly minimizing others because all cannot be achieved at the same time.

While each ethical quandary is unique, here are steps that will help you arrive at the best decision.

Step 1. Define the problem.

Step 2. Acknowledge the context in which the problem arose in order to identify all stakeholders.

Step 3. Identify the values at stake. Use the acronym CHAPELFIRZ to remember the ten core values:

> Caring
> Honesty
> Accountability
> Promise keeping
> Pursuit of excellence
> Loyalty
> Fairness
> Integrity
> Respect for others
> Responsible citizenship

Step 4. Select the most important values to maximize in this situation.

Step 5. Consider all possible ways to resolve the problem. Then select the alternative that maximizes the essential values identified in step 4 and minimizes as few other values as possible.

Step 6. Assure that the consequences of the decision will be ethical with regard to both its short-term and long-term consequences.

Step 7. Implement the decision.

Step 8. Own the decision. Be prepared to justify it by explaining your choice of trade-offs among the values.

Hands-On Activity

Develop confidence in your ability to explain the trade-offs in your decisions. To practice this, recall a recent ethical decision that you made. Articulate the values that your choice maximized and the values that were minimized in the process. Explain why you judged this to be the best choice.

NOTES

1. Thad Moore, "Taking on the Blue Wall," *The Post and Courier* (May 26, 2012), http://www.postandcourier.com/article/20120527/PC1204/120529368.

2. Dennis F. Thompson, "The Possibility of Administrative Ethics," *Public Administration Review* 45, no. 5 (1985): 555–561.

3. Paul H. Douglas, *Ethics in Government* (Cambridge, MA: Harvard University Press, 1952), 19.

4. American Society for Public Administration, *Code of Ethics*, last modified 2017, http://aspanet.org/ASPA/Code-of-Ethics/ASPA/Code-of-Ethics/Code-of-Ethics.aspx?hkey=5b8f046b-dcbd-416d-87cd-0b8fcfacb5e7.

5. J.A. Rohr, *Ethics for Bureaucrats: An Essay on Law and Values*, 2nd ed. (New York: Marcel Dekker, 1989).

6. Woodrow Wilson, "The Study of Administration," *Political Science Quarterly* 2, no. 2 (1887): 197–222.

7. John Rawls, *A Theory of Justice* (Cambridge, MA: Belknap Press, 1971).

8. J.B. Wogan, "How Cities Are Ending Unintentional Racial Discrimination," *Governing* (August 11, 2016), www.governing.com/topics/mgmt/gov-racial-equity-center-social-inclusion.html.

9. Basic Obligation of Public Service, 5 C.F.R. § 2635.101 (2005), http://www.ecfr.gov/cgi-bin/text-idx?c=ecfr&SID=06f812f26e7ed9f364bb87944757b912&rgn=div5&view=text&node=5:3.0.10.10.9&idno=5#sp5.3.2635.b.

10. Robert W. Smith, "Enforcement or Ethical Capacity: Considering the Role of State Ethics Commissions at the Millennium," *Public Administration Review* 63, no. 3 (2003): 283–295.

11. American Civil Liberties Union of Kentucky (ACLU), "ACLU Files Motion for Legal Fees in Rowan County Marriage License Case," (September 23, 2016), http://www.aclu-ky.org/articles/aclu-files-motion-for-legal-fees-in-rowan-county-marriage-license-case/.

12. David H. Rosenbloom, "Public Administrative Theory and the Separation of Powers," *Public Administration Review* 43, no. 3 (1983): 219–227.

13. Rowan County Kentucky Clerk Kim Davis website, last modified 2015, http://rowancountyclerk.com.

14. U.S. Const. amend. IV, § 1.

15. "Social Equity in Governance," National Academy of Public Administration (NAPA) (n.d.), http://www.napawash.org/fellows/standing-panels/social-equity-in-governance.html.

16. Herman Finer, "Administrative Responsibility in Democratic Government," *Public Administration Review* 1, no. 4 (1941): 335–350; and Carl J. Friedrich, "Public Policy and the Nature of Administrative Responsibility," in *Public Policy*, ed. Carl J. Friedrich and Edward S. Mason (Cambridge, MA: Harvard University Press, 1940), 3–24.

17. Anthony Bertelli and Laurence E. Lynn, Jr., "Managerial Responsibility," *Public Administration Review* 63, no. 3 (2003): 259–268; and Frederick C. Mosher, *Democracy and the Public Service* (New York, NY: Oxford University Press, 1968).

18. Eleanor Roosevelt, *The Moral Basis of Democracy* (New York: Howell, Soskin & Co., 1940).

19. Herbert A. Simon, *Reason in Human Affairs* (Stanford, CA: Stanford University Press, 1983), 7–8.

20. Mary E. Guy, *Ethical Decision Making in Everyday Work Situations* (Westport, CT: Quorum Books, 1990).

21. Albert O. Hirschman, *Exit, Voice, and Loyalty: Responses to Decline in Firms, Organizations, and States* (Cambridge, MA: Harvard University Press, 1990).

22. Guy B. Adams and Danny L. Balfour, *Unmasking Administrative Evil*, 4th ed. (New York, NY: Routledge, 2014).

23. *Ask Me Why I Care: Public Service Stories*, video, directed by Mary R. Hamilton and Rita Paskowitz (Omaha, Nebraska: College of Public Affairs and Community Service), accessed May 26, 2017 at http://www.unomaha.edu/college-of-public-affairs-and-community-service/community-engagement/pss-janet-norwood.php.

24. Michael J. Mishak, "Drinks, Junkets and Jobs: How the Insurance Industry Courts State Commissioners," *Washington Post* (October 2, 2016), https://www.washingtonpost.com/investigations/drinks-junkets-and-jobs-how-the-insurance-industry-courts-state-commissioners/2016/10/02/1069e7a0-6add-11e6-99bf-f0cf3a6449a6_story.html?utm_term=.6077a6ecf715.

ADDITIONAL RESOURCES

Hopson, Justin. 2012. *Breaking the Blue Wall: One Man's War Against Police Corruption.* Bloomington, IN: Westbow Press.

Johnson, Norman J., and James H. Svara. 2011. *Justice for All: Promoting Social Equity in Public Administration.* Armonk, NY: M.E. Sharpe, Inc.

O'Leary, Rosemary. 2006. *The Ethics of Dissent: Managing Guerrilla Government.* Washington, DC: CQ Press.

Visit this website to see the range of U.S. government entities that have authority over ethics related issues: https://www.oge.gov/Web/OGE.nsf/Mission%20and%20 Responsibilities/CB90868111677A6F85257EA6006557BA/$FILE/836ef6c81 aa84d9db6ff3e13db6728061.pdf?open.

Public Productivity and Performance

The imperatives of public service are economy, efficiency, effectiveness, and equity. Balancing these imperatives is challenging. They are achieved with constant awareness of the wants and needs of the public being served and a commitment to continuous improvement. These chapters discuss this focus.

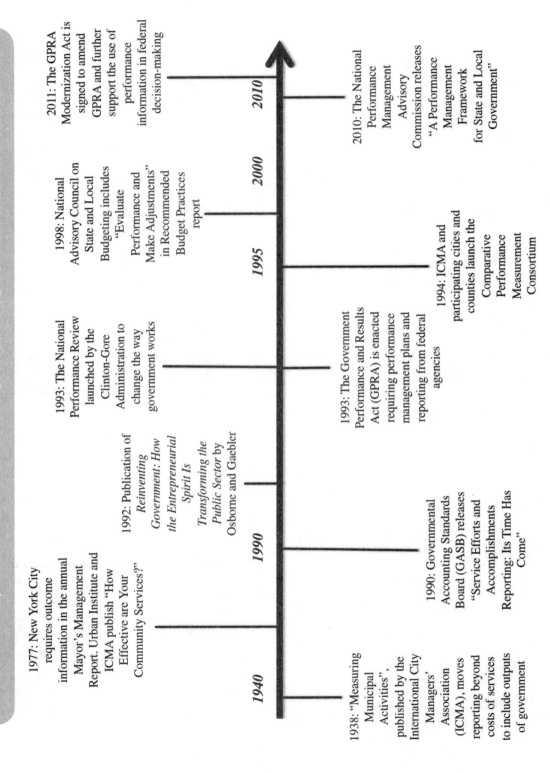

Chapter 14 Timeline: Measuring And Managing For Performance

1938: "Measuring Municipal Activities", published by the International City Managers' Association (ICMA), moves reporting beyond costs of services to include outputs of government

1977: New York City requires outcome information in the annual Mayor's Management Report. Urban Institute and ICMA publish "How Effective are Your Community Services?"

1990: Governmental Accounting Standards Board (GASB) releases "Service Efforts and Accomplishments Reporting: Its Time Has Come"

1992: Publication of *Reinventing Government: How the Entrepreneurial Spirit Is Transforming the Public Sector* by Osborne and Gaebler

1993: The National Performance Review launched by the Clinton-Gore Administration to change the way government works

1993: The Government Performance and Results Act (GPRA) is enacted requiring performance management plans and reporting from federal agencies

1994: ICMA and participating cities and counties launch the Comparative Performance Measurement Consortium

1998: National Advisory Council on State and Local Budgeting includes "Evaluate Performance and Make Adjustments" in Recommended Budget Practices report

2010: The National Performance Management Advisory Commission releases "A Performance Management Framework for State and Local Government"

2011: The GPRA Modernization Act is signed to amend GPRA and further support the use of performance information in federal decision-making

1940   *1990*   *1995*   *2000*   *2010*

MEASURING AND MANAGING FOR PERFORMANCE

WHAT YOU WILL LEARN

Reasons to measure performance

Categories and criteria for performance measures

Translating measures into management

Performance in the nonprofit context

Barriers to performance management

Skillbox: Essentials of program evaluation

In 2003, scholar Robert Behn asked the seemingly simple question, "Why measure performance?" The short answer, he argued, is to "improve."[1] This chapter details the complexity behind the desire to measure, monitor, and manage organizational performance with this noble goal of performance improvement.

The public sector has always struggled with the perception of poor performance. In the absence of a clear outcome like profitability, government and nonprofit organizations have a heavier burden to demonstrate achievements. The expectation of low quality public services has even seeped into everyday vernacular.

Shoddy public service is often considered "close enough for government work." Encountering outdated government technology is greeted with the cynical observation that "it's not state of the art, it's state." Even former President Harry S. Truman acknowledged systemic barriers to high performance when he quipped, "Whenever you have an efficient government you have a dictatorship."[2] Reversing long-standing perceptions does not happen overnight. Measuring performance is a first step toward improving public service. The following case describes the challenges of measuring performance in a setting familiar to most everyone: education.

HIGH-STAKES PERFORMANCE MEASUREMENT IN PUBLIC SCHOOLS

Nearly 40 percent of state and local government employees in the United States work in elementary and secondary education.[3] The performance of schools is as scrutinized as any public service. And while everybody agrees on the need for "good" schools, the meaning of "good" is subjective and differs across stakeholders.

In the early 2000s, the focus of school performance was on students meeting a minimum level of "proficiency" on state assessment tests as directed in the federal government's No Child Left Behind (NCLB) legislation. More recently, measuring the performance of schools and teachers has shifted to "growth" in student learning. The "proficiency" and "growth" approaches are both reasonable representations of learning, but one is an absolute measure based on existing standards of mastery while the other represents the relative change from a student's prior mastery of subject matter.[4]

A proficiency approach might focus on the share of students in a school who score in the proficient or advanced range on a state test for math. The proficiency perspective requires teachers to focus on the minimum acceptable student performance. The growth approach might look to the per-centage change in standardized test scores for each student over the course of the year. Growth targets recognize the progress made by students over time, but do not guarantee accountability for proficiency.

Others argue that subject matter tests fail, altogether, to capture critical aspects of learning that occur in schools or are biased toward certain subgroups. This has led to efforts to measure social and emotional learning (SEL) in schools, including a recent federal requirement that states introduce "nonacademic measures" in assessing school performance.[5] Even some supporters of the importance of SEL have pushed back on the use of such measures to evaluate school performance. For example, Professor Angela Duckworth recalls writing a paper on the challenges of generating reliable SEL measures where the "working title" of the paper was "all measures suck, and they all suck in their own way."[6]

The choice of performance measures has serious implications for student learning, teacher and principal compensation and retention, and even school closures. The high stakes are apparent in well-publicized, but infrequent, scandals across the United States where teachers and administrators physically changed students' answers on standardized tests. Atlanta Public Schools in Georgia was a prominent example, where the successes in the classroom had been rewarded with praise, a national superintendent of the year award, and financial support from major foundations. In 2011, an investigation concluded that there "were teachers and principals in forty-four schools erasing and changing test answers," particularly in critical testing grades.[7]

Questions to Ponder

1. Measuring school quality highlights the challenges of selecting ideal performance measures. What are the strengths and weaknesses of the proficiency and growth measures of student or school-level performance? How does the selection of measures impact different groups of students?

2. Is it realistic to believe that any single performance measure can capture the complex goals of public programs?

3. Which is a greater concern: Using performance measures for high-stakes purposes (such as compensation) or having performance measures that lack incentives for improvement?

REASONS TO MEASURE PERFORMANCE

Before addressing the "why" of performance measurement, it is useful to define the relevant terms. Researchers broadly assume an implicit understanding of "performance" and focus instead on its meaning when paired with "measurement." Reflecting on the meaning of performance is useful, though, as a reminder that it is the actions and accomplishments of the public sector that are being scrutinized with hopes of improvement.

The federal Government Accountability Office (GAO) defines performance measurement as "the ongoing monitoring and reporting of program accomplishments, particularly progress toward pre-established goals . . . typically conducted by program or agency management."[8] A handful of concepts are noteworthy in the definition. First, performance measurement is considered a recurring process, rather than a one-time act. In other words, there is a time element reflected in conducting performance measurement. Depending on the activity, performance measures might be generated daily, annually, or any iteration in between.

Second, performance measures must be monitored to serve a useful function. Third, performance measures require goals with which to be compared. In the absence of explicit goals, measures from previous time periods serve as implicit comparisons for performance. Finally, the parties responsible for carrying out performance measurement are usually within the organization as opposed to the fairly common use of external contractors to conduct discrete and in-depth evaluations of programs and activities.

Performance measurement has become ubiquitous in state and local governments in the United States, while more limited expansion across the globe is also apparent.[9] Performance measurement approaches are tailored to each government's objectives and resources. The city of Portland, Oregon's performance measurement system is used throughout the chapter to illustrate various concepts. The following provides background on Portland's experience with performance improvement before discussing the reasons for measuring performance.

GAUGING SUCCESS IN THE PACIFIC NORTHWEST: PORTLAND'S PERFORMANCE

Why Portland, Oregon? The city of Portland has engaged in formal performance management initiatives since the early 1970s, including integrating performance measures into the annual budget beginning in 1977.[10] The adoption of *The Portland Plan* (the Plan) in 2012 provides a strategic template for the purposes of performance measurement. In recent years, the use of key performance measures has been expanded to all bureaus (departments) in addition to the citywide measures of success set forth in the Plan.

The city also has embraced a series of best practices including the presentation of performance information via online dashboards and participation in learning communities such as the Bloomberg Philanthropies' What Works Cities and the World Council on City Data. Portland embraces "data-driven executive level performance management meetings" to address hard-to-solve issues and to empower employees to initiate performance improvement efforts. The city offers structured performance management assistance to departments through its budget office.[11]

The Plan, as a comprehensive strategic planning document, established a set of core principles (prosperity, education, health, and equity) around which performance measurements are developed at the citywide level. The Plan sets forth a compelling argument for the critical link between measurement and performance improvement, noting "you can't track what you don't measure, and what you don't measure rarely gets done."[12]

The rationale for adopting performance measures is apparent in scholar Harry Hatry's description of performance management as "the practice of public service managers using performance data to help them make decisions so as to continually improve services to their customers."[13] To reiterate, improvement in doing whatever government does is the overarching reason for measuring and monitoring performance. There are a number of other justifications for performance measurement from the perspective of the public manager that are distinct, but supportive, of the goal of improvement. Table 14.1 presents one especially thoughtful list, from Robert Behn, of the purposes of measuring performance and the associated questions addressed by performance measures.

TABLE 14.1 REASONS TO ENGAGE IN PERFORMANCE MEASUREMENT[14]

Reason	Questions answered by performance measures
Evaluate	How well is my public agency performing?
Control	How can I ensure that my subordinates are doing the right thing?
Budget	On what programs, people, or projects should my agency spend the public's money?
Motivate	How can I motivate line staff, middle managers, nonprofit and for-profit collaborators, stakeholders, and citizens to do the things necessary to improve performance?
Promote	How can I convince political superiors, legislators, stakeholders, journalists, and citizens that my agency is doing a good job?
Celebrate	What accomplishments are worthy of the important organizational ritual of celebrating success?
Learn	Why is what working or not working?
Improve	What exactly should who do differently to improve performance?

The breadth of purposes for measuring performance is unsurprising given the many hats worn by public managers. Performance measures are used for comparison, monitoring staff, assessing trade-offs in allocating resources, as incentives, for publicity, for acknowledgment, and to better understand public services; all in the name of continuous improvement. Even this list is not exhaustive, as measuring performance supports transparency and accountability for the public even in the absence of performance improvement.[15] The purposes can be related to even broader notions of performance that overlay the entire field of public administration.

THE PILLARS OF PERFORMANCE

The National Academy of Public Administration has adopted economy, efficiency, effectiveness, and equity as the four pillars of public administration.[16] The pillars represent the overarching objectives of the public sector as identified by leaders in the field. Performance measures represent an effort to gauge the success of government in supporting economy, efficiency, effectiveness, or equity goals.

Economy and efficiency are closely related and refer to using limited public resources to provide expected services at the lowest cost. Effectiveness represents government actually accomplishing intended results. Without being effective, a government cannot simultaneously be economical and efficient. Equity focuses on the fair and just operation of government and distribution of government services.[17] Of the pillars, equity is the latest edition and, arguably, least developed in the performance measurement field.

CONCEPTUALIZING PUBLIC PERFORMANCE

Underlying performance measurement are key concepts that comprise the logic of public sector activities. For each public service function, there are resources allocated to that purpose. These resources are collectively referred to as "inputs." Inputs represent labor and capital, which might include money, people, equipment, and buildings, all dedicated to the delivery of a specific good or service. As an example, consider primary and secondary education. The inputs include teachers, teachers' aides, counselors, school principals, district superintendents, buses, bus drivers, school buildings (with cafeterias, gyms, auditoriums, and science labs), janitors, nurses, special education co-ordinators, and so on. All of these inputs can also be represented as a dollar amount indicating the associated costs of education.

The public sector cannot operate without inputs. They are the basis for delivering "outputs," which are what a "program actually does"[18] or the "direct products and services delivered" by an organization or program.[19] Continuing with the education example, primary outputs are the number of students educated or enrolled, a count of graduated students, along with a series of secondary outputs, such as the number of students served by after-school activities or new programs.

Outputs versus Outcomes

Outputs produce results, which are called "outcomes." These represent the change in conditions resulting from the activities. The difference between outputs and outcomes is the basis for much confusion in performance measurement, but "managers who are concerned with overall performance must look beyond outputs to outcomes because they represent program effectiveness."[20] Indeed, a shift started in the 1970s from focusing "on measuring finances (inputs) and sometimes outputs, (the amount of work completed by the organization)" to measuring outcomes.[21] The Governmental Accounting Standards Board (GASB), in 1989, started issuing a series of influential and somewhat contentious publications on the need for state and local government reporting of "service efforts and accomplishments." Service accomplishments represented both outputs and outcomes.[22] Notable state efforts to embark on strategic planning using performance indicators subsequently emerged, including the Oregon Shines plan (and associated Oregon Benchmarks)[23] and Minnesota Milestones, which launched in 1991.[24]

Enthusiasm around outcome-based performance measurement accelerated through the early 1990s. In 1992, publication of the influential book *Reinventing Government: How the Entrepreneurial Spirit Is Transforming the Public Sector* (David Osborne and Ted Gaebler) showcased an appealing performance and customer-oriented approach to government. From a legislative perspective, the watershed event was enactment of the Government Performance and Results Act of 1993 (GPRA), which ushered in strategic planning and performance reporting for federal agencies. At the same time, the

Clinton Administration's National Performance Review was inspired by *Reinventing Government*. The governmentwide initiative was overseen by Vice President Al Gore and launched in March 1993 with the goal of a government that "works better and costs less." The growing saliency of outcomes mirrored the interest in New Public Management trends such as "managing for results," "total quality management," and "reinventing government."

Scholar Theodore Poister and colleagues provide clarity to the distinction between outputs and outcomes with concrete examples:

> Outputs often represent the amount of work performed or the volume of activity completed . . . Sometimes outputs are measured in terms of the number of clients or cases treated . . . Outcomes are the substantive results generated by producing these outputs. Criminal investigations and arrests do not really count for much—for instance, if the police are not able to solve the crimes they are working on, and reconstructed highway segments do not serve any particular public interest or create value if they do not result in improved flow of traffic and reduced travel times for the motorists using them . . . Outcomes are the ultimate criteria for gauging program effectiveness, but as direct products of program activity, outputs are critical for achieving intended outcomes.[25]

Returning again to the example of elementary and secondary education, the primary outcomes of education include learning achievement (rather than just completing classes) and college and career readiness (instead of just graduation). The relationship between inputs, outputs, and outcomes is the basis for program logic models that are used in evaluation. Figure 14.1 displays this. Such models are adapted to reflect the actual inputs, activities performed, outputs that result, and outcomes that are achieved.

Figure 14.1 makes clear that outcomes are sometimes distinguished by time. In the education example, the number of students matriculating to college after high school graduation may be an initial outcome of success, but more important is whether the students were adequately prepared to succeed in and graduate from college (an intermediate outcome), and ultimately be successful in society and the labor market (a long-term outcome). The ability for any program to claim credit for outcomes diminishes as time increases between the time services were received and measurement occurs.

It is not unusual for one program's outcome to be another program's output. For example, a state education department with stringent high school graduation requirements might count an increasing proportion of students who graduate as an outcome. Alternately, the number of high school graduates is more an output than an outcome in

FIGURE 14.1: BASIC PROGRAM LOGIC MODEL[26]

Inputs $\longrightarrow$ Activities $\longrightarrow$ Outputs $\longrightarrow$ Initial Outcomes $\longrightarrow$ Intermediate Outcomes $\longrightarrow$ Long-term Outcomes

states with high shares of graduates in need of remedial education before matriculating to higher education. The next section reviews how the components of performance (inputs, outputs, and outcomes) are used as performance measures.

TYPOLOGY OF PERFORMANCE MEASURES

Performance measures fall into a number of categories based on the focus of measurement. The most relevant categories for public sector managers include measures of output, efficiency, outcomes, and cost-effectiveness. The major types of measures are presented in Table 14.2 along with associated characteristics and examples related to a human resources department's hiring activities.

Inputs—resources used to deliver public services—are represented in Table 14.2 despite not directly measuring performance, because they are building blocks used to generate efficiency measures.[27] Inputs can also be used to measure resource use over time.

Output measures are frequently synonymous with workload and represent the activities carried out by the program or organization. As previously described, outputs are often represented by the volume or counts of activities. Output measures are incapable of addressing service "quality or efficiency," but can signify changes in service demand over time.[28] Despite the sometimes zealous push to measure outcomes, output measures have not lost their utility because, compared to outcomes, they are easier to collect, are more directly influenced by the organization, and provide useful operational information to managers and decision makers.[29]

Efficiency measures combine inputs and outputs to represent the amount of resources required to complete an activity or provide a service. The inputs are typically the total cost or staff time of the activity and are communicated as per unit amounts. An alternative approach to measuring efficiency uses the time needed to perform a given activity.

Outcome measures reflect effectiveness and are tied directly to the goals of a program or activity. Direct measurement of outcomes is preferred, but in many cases it is difficult to operationalize outcomes. Outcomes in the public sector are sometimes measured as "responsiveness," when the speed with which a service is delivered is a primary product of the activity, such as in emergency medical response. When perceptions of service quality are important, satisfaction surveys are commonly used.[30]

Measures of cost-effectiveness relate costs to outcome measures.[31] The appeal of such measures is obvious for planning, since a manager can determine the cost of achieving better results. In practice, such precision is difficult to achieve. Economy, efficiency, and effectiveness, three of the four pillars of public administration, are prominently captured by the standard categories of performance measures. Equity, on the other hand, is not explicitly represented. Equity can most readily be integrated into performance measurement systems as outcome measures that assess whether identified programs achieve procedural fairness to all groups or, for example, result in intended and effective redistribution of resources.

TABLE 14.2 PRIMARY PERFORMANCE MEASURE CATEGORIES[32]

Components of Measure	Aspect of Performance	Relative Difficulty in Collecting	Example Measures (Hiring activity by an HR department)*
Inputs		Low	Department spending (time and materials) for hiring function
Outputs	Workload	Low	Job applications received and processed; vacant jobs filled
Inputs/Outputs	Efficiency	Medium	Cost-per-application processed; cost-per-vacant job filled
Outcomes	Effectiveness	High	Percentage of vacant job openings successfully filled
Inputs/Outcomes or Change in Inputs/ Change in Outcomes	Cost-effectiveness	High	Cost-per-job opening successfully filled

*Note: "Successfully filled" means that the new hires completed the probationary period and are performing adequately after six months.

The different categories of performance measures have advantages and disadvantages. Foremost, there is a clear trade-off between the ease with which a performance measure is devised and put into operation and the strategic usefulness of that measure. In other words, input and output measures are fairly easy to identify and gather, because they are often already collected in the course of operations. Outcome measures are often more difficult to collect, since the impacts are frequently external to the organization. Efficiency and cost-effectiveness measures demand additional granularity in how resources are used in the organization and for which activities. Such information comes ideally from cost accounting systems, which may be more common in larger organizations with greater management capacity. Related to ease of collection, the next section details criteria to consider when designing and adopting performance measures.

CRITERIA FOR PERFORMANCE MEASURES

No single performance measure is adequate for all purposes.[33] Multiple measures, within reason, compensate for weaknesses in any single performance indicator. A number of common-sense criteria have been identified for designing useful performance measures.[34]

Valid and Reliable

Each should be assessed for validity and reliability. Validity means that the indicator measures what it is intended to measure. Reliability refers to accuracy of the measure and its ability to be consistent over repeated measurement.

Understandable

Measures need to be understandable to users, whether they are elected officials, managers, front-line staff, or citizens. With some programs, performance is viewed differently by citizens as compared to agency officials or elected representatives. A 2005 report on citizen engagement and performance measurement confirmed this, finding:

> When municipal governments do not hear or understand the ways in which their constituencies evaluate their performance, a "disconnect" ensues: government is evaluating its effectiveness using one set of criteria; the public may be applying quite another.[35]

The takeaway from this is that, although more complex measures may be appealing, all uses and users must be considered. A compromise is to use more complex measures for internal management purposes, while using "meta-measures" to communicate performance in a simpler manner to the public.[36] The use of metameasures is demonstrated in Portland since, "while there are hundreds of data points within the Plan to track progress, it is simply not feasible to measure everything. Instead, the Plan identifies twelve core measures—each serves as an indicator about the city."[37]

> *"While people are interested in government and what it is doing, if you were to call them and say, 'Do you want to see some performance measures of government?' they would probably hang up on you."*
>
> —Barbara Cohn

Timely

Even measures satisfying the above criteria are of little use if they fail to be timely, so measures should be selected that can be collected and reported before becoming stale or irrelevant to decision making.

Resistant to Gaming

Good performance measures are also resistant to perverse behavior or gaming, including misreporting. Performance measures are intended to incentivize changes in behavior that improve services, but measures that can be influenced without related positive changes in service quality are counterproductive.

Targeted to Mission

The selected measures should collectively provide a comprehensive view of the organization's or service's most important performance areas. The temptation to choose performance measures that are easily gathered but of minor importance is shortsighted and subverts the value of the assessment. And using multiple and redundant measures needlessly complicates collection and interpretation of the information. Ideally, each performance measure "contributes something distinctive."[38]

Cost Effective

Data collection costs must be taken into consideration when choosing measures. Even when the ideal measure is unavailable, there are likely to be proxies among existing information that is already collected by the organization or surrogate measures that are available without great cost.

Usable Information

If performance improvement is the primary reason for using performance measures, then they should reflect activities that can be controlled, or at least influenced, by the organization's actions. In other words, collect data that can be used to identify problems and make improvements. This is the hallmark of learning organizations.

The Portland Plan's twelve primary indicators represent overarching performance priorities for the city and range from "equity and inclusion" to "healthy watersheds." The priorities and associated measures are presented in Table 14.3. While city policies and programs directly and indirectly influence all of the measures, there are some areas over which the city has more control than others. Holding the city accountable for graduation rates to support the goal of "educated youth," for example, is tough because independent school districts with their own elected school boards are in charge of delivering education. Indeed, at times, performance measures are effectively used to elevate a topic in importance and to bring pressure on the responsible parties to act. The Plan compares its overall indicators to "medical vital signs, like, heartbeat, temperature, and blood pressure. Each vital sign is an indicator of overall health. If one or more is not what it is expected to be, further diagnosis is needed."[39] The overall indicators are then reinforced by performance measures focused on the direct activities of Portland's city government.

TABLE 14.3 CITY OF PORTLAND, OREGON'S MEASURES OF SUCCESS, 2012[40]

Area	Measures
1. Equity and inclusion	Income distribution; diversity index
2. Resident satisfaction	Percent satisfied living in the city
3. Educated youth	High school on-time graduation rate
4. Prosperous households	Percent above self-sufficiency
5. Growing business	Export value, city rank
6. Job growth	Number of jobs
7. Transit and active transportation	Percent who take transit, walk, bike, or less polluting options to work
8. Reduced carbon emissions	Percent below 1990 levels
9. Complete neighborhoods	Complete neighborhood index; access to healthy food; access to parks
10. Healthier people	Adults at a healthy weight; eighth graders at a healthy weight
11. Safer city	Percent who feel safe walking alone at night in their neighborhood; serious crimes per 1,000
12. Healthy watersheds	Water quality index; tree canopy

More general guidance for developing performance measures comes from the National Performance Management Advisory Commission. The commission recommends measures be informative, well understood, and relevant, with a pragmatic focus on improving decision making, performance improvement, and public accountability based on the collected information. Performance measures ideally "serve multiple audiences" and are kept simple,[41] although both of these objectives are sometimes easier said than done. Finally, public sector employees frequently lack control in selecting and defining the performance measures applied to their work. Such decisions can be political and measures may be "imposed" by other stakeholders.[42] The next section moves beyond the design of performance measures to understand how providing information in the form of measures can translate to managing performance.

TRANSLATING MEASURES INTO MANAGEMENT

Just adopting performance measures does not guarantee that performance improvement follows. A certain degree of accountability does accompany performance measurement if the results are continuously made public, since the media and citizens provide scrutiny. An accessible way to present performance data online is by using dashboards that are color coded to represent whether existing targets or performance standards were achieved.

For performance improvement to occur, the information from measures must be acted upon. The city of Portland recognizes this in their Performance Management Manual, noting the city "seeks to hasten the transition from measuring and reporting on performance data, to managing and improving services through the use of performance data."[43] Performance management is the continuous use of performance information to identify operational areas in need of attention or improvement and to guide strategic decision making.

> *"If you ignore performance and don't use the tools you have to reshape government to meet the demands of a new world and a new economy, you will lose."*
>
> —Roy Barnes

Strategic Planning

The strategic planning process guides organizational performance. Through strategic planning, an organization establishes or refines its mission, along with the goals and objectives that guide day-to-day operations. Performance measures are instrumental for fulfilling a plan because goal formulation can be linked to tangible outcomes reflected by performance measures.

Professor David Ammons argues that "a good set [of performance measures] inspires managerial thinking by providing crucial performance data that cannot be ignored."[44] When integrated with a strategic plan, the elevated and formalized role of performance measures makes the data more difficult to overlook. Poister and colleagues contend that "usually the most meaningful performance measures are derived from the mission, goals, objectives, and, sometimes, service standards that have been established for a particular program."[45]

Budgeting

Integration of performance information into budget deliberations has long been promoted as a way to improve organizational decision making. Rather than ascribing to incremental changes in annual budget allocations, performance measurement can present opportunities for thoughtful redistribution based on actual outputs and outcomes. To some degree, performance information can help reduce the information asymmetries between legislators, the budget office, and managers of programs and departments, and can introduce incentives for greater efficiency.

The optimism over performance-based budgeting has become more modest over time as the political nature of budgeting has become more obvious. Professor Phil Joyce reasonably suggests that "performance-informed budgeting" is a more useful label for injecting performance information into the political process of budgeting.[46] The federal government has a long history of performance-oriented budget and management reforms, including Planning, Programming, and Budgeting System (PPBS), Management by Objective (MBO), and Zero-Based Budgeting (ZBB).[47] Most state governments incorporate some degree of performance information into the budgeting process and local governments frequently present performance measures alongside financial information in annual budgets.[48] Budgeting is one of the venues where performance measures can be translated into decision making, but convincing legislators to make budget decisions primarily on the basis of performance data has been met with limited success.

Standards, Targets, and Goals

On their own, performance measures provide little value. Their utility derives from the ability to compare collected measures to a performance standard, target, or goal.[49] Only then does a performance measure convey actionable information. The simplest approach, and often the most logical, is to compare current performance measures to past values. Over time, such a use provides trend data that indicate improvement, stability, or decline. This is useful information that informs managers about actions that are effective or that need to be modified.

A second option for determining performance targets or goals is referred to as benchmarking. Benchmarking looks to peer organizations to determine what represents average and, perhaps, aspirational performance. The performance of peer organizations is then used as the basis for determining internal performance goals. A considerable challenge of benchmarking is determining the appropriate comparison group, where conditions are similar enough to provide reasonable guidance. Professional standards are also used as benchmarks for services, but the standards are typically a form of benchmarking based on best practices. For example, national standards for response times are commonly used as targets for emergency services like fire, police, and ambulance.

> *"It's one of the ways you can tell how well you're doing . . . If all you have is your own number and you don't have a comparison, you can't know if you are doing well."*
>
> —Harry P. Hatry

Determining performance goals for specific measures is a subjective process that reflects the priorities and expectations of decision makers. Typically, department managers work with budget staff to identify both the appropriate performance measures and the targets by which to be assessed. A political tension exists between setting goals that are easily achievable, such as maintaining existing levels of performance, and challenging managers with stretch goals that risk failure. The city of Portland openly addresses this trade-off in setting targets for performance measures, noting that "by 2035 we want to see 90 percent of high school students graduate on time and have 70 percent of Portlanders take transit, walk, bike, carpool to work or work from home. At first glance, these goals may seem overly ambitious. They are intentionally set as stretch goals to inspire creativity and hard work."[50]

The belief that combining performance measures with performance goals will incentivize staff toward improvement is powerful. Regardless of how the target is set, managers and front-line staff are usually given some degree of discretion to meet the goal. Without any budgetary or operational discretion, changes in performance are unrealistic. In some cases, the use of program evaluation is needed to determine how a program or activity can be modified and improved. The following are examples of department-level performance measures in the city of Portland. They reflect the types of performance measures described earlier and the use of targets to assess year-to-year changes.

HOUSING AND FIRE: KEY PERFORMANCE MEASURES AND TARGETS

The city of Portland presents each bureau's key performance measures (KPMs) online. Managed centrally by the City Budget Office, performance management "(1) provides Council and City leaders with critical information for decision making, (2) ensures that bureau missions, strategic direction, and programs are aligned with City priorities and intended results, and (3) allows the City to better communicate the quality and breadth of services it provides."[51]

Three consecutive years of measures are presented, along with targets for the most recently completed year and subsequent year. Doing so allows readers to assess trends in the measures and determine how the targets are changing. As is common, the most recent year's measures are compared to the target. A measure that meets its target is represented with a green circle,

while those that fall short of the target are indicated with a red "X."

The Portland Housing Bureau's (PHB) mission is to "solve the unmet housing needs of the people of Portland."[52] Seven performance measures that are focused mainly on affordable housing, homelessness, and PHB programming are presented in 2016 (see Table 14.4 for details). PHB met six of the seven targets. The measures represent a range of outcomes from expanding the affordable housing stock to the number of individuals prevented from becoming homeless.

Other measures capture the effectiveness of PHB's activities including the percentages of households receiving home repairs and retaining their homes twelve months after services, households receiving homebuyer education or counseling and subsequently purchasing a home, and retention rate of households placed in permanent housing at twelve months. A couple of the measures look like outputs, but represent mission-based results. For targets met, PHB exceeded the 2016 targets by an average of 32 percent, suggesting the goal setting was too conservative. In contrast, the 2017 targets have more than compensated with average increases of more than 50 percent.

TABLE 14.4 PORTLAND HOUSING BUREAU PERFORMANCE MEASURES[53]

2016 to Target	Key Performance Measure	2014	2015	2016 Target	2016	2017 Target
Met	Housing units opened that are newly affordable	279	182	251	362	753
Met	Number of individuals prevented from becoming homeless	4,023	3,522	2,600	3,922	4,900
Met	Percentage of households receiving home repairs and retaining their homes twelve months after services	80%	83%	80%	80%	80%
Did not meet	Percentage of households receiving homebuyer education or counseling and subsequently purchasing a home	27%	28%	27%	10%	28%
Met	Percentage utilization of minority contracts in housing construction (contract $ awarded)	15%	13%	15%	19%	15%
Met	Retention rate of households placed in permanent housing at twelve months	77%	78%	70%	74%	85%
Met	Total number of homeless individuals placed in permanent housing	3,402	3,909	2,430	4,049	4,324

Portland Fire & Rescue (PF&R) "aggressively and safely protects life, property, and the environment."[54] Seven performance measures are used to assess achievement of this mission focused mainly on incident responsiveness, reductions in loss of life and property, and citizen outreach (see Table 14.5 for details). PF&R met only one of the seven performance measure targets in 2016. The measures represent a range of outputs and outcomes, from number of incidents, for which a larger number is considered "worse," and community outreach activities (outputs) to the rate of successful resuscitation from cardiac arrest and the proportion of fires where the flames were limited to the room of origin (outcomes). The response time and unit availability measures represent outcomes based on the expectation that a faster response is more effective in saving lives and property.

TABLE 14.5 PORTLAND FIRE & RESCUE PERFORMANCE MEASURES[55]

2016 to Target	Key Performance Measure	2014	2015	2016 Target	2016	2017 Target
Did not meet	Total number of incidents	72,023	77,581	73,260	81,038	83,350
Met	Time lost to on-duty injury (in full-time equivalent employees)	13.50	10.30	10.40	10.10	10.00
Missing	Successful cardiac arrest resuscitation rate	46%	49%	50%	-	50%
Did not meet	Percentage of time unit from closest station is available for response	92%	92%	93%	92%	92%
Did not meet	Percentage of structural fires where flamespread was confined to room of origin	78%	76%	80%	76%	77%
Did not meet	Maximum response time to 90 percent of high priority calls	7.12	7.12	7.11	7.19	7.10
Did not meet	Citizens contacted during community outreach/partnership activities	121,702	108,600	120,000	103,200	120,000

Unlike the PHB, PF&R had around a 14 percent success rate in meeting performance targets. Does this mean that they performed poorly in 2016? Not necessarily. A look at the measures shows that some of the misses were by amounts that may not be important from a practical perspective. Although every second counts in emergency response, the difference between the actual "maximum response time to 90 percent of high priority calls" exceeded the target time by only 0.08 minutes or 4.8 seconds. Similarly, 92 percent of the time a unit from the closest station was available for response to an incident, which fell just shy of the 93 percent target.

Given the inability to meet most of the targets in 2016, targets were either maintained or made more lenient in 2017 with the exception of the target that was easily achieved. The continuous decline in citizen outreach deserves further investigation. Lowering the performance target would make sense if the activity is no longer prioritized as it was in 2014.

These examples illustrate the challenge of identifying valid, reliable, meaningful performance measures and setting targets that make sense and represent important dimensions of performance. A number of effectiveness measures are presented, although neither of the bureaus use any measures of efficiency or cost-effectiveness. To do so, the bureaus would have divided the reported output and outcome measures by the associated costs to produce them. One of the key performance measures for the City Budget Office is the "Percentage of City KPMs with positive year-over-year results." The 2016 target of 52.5 percent was not met, but there is always hope for next year (with a new target of 33.7 percent).[56]

PERFORMANCE IN THE NONPROFIT CONTEXT

The nature of nonprofit organizations suggests fundamental challenges to performance management efforts. In stark contrast to businesses, nonprofits have a less well-defined "primary interest group" (no owners), goals are complex, mission-based, and difficult to capture in readily-available performance measures, and they often serve a diverse set of stakeholders.[57]

Nevertheless, the continued professionalization of the nonprofit sector guarantees that measuring, monitoring, and managing performance will continue to be prioritized.

Performance measurement has been used by nonprofit organizations for decades. The primary approaches include measures of financial accountability, program products (outputs), adherence to standards (including professional certification and accreditation), participant-focused measures (who are receiving services), key performance indicators, and client satisfaction (surveys of service recipients).[58]

Similar to the experience of governments, the early-1990s witnessed a push for outcome-based performance measurement. The shift to outcome-focused performance measurement by nonprofit organizations is often attributed to the release of the United Way of America's report, *Measuring Program Outcomes: A Practical Approach*, in 1996.[59] The subsequent growth in the use of performance measures for outcomes resulted, in part, from large, national organizations embracing the approach. The demands for tracking outcomes trickled down to local organizations, particularly in response to more rigorous performance standards for grantees and contractors. More recently, the focus on outcomes of nonprofit activities has accelerated under the label of measuring social impact.

BUCKS AND ACRES: MEASURING PERFORMANCE AT THE NATURE CONSERVANCY

The transition to more sophisticated, outcome-oriented systems of performance measurement by nonprofits is reflected in the oft-used example of The Nature Conservancy. The Nature Conservancy, founded in 1951, has the grand mission "to conserve the lands and waters on which all life depends."[60] The Conservancy's longtime measures of performance were referred to as "bucks and acres." The "bucks" represented donations received and "acres" indicated the amount of land protected each year. As a system of performance measurement, the two measures were simple, straightforward, and useful to both internal and external stakeholders.

A disconnect between measures and mission became clear in the 1990s when staff realized that biodiversity continued to decline on some "protected" Conservancy lands. Individuals involved in rethinking the organization's measures of success noted that "the Conservancy's goal, after all, isn't to buy land or raise money; it is to preserve the diversity of life on Earth."[61] Concerns over mission fulfillment resulted in a shift in the organization's strategy to focus more broadly on "preserving larger ecosystems"

rather than solely acquiring land parcels with biodiversity value.[62] A peripheral benefit of undertaking performance measurement is that it clarifies the linkage between activities and goals, which in this case resulted in strategic change.

Beginning in 1996, The Nature Conservancy experimented with alternative performance measures and ultimately replaced "bucks and acres" with a "family of measures" approach. A manageable number of measures were adopted across three areas: capacity, activity, and impact. Capacity measures reflect an expansion of the original "bucks" focus by including membership, public support for projects, private fund-raising growth, and share of the market. Activity is represented by the number of projects initiated and protected areas, somewhat akin to the old "acres" measure. The impact measures directly tie to the organization's mission by capturing "biodiversity health" and "threat abatement" resulting from their activities.[63] The adopted capacity measures reflect the critical resources needed to support the organization's measured activities, which in turn drive whether the objectives and mission are met.

For nonprofit leaders John Sawhill and David Williamson, the experience with The Nature Conservancy and other nonprofit organizations suggests that nonprofits require three types of complementary performance measures. First, measures to gauge success in raising resources for the organization, like contract or grant revenue. Second, the organization's activities, including outputs like the number of people counseled or the number of meals served, are measured as indicators of activity. Third, and most challenging for nonprofits with broad missions, are measures related to mission fulfillment. To establish performance measures that capture mission achievement, the suggested strategy is to "develop micro-level goals that, if achieved, would imply success on a grander scale."[64]

Balanced Scorecard

Despite emerging in the 1990s for use in business, the balanced scorecard remains a visible and relevant performance measurement and management approach for nonprofit organizations. The balanced scorecard incorporates nonfinancial performance measures that give an internal perspective, customer perspective, and learning and growth perspective, alongside the traditional financial perspective of performance. These measures combine to assess the ongoing success of the organization against established objectives and targets.[65]

The balanced scorecard approach, and similar performance measurement initiatives, represent a push to move beyond financial measures of performance. It is especially warranted for nonprofits because financial reporting requirements and the interests of donors have resulted in the use of spending allocations as a prominent but flawed measure for both efficiency and effectiveness. Specifically, the program services ratio represents the share of spending directed to programs (mission-based activities) as opposed to support services (such as fund-raising and administration). The following section discusses the prime challenges to using performance measures effectively for management in the public sector.

BARRIERS TO PERFORMANCE MANAGEMENT

The popularity and spread of performance measures in the public sector suggests unbridled success in their use to inform management. To the contrary, Hatry suggests that, "for the most part, the information provided by performance measurement systems has been both shallow and not always as timely as is needed to help managers operate throughout the year."[66] Poister and colleagues observe that, "although many public and nonprofit agencies have workable systems in place, others see their measurement systems fall apart before being completed, and still others end up installing systems that are not particularly helpful or are simply not used effectively."[67] Practitioners complain that performance measurement systems lose relevance but are hard to change, lack flexibility, incentivize inflating measured activities and focus on already successful practices, and are sometimes imposed by outsiders with limited understanding of the organization's day-to-day operations.[68]

The academic literature also points to a number of challenges for performance measurement. These include (a) a tendency to adopt measures but not meaningfully use them; (b) the fact that the focus on measurement artificially narrows the aspects of performance considered important (especially favoring efficiency); (c) added complexities that are introduced for monitoring performance under contracting arrangements; (d) gaming of performance measures; and (e) the potential to punish managers and programs based on performance measures even when the outcome is out of their control.[69] Other limitations relate to the application of measures to activities that overlap multiple departments. This happens because performance measures and the managers responsible for them do not always align neatly into predetermined organizational silos.

The sustainability of performance management is especially problematic in the public sector where the turnover of elected leaders, as well as appointed officials serving at the pleasure of the elected, is a cherished characteristic of democracy. Whether due to a newly-elected executive's desire to brand their own performance initiative or a tendency to want to distance themselves from previous office-holders' efforts, leadership turnover is a frequent predictor of lapsed performance management efforts. In contrast, the lasting influence of GPRA at the federal level, and the subsequent 2010 amendments known as the Government Performance and Results Modernization Act, demonstrates the staying power when performance management is institutionalized as law.

Resistance to adopting performance management systems comes from two fundamental assertions made at the organizational level. First, many organizations insist that they are unique and the application of benchmarking or performance standards will misrepresent their performance. There is some truth to the claim of uniqueness, but the inherent differences between organizations should not discourage comparisons with standards generated externally. Without a standard for comparison, organizations are left unaware of areas for potential improvement. Second, the National Performance Management Advisory Commission strongly argues against the frequent assertion that "you can't measure what we do."[70]

Many of these barriers to sustainable performance management can be addressed with a willingness to periodically revisit existing performance measures for relevance with both front-line staff and managers. For example, the focus on easily-measurable activities is seductive but it distracts from meaningful priorities. Measures—even if imperfect—which capture a broader range of performance outcomes, including equity concerns, are worth pursuing.

An effective performance management system should explicitly demonstrate its value as a justification for its continued use. Decoupling performance management initiatives from specific leaders and instead associating the effort with the organization, itself, is a maneuver that improves its staying power. Even when not used regularly for decision making and service improvement, the continuous nature of performance management still "can serve as an early warning system to management and as a vehicle for improving accountability to the public."[71]

Ask Me Why I Care: Phin Xaypagna, organization development consultant for Mecklenburg County, North Carolina[72]

Phin Xaypangna works for Mecklenburg County government where her work revolves around team development, diversity and inclusion consulting, leadership development, facilitation, and strategic planning. She has served on the board of the Carolinas Asian Chamber of Commerce and as president of the Charlotte Asian Heritage Association. Phin is a native of Laos and is fluent in Laotian and Thai. Access her story at https://www.unomaha.edu/college-of-public-affairs-and-community-service/community-engagement/pss-phin-xaypangna.php.

SUMMARY

As seen in the education case at the beginning of the chapter, no single performance measure can capture the multifaceted objectives of complex organizations. Do schools want students to be proficient in different subjects? Show growth in the subjects? Be prepared for college or careers? Develop nonacademic social skills? Most would answer with a resounding "yes" to all of these goals, but accurately measuring and understanding how to improve these outcomes is no easy feat.

Performance measurement is an appealing public sector tool to continuously inform managers and citizens about "how things are going." Measuring and monitoring what matters in an organization sounds deceptively simple, but capturing the intended results of programs and services through outcome measures can be hard. Taking that information and using it to spur improvement is the fundamental role of performance management.

KEY TERMS

Benchmarking – the act of looking externally to peer organizations to determine what represents average and, perhaps, aspirational performance.

Cost-effectiveness – a measure that relates costs to outcome measures.

Effectiveness – refers to the accomplishment of intended results or goals.

Efficiency – a measure that combines inputs and outputs to represent the amount of resources required to complete an activity or provide a service.

Inputs – resources used in an activity; used to generate efficiency measures or to measure resource use over time.

Logic model – a representation of the relationship between program inputs, outputs, and outcomes; primarily used in evaluation.

Outcomes – the results produced by public sector outputs; they represent the change in conditions resulting from activities.

Outputs – the goods/services delivered or produced by an organization or program.

Performance management – refers to the use of performance information by public managers to improve the work of their organizations.

DISCUSSION QUESTIONS

1. Reflect on the reasons for performance measurement from Table 14.1. Which do you find most compelling from the perspective of the public manager? Would the reasons differ from the perspective of a program participant or service recipient?

2. Have you ever used performance measures from a government or nonprofit organization? If so, for what and did they prove useful? If not, provide one to two examples of when you think they would come in handy.

3. Think about a public service program. Consider how you would benchmark the program by comparing activities and performance levels within or across organizations. On what characteristics would you select a comparison group? What would be some of the key performance measures for comparison?

4. Review the barriers and challenges to sustaining the use of performance management in an organization. In your opinion, what are the two most critical challenges and why?

EXERCISES

1. Look for the existing performance measures for three peer government or nonprofit organizations of interest. Reporting of performance measures may often be found in the annual report for nonprofit organizations. Write a one-to-two-page professional memo that addresses the following questions: What were the selected organizations? Were explicit performance measures located for each organization? If found, where was the performance information for each organization (e.g., annual report, dedicated

webpage, annual budget)? Are the performance measures explicitly connected to each organization's mission or strategic plan? Do the measures generally represent inputs, outputs, or outcomes for the organization? Overall, do the performance measures make sense as representations of the stated performance element or do they just seem convenient?

2. Pick an organization that you either work for or would have an interest in working for in the future. For a nonprofit organization, use the mission statement and description of key programs (from the annual report, website, or IRS Form 990) to propose a series of key performance measures for either the organization as a whole or for a selected program. If a state or local government is selected, pick a major function and propose a series of key performance measures. If a federal government agency is selected, locate the GPRA performance report/plan. For the selected organizations, would each of the proposed measures be easy or difficult to collect? Would your proposed measures be categorized as output, efficiency, or outcome measures as described in the chapter, or something else?

BUILD YOUR SKILLS

Well-crafted performance measurement promises the ability to track the ups and downs of public service outcomes over time. Performance management uses the measures as a guide for areas that need attention and improvement. Unfortunately, measures that are lagging expectations do not come with an instruction manual that explains the underlying reasons for poor performance. Nor do performance measures explain the best way to go about improving the services or programs expected to influence the outcome under scrutiny.

Although performance management systems can dig deeper into areas presenting troubling measures, program evaluation is a commonly used tool to uncover the "why" and "how" of program operations and effectiveness. Across government and nonprofit organizations, skilled program evaluators are highly valued for their ability to assess the effectiveness of public programs and diagnose areas for improvement. Here is an introduction to program evaluation, along with guidance on how an evaluation is conducted.

SKILLBOX: ESSENTIALS OF PROGRAM EVALUATION

Is the Program Working?

This is a common question asked by those working in public service. Whether trying to determine if a program is operating as planned or achieving its expected outcomes, a formal response to the question comes from conducting a program evaluation. Taking an entire course on program evaluation is a good idea, but the following provides an introduction to the subject and a step-by-step guide to conducting evaluation.

What Is Program Evaluation?

Program evaluation is a discrete study intended "to assess how well a program is working."[1] Program is a misnomer, though, since program evaluation is conducted broadly for any activity or policy with a defined purpose. The details of program evaluation vary dramatically based on the setting. A common distinction separates process evaluations from outcome evaluations.

Process evaluation has a procedural focus and determines whether a program is being implemented according to expectations. Outcome evaluation focuses on determining if the program is effective in accomplishing objectives.[2] An evaluation does not usually result in a clear finding that a program is a success or failure. Rather, a useful evaluation answers "how effective" a program is and "why," so that recommendations can be made to improve performance.

How Does Program Evaluation Differ from Performance Measurement?

Program evaluation supplements performance measurement. Whereas performance measurement regularly monitors an organization's status with regard to goals, program evaluation represents an effort to explain the mechanisms by which programs are succeeding or failing. Program evaluation informs program improvement and supports accountability by determining whether objectives are being met.[3]

Major Steps to Program Evaluation

The following steps represent the actions taken to design and conduct a program evaluation.

1) Determine the need for and focus of the program evaluation.
   - **Prioritize.** Evaluation and continuous improvement are always necessary, but there are never enough resources (time or money) to provide in-depth evaluations of all activities. Because a small number of pro-

grams typically consume a majority of an organization's resources, set priorities on the most important ones.

- **Plan.** Critical programs deserve to be evaluated on at least a semi-regular basis. Ideally, evaluation is built into the planning for new and existing programs. Rather than evaluation as an afterthought, providing authority and resources for systematic evaluation upfront helps guarantee that program assessment and improvement take place. Designing programs with an integrated evaluation component allows for more rigorous evaluation approaches and measures compared to after-the-fact designs. Including a plan for program evaluation in grant applications is common practice.
- **React.** In the absence of proactive planning, program evaluation is a reactive tool targeted for programs that appear to be performing below expectations or lack evidence of effectiveness. This reactive approach is especially common in organizations that are resource constrained.

2) Decide who will conduct the program evaluation.
- The **purpose** and **audience** for the program evaluation, along with the size of the organization, dictate who actually conducts the evaluation work.
- **In-house.** If the purpose of the evaluation is primarily for process improvement, the audience is internal, and the organization is large, then conducting the evaluation in-house is reasonable. The choice to perform an evaluation with internal resources does not mean that objectivity is sacrificed. Large organizations often house evaluation departments, which operate with some independence from programs. A best practice is to involve program managers in the design of the evaluation. To reduce the possibility of bias, staff who do not have a vested interest in the program are assigned to direct and conduct the evaluation.
- **External.** If the purpose of the evaluation is to determine program effectiveness or impact, the audience includes external parties like grant makers, taxpayers, or donors, and the organization lacks internal evaluation expertise, then contracting out for the evaluation makes sense. External evaluators are especially advisable when a program is faced with controversy or when the objectivity and independence of the evaluation team is paramount. The decision to use external evaluators may cost more but it will result in greater objectivity.

> ➤ An example: Mathematica Policy Research was hired to conduct the Evaluation of Adolescent Pregnancy Prevention Approaches from 2008 to 2016 for the U.S. Department of Health and Human Services, Office of Adolescent Health. The project included process evaluations of seven sites across the country that were implementing different pregnancy prevention approaches. The evaluators also completed sophisticated outcome evaluations to gauge program effectiveness for all but one site.[4]

- **Hybrid.** The reality is that program evaluation, even when conducted primarily by an external party, still requires extensive involvement by the organization itself. A respectful relationship between evaluators and those being evaluated starts with a clear articulation for the purpose of the evaluation. Open communication can limit turf wars and problems encountered during information gathering.

3) Define the program being evaluated and identify expected outcomes.
- **Clarify.** Make sure the program under consideration is well defined. What activities are part of the program? Make sure the program's goals are clear and agreed upon by stakeholders, both internal and external, as they form the basis for evaluation. In other words, how is the program expected to function? What is the program expected to accomplish?
- **Logic model.** Once the goals are clear, document how the program activities are theoretically connected to achieving those goals. This is done by developing a logic model that details how a program's inputs, such as personnel and other resources, generate program activities and outputs, such as individuals served or emergency responses. Program evaluation is especially concerned with how the outputs of a program translate into outcomes, such as improved health or economic development, which support the stated goals. The logic model serves as a visual guide to designing the evaluation and ensures that a coherent set of outcomes are identified.

4) Based on the evaluation objectives established by stakeholders, compile a set of questions to be answered.

5) Determine the evaluation technique or techniques to address each question.
- **Appropriateness.** Program evaluation is applied research, but the level of methodological sophistication depends on (1) the nature of the program under consideration, (2) the type of information that can be collected, and (3) the available resources dedicated to the evaluation, meaning time, money, and expertise. Regardless of resource lim-

itations, the chosen methods should be objective and appropriate to answer the evaluation questions.

- **Options.** Evaluators use a variety of methods and approaches tailored to their questions. The American Evaluation Association provides a partial list of program evaluation approaches including case studies, surveys, quasi-experimental designs, cost-benefit and cost-effectiveness analyses, and meta-analysis.[5] Other options include document analysis, participant observation, and the use of focus groups.

  - ➤ A distinction is often made between quantitative and qualitative evaluation approaches, but well-designed evaluations reflect both elements. For example, interviews with program managers and participants might provide a qualitative complement to statistical analysis of customer outcome data.

  - ➤ When possible, the evaluation approach should be as simple as possible. Simplicity makes the evaluation more transparent, understandable to stakeholders, and less costly.

- **Causation.** As with most social science research, it is a challenge to isolate the impact of a program from other confounding, and often external, explanations for changes in outcomes. The ability to draw causal conclusions is a distinction between outcome evaluation and the more rigorous impact evaluation. Random assignment of participants to a program is an ideal technique to eliminate bias from evaluation. Where possible, identify and use a comparison group to help isolate the program's effects on participants. An ideal comparison group, whether people, cities, or nonprofit organizations, is similar to the program participants in all ways except for exposure to the program or policy. Asserting causation is difficult, and evaluators must take into account sources of bias when adopting an evaluation approach in order to avoid misrepresenting outcomes.

6) Gather information and data to support the evaluation.

- **Collect.** Data collection is the most labor intense stage of an evaluation. It may include interviews of program managers, surveys of participants, or aggregating data from internal and external sources.

- **Privacy.** Be especially sensitive to data collection that involves personal information. All evaluators should be familiar with the subtle difference between promising anonymity and promising confidentiality to evaluation participants. With anonymity, a participant's survey response (or their program data) cannot be linked back to them even by the evaluators themselves. Confidentiality, on the other hand, exists when evaluators can identify the participant, but the evaluation provides analysis at only an aggregated level where no individuals are openly identified.

7) Review and assess the data to generate findings.
   - **Process.** Data are organized and processed for analysis. This will entail transcribing interviews or recoding administrative data.
   - Analyze. Applying the selected methodological approach to the collected data is the heart of the evaluation and is intended to answer the evaluation questions.

8) Document and publicize results to stakeholders.
   - **Review.** Although independence is an admirable quality of evaluation, the initial findings should be reviewed with key stakeholders before broad release to guarantee that the interpretation of the data and conclusions makes sense to those closest to the program.
   - **Summarize.** Program evaluation reports should include a concise summary of findings in an executive summary and a separate "results in brief" report. The use of charts and figures to effectively communicate the evaluation's findings is desirable.
   - **Document.** The final report should clearly connect the objectives of the evaluation, the goals of the program, the evaluation's results, and any recommendations based on the findings. The program evaluation process must be adequately detailed to support the credibility of the analysis. The evaluation should be released to all key stakeholders identified at the beginning of the process.

Hands-On Activities

1. Given the following scenario, use the steps given earlier to draft and propose an evaluation plan to your supervisors in the form of a two-page memo. Think through the types of data needed to answer your identified evaluation questions, how the data might be acquired, and how it would be analyzed. Be sure to recognize the main challenges of evaluating such a program.

An aging city experienced a number of highly visible instances of perceived police misconduct in recent years. The mayor launched a new program a year ago named "On the Beat," to highlight the return to more connected neighborhood policing. The program's goal is to improve police-citizen relations without sacrificing public safety. The program included the elimination of stop-and-frisk policies, the introduction of monthly public meetings held by police department representatives in each neighborhood, and the appointment of a volunteer citizen-police liaison by neighborhood.

2. Find a completed program evaluation online. A starting point could be the many national and local evaluation firms. Some national examples include Abt Associates, American Institutes for Research, Mathematica Policy Research, and Westat. Review the final evaluation report paying special attention to the adopted methodological approach. In a one-page memo directed to the organization for whom the evaluation was conducted, explain the goal of the evaluation, whether the evaluation adequately satisfied the objectives, summarize the findings, provide an overview of the evaluation design, detail any challenges experienced during the evaluation, and discuss whether any recommendations made are clearly connected to the findings.

Notes

1. United States Government Accountability Office (GAO). *Performance Measurement and Evaluation: Definitions and Relationships.* GAO-11-646SP: May 2, 2011. https://www.ise.gov/gao-11-646sp-performance-measurement-and-evaluation-definitions-and-relationships.

2. GAO, 2011.

3. Stephanie Shipman. "Program Evaluation: Definitions and Uses." GAO Applied Research and Methods Team. April 16, 2010. http://www.cesu.psu.edu/meetings_of_interest/Interagency_SS_roundtables/041610/TALK_INTRO_TO_EVAL.pdf.

4. U.S. Department of Health and Human Services, Office of Adolescent Health. "Evaluation of Adolescent Pregnancy Prevention Approaches (PPA)." December 8, 2016. http://www.hhs.gov/ash/oah/oah-initiatives/evaluation/federal-led-evaluation/ppa-study.html#.

5. American Evaluation Association. *An Evaluation Roadmap for a More Effective Government.* October 2013. www.eval.org/d/do/472. file:///C:/Users/Owner/Downloads/An%20Evaluation%20Roadmap%20for%20a%20More%20Effective%20Government%20-%2011-25-2013.pdf

For Additional Information

U.S. Government Accountability Office. *Designing Evaluations.* GAO-12-208G: January 2012. http://www.gao.gov/assets/590/588146.pdf.

NOTES

1. Robert D. Behn, "Why Measure Performance? Different Purposes Require Different Measures," *Public Administration Review* 63, no. 5 (2003): 586–606.

2. Harry S. Truman, "Lecture at Columbia University" (speech, New York, April 28, 1959).

3. Based on, U.S. Census Bureau, "Total March Full-Time and Part-Time Employment," *2015 Annual Survey of Public Employment and Payroll* (March 2015), http://factfinder.census.gov/bkmk/table/1.0/en/GEP/2015/00A4.

4. Lisa Lachlan-Haché and Marina Castro, *Proficiency or Growth? An Exploration of Two Approaches for Writing Student Learning Targets*, American Institutes for Research (April 2015), http://www.air.org/sites/default/files/Exploration-of-Two-Approaches-Student-Learning-Targets-April-2015.pdf.

5. Kate Zernike, "Testing for Grit? Schools Pushed on Social Skills," *New York Times* (March 1, 2016), A1.

6. Ibid.

7. Patrik Jonsson, "America's Biggest Teacher and Principal Cheating Scandal Unfolds in Atlanta," *Christian Science Monitor* (July 5, 2011), http://www.csmonitor.com/USA/Education/2011/0705/America-s-biggest-teacher-and-principal-cheating-scandal-unfolds-in-Atlanta.

8. U.S. Government Accountability Office, *Performance Measurement and Evaluation: Definitions and Relationships*, GAO-11-646SP (May 2, 2011), http://www.gao.gov/products/GAO-11-646SP.

9. Harry P. Hatry, *Transforming Performance Measurement for the 21st Century*, The Urban Institute (July 2014), http://www.urban.org/sites/default/files/publication/22826/413197-transforming-performance-measurement-for-the-21st-century.pdf.

10. The City of Portland, Oregon, City Budget Office, *Performance Management Manual: Transitioning the City from Measurement and Reporting to Management and Improving* (December 2014), 5, https://www.portlandoregon.gov/cbo/article/513721.

11. The City of Portland, Oregon, City Budget Office, *Performance Management Toolkit*, https://www.portlandoregon.gov/cbo/article/636524.

12. The City of Portland, Oregon, *The Portland Plan* (April 25, 2012), 12–13, http://www.portlandonline.com/portlandplan/index.cfm?c=58776&a=398384.

13. Hatry, *Transforming Performance*.

14. Adapted from Table 1 in Behn, "Why Measure."

15. U.S. Government Accountability Office, *Performance Measurement.*

16. National Academy of Public Administration, *Strategic Plan* (Spring 2005), http://www.napawash.org/wp-content/uploads/2005/05-14.pdf.

17. Kristen Norman-Major, "Balancing the Four Es; or Can We Achieve Equity for Social Equity in Public Administration?" *Journal of Public Affairs Education* 17, no. 2 (2011): 233–252; and, H.G. Frederickson, *Social Equity and Public Administration: Origins, Developments and Applications* (Armonk, NY: M.E. Sharpe, 2010).

18. Theodore H. Poister, Maria P. Aristigueta, and Jeremy L. Hall, *Managing and Measuring Performance in Public and Nonprofit Organizations: An Integrated Approach* (San Francisco, CA: Jossey-Bass, 2014), 57.

19. U.S. Government Accountability Office, *Performance Measurement.*

20. Poister, Aristigueta, and Hall, *Managing.*

21. Hatry, *Transforming Performance.*

22. Governmental Accounting and Standards Board (GASB), *GASB Summary of Concepts Statement No. 2: Service Efforts and Accomplishments Reporting* (April 1994), http://www.gasb.org/st/concepts/gconsum2.html.

23. Government Innovators Network, "Oregon Benchmarks," https://www.innovations.harvard.edu/oregon-benchmarks.

24. State of Minnesota, *Minnesota Milestones*, https://mn.gov/admin/assets/1992-minnesota-milestones-original-report_tcm36-220250.pdf.

25. Poister, Aristigueta, and Hall, *Managing*, 58.

26. Based on Figure 2.1 in Margaret C. Plantz, Martha Taylor Greenway, and Michael Hendricks, "Outcome Measurement: Showing Results in the Nonprofit Sector," *New Directions for Evaluation* 75 (1997): 19.

27. David N. Ammons, "Performance Measurement in Local Government," in *Accountability for Performance: Measurement and Monitoring in Local Government*, ed. David N. Ammons, (Washington, D.C.: International City/County Management Association, 1995), 20.

28. Ibid.

29. Hatry, *Transforming Performance.*

30. Ammons, "Performance Measurement."

31. Poister, Aristigueta, and Hall, *Managing.*

32. Ammons, "Performance Measurement."

33. Behn, "Why Measure."

34. The criteria for good performance measures come from Ammons, "Performance Measurement."

35. Barbara J. Cohn Berman, *Listening to the Public: Adding the Voices of the People to Government Performance Measurement and Reporting*, Fund for the City of New York, Center on Municipal Government Performance (2005), 6.

36. Robert L. Bland, *A Budgeting Guide for Local Government*, 2nd ed. (Washington, DC: International City County Management Association, 2007), 140.

37. The City of Portland, *The Portland Plan*, 105.

38. Ammons, "Performance Measurement," 21.

39. The City of Portland, *The Portland Plan*, 106.

40. Ibid., 12–13.

41. National Performance Management Advisory Commission, *A Performance Management Framework for State and Local Government: From Measurement and Reporting to Management and Improving* (Chicago, IL: National Performance Management Advisory Commission, 2010).

42. Behn, "Why Measure."

43. The City of Portland, *Performance Management Manual*, 4.

44. Ammons, "Performance Measurement," 5.

45. Poister, Aristigueta, and Hall, *Managing*, 88.

46. Philip G. Joyce, "The Obama Administration and PBB: Building on the Legacy of Federal Performance-Informed Budgeting?" *Public Administration Review* 71, no. 3 (2011): 356–367.

47. Patria De Lancer Julnes, "Performance Measurement: An Effective Tool for Government Accountability? The Debate Goes On," *Evaluation* 12, no. 2 (2006): 219–235.

48. Yi Lu and Katherine Willoughby, *Performance Budgeting in the States: An Assessment*, IBM Center for the Business of Government (2012), http://www.businessofgovernment.org/sites/default/files/Viewpoints_Lu.pdf.

49. Behn, "Why Measure."

50. The City of Portland, *The Portland Plan*, 106.

51. The City of Portland, City Budget Office, "Performance Management," last modified 2017, https://www.portlandoregon.gov/cbo/67122.

52. City of Portland, Portland Housing Bureau, "Mission, Vision & Values," last modified 2017, https://www.portlandoregon.gov/phb/article/426675.

53. City of Portland, City Budget Office, "Portland Housing Bureau," last modified 2017, https://www.portlandoregon.gov/cbo/article/523267.

54. City of Portland, Portland Fire & Rescue, "Mission, Vision & Principles," last modified 2017, https://www.portlandoregon.gov/fire/article/7737.

55. City of Portland, City Budget Office, "Portland Fire and Rescue," last modified 2017, https://www.portlandoregon.gov/cbo/article/523268.

56. The City of Portland, City Budget Office, "City Budget Office," last modified 2017, https://www.portlandoregon.gov/cbo/article/523301.

57. Gerhard Speckbacher, "The Economics of Performance Management in Nonprofit Organizations," *Nonprofit Management & Leadership* 13, no. 3 (Spring 2003): 267–268.

58. Margaret C. Plantz, Martha Taylor Greenway, and Michael Hendricks, "Outcome Measurement: Showing Results in the Nonprofit Sector," *New Directions for Evaluation* 75 (1997): 15–30.

59. National Performance Management Advisory Commission, *A Performance.*

60. The Nature Conservancy, "About Us," last modified 2017, https://www.nature.org/about-us/.

61. John Sawhill and David Williamson, "Measuring What Matters in Nonprofits," *McKinsey Quarterly* (May 2001), http://www.mckinsey.com/industries/social-sector/our-insights/measuring-what-matters-in-nonprofits.

62. Ibid.

63. Ibid.

64. Ibid.

65. Robert S. Kaplan, "Strategic Performance Measurement and Management in Nonprofit Organizations," *Nonprofit Management & Leadership* 11, no. 3 (2001): 354.

66. Hatry, *Transforming Performance.*

67. Poister, Aristigueta, and Hall, *Managing*, 25.

68. John Buntin, "25 Years Later, What Happened to 'Reinventing Government'?" *Governing* (September 2016), http://www.governing.com/topics/mgmt/gov-reinventing-government-book.html.

69. This summary is based on Poister, Aristigueta, and Hall, *Managing*. For a more detailed discussion of the academic literature, see Poister, Aristigueta, and Hall, *Managing*, 25–27.

70. National Performance Management Advisory Commission, *A Performance*, 39.

71. U.S. Government Accountability Office, *Performance Measurement*.

72. *Ask Me Why I Care: Public Service Stories*, video, directed by Mary R. Hamilton and Rita Paskowitz (Omaha, Nebraska: College of Public Affairs and Community Service), https://www.unomaha.edu/college-of-public-affairs-and-community-service/community-engagement/pss-phin-xaypangna.php.

ADDITIONAL RESOURCES

Behn, Robert D, "Why Measure Performance? Different Purposes Require Different Measures," *Public Administration Review* 63, no. 5 (2003): 586–606.

Forsythe, Dall, ed. 2001. *Quicker, Better, Cheaper? Managing Performance in American Government* (Albany, NY: Rockefeller Institute Press).

National Performance Management Advisory Commission. 2010. *A Performance Management Framework for State and Local Government: From Measurement and Reporting to Management and Improving* (Chicago, IL: National Performance Management Advisory Commission).

Poister, Theodore H., Maria P. Aristigueta, and Jeremy L. Hall. 2014. *Managing and Measuring Performance in Public and Nonprofit Organizations: An Integrated Approach* (San Francisco, CA: Jossey-Bass).

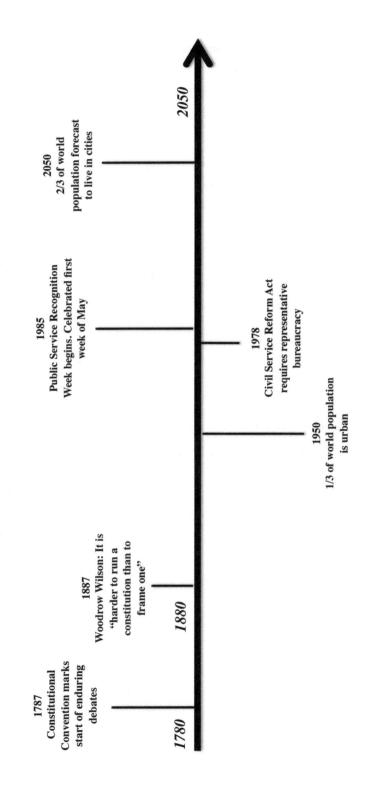

Chapter 15 Timeline: Public Services, Well Delivered

1787
Constitutional Convention marks start of enduring debates

1887
Woodrow Wilson: It is "harder to run a constitution than to frame one"

1985
Public Service Recognition Week begins. Celebrated first week of May

2050
2/3 of world population forecast to live in cities

1950
1/3 of world population is urban

1978
Civil Service Reform Act requires representative bureaucracy

1780

1880

2050

PUBLIC SERVICES, WELL DELIVERED

WHAT YOU WILL LEARN

The public service landscape

Jeffersonian vs. Hamiltonian ideals

Contemporary challenges

Being a public service professional

Adaptive nature of public administration

Skillbox: Is public service the right career for you?

Public scrutiny is a hallmark of good government but it can complicate administrative work. For example, as the air traffic control case demonstrates, there is an ironic twist when public entities strive to be learning organizations—to learn from their errors in order to improve performance. Because data are publicly available, learning from errors can send a misleading message.

AIR TRAFFIC CONTROL PERFORMANCE IMPROVEMENT PROJECT[1]

The Federal Aviation Administration's Air Traffic Organization (ATO) employs over 16,000 air traffic controllers who manage 7,000 aircraft flying over the United States at any given time. Their job is to make sure that planes maintain a safe distance between each other to minimize the risk of collision. When the safe distance is not maintained, an operational error occurs. These may be caused by pilot mistake, air traffic controller error, or outdated or inaccurate procedures.

In order to learn the cause of errors, the ATO needed air traffic controllers to report each mistake. As with many performance measures, it was a challenge to gather data because there was a disincentive for controllers to document mishaps. To do so would subject them to disciplinary action. Moreover, managers at the ATO facilities were reluctant to report because their raises and bonuses were tied to reducing, not increasing, the number of errors. To overcome the reluctance to report, the ATO implemented a voluntary reporting system that encouraged detailed and frequent reporting of safety hazards in exchange for immunity from punitive action.

Once the incentive system had been changed to reward error reporting rather than to punish it, the overall number of errors jumped from 1,895 in 2011 to 4,394 in 2012. This provided the data needed to identify causes and to implement preventive measures.

Error information was used to help the organization learn and improve procedures. Air traffic safety was made safer because of it, but there was an outcry from the public when they learned of the dramatic increase in errors. The increase was interpreted as real, rather than simply an increase in reporting, which was a nuance difficult to communicate in short press releases and brief news snippets.

The irony is that a successful process improvement procedure gave the appearance of process failure. While transparency contributes to better government in many ways, public scrutiny presents a challenge to the image of the organization. While business does not have to reveal information about internal operations, public organizations do. And news that communicates a negative message is difficult to counter.

Questions to Ponder

1. How does the human element contribute to, or hinder, performance measurement and process improvement strategies?
2. Because of the publicness of government operations, there was a public outcry when the errors increased from 1,895 incidents to 4,394 in one year. The truth is that errors had not increased. What had increased was the honest reporting of them. What skills are necessary in order to provide performance measurement data to the public in a way that is accurate and prevents misunderstanding?
3. Contrast the image of public organizations to that of business organizations. How does the presence or absence of transparency requirements affect the image of each?

ADVANCING THE PUBLIC INTEREST

A thriving democracy is the product of a combination of elements. These include a constitution that sets the rules, an engaged citizenry that subscribes to constitutional values, a vibrant business community that creates jobs and wealth, a dynamic non-profit sector that pushes, prods, and pulls in a way that gives voice to interests that are otherwise not loud enough to be heard in the halls of government, and a public service workforce that is committed to advancing quality of life through equitable, effective, well-managed programs.

By engaging in collective action, the pursuit of public purposes begins. For the biggest, thorniest problems, action by government is required. Working through elected representatives, ideas become policy inputs, which are shaped into legislation. The provisions of the legislation are then transformed into programs through administrative processes, and programs are built that produce outputs. While more is visible in the policy process than in the "black box" of administration, it is in the black box that legislation comes alive: rules are written that prescribe how policy shall be transformed into action, the program is implemented and managed, and services are delivered. Those who make a career of public service are the hands and feet of government, the catalysts that encourage citizens to get involved, and the service providers who deliver performance. Figure 15.1 shows the link between policy, administration, and programs.

> *"I can assure you, public service is a stimulating, proud and lively enterprise. It is not just a way of life, it is a way to live fully. Its greatest attraction is the sheer challenge of it—struggling to find solutions to the great issues of the day"*
>
> —Lee H. Hamilton

FIGURE 15.1 MAKING PROGRAMS HAPPEN

Running a constitution, as Woodrow Wilson[2] described it, involves engaging the public in problem identification, policy formation, program design and delivery, and evaluation of outcomes. Public service professionals are agents of stability and change in every community in the nation. By providing leadership and knowing how to bring strangers together to achieve a mission that no one can achieve by acting alone, savvy administrators make things happen. Hiring the right people with the right skills, equipping them with the resources necessary to get the job done, and communicating effectively, are benchmarks of good public service.

To execute the public will, tax policy is important because it influences economic growth, funds government, and provides the resources for public agencies to procure the goods and services they need from nonprofit service providers and private sector vendors. Performance management provides measures to monitor outcomes for both effectiveness and equity. Public integrity requires that government act in citizens' best interest. Administrative law sets the rules for how operations are to be conducted and how citizens can file appeals when they wish to grieve actions they believe to be unfair. These dimensions exist within a public service environment that requires transparency so that citizens can monitor government operations.

All dimensions of public service are interconnected in a system of governance built on enduring tensions. Debates that the founding fathers engaged in as they crafted the Constitution embody the opposing points of view of rural and urban constituencies, business and citizen interests, and trust versus suspicion of centralized power. These tensions continue to manifest themselves today in partisan debates during election campaigns and during policy debates in legislative bodies. Savvy administrators stay informed so that they can steer their programs around the rocks and shoals that arise because of these tensions.

THOMAS JEFFERSON VERSUS ALEXANDER HAMILTON

Public administration is contextual and is rooted in the political culture of each nation. The United States, for example, is the child of two different fathers: Thomas Jefferson and Alexander Hamilton. Their views mark opposite poles of the American experiment: rural versus urban; decentralized versus centralized; legislative versus executive; and trust in the masses versus reliance on the judgment of elites.[3] These competing perspectives are sewn into the Constitution and create a dynamic tension in the structure of government, in policy debates, and in the design of public programs.

The House of Representatives, with representation proportional to population, and the Senate, with equal representation for each state regardless of population, reflect the compromise between urban and rural states. The electoral college removes the selection of president from the voters such that a small group of political elites actually make the selection based on which candidate wins the majority of votes in each state. This gives the appearance of trust in the electorate while actually relying on the judgment of elites.

In other words, the Constitution reflects compromises that were necessary in order to secure ratification. The debates and tensions of 1787 repeat themselves in policy debates today. Who gets to decide: elites or the general public? Urban dwellers or farmers? It is up to elected leaders and career public executives to make the system work by balancing competing views and the tensions that exist. Effective administration that balances competing values legitimizes the political system and government itself.

The interplay of politics and administration shapes the approaches to environmental, social, and economic challenges now, just as it did when George Washington initiated the administrative machinery of the executive branch. Public management requires awareness of the tensions that are built into the system so that programs succeed despite the tension.

The irony of American government is that it works better in practice than in theory. This means that while the in-built tensions should stymie public performance and collaboration, Americans have found a way to make it work. It is not always pretty, and success is marked by fits and starts, but U.S. democracy has survived longer than any other nation with a similar structure. The obligation of those who plan, implement, and deliver public service is to embrace both fathers while keeping them in balance. It is through public administration that the nation's motto, *E Pluribus Unum* (from the many, one) is realized.

CHALLENGES

As Woodrow Wilson noted, running a constitution is easier said than done.[4] At its most basic, government in a capitalist democracy is the institution that is responsible for creating and sustaining markets, enforcing contracts, protecting private property, producing systems of education and infrastructure that allow commerce to flourish, providing for the defense of the nation, and maintaining a safety net of services for those who need them. Government serves as the referee and the balancing agent to keep markets fair and to advance opportunity. These functions come with challenges that change with the times. Contemporary issues revolve around social equity concerns, whether or not to outsource services, the intersectionality of public problems, questions of how to harness information technology for constructive purposes, and quandaries about how to ensure representativeness and how to encourage citizen engagement. These are discussed next.

Social Equity

While economic theory is used to forecast costs and benefits of public policies, there is a better way to assess equity. Talk of costs and savings populates conversations about public spending, but a cost for one set of stakeholders is a benefit to others and a waste to still others. In contrast, couching policy proposals in terms of who wins and who loses quickly brings the focus to fairness and how programs differentially affect stakeholders.[5]

Better policing, better schools, better public transit, affordable housing, and good jobs, go a long way to advancing social equity. The health insurance guarantees in the Affordable Care Act, Medicare, and Medicaid, provide additional examples, as do public education and school voucher programs. Even natural disasters provide a framework for identifying winners and losers, where flooding devastates the homes of the poorest and the construction industry benefits during the rebuilding process. Similar debates are appropriate for affordable housing programs and laws restricting where the homeless can sleep.

The "who wins, who loses" question also belongs in debates about federalism and which level of government is responsible for what. For example, the effects of Hurricane Katrina in 2005 continue to reverberate. While local governments want the federal government to stay out of their affairs, everyone wants the resources of the Federal Emergency Management Agency (FEMA) when devastation strikes. The benefit of FEMA resources comes with the price of the federal government dictating mitigation requirements such as stronger building codes and rules about building in floodplains. Such rules limit damage the next time disaster strikes but local governments and developers lose autonomy.

> "Equality is the soul of liberty; there is, in fact, no liberty without it."
>
> —Frances Wright

Another "who wins, who loses" question arises when examining whether government should provide services directly or contract with nonprofit or for-profit providers. Known as the "insourcing versus outsourcing" question, there are winners and losers for each decision.

Balancing Act: Outsourcing and Equity

Governments at all levels have relied on contracting to business and nonprofits to deliver some of their services. While some outsourcing has been used throughout American history, recent decades have seen the greatest amount for reasons that range from economics to available expertise to political ideology. There are several reasons why outsourcing runs the risk of widening the gap between the haves and the have-nots unless contracts are carefully crafted to prevent unintended consequences.[6] Problems can be accentuated when contracting to for-profit entities because, while nonprofits simply need their costs covered by the contract, for-profit enterprises have an obligation to return profits to investors. Increased user fees, decreased quality of services, and workers with low wages and no benefits add fuel to the fire of the "who wins, who loses" question.

New User Fees and Increased User Fees. Private contractors often charge new fees to users or increase existing fees. Steep price increases affect minimum wage earners more than high wage earners. Privatized services that are critical, such as water or transit or toll roads provide examples. For example, in Texas, a driver's failure to pay $7.50 in highway tolls ballooned to $157.50 due to administrative fees and other charges from a debt collections contractor. In Dillon Beach, California, residents' water bills from the investor-owned utility Cal Water were up to six times as expensive in 2013 when compared with nearby towns billed by the public water district. Residents on fixed incomes reported extreme water conservation efforts such as bathing only once a week and reusing water from the shower to wash dishes.[7] Although these examples are egregious, they represent the unintended consequences that must be guarded against.

Privatized Human Services. Because human service programs assist those who have little to no political power, they are favorites for outsourcing and disproportionately affect the poorest constituencies. Lacking political efficacy, their voices are not heard at city council meetings. Providers have little incentive to go the extra mile with the neediest clientele, which are often the most costly to serve. In California, for example, where a large percentage of foster care is privatized, children living in homes run by private agencies have been found to be one-third more likely to be victims of abuse than children in state supervised homes.[8] Another example is for-profit prisons. In 2016, the U.S. Department of Justice issued a scathing report of problems at privately-managed federal prisons.[9] Compared to government-managed prisons, the contract prisons had higher rates of assaults by inmates on other inmates as well as by inmates on staff, more contraband, more lockdowns, and more grievances. In fact, in 2016 the U.S. Department of Justice issued a directive to reduce reliance on private prisons, explaining that "They simply do not provide the same level of correctional services, programs, and resources; they do not save substantially on costs; and . . . they do not maintain the same level of safety and security."[10]

Decreased Wages and Absent Benefits. Privatization often results in lower wages to those who work for contractors, along with less job security, and fewer health and retirement benefits. This means that, in many cases, minimum-wage jobs result. This is a problem primarily in contracts with for-profit entities because nonprofits tend to have comparable salaries and benefits to the public sector.

Outsourcing works best when it is done thoughtfully to ensure that it does not result in a greater burden for those least able to afford services. When a contractor promises to do it "better, faster, cheaper," there are two questions to ask. First, what will the contractor spend less money on? Second, how much is being diverted to profit that is not being spent on service? Writing minimum levels of wages into the contract, setting limits on fees, and insisting on transparency and accountability are steps that help to overcome the equity concerns that arise with outsourcing.

Intersectionality of Problems

Although public programs are categorized into silos, such as housing, family and children services, transportation, health care, job training, mental health services, and more, those in need usually live lives where one problem compounds another. The intersection of multiple problems complicates the remedy. Combining service delivery in a way that is conducive to collaboration among providers as well as accessible to those in need remains a challenge but holds promise for those who need access.

A service innovation that is being tried in some places is the office of Ombud. This is a position whose mission is to help people find the services they need. Used on many college campuses as a place where everyone can go to seek assistance, it is being tried in cities and states with the goal of making it easier for residents to navigate that which, for many, is the too-complicated world of public services.

Another approach to the intersectionality of problems is a one-stop shop where multiple providers are officed together. Rather than being sent across town from one agency to another, those seeking services can access most of what they need at one location. In this way, bureaucratic silos are changing to collaborations between agencies, with networks that link service providers, whether governmental or contracted.

Information Age Government

The development of the Internet, a successful project of the U.S. Department of Defense, has transformed the globe by enabling instantaneous communication. It affects governance in multiple ways: the rapidity of news and social media that relay events minute by minute, the capacity for government to connect to citizens and vice versa, and the proliferation and transfer of large datasets that have the potential to provide information and insights. Simultaneously, the ease of communication has introduced another set of challenges. Hysteria fanned by fake news and breaches of personal information by cybercrime are foremost among them.

News Media

There are three categories that capture the connection between media and governance: public relations, agenda building, and the effect of media logic.[11] Public relations refers to how public information officers use media to communicate to the public and inform them of government actions. Agenda building refers to the use of media to broadcast public problems and policy ideas with the goal of shaping opinion in a way that will affect legislation and program design. The third category is the effect of media logic. Stories that have drama and sensationalism will grab headlines and get greater readership than stories of routine events. And stories that are captured by photographs and videos will grab more attention than text only. For better or for worse, public information officers must frame their organization's stories so that each one reflects well on the agency.

The case of Air Traffic Controllers and error rates provides an example of media logic. The essence of the story from the agency's perspective was that they were using data to improve performance and make air travel safer. But the story that made headlines was that air traffic control errors had skyrocketed. Another example of framing happens when a child under the care of a child welfare agency is killed by an abusive family. The story will be sensationalized in a way that reflects badly on the agency's work and on the caseworkers, regardless of the realities that resulted in the death. Administrators are responsible not only for making stories but for managing stories.

Social Media

The capacity for public entities to host websites and Facebook sites allows them to communicate instantaneously, posting documents and emergency notices as well as inviting feedback. And the capacity to monitor sites in order to track public opinion is a benefit. At the same time, the firestorm that erupts based on an inaccurate post is hard to extinguish. In sum, social media is an administrative asset that can also be a burden to manage.

In an era of fake news, Facebook, Twitter, Google, and search engines are trying to determine how to respond to postings that are not true. Misinformation travels as fast as accurate information. For government, balancing freedom of the press against sanctions for propagating news hoaxes presents a perplexing problem. This amplifies the fact that the potential of information technology is staggering, just as are the administrative burdens and benefits.

Information and communication technology is a primary driver of the collaborative and networked services that dot the landscape of public service and of intersectoral collaboration. It enables greater collaboration by removing the need for top-down hierarchies and it decentralizes power. But the downside is that the decentralization makes it difficult to determine who is accountable for what, and whether postings are legitimate.

Big Data

The proliferation of data has brought decision makers to the point that they are drowning in information while starving for certainty. There are massive quantities of data produced by and about people and their interactions. From body camera videos to Internet clicks, to user-generated content, to sensor networks, to traditional datasets, the challenge is about making information usable so that decision makers take advantage of it.

Translating data into usable information is an important skill.[12] Conclusions provided by statisticians, complete with caveats and confidence intervals, cause many to look with suspicion on data that contradict personal experience. Unless findings from large data sets are easily interpretable, decision makers will rely on "ordinary" knowledge based on experience and common sense. To be heard, policy analysts must speak in the language of the policy maker, whether that is easy-to-interpret graphical presentations or clear-cut answers to policy questions. Big data present opportunity for better decision making, but that will not happen unless effective translation occurs.

Procurement

Procurement is at the heart of most that government does, and some jurisdictions manage this better than others.[13] Those at the cutting edge spend money responsibly while also pursuing innovations in contract management and promoting goals of diversity and inclusiveness. Rather than a process of simply following rules, procurement is taking its place alongside information management and human capital management to become a strategic vehicle of government action. By centering procurement as a means for aiding economic development and engaging diverse constituencies, the pursuit of public goals extends beyond internal operations to collaboration with the entire community, such that residents, interest groups, and businesses see government as "us" rather than "them."

The theory of market dynamics is that competition drives down prices. For this reason, it is in government's interest when vendors compete to sell to it. For many vendors, however, the sell-to-government market is not a level playing field. In large jurisdictions, each agency has different rules, such as varying dollar thresholds for different types of bids, different definitions for what constitutes an emergency procurement that is eligible to skip the regular bidding process, and different regulations and forms. When procurement systems require too much staff time and too many delays to make sales profit-worthy, small vendors leave the market because selling to government is too labor-intensive and too time-consuming. This, in turn, favors larger vendors. As competition declines, prices the government is charged increase. Standardized purchasing processes are one solution that the city of Chicago has found fruitful because it makes it easier for businesses to understand requirements and to comply with them.[14] Similar procurement reform is going on in other cities and counties around the nation with the goal of making it simpler for vendors to sell to government and for government to collaborate with more stakeholders.

Unintended Consequences

Unintended consequences of well-intended actions are every manager's curse. Although unintended consequences can follow any action, whether of a business or a government entity, it is more likely to happen in government because public organizations live longer and their actions last longer. Thus, there is more time for consequences to develop. In contrast, the average lifespan of the best businesses—those listed on the S&P 500 index of leading U.S. companies—is only fifteen years.[15]

An example of unintended consequences is found in urban arbors. Many cities planted trees years ago for environmental and aesthetic reasons. They beautify sidewalks and they help the environment. Now those trees have matured and, in some cases, their roots have damaged sewer lines or destroyed sidewalks.[16] Moreover, during financially lean years, cities such as New York shifted budget allocations and reduced tree pruning as a cost-cutting measure. And starting around 2006, the city noticed a steady rise in the number of tree-related legal claims. The city had to double its tree pruning budget to see the number of claims decline. Examples such as these—planting trees in urban environments—show how a good idea can still produce expensive problems down the road. Challenges never cease. Managing them effectively is the answer.

Transparency

Transparency is foremost among the differences between government and business. Government is the instrument for achieving public purposes. For this reason, citizens have a right to know what it does and how it does it. This means that public executives must budget for the nonmission-based work of keeping the public informed about operations, responding to requests for information, and following formal administrative procedures for setting rules, hearing grievances, and issuing public notices.

To follow procedures designed to ensure that government actions are transparent requires that delays are built into processes. This presents challenges when speedy action is sought but protocol requires step-by-step procedures to be followed. The delay is a necessary price to pay in order for citizens to have confidence in government, but it complicates the work for administrators. It is a "comes with" for public service.

Representativeness

For many purposes—inclusion of all viewpoints, embracing diversity, achieving consensus across groups, enriching decision-making processes, and communicating a sense of ownership—it is essential that those making decisions and delivering programs resemble the people who are affected by the decisions and who receive the services. More durable decisions and processes arise when diverse points of view are taken into account. Representative bureaucracy is the term used for this.

The Civil Service Reform Act of 1978 codifies the requirement for the federal workforce to mirror the American people. This is an important value at the state and local levels of government, as well. From a management perspective, this means that jobs must be publicly posted in enough different outlets that jobseekers have an opportunity to learn about the job and how to apply. It is important that decision making reflects the views of all and that service delivery is performed by people who are representative of those being served.

Citizen Engagement

Democracies thrive when citizens trust their government. They falter when citizens lack confidence that government action is in their best interest. This is why it is imperative that citizens engage with government and see it as a constructive vehicle for achieving public goals. This is also why governments engage with citizens to ensure that public actions are consistent with public opinion.

While all organizations have politics within them, public administration *is* politics. Although election campaigns are the most apparent window of opportunity for policy preferences to be expressed, voting behavior is less like real engagement and more like drive-by participation. Because campaign rhetoric exaggerates claims of what can be achieved, expectations are more often dashed than achieved after campaigns have concluded and this risks cynicism. It falls to the executive function of government to provide a steady hand and steer the nation's efforts down a middle path even in the most turbulent times, resisting the whipsaw effect of partisan ideology. It is the nation's institutions that maintain the character of the republic. And it is public service professionals who maintain the institutions.

Change occurs with gradual—not radical—bends to the right or left. This is because administrative machinery is designed to adhere to processes prescribed by law. Having said this, innovation happens and often it is as a result of collaboration with public service-minded nonprofits. They provide a way for citizens to band together, innovate, and persuade government to embrace their initiative. The growing popularity of farm-to-market fresh food provides an example.

The locally grown food initiatives around the nation demonstrate the resilience of citizens using government to help them achieve public-minded goals. Whether organized into nonprofit advocacy groups, vocal neighborhood associations, or created by public agencies reaching out to their clientele, citizen engagement means government working hand-in-glove with citizen groups to adjust to current needs and circumstances.

LOCALLY GROWN FOOD[17]

Driven by a desire to increase urban farming and connect it to local markets, nonprofits and local governments are taking the lead and states are following by modifying laws that advance the effort. In the past, food policy was left to the federal government and long supply chains with mass produced food predominated. Now farm-to-school fresh food programs, blighted urban neighborhoods being replaced by gardens, and food stamps being accepted in local farmers markets, are examples of innovations that help to make locally produced fresh food more accessible. From Baltimore to Chicago to Denver, small changes pave the way for significant change.

This is an example of how nonprofits with a mission to encourage farm-to-table programs and producing locally-grown crops have embraced food safety and environmental concerns. They have convinced local governments to cooperate by enabling urban gardens and farmers markets. In turn, cities have pressed their state legislatures to change laws in order to enable production and sale of fresh produce.

Running a Constitution with Integrity

From engaging citizens in the initiation, design, and redesign of services, to ensuring transparency in all facets of policy deliberation and program operations, to ensuring social equity, to balancing the Jeffersonian and Hamiltonian visions for America, to managing information, people, and money, the challenge of public administration is to make the values of the Constitution come to life. This happens episodically with election management in every precinct on election day; daily with ensuring safe water and air, and access to education and health care; and, during crises, with emergency response, law enforcement, and national defense. And it extends from a pinpoint focus on neighborhoods, to the national level and beyond. The scope is vast and the career opportunities are immense.

Lead, Solve, Change

Being an effective public service professional requires leadership, which means taking the initiative to get things done. It also requires accepting responsibility for decisions, behavior, and results while acting with personal integrity. Effective leaders grow in the job by improving their knowledge and skills and collaborating with those who have differing points of view. Solving problems is part of the job, as the case of the bike share program demonstrates.

BIKE SHARE PROGRAMS[18]

Changing outmoded procedures and replacing them with systems that work better is part of the job. Change requires the courage to leave tried and true procedures behind and take the risk that a new system will make things work better. Bike share programs in cities across the country are examples of an innovation that addresses transit needs differently than in the past.

Bike share schemes are a low cost transit program that encourages bicycling. They allow commuters and tourists to borrow a bike from point "A" and drop it off at point "B." These programs offer affordable access to bicycles for short-distance trips as an alternative to buses and cars, thereby reducing traffic snarls, noise, and air pollution. In many cities, smartphone apps show stations with available bikes and open docks, which enable several riders to use the same bike in the same day.

Although bike sharing was implemented in Europe and Asia decades ago, it began in the United States more recently, starting in Denver, Washington, DC, and Minneapolis. Estimates are that there are now close to 100 cities that offer the program, or plan to offer it. Like all public transportation systems, bike share programs do not always make a profit or cover all their costs, but partnerships between city governments and nonprofit bicycling groups have worked to spread the cost and keep them going.

LOOKING FORWARD

For public executives, success lies in creating order out of chaos. But much of what complicates the workday in public service is neither predictable nor controllable. Natural disasters are the easy part, relatively speaking. Although terribly destructive, the aftermath of hurricanes, floods, earthquakes, wildfires, and tornadoes can be mitigated by planning. Emergency preparedness occurs at all levels of government and helps to lessen the impact. On the other hand, macrodynamics—in the form of large forces—bring elusive swings in public priorities that affect public service at all levels and occur in ways that defy preparation.

Large Forces[19]

Like a tsunami, large forces resulting from a mix of cultural, economic, political, technological, and philosophical change, well up around the world and take hold of public opinion in ways that are unstoppable. Governments are required to adjust to them, lest populist revolt happens. For example, in recent years tension between isolationism and globalism is arousing significant debate.

As pressures for globalization rise, contrary pressures for localism mount. Internationally, this irony is captured as tribalism versus nationalism and nationalism versus globalism. The inward desire for neighborhoods and communities to create their own identity, to determine their own fate, to self-govern, and to build their own economies, parallels the outward focus on globalization. Balancing the tension between parochial interests and global pressures is a high-wire act between international interests and nation states; federal versus state versus local governments; and neighborhoods versus cities versus counties.

As much as air travel and the Internet have made it easy to navigate around the world and to communicate with anyone anywhere, Great Britain's vote to exit the European Union (EU) is emblematic of a large force. The EU is credited with keeping the peace in Western Europe for over fifty years, and Great Britain has been a beneficiary of this, just as other member states have. But faced with increasing waves of refugees, and the threat of global terrorism, Great Britain's government was stunned by an uprising of voters who preferred to retreat from collaboration and return to a time when each European nation was independent. Debates during the vitriolic Clinton versus Trump presidential campaign with regard to international trade and immigration present a similar refrain. The result was a political campaign that hardened attitudes and made it more difficult to find common ground.

The twenty-first century has been punctuated by the 9/11 attacks, global financial crises, terrorism, climate change, advances in information technology and information breaches, and a change in identity politics from the predominance of male/female and white/other to a host of racial, ethnic, and gender identities. Moreover, a rapid shift is happening in the world's population. In 1950, one-third of all people lived in urban areas. It is now projected that by 2050, almost two-thirds of the world's population will live in cities.[20] Urbanization increases demand for jobs, housing, energy, clean water, food, transportation infrastructure, and human services. As the population grows denser, air pollution, water shortages, and environmental hazards increase.[21] Creative solutions are called for and it will be public service professionals who will make them happen.

These macrodynamics affect public opinion and the way the populace rank priorities. The forces manifest themselves in the political sphere in debates about job protections, tariffs, and immigration policy. In the public management sphere, they play out in a proliferation of programs designed to attack a panoply of challenges. Meanwhile, reliance on the rule of law serves as a rudder, maintaining a predictability to public action by adherence to procedures, functioning with transparency, and using precedents as guideposts. When discontinuities occur, they are more often five-degree rather than ninety-degree turns. The constitutional forces and tensions that mold the way that public administration functions are persistent and enduring and protective of the American system.

The Adaptive Nature of Public Administration

Public administration is an adaptive field that adjusts to forces, whether large or small. It must do this in order to express and enact the public will. Hierarchy (top-down authority) is morphing into heterarchy (multiple power centers working collaboratively) as information technology speeds communication. The instruments through which administrative ends are met—organizations—adapt also. Rather than a unitary public agency controlling each policy area, the pursuit of public goals is atomized across a mix of governmental and nonprofit agencies, and to a lesser extent, for-profit social enterprise pursuits, whether the subject is housing, defense, preservation of endangered species, or health care.

Cities that can no longer afford to provide all of the services demanded by their residents are forming regional procurement, taxing, and service districts to achieve economies of scale. Cash-strapped states are forming regional cooperative pacts to provide benefits to residents without having to directly deliver them. An example is the case of regional higher education compacts that allow students to attend another state's university but pay in-state tuition when pursuing a major that is not provided in their own state.

The problems that come to government are complex administrative problems that require sophisticated judgments on questions whose answers are elusive. The question for administrators is how to organize in multiplex settings, where power is shared, boundaries are hazy, accountability is ambiguous, goals are conflicting, and resources are never sufficient to do all that is needed. As interconnections inexorably spread, it will become difficult to define where government begins and where it ends. Yet govern we must, within a constitutional framework, and in a context that marries politics, management, and the law. Amid all of this, justice and social equity remain on center stage, for it always falls on government, the biggest of the actors in governance, to be responsible for leveling the playing field and ensuring that everyone is treated fairly.

Governance is a complexly fragmented pursuit, relying on the interactions of government, business, and nonprofits. The actions of administrators are rooted in a constitution that is built to engender and resolve conflict simultaneously. To this end, public administration is a resilient, dynamic pursuit, designed to advance rather than impede individual rights, business interests, and the initiatives of public service-minded nonprofits.

It is hard to overstate the importance of public administration and its complexity. Public administration has the awesome responsibility to breathe life and meaning into democracy. Its language speaks of networked alliances, global interconnections, and a field without bounds. Its enduring elements are citizen engagement, accountability, and regime values, just as they have always been.

BEING A PUBLIC SERVICE PROFESSIONAL

The human side of public service is where things get real. Talent, leadership, commitment, communications, work culture, acumen, innovation, and strategy combine to produce public action. The case of Rachel Lyon, a park supervisor in Independence, Kansas demonstrates the intrinsic rewards of public service.

Ask Me Why I Care: Rachel Lyon, Park Supervisor, Park Department, City of Independence, Kansas[22]

"When your job is to create beauty and happy occasions, well, there aren't many things better than that."—Rachel Lyon

As a Certified Master Gardener, Rachel works for the Park Department in Independence, Kansas. She describes her work as creative problem-solving and considers herself lucky to be someone who is excited to go to work every day. As a park supervisor, her work at Riverside Park allows her to satisfy her technical curiosity because she is charged with maintaining the structural and mechanical integrity of several historic buildings as well as a vintage carousel and miniature train. Combined with the design and maintenance of all the park's planting areas, she is gratified that her work serves as a backdrop to countless memories for the city's residents who use the park for weddings, family gatherings, and entertainment. Access Rachel's story at http://www.unomaha.edu/college-of-public-affairs-and-community-service/community-engagement/pss-rachel-lyon.php.

SUMMARY

A career as a public service professional can take many shapes, focus on national, state, regional, or neighborhood issues, involve all sectors of the economy, and provide a lifetime of rewards. Whether one is interested in human services, transit, tax policy, energy, housing, law enforcement, defense, parks and recreation, data analysis, emergency management, public works, or environmental quality, there are always challenges to be met. Whether one prefers to work in large organizations with proud traditions that extend over decades, or small grassroots nonprofits, there are settings that provide the opportunity to get involved and make a difference. Regardless of the context, they all require stewardship that is effective and ethical.

As the air traffic control case demonstrates, the public service landscape can be rocky. Transparency brings with it public scrutiny. The United States was founded on the notion that the public must be informed about government action. If it is true that bank robbers rob banks because that is where the money is, it is equally true that the media report on government because that is where the information is. Plain and simple, government is different from business, not just in the unimportant ways, but in the important ways as well.

Those who make a career of public service have the noble task of exercising discretion in a way that affirms and advances democracy. Whether functioning as a pragmatist, a facilitator, an expert professional, or an agent of the people, the work of public administrators legitimizes and sculpts the pursuit of public purposes. And administration, itself, is the human process through which society expresses and realizes its values.

KEY TERMS

Citizen engagement – citizen participation, inspired by a sense of duty and/or efficacy, and fostered by an open, democratic government.

Hamiltonian ideals – emphasizes the superiority of urban society, centralized government, importance of the executive function, and trust in the elites.

Insourcing – regarding public services, this refers to direct provision of services by the government.

Jeffersonian ideals – emphasizes the superiority of rural society, decentralized government, importance of the legislative function, and trust in the masses.

Learning organization – organizations that adapt to changes by identifying problems, self-correcting, monitoring, and making subsequent adjustments, as needed.

Outsourcing – regarding public services, this refers to contracting with private or non-profit providers for production of services.

Social equity – refers to the presence of fairness, justice, and equitable outcomes in public administration.

Stewardship – responsible planning and management of duties or resources.

DISCUSSION QUESTIONS

1. Explain what this sentence means: "The actions of administrators are rooted in a constitution that is built to engender and resolve conflict simultaneously." What implications does this have for the work of administrators?

2. List and describe three differences between government and business.

3. Think of a challenge that complicates the work of public administrators. Is this a new challenge, or a long-standing one?

4. Think of a story in the news or a time in your own work when an unintended consequence resulted from a policy. How did administrators adapt to manage such a challenge?

5. Find a local public service provider online. What types of services do they provide to individuals? Where are they provided? Are these services all located in one building and accessible by public transit?

BUILD YOUR SKILLS

The range of career choices within public service is extraordinary, as are choices of location and setting. Whether in grassroots nonprofit organizations, large state and federal agencies, town halls or special districts, public health clinics, or policy analysis think tanks, the choices are many. Here is guidance as you consider your career path.

SKILLBOX: IS PUBLIC SERVICE THE RIGHT CAREER FOR YOU?

It is as important to know what you do NOT want to do as it is to know what you DO want to do. Here is information to help determine if public service is right for you.

Challenging Work/Abundant Opportunities

Public service takes place amid a web of relationships that respond to public needs. Whether in government, in public-service-minded nonprofits, or in businesses that contract with government, careers range from vital daily services, to tackling wicked problems that defy quick solutions, to preparing for and responding to emergencies.

Public service professionals tackle challenging problems that define the public agenda and call for talented individuals. Whether working to provide housing for the homeless, ensuring water quality, defending the nation, providing safe and enjoyable parks and recreation areas, addressing public health threats, ensuring safe roads and bridges, helping former prisoners adjust to life in society again, or fighting terrorism, the career opportunities are many. Implementing information technologies that better connect citizens to their governments, improving readiness and responses to natural disasters, expanding services to meet the needs of changing populations without raising taxes—all of these contexts require leadership, human resource management, financial management, and information management.

Job opportunities exist in every city, every state, and around the globe. These opportunities offer challenging work, good pay and benefits, and many choices of where to live and work.

Public Service Is NOT for Those Who

- Measure success by profit margins
- Think that government is the same as business
- Need to have total control over policy direction
- Like to work unilaterally

Public Service IS for Those Who

- Value working with people of different backgrounds
- Enjoy the stimulation of diverse points of view
- Want meaningful work that makes a difference in people's lives
- Enjoy working collaboratively with multiple entities and interests
- Find meaning in tackling large problems

Public Service Requires

- Commitment
- Competence
- Integrity

Where to Find Information about Public Service Jobs

Go to this link to find information about career resources and jobs in public service: http://publicservicecareers.org/.

Go to this link to access the *Occupational Outlook Handbook* and browse descriptions for all occupations: https://www.bls.gov/ooh/.

Hands-On Activity

1. Assume you are thinking about starting your career as a budget analyst. Browse the *Occupational Outlook Handbook* (https://www.bls.gov/ooh/) and find information about the job's average salary, similar occupations, work environment, and occupational outlook.

2. Conduct a self-assessment. Visit the U.S. Department of Labor's O*NET website at https://www.mynextmove.org/explore/ip to assess your occupational interests. After generating your profile, scroll through jobs listed on the O*NET site (https://www.onetonline.org/) to find jobs that are highly rated on your profile and learn more about them. Many will be found in public service organizations.

NOTES

1. Russell W. Mills, *Incident Reporting Systems: Lessons from the Federal Aviation Administration's Air Traffic Organization*, IBM Center for The Business of Government (2013), http://www.businessofgovernment.org/sites/default/files/Incident%20Reporting%20Systems.pdf.

2. Woodrow Wilson, "The Study of Administration," *Political Science Quarterly* 2, no. 2 (June 1887): 197–222.

3. James Keene, "American Governance's Fundamental Tension," *Governing* (September 29, 2016), http://www.governing.com/gov-institute/voices-col-jefferson-hamilton-fundamental-tension-american-governance.html?utm_term=American%20Governance%26rsquo%3Bs%20Fundamental%20Tension&utm_campaign=How%20Unregulated%20Dark%20Money%20Is%20Reshaping%20State%20Politics&utm_content=email&utm_source=Act-On+Software&utm_medium=email.

4. Wilson, "The Study."

5. Alan Ehrenhalt, "Winner and Loser Economics," *Governing* (November 2015), 14–15.

6. Liz Farmer, "Privatization May Be Worsening Inequality: A New Study Suggests Out-

sourcing Government Services Can Disproportionately Impact Low-Income Users' Finances, Health and Safety," *Governing* (October 13, 2016), http://www.governing.com/topics/finance/gov-privatization-inequality.html; and In the Public Interest, *Report: How Privatization Increases Inequality* (September 28, 2016), https://www.inthepublicinterest.org/report-how-privatization-increases-inequality-2/.

7. In the Public Interest, Report.

8. Ibid.

9. U.S. Department of Justice, Office of the Inspector General, *Review of the Federal Bureau of Prisons' Monitoring of Contract Prisons* (August 2016), https://oig.justice.gov/reports/2016/e1606.pdf.

10. U.S. Department of Justice 2016, Office of the Deputy Attorney General, memorandum, August 18, 2016, "Reducing Our Use of Private Prisons," https://assets.documentcloud.org/documents/3027877/Justice-Department-memo-announcing-announcing.pdf.

11. Erik H. Klijn, Mark van Twist, Martijn van der Steen, and Stephen Jeffares, "Public Managers, Media Influence, and Governance: Three Research Traditions Empirically Explored," *Administration & Society* 48, no. 9 (2016): 1036–1058.

12. Donald F. Kettl, "Making Data Speak: Lessons for Using Numbers for Solving Public Policy Puzzles," *Governance* 29, no. 4 (2016): 573–579.

13. Liz Farmer, "Purchase Power," *Governing* (March, 2016), 47–52.

14. Katherine Barrett and Richard Greene, "Better Buyers," *Governing* (August 2016), 58–59.

15. Kim Gittleson, "Can a Company Live Forever?" *BBC News New York* (January 19, 2012), http://www.bbc.com/news/business-16611040.

16. Mike Maciag, "From Police Shootings to Playground Injuries, Lawsuits Drain Cities' Budgets," *Governing* (November, 2016), http://www.governing.com/topics/finance/gov-government-lawsuits-settlements.html?utm_term=From%20Police%20Shootings%20to%20Playground%20Injuries%2C%20Lawsuits%20Drain%20Cities%27%20Budgets&utm_campaign=From%20Police%20Shootings%20to%20Playground%20Injuries%2C%20Lawsuits%20Drain%20Cities%27%20Budgets&utm_content=email&utm_source=Act-On+Software&utm_medium=email.

17. Sarah Breitenbach, "Beyond Farmers Markets: Cities, States Champion Locally Grown Food," *Stateline* (November 7, 2016), http://www.pewtrusts.org/en/research-and-analysis/blogs/stateline/2016/11/07/beyond-farmers-markets-cities-states-champion-locally-grown-food.

18. Rebecca Beitsch, "Despite Popularity, Bike Share Programs Often Need Subsidies," *Stateline* (March 24, 2016), http://www.pewtrusts.org/en/research-and-analysis/blogs/stateline/2016/03/24/despite-popularity-bike-share-programs-often-need-subsidies.

19. Alisdair Roberts, *Large Forces: What's Missing in Public Administration* (self-published,

2014).

20. United Nations, Department of Economic and Social Affairs, Population Division, *World Urbanization Prospects: The 2014 Revision*, Highlights (2014), https://esa.un.org/unpd/wup/Publications/Files/WUP2014-Highlights.pdf.

21. John McIlwain, *Housing in America: The Next Decade* (Washington, DC: Urban Land Institute, 2010), http://uli.org/report/housing-in-america-the-next-decade/.

22. *Ask Me Why I Care: Public Service Stories* video, directed by Mary R. Hamilton and Rita Paskowitz (Omaha, Nebraska: College of Public Affairs and Community Service), http://www.unomaha.edu/college-of-public-affairs-and-community-service/community-engagement/pss-rachel-lyon.php.

ADDITIONAL RESOURCES

Guy, Mary E. and Marilyn M. Rubin. 2015. *Public Administration Evolving: From Foundations to the Future.* New York, NY: Routledge.

APPENDIX

U.S. CONSTITUTION AND AMENDMENTS[1]

Written in 1787, ratified in 1788, and in effect since 1789, the U.S. Constitution is the world's longest surviving written charter of government. It has remained in force for over two centuries and successfully separates and balances governmental powers in a way that (a) safeguards majority rule while protecting minority rights, (b) preserves individual liberty and equality, and (c) sets the boundaries for federal versus state powers. More a concise statement of national principles than a detailed plan of operation, interpretation of the Constitution continually evolves to meet the changing needs of a society profoundly different from the eighteenth-century world of its creation. The Constitution has been amended twenty-seven times, most recently in 1992. The first ten amendments are called the Bill of Rights.

PREAMBLE

We the People of the United States, in Order to form a more perfect Union, establish Justice, insure domestic Tranquility, provide for the common defence, promote the general Welfare, and secure the Blessings of Liberty to ourselves and our Posterity, do ordain and establish this Constitution for the United States of America.

ARTICLE I

Section 1

All legislative Powers herein granted shall be vested in a Congress of the United States, which shall consist of a Senate and House of Representatives.

Section 2

The House of Representatives shall be composed of Members chosen every second Year by the People of the several States, and the Electors in each State shall have the Qualifications requisite for Electors of the most numerous Branch of the State Legislature.

No Person shall be a Representative who shall not have attained to the Age of twenty five Years, and been seven Years a Citizen of the United States, and who shall not, when elected, be an Inhabitant of that State in which he shall be chosen.

Representatives and direct Taxes shall be apportioned among the several States which may be included within this Union, according to their respective Numbers, which shall be determined by adding to the whole Number of free Persons, including those bound to Service for a Term of Years, and excluding Indians not taxed, three fifths of all other Persons. The actual Enumeration shall be made within three Years after the first Meeting of the Congress of the United States, and within every subsequent Term of ten Years, in such Manner as they shall by Law direct. The Number of Representatives shall not exceed one for every thirty Thousand, but each State shall have at Least one Representative; and until such enumeration shall be made, the State of New Hampshire shall be entitled to chuse three, Massachusetts eight, Rhode-Island and Providence Plantations one, Connecticut five, New York six, New Jersey four, Pennsylvania eight, Delaware one, Maryland six, Virginia ten, North Carolina five, South Carolina five, and Georgia three.

When vacancies happen in the Representation from any State, the Executive Authority thereof shall issue Writs of Election to fill such Vacancies.

The House of Representatives shall chuse their Speaker and other Officers; and shall have the sole Power of Impeachment.

Section 3

The Senate of the United States shall be composed of two Senators from each State, chosen by the Legislature thereof, for six Years; and each Senator shall have one Vote.

Immediately after they shall be assembled in Consequence of the first Election, they shall be divided as equally as may be into three Classes. The Seats of the Senators of the first Class shall be vacated at the Expiration of the second Year, of the second Class at the Expiration of the fourth Year, and of the third Class at the Expiration of the sixth Year, so that one third may be chosen every second Year; and if Vacancies happen by Resignation, or otherwise, during the Recess of the Legislature of any State, the Executive thereof may make temporary Appointments until the next Meeting of the Legislature, which shall then fill such Vacancies.

No Person shall be a Senator who shall not have attained to the Age of thirty Years, and been nine Years a Citizen of the United States, and who shall not, when elected, be an Inhabitant of that State for which he shall be chosen.

The Vice President of the United States shall be President of the Senate, but shall have no Vote, unless they be equally divided.

The Senate shall chuse their other Officers, and also a President pro tempore, in the Absence of the Vice President, or when he shall exercise the Office of President of the United States.

The Senate shall have the sole Power to try all Impeachments. When sitting for that Purpose, they shall be on Oath or Affirmation. When the President of the United States is tried, the Chief Justice shall preside: And no Person shall be convicted without the Concurrence of two thirds of the Members present.

Judgment in Cases of Impeachment shall not extend further than to removal from Office, and disqualification to hold and enjoy any Office of honor, Trust or Profit under the United States: but the Party convicted shall nevertheless be liable and subject to Indictment, Trial, Judgment and Punishment, according to Law.

Section 4

The Times, Places and Manner of holding Elections for Senators and Representatives, shall be prescribed in each State by the Legislature thereof; but the Congress may at any time by Law make or alter such Regulations, except as to the Places of chusing Senators.

The Congress shall assemble at least once in every Year, and such Meeting shall be on the first Monday in December, unless they shall by Law appoint a different Day.

Section 5

Each House shall be the Judge of the Elections, Returns and Qualifications of its own Members, and a Majority of each shall constitute a Quorum to do Business; but a smaller Number may adjourn from day to day, and may be authorized to compel the Attendance of absent Members, in such Manner, and under such Penalties as each House may provide.

Each House may determine the Rules of its Proceedings, punish its Members for disorderly Behaviour, and, with the Concurrence of two thirds, expel a Member.

Each House shall keep a Journal of its Proceedings, and from time to time publish the same, excepting such Parts as may in their Judgment require Secrecy; and the Yeas and Nays of the Members of either House on any question shall, at the Desire of one fifth of those Present, be entered on the Journal.

Neither House, during the Session of Congress, shall, without the Consent of the other, adjourn for more than three days, nor to any other Place than that in which the two Houses shall be sitting.

Section 6

The Senators and Representatives shall receive a Compensation for their Services, to be ascertained by Law, and paid out of the Treasury of the United States. They shall in all Cases, except Treason, Felony and Breach of the Peace, be privileged from Arrest during their Attendance at the Session of their respective Houses, and in going to and returning from the same; and for any Speech or Debate in either House, they shall not be questioned in any other Place.

No Senator or Representative shall, during the Time for which he was elected, be appointed to any civil Office under the Authority of the United States, which shall have been created, or the Emoluments whereof shall have been encreased during such time; and no Person holding any Office under the United States, shall be a Member of either House during his Continuance in Office.

Section 7

All Bills for raising Revenue shall originate in the House of Representatives; but the Senate may propose or concur with Amendments as on other Bills.

Every Bill which shall have passed the House of Representatives and the Senate, shall, before it become a Law, be presented to the President of the United States: If he approve he shall sign it, but if not he shall return it, with his Objections to that House in which it shall have originated, who shall enter the Objections at large on their Journal, and proceed to reconsider it. If after such Reconsideration two thirds of that House shall agree to pass the Bill, it shall be sent, together with the Objections, to the other House, by which it shall likewise be reconsidered, and if approved by two thirds of that House, it shall become a Law. But in all such Cases the Votes of both Houses shall be determined by Yeas and Nays, and the Names of the Persons voting for and against the Bill shall be entered on the Journal of each House respectively. If any Bill shall not be returned by the President within ten Days (Sundays excepted) after it shall have been presented to him, the Same shall be a Law, in like Manner as if he had signed it, unless the Congress by their Adjournment prevent its Return, in which Case it shall not be a Law.

Every Order, Resolution, or Vote to which the Concurrence of the Senate and House of Representatives may be necessary (except on a question of Adjournment) shall be presented to the President of the United States; and before the Same shall take Effect, shall be approved by him, or being disapproved by him, shall be repassed by two thirds of the Senate and House of Representatives, according to the Rules and Limitations prescribed in the Case of a Bill.

Section 8

The Congress shall have Power To lay and collect Taxes, Duties, Imposts and Excises, to pay the Debts and provide for the common Defence and general Welfare of the

United States; but all Duties, Imposts and Excises shall be uniform throughout the United States;

To borrow Money on the credit of the United States;

To regulate Commerce with foreign Nations, and among the several States, and with the Indian Tribes;

To establish an uniform Rule of Naturalization, and uniform Laws on the subject of Bankruptcies throughout the United States;

To coin Money, regulate the Value thereof, and of foreign Coin, and fix the Standard of Weights and Measures;

To provide for the Punishment of counterfeiting the Securities and current Coin of the United States;

To establish Post Offices and post Roads;

To promote the Progress of Science and useful Arts, by securing for limited Times to Authors and Inventors the exclusive Right to their respective Writings and Discoveries;

To constitute Tribunals inferior to the supreme Court;

To define and punish Piracies and Felonies committed on the high Seas, and Offences against the Law of Nations;

To declare War, grant Letters of Marque and Reprisal, and make Rules concerning Captures on Land and Water;

To raise and support Armies, but no Appropriation of Money to that Use shall be for a longer Term than two Years;

To provide and maintain a Navy;

To make Rules for the Government and Regulation of the land and naval Forces;

To provide for calling forth the Militia to execute the Laws of the Union, suppress Insurrections and repel Invasions;

To provide for organizing, arming, and disciplining, the Militia, and for governing such Part of them as may be employed in the Service of the United States, reserving to the States respectively, the Appointment of the Officers, and the Authority of training the Militia according to the discipline prescribed by Congress;

To exercise exclusive Legislation in all Cases whatsoever, over such District (not exceeding ten Miles square) as may, by Cession of particular States, and the Acceptance of Congress, become the Seat of the Government of the United States, and to exercise like Authority over all Places purchased by the Consent of the Legislature of the State in which the Same shall be, for the Erection of Forts, Magazines, Arsenals, dock-Yards, and other needful Buildings;—And

To make all Laws which shall be necessary and proper for carrying into Execution the foregoing Powers, and all other Powers vested by this Constitution in the Government of the United States, or in any Department or Officer thereof.

Section 9

The Migration or Importation of such Persons as any of the States now existing shall think proper to admit, shall not be prohibited by the Congress prior to the Year one thousand eight hundred and eight, but a Tax or duty may be imposed on such Importation, not exceeding ten dollars for each Person.

The Privilege of the Writ of Habeas Corpus shall not be suspended, unless when in Cases of Rebellion or Invasion the public Safety may require it.

No Bill of Attainder or ex post facto Law shall be passed.

No Capitation, or other direct, Tax shall be laid, unless in Proportion to the Census or enumeration herein before directed to be taken.

No Tax or Duty shall be laid on Articles exported from any State.

No Preference shall be given by any Regulation of Commerce or Revenue to the Ports of one State over those of another; nor shall Vessels bound to, or from, one State, be obliged to enter, clear, or pay Duties in another.

No Money shall be drawn from the Treasury, but in Consequence of Appropriations made by Law; and a regular Statement and Account of the Receipts and Expenditures of all public Money shall be published from time to time.

No Title of Nobility shall be granted by the United States: And no Person holding any Office of Profit or Trust under them, shall, without the Consent of the Congress, accept of any present, Emolument, Office, or Title, of any kind whatever, from any King, Prince, or foreign State.

Section 10

No State shall enter into any Treaty, Alliance, or Confederation; grant Letters of Marque and Reprisal; coin Money; emit Bills of Credit; make any Thing but gold and silver Coin a Tender in Payment of Debts; pass any Bill of Attainder, ex post facto Law, or Law impairing the Obligation of Contracts, or grant any Title of Nobility.

No State shall, without the Consent of the Congress, lay any Imposts or Duties on Imports or Exports, except what may be absolutely necessary for executing its inspection Laws: and the net Produce of all Duties and Imposts, laid by any State on Imports or Exports, shall be for the Use of the Treasury of the United States; and all such Laws shall be subject to the Revision and Control of the Congress.

No State shall, without the Consent of Congress, lay any Duty of Tonnage, keep Troops, or Ships of War in time of Peace, enter into any Agreement or Compact with another State, or with a foreign Power, or engage in War, unless actually invaded, or in such imminent Danger as will not admit of delay.

ARTICLE II

Section 1

The executive Power shall be vested in a President of the United States of America. He shall hold his Office during the Term of four Years, and, together with the Vice President, chosen for the same Term, be elected, as follows:

Each State shall appoint, in such Manner as the Legislature thereof may direct, a Number of Electors, equal to the whole Number of Senators and Representatives to which the State may be entitled in the Congress: but no Senator or Representative, or Person holding an Office of Trust or Profit under the United States, shall be appointed an Elector.

The Electors shall meet in their respective States, and vote by Ballot for two Persons, of whom one at least shall not be an Inhabitant of the same State with themselves. And they shall make a List of all the Persons voted for, and of the Number of Votes for each; which List they shall sign and certify, and transmit sealed to the Seat of the Government of the United States, directed to the President of the Senate. The President of the Senate shall, in the Presence of the Senate and House of Representatives, open all the Certificates, and the Votes shall then be counted. The Person having the greatest Number of Votes shall be the President, if such Number be a Majority of the whole Number of Electors appointed; and if there be more than one who have such Majority, and have an equal Number of Votes, then the House of Representatives shall immediately chuse by Ballot one of them for President; and if no Person have a Majority, then from the five highest on the List the said House shall in like Manner chuse the President. But in chusing the President, the Votes shall be taken by States, the Representatives from each State having one Vote; a quorum for this Purpose shall consist of a Member or Members from two thirds of the States, and a Majority of all the States shall be necessary to a Choice. In every Case, after the Choice of the President, the Person having the greatest Number of Votes of the Electors shall be the Vice President. But if there should remain two or more who have equal Votes, the Senate shall chuse from them by Ballot the Vice-President.

The Congress may determine the Time of chusing the Electors, and the Day on which they shall give their Votes; which Day shall be the same throughout the United States.

No Person except a natural born Citizen, or a Citizen of the United States, at the time of the Adoption of this Constitution, shall be eligible to the Office of President; neither shall any person be eligible to that Office who shall not have attained to the Age of thirty five Years, and been fourteen Years a Resident within the United States.

In Case of the Removal of the President from Office, or of his Death, Resignation, or Inability to discharge the Powers and Duties of the said Office, the Same shall devolve on the Vice President, and the Congress may by Law provide for the Case of

Removal, Death, Resignation or Inability, both of the President and Vice President, declaring what Officer shall then act as President, and such Officer shall act accordingly, until the Disability be removed, or a President shall be elected.

The President shall, at stated Times, receive for his Services, a Compensation, which shall neither be encreased nor diminished during the Period for which he shall have been elected, and he shall not receive within that Period any other Emolument from the United States, or any of them.

Before he enter on the Execution of his Office, he shall take the following Oath or Affirmation:—"I do solemnly swear (or affirm) that I will faithfully execute the Office of President of the United States, and will to the best of my Ability, preserve, protect and defend the Constitution of the United States."

Section 2

The President shall be Commander in Chief of the Army and Navy of the United States, and of the Militia of the several States, when called into the actual Service of the United States; he may require the Opinion, in writing, of the principal Officer in each of the executive Departments, upon any Subject relating to the Duties of their respective Offices, and he shall have Power to Grant Reprieves and Pardons for Offences against the United States, except in Cases of Impeachment.

He shall have Power, by and with the Advice and Consent of the Senate, to make Treaties, provided two thirds of the Senators present concur; and he shall nominate, and by and with the Advice and Consent of the Senate, shall appoint Ambassadors, other public Ministers and Consuls, Judges of the supreme Court, and all other Officers of the United States, whose Appointments are not herein otherwise provided for, and which shall be established by Law: but the Congress may by Law vest the Appointment of such inferior Officers, as they think proper, in the President alone, in the Courts of Law, or in the Heads of Departments.

The President shall have Power to fill up all Vacancies that may happen during the Recess of the Senate, by granting Commissions which shall expire at the End of their next Session.

Section 3

He shall from time to time give to the Congress Information on the State of the Union, and recommend to their Consideration such Measures as he shall judge necessary and expedient; he may, on extraordinary Occasions, convene both Houses, or either of them, and in Case of Disagreement between them, with Respect to the Time of Adjournment, he may adjourn them to such Time as he shall think proper; he shall receive Ambassadors and other public Ministers; he shall take Care that the Laws be faithfully executed, and shall Commission all the Officers of the United States.

Section 4

The President, Vice President and all Civil Officers of the United States, shall be removed from Office on Impeachment for, and Conviction of, Treason, Bribery, or other high Crimes and Misdemeanors.

ARTICLE III

Section 1

The judicial Power of the United States, shall be vested in one supreme Court, and in such inferior Courts as the Congress may from time to time ordain and establish. The Judges, both of the supreme and inferior Courts, shall hold their Offices during good Behaviour, and shall, at stated Times, receive for their Services, a Compensation, which shall not be diminished during their Continuance in Office.

Section 2

The judicial Power shall extend to all Cases, in Law and Equity, arising under this Constitution, the Laws of the United States, and Treaties made, or which shall be made, under their Authority;—to all Cases affecting Ambassadors, other public ministers and Consuls;—to all Cases of admiralty and maritime Jurisdiction;—to Controversies to which the United States shall be a Party;—to Controversies between two or more States;—between a State and Citizens of another State;—between Citizens of different States;—between Citizens of the same State claiming Lands under Grants of different States, and between a State, or the Citizens thereof, and foreign States, Citizens or Subjects.

In all Cases affecting Ambassadors, other public Ministers and Consuls, and those in which a State shall be Party, the supreme Court shall have original Jurisdiction. In all the other Cases before mentioned, the supreme Court shall have appellate Jurisdiction, both as to Law and Fact, with such Exceptions, and under such Regulations as the Congress shall make.

The Trial of all Crimes, except in Cases of Impeachment, shall be by Jury; and such Trial shall be held in the State where the said Crimes shall have been committed; but when not committed within any State, the Trial shall be at such Place or Places as the Congress may by Law have directed.

Section 3

Treason against the United States, shall consist only in levying War against them, or in adhering to their Enemies, giving them Aid and Comfort. No Person shall be convicted of Treason unless on the Testimony of two Witnesses to the same overt Act, or on Confession in open Court.

The Congress shall have Power to declare the Punishment of Treason, but no Attainder of Treason shall work Corruption of Blood, or Forfeiture except during the Life of the Person attainted.

ARTICLE IV

Section 1

Full Faith and Credit shall be given in each State to the public Acts, Records, and judicial Proceedings of every other State. And the Congress may by general Laws prescribe the Manner in which such Acts, Records and Proceedings shall be proved, and the Effect thereof.

Section 2

The Citizens of each State shall be entitled to all Privileges and Immunities of Citizens in the several States.

A Person charged in any State with Treason, Felony, or other Crime, who shall flee from Justice, and be found in another State, shall on Demand of the executive Authority of the State from which he fled, be delivered up, to be removed to the State having Jurisdiction of the Crime.

No Person held to Service or Labour in one State, under the Laws thereof, escaping into another, shall, in Consequence of any Law or Regulation therein, be discharged from such Service or Labour, but shall be delivered up on Claim of the Party to whom such Service or Labour may be due.

Section 3

New States may be admitted by the Congress into this Union; but no new State shall be formed or erected within the Jurisdiction of any other State; nor any State be formed by the Junction of two or more States, or Parts of States, without the Consent of the Legislatures of the States concerned as well as of the Congress.

The Congress shall have Power to dispose of and make all needful Rules and Regulations respecting the Territory or other Property belonging to the United States; and nothing in this Constitution shall be so construed as to Prejudice any Claims of the United States, or of any particular State.

Section 4

The United States shall guarantee to every State in this Union a Republican Form of Government, and shall protect each of them against Invasion; and on Application of the Legislature, or of the Executive (when the Legislature cannot be convened) against domestic Violence.

ARTICLE V

The Congress, whenever two thirds of both Houses shall deem it necessary, shall propose Amendments to this Constitution, or, on the Application of the Legislatures of two thirds of the several States, shall call a Convention for proposing Amendments, which, in either Case, shall be valid to all Intents and Purposes, as Part of this Constitution, when ratified by the Legislatures of three fourths of the several States, or by Conventions in three fourths thereof, as the one or the other Mode of Ratification may be proposed by the Congress; Provided that no Amendment which may be made prior to the Year One thousand eight hundred and eight shall in any Manner affect the first and fourth Clauses in the Ninth Section of the first Article; and that no State, without its Consent, shall be deprived of its equal Suffrage in the Senate.

ARTICLE VI

All Debts contracted and Engagements entered into, before the Adoption of this Constitution, shall be as valid against the United States under this Constitution, as under the Confederation.

This Constitution, and the Laws of the United States which shall be made in Pursuance thereof; and all Treaties made, or which shall be made, under the Authority of the United States, shall be the supreme Law of the Land; and the Judges in every State shall be bound thereby, any Thing in the Constitution or Laws of any state to the Contrary notwithstanding.

The Senators and Representatives before mentioned, and the Members of the several State Legislatures, and all executive and judicial Officers, both of the United States and of the several States, shall be bound by Oath or Affirmation, to support this Constitution; but no religious Test shall ever be required as a Qualification to any Office or public Trust under the United States.

ARTICLE VII

The Ratification of the Conventions of nine States, shall be sufficient for the Establishment of this Constitution between the States so ratifying the Same.

Done in Convention by the Unanimous Consent of the States present the Seventeenth Day of September in the Year of our Lord one thousand seven hundred and Eighty seven and of the Independence of the United States of America the Twelfth In Witness whereof We have hereunto subscribed our Names,

G. Washington, Presidt and deputy from Virginia

[signors]

AMENDMENT I (1791)

Congress shall make no law respecting an establishment of religion, or prohibiting the free exercise thereof; or abridging the freedom of speech, or of the press; or the right of the people peaceably to assemble, and to petition the Government for a redress of grievances.

AMENDMENT II (1791)

A well regulated Militia, being necessary to the security of a free State, the right of the people to keep and bear Arms, shall not be infringed.

AMENDMENT III (1791)

No Soldier shall, in time of peace be quartered in any house, without the consent of the Owner, nor in time of war, but in a manner to be prescribed by law.

AMENDMENT IV (1791)

The right of the people to be secure in their persons, houses, papers, and effects, against unreasonable searches and seizures, shall not be violated, and no Warrants shall issue, but upon probable cause, supported by Oath or affirmation, and particularly describing the place to be searched, and the persons or things to be seized.

AMENDMENT V (1791)

No person shall be held to answer for a capital, or otherwise infamous crime, unless on a presentment or indictment of a Grand Jury, except in cases arising in the land or naval forces, or in the Militia, when in actual service in time of War or public danger; nor shall any person be subject for the same offence to be twice put in jeopardy of life or limb; nor shall be compelled in any criminal case to be a witness against himself, nor be deprived of life, liberty, or property, without due process of law; nor shall private property be taken for public use, without just compensation.

AMENDMENT VI (1791)

In all criminal prosecutions, the accused shall enjoy the right to a speedy and public trial, by an impartial jury of the State and district wherein the crime shall have been committed, which district shall have been previously ascertained by law, and to be informed of the nature and cause of the accusation; to be confronted with the witnesses against him; to have compulsory process for obtaining witnesses in his favor, and to have the Assistance of Counsel for his defence.

AMENDMENT VII (1791)

In Suits at common law, where the value in controversy shall exceed twenty dollars, the right of trial by jury shall be preserved, and no fact tried by a jury, shall be otherwise re-examined in any Court of the United States, than according to the rules of the common law.

AMENDMENT VIII (1791)

Excessive bail shall not be required, nor excessive fines imposed, nor cruel and unusual punishments inflicted.

AMENDMENT IX (1791)

The enumeration in the Constitution, of certain rights, shall not be construed to deny or disparage others retained by the people.

AMENDMENT X (1791)

The powers not delegated to the United States by the Constitution, nor prohibited by it to the States, are reserved to the States respectively, or to the people.

AMENDMENT XI (1795)

(note: Article III, section 2 was modified by this amendment.)

The Judicial power of the United States shall not be construed to extend to any suit in law or equity, commenced or prosecuted against one of the United States by Citizens of another State, or by Citizens or Subjects of any Foreign State.

AMENDMENT XII (1804)

(note: A portion of Article II, section 1 was superseded by this amendment).

The Electors shall meet in their respective states and vote by ballot for President and Vice-President, one of whom, at least, shall not be an inhabitant of the same state with themselves; they shall name in their ballots the person voted for as President, and in distinct ballots the person voted for as Vice-President, and they shall make distinct lists of all persons voted for as President, and of all persons voted for as Vice-President, and of the number of votes for each, which lists they shall sign and certify, and transmit sealed to the seat of the government of the United States, directed to the President of the Senate;—The President of the Senate shall, in the presence of the Senate and House of Representatives, open all the certificates and the votes shall then be counted;—The person having the greatest Number of votes for President, shall be the President, if such number be a majority of the whole number of Electors appointed; and if no person have such majority, then from the persons having the highest numbers not exceeding three on the list of those voted for as President, the House of Representatives shall choose immediately, by ballot, the President. But in choosing the President, the votes shall be taken by states, the representation from each state having one vote; a quorum for this purpose shall consist of a member or members from two-thirds of the states, and a majority of all the states shall be necessary to a choice. And if the House of Representatives shall not choose a President whenever the right of choice shall devolve upon them, before the fourth day of March next following, then the Vice-President shall act as President, as in the case of the death or other constitutional disability of the President (note: superseded by section 3 of the 20th amendment.)—The person having the greatest number of votes as Vice-President, shall be the Vice-President, if such number be a majority of the whole number of Electors appointed, and if no person have a majority, then from the two highest numbers on the list, the Senate shall choose the Vice-President; a quorum for the purpose shall consist of two-thirds of the whole number of Senators, and a majority of the whole number shall be necessary to a choice. But no person constitutionally ineligible to the office of President shall be eligible to that of Vice-President of the United States.

AMENDMENT XIII (1865)

(note: a portion of Article IV, section 2 was superseded by this amendment)

Section 1. Neither slavery nor involuntary servitude, except as a punishment for crime whereof the party shall have been duly convicted, shall exist within the United States, or any place subject to their jurisdiction.

Section 2. Congress shall have power to enforce this article by appropriate legislation.

AMENDMENT XIV (1868)

(note: Article I, section 2 was modified by section 2 of this amendment)

Section 1. All persons born or naturalized in the United States and subject to the jurisdiction thereof, are citizens of the United States and of the State wherein they reside. No State shall make or enforce any law which shall abridge the privileges or immunities of citizens of the United States; nor shall any State deprive any person of life, liberty, or property, without due process of law; nor deny to any person within its jurisdiction the equal protection of the laws.

Section 2. Representatives shall be apportioned among the several States according to their respective numbers, counting the whole number of persons in each State, excluding Indians not taxed. But when the right to vote at any election for the choice of electors for President and Vice President of the United States, Representatives in Congress, the Executive and Judicial officers of a State, or the members of the Legislature thereof, is denied to any of the male inhabitants of such State, being twenty-one years of age (changed by section 1 of the 26th amendment), and citizens of the United States, or in any way abridged, except for participation in rebellion, or other crime, the basis of representation therein shall be reduced in the proportion which the number of such male citizens shall bear to the whole number of male citizens twenty-one years of age in such State.

Section 3. No person shall be a Senator or Representative in Congress, or elector of President and Vice President, or hold any office, civil or military, under the United States, or under any State, who, having previously taken an oath, as a member of Congress, or as an officer of the United States, or as a member of any State legislature, or as an executive or judicial officer of any State, to support the Constitution of the United States, shall have engaged in insurrection or rebellion against the same, or given aid or comfort to the enemies thereof. But Congress may by a vote of two-thirds of each House, remove such disability.

Section 4. The validity of the public debt of the United States, authorized by law, including debts incurred for payment of pensions and bounties for services in suppressing insurrection or rebellion, shall not be questioned. But neither the United States nor any State shall assume or pay any debt or obligation incurred in aid of insurrection or rebellion against the United States, or any claim for the loss or emancipation of any slave; but all such debts, obligations and claims shall be held illegal and void.

Section 5. The Congress shall have power to enforce, by appropriate legislation, the provisions of this article.

AMENDMENT XV (1870)

Section 1. The right of citizens of the United States to vote shall not be denied or abridged by the United States or by any State on account of race, color, or previous condition of servitude.

Section 2. The Congress shall have power to enforce this article by appropriate legislation.

AMENDMENT XVI (1913)

(note: Article I, section 9 was modified by this amendment)

The Congress shall have power to lay and collect taxes on incomes, from whatever source derived, without apportionment among the several States, and without regard to any census or enumeration.

AMENDMENT XVII (1913)

(note: Article I, section 3 was modified by this amendment)

The Senate of the United States shall be composed of two Senators from each State, elected by the people thereof, for six years; and each Senator shall have one vote. The electors in each State shall have the qualifications requisite for electors of the most numerous branch of the State legislatures.

When vacancies happen in the representation of any State in the Senate, the executive authority of such State shall issue writs of election to fill such vacancies: Provided, That the legislature of any State may empower the executive thereof to make temporary appointments until the people fill the vacancies by election as the legislature may direct.

This amendment shall not be so construed as to affect the election or term of any Senator chosen before it becomes valid as part of the Constitution.

AMENDMENT XVIII (1919)

(note: this amendment was repealed by amendment 21)

Section 1. After one year from the ratification of this article the manufacture, sale, or transportation of intoxicating liquors within, the importation thereof into, or the exportation thereof from the United States and all territory subject to the jurisdiction thereof for beverage purposes is hereby prohibited.

Section 2. The Congress and the several States shall have concurrent power to enforce this article by appropriate legislation.

Section 3. This article shall be inoperative unless it shall have been ratified as an amendment to the Constitution by the legislatures of the several States, as provided in the Constitution, within seven years from the date of the submission hereof to the States by the Congress.

AMENDMENT XIX (1920)

The right of citizens of the United States to vote shall not be denied or abridged by the United States or by any State on account of sex.

Congress shall have power to enforce this article by appropriate legislation.

AMENDMENT XX (1933)

(note: Article I, section 4 was modified by section 2 of this amendment)

Section 1. The terms of the President and Vice President shall end at noon on the 20th day of January, and the terms of Senators and Representatives at noon on the 3d day of January, of the years in which such terms would have ended if this article had not been ratified; and the terms of their successors shall then begin.

Section 2. The Congress shall assemble at least once in every year, and such meeting shall begin at noon on the 3d day of January, unless they shall by law appoint a different day.

Section 3. If, at the time fixed for the beginning of the term of the President, the President elect shall have died, the Vice President elect shall become President. If a President shall not have been chosen before the time fixed for the beginning of his term, or if the President elect shall have failed to qualify, then the Vice President elect shall act as President until a President shall have qualified; and the Congress may by law provide for the case wherein neither a President elect nor a Vice President elect shall have qualified, declaring who shall then act as President, or the manner in which one who is to act shall be selected, and such person shall act accordingly until a President or Vice President shall have qualified.

Section 4. The Congress may by law provide for the case of the death of any of the persons from whom the House of Representatives may choose a President whenever the right of choice shall have devolved upon them, and for the case of the death of any of the persons from whom the Senate may choose a Vice President whenever the right of choice shall have devolved upon them.

Section 5. Sections 1 and 2 shall take effect on the 15th day of October following the ratification of this article.

Section 6. This article shall be inoperative unless it shall have been ratified as an amendment to the Constitution by the legislatures of three-fourths of the several States within seven years from the date of its submission.

AMENDMENT XXI (1933)

Section 1. The eighteenth article of amendment to the Constitution of the United States is hereby repealed.

Section 2. The transportation or importation into any State, Territory, or possession of the United States for delivery or use therein of intoxicating liquors, in violation of the laws thereof, is hereby prohibited.

Section 3. This article shall be inoperative unless it shall have been ratified as an amendment to the Constitution by conventions in the several States, as provided in the Constitution, within seven years from the date of the submission hereof to the States by the Congress.

AMENDMENT XXII (1951)

Section 1. No person shall be elected to the office of the President more than twice, and no person who has held the office of President, or acted as President, for more than two years of a term to which some other person was elected President shall be elected to the office of the President more than once. But this Article shall not apply to any person holding the office of President, when this Article was proposed by the Congress, and shall not prevent any person who may be holding the office of President, or acting as President, during the term within which this Article becomes operative from holding the office of President or acting as President during the remainder of such term.

Section 2. This article shall be inoperative unless it shall have been ratified as an amendment to the Constitution by the legislatures of three-fourths of the several States within seven years from the date of its submission to the States by the Congress.

AMENDMENT XXIII (1961)

Section 1. The District constituting the seat of Government of the United States shall appoint in such manner as the Congress may direct:

A number of electors of President and Vice President equal to the whole number of Senators and Representatives in Congress to which the District would be entitled if it were a State, but in no event more than the least populous State; they shall be in addition to those appointed by the States, but they shall be considered, for the purposes of the election of President and Vice President, to be electors appointed by a State; and they shall meet in the District and perform such duties as provided by the twelfth article of amendment.

Section 2. The Congress shall have power to enforce this article by appropriate legislation.

AMENDMENT XXIV (1964)

Section 1. The right of citizens of the United States to vote in any primary or other election for President or Vice President for electors for President or Vice President, or for Senator or Representative in Congress, shall not be denied or abridged by the United States or any State by reason of failure to pay any poll tax or other tax.

Section 2. The Congress shall have power to enforce this article by appropriate legislation.

AMENDMENT XXV (1967)

(note: Article II, section 1 was affected by this amendment)

Section 1. In case of the removal of the President from office or of his death or resignation, the Vice President shall become President.

Section 2. Whenever there is a vacancy in the office of the Vice President, the President shall nominate a Vice President who shall take office upon confirmation by a majority vote of both Houses of Congress.

Section 3. Whenever the President transmits to the President pro tempore of the Senate and the Speaker of the House of Representatives his written declaration that he is unable to discharge the powers and duties of his office, and until he transmits to them a written declaration to the contrary, such powers and duties shall be discharged by the Vice President as Acting President.

Section 4. Whenever the Vice President and a majority of either the principal officers of the executive departments or of such other body as Congress may by law provide, transmit to the President pro tempore of the Senate and the Speaker of the House of Representatives their written declaration that the President is unable to discharge the powers and duties of his office, the Vice President shall immediately assume the powers and duties of the office as Acting President.

Thereafter, when the President transmits to the President pro tempore of the Senate and the Speaker of the House of Representatives his written declaration that no inability exists, he shall resume the powers and duties of his office unless the Vice President and a majority of either the principal officers of the executive department or of such other body as Congress may by law provide, transmit within four days to the President pro tempore of the Senate and the Speaker of the House of Representatives their written declaration that the President is unable to discharge the powers and duties of his office. Thereupon Congress shall decide the issue, assembling within forty-eight hours for that purpose if not in session. If the Congress, within twenty-one days after receipt of the latter written declaration, or, if Congress is not in session, within twenty-one days after Congress is required to assemble, determines by two-thirds vote of both Houses that the President is unable to discharge the powers and duties of his office, the Vice President shall continue to discharge the same as Acting President; otherwise, the President shall resume the powers and duties of his office.

AMENDMENT XXVI (1971)

(note: Amendment 14, section 2 was modified by section 1 of this amendment)

Section 1. The right of citizens of the United States, who are eighteen years of age or older, to vote shall not be denied or abridged by the United States or by any State on account of age.

Section 2. The Congress shall have power to enforce this article by appropriate legislation.

AMENDMENT XXVII (1992)

No law varying the compensation for the services of the Senators and Representatives shall take effect, until an election of Representatives shall have intervened.

NOTES

1. Sources for the introductory comments and the document are the websites of the U.S. Senate, accessed at https://www.senate.gov/civics/constitution_item/constitution .htm and National Archives, accessed at https://www.archives.gov/founding-docs/ constitution-transcript.

NOTES ON QUOTATIONS

233   Abraham Lincoln, U.S. President (1861–1865)

234   Donald F. Kettl, former dean of the School of Public Policy, University of Maryland

244   Alan Berube, Brookings Institution Metropolitan Policy Program Senior Fellow and Deputy Director

305   Art Taylor, President and CEO, BBB Wise Giving Alliance; Jacob Harold, President and CEO, GuideStar; and Ken Berger, CEO, Charity Navigator

311   Susan Urahn, Managing Director, Pew Center on the States

332   Thad Allen, Admiral and former Commandant of the United States Coast Guard

342   John D. Donahue, Raymond Vernon Lecturer in Public Policy, Harvard University

364   The New Jersey Privatization Task Force, created in 2010 to review opportunities for, and impediments to, opportunities for privatization

377   Gavin Newsom, former mayor of San Francisco and lieutenant governor of California

404   Jonathan Turley, Shapiro Professor of public interest law at George Washington University

422   Paul H. Douglas, served as U.S. Senator (IL) from 1949 to 1967

428   Joe Biden, served as U.S. Vice President from 2009 to 2017

430   Walter M. Shaub, served as Director of the U.S. Office of Government Ethics from 2013 to 2017

437   Eleanor Roosevelt, author of *The Moral Basis of Democracy* and U.S. First Lady from 1933 to 1945

462   Barbara Cohn, director of the Fund for the City of New York's Center on Government Performance

465   Roy Barnes, former governor, State of Georgia

466   Harry P. Hatry, distinguished fellow and director of the Public Management Program, Urban Institute

491   Lee H. Hamilton, former U.S. representative (IN) and vice-chair of the 9/11 Commission

494   Frances Wright, writer

INDEX

Boldface page references indicate photographs. *Italic* references indicate figures and boxed text.

ABOUT THE AUTHORS

Mary E. Guy worked in government for the first decade of her career and has been teaching and writing about public service ever since. Focusing on the human processes involved, she has lectured around the world on the subject of democratic administration and the everyday experience of public service professionals. With a focus on frontline workers, she studies the work lives of street-level public servants to learn how they cope with emotionally intense work, such as that encountered by disaster response teams who respond to unpredictable horrors, emergency dispatchers who answer 911 calls, detectives and social workers who must remove children from abusive families, and law enforcement officers who must respond to whatever situation arises, often amid chaotic circumstances. Their experiences illuminate the daily demands of public service and inform Professor Guy's work. Winner of the 2018 Dwight Waldo Award, she has also been honored with the 2012 Distinguished Research Award, given jointly by the American Society for Public Administration and the Network of Schools of Public Policy, Affairs, and Administration, an award that acknowledges research that has changed the way scholars think about the field, and she delivered the 2009 Stone Lecture for the American Society for Public Administration. She is past editor-in-chief of the *Review of Public Personnel Administration,* a fellow of the National Academy of Public Administration, and past president of the American Society for Public Administration. She is Professor in the School of Public Affairs at the University of Colorado Denver and taught previously at the Askew School of Public Administration and Policy at Florida State University and at the University of Alabama at Birmingham.

Todd L. Ely is associate professor in the School of Public Affairs at the University of Colorado Denver and Director of the Center for Local Government Research and Training. His research and teaching focus on the financing of state and local public services, municipal debt, education finance and policy, and public and nonprofit financial management. While earning an MPA degree, he gained a broad perspective on public service with early work experience at multiple levels of government. With an

MPA in hand, he went to work in the private sector as a management consultant. After transitioning back to public service through a stint with AmeriCorps in rural Indiana, he became the program coordinator for the MPA program at the University of Arizona where he was responsible for the recruiting, retention, and career services of MPA students. He joined the faculty at the University of Colorado Denver after earning his PhD in public administration from New York University's Robert F. Wagner Graduate School of Public Service. He has since received school-level awards for his teaching, service, and research. His writing targets both practice and theory, with grant-funded research from the American Educational Research Association, Ford Foundation, and Governmental Accounting Standards Board. Recent publications can be found in *The American Review of Public Administration*, *Municipal Finance Journal*, *National Tax Journal*, *Nonprofit and Voluntary Sector Quarterly*, *Public Administration Review*, *Public Budgeting & Finance*, *State and Local Government Review*, and *Urban Affairs Review*. Media outlets and public agencies frequently call on his research and expertise.